THE

HISTORY OF THE REFORMATION

OF THE

CHURCH OF ENGLAND.

THE

HISTORY OF THE REFORMATION

OF THE

CHURCH OF ENGLAND

BY

GILBERT BURNET, D.D.

BISHOP OF SALISBURY.

A NEW EDITION CAREFULLY REVISED, AND THE RECORDS
COLLATED WITH THE ORIGINALS,

BY

NICHOLAS POCOCK, M.A.

LATE MICHEL FELLOW OF QUEEN'S COLLEGE.

VOL. II.

OXFORD
AT THE CLARENDON PRESS
MDCCCLXV

Complete set — S.B.N. — GB: 576.78546.6
This volume — S.B.N. — GB: 576.78931.3

Republished in 1969 by Gregg International Publishers Limited
Westmead, Farnborough, Hants., England

Printed in Holland

THE SECOND PART.

OF THE PROGRESS MADE IN THE REFORMATION

TILL THE SETTLEMENT OF IT

IN THE BEGINNING OF

QUEEN ELIZABETH'S REIGN.

THE PREFACE.

THE favourable reception which the former part of this work had, together with the new materials that were sent me from noble and worthy hands, have encouraged me to prosecute it, and to carry down the History of the Reformation of this Church till it was brought to a complete settlement in the beginning of queen Elizabeth's reign; which I now offer to the world.

The great zeal of this age for what was done in that, about religion, has made the History of it to be received and read with more than ordinary attention and care : and many have expressed their satisfaction in what was formerly published, by contributing several papers of great consequence to what remained. And since I found no part of the first volume was more universally acceptable, than that wherein I was only a transcriber ; I mean the Collection of Records and authentic Papers, which I had set down in confirmation of the more remarkable and doubtful parts of the History ; I continue the same method now. I shall repeat nothing here that was in my former preface ; but refer the reader to such things as concern this History in general, and my encouragement in the undertaking and prosecution of it, to what is there premised to the whole work : and therefore I shall now enlarge on such things as do more particularly relate to this volume.

The papers, that were conveyed to me from several hands, are referred to, as the occasion to mention them occurs in the History, with such acknowledgments as I thought best became this way of writing, though far short of the merits of those who furnished me with them. But the storehouse from whence I drew the greatest part both of the History and Collection, is the often celebrated Cotton library, out of which, by the noble favour of its truly learned owner, sir John Cotton, I gathered all that was necessary for composing this part, together with some few things which had escaped me in my former search, and belong to the first part; and those I have mixed in the Collection added to this volume, upon such occasions as I thought most pertinent. But among all the remains of the last age, that are with great industry and order laid up in that treasury, none pleased me better, nor were of more use to me, than the Journal of king Edward's reign, written all with his own hand; with some other papers of his, which I have put by themselves in the beginning of the Collection: of these I shall say nothing here, having given a full account of them in the History of his reign, to which I refer the reader. I find most of our writers have taken parcels out of them, and sir John Hayward [1] has transcribed from them the greatest part of his book; therefore I thought this a thing of such consequence, that upon good advice I have published them all faithfully copied from the originals.

But as others assisted me towards the perfecting this part, so that learned divine, and most exact inquirer into historical learning, Mr. Fulman, rector of Hampton-Meysey in Gloucestershire, did most signally oblige me, by a collection of some mistakes I had made in the former work. He had for many years applied his thoughts with a very searching care to the same subject, and so was able to judge more critically of it than other readers. Some of those had escaped me, others had not come within my view; in some particulars my vouchers were not good, and in others I had mistaken my authors. These I publish at the end [2] of this volume, being neither ashamed to confess my faults, nor unwilling to acknowledge from what hand I received better information. My design in writing is to discover truth, and to deliver it down impartially to the next age; so I should think it both a mean and criminal piece of vanity to suppress this discovery of my errors. And though the number and consequence of them had been

[1] [Hayward (Sir John) The life and raigne of King Edward VI; with the beginning of the raigne of Queen Elizabeth. London 1636. 12mo. first published in 4to. 1630. The references made in this volume are to the edition published in the second volume of Kennett's History of England, ed. 1719.]

[2] [In the present edition they are inserted in the notes to the places to which they refer, and are distinguished by the addition of the letter [F].]

greater than it is, I should rather have submitted to a much severer penance, than have left the world in the mistakes I had led them into: yet I was not a little pleased to find that they were neither many, nor of importance to the main parts of the History; and were chiefly about dates, or small variations in the order of time. I hope this part has fewer faults, since that worthy person did pursue his former kindness so far as to review it beforehand; and with great judgment to correct such errors as he found in it: those I had formerly fallen into made me more careful in examining even the smallest matters. Yet if, after all my care, and the kind censures of those who have revised this work, there is any thing left that may require a further retractation, I shall not decline to make it so soon as I see there is need of it; being, I hope, raised above the poor vanity of seeking my own reputation, by sacrificing truth to it.

Those to whose censure I submitted this whole History in both its parts, were chiefly three great divines, whose lives are such examples, their sermons such instructions, their writings such unanswerable vindications of our church, and their whole deportment so suitable to their profession, that, as I reckon my being admitted into some measure of friendship with them among the chief blessings of my life, so I know nothing can more effectually recommend this work than to say, that it passed with their hearty approbation, after they had examined it with that care, which their great zeal for the cause concerned in it, and their goodness to the author, and freedom with him, obliged them to use. They are so well known, that, without naming them, those of this age will easily guess who they are; and they will be so well known to posterity by their excellent writings, that the naming them is so high an advantage to my book, that I much doubt whether it is decent for me to do it. One of them, Dr. Lloyd[3], is now, while I am writing, by his majesty's favour, promoted to the bishopric of St. Asaph: a dignity to which how deservedly soever his great learning, piety, and merit, has advanced him, yet I particularly know how far he was from any aspirings to it; it was he I described in my former preface, that engaged me first to this design, and

---

[3] [He was consecrated bishop of St. Asaph Oct. 3rd, 1680; and was afterwards Bishop of Lichfield and Coventry, and finally of Worcester.]

for that reason he has been more than ordinary careful to examine it with that exactness that is peculiar to him. The other two are the reverend, learned, and judicious deans of Canterbury and St. Paul's, Dr. Tillotson and Dr. Stillingfleet, too well known to receive any addition from the characters I can give of them.

Others gave me supplies of another sort, to enable me to go through with an undertaking that put me to no small expense. I am not ashamed to acknowledge, that the straitness of my condition made this uneasy to me, being destitute of all public provision : but I should be much ashamed of my ingratitude, if I did not celebrate their bounty who have taken such care of me, as not to leave this addition of charge on one who lives not without difficulties. I must again repeat my thanks for the generous kindness, protection, and liberal supplies of sir Harbottle Grimstone, master of the rolls, this being the sixth [4] year of my subsistence under him, to whom I must ever acknowledge that I am more beholden than to all men living. The noble Mr. Boyle, as he employs both his time and wealth for the good of mankind, (for which he considers himself as chiefly born, and which he has promoted not only in his own excellent writings, that have made him so famous over all the world, but in many other designs that have been chiefly carried on at his cost,) so hath he renewed his kindness to me in largesses suitable to so great a mind. Others were also pleased to join their help. The right honourable the lord Finch, now lord high chancellor of England, whose great parts, and greater virtues, are so conspicuous, that it were a high presumption in me to say any thing in his commendation, being in nothing more eminent than in his zeal for, and care of this church, thought it might be of some importance to have its history well digested ; and therefore, as he bore a large share of my expense, so he took it more particularly under his care, and, under all the burdens of that high employment which he now bears, yet found time for reading it in manuscript, of which he must have robbed himself, since he never denies it to those who have a right to it on any public account; and hath added such remarks and corrections as are no small part of any finishing it

[4] [The author had been appointed preacher at the Rolls' Chapel by sir Harbottle Grimstone in 1675.]

may be judged to have. The lord Russell, the inheritor of that
zeal for true religion, and the other virtues that have from the
first beginnings of the reformation, in a continued entail,
adorned that noble family of Bedford, beyond most others of
the kingdom, did espouse the interest of the protestant religion
in this particular, as he has done on all other more public occasions; and by a most liberal supply encouraged me to prosecute this undertaking. That worthy counsellor, whose celebrated integrity and clear judgment have raised him so high
in his profession, Anthony Keck, esq. did also concur in easing
me of the charge that searching, copying, and gathering materials, put me to : and having received as much from these my
noble benefactors as did enable me to carry on my design, I
did excuse myself at other persons' hands, who very generously
offered to supply me in the expense which this work brought
with it. That was done in a most extraordinary manner by
the right honourable the earl of Halifax, whom if I reckon
among the greatest persons this age has produced, I am sure
all that know him will allow that I speak modestly of him : he
indeed offered me the yearly continuance of a bounty, that
would not only have defrayed all this expense, but have been
an entire and honourable subsistence to me.; and though my
necessities were not so pressing as to persuade me to accept it,
yet so unusual a generosity doth certainly merit the highest
acknowledgments I can make for it.

But I now turn to that which ought to be the chief subject
of this preface ; to remove the prejudices, by which weak and
unwary persons have been prepossessed in their judgments
concerning the reformation, during that period of it that falls
within this volume. I know the duty of an historian leads
him to write as one that is of neither party, and I have endeavoured to follow it as carefully as I could, neither concealing
the faults of the one party, nor denying the just praises that
were due to any of the other side, and have delivered things
as I found them, making them neither better nor worse than
indeed they were: but now that I am not yet entered into
that province, and am here writing my own thoughts, and not
relating the actions of other men, I hope it will be judged no
indecent thing to clear the reader's mind of those impressions,
which may either have already biassed him too much, or may,

upon a slight reading of what follows, arise in his thoughts: unless he were prepared and armed with some necessary reflections, which every one that may possibly read this History has not had the leisure, or other opportunities, to make to such a degree as were needful.

It is certainly an unjust way of proceeding, in any that is to be a judge, to let himself be secretly possessed with such impressions of persons and things as may bias his thoughts: for where the scales are not well adjusted, the weight cannot be truly reckoned. So that it is an indirect method to load men's minds with prejudices, and not to let them in to the trial of truth till their inclinations are first swayed such a way. I deny not but in matters of religion most commonly men receive such notions, before they can well examine them, as do much determine them in the inquiries they make afterwards, when their understandings grow up to a fuller ripeness: but those preoccupations, if rightly infused, are rather such as give them general notions of what is good and honest in the abstracted ideas, than concerning matters of fact: for every wise and pious man must avoid all such methods of instruction as are founded on falsehood and craft: and he that will breed a man to love truth, must form in him such a liking of it, that he may clearly see he would bribe him into no opinion or party by false or indirect arts. But since men are generally so apt to let some easy notions enter into their minds, which will preengage their affections, and for most part those who set themselves to gain proselytes, do begin with such arts; it will not be amiss to give the reader such an account of these, as may prepare him against them, that so he may with a clearer mind consider what is now to be delivered to him, concerning the reformation of religion among us.

I shall begin with that which is most commonly urged; that the whole church being one body, the changes that were made in religion did break that unity, and dissolve the bond by which the catholic church is to be knit together; and that therefore the first reformers began, and we still continue, a schism in the church.

In answer to this, it is to be considered, that the bishops and pastors of the church are obliged to instruct their people in the true faith of Christ, according to the scriptures: the nature of their function, being a sacred trust, binds them to this; they were also at their consecration engaged to it by a formal sponsion, according to the questions and answers that are in the Roman Pontifical to this day. Pastors owe it as a debt to their people to teach them according to the scriptures: they owe a charity to their brethren, and are to live with them in the terms of brotherly love and friendly correspondence; but if that cannot be had on easier terms than the concealing necessary truths, and the delivering gross errors to those committed to their charge, it is certain that they ought not to purchase it at so dear a rate. When the pastors of this church saw it overrun with errors and corruptions, they were obliged, by the duty they owed to God and to their people, to discover them, and to undeceive their misled flocks. It is of great importance to maintain peace and unity; but if a party in the church does set up some doctrines and practices, that do much endanger the salvation of souls, and makes advantages by these, so that there is no hope left to gain them by rational and softer methods; then, as St. Peter was to be withstood to his face in a lesser matter, much more are those, who pretend no higher than to be his successors, to be withstood, when the things are of great moment and consequence. When heresies sprung up in the primitive church, we find the neighbouring bishops condemned them without staying for the concurrence of other churches; as in the case of Samosatenus, Arius, and Pelagius: and even when the greatest part of the church was become Semi-Arian, and many great councils, chiefly that at Ariminum, consisting of above eight hundred bishops, as some say, had through ignorance and fear complied, the orthodox bishops did not forbear to instruct those committed to their care according to the true faith. A general concurrence is a thing much to be laboured for; but when it cannot be had, every bishop must then do his duty so as to be answerable to the chief bishop of souls.

So that, instead of being led away by so slight a prejudice, we must turn our inquiries to this, Whether there were really such abuses in the church, as did require a reformation? and whether there was any reason to hope for a more general concurrence in it? In the following History the reader will see what corruptions were found to be both in the doctrine and

worship of this church : from whence he may infer what need
there was of reformation. And it is very plain, that they
had no reason to expect the concurrence of other churches;
for the council of Trent had already made a great progress,
and it was very visible, that, as the court of Rome governed
all things there, so they were resolved to admit of no effectual
reformation of any considerable matters; but to establish, by
a more formal decision, those errors and abuses that had
given so much scandal to the Christian world for so many
ages.

This being the true state of the case, it is certain, that if
there were really great corruptions, either in belief or manners, in this church, then the bishops were bound to reform
them : since the backwardness of others in their duty could
not excuse them from doing theirs, when they were clearly
convinced of it. So that the reader is to shake off this prejudice, and only to examine whether there was really such
need of a reformation ; since, if that be true, it is certain the
bishops of this, as well as of other churches, were bound to set
about it; and the faultiness of some could be no excuse to the
rest.

The second prejudice is, that the reformation was begun
and carried on, not by the major part of the bishops and
clergy, but by a few selected bishops and divines, who being
supported by the name of the king's authority, did frame
things as they pleased ; and by their interest at court got
them to be enacted in parliament : and after they had removed such bishops as opposed them, then they procured the
convocation to consent to what was done : so that upon the
matter, the reformation was the work of Cranmer, with a few
more of his party, and not of this church, which never agreed
wholly to it, till the bishops were so modelled as to be compliant to the designs of the court. In short, the resolution of
this is to be taken from a common case ; when the major part
of a church is, according to the conscience of the supreme civil
magistrate, in an error, and the lesser part is in the right.
The case is not hard, if well understood ; for in the whole
scripture there is no promise made to the major part of the
pastors of the church ; and there being no divine promise
made about it, it is certain that the nature of man is such, that

truth, separated from interest, hath few votaries : but when it is opposite to it, it must have a very small party. So that most of those things which needed reformation, being such as added much to the wealth and power of the clergy, it had been a wonder indeed, if the greater part had not opposed it. In that case, as the smaller part were not to depart from their sentiments, because opposed in them by a more numerous party that was too deeply concerned in the matter ; so it was both natural for them, and very reasonable, to take sanctuary in the authority and protection of the prince and the law. That princes have an authority in things sacred, was so universally agreed to in king Henry's reign, and was made out upon such clear evidence of reason and precedents, both in the Jewish state, and in the Roman empire, when it turned Christian, that this ground was already gained. It is the first law in Justinian's Code, made by Theodosius when he came to the empire, That all should every where, under severe pains, follow that faith which was received by Damasus bishop of Rome, and Peter of Alexandria. And why might not the king and laws of England give the like authority to the archbishops of Canterbury and York ?

When the empire, and especially the eastern part of it, had been, during the reign of Constantius, and Valens succeeding him after a short interval, so overspread with Arianism, it is scarce to be imagined how it could have been reformed in any other manner : for they durst not at first trust it to the discretion of a synod ; and yet the question then on foot was not so linked with interest, being a speculative point of divinity, as those about which the contests were in the beginnings of the reformation.

It is not to be imagined how any changes in religion can be made by sovereign princes, unless an authority be lodged with them of giving the sanction of a law to the sounder, though the lesser part of a church : for as princes and lawgivers are not tied to an implicit obedience to clergymen, but are left to the freedom of their own discerning, so they must have a power to choose what side to be of, where things are much inquired into. The jurisdiction of synods or councils is founded either on the rules of expediency and brotherly correspondence, or on the force of civil laws : for when the Christian belief had not the support of law, every bishop taught his own flock the best he could, and gave his neighbours such an account of his faith, at, or soon after, his consecration, as satisfied them, and so maintained the unity of the church. The formality of synods grew up in the church from the division of the Roman empire, and the dignity of the several cities; which is a thing so well known, and so plainly acknowledged by the writers of all sides, that it were a needless imposing on the reader's patience to spend time to prove it. Such as would understand it more perfectly, will find it in De Marca, the late archbishop of Paris' books *De Concordiâ Imperii et Sacerdotii* [5], and in Blondel's works, *De la Primauté de l'Eglise* [6]. None can imagine there is a divine authority in that which sprang from such a beginning. The major part of synods cannot be supposed to be, in matters of faith, so assisted from Heaven, that the lesser part must necessarily acquiesce in their decrees, or that the civil powers must always measure their laws by their votes: especially where interest does visibly turn the scales. And this may satisfy any reasonable man as to this prejudice; that if archbishop Cranmer and Holgate, the two primates and metropolitans of this church, were in the right, in the things that they procured to be reformed, though the greater part of the bishops, being biassed by base ends, and generally both superstitious and little conversant in the true theological learning, did oppose them, and they were thereby forced to order matters so, that at first they were prepared by some selected bishops and divines, and afterwards enacted by king and parliament, this is no just exception to what was so managed. And such a *reformation* can no more be blasted by being called a *parliament religion*, than the *reformations* made by the kings of Israel, without or against the majority of the priests, could be blemished by being called *the king's religion*.

A third prejudice is, that the persons who governed the affairs at court were weak or ill men: that the king being under age, things were carried by those who had him in their

---

[5] [Marca (Petrus de), Dissertationum de Concordiâ Sacerdotii et Imperii &c. lib. 8. ed. tertia auctior. Par. 1704. fol.]

[6] [Blondellus (David) De la Primauté en l'Eglise &c. Genev. 1641. fol.]

power. And for the two great ministers of that reign, or rather the administrators of it, the dukes of Somerset and Northumberland, as their violent and untimely deaths may seem to be effects of the indignation of Heaven for what they did; so they were both eminently faulty in their administration, and are supposed to have sought too much their own ends. This seems to cast a blemish on their actions, and to give some reason to suspect the things were not good which had such instruments to advance them.

But this prejudice, compounded of many particulars when taken to pieces, will appear of no force to blast the credit of what they did. By our law, the king never dies, and is never young nor old; so that the authority of the king is the same, whether administered by himself or by his governors, when he is under age: nor are we to judge of men by the events that befal them. These are the deepest secrets of Divine Providence, into which it is impossible for men of limited understandings to penetrate: and if we make judgments of persons and things by accidents, we shall very often most certainly conclude falsely. Solomon made the observation, which the series of human affairs ever since hath fully justified, *that there are just men, to whom it happens according to the work of the wicked; and wicked men, to whom it happens according to the work of the righteous:* and the inquiring into these seemingly unequal steps of God's governing the world, *is a vanity.* As for the duke of Northumberland, the reformation is not at all concerned in him; for if we believe what he said, when there was the least reason to suspect him, on the scaffold, he was all the while a papist in his heart: and so no wonder if such a man, striking in for his own ambitious ends with that which was popular, even against the persuasions of his conscience, did very ill things. The duke of Somerset was indeed more sincere; and though he was not without his faults, (which we may safely acknowledge, since the man of infallibility is not pretended to be without sin,) yet these were not such heinous transgressions, but rather such as human infirmity exposes most men to, when they are raised to an high condition. He was too vain, too much addicted to his own notions, and, being a man of no extraordinary parts, he was too much at the disposal of those, who by flatteries and submissions insinuated themselves into him; and he made too great haste to raise a vast estate to be altogether innocent: but I never find him charged with any personal disorders, nor was he ever guilty of falsehood, of perverting justice, of cruelty, or of oppression. He was so much against the last of these, that he lost the affections of the nobility for being so careful of the commons, and covering them from the oppression of their landlords. The business of his brother, though it has a very ill appearance, and is made to look worse by the lame account our books give of it, seems to have been forced on him: for the admiral was a man of most incurable ambition, and so inclined to raise disturbance, that, after so many relapses and such frequent reconciliations, he still breaking out into new disorders, it became almost necessary to put him out of a capacity of doing more mischief. But if we compare the duke of Somerset with the great ministers even in the best courts, we shall find him better than most of them: and if some few have carried their prosperity better, many more, even of those who are otherwise recorded for extraordinary persons, have been guilty of far greater faults. He who is but a little acquainted with history, or with the courts of princes, must needs know so much of this argument, that he will easily cure himself of any ill effects which this prejudice may have on him.

A fourth prejudice is raised from the great invasions which were then made upon the church-lands, and things dedicated to pious uses; which is a thing hated by men of all religions, and branded with the odious names of *sacrilege*, and *robbing of God;* so that the spoils of religious houses and churches seem to have been the secret motives that at first drew in, and still engage, so many to the reformation. This has more weight in it than the former, and therefore deserves to be more fully considered.

The light of nature teaches, that those who are dedicated to the service of God, and for instructing the people, ought to be so well provided for, that they may be delivered from the distractions of secular cares, and secured from the contempt which follows poverty; and be furnished with such means as may both enable them to know that well wherein they are to instruct others, and to gain such an interest in the affections of those among whom they labour, as modest hospitality and liberal almsgiving may procure. In this all nations and religions have so generally agreed, that it may be well called a law of nations, if not of nature. Had churchmen been contented with this measure, it is very probable things had never run to the other extreme so much as they have done. But as the pope got to himself a great principality, so the rest of his clergy designed to imitate him in that as much as was possible: they spared no pains, nor thought they any methods too bad, that could set forward these projects. The belief of purgatory, and the redeeming of souls out of it by masses, with many other public cheats imposed on the world, had brought the wealth of this and other nations into their hands. Upon the discovery of this imposture, it was but a reasonable and just proceeding of the government to reassume those lands, and dispose otherwise of them, which had been for most part fraudulently drawn from the former ages: for indeed the best part of the soil of England being in such ill hands, it was the interest of the whole kingdom to have it put to better uses. So that the abbeys being generally raised and endowed by the efficacy of those false opinions, which were infused into the people, I can see no just exception against the dissolution of them, with the chantries, and other foundations of like superstition; and the fault was not in taking them away, but in not applying a greater part of them to uses truly religious.

But most of these monasteries had been enriched by that, which was indeed the spoil of the church: for in many places the tithes which belonged to the secular clergy were taken from them, and by the authority of papal bulls were given to the monasteries. This was the original of the greatest mischief that came on this church at the reformation: the abbots having possessed themselves of the tithes, and having left to those who served the cure, either some small donative or stipend, and at best the small tithes or vicarage, those who purchased the abbey-lands from the crown in the former reign, had them with no other charge reserved for the incumbents but that small pittance that the abbots had formerly given them: and this is now a much less allowance than the curates had in the times of popery; for though they have now the same right by their incumbency that they then had, yet in the time of superstition, the fees of obits, exequies, soul-masses, and such other perquisites, did furnish them so plentifully, that, considering their obligation to remain unmarried, they lived well, though their certain maintenance was but small: but these things falling off by the reformation, which likewise leaves the clergy at liberty in the matter of marriage, this has occasioned much ignorance and scandal among the clergy. I shall not enter into the debate about the divine right of tithes: this I am sure of, a decent maintenance of the clergy is of natural right, and that it is not better looked to is a public reproach to the whole nation; when, in all other religions and nations, those who serve at the altar live by it. The ancient allowances for the curates in market towns being generally so small, because the number and wealth of the people made the perquisites so considerable, has made those places to be too often but ill supplied: and what way this makes for the seducers of all hands, when the minister is of so mean a condition, and hath so incompetent a maintenance, that he can scarce secure himself from extreme want and great contempt, I leave it to every man to judge.

This is as high a contempt of religion and the gospel as any can be, and is one of those things for which this nation has much to answer to God; that now, in one hundred and twenty years' time[7], so little has been done by public authority for the redress of such a crying oppression. Some private persons have done great things this way, but the public has yet done nothing suitable to the occasion: though their neighbour nation of Scotland has set them a very good example; where, by the great zeal and care of king James, and the late blessed king, acts and orders of parliament have been made for examining the whole state of the clergy, and for supplying all poor livings so plentifully, that in glebe and tithes all benefices are now raised to at least fifty pounds sterling yearly. What greater scorn can be put upon religion, than to provide so scantly for those that are trusted with the care of souls, that some hundreds of parishes in England pay not ten pounds a year to their pastors, and perhaps some thousands not fifty? This is to be numbered among those crying sins that are bringing down vengeance on us, since by this many souls are

---

[7] [The date of the first publication of this was 1681.]

left to perish, because it is not possible to provide them with able and faithful shepherds. I shall not examine all the particular reasons that have obstructed the redress of this mischief; but those concerned in it may soon find some of them out in themselves. And here I acknowledge a great and just prejudice lies against our reformation, which no man can fully answer. But how faulty soever we may be in this particular, they of the church of Rome have little reason to object it to us, since the first and true occasion of it was of their own doing. Our fault is, that, at the dissolution of the monasteries, restitution was not made to the parish priests of what the popes had sacrilegiously taken from them. And now that we are upon the utter extirpation of popery, let us not retain this relic of it. And I pray God to inspire and direct his majesty and his two houses of parliament effectually to remove this just, and, for aught I know, only great scandal of our English reformation.

A fifth prejudice, which seems to give ill impressions of our reformation, is, that the clergy have now no interest in the consciences of the people, nor any inspection into their manners; but they are without yoke or restraint. All the ancient canons for the public penance of scandalous offenders are laid aside, and our clergy are so little admitted to know or direct the lives and manners of their flocks, that many will scarce bear a reproof patiently from them: our ecclesiastical courts are not in the hands of the bishops and their clergy, but put over to the civilians, where too often fees are more strictly looked after than the correction of manners. I hope there is not cause for so great a cry; but so it is, these courts are much complained of; and public vice and scandal is but little inquired after, or punished: excommunication is become a kind of secular sentence, and is hardly now considered as a spiritual censure, being judged and given out by laymen, and often upon grounds, which, to speak moderately, do not merit so severe and dreadful a sentence. There are, besides this, a great many other abuses, brought in in the worst times, and now purged out of some of the churches of the Roman communion, which yet continue, and are too much in use among us; such as pluralities, non-residences, and other things of that nature: so that it may be said, that some of the manifest corruptions of popery, where they are recommended by the advantages that accompany them, are not yet throughly purged out, notwith-standing all the noise we have made about reformation in matters much more disputable, and of far less consequence.

This whole objection, when all acknowledged, as the greatest part of it cannot be denied, amounts indeed to this; that our reformation is not yet arrived at that full perfection that is to be desired. The want of public penance, and penitentiary canons, is indeed a very great defect: our church does not deny it, but acknowledges it in the Preface to the office of Commination. It was one of the greatest glories of the primitive church, that they were so governed, that none of their number could sin openly without public censure, and a long separation from the holy communion; which they judged was defiled by a promiscuous admitting of all persons to it. Had they consulted the arts of policy, they would not have held in converts by so strict a way of proceeding, lest their discontent might have driven them away; at a time when to be a Christian was attended with so many discouragements, that it might seem dangerous, by so severe a discipline, to frighten the world out of their communion. But the pastors of that time resolved to follow the rules delivered them by the apostles, and trusted God with the success, which answered and exceeded all their expectations: for nothing convinced the world more of the truth of that religion, than to see those trusted with the care of souls watch so effectually over their manners, that for some sins, which in these loose ages in which we live pass but for common effects of human frailty, men were made to abstain from the communion for many years, and did cheerfully submit to such rules as might be truly medicinal for curing those diseases in their minds.

But, alas! the churchmen of the latter ages being once vested with this authority, to which the world submitted as long as it saw the good effects of it, did soon learn to abuse it; and to bring the people to a blind subjection to them. It was one of the chief arts by which the papacy swelled to its height: for confessors, instead of bringing their penitents to open penance, set up other things in the room of it; pretending they could commute it, and in the name of God accept of one thing for another: and they accepted of a penitent's going either to the holy war, or, which was more holy of the two, to one of the pope's wars against heretics, or deposed princes; and gave full pardons to those who thus engaged in their designs. Afterwards (when the pope had no great occasion to kill men, or the people no great mind to be killed in his service) they accepted of money, as an alms to God: and so all public penance was laid down, and murder or merchandise was set up in its room. This being the state of things at the reformation, it is no wonder if the people could not be easily brought to submit to public penance; which had been for some ages entirely laid aside: and there was reason why they should not be forward to come under the yoke of their priests, lest they should have raised upon that foundation such a tyrannical dominion over them, as others had formerly exercised. This made some reformed churches beyond sea bring in the laity with them into their courts, which if they had done merely as a good expedient for removing the jealousy which the world then had of ecclesiastical tyranny, there was no great objection to have been made to it; but they made the thing liable to very great exception, when they pretended a divine institution for those lay-elders. Here in England, it is plain the nation would not bear such authority to be lodged with the clergy at first: but it will appear in the following work, that a platform was made of an ecclesiastical discipline, though the bishops had no hope of reducing it into practice till the king should come to be of age, and pass a law for the authorizing of it; but he dying before this was effected, it was not prosecuted with that zeal that the thing required in queen Elizabeth's time: and then those who in their exile were taken with the models beyond seas, contending more to get it put in the method of other churches than to have it set up in any other form, that contention begat such heat, that it took men off from this and many other excellent designs. And whereas the presbyters were found to have had anciently a share in the government of the churches, as the bishop's council and assistants; some of them, that were of hot tempers, demanding more than their share, they were by the immoderate use of the counterpoise kept out of any part of ecclesiastical discipline; and all went into those courts commonly called the *spiritual courts;* without making distinction between those causes of testaments, marriages, and such other suits that re-

quire some learning in the civil and canon law, and the other
causes of the censures of the clergy and laity, which are of a
more spiritual nature, and ought indeed to be tried only by the
bishops and clergy; for they are no small part of the care
of souls, which is incumbent on them: and by them only ex-
communications ought to be made, as being a suspension
from the sacred rites of Christians, of which none can be the
competent judges, but those to whom the charge of souls is
committed. The worst that can be said of all these abuses
is, that they are relics of popery, and we owe it to the unhappy
contests among ourselves that a due correction has not been
yet given to them.

From hence one evil has followed, not inferior to these,
from whence it flows; that the pastoral charge is now looked
on by too many, rather as a device only for instructing people,
to which they may submit as much as they think fit, than as a
care of souls, as indeed it is. And it is not to be denied but
the practice of not a few of us of the clergy has confirmed the
people in this mistake; who consider our function as a method
of living, by performing divine offices, and making sermons,
rather than as a watching over the souls of the flocks committed
to us, visiting the sick, reproving scandalous persons, reconciling differences, and being strict at least in governing the poor,
whose necessities will oblige them to submit to any good rules
we shall set them for the better conduct of their lives. In
these things does the pastoral care chiefly consist, and not only
in the bare performing of offices, or pronouncing sermons,
which every one almost may learn to do after some tolerable
fashion. If men had a just notion of this holy function, and a
right sense of it before they were initiated into it, those scandalous abuses of plurality of benefices with cure, (except where
they are so poor and contiguous, that both can scarce maintain
one incumbent, and one man can discharge the duty of both very
well,) non-residences, and the hiring out that sacred trust to piti-
ful mercenaries at the cheapest rates, would soon fall off. These
are things of so crying a nature, that no wonder if the wrath
of God is ready to break out upon us. These are abuses that
even the church of Rome, after all her impudence, is ashamed
of; and are at this day generally discountenanced all France
over. Queen Mary here in England, in the time of popery,
set herself effectually to root them out: and that they should

be still found among protestants, and in so reformed a church, is a scandal that may justly make us blush. All the honest prelates at the council of Trent endeavoured to get residence declared to be of divine right, and so not to be dispensed with upon any consideration whatsoever. And there is nothing more apparently contrary to the most common impressions, which all men have about matters of religion, than that benefices are given for the office to which they are annexed: and if in matters of men's estates, or of their health, it would be a thing of high scandal for one to receive the fees, and commit the work to the care of some inferior or raw practitioner, how much worse is it to turn over so important a concernment as the care of souls must be confessed to be, to mean hands! And, to conclude, those who are guilty of such disorders have much to answer for; both to God, for the neglect of those souls for which they are to give an account; and to the world, for the reproach they have brought on this church, and on the sacred functions, by their ill practices. Nor could the divisions of this age ever have risen to such a height, if the people had not been possessed with ill impressions of some of the clergy, from those inexcusable faults that are so conspicuous in too many that are called shepherds ; *who clothe themselves with the wool, but have not fed the flock ; that have not strengthened the diseased, nor healed the sick, nor bound up that which was broken, nor brought again that which was driven away, nor sought that which was lost, but have ruled them with force and cruelty.* And if we would look up to God who is visibly angry with us, and has *made us base and contemptible among the people,* we should find great reason to reflect on those words of Jeremy, *The pastors are become brutish, and have not sought the Lord ; therefore they shall not prosper, and all their flocks shall be scattered.*

But I were very unjust, if, having ventured on so plain and necessary a reprehension, I should not add, that God has not so left this age and church, but there is in it a great number in both the holy functions, who are perhaps as eminent in the exemplariness of their lives, and as diligent in their labours, as has been in any one church in any age since miracles ceased. The humility and strictness of life in many of our prelates, and some that were highly born, and yet have far outgone some others, from whom more might have been expected, raises them far above censure, though perhaps not above envy. And when such think not the daily instructing their neighbours a thing below them, but do it with as constant a care as if they were to earn their bread by it; when they are so affable to the meanest clergymen that come to them; when they are so nicely scrupulous about those whom they admit into holy orders, and so large in their charities, that one would think they were furnished with some unseen ways; these things must raise great esteem for such bishops, and seem to give some hopes of better times. Of all this I may be allowed to speak the more freely, since I am led to it by none of those bribes, either of gratitude, or fear, or hope, which are wont to corrupt men to say what they do not think. But I were much to blame, if, in a work that may perhaps live some time in the world, I should only find fault with what is amiss, and not also acknowledge what is so very commendable and praiseworthy. And when I look into the inferior clergy, there are, chiefly about this great city of London, so many, so eminent, both for the strictness of their lives, the constancy of their labours, their excellent and plain way of preaching, (which is now perhaps brought to as great a perfection as ever was since men spoke as they received it immediately from the Holy Ghost,) the great gentleness of their deportment to such as differ from them, their mutual love and charity, and, in a word, for all the qualities that can adorn ministers or Christians, that if such a number of such men cannot prevail with this debauched age, this one thing to me looks more dismally than all the other affrighting symptoms of our condition; that God having sent so many faithful teachers, their labours are still so ineffectual.

I have now examined all the prejudices that either occur to my thoughts, or that I have met with in books or discourses, against our reformation; and I hope, upon a free inquiry into them, it will be found that some of them are of no force at all, and that the other, which are better grounded, can amount to no more than this, that things were not managed with that care, or brought to that perfection, that were to be desired; so that all the use we ought to make of these objections is, to be directed by them to do those things which may complete

and adorn that work, which was managed by men subject to
infirmities, who neither could see every thing, nor were able
to accomplish all that they had projected, and saw fit to be
done.

But from the matter of the following History another objection of another sort may arise, which, though it has no relation
to the reformation, yet leaves no small imputation on the nation, as too apt to change, and be carried about with every religion in vogue; since in little more than twenty years' time
there were four great changes made in religion : and in all
these the main body of the nation turned with the stream, and
it was but a small number that stood firm, and suffered for
their consciences. But if the state of the nation be well considered, there will be nothing in all this so strange as at first
view it may perhaps appear : for in the times of popery the
people were kept in such profound ignorance, that they knowing
nothing of religion beyond the outward forms and pageantry,
and being highly dissatisfied with the ill lives of the clergy,
and offended with their cruelty against those that contradicted
their opinions, it is no wonder that they were inclined to hear
preachers of any sort, who laid out to them the reasons of the
doctrine they delivered, and did not impose it on them in
gross, as the others had done. These teachers, being also men
of innocent tempers and good lives, and being recommended to
the compassion of the nation by their sufferings, and to their
esteem by their zeal and readiness to run all hazards for their
consciences, had great advantages to gain on the belief and affections of the people. And, to speak freely, I make no doubt
but if the reformation had been longer a hatching under the
heat of persecution, it had come forth perfecter than it was.
This disposition of the people, and king Henry's quarrelling
with the pope, made the way easy for the first change : but
then the severities about the supremacy on one hand, and the
six articles on the other, made people to stagger and reel between the two religions. And all people being fond of new
things, and the discoveries of the impostures of the priests and
lewdness of the monks increasing their dislike of them, it was
no wonder the reformation went on with so little tumult and
precipitation till king Edward's time. But though there were
then very learned and zealous divines, who managed and car-

ried on the changes that were made, yet still the greater part of the clergy was very ignorant and very corrupt; which was occasioned by the pensions that were reserved out of the rents of the suppressed monasteries to the monks during their lives, or till they were provided with livings. The abbey-lands that were sold, with the charge of these annexed to them, coming into the hands of persons who had no mind to have that burden lie longer on them, they got these monks provided with benefices, that so they might be eased of that charge[8]. And for the other abbeys that still remained with the crown, the same course was taken; for the monks were put into all the small benefices that were in the king's gift. So that the greatest part of the clergy were such as had been formerly monks or friars, very ignorant for most part, and generally addicted to their former superstition; though otherwise men that would comply with any thing rather than forfeit their livings. Under such incumbents nothing but ignorance and unconcernedness in religion could prevail. By this means it was that the greater part of the nation was not well instructed, nor possessed with any warmth and sincere love to the reformation; which made the following change under queen Mary more easily effected. The proceedings in king Edward's time were likewise so gentle and moderate, flowing from the calm temper of archbishop Cranmer, and the policy of others, who were willing to accept of any thing they could obtain, hoping that time would do the business, if the overdriving it did not precipitate the whole affair; that it was an easy thing for a concealed papist to weather the difficulties of that reign. There were also great scandals given by the indiscretion of many of the new preachers. The misgovernment of affairs under the duke of Somerset, with the restless ambition of the duke of Northumberland, did alienate the nation much from them: and a great aversion commonly begets an universal dislike of every thing that is done by those whom we hate.

All these things concurred to prepare the minds of the people to the change made by queen Mary. But in her reign popery did more plainly discover itself in the many repeated burnings, and the other cruelties then openly exercised: the nation was

[8] [See page 24, infra.]

also in such danger of being brought under the uneasy yoke of Spanish government; and they were many of them in fear of losing their new-gotten church-lands. These things, together with the loss of Calais in the end of her reign, which was universally much resented as a lasting dishonour to the nation, raised in them a far greater aversion to her government, and to every thing that had been done in it, than they had to the former. The genius of the English leads them to hate cruelty and tyranny; and when they saw these were the necessary concomitants of popery, no wonder it was thrown out with so general an agreement, that there was scarce any considerable opposition made to it, except by some few of their clergy, who, having changed so oft, were ashamed of such repeated recantations, and so resolved at last to stand their ground; which was the more easy to resolve on under so merciful a prince, who punished them only by a forfeiture of their benefices, and, that being done, took care of their subsistence for the rest of their lives; Bonner himself not being excepted, though so deeply dyed in the blood of so many innocents.

All these things laid together, it will not seem strange that such great alterations were so easily brought about in so short a time. But from the days of queen Elizabeth, that the old monks were worn out, and new men better educated were placed in churches, things did generally put on a new visage: and this church has since that time continued to be the sanctuary and shelter of all foreigners, and the chief object of the envy and hatred of the popish church, and the great glory of the reformation; and has wisely avoided the splitting asunder on the high points of the divine decrees, which have broken so many of the reformed beyond sea; but in these has left divines to the freedom of their several opinions: nor did she run on that other rock, of defining at first so peremptorily the manner of Christ's presence in the sacrament, which divided the German and the Helvetian churches; but in that did also leave a latitude to men of different persuasions. From this great temper it might have reasonably been expected, that we should have continued united at home; and then for things sacred, as well as civil, we had been out of the danger of what all our foreign enemies could have contrived or done against us.

But the enemy, while the watchmen slept, sowed his tares

even in this fruitful field ; of which it may be expected I should give some account here ; and the rather, because I end this work at the time when those unhappy differences first arose, so that I give them no part in this History : and yet I have, in the search I made, seen some things of great importance, which are very little known, that give me a clearer light into the beginnings of these differences than is commonly to be had ; of which I shall discourse so as becomes one who has not blindly given himself up to any party, and is not afraid to speak the truth even in the most critical matters.

There were many learned and pious divines in the beginning of queen Elizabeth's reign, who, being driven beyond sea, had observed the new models set up in Geneva, and other places, for the censuring of scandalous persons, of mixed judicatories of the ministers and laity ; and these, reflecting on the great looseness of life which had been universally complained of in king Edward's time, thought such a platform might be an effectual way for keeping out a return of the like disorders. There were also some few rites reserved in this church, that had been either used in the primitive church, or, though brought in of later time, yet seemed of excellent use to beget reverence in holy performances ; which had also this to be said for them, that the keeping these still was done in imitation of what Christ and his apostles did, in symbolizing with the Jewish rites, to gain the Jews thereby as much as could be ; so it was judged necessary to preserve these, to let the world see, that, though corruptions were thrown out, yet the reformers did not love to change only for change sake, when it was not otherwise needful : and this they hoped might draw in many, who otherwise would not so easily have forsaken the Roman communion. Yet these divines excepted to those, as compliances with popery ; and though they professed no great dislike to the ceremonies themselves, or doubt of their lawfulness, yet were they against their continuance upon that single account, which was indeed the chief reason why they were continued. But all this debate was modestly managed, and without violent heat or separation : afterwards some of the queen's courtiers had an eye to the fair manors of some of the greater sees, and, being otherwise men of ill tempers and lives, and probably of no religion, would have persuaded the queen, that nothing could unite all the reformed churches so effectually, as to bring the English church to the model beyond sea; and that it would much enrich the crown, if she took the revenues of bishoprics and cathedrals into her own hands. This made those on the other hand (who laid to heart the true interest of the protestant religion, and therefore endeavoured to preserve this church in that strong and well modelled frame to which it was brought, particularly the lord Burleigh, the wisest statesman of that age, and perhaps of any other,) study how to engage the queen out of interest to support it: and they demonstrated to her, that these new models would certainly bring with them a great abatement of her prerogative; since, if the concerns of religion came into popular hands, there would be a power set up distinct from hers, over which she could have no authority.

This she perceived well, and therefore resolved to maintain the ancient government of the church: but by this means it became a matter of interest; and so these differences, which might have been more easily reconciled before, grew now into formed factions: so that all expedients were left unattempted which might have made up the breach: and it becoming the interest of some to put it past reconciling, this was too easily effected. Those of the division, finding they could not carry their main design, raised all the clamours they could against the churchmen; and put in bills into the parliament against the abuses of pluralities, non-residences, and the excesses of the spiritual courts. But the queen being possessed with this, that the parliament's meddling in these matters tended to the lessening of her authority, of which she was extremely sensible, got all these bills to be thrown out. If the abuses, that gave such occasion to the malcontented to complain, had been effectually redressed, that party must have had little to work on: but these things furnished them with new complaints still. The market-towns being also ill provided for, there were voluntary contributions made for lectures in these places. The lecturers were generally men that overtopped the incumbents in diligent and zealous preaching; and they depending on the bounty of the people for their subsistence, were engaged to follow the humours of those who governed those voluntary contributions.

All these things tended to the increase of the party; which owed its chief growth to the scandalous maintenance of the ministers of great towns, for which reason they were seldom of great abilities; and to the scandals given by the pluralities and non-residences of others that were overprovided. Yet the government in civil matters was so steady all the queen's reign, that they could do no great thing, after she once declared herself so openly and resolutely against them.

But upon king James' coming to the crown, and the divisions that came to be afterwards in parliaments, between the too often named parties for the court and country, and clergymen being linked to the interests of the crown; all those who in civil matters opposed the designs of the court resolved to cherish those of the division, under the colour of their being hearty protestants, and that it was the interest of the reformed religion to use them well, and that all protestants should unite: and indeed the differences between them were then so small, that if great art had not been used to keep them asunder, they had certainly united of their own accord. But the late unhappy wars engaged those who before only complained of abuses into a formed separation; which still continues, to the great danger and disgrace of the protestant religion. I shall not make any observations on latter transactions, which fall within all men's view; but it is plain, that from the beginning there have been laboured designs to make tools of the several parties, and to make a great breach between them, which lays us now so open to our common enemy. And it looks like a sad forerunner of ruin, when we cannot, after so long experience of the mischievous effects of these contests, learn to be so wise as to avoid the running on those rocks, on which our fathers did so unfortunately split: but, on the contrary, many steer as steadily towards them, as if they were the only safe harbours, where they may securely weather every storm.

But being now to lead the reader into so agreeable a prospect, as I hope the reformation of the church will be to him, I will hold him yet a little longer before I open it; and desire him, for his better preparation to it, to reflect on the nature of religion in general, and of the Christian in particular. That religion is chiefly designed for perfecting the nature of man, for improving his faculties, governing his actions, and securing the peace of every man's conscience, and of the societies of mankind in common, is a truth so plain, that, without further arguing about it, all will agree to it. Every part of religion is then to be judged by its relation to the main ends of it: and since the Christian doctrine was revealed from Heaven, as the most perfect and proper way that ever was for the advancing the good of mankind, nothing can be a part of this holy faith but what is proportioned to the end for which it was designed. And all the additions that have been made to it, since it was first delivered to the world, are justly to be suspected; especially where it is manifest at first view that they were intended to serve carnal and secular ends. What can be reasonably supposed in the papacy, where the popes are chosen by such intrigues, either of the two crowns, the nephews of the former pope, or the craft of some aspiring men, to entitle them to infallibility or universal jurisdiction? What can we think of redeeming souls out of purgatory, or preserving them from it, by tricks, or some mean pageantry, but that it is a foul piece of merchandise? What is to be said of implicit obedience, the priestly dominion over consciences, the keeping the scriptures out of the people's hands, and the worship of God in a strange tongue, but that these are so many arts to hoodwink the world, and to deliver it up into the hands of the ambitious clergy? What can we think of the superstition and idolatry of images, and all the other pomp of the Roman worship, but that by these things the people are to be kept up in a gross notion of religion, as a splendid business, and that the priests have a trick of saving them, if they will but take care to humour them, and leave that matter wholly in their hands? And, to sum up all, what can we think of that constellation of prodigies in the sacrament of the altar, as they pretend to explain it, and all really to no purpose, but that it is an art to bring the world by wholesale to renounce their reason and sense, and to have a most wonderful veneration for a sort of men, who can with a word perform the most astonishing thing that ever was?

I should grow too large for a preface, if I would pursue this argument as far as it will go. But if, on the other hand, we reflect on the true ends of this holy religion, we must needs be convinced, that we need go no where else out of this church to find them; but are completely instructed in all parts of it, and furnished with all the helps to advance us to that which is indeed *the end of our faith, the salvation of our souls.* Here we have the rules of holy obedience, and the methods of repentance and reconciliation for past sins, clearly set before us : we believe all that doctrine which Christ and his apostles delivered, and the primitive church received : we have the comfort of all those sacraments which Christ instituted, and in the same manner that he appointed them : all the helps to devotion that the gospel offers are in every one's hand. So what can it be that should so extravagantly seduce any who have been bred up in a church so well constituted, unless a blind superstition in their temper, or a desire to get heaven in some easier method than Christ has appointed, do strangely impose on their understandings, or corrupt their minds. Indeed the thing is so unaccountable, that it looks like a curse from Heaven on those who are given up to it for their other sins ; for an ordinary measure of infatuation cannot' carry any one so far in folly. And it may be laid down for a certain maxim, that such as leave us have never had a true and well formed notion of religion, or of Christianity in its main and chief design ; but take things in parcels, and without examining them suffer themselves to be carried away by some prejudices which only darken weaker judgments.

But if it is an high and unaccountable folly for any to forsake our communion, and go over to those of Rome, it is at the same time an inexcusable weakness in others, who seem full of zeal against popery, and yet upon some inconsiderable objections do depart from the unity of this body, and form separated assemblies and communions, though they cannot object any thing material either to our doctrine or worship. But the most astonishing part of the wonder is, that in such differences there should be so little mutual forbearance or gentleness to be found ; and that these should raise such heats as if the substance of religion were concerned in them. This is of God, and is a stroke from Heaven on both sides for their other sins : we of the church communion have trusted too much to the supports we receive from the law, we have done our duties too slightly, and have minded the care of souls too little ; therefore God, to punish and awaken us, has suffered so many of our people to be wrested out of our hands : and those of the separation have been too forward to blood and war, and thereby have drawn much guilt on themselves, and have been too compliant with the leaders of their several factions, or rather apt to outrun them. It is plain, God is offended with us all, and therefore we are punished with this fatal blindness, not to see at this time the things that belong to our peace.

And this leads me to reflections of another sort, with which I shall conclude this preface, which I have now drawn out to a greater length than at first I intended. It is apparent, the wrath of God hangs over our heads, and is ready to break out upon us. The symptoms of our ill condition are as sad as they are visible: and one of the worst is, that each sort and party is very ready to throw the guilt of it off themselves, and cast it on others, with whom they are displeased; but no man says, *What have I done?* The clergy accuse the laity, and the laity condemn the clergy; those in the city charge the country, and the country complains of the city: every one finds out somewhat wherein he thinks he is least concerned, and is willing to fix on that all the indignation of Heaven; which, God knows, we ourselves have kindled against ourselves. It cannot be denied, since it is so visible, that universally the whole nation is corrupted, and that the gospel has not had those effects among us which might have been expected, after so long and so free a course as it has had in this island. Our wise and worthy progenitors reformed our doctrine and worship; but we have not reformed our lives and manners: what will it avail us to understand the right methods of worshipping God, if we are without true devotion, and coldly perform public offices, without sense and affection; which is as bad as a beadroll of prayers, in whatever language they be pronounced? What signifies our having the sacraments purely administered among us, if we either contemptuously neglect them, or irreverently handle them, more perhaps in compliance with law, than out of a sense of the holy duties incumbent on us? For what end are the scriptures put in our hands, if we do not read them with great attention, and order our lives according to them? And what does all preaching signify, if men go to church merely for form, and hear sermons only as set discourses, which they will censure or commend as they think they see cause; but are resolved never to be the better for them? If to all these sad considerations we add the gross sensuality and impurity, that is so avowedly practised that it is become a fashion, so far is it from being a reproach; the oppression, injustice, intemperance, and many other immoralities among us; what can be expected, but that these abominations receiving the highest aggravation they are capable of from the clear light of the gospel which we have so long enjoyed, the just judgments of Heaven should fall on us so signally, as to make us a reproach to all our neighbours? But as if all this were not enough to fill up the measure of our iniquities, many have arrived at a new pitch of impiety, by defying Heaven itself with their avowed blasphemies and atheism: and if they are driven out of their atheistical tenets, which are indeed the most ridiculous of any in the world, they set up their rest on some general notions of morality and natural religion, and do boldly reject all that is revealed; and, where they dare vent it, (alas! where dare they not do it?) they reject Christianity and the scriptures with open and impudent scorn, and are absolutely insensible of any obligation of conscience in any thing whatsoever: and even in that morality which they for decency's sake magnify so much, none are more barefacedly and grossly faulty. This is a direct attempt against God himself; and can we think that he will not visit for such things, nor be avenged on such a nation? And yet the hypocrisy of those who disguise their flagitious lives with a mask of religion is perhaps a degree above all; though not so scandalous till the mask falls off, and that they appear to be what they truly are. When we are all so guilty, and when we are so alarmed by the black clouds that threaten such terrible and lasting storms, what may be expected but that we should be generally struck with a deep sense of our crying sins, and turn to God with our whole souls? But if, after all the loud awakenings from Heaven, we will not hearken to that voice, but will still go on in our sins, we may justly look for unheard-of calamities, and such miseries as shall be proportioned to our offences; and then we are sure they will be great and wonderful.

Yet if, on the other hand, there were a general turning to God, or at least if so many were rightly sensible of this, as, according to the proportion that the mercies of God allow, did some way balance the wickedness of the rest; and if these were as zealous in the true methods of imploring God's favour, as others are in procuring his displeasure, and were not only mourning for their own sins, but for the sins of others; the prayers and sighs of many such might dissipate that dismal cloud which our sins have gathered, and we might yet hope to see the gospel take root among us: since that God, who is the Author of it, is merciful, and full of compassion, and ready to forgive; and this holy religion, which by his grace is planted among us, is still so dear to him, that if we by our own unworthiness do not render ourselves incapable of so great a blessing, we may reasonably hope that he will continue that which at first was by so many happy concurring providences brought in, and was by a continued series of the same indulgent care advanced by degrees, and at last raised to that pitch of perfection which few things attain in this world. But this will best appear in the ensuing History, from which I fear I may have too long detained the reader.

September 10, 1680.

according to the proportion that the mercies of God allow, did some way balance the wickedness of the rest; and if these were as zealous in the true methods of imploring God's favour, as others are in procuring his displeasure, and were not only mourning for their own sins, but for the sins of others; the prayers and sighs of many such might dissipate that dismal cloud which our sins have gathered, and we might yet hope to see the gospel take root among us: since that God, who is the Author of it, is merciful, and full of compassion, and ready to forgive; and this holy religion, which by his grace is planted among us, is still so dear to him, that if we by our own unworthiness do not render ourselves incapable of so great a blessing, we may reasonably hope that he will continue that which at first was by so many happy concurring providences brought in, and was by a continued series of the same indulgent care advanced by degrees, and at last raised to that pitch of perfection which few things attain in this world. But this will best appear in the ensuing History, from which I fear I may have too long detained the reader.

September 10, 1680.

THE HISTORY

OF

THE REFORMATION

OF

THE CHURCH OF ENGLAND.

PART II.—BOOK I.

Of the Life and Reign of King Edward the Sixth.

EDWARD, the sixth king of England of that name, was the only son of king Henry the Eighth, by his best beloved queen Jane Seymour, or St. Maur, daughter to sir John Seymour, who was descended from Roger St. Maur, that married one of the daughters and heirs of the lord Beauchamp of Hache. Their ancestors came into England with William the Conqueror, and had at several-times made themselves considerable by the noble acts they did in the wars. He was born at Hampton-Court on the twelfth day of October, being St. Edward's eve in the year 1537, and lost his mother the day[1] after

Edw. VI. born, Oct. 12, 1537.

---

[1] Yourself say Two days after in the Appendix of tom. i. p. 295. His journal says a few days after. [G]

The king's journal, printed by your lordship, says, 'within few days after the birth of her son, died.' George Lilly, who lived at the same time, and near the place—*Duodecimo post die moritur.*— Chron. And so the continuation of Fabian, October 23. These seem to be the

best authorities. [B]

Queen Jane died the 24th of October, in a journal written by Cecil, that was in twelve days after King Edward's birth. So it is in the Herald's Office. [S]

[The 12th of October in 1537 fell on a Friday. A letter printed in State Papers, i. 572, dated 'this Wednesday mornyng,' speaks of the Queen's confessor ' preparing to ministre to

[Hayward, p. 273 from Sanders.] he was born[2]; who died, not by the cruelty of the chirurgeons ripping up her belly to make way for the prince's birth, (as some writers gave out, to represent king Henry barbarous and cruel in all his actions; whose report has been since too easily followed;) but, as the original letters that are yet extant, shew, she was well delivered of him, and the day following was taken with a distemper incident to women in that condition, of which she died.

And christened. He was soon after christened; the archbishop of Canterbury, and the dukes of Norfolk and Suffolk[3], being his godfathers, [Hall, p. 825.] according to his own journal; though Hall says, the last was only his godfather when he was bishopped. He continued [Hayward, p. 274.] under the charge and care of the women till he was six years old; and then he was put under the government of Dr. Cox and Mr. Cheke: the one was to be his preceptor for his manners, and the knowledge of philosophy and divinity; the other for the tongues and mathematics. And he was also provided with masters for the French, and all other things becoming a prince, the heir of so great a crown.

His disposition. He gave very early many indications of a good disposition to learning, and of a most wonderful probity of mind; and, above all, of great respect to religion, and every thing relating

her grace the sacrament of unction. There can be no doubt this was Wednesday Oct. 24. And the following extract from a contemporary diary is conclusive: ' On Saynte Edwardes eve Fryday in the mornyng, was prince Edward boorn, the trew son of K. H. the viii. and quene Jane his mothur in Hamton Corte. His godffathurs was the deuke of Norfock, and the deuke of Suffocke, and the Bisschop of Caunterbery; and his godmothur was his owne sister, which was dooughter of quene Kataryn a fore sayd. On Saynte Crispyns 'eve Wensday, dyid quene Jane in childbed, and is beryid in the castelle of Wynsor.'
      Extract from p. 11. of the London Chronicle during the reigne of Henry the Seventh and Henry the Eighth—printed for the Camden Society, 1859, from Cotton MSS. Vesp. A. xxv. fol. 38–46.]

[2] The queen died on the 14th, say Hall [p. 825], Stow [p. 575], Speed [p. 1039], and Herbert [p. 492], [and Holinshed, p. 944]; on the 15th, saith Henninges, [Theatrum Genealogicum, tom. 4. par. 3. p. 105]; on the 17th, if the letter of the physicians be true, in Fuller's Church Hist. [lib. 7] p. 422. Cotton. Libr. [Nero C. x. fol. 2.]
      It was copied from its original in the Cotton Library, and yourself gave credit to them in the forecited place of your Appendix. [part i. p. 295. G]

[3] The Duke of Suffolk was godfather at his confirmation, not at his baptism. [S]

to it. So that, when he was once in one of his childish diver- [Fuller, vii. 424.] sions, somewhat being to be reached at, that he and his companions were too low for, one of them laid on the floor a great Bible that was in the room to step on; which he beholding with indignation, took up the Bible himself, and gave over his play for that time. He was in all things subject to the orders laid down for his education, and profited so much in learning, that all about him conceived great hopes of extraordinary things from him, if he should live: but such unusual beginnings seemed rather to threaten the too early end of a life, that by all appearance was likely to have produced such astonishing things. He was so forward in his learning, that, before he was [Cotton MSS. Nero. C. x. fol. 1, sqq. and Fuller, vii. 423.] eight years old, he wrote Latin letters to his father, who was a prince of that stern severity, that one can hardly think those about his son durst cheat him by making letters for him. He used also at that age to write both to his godfather the archbishop of Canterbury, and to his uncle, who was first made viscount Beauchamp, as descended from that family, and soon after earl of Hertford. It seems queen Catharine Parr understood Latin, for he wrote to her also in the same language. But the full character of this young prince is given us by Car- [Ibid.] dan, who writ it after his death, and in Italy, where this prince was accounted an heretic; so that there was nothing to be got or expected by flattering him: and yet it is so great, and withal so agreeing in all things to truth, that, as I shall begin my Collection of Papers at the end of this volume with his Collect. Numb. 1. words in Latin, so it will be very fit to give them here in English.

" All the graces were in him. He had many tongues when Cardan's character of him. " he was yet but a child: together with the English, his na- " tural tongue, he had both Latin and French. Nor was he " ignorant, as I hear, of the Greek, Italian, and Spanish, and " perhaps some more: but for the English, French, and Latin, " he was exact in them; and apt to learn every thing. Nor " was he ignorant of logic, of the principles of natural philo- " sophy, nor of music. The sweetness of his temper was such " as became a mortal, his gravity becoming the majesty of a " king, and his disposition suitable to his high degree. In sum, " that child was so bred, had such parts, was of such expecta- " tion, that he looked like a miracle of a man. These things

" are not spoken rhetorically, and beyond the truth, but are
" indeed short of it." And afterwards he adds, " He was a
" marvellous boy. When I was with him, he was in the fif-
" teenth year of his age, in which he spake Latin as politely
" and as promptly as I did : he asked me what was the subject
" of my books, *de Rerum Varietate*, which I had dedicated to
" him. I answered, that in the first chapter I gave the true
" cause of comets, which had been long inquired into, but was 3
" never found out before. What is it ? said he. I said, it was
" the concourse of the light of wandering stars. He answered,
" How can that be, since the stars move in different motions ?
" how comes it that the comets are not soon dissipated, or do
" not move after them according to their motions ? To this I
" answered, They do move after them, but much quicker than
" they, by reason of the different aspect, as we see in a crystal,
" or when a rainbow rebounds from the wall : for a little
" change makes a great difference of place. But the king
" said, How can that be, where there is no subject to receive
" that light, as the wall is the subject for the rainbow ? To
" this I answered, that this was as in the milky-way, or where
" many candles were lighted, the middle place where their
" shining met was white and clear. From this little taste it
" may be imagined what he was. And indeed the ingenuity
" and sweetness of his disposition had raised in all good and
" learned men the greatest expectation of him possible. He
" began to love the liberal arts before he knew them; and to
" know them before he could use them : and in him there was
" such an attempt of nature, that not only England, but the
" world, has reason to lament his being so early snatched
" away. How truly was it said of such extraordinary persons,
" that their lives are short, and seldom do they come to be
" old. He gave us an essay of virtue, though he did not live
" to give a pattern of it. When the gravity of a king was
" needful, he carried himself like an old man; and yet he was
" always affable and gentle, as became his age. He played on
" the lute : he meddled in affairs of state : and for bounty, he
" did in that emulate his father ; though he, even when he en-
" deavoured to be too good, might appear to have been bad :
" but there was no ground of suspecting any such thing in the
" son, whose mind was cultivated by the study of philosophy."

It has been said[4], in the end of his father's life, that he then A design to create him prince of Wales. designed to create him prince of Wales: for though he was called so, as the heirs of this crown are, yet he was not by a formal creation invested with that dignity. This pretence was made use of to hasten forward the attainder of the duke of Norfolk, since he had many offices for life, which the king intended to dispose of; and desired to have them speedily filled, in order to the creating of his son prince of Wales. In the mean time his father died; and the earl of Hertford and sir Anthony Browne were sent by the council to give him notice of King Henry dies. it, being then at Hertford[5], and to bring him to the Tower of London; and, having brought him to Enfield, with his sister the lady Elizabeth, they let him know of his father's death, and that he was now their king. On the thirty-first of January Jan. 31. [Hayward, 271.] the king's death was published in London, and he proclaimed king.

At the Tower, his father's executors, with the rest of the King Edward came to the Tower. privy-council, received him with the respects due to their king: so tempering their sorrow for the death of their late master, with their joy for his son's happy succeeding him, that by an excess of joy they might not seem to have forgot the one so soon, nor to bode ill to the other by an extreme grief. The first thing they did was, the opening king Henry's will: King Henry's will opened. [Rymer xv. p. 110.] by which they found, he had nominated sixteen persons to be his executors, and governors to his son, and to the kingdom, till his son was eighteen years of age. These were, the archbishop of Canterbury; the lord Wriothesley, lord chancellor;
4 the lord St. John, great master[6]; the lord Russell, lord privy seal; the earl of Hertford, lord great chamberlain; the viscount Lisle, lord admiral; Tunstall, bishop of Durham; sir Anthony Browne, master of the horse; sir William Paget, secretary of state; sir Edward North, chancellor of the court of augmentations; sir Edward Montague, lord chief justice of the common pleas; judge Bromley, sir Anthony Denny, and sir William Herbert, chief gentlemen of the privy-chamber; sir Edward Wotton, treasurer of Calais; and Dr. Wotton, dean of Canter-

4 [See part I. p. 347.]
5 [Holinshed says Hatfield. Hertford is taken from king Edward's Journal.]

6 Supply, *of the household.* [G.] [The original document has, 'of our house.' Rymer xv. 115. The council book, p. 1, has 'of the household.']

bury and York. These, or the major part of them, were to execute his will, and to administer the affairs of the kingdom. By their consent were the king and his sisters to be disposed of in marriage : but with this difference ; that it was only ordered that the king should marry by their advice ; but the two sisters were so limited in their marriage, that they were to forfeit their right of succession, if they married without their consent ; it being of far greater importance to the peace and interest of the nation who should be their husbands, if the crown did devolve on them, than who should be the king's wife.   And by the act passed in the thirty-fifth year of king Henry, he was empowered to leave the crown to them, with

[Ibid. p. 116.] what limitations he should think fit.   To the executors, the king added by his will a privy-council, who should be assisting to them.   These were, the earls of Arundel and Essex ; sir Thomas Cheyney, treasurer of the household ; sir John Gage, comptroller ;   sir Anthony Wingfield, vice-Chamberlain ;   sir William Petre, secretary of state ; sir Richard Rich, sir John Baker, sir Ralph Sadler, sir Thomas Seymour, sir Richard Southwell, and sir Edmund Peckham.   The king also ordered, that, if any of the executors should die, the survivors, without giving them a power of substituting others, should continue to administer affairs.   He also charged them to pay all his debts, and the legacies he left, and to perfect any grants he had begun, and to make good every thing that he had promised.

[Council Book, p. 3.] The will being opened, and read, all the executors, judge Bromley and the two Wottons only excepted, were present, and did resolve to execute the will in all points, and to take an oath for their faithful discharge of that trust.

Debate about choosing a protector. But it was also proposed, that, for the speedier despatch of things, and for a more certain order and direction of all affairs, there should be one chosen to be head of the rest, to whom

[Ibid. p. 5.] ambassadors and others might address themselves.   It was added, to caution this, that the person to be raised to that dignity should do nothing of any sort without the advice and consent of the greater part of the rest.   But this was opposed by the lord chancellor, who thought, that, the dignity of his office setting him next the archbishop of Canterbury, who did not much follow secular affairs, he should have the chief stroke in the government ; therefore he pressed, that they might not

depart from the king's will in any particular, neither by adding
to it nor taking from it : it was plain, the late king intended
they should. be all alike in the administration, and the raising
one to a title or degree above the rest was a great change
from what he had ordered. And whereas it was now said,
that the person to be thus nominated was to have no manner
of power over the rest, that was only to exalt him into an high
dignity with the less envy or apprehension of danger ; for it
was certain great titles always make way for high power. But
the earl of Hertford had so great a party among them, that it
was agreed to ; the lord chancellor himself consenting, when
5 he saw his opposition was without effect, that one should be
raised over the rest in title, to be called the *protector of the
king's realms, and the governor of his person.* The next
point held no long debate, who should be nominated to this
high trust ; for they unanimously agreed, that the earl of
Hertford, by reason of his nearness of blood to the king, and The earl of
the great experience he had in affairs, was the fittest person. Hertford
" So he was declared protector of the realm, and governor to [Council
" the king's person ; but with that special and express condi- Book, p. 6.]
" tion, that he should not do any act but by the advice and
" consent of the other executors, according to the will of the
" late king." Then they all went to take their oaths ; but it
was proposed, that it should be delayed till the next day, that
so they might do it upon better consideration. More was not
done that day, save that the lord chancellor was ordered to
deliver up the seals to the king, and to receive them again [Ibid. p. 7.]
from his hands ; for king Henry's seal was to be made use of,
either till a new one was made, or till the king was crowned :
he was also ordered to renew the commissions of the judges,
the justices of peace, the presidents of the north, and of Wales,
and of some other officers. This was the issue of the first
council-day under this king : in which, the so easy advancement of the earl of Hertford to so high a dignity gave great
occasion to censure ; it seeming to be a change of what king
Henry had designed [7]. But the king's great kindness to his
uncle made it pass so smoothly ; for the rest of the executors,
not being of the ancient nobility, but courtiers, were drawn in

---

[7] [E. Hertford signs before all the others on this first day.]

easily to comply with that which was so acceptable to their young king. Only the lord chancellor, who had chiefly opposed it, was to expect small favour at the new protector's hands. It was soon apparent what emulation there was between them : and the nation being then divided between those who loved the old superstition, and those who desired a more complete reformation ; the protector set himself at the head of the one, and the lord chancellor at the head of the other party.

Which is declared in council. [Ibid. p. 9.]

The next day the executors met again, and first took their oaths most solemnly for their faithful executing the will. They also ordered all those who were by the late king named privy counsellors to come into the king's presence, and there they declared to the king the choice they had made of his uncle ; who gave his assent to it. It was also signified to the lords of the

[Ibid. p. 10.]

council, who likewise with one voice gave their consent to it. And despatches were ordered to be sent to the emperor, the French king, and the regent of Flanders, giving notice of the

[Ibid. p. 11.]

king's death, and of the constitution of the council, and the nomination of the protector during the minority of their young king. All despatches were ordered to be signed only by the

[Ibid. p. 12.]

protector ; and all the temporal lords, with all the bishops about the town, were commanded to come and swear allegiance

Feb. 2.

to the king. On the second of February the protector was declared lord treasurer and earl marshal, these places having been designed for him by the late king upon the duke of Norfolk's attainder. Letters were also sent to Calais, Boulogne, Ireland, the marches of Scotland, and most of the counties of England, giving notice of the king's succession, and of the order now settled. The will was also ordered to be enrolled, and every of the executors was to have an exemplification of it 6 under the great seal : and the clerks of the council were also ordered to give to every of them an account of all things done

The bishops take out commissions for their bishoprics. [Council Book, p. 21.]

in council under their hands and seals. And the bishops were required to take out new commissions of the same form with those they had taken out in king Henry's time ; (for which, see the former part, vol. i. p. 267 ;) only with this difference, that there is no mention made of a vicar-general in these commissions, as was in the former, there being none after Cromwell advanced to that dignity. Two of these commissions are yet

extant; one taken out by Cranmer, the other taken out by
Bonner. But this was only done by reason of the present
juncture, because the bispops being generally addicted to the
former superstition, it was thought necessary to keep them
under so arbitrary a power as that subjected them to; for they
hereby held their bishoprics only during the king's pleasure,
and were to exercise them as his delegates in his name, and by
his authority. Cranmer set an example to the rest, and took out
his commission; which is in the Collection. But this was after- Collect.
wards judged too heavy a yoke; and therefore the new bishops Numb. 2.
that were made by this king were not put under it; (and so
Ridley, when made bishop of London in Bonner's room, was
not required to take out any such commission;) but they were
to hold their bishoprics during life.

There was a clause in the king's will, requiring his executors [Rymer xv.
to make good all that he had promised in any manner of ways. p. 115.]
Whereupon sir William Paget, sir Anthony Denny, and sir Book,
William Herbert were required to declare what they knew of p. 25.]
the king's intentions and promises; the former being the secre- of the new
tary whom he had trusted most, and the other two, those that many no-
attended on him in his bedchamber during his sickness; though blemen.
they were called gentlemen of the privychamber; for the service of the gentlemen of the bedchamber was not then set up.
Paget declared, that, when the evidence appeared against the
duke of Norfolk and his son the earl of Surrey, the king, who [Ibid.
used to talk oft in private with him alone, told him, that he in- p. 26.]
tended to bestow their lands liberally : and since by attainders,
and other ways, the nobility were much decayed, he intended
to create some peers ; and ordered him to write a book of such
as he thought meetest: who thereupon proposed the earl of
Hertford to be a duke; the earl of Essex to be a marquis; the
viscount Lisle to be an earl, the lords St. John, Russell, and
Wriothesley, to be earls; and sir Thomas Seymour, sir Thomas Cheyney, sir Richard Rich, sir William Willoughby, sir
Thomas Arundel, sir Edmund Sheffield, sir John St. Leger, sir
— Wymbish, sir — Vernon of the Peak, and sir Christopher
Danby, to be barons. Paget also proposed a distribution of [Ibid.
the duke of Norfolk's estate. But the king liked it not, and p. 27.]
made Mr. Gates bring him the books of that estate; which being
done, he ordered Paget *to tot upon my lord of Hertford's head*

(these are the words of his deposition) a thousand marks; on the lord Lisle, St. John, and Russell, 200*l.* a year; to the lord Wriothesley 100*l.* and for sir Thomas Seymour 300*l.* a year. But Paget said it was too little; and stood long arguing it with him: yet the king ordered him to propose it to the persons concerned, and see how they liked it. And he putting the king in mind of Denny, who had been oft a suitor for him, but he had never yet in lieu of that obtained any thing for Denny, the king ordered 200*l.* for him, and four hundred marks for 7 sir William Herbert; and remembered some others likewise.

[Ibid. p. 28.]

But Paget having, according to the king's commands, spoken to these who were to be advanced, found that many of them desired to continue in their former ranks, and thought the lands the king intended to give were not sufficient for the maintenance of the honour to be conferred on them: which he reported to the best advantage he could for every man, and endeavoured to raise the king's favour to them as high as he could. But while this was in consultation, the duke of Norfolk, very prudently apprehending the ruin of his posterity if his lands were divided into many hands, out of which he could not so easily recover them; whereas, if they continued in the crown, some turn of affairs might again establish his family; and intending also to oblige the king by so unusual a compliment, sent a desire to him, that he would be pleased to settle all his lands on the prince, (the now king,) and not give them away: for, said he, according to the phrase of that time, *they are goodly and stately gear.* This wrought so far on the king, that he resolved to reserve them for himself, and to reward his servants some other way. Whereupon Paget pressed him once to resolve on the honours he would bestow, and what he would give with them, and they should afterwards consider of the way how to give it. The king growing still worse, said to him, "that, if aught came to him but good, as he thought " he could not long endure, he intended to place them all about " his son, as men whom he trusted and loved above all other: " and that therefore he would consider them the more." So, after many consultations, he ordered the book to be thus filled

[Ibid. p. 29.]

up: " The earl of Hertford to be earl marshal and lord trea- " surer, and to be duke of Somerset, Exeter, or Hertford; and " his son to be earl of Wiltshire, with 800*l.* a year of land, and

" 300*l.* a year out of the next bishop's land that fell void; the
" earl of Essex to be marquis of Essex; the viscount Lisle to
" be earl of Coventry; the lord Wriothesley to be earl of Win-
" chester; sir Thomas Seymour to be a baron and lord admiral;
" sir Richard Rich, sir John St. Leger, sir William Willoughby,
" sir Edmund Sheffield, and sir Christopher Danby, to be
" barons: with yearly revenues to them, and several other
" persons." And having at the suit of sir Edward North, promised to give the earl of Hertford six of the best prebends that
should fall in any cathedral, except deaneries and treasurer-
ships; at his suit he agreed, that a deanery and a treasurership should be instead of two of the six prebendaries.
And thus, all this being written as the king had ordered it, the [Ibid.
king took the book, and put it in his pocket, and gave the se- p. 30.]
cretary order to let every one know what he had determined
for them. But before these things took effect the king died:
yet, being on his death-bed put in mind of what he had promised, he ordered it to be put in his will, that his executors
should perform every thing that should appear to have been promised by him. All this Denny and Herbert confirmed; for they [Ibid.
then waited in his chamber: and when the secretary went out, p. 31.]
the king told them the substance of what had passed between
them, and made Denny read the book over again to him; whereupon Herbert observed, that the secretary had remembered all
but himself: to which the king answered, he should not forget
him; and ordered Denny to write 400*l.* a year for him. All these
8 things being thus declared upon oath, and the greatest part of
them having been formerly signified to some of them, and the
whole matter being well known and spread abroad, the executors, both out of conscience to the king's will, and for their own [Ibid.
honours, resolved to fulfil what the king had intended, but was p. 32.]
hindered by death to accomplish. But, being apprehensive both
of wars with the emperor and French king, they resolved not to
lessen the king's treasure nor revenue, nor to sell his jewels or
plate but to find some other ways to pay them; and this put
them afterwards on selling the chantry lands.

The business of Scotland was then so pressing, that Bal- The affairs
naves, who was agent for those that had shut themselves within of Scotland.
the castle of St. Andrew's, had this day 1180*l.* ordered to be [Council
Book,
carried to them for an half year's pay to the soldiers of that p. 17.]

[Ibid.
p. 19.]

Feb. 6,
1547.
the king
knighted.
[Stow, p.
593.]
[Council
Book,
p. 22.]

garrison : there were also pensions appointed for the most leading men in that business. The earl of Rothes' eldest son had 280*l.*, sir James Kircaldy had 200*l.*, and many others had smaller pensions allowed them, *for their amity*, as it is expressed in the council-books. That day the lord protector knighted the king, being authorized to do it by letters patents. So it seems, that as the laws of chivalry required that the king should receive knighthood from the hand of some other knight; so it was judged too great a presumption for his own subject to give it, without a warrant under the great seal. The king at the same time knighted sir John Hublethorn, the lord mayor of London. When it was known abroad what a distribution of honour and wealth the council had resolved on, it was much censured: many saying, that it was not enough for them to have drained the dead king of all his treasure, but that the first step of their proceedings in their new trust was to provide honour and estates for themselves: whereas it had been a more decent way for them to have reserved their pretensions till the king had come to be of age. Another thing in the attestations seemed much to lessen the credit of the king's will, which was said to be signed the thirtieth of December, and so did bear date: whereas this narration insinuates, that it was made a very little while before he died, not being able to accomplish his design in these things which he had projected: but it was well known that he was not so ill on the thirtieth of December.

Secular
men had
their eccle-
siastical
dignities.

It may perhaps seem strange, that the earl of Hertford had six good prebends promised him; two of these being afterwards converted into a deanery and a treasurership. But it was ordinary at that time. The lord Cromwell had been dean of Wells; and many other secular men had these ecclesiastical benefices without cure conferred on them. For which, there being no charge of souls annexed to them, this might seem to be an excuse. Yet even those had a sacred charge incumbent on them in the cathedrals; and were just and necessary encouragements, either for such as by age, or other defects, were not fit for a parochial charge, and yet might be otherwise capable to do eminent service in the church; or for the support of such as in their parochial labours did serve so well as to merit preferment, and yet perhaps were so meanly provided

for, as to need some further help for their subsistence. But
certainly they were never intended for the enriching of such
lazy and sensual men, who, having given themselves up to a
secular course of life, had little of a churchman but the habit
and name; and yet used to rail against sacrilege in others,
9 not considering how guilty themselves were of the same crime,
enriching their families with the spoils of the church, or with
the goods of it, which were put into their hands for better
uses. And it was no wonder, that, when clergymen had thus
abused these endowments, secular men broke in upon them;
observing plainly, that the clergy who enjoyed them made no
better use of them than laics might do: though, instead of
reforming an abuse that was so generally spread, they, like
men that minded nothing more than the enriching of themselves, took a certain course to make the mischief perpetual,
by robbing the church of those endowments and helps it had
received from the munificence of the founders of its cathedrals,
who were generally the first Christian kings of this nation;
which, had it been done by law, would have been a thing of
very bad consequence; but as it was done, was directly contrary to the *magna charta*, and to the king's coronation oath.

But now they that were weary of the popish superstitions,
observing that archbishop Cranmer had so great a share of the
young king's affection, and that the protector and he were in
the same interests, began to call for a further reformation of
religion, and some were so full of zeal for it, that they would
not wait on the slow motions of the state. So the curate and
churchwardens of St. Martin's in Ironmonger-lane, in London,
took down the images and pictures of the saints, and the crucifix, out of their church, and painted many texts of scripture
upon the walls; some of them *according to a perverse translation*, as the complaint has it: and in the place where the crucifix was, they set up the king's arms, with some texts of scripture about it.   Upon this, the bishop and lord mayor of London complained to the council. And the curate and churchwardens being cited to appear, answered for themselves, that
the roof of their church being bad, they had taken it down;
and that the crucifix and images were so rotten, that, when
they removed them, they fell to powder: that the charge they
had been at in repairing their church was such, that they could

Images removed without authority out of one church in London. [Council Book, p. 40.]

not buy new images: that they had taken down the images in the chancel, because some had been guilty of idolatry towards them. In conclusion, they said, what they had done was with a good intention; and if they had in any thing done amiss, they asked pardon, and submitted themselves. Some were for punishing them severely: for all the papists reckoned, that this would be a leading case to all the rest of this reign: and if this was easily passed over, others would be, from that remissness, animated to attempt such things every where. But on the other hand, those at court, who had designed to set forward a reformation, had a mind only so far to check the heat of the people, as to keep it within compass, but not to dishearten their friends too much. Cranmer and his party were for a general removing of all images; and said, that in the late king's time, order being given to remove such as were abused to superstition; upon that, there were great contests in many places, what images had been so abused, and what not; and that these disputes would be endless, unless all were taken away.

An account of the progress of image-worship. [A.D. 277.]   In the purest times of Christianity they had no images at all in their churches. One of the first councils, namely, that at Elvira in Spain, made a canon against the painting what they worshipped on the walls. Epiphanius was highly offended when he saw a veil hanging before the door of a church, with a picture on it; which he considered so little, as not to know 10 well whose picture it was, but thought it might be Christ's, or some other saint's; yet he tore it, and gave them of that place money to buy a new veil in its room. Afterwards, with the rest of the pomp of heathenism, images came to be set up in churches; yet so as that there was no sort of worship paid to [Fox, lib. ix. p. 71.] them. But, in the time of pope Gregory the First, many went into extremes about them; some were for breaking them, and others worshipped them. That pope thought the middle way best; neither to break, nor to worship them; but to keep them only to put the people in mind of the saints. Afterwards, there being subtle questions started about the unity of Christ's person and will, the Greek emperors generally inclined to have the animosities raised by these removed by some comprehensive words, to which all might consent; which the interest of state, as well as religion, seemed to require: for their empire every day declining, all methods for uniting it were thought good and prudent. But the bishops were stiff and peremptory: so, in the sixth general council, they condemned all who dif- [A.D. 680.] fered from them. Upon this, the emperors that succeeded would not receive that council; but the bishops of Rome ordered the pictures of all the bishops, who had been at that council, to be set up in the churches : upon which the emperors contended against these, or any pictures whatsoever in churches. And herein that happened which is not unusual; that one controversy rising occasionally out of another, the parties forsake the first contest, and fall into sharp conflicts about the occasional differences. For now the emperors and popes quarrelled most violently about the use of images; and ill names going a great way towards the defaming an opinion, the popes and their party accused all that were against images as favouring Judaism, or Mahometanism, which was then much spread in Asia and Africa : the emperors and their party accusing the others of Gentilism and heathenish idolatry. Upon [Fox, vol. i. this occasion, Gregory III. first assumed the rebellious preten- p. 143.] sion to a power to depose Leo the emperor from all his dominions in Italy. There was one general council at Constanti- [A.D. 786.] nople, that condemned the use or worship of images; and, soon after, another at Nice did establish it. And yet, at the [A.D. 787.] same time, Charles the Great, though not a little linked in interest to the bishops of Rome, holding both the French and imperial crowns by the favour of the popes, wrote, or employed Alcuinus (a most learned countryman of ours, as these times went) to write in his name, against the worship of images. And in a council at Frankfort it was condemned; which was [A.D. 794.] also done afterwards in another council at Paris. But, in such [A.D. 825.] ages of ignorance and superstition, any thing that wrought so [Fox, lib. much on the senses and imaginations of the people, was sure ix. p. 71.] to prevail in conclusion. And this had, in a course of seven more ages, been improved (by the craft and impostures of the monks) so wonderfully, that there was no sign of divine adoration that could be invented, that was not applied to these images. So in king Henry's time that temper was found, that such images as had been abused to superstition should be removed; and for other images, external worship (such as kneeling, censing, and praying before them) was kept up; but the people were to be taught, that these were not at all intended to the image, but to that which was represented by it. And upon this there was much subtle arguing. Among Cranmer's papers, I have seen several arguments for a moderate use of 11 images. But to all these they opposed the second Commandment, as plainly forbidding all visible objects of adoration, together with what was in the scriptures against the idolatry of the heathens, and what the fathers had written against the gentiles. And they added, that how excusable soever that practice might have been in such dark and barbarous ages, in which the people knew little more of divine matters than what they learned from their images; yet the horrible abuses that followed, on the bringing them into churches, made it necessary now to throw them all out. It was notorious, that the people every where doted on them, and gave them divine honour. Nor did the clergy, who were generally too guilty themselves of such abuses, teach them how to distinguish aright: and the acts of worship, that were allowed, were such, that, beside the scandal such worship had in it, and the danger of drawing people into idolatry, it was in itself inexcusable to offer up such external parts of religious adoration to gold or silver, wood or stone. So Cranmer and others, being resolved to purge the church of this abuse, got the worst part of the sentence, that some had designed against the curate and churchwardens, to be mitigated into a reprimand; and, as it is entered in the council-books, "In respect of their submission, and of some " other reasons, which did mitigate their offence," (these were Cranmer's arguments against images,) "they did pardon their " imprisonment, which was at first determined; and ordered " them to provide a crucifix, or at least some painting of it, " till one were ready; and to beware of such rashness for the " future." But no mention is made of the other images.

Many begin to pull down images;

The carriage of the council in this matter discovering the inclinations of the greatest part of them, and Dr. Ridley having in his Lent sermon preached against the superstition that was generally had to images and holy water, it raised a great heat over England: so that Gardiner, hearing that on May-day the people of Portsmouth had removed and broken the images of Christ and the saints, writ about it, with great warmth, to one captain Vaughan, that waited on the protector, and was then

At which Gardiner is much offended.
[Fox, lib. ix. p. 54.]

at Portsmouth. " He desired to know whether he should send
" one to preach against it; though he thought that was the cast-
" ing precious stones to hogs, or worse than hogs, as were these
" Lollards. He said, that Luther had set out a book against
" those who removed images, and himself had seen them still
" in the Lutheran churches: and he thought the removing
" images was on design to subvert religion and the state of the
" world : he argues for them from the king's image on the
" seal, Cæsar's image on the coin brought to Christ, the king's
" arms carried by the heralds : he condemns false images : but
" for those that were against true images, he thought they
" were possessed with the Devil."   Vaughan sent his letter to
the protector, with one from Gardiner to himself; who, finding
the reasoning in it not so strong but that it might be answered,
wrote to him himself, " that he allowed of his zeal against in- The pro-
" novations, but that there were other things that needed to tector writ
" be looked to as much.   Great difference there was between about it.
" the civil respect due to the king's arms, and the worship
" given to images.   There had been a time, in which the abuse The letters
" of the scriptures was thought a good reason to take them are in
" from the people ; yea, and to burn them : though he looked and Monu-
" on them as more sacred than images; which, if they stood ments.
12 " merely as remembrancers, he thought the hurt was not [p. 55 sqq.]
" great : but it was known that for the most part it was other-
" wise : and upon abuse the brazen serpent was broken, though
" made at God's commandment: and it being pretended that
" they were *the books of the people,* he thought the Bible a
" much more intelligible and useful book.   There were some
" too rash, and others too obstinate : the magistrate was to
" steer a middle course between them ; not considering the
" antiquity of things so much as what was good and expe-
" dient."   Gardiner writ again to the protector, " complaining [Ibid. p.
" of Bale and others, who published books to the dishonour of 56.]
" the late king; and that all were running after novelties ;
" and often inculcates it, that things should be kept in the
" state they were in till the king were of age : and in his letters
" reflects both on the archbishop of Canterbury and the bishop
" of Durham for consenting to such things."

But, finding his letters had no effect on the protector, he Gardiner
wrote to Ridley, " that by the law of Moses we were no more writ to
Ridley,

BURNET, PART II.   E

who had
preached
against
images.
[ibid. p.
71.]

" bound not to have images than not to eat blood-puddings.
" Image and idol might have been used promiscuously in
" former times, as king and tyrant were; yet there was a
" great difference between these, according to the notions we
" now have. He cites pope Gregory, who was against both
" adoring and breaking them: and says, the worship is not
" given to the image, so there is no idolatry; but to him re-
" presented by it: and as the sound of speech did by the ear
" beget notions in us, so he did not see but the sight of an
" image might stir up devotion. He confessed there had been
" abuses, as there is in every thing that is in men's hands: he
" thinks imagery and graving to be of as good use for instruc-
" tion, as writing or printing: and, because Ridley had also
" preached against the superstition of holy water to drive
" away devils, he added, that a virtue might be in water as
" well as in Christ's garment, St. Peter's shadow, or Elisha's

[Ibid. p.
72.]

" staff. Pope Marcellus ordered Equitius to use it: and the
" late king used to bless cramp-rings, both of gold and silver,
" which were much esteemed every where; and when he was
" abroad, they were often desired from him. This gift he
" hoped the young king would not neglect. He believed the
" invocation of the name of God might give such a virtue to

[Ibid. p.
73.]

" holy water as well as to the water of baptism." For Ridley's
answer to this, I never saw it; so these things must here pass
without any reply: though it is very probable an ordinary
reader will, with a very small measure of common sense and
learning, see how they might have been answered. The thing
most remarkable here is about these cramp-rings, which king
Henry used to bless, of which I never met with any thing be-

[Part ii. p.
321. and
Records, p.
294, 5.]

fore I saw this letter: but since I understand the office of
blessing of these rings is extant, as it was prepared for queen
Mary's use, as shall be told in her reign; it must be left to
conjecture, whether he did it as a practice of former kings, or
whether, upon his being made supreme head, he thought fit to
take on him, as the pope did, to consecrate such things, and
send them about: where, to be sure, fancy and flattery would
raise many stories of the wonderful effects of what he had so
blessed; and perhaps these might have been as true as the
reports made of the virtues of Agnus Dei's, touched beads,
blessed pebbles, with such other goodly ware, which the friars

are wont to carry about, and distribute to their benefactors, as
13 things highly sanctified. This I set down more fully, and have
laid some things together that fell not out till some months
after this, being the first step that was made towards a reformation in this reign.

Upon this occasion, it is not unlikely that the council wrote
their letters to all the justices of peace of England, on the
twelfth of February, letting them know, that they had sent
down new commissions to them for keeping the peace: ordering
them to assemble together, and first to call earnestly on God
for his grace to discharge their duties faithfully, according to
the oaths which they were to take; and that they should impartially, without corruption or sinister affection, execute their
office, so that it might appear that they had God, and the good
of their king and country, before their eyes; and that they
should divide themselves into the several hundreds, and see to
the public peace; and that all vagabonds and disturbers of the
peace should be duly punished; and that once every six weeks
they should write to the lord protector and council, the state
in which the county was, till they were otherwise commanded.
That which was sent into the county of Norfolk will be found
in the Collection.

Feb. 12,
1547.
The com-
mission of
the justices
of the
peace.
[Council
Book,
p. 46.]

Collect.
Numb. 3.

But now the funeral of the deceased king, and the coronation of his son, were to be despatched. In the coronation ceremonies that had been formerly used, there were some things
that did not agree with the present laws of the land; as the
promise made to the abbots for maintaining their lands and
dignities: they were also so tedious, that a new form was ordered to be drawn, which the reader will find in the Collection.
The most material thing in it is the first ceremony, whereby
the king being shewed to the people at the four corners of the
stage, the archbishop was to demand their consent to it; and
yet in such terms as should demonstrate he was no elective
prince: "for he being declared the rightful and undoubted
" heir both by the laws of God and man, they were desired to
" give their good-wills and assents to the same, as by their
" duty of allegiance they were bound to do." This being
agreed on the thirteenth of February, on the day following
king Henry's body was, with all the pomp of a royal funeral,

Collect.
Numb.

Feb. 13,
1547.
King Hen-
ry buried.

[Hayward, p. 271.] removed to Shene[8], in the way to Windsor.   There great observation was made on a thing that was no extraordinary matter : he had been extreme corpulent, and, dying of a dropsy, or something like it, it was no wonder if a fortnight after, upon so long a motion, some putrid matter might run through the coffin.   But Shene[9] having been a house of religious women, it was called a signal mark of the displeasure of Heaven, that some of his blood and fat dropped through the lead in the night : and, to make this work mightily on weak people, it was said, that the dogs licked it next morning.   This was much magnified in commendation of friar Peto, afterwards made cardinal, who (as was told, p.151 of the former part,) had threatened him, in a sermon at Greenwich, *that the dogs should lick his blood :* though, to consider things more equally, it had been a wonder indeed if it had been otherwise.   But having met with this observation in a manuscript written near that

[Feb. 15.] time, I would not envy the world the pleasure of it.   Next day
[Feb. 16.] he was brought to Windsor, and interred in St. George's chapel.   And he having by his will left that church 600*l.* a year for ever, for two priests to say mass at his tomb daily, for four obits yearly, and a sermon at every obit, with 10*l.* to the poor, 14 and for a sermon every Sunday, together with the maintenance of thirteen poor knights ; the judges were consulted how this should be well settled in law : who advised, that the lands, which the king had given, should be made over to that college by indentures tripartite ; the king being one party ; the protector, and the other executors, a second ; and the dean and chapter of Windsor, a third party.   These were to be signed with the king's hand, and the great seal put to them, with the hands and seals of all the rest : and then patents were to be given for the lands, founded on the king's testament, and the indentures tripartite.

Soul-masses examined.   But the pomp of this business ministered an occasion of inquiring into the use and lawfulness of soul-masses and obits, which came to be among the first things that were reformed. Christ had instituted the sacrament to be celebrated in remem-

---

[8] For Shene read Syon. [S.]   Syon was a nunnery.   (Ibid. p. 29.)
[9] [Shene was a monastery. Vide   The author copies the mistake from
Dugdale's Monasticon, vi. 540.—   Hayward, p. 271.]

brance of his death, and it was a sacrament only to those who
did participate in it : but that the consecrating the sacrament
could be of any use to departed souls, seemed a thing not easy
to be conceived; for if they are the prayers of the living that
profit the dead, then these would have done as well without a
mass.   But the people would not have esteemed bare prayers
so much, nor have paid so dear for them : so that the true
original of soul-masses was thought to have been only to increase the esteem and wealth of the clergy.   It is true, in the
primitive church there was a commemoration of the saints departed in the *daily sacrifice;* so they termed the communion ;
and such as had given any offence at their death were not remembered in it : so that for so slight an offence as the leaving
a priest tutor to one's children, which might distract them from
their spiritual care, one's name was to be left out of that commemoration in Cyprian's time ; which was a very disproportioned punishment to that offence, if such commemorations had
been thought useful or necessary to the souls departed.   But
all this was nothing to the private masses for them, and was
indeed nothing at first but an honourable mention of such as
had died in the faith.   And they believing then generally that
there was a glorious thousand years to be on earth, and that
the saints should rise, some sooner, and some later, to have
their part in it; they prayed in general for their quiet rest,
and their speedy resurrection.   Yet these prayers growing, as
all superstitious devices do, to be more considered, some began
to frame an hypothesis to justify them by; that of the thousand years being generally exploded.   And in St. Austin's time
they began to fancy there was a state of punishment, even for
the good, in another life; out of which, some were sooner, and
some later freed, according to the measure of their repentance
for their sins in this life.   But he tells us, this was taken up
without any sure ground; and that it was no way certain.   Yet
by visions, dreams, and tales, the belief of it was so far promoted, that it came to be generally received in the next age
after him: and then, as the people were told that the saints in-
terceded for them, so it was added, that they might intercede
for their departed friends.   And this was the foundation of all
that trade of soul-masses and obits.   Now the deceased king
had acted like one who did not believe that these things signi-

fied much ; otherwise, he was to have but ill reception in purgatory, having by the subversion of the monasteries deprived
the departed souls of the benefit of the many masses that were 15
said for them in these houses: yet it seems at his death he
would make the matter sure ; and, to shew he intended as
much benefit to the living, as to himself being dead, he took
care that there should be not only masses and obits, but so
many sermons at Windsor, and a frequent distribution of alms
for the relief of the poor.   But upon this occasion it came to
be examined, what value there was in such things.   Yet the
archbishop plainly saw that the lord chancellor would give
great opposition to every motion that should be made for any
further alteration, for which he, and all that party, had this
specious pretence always in their mouths ; that their late glorious king was not only the most learned prince, but the most
learned divine in the world; (for the flattering him did not end
with his life ;) and that therefore they were at least to keep all
things in the condition wherein he had left them, till the king
were of age.   And this seemed also necessary on considerations
of state : for changes in matter of religion might bring on commotions and disorders, which they, as faithful executors, ought
to avoid.   But to this it was answered, that as their late king
was infinitely learned, (for both parties flattered him dead as
well as living,) so he had resolved to make great alterations,
and was contriving how to change the mass into a communion:
that therefore they were not to put off a thing of such consequence, wherein the salvation of people's souls was so much
concerned, but were immediately to set about it.   But the lord
chancellor gave quickly great advantage against himself to his
enemies, who were resolved to make use of any error he might
be guilty of, so far as to ease themselves of the trouble he was
like to give them.

The crea-
tion of
peers.

The king's funeral being over, order was given for the
creation of peers.   The protector was to be duke of Somerset ;
the earl of Essex to be marquis of Northampton ; the viscount
Lisle to be earl of Warwick; the lord Wriothesley earl of
Southampton ; besides the new creation of the lords Seymour,
Rich, Willoughby of Parham, and Sheffield : the rest it seems
excusing themselves from new honours, as it appeared from
the deposition of Paget, that many of those, on whom the late

king had intended to confer titles of honour, had declined it
formerly.   On the twentieth of February, being Shrove- Feb. 20,
Sunday, the king was crowned by the archbishop of Canter- 1547. Coro-
nation.
bury, according to the form that was agreed to : the protector
serving in it as lord steward ; the marquis of Dorset as lord
constable ; and the earl of Arundel as earl marshal, deputed
by the protector.   A pardon was proclaimed, out of which the
duke of Norfolk, cardinal Pole, and some others, were excepted.

The first business of importance after the coronation was The lord
chancellor
the lord chancellor's fall : who, resolving to give himself is removed
wholly to matters of state, had on the eighteenth of February from his
office.
put the great seal to a commission, " directed to sir Richard [10] [Collect.
" Southwell, master of the rolls ; John Tregonwel, esq. master Numb. 5.]
" of chancery ; and to John Oliver, and Anthony Bellasis,
" clerks, masters of chancery ; setting forth, that the lord
" chancellor being so employed in the affairs of state that he
" could not attend on the hearing of causes in the court of
" chancery, these three masters, or any two of them, were
" empowered to execute the lord chancellor's office in that
" court in as ample manner as if he himself were present ;
" only their decrees were to be brought to the lord chancellor
" to be signed by him, before they were enrolled."   This being
16 done without any warrant from the lord protector, and the
other executors, it was judged a high presumption in the lord
chancellor thus to devolve on others that power which the law
had trusted in his hands.   The persons named by him increased the offence which this gave, two of them being canonists ; so that the common lawyers looked upon this as a precedent of very high and ill consequence : and, being encouraged
by those who had no good-will to the chancellor, they petitioned the council in this matter, and complained of the evil
consequences of such a commission ; and set forth the fears
that all the students of the law were under, of a change that
was intended to be made of the laws of England.   The council
remembered well they had given no warrant at all to the lord
chancellor for the issuing out any such commission ; so they
sent it to the judges, and required them to examine the com-

[10] For Richard read Robert [S.]   [For an explanation of this mistake,
see Part iii. p. 169.]

mission, with the petition grounded upon it: who delivered their opinions on the last of February, that the lord chancellor ought not, without warrant from the council, to have set the seal to it; and that, by his so doing, he had by the common law forfeited his place to the king, and was liable to fine and imprisonment at the king's pleasure. This lay sleeping till the

sixth of March, and then the judges' answer being brought to the council, signed with all their hands, they entered into a debate how far it ought to be punished. The lord chancellor carried it very high; and, as he had used many menaces to those who had petitioned against him, and to the judges for giving their opinions as they did, so he carried himself insolently to the protector, and told him, he held his place by a better authority than he held his: that the late king, being empowered to it by act of parliament, had made him not only chancellor, but one of the governors of the realm during his son's minority; and had by his will given none of them power over the rest to throw them out at pleasure, and that therefore they might declare the commission void if they pleased, to which he should consent; but they could not for such an error turn him out of his office, nor out of his share of the government. To this it was answered, that, by the late king's will, they, or the major part of them, were to administer till the king was of age; that this subjected every one of them in particular to the rest; that otherwise, if any of them broke out into rebellion, he might pretend he could not be attainted nor put from the government; therefore it was agreed on, that every of them in particular was subject to the greater part. Then the lord chancellor was required to shew what warrant he had for that he had done. Being now driven from that which he chiefly relied on, he answered for himself, that he had no warrant; yet he thought by his office he had power to do it; that he had no ill intention in it, and therefore

submitted himself to the king's mercy, and to the gracious consideration of the protector and the council; and desired, that, in respect of his past services, he might forego his office with as little slander as might be; and that, as to his fine and imprisonment, they would use moderation: so he was made to withdraw. "The counsellors, (as it is entered in the council-" book,) considering in their consciences his abuses sundry

" ways in his office, to the great prejudice and utter decay of
" the common laws, and the prejudice that might follow by the
" seals continuing in the hands of so stout and arrogant a [Ibid. p.
" person, who would as he pleased put the seals to such com- 103.]
17 " missions without warrant, did agree, that the seal should
" be taken from him, and he be deprived of his office, and
" be further fined, as should be afterwards thought fitting ;
" only they excused him from imprisonment." So he being
called in, and heard say all he could think of for his own
justification, they did not judge it of such importance as might
move them to change their mind. Sentence was therefore [Ibid. p.
given, that he should stay in the council-chamber and closet 104.]
till the sermon was ended; that then he should go home with
the seal to Ely House, where he lived ; but that, after supper,
the lord Seymour, sir Anthony Browne, and sir Edward North, [Ibid. p.
should be sent to him, and that he should deliver the seal into 105.]
their hands ; and be from that time deprived of his office, and
confined to his house during pleasure, and pay what fine should
be laid on him. To all which he submitted, and acknowledged
the justice of their sentence. So the next day the seal was put [March 7.
into the lord St. John's hands[11], till they should agree on a Council
fit man to be lord chancellor; and it continued with him 107.]
several months. On the day following, the late king's will [Ibid. p.
being in his hands for the granting of exemplifications of it 109.]
under the great seal, it was sent for, and ordered to be laid up
in the treasury of the exchequer : and the earl of Southampton
continued in his confinement till the twenty-ninth of June, but
then he entered into a recognizance of four thousand pounds to
pay what fine they should impose on him, and upon that he
was discharged of his imprisonment. But in all this sentence
they made no mention of his forfeiting his being one of the
late king's executors, and of the present king's governors;
either judging, that, being put in these trusts as he was lord
chancellor, the discharging him of his office did by consequence
put an end to them : or perhaps they were not willing to do
any thing that might seem to change the late king's will ; and
therefore, by keeping him under the fear of a severe fine, they

[11] 29 Junii, Sigillum magnum   Edw. 6. p. 4., Dugdale, Orig. Jurid.
Will. Paulet Militi, Domino S. Jo.   [B.]
de Basing liberatum fuit. Pat. 1.

chose rather to oblige him to be absent, and to carry himself quietly, than by any sentence to exclude him from his share in that trust.   Which I incline the rather to believe, because I find him afterwards brought to council without any order entered about it : so that he seems to have come thither rather on a former right, than on a new choice made of him.   Thus fell the lord chancellor, and in him the popish party lost their chief support, and the protector his most emulous rival.   The reader will find the commission, with the opinion of the judges

Collect.
Numb. 5.

about it, in the Collection ; from which he will be better able to judge of these proceedings against him, which were summary and severe, beyond the usage of the privy-council, and without the common forms of legal processes.   But the council's authority had been raised so high by the act mentioned, page 263 of the former part, that they were empowered sufficiently for matters of that nature.

The pro-
tector holds
his office
by patent.

That which followed a few days after made this be the more censured, since the lord protector, who hitherto held his office but by the choice of the rest, and under great restrictions, was now resolved to hold it by patent, to which the late chancellor had been unwilling to consent.   The pretence for it was, that the foreign ministers, the French ambassador in particular, desired to be satisfied concerning his power, and how far they might treat with him, and depend on the assurances and promises he gave.   So the protector and council did on the

March 13.
[Council
Book, p.
117.]

thirteenth of March petition the king, that they might act by a commission under the great seal, which might empower and justify them in what they were to do.   And that was to be 18 done in this manner : the king and the lords were to sign the warrant for it, upon which the lord St. John (who, though he had the keeping of the great seal, was never designed to be lord keeper, nor was empowered to hear causes) should set the seal to it.   The original warrant was to be kept by the protector, and exemplifications of it were to be given to foreign

[Ibid. p.
121.]

ministers.   To this order sir Thomas Cheyney set his hand ; upon what authority I do not so clearly see, since he was none of the executors.   By this commission (which will be found in

Collect.
Numb. 6.

the Collection) it is set forth, " that the king, being under age, " was desired, by divers of the nobles and prelates of the " realm, to name and authorize one above all others to have

" the charge of the kingdom, with the government of his
" person ; whereupon he had formerly by word of mouth
" named his uncle to be protector and governor of his person ;
" yet, for a more perfect declaration of that, he did now ratify
" and approve all he had done since that nomination, and con-
" stituted him his governor, and the protector of his kingdom,
" till he should attain the full age of eighteen years ; giving
" him the full authority that belonged to that office, to do
" every thing as he by his wisdom should think for the honour,
" good, and prosperity of the king and kingdom : and, that
" he might be furnished with a council for his aid and assist-
" ance, he did, by the advice of his uncle and others, nobles,
" prelates, and wise men, accept of these persons for his coun-
" sellors : the archbishop of Canterbury ; the lord St. John,
" president ; the lord Russell, lord privy-seal ; the marquis of
" Northampton, the earls of Warwick and Arundel, the lord
" Seymour, the bishop of Durham, the lord Rich, sir Thomas
" Cheyney, sir John Gage, sir Anthony Browne, sir Anthony
" Wingfield, sir William Paget, sir William Petre, sir Ralph
" Sadler, sir John Baker, doctor Wotton, sir Anthony Denny,
" sir William Herbert, sir Edward North, sir Edward Mon-
" tague, sir Edward Wotton, sir Edmund Peckham, sir Thomas
" Bromley, and sir Richard Southwell ; giving the protector
" power to swear such other commissioners as he should think
" fit : and that he, with so many of the council as he should
" think meet, might annul and change what they thought
" fitting ; restraining the council to act only by his advice and
" consent."   And thus was the protector fully settled in his
power, and no more under the curb of the coexecutors, who were
now mixed with the other counsellors, that by the late king's
will were only to be consulted with as they saw cause.   But,
as he depressed them to an equality with the rest of the counsellors, so he highly obliged the others, who had been formerly
under them, by bringing these equally with them into a share
of the government.   He had also obtained to himself an high
authority over them, since they could do nothing without his
consent ; but he was only bound to call for so many of them
as he thought meet, and was not limited to act as they advised,
but clothed with the full regal power ; and had it in his hands
to oblige whom he would, and to make his party greater by

calling into the council such as he should nominate. How far
this was legal, I shall not inquire. It was certainly contrary
to king Henry's will. And that being made upon an act
of parliament, which empowered him to limit the crown and
the government of it at his pleasure, this commission, that did
change the whole government during the king's minority,
seems capable of no other defence, but that, it being made by 19
the consent of the major part of the executors, it was still
warrantable even by the will, which devolved the government
on them, or the major part of them.

All this I have opened the more largely, both because none
of our historians have taken any notice of the first constitution
of the government during this reign, and, being ignorant of the
true account of it, they have committed great errors: and
because, having obtained, by the favour of that most industrious
collector of the transactions of this age, Mr. Rushworth, the
original council-book for the two first years of this reign, I had
a certain authority to follow in it; the exactness of that book
being beyond any thing I ever met with in all our records.
For every council-day the privy counsellors that were present
set their hands to all that was ordered: judging so great
caution necessary when the king was under age. And therefore I thought this a book of too great consequence to lie in
private hands; so, the owner having made a present of it to
me, I delivered it to that noble and virtuous gentleman sir
John Nicolas, one of the clerks of the council, to be kept with
the rest of their books.

The state
of affairs in
Germany.
[Council
Book, p.
83.]

And having now given the reader a clear prospect of the
state of the court, I shall next turn to the affairs that were
under their consideration. That which was first brought
before them was concerning the state of Germany. Francis
Burgartus, chancellor to the duke of Saxe, with others, from
the other princes and cities of the empire, were sent over, upon
the news of the former king's death, to solicit for aids from the
new king toward the carrying on the war with the emperor. In
order to the clearing of this, and to give a just account of our
councils in reference to foreign affairs, especially the cause
being about religion, I shall give a short view of the state
of Germany at this time. The emperor, having formed a
design of an universal monarchy, laid hold on the differences of

religion in Germany, as a good mean to cover what he did, with the specious pretence of punishing heresy, and protecting the catholics. But, before he had formed this design, he procured his brother to be chosen king of the Romans, and so declared his successor in the empire; which he was forced to do, being obliged to be much in Spain and his other hereditary dominions; and being then so young as not to enter into such deep counsels as he afterwards laid. But his wars in Italy put him oft in ill terms with the pope; and, being likewise watched over in all his motions by Francis the First and Henry the Eighth, and the Turk often breaking into Hungary and Germany, he was forced to great compliances with the princes of the empire; who, being animated by the two great crowns, did enter into a league for their mutual defence against all aggressors. And at last, in the year 1544, in the diet held at Spire, the emperor, being engaged in war with France and the Turk, both to secure Germany, and to obtain money of the princes, was willing to agree to the edict made there; which was, that, till there was a free council in Germany, or such an assembly in which matters of religion might be settled, there should be a general peace, and none was to be troubled for religion; the free exercise of both religions being allowed; and all things were to continue in the state they were then in. And the imperial chamber at Spire was to be reformed; for the judges of that court being all papists, there were many processes depending at the suit of the ecclesiastics against the protestant princes, who had driven them out of their lands: and the princes expecting no fair dealing from them, all these processes were now suspended, and the chamber was to be filled up with new judges, that should be more favourable to them. They obtaining this decree, contributed very liberally to the wars the emperor seemed to be engaged in : who, having his treasure thus filled, presently made peace both with France and the grand signior, and resolved to turn his wars upon the empire, and to make use of that treasure and force they had contributed, to invade their liberties, and to subdue them entirely to himself. Upon this he entered into a treaty with the pope, that a council should be opened in Trent; upon which he should require the princes to submit to it, which if they refused to do, he should

Jan. 11. 1531. Ferdinand crowned king of the Romans. [Sleidan, fol. 117.]

Feb. 20. 1544. Diet began at Spire. [Sleidan, fol. 235.]

Sept. 24. 1544. Emperor has peace with France. [ibid. fol. 243.]

Oct. 1545. Peace with the Turk.

make war on them. The pope was to assist him with ten thousand men, besides heavy taxes laid on his clergy ; to which he willingly consented. But the emperor, knowing that if religion were declared to be the ground of the war, all the protestants would unite against him, who were the much greater number of the empire, resolved to divide them among themselves, and to pretend somewhat else than religion as the cause of the war. There were then four of the electors of that religion ; the count palatine, the duke of Saxe, the marquis of Brandenburg, and the archbishop of Cologne ; besides the landgrave of Hesse, the duke of Wurtemberg, and many lesser princes, and almost all the cities of the empire. Bohemia, and the other hereditary dominions of the house of Austria, were also generally of the same religion. The northern kings and the Swiss cantons were firmly united to them : the two crowns of England and France were likewise concerned in interest to support them against the Austrian family. But the emperor got France and England engaged in a war between themselves, so that he was now at leisure to accomplish his designs on the empire ; where, some of the princes being extreme old, as the count palatine, and Herman, archbishop of Cologne ; others, being of soft and inactive tempers, as the marquis of Brandenburg ; and others discontented and ambitious, as Maurice of Saxony, and the brothers of Brandenburg ; he had indeed none of the first rank to deal with, but the duke of Saxe and the landgrave of Hesse, who were both great captains, but of such different tempers, that, where they were in equal command, there was no great probability of success. The former was a prince of the best composition of any in that age ; he was sincerely religious, and one of the most equally tempered men that was then alive, neither lifted up with success, nor cast down with misfortunes ; he had a great capacity, but was slow in his resolutions. The landgrave, on the other hand, had much more heat, was a quicker man, and of an impatient temper, on which the accidents of life made deep impressions.

When the emperor began to engage in this design, the pope, being jealous of his greatness, and desirous to entangle him in a long and expenseful war, published the secret ends of the league ; and opened the council in Trent in November 1545, where a few bishops and abbots, with his legates presiding over

them, usurped the most glorious title of *the most holy œcume-* [History
nical council, representing the catholic church.   They entered, of the
                                                                  Council
by such slow steps as were directed from Rome, into the dis- of Trent,
21 cussion of articles of doctrine; which were, as they were p. 127 sqq.]
pleased to call it, explained to them by some divines, for most
part friars, who amused the more ignorant bishops with the
nice speculations with which they had been exercised in the
schools; where hard and barbarous words served in good stead
to conceal some things not so fit to be proposed barefaced, and
in plain terms.   The emperor, having done enough towards his
design, that a council was opened in Germany, endeavoured to
keep them from determining points of doctrine, and pressed
them to examine some abuses in the government of the church,
which had at least given occasion to that great alienation of so
many from the see of Rome and the clergy.   There were also
divers wise and learned prelates, chiefly of Spain, who came
thither full of hopes of getting these abuses redressed.   Some
of them had observed, that in all times heresies and schisms did
owe their chief growth to the scandals, the ignorance, and
negligence of the clergy, which made the laity conceive an ill
opinion of them, and so disposed them, both in inclination and
interest, to cherish such as opposed them; and therefore they
designed to have many great corruptions cast out: and observing that bishops' nonresidence was a chief occasion of all
those evils, they endeavoured to have residence declared to be
of divine right; intending thereby to lessen the power of the
papacy, which was grown to that height, that they were slaves
to that see, taxed by it at pleasure, and the care of their
dioceses extorted out of their hands by the several ranks of
exempted priests : and also to raise the episcopal authority to
what it was anciently, and to cut off all these encroachments
which the see of Rome had made on them, at first by craft,
and which they still maintained by their power.   But the
court of Rome was to lose much by all reformations ; and some
cardinals openly declared, that every reformation gave the
heretics great advantages, and was a confession that the church
had erred, and that these very things, so much complained of,
were the chief nerves of the popedom ; which being cut, the
greatness of their court must needs fall : and therefore they
did oppose all these motions, and were still for proceeding in

establishing the doctrine. And though the opposing a decree to oblige all to residence was so grossly scandalous that they were ashamed of it, yet they intended to secure the greatness of the court by a *salvo* for the pope's privilege and dignity in granting dispensations. These proceedings at Trent discovered what was to be expected from that council, and alarmed all the protestants to think what they were to look for, if the emperor should force them to submit to the decrees of such an assembly, where those whom they called heretics could expect little, since the emperor himself could not prevail so far as to obtain or hinder delays, or to give preference for matters of discipline to points of doctrine. So the protestants met at Frankfort, and entered into councils for their common safety, in case any of them should be disturbed about religion; chiefly for preserving the elector of Cologne, whom the pope had cited to Rome for heresy. They wrote to the emperor's ministers, that they heard from all hands, that the emperor was raising great forces, and designing a war against them; who thought themselves secured by the edict of Spire, and desired nothing but the confirmation of that, and the regulation of the imperial chamber, as was then agreed on. A meeting being proposed between the emperor and the landgrave, the landgrave went to 22 him to Spire, where the emperor denied he had any design of a war, with which the other charged him; only he said, he had with great difficulty obtained a council in Germany, and therefore he hoped they would submit to it. But, after some expostulations on both hands, the landgrave left him; and now the thing was generally understood, though the emperor did still deny it, and said he would make no war about religion, but only against the disturbers of the peace of the empire. By this means he got the elector palatine to give little or no aid to the other princes. The marquis of Brandenburg was become jealous of the greatness of Saxe, and so was at first neuter; but afterwards openly declared for the emperor. But Maurice, the duke of Saxe's near kinsman, who by that duke's means was settled in a fair principality, which his uncle George had left him only on condition that he turned papist, notwithstanding which he got him to be possessed of it, was made use of by the emperor as the best instrument to work his ends. To him therefore he promised the electoral dignity, with the

[margin note:] January, 1546, princes meet at Frankfort.

dominions belonging to the duke of Saxe, if he would assist him
in the war against his kinsman, the present elector; and gave
him assurance, under his hand and seal, that he would make
no change in religion, but leave the princes of the Augsburg
Confession the free exercise of their religion.   And thus the
emperor singled out the duke of Saxe and the landgrave from
the rest, reckoning wisely, that, if he once mastered them, he
should more easily overcome all the rest.   He pretended some
other quarrels against them, as that of the duke of Brunswick,
who, having begun a war with his neighbours, was taken
prisoner, and his dominions possessed by the landgrave. That,
with some old quarrels, was pretended the ground of the
war.   Upon which the princes published a writing to shew
that it was religion only, and a secret design to subdue Germany, that was the true cause of the war; and those alleged
were sought pretences to excuse so infamous a breach of faith,
and of the public decrees; that the pope, who designed the
destruction of all of that confession, had set on the emperor to
this, who easily laid hold on it, that he might master the
liberty of Germany; therefore they warned all the princes of
their danger.   The emperor's forces being to be drawn together out of several places in Italy, Flanders, Burgundy, and
Bohemia, they whose forces lay nearer had a great advantage,
if they had known how to use it; for in June they brought June,
into the field seventy thousand foot and fifteen thousand horse, 1546,
and might have driven the emperor out of Germany, had they and land-
proceeded vigorously at first: but the divided command was [Thuanus,
fatal to them; for when one was for action, the other was lib. ii. cap.
against it.   So they lost their opportunity, and gave the em- p. 69.]
peror time to gather all his forces about him, which were far
inferior to theirs in strength: but the emperor gained by
time; whereas they, who had no great treasure, lost much.
All the summer, and a great deal of the winter, was spent
without any considerable action, though the two armies were
oft in view one of another.   But in the beginning of the July 20,
winter, the emperor, having proscribed the duke of Saxe, and 1546,
promised to bestow the principality on Maurice, he fell into Saxe and
Saxony, and carried a great many of the cities, which were landgrave
not prepared for any such impression. This made the duke [Sleidan,
separate his army, and return to the defence of his own fol, 281.]

the elector
returns into
Saxony.
[Ibid. fol.
297.]
Jan. 7,
1546,
peace con-
cluded be-
tween Eng-
land and
France.

country, which he quickly recovered, and drove Maurice almost out of all his own principality. The states of Bohemia 23 also declared for the elector of Saxony.

This was the state of affairs there. The princes thought they had a good prospect for the next year, having mediated a peace between the crowns of England and France, whose forces falling into Flanders must needs have bred a great distraction in the emperor's councils. But king Henry's death gave them great apprehensions, and not without cause; for when they sent hither for an aid in money to carry on the war, the protector and council saw great dangers on both hands: if they left the Germans to perish, the emperor would be then so lifted up, that they might expect to have an uneasy neighbour of him; on the other hand, it was a thing of great consequence to engage an infant king in such a war; therefore their succours from hence were like to be weak and very slow. Howsoever, the council ordered Paget to assure them, that within three or four months they should send fifty thousand crowns to their assistance, which was to be covered thus: the merchants of the Stillyard were to borrow so much of the king, and to engage to bring home stores to that value; they having the money, should send it to Hamburg, and so to the duke of Saxe. But the princes received a second blow in the loss of Francis the First of France, who having lived long in a familiarity and friendship with king Henry, not ordinary for crowned heads, was so much affected with the news of his death, that he was never seen cheerful after it. He made royal funeral rites to be performed to his memory in the church of Notre Dame, to which the clergy (who, one would have thought should have been glad to have seen his funerals celebrated in any fashion) were very averse; but that king had emancipated himself to a good degree from a servile subjection to them, and would be obeyed: he outlived the other not long, for he died the last of March. He was the chief patron of learned men, and advancer of learning, that had been for many ages: he was generally unsuccessful in his wars, and yet a great commander. At his death he left his son an advice, to beware of the brethren of Lorraine, and to depend much on the counsellors whom he had employed. But his son, upon his coming to the crown, did so deliver himself

[Council
Book, p.
83.]

[10 March,
Council
Book, p.
112.]

[Ibid. p.
113.]

March 31,
1547,
Francis I.
died.

up to the charms of his mistress Diana, that all things were
ordered as men made their court to her; which the ministers
that had served the former king scorning to do, and the brothers of the house of Lorraine doing very submissively, the
one were discharged of their employments, and the other
governed all the councils. Francis had been oft fluctuating in
the business of religion. Sometimes he had resolved to shake
off the pope's obedience, and set up a patriarch in France, and
had agreed with Henry the Eighth to go on in the same
counsels with him. But he was first diverted by his alliance
with Clement the Seventh; and afterwards by the ascendant
which the cardinal of Tournon had over him, who engaged
him at several times into severities against those that received
the reformation; yet he had such a close eye upon the emperor's motions, that he kept a constant good understanding
with the protestant princes, and had no doubt assisted them if
he had lived. But upon his death new counsels were taken
the brothers of Lorraine were furiously addicted to the interests of the papacy, one of them being a cardinal, who persuaded the king rather to begin his reign with the recovery of
24 Boulogne out of the hands of the English; so that the state of
Germany was almost desperate before he was aware of it.
And indeed the Germans lost so much in the death of these
two kings, upon whose assistance they had depended, that it
was no wonder they were easily overrun by the emperor.
Some of their allies, the cities of Ulm and Frankfort, and the
duke of Wurtemberg, submitting themselves to the emperor's
mercy, the rest were much disheartened; which is a constant
forerunner of the ruin of a confederacy. Such was the state of
religion abroad.

At home, men's minds were much distracted. The people, The design laid for a further re-formation at home.
especially in market-towns and places of trade, began generally
to see into many of the corruptions of the doctrine and worship,
and were weary of them. Some preached against some abuses:
Glasier, at Paul's Cross, taught, that the observance of Lent [April, Stow, p. 594.]
was only a positive law; others went further, and plainly con-
demned most of the former abuses. But the clergy were as
much engaged to defend them. They were for the most part
such as had been bred in monasteries and religious houses: for
there being pensions reserved for the monks, when their houses

were surrendered and dissolved, till they should be otherwise provided, the court of augmentations took care to ease the king of that charge, by recommending them to such small benefices as were at the king's disposal; and such as purchased those lands of the crown, with that charge of paying the pensions to the monks, were also careful to ease themselves by procuring benefices for them. The benefices were generally very small, so that in many places three or four benefices could hardly afford enough for the maintenance of one man. And this gave some colour for that abuse of one man's having many benefices that have a care of souls annexed to them; and that not only where they are so contiguous, that the duty can be discharged by one, and so poor that the maintenance of both will scarce serve for the encouragement of one person, but even where they are very remote, and of considerable value. This corruption, that crept in in the dark ages of the church, was now

[Cap. 13. 21 Henry 8. Statutes, vol. 3. p. 294.]

practised in England out of necessity. By an act made in king Henry the Eighth's time, none might hold two benefices without a dispensation, but no dispensation could enable one to hold three[12]; yet that was not at this time much considered. The excuses made for this were, that in some places they could not find good men for the benefices, but in most places the livings were brought to nothing. For while the abbeys stood, the abbots allowed those whom they appointed to serve the cure in the churches that belonged to them (which were in value above the half of England) a small stipend, or some little part of the vicarage tithes[13]; and they were to raise their subsistence out

[12] ["The contrary of this appears from the register of faculties granted by archbishop Parker; wherein may be found very many dispensations of triality of benefices with cure of souls, enabling the grantee to hold any third living with two, or any two with one already possessed; or to hold any three hereafter to be obtained." Harmer, p. 66.]

[13] ["The case of vicars was not so bad before the reformation as after. Before it, the fees of sacraments, sacramentals, *diriges*, &c., were very great; since, very inconsiderable. Before the reformation,

bishops could from time to time increase their allowance out of the tithes of the benefice, in what proportion they pleased, even beyond the first dotation of it. The bishops indeed have the same right still, as Dr. Ryve (Vicar's plea) hath fully proved; but the interposition of the common law would now hinder the execution of it. The vicars then were not left to the pleasure of the abbot or religious house, to whom the church belonged. But the bishops endowed the vicarages with what proportion of tithes and emoluments they thought fit; in many

of the fees they had by the sacraments, and other sacramentals;
and chiefly by the singing masses for the poor that died; for the
abbeys had the profit of it from the rich. And masses went
generally for two-pence; a groat was thought a great bounty.
So they all concluded themselves undone, if these things were
withdrawn. This engaged them against any reformation, since
every step that was made in it took their bread out of their
mouths. But they, being generally very ignorant, could oppose nothing with the force of reason or learning. So, although
they were resolved to comply with any thing, rather than forfeit
25 their benefices; yet in their hearts they abhorred all reformation, and murmured against it where they thought they might
do it safely: some preached as much for the old abuses, as
others did against them. Dr. Pern, at St. Andrew's Under-
shaft, justified the worship of images on the twenty-third of
April; yet on the nineteenth of June he preached a recantation [Stow, p.
of that sermon. Besides these, there were great prelates, as 594.]
Gardiner, Bonner, and Tunstall, whose long experience in affairs, they being oft employed in foreign embassies, together
with their high preferment, gave them great authority; and
they were against all alterations in religion. But that was not
so decent to profess; therefore they set up on this pretence;
that, till the king, their supreme head, were of age, so as to
consider things himself, all should continue in the state in which
king Henry had left them: and these depended on the lady
Mary, the king's eldest sister, as their head, who now professed
herself to be in all points for what her father had done; and
was very earnest to have every thing enacted by him, but
chiefly the six articles, to continue in force.

places reserved to the vicar one half
of all manner of tithes, and the whole
fees of all sacraments, sacramentals,
&c., in most places reserved to them,
not some little part of, but all the
vicarage tithes, and in other places
appointed to them an annual pension of money. In succeeding times,
when the first endowments appeared
too slender, they increased them at
their pleasure. Of all which, our
ancient registers and records give
abundant testimony. This was the
case of all vicarages. As for those
impropriated livings, which have
now no settled endowment, and are
therefore called, not vicarages, but
perpetual, or sometimes arbitrary
curacies, they are such as belonged
formerly to those orders who could
serve the cure of them in their own
persons, as the canons regular of
the order of St. Austin, which being
afterwards devolved into the hands
of laymen, they hired poor curates
to serve them at the cheapest rate
they could, and still continue to do
so." Harmer, p. 66.]

On the other hand, Cranmer, being now delivered from that too awful subjection that he had been held under by king Henry, resolved to go on more vigorously in purging out abuses. He had the protector firmly united to him in this design. Dr. Cox and Mr. Cheke, who were about the young king, were also very careful to infuse right principles of religion into him; and, as he was very capable of understanding what was laid before him, so he had an early liking to all good and generous principles; and was of so excellent a temper of mind, that, as he naturally loved truth, so the great probity of his manners made him very inclinable to love and cherish true religion. Cranmer had also several bishops of his side; Holgate of York, Holbeche of Lincoln, Goodrich of Ely, and, above all, Ridley elect of Rochester, designed for that see by

[Sept. 5.] king Henry[14], but not consecrated till September this year. Old Latimer was now discharged of his imprisonment, but had no mind to return to a more public station, and did choose rather to live private, and employ himself in preaching. He was kept by Cranmer at Lambeth, where he spent the rest of his days, till he was imprisoned in queen Mary's time, and attained the glorious end of his innocent and pious life. But the apprehensions of his being restored again to his old bishopric, put Heath, then bishop of Worcester, into great anxieties; sometimes he thought, if he consented to the reformation, then Latimer, who left his bishopric on the account of the six articles, must be restored, and this made him join with

Journal of the house of commons. [p. 6. January 8, 1549.] the popish party: at other times, when he saw the house of commons moved to have Latimer put in again, then he joined in the counsels for the reformation, to secure friends to himself by that compliance. Others of the bishops were ignorant and weak men, who understood religion little, and valued it less; and so, although they liked the old superstition best, because

[14] Quære How? When in the commission granted for, the examination whether the marquis of Northampton could lawfully marry after the divorcement of his wife Anne for adultery, bearing date three months after the death of king Henry, even May the 7th, 1 Edward VI. Holbeche was bishop of Rochester, and not at that time translated to Lincoln. [G] [This mistake has also been noticed by Wharton in the 'Specimen of Errors', p. 68, where he says, that Henry VIII. died Jan. 28, 1547, and that the vacancy at Rochester was caused by the translation of Holbeche of Rochester to Lincoln August 9th, 1547.]

it encouraged ignorance most, and that was the only sure support of their power and wealth, yet they resolved to swim with the stream. It was designed by Cranmer and his friends to carry on the reformation but by slow and safe degrees, not hazarding too much at once. They trusted in the providence of God, that he would assist them in so good a work. They knew the corruptions they were to throw out to be such, that they should easily satisfy the people with what they did; and 26 they had many learned men among them, who had now for divers years been examining these matters. There were also many that declared they had heard the late king express his great regret for leaving the state of religion in so unsettled a condition; and that he had resolved to have changed the mass into a communion, besides many other things. And in the act of parliament which he had procured (see page 263, first part) for giving force and authority to his proclamation a proviso was added, that his son's counsellors, while he should be under age, might set out proclamations of the same authority with these which were made by the king himself. This gave them a full power to proceed in that work; in which they resolved to follow the method begun by the late king, of sending visitors over England with injunctions and articles. A visitation is made over England. They ordered them six several circuits or precincts. The first was, London, Westminster, Norwich, and Ely. The second, Rochester, Canterbury, Chichester, and Winchester. The third, Sarum, Exeter, Bath, Bristol, and Gloucester. The fourth, York, Durham, Carlisle, and Chester. The fifth Peterborough, Lincoln, Oxford, Coventry, and Lichfield. And the sixth, Wales, Worcester, and Hereford. For every circuit there were two gentlemen, a civilian, a divine [15], and a register. They were designed to be sent out in the beginning of May, as appears by a letter, to be found in the Collection, written the fourth of May to the archbishop of York. (There is also in the registers of London another of the same strain.) Yet the visitation being put off for some months, this inhibition was suspended, on the sixteenth of May, till it should be again renewed. The letter sets forth, that the king being speedily Collect. Numb. 7. [Bonner's Register, fol. 105. Tunstall's Register, fol. 38.]

---

[15] This rule was not observed; in some circuits there were four visitors; in others six; in some no civilian; in some two divines; in some one gentleman, and in some three. See Cranmer's Mem. p. 136. [S.]

to order a visitation over his whole kingdom, therefore neither
the archbishop, nor any other, should exercise any jurisdiction
while that visitation lasted. And since the minds of the people
were held in great suspense by the controversies they heard
so variously tossed in the pulpits, that, for quieting these, the
king did require all bishops to preach no where but in their
cathedrals; and that all other clergymen should not preach
but in their collegiate or parochial churches, unless they obtained a special license from the king to that effect. The
design of this was, to make a distinction between such as
preached for the reformation of abuses, and such as did it not.
The one were to be encouraged by licenses to preach wherever
they desired to do it; but the others were restrained to the
places where they were incumbents. But that which of all
other things did most damp those who designed the reformation, was the misery to which they saw the clergy reduced,
and the great want of able men to propagate it over England.
For the rents of the church were either so swallowed up by
the suppression of religious houses, to whom the tithes were
generally appropriated, or so basely alienated by some lewd
or superstitious incumbents, who, to preserve themselves, being
otherwise obnoxious, or to purchase friends, had given away
the best part of their revenues and benefices, that there was
very little encouragement left for those that should labour in
the work of the gospel. And though many projects were
thought on for remedying this great abuse, yet those were all
so powerfully opposed, that there was no hope left of getting it
remedied, till the king should come to be of age, and be able
by his authority to procure the churchmen a more proportioned maintenance.

Some homi-
lies com-
piled.
        Two things only remained to be done at present. The one 27
was, to draw up some homilies for the instruction of the people,
which might supply the defects of their incumbents, together
with the providing them with such books as might lead them
into the understanding of the scripture. The other was, to
select the most eminent preachers they could find, and send
them over England with the visitors, who should with more
authority instruct the nation in the principles of religion.
Therefore some were appointed to compile those homilies; and
twelve were at first agreed on, being about those arguments

which were in themselves of the greatest importance. The
1st [16] was, about the Use of the Scriptures. The 2nd, Of the
Misery of Mankind by Sin. 3rd, Of their Salvation by Christ,
4th, Of True and Lively Faith. 5th, Of Good Works. 6th, Of
Christian Love and Charity. 7th, Against Swearing, and
chiefly Perjury. 8th, Against Apostasy, or declining from
God. 9th, Against the Fear of Death. 10th, An Exhortation
to Obedience. 11th, Against Whoredom and Adultery, setting
forth the State of Marriage, how necessary and honourable it
was. And the 12th, Against Contention, chiefly about Matters
of Religion. They intended to set out more afterwards; but
these were all that were at this time finished. The chief design in them was, to acquaint the people with the method of
salvation according to the gospel; in which there were two
dangerous extremes at that time that had divided the world.
The greatest part of the ignorant commons seemed to consider
their priests as a sort of people who had such a secret trick of
saving their souls, as mountebanks pretend in the curing of
diseases; and that there was nothing to be done but to leave
themselves in their hands, and the business could not miscarry.
This was the chief basis and support of all that superstition
which was so prevalent over the nation. The other extreme
was, of some corrupt gospellers, who thought, if they magnified Christ much, and depended on his merits and intercession, they could not perish, which way soever they led their
lives. In these homilies therefore special care was taken to
rectify these errors. And the salvation of mankind was on
the one hand wholly ascribed to the death and sufferings of
Christ, to which sinners were taught to fly, and to trust to it
only, and to no other devices for the pardon of sin. They
were at the same time taught, that there was no salvation
through Christ but to such as truly repented, and lived according to the rules of the gospel. The whole matter was so
ordered, to teach them, that, avoiding the hurtful errors on
both hands, they might all know the true and certain way of
attaining eternal happiness. For the understanding the New
Testament, Erasmus' Paraphrase, which was translated into
English, was thought the most profitable and easiest book.

[16] These titles are not as they are in the original book. They are only
abridged. [S.]

Therefore it was resolved, that, together with the Bible, there should be one [17] of these in every parish church over England. They next considered the articles and injunctions that should be given to the visitors. The greatest part of them were only the renewing what had been ordered by king Henry during Cromwell's being vicegerent, which had been much neglected since his fall. For as there was no vicegerent, so there was few visitations appointed after his death by the king's authority : but the executing former injunctions was left to the several bishops, who were for the most part more careful about the six articles, than about the injunctions.

Articles
and injunc-
tions for
the visita-
tion. [Fox,
lib. ix. p. 5.]

" [18] So now, all the orders about renouncing the pope's power, 28 " and asserting the king's supremacy ; about preaching, teach- " ing the elements of religion in the vulgar tongue ; about the " benefices of the clergy, and the taxes on them for the poor, " for scholars, and their mansion-houses ; with the other in- " junctions for the strictness of churchmen's lives ; and against " superstitions, pilgrimages, images, or other rites of that kind, " and for register-books ; were renewed. And to these many " others were added ; as, that curates should take down such " images as they knew were abused by pilgrimages or offerings " to them ; but that private persons should not do it. That in " the confessions in Lent they should examine all people whe- " ther they could recite the elements of religion in the English " tongue. That at high mass they should read the Epistle " and Gospel in English ; and every Sunday and holyday they " should read at matins one chapter out of the New Testa- " ment, and at even-song, another out of the Old, in English. " That the curates should often visit the sick, and have many " places of the scripture in English in readiness, wherewith to " comfort them. That there should be no more processions " about churches, for avoiding contention for precedence in " them. And that the Litany, formerly said in the processions, " should be said thereafter in the choir in English, as had

[Ibid. p. 6.] " been ordered by the late king. That the holyday being insti- " tuted at first that men should give themselves wholly to God ; " yet God was generally more dishonoured upon it than on the

---

17 [The Paraphrase of Erasmus upon the Newe Testamente. Lond. by Edw. Whytchurch, 1548, 9. fol.

2 vols.]

18 The injunctions are only abstracted, not the articles. [S.]

" other days, by idleness, drunkenness, and quarrelling, the
" people thinking that they sufficiently honoured God by hearing
" mass at matins, though they understood nothing of it to
" their edifying; therefore thereafter the holyday should be
" spent, according to God's holy will, in hearing and reading
" his holy word, in public and private prayers, in amending
" their lives, receiving the communion, visiting the sick, and
" reconciling themselves to their neighbours. Yet the curates
" were to declare to their people, that in harvest-time they
" might upon the holy and festival days labour in their har-
" vest. That curates were to admit none to the communion
" who were not reconciled to their neighbours. That all dig-
" nified clergymen should preach personally twice a year.
" That the people should be taught not to despise any of the
" ceremonies not yet abrogated, but to beware of the supersti-
" tion of sprinkling their beds with holy water, or the ringing
" of bells, or using of blessed candles for driving away devils.
" That all monuments of idolatry should be removed out of the
" walls or windows of churches, and that there should be a
" pulpit in every church for preaching. That there should be
" a chest with a hole in it for the receiving the oblations of the
" people for the poor; and that the people should be exhorted
" to almsgiving, as much more profitable than what they for-
" merly bestowed on superstitious pilgrimages, trentals, and
" decking of images. That all patrons who disposed of their
" livings by simoniacal pactions should forfeit their right for
" that vacancy to the king. That the Homilies should be read.
" That priests should be used charitably and reverently for
" their office' sake. That no other primer should be used but
" that set out by king Henry. That the prime and the hours
" should be omitted where there was a sermon or homily. That
" they should in bidding the prayers remember the king their
29 " supreme head, the queen dowager, the king's two sisters,
" the lord protector and the council, the lords, the clergy, and
" the commons of the realm; and to pray for souls departed
" this life, that at the last day we with them may rest both
" body and soul. All which injunctions were to be observed,
" under the pains of excommunication, sequestration, or depri-
" vation, as the ordinaries should answer it to the king, the
" justices of peace being required to assist them."

Injunctions
to the bi-
shops.
[Fox, vol.
ii. lib. ix.
p. 6.]

Besides these, there were other injunctions given to the
bishops, " that they should see the former put in execution,
" and should preach four times a year in their dioceses; once
" at their cathedral, and three times in other churches, unless
" they had a reasonable excuse for their omission.   That their
" chaplains should be able to preach God's word, and should
" be made labour oft in it: that they should give orders to
" none but such as would do the same; and if any did other-
" wise, that they should punish them, and recal their license."
These are the chief heads of the injunctions, which being so
often printed, I shall refer the reader, that would consider
them more carefully, to the Collection of these. and other such
curious things, made by the right reverend father in God Anthony Sparrow, now lord bishop of Norwich[19].

These being published[20], gave occasion to those who censured all things of that nature to examine them.

The removing images that had been abused gave great occasion of quarrel; and the thing being to be done by the
clergy only, it was not like that they, who lived chiefly by such
things, would be very zealous in the removing them.   Yet, on
the other hand, it was thought necessary to set some restraints
to the heats of the people, who were otherwise apt to run too
far, where bounds were not set to them.

The article about the strict observance of the holyday seemed
a little doubtful; whether by the holyday was to be understood
only the Lord's-day, or that and all other church-festivals.
The naming it singularly the holyday, and in the end of that
article adding festival-days to the holyday, seemed to favour
their opinion that thought this strict observance of the holyday was particularly intended for the Lord's-day, and not for
the other festivals.   And indeed the setting aside of large portions of time on that day for our spiritual edification, and for
the service of God, both in public and private, is so necessary

[19] These articles are not in bishop Sparrow's Collection, but were
printed anno 1547. [S.]

[20] [" Injunccions geven by the
moste excellent Prince Edward the
sixte, &c., to all and singuler his
loving subjectes, as wel as of the
Clergie, as of the Laietie." London,
by Rich. Grafton, 1547, 4to.   At the
end of the volume are, " Articles
to bee enquired of in the kynges
majestie's visitacion." These, which
are omitted by Sparrow, are printed
in Strype, Eccles. Memor. vol. 2. p.
48. sqq.]

for the advancement of true piety, that great and good effects must needs follow on it. But some came afterwards, who, not content to press great strictness on that day, would needs make a controversy about the morality of it, and about the fourth Commandment, and framed many rules for it, which were stricter than themselves or any other could keep, and so could only load men's consciences with many scruples. This drew an opposition from others, who could not agree to these severities; and these contests were, by the subtilty of the enemies of the power and progress of religion, so improved, that, instead of all men's observing that time devoutly as they ought, some took occasion, from the strictness of their own way, to censure all as irreligious who did not in every thing agree to their notion concerning it; others, by the heat of contradiction, did too much slacken this great bond and instrument of religion, which is since brought under so much neglect that it 30 is for most part a day only of rest from men's bodily labours, but perhaps worse employed than if they were at work : so hard a thing it is to keep the due mean between the extremes of superstition on the one hand, and of irreligion on the other.

The corruption of lay-patrons in their simoniacal bargains was then so notorious, that it was necessary to give a check to it, as we find there was by these injunctions. But whether either this, or the oath afterwards appointed to be taken, has effectually delivered this church of that great abuse, I shall not determine. If those who bestow benefices did consider, that, the charge of souls being annexed to them, they shall answer to God severely for putting so sacred a trust in mean or ill hands, upon any base or servile accounts. it would make them look a little more carefully to a thing of so high consequence, and neither expose so holy a thing to sale, nor gratify a friend or servant by granting them the next advowson, or be too easily overcome with the solicitations of impudent pretenders.

The form of bidding prayer was not begun by king Henry, as some have weakly imagined, but was used in the times of popery, as will appear by the form of bidding the beads in king Henry the Seventh's time, which will be found in the Collection ; where the way was, first, for the preacher to name and open his text, and then to call on the people to go to their

Collect.
Numb. 8.

prayers, and to tell them what they were to pray for; after which, all the people said their beads in a general silence, and the minister kneeled down likewise and said his. All the change king Henry the Eighth made in this was, that, the pope and cardinals' names being left out, he was ordered to be mentioned with the addition of his title of Supreme Head, that the people, hearing that oft repeated by their priests, might be better persuaded about it; but his other titles were not mentioned. And this order was now renewed; only the prayer for departed souls was changed from what it had been. It was formerly in these words: "Ye shall pray for the souls that be departed, " abiding the mercy of Almighty God, that it may please him, " the rather at the contemplation of our prayers, to grant them " the fruition of his presence:" which did imply their being in a state where they did not enjoy the presence of God, which was avoided by the more general words now prescribed,

The injunctions given the bishops directed them to that, which, if followed carefully, would be the most effectual means of reforming, at least the next age, if not that wherein they lived. For if holy orders were given to none but to those who are well qualified, and seem to be internally called by a divine vocation, the church must soon put on a new face: whereas, when orders are too easily given, upon the credit of emendicated recommendations or titles, and after a slight trial of the knowledge of such candidates, without any exact scrutiny into their sense of things, or into the disposition of their minds; no wonder, if, by the means of clergymen so ordained, the church lose much in the esteem and love of the people, who, being possessed with prejudices against the whole society for the faults which they see in particular persons, become an easy prey to such as divide from it.

August, the protector went into Scotland. [Stow, p. 594.]

Thus were the visitors instructed, and sent out to make their 31 circuits in August, about the time that the protector made his expedition into Scotland. For the occasion of it I shall refer the reader to what is already said in the former part of this work. Before they engaged deeper in the war, sir Francis Brian was sent over to France, to congratulate the new king, and to see if he would confirm these propositions that were agreed to during his father's life, and if he would pay the pension that was to be given yearly till Boulogne was restored;

and chiefly to obtain of him to be neutral in the war of Scot- Thuanus, [lib. iii. cap. 10. vol. i. p. 113.]
land, complaining of that nation, that had broken their faith
with England in the matter of the marriage. To all which the
French king answered, that for these articles they mentioned,
he thought it dishonourable for him to confirm them ; and said,
his father's agent. Poligny had no warrant to yield to them,
for by them the English were at liberty to fortify what they
had about Boulogne, which he would never consent to : that he
was willing to pay what was agreed to by his father, but would
have first the conditions of the delivery of Boulogne made more
clear. As for the Scots, they were his perpetual allies, whom
he could not forsake if they were in any distress. And when Questions made, whether Scotland was a free kingdom, or subject to England.
it was pressed on him, and his ambassador at London, that
Scotland was subject to the crown of England; they had no
regard to it. When the council desired the French ambassador
to look on the records which they should bring him for proving
their title, he excused himself, and said, his master would not
interpose in a question of that nature, nor would he look back
to what was pretended to have been done two or three hundred
years ago, but was to take things as he found them ; and that
the Scots had records likewise to prove their being a free kingdom. So the council saw they could not engage in the war
with Scotland, without drawing on a war with France, which
made them try their interest with their friends this year to see
if the marriage could be obtained. But the castle of St. Andrew's was now lost by the assistance that Leo Strozzi brought
from France. And though they in England continued to send
pensions to their party, (for in May 1300l. [21] was sent down by
Henry Balnaves, and in June 125l. was sent to the earl of [May 4.] [June 2. Council Book, p. 178.]
Glencairn for an half year's payment of his pension,) yet they
could gain no ground there, for the Scots now thought themselves safer than formerly ; the crown of England being in the
hands of a child, and the court of France being much governed
by their queen-dowager's brothers. They gave way to the
borderers to make inroads, of whom about two thousand fell into
the western marches, and made great depredations. The Scots
in Ireland were also very ill neighbours to the English there.
There were many other complaints of piracies at sea, and of a [Sept. 25. Council Book, p. 228.]
ship-royal that robbed many English ships : but how these

[21] [The sum is 1279l. in the Council Book, p. 163.]

came to be complained of, I do not see; for they were in open war, and I do not find any truce had been made. The French agent at London pressed much that there might be a treaty on the borders before the breach were made wider. But now the protector had given orders for raising an army, so that he had no mind to lose that summer. Yet, to let the French king see how careful they were of preserving his friendship, they appointed the bishop of Durham, and sir Robert Bowes, to give the Scotch commissioners a meeting on the borders the fourth of August; but with these secret instructions, that, if the Scots would confirm the marriage, all other things should be presently forgiven, and peace be immediately made up; but if they were not empowered in that particular, and offered only to treat about restitutions, that then they should immediately break off the treaty. The bishop of Durham was also ordered to carry down with him the exemplifications of many records, to prove the subjection of the crown of Scotland to England; some of these are said to have been under the hands and seals of their kings, their nobles, their bishops, abbots, and towns. He was also ordered to search for all the records that were lying at Durham, where many of them were kept, to be ready to be shewed to the Scots upon any occasion that might require it. The meeting on the borders came to a quick issue, for the Scottish commissioners had no power to treat about the marriage. But Tunstall, searching the registers of his see, found many writings of great consequence to clear that subjection, of which the reader will see an account in a letter he writ to the

Collect.
Numb. 9.

council in the Collection of papers. The most remarkable of these was, the homage king William of Scotland made to Henry the Second, by which he granted, that all the nobles of his realm should be his subjects, and do homage to him; and that all the bishops of Scotland should be under the archbishops of York; and that the king of England should give all the abbeys and honours in Scotland, at the least they should not be given without his consent; with many other things of the like nature. It was said, that the monks in those days, who generally kept the records, were so accustomed to the forging of stories and writings, that little credit was to be given to such records as lay in their keeping. But having so faithfully acknowledged what was alleged against the freedom of Scotland, I may be allowed to set down a proof on the other side for my native country, copied from the original writing yet extant under the hands and seals of many of the nobility and gentry of that kingdom. It is a letter to the Pope; and it was ordinary, that of such public letters there were duplicates signed; the one of which was sent, and the other laid up among the records : of which I have met with several instances. So that of this letter, the copy which was reserved, being now in noble hands, was communicated to me, and is in the Collection.   It was upon the pope's engaging with the king of England to assist him to subdue Scotland that they writ to him, and did assert most directly, that their kingdom was at all times free and independent.   But now, these questions being waived, the other difference about the marriage was brought to a sharper decision. *Collect. Numb. 10.*

On the twenty-first of August the protector took out a commission to be general, and to make war on Scotland ; and did devolve his power during his absence on the privy-council ; and appointed his brother to be lord lieutenant for the south, and the earl of Warwick (whom he carried with him) lord lieutenant for the north ; and left a commission of array to the marquis of Northampton for Essex, Suffolk, and Norfolk ; to the earl of Arundel for Sussex, Surrey, Hampshire, and Wiltshire ; and to sir Thomas Cheyney for Kent. All this was in case of an invasion from France. Having thus settled affairs during his absence, he set out for Newcastle, having ordered his troops to march thither before ; and, coming thither on the twenty-seventh of that month, he saw his army mustered on the twenty-eighth, and marched forward to Scotland.   The lord Clinton commanded the ships, that sailed on as the army marched ; which was done, that provisions and ammunition might be brought by them from Newcastle or Berwick, if the enemy should at any time fall in behind their army. He entered into Scotch ground the second of September, and advanced to the Paths the fifth ; where, the passage being narrow and untoward, they looked for an enemy to have disputed it, but found none ; the Scots having only broken the ways, which, in that dry season, signified not much but to stop them some hours in their march. When they had passed these, some little castles, Dunglass, Thornton, and Innerwick, having but a few ill-provided men in them, surrendered to them.   On the ninth they came to *August 21. [Council Book p. 208.]*   *[Ibid. p. 212 sqq.]*   *August 27, 28. [Patten, A, ii.]*   *Sept. 2.*   *[Sept. 5. Ibid. B ii.]*   *Sept. 9. [Ibid. E. i.]*

33

Falside, where there was a long fight in several parties, in
which there were one thousand three hundred of the Scots
slain.   And now they were in sight of the Scotch army, which
was, for numbers of men, one of the greatest that they had
ever brought together, consisting of thirty thousand men; of
which ten thousand were commanded by the governor, eight
thousand by the earl of Angus, eight thousand by the earl of
Huntley, and four thousand by the earl of Argyle, with a fair
train of artillery, nine brass, and twenty-one iron guns.   On
the other side, the English army consisted of about fifteen
thousand foot and three thousand horse, but all well appointed.
The Scots were now heated with the old national quarrel to
England.   It was given out, that the protector was come with
his army to carry away their queen, and to enslave the kingdom.   And, for the encouraging the army, it was also said,
that twelve galleys and fifty ships were · on the sea from
France, and that they looked for them every day.

The pro-
tector's of-
fers to the
Scots.
[Spots-
wood, p.
88.
Godwin,
p. 125.]

The protector, finding an army brought together so soon,
and so much greater than he expected, began to be in some
apprehension, and therefore he writ to the Scots to this effect:
that they should remember they were both Christians, and so
should be tender of the effusion of so much blood; that this
war was not made with any design, but for a perpetual peace,
by the marriage of their two princes, which they had already
agreed, and given their public faith upon it; and that the
Scots were to be much more gainers by it than the English;
the island seemed made for one empire; it was pity it should
be more distracted with such wars, when there was so fair and
just a way offered for uniting it; and it was much better for
them to marry their queen to a prince of the same language,
and on the same continent, than to a foreigner: but if they
would not agree to that, he offered that their queen should be
bred up among them, and not at all contracted, neither to the
French, nor to any other foreigner, till she came of age, that
by the consent of the estates she might choose a husband for
herself.   If they would agree to this, he would immediately
return with his army out of Scotland, and make satisfaction
for the damages the country had suffered by the invasion.

[Buchn.-
nan, i. p.
298.]

This proposition seems to justify what the Scotch writers say,
though none of the English mention it, that the protector,

what for want of provisions, and what from the apprehensions
he had of so numerous an army of the Scots, was in great
straits, and intended to have returned back to England without
hazarding an engagement. But the Scots thought they were
so much superior to the English, and that they had them now
at such a disadvantage, that they resolved to fall upon them
next day. And, that the fair offers made by the protector
34 might not raise division among them, the governor having
communicated these to a few whom he trusted, was by their
advice persuaded to suppress them: but he sent a trumpeter Rejected
to the English army with an offer to suffer them to return ^{by them.}
without falling upon them; which the protector had reason to
reject, knowing that so mean an action in the beginning of
his administration would have quite ruined his reputation.
But to this, another, that came with the trumpeter, added a [Hayward,
message from the earl of Huntley, that the protector and he, p. 282.]
with ten or twenty of a side, or singly, should decide the
quarrel by their personal valour. The protector said, this was
no private quarrel, and the trust he was in obliged him not to
expose himself in such a way; and therefore he was to fight
no other way but at the head of his army. But the earl of
Warwick offered to accept the challenge. The earl of Huntley
sent no such challenge, as he afterwards purged himself when
he heard of it. For as it was unreasonable for him to expect
the protector should have answered it, so it had been an
affronting the governor of Scotland to have taken it off of his
hands, since he was the only person that might have challenged the protector on equal terms. The truth of the matter
was, a gentleman, that went along with the trumpeter, made
him do it without warrant, fancying the answer to it would
have taken up some time, in which he might have viewed the
enemy's camp.

On the tenth of September the two armies drew out, and Sept. 10,
fought in the field of Pinkey, near Musselburgh. The English the battle
had the advantage of the ground. And in the beginning of near Mus-
the action a cannon ball from one of the English ships killed [Hayward,
the lord Grame's eldest son, and twenty-five men more; which 286.]
put the earl of Argyle's Highlanders into such a fright, that vi.]
they could not be held in order. But, after a charge given by
the earl of Angus, in which the English lost some few men, the

Scots gave ground; and the English observing that, and breaking in furiously upon them, the Scots threw down their arms and fled; the English pursued hard, and slew them without mercy. There were reckoned to be killed about fourteen thousand, and fifteen hundred taken prisoners, among whom was the earl of Huntley, and five hundred gentlemen; and all the artillery was taken. This loss quite disheartened the Scots, so that they all retired to Stirling, and left the whole country to the protector's mercy: who the next day went and took Leith; and the soldiers in the ships burnt some of the sea-towns of Fife, and retook some English ships that had been taken by the Scots, and burnt the rest. They also put a garrison in the isle of St. Columba in the Frith, of about two hundred soldiers, and left two ships to wait on them. He also sent the earl of Warwick's brother, sir Ambrose Dudley, to take Broughty, a castle in the mouth of Tay; in which he put two hundred soldiers. He wasted Edinburgh, and uncovered the abbey of Holyrood-house, and carried away the lead and the bells belonging to it. But he neither took the castle of Edinburgh, nor did he go on to Stirling, where the queen, with the stragglers of the army, lay. And it was thought, that, in the consternation wherein the late defeat had put them, every place would have yielded to him. But he had some private reasons that pressed his return, and made him let go the advantages that were now in his hands, and so gave the Scots time to bring succours out of France; whereas he might easily have made an end of the war now at once, if he had followed his success vigorously. The earl of Warwick, who had a great share in the honour of the victory, but knew 53 that the errors in conduct would much diminish the protector's glory, which had been otherwise raised to an unmeasurable height, was not displeased at it. So, on the eighteenth of September, the protector drew his army back into England; and, having received a message from the queen and the governor of Scotland, offering a treaty, he ordered them to send commissioners to Berwick to treat with those he should appoint. As he returned through the March and Teviotdale, all the chief men in these counties came in to him, and took an oath to king Edward, the form whereof will be found in the Collection; and delivered into his hands all the places of strength in their

[Patten, L. vii.]

[Sept. 21, Holinshed, p. 990.]

Sept. 18.

Collect. Numb. 11.

counties.   He left a garrison of two hundred in Home-castle, under the command of sir Edward Dudley ; and fortified Rox-burgh, where, for encouraging the rest, he wrought two hours with his own hands, and put three hundred soldiers and two hundred pioneers into it, giving sir Ralph Bulmer the command. At the same time the earl of Lennox and the lord Wharton made an inroad by the west marches ; but with little effect.

On the twenty-ninth of September the protector returned into England full of honour, having in all that expedition lost not above sixty men, as one[22] that then writ the account of it says : the Scotch writers say, he lost between two and three hun-dred. He had taken eighty pieces of cannon, and bridled the two chief rivers of the kingdom by the garrisons he left in them ; and had left many garrisons in the strong places on the frontier.   And now it may be easily imagined how much' this raised his reputation in England ; since men commonly make auguries of the fortune of their rulers from the successes of the first designs they undertake.   So now they remembered what he had done formerly in Scotland ; and how he had in France, with seven thousand men, raised the French army of twenty thousand, that was set down before Boulogne, and had forced them to leave their ordnance, baggage, and tents, with the loss of one man only, in the year 1544 ; and that, next year, he had fallen into Picardy, and built New-Haven, with two other forts there.   So that they all expected great success under his government.   And indeed, if the breach between his brother and him, with some other errors, had not lost him the advantages he now had, this prosperous action had laid the foundation of great fortunes to him.

He left the earl of Warwick to treat with those that should be sent from Scotland.   But none came ; for that proposition had been made only to gain time.   The queen-mother there was not ill pleased to see the interest of the governor so much

Sept. 29.
the pro-
tector re-
turned to
England.
[Patten,
P. vi.]

---

[22] [The Expedicion into Scotlãde of the most woorthely fortunate prince Edward, Duke of Soomerset, uncle unto our most noble souereign lord ye kĩges maiestie Edward the VI. Goouernour of hys hyghnes persone, and Protectour of hys graces realmes, dominions and subjectes : made in the first yere of his Ma-iesties most prosperous reign, and set out by way of diarie, by W. Patten, Londoner.   Vivat Victor.

This volume, of which there is a copy in the King's Library, is not paged or foliated, but is dated on the last leaf, 1548.]

impaired by that misfortune, and persuaded the chief men of
that kingdom to cast themselves wholly into the arms of
France, and to offer their young queen to the dauphin, and to
think of no treaty with the English. So the earl of Warwick
returned to London, having no small share in the honour of
this expedition. He was son to that Dudley, who was attainted
and executed the first year of king Henry the Eighth's reign.
But whether it was that the king afterwards repented of his
severity to the father, or that he was taken with the qualities

[Mar. 12,
1543.]

of the son, he raised him by many degrees to be admiral, and
viscount Lisle. He had defended Boulogne, when it was in no
good condition, against the dauphin, whose army was believed
fifty thousand strong; and when the French had carried the
basse-town, he recovered it, and killed eight hundred of their
men. The year after that, being in command at sea, he offered 36
the French fleet battle; which they declining, he made a descent upon Normandy with five thousand men, and, having
burnt and spoiled a great deal, he returned to his ships with the
loss only of one man. And he shewed he was as fit for a court
as a camp; for being sent over to the French court·upon the
peace, he appeared there with much splendour, and came off
with great honour. He was indeed a man of great parts, had
not insatiable ambition, with profound dissimulation, stained his
other noble qualities.

The protector at his return was advised presently to meet
the parliament, (for which the writs had been sent out before
he went into Scotland,) now that he was so covered with glory,
to get himself established in his authority, and to do those other

The visitors
execute the
injunctions
things which required a session. He found the visitors had
performed their visitation, and all had given obedience. And
those who expounded the secret providences of God with an
eye to their own opinions, took great notice of this; that on

Acts and
Monu-
ments,
[lib. ix.
p. 17. and
Godwin,
p. 127.]
the same day in which the visitors removed, and destroyed most
of the images in London, their armies were so successful in
Scotland in Pinkey-field. It is too common to all men to magnify such events much, when they make for them; but if they
are against them, they turn it off by this, that God's ways are
past finding out. So partially do men argue where they are
once engaged. Bonner and Gardiner had shewed some dislike
of the Injunctions. Bonner received them with a protestation

that he would observe them, if they were not contrary to God's
law, and the ordinances of the church. Upon which sir Anthony
Cook, and the other visitors, complained to the council. So But they
Bonner was sent for, where he offered a submission, but full of were not well receiv-
vain *quiddities;* (so it is expressed in the council-book.) But ed by Bon-
they not accepting of that, he made such a full one as they de- ner.
sired, which is in the Collection. Yet, for giving terror to [Council Book, p. 221.]
others, he was sent to lie for some time in a prison called the Collect.
Fleet. Gardiner seeing the Homilies, was also resolved to pro- Numb. 12.
test against them. Sir John Godsalve, who was one of the vi- Nor by
sitors, wrote to him not to ruin himself, nor lose his bishopric Gardiner.
by such an action. To whom he wrote a letter, that has more
of a Christian and of a bishop in it than any thing I ever saw
of his. He expresses, in handsome terms, a great contempt of
the world, and a resolution to suffer any thing rather than depart from his conscience. Besides that, (as he said,) the things
being against law, he would not deliver up the liberties of his
country, but would petition against them. This letter will be
found in the Collection, for I am resolved to suppress nothing Collect.
of consequence, on what side soever it may be. On the twenty- Numb. 13.
fifth of September, it being informed to the council that Gar- Sept. 25.
diner had written to some of that board, and had spoken to [Council Book p. 229.]
others, many things in prejudice and contempt of the king's
visitation, and that he intended to refuse to set forth the Homilies and Injunctions; he was sent for to the council: where,
being examined, he said he thought they were contrary to the
word of God, and that his conscience would not suffer him to
observe them. He excepted to one of the homilies, that it did
exclude charity from justifying men, as well as faith. This he [Vide Part
said was contrary to the book set out in the late king's time, iii. p. 187.]
which was afterwards confirmed in parliament in the year 1542.
He said further, that he could never see one place of scripture,
nor any ancient doctor, that favoured it. He also said, Eras-
37 mus' Paraphrase was bad enough in Latin, but much worse in
English; for the translator had oft out of ignorance, and oft
out of design, misrendered him palpably, and was one that neither understood Latin nor English well. He offered to go to
Oxford to dispute about justification, with any they should send
him to; or to enter in conference with any that would undertake his instruction in Town. But this did not satisfy the coun-

cil; so they pressed him to declare what he intended to do when the visitors should be with him. He said, he did not know; he should further study these points: for it would be three weeks before they could be with him; and he was sure he would say no worse, than that he should obey them as far as could consist with God's law and the king's. The council urged him to promise, that he would without any limitation set forth the Homilies and the Injunctions: which he refusing to

[Ibid. p. 229.]

do, was sent to the Fleet. Some days after that, Cranmer went to see the dean of St. Paul's, having the bishops of Lincoln and Rochester, with Dr. Cox, and some others, with him. He sent for Gardiner thither, and entered into discourse with him about that passage in the homily, excluding charity out of our justification; and urged those places of St. Paul,

[Rom iii. 20, Gal. ii. 16.]

That we are justified by faith without the works of the law. He said his design in that passage was only to draw men from trusting in any thing they did, and to teach them to trust only to Christ. But Gardiner had a very different notion of justification; for, as he said, infants were justified by baptism, and penitents by the sacrament of penance; and, that the conditions of the justifying of those of age were charity as well as faith; as the three estates make a law all joined together: for by this simile he set it out in the report he writ of that discourse to the lord protector, reckoning the king one of the three estates; (a way of speech very strange, especially in a bishop and a lawyer.) For Erasmus it was said, that, though there were faults in his Paraphrase, as no book besides the scriptures is without faults, yet it was the best for that use they could find; and they did choose rather to set out what so learned a man had written, than to make a new one, which might give occasion to more objections; and he was the most indifferent writer they knew. Afterwards Cranmer, knowing what was likely to work most on him, let fall some words (as Gardiner writ to the protector) of bringing him into the privy-council, if he would concur in what they were carrying on. But that not having its ordinary effect on him, he was carried back to the Fleet.

There were also many complaints brought by some clergymen, of such as had used them ill for their obeying the king's Injunctions, and for removing images. Many were upon their submission sent away with a severe rebuke; others, that

offended more heinously, were put in the Fleet for some time,
and afterwards, giving bond for their good behaviour, were
discharged.   But, upon the protector's return, the bishop of [Fox, vol.
Winchester writ him a long letter in his own vindication. ii. lib. ix.
" He complained of the visitors proceeding in his absence in so p. 63.]
" great a matter.   He said the Injunctions were contrary to
" themselves; for they appointed the Homilies to be read,
" and Erasmus' Paraphrase to be put in all churches: so he
" selected many passages out of these that were contrary to
" one another.   He also gathered many things out of Erasmus'
" Paraphrase that were contrary to the power of princes, and
" several other censurable things in that work, which Erasmus
38 " wrote when he was young, being of a far different strain
" from what he writ when he grew older, and better ac-
" quainted with the world.   But he concluded his letter with Collect.
" a discourse of the extent of the king and council's power, Numb. 14.
" which is all I transcribed of it, being very long, and full of
" things of no great consequence.   He questions how far the
" king could command against common or statute law, of
" which himself had many occasions to be well informed.
" Cardinal Wolsey had obtained his legatine power at the
" king's desire, but, notwithstanding that, he was brought into
" a *præmunire;* and the lawyers upon that argument cited
" many precedents of judges that were fined when they trans-
" gressed the laws, though commanded by warrants from the
" king; and earl Tiptoft, who was chancellor, lost his head
" for acting upon the king's warrant against law.   In the late
" king's time, the judges would not set fines on the breakers of
" the king's proclamations, when they were contrary to law,
" till the act concerning them was passed, about which there
" were many hot words when it was debated.   He mentions a
" discourse that passed between him and the lord Audley in
" the parliament concerning the king's supremacy.   Audley
" bid him look the act of supremacy, and he would see the
" king's doings were restrained to spiritual jurisdiction.   And
" by another act no spiritual law could take place against the [Ibid.
" common law, or an act of parliament; otherwise the bishops p. 64.]
" would strike in with the king, and, by means of the supre-
" macy, would order the law as they pleased; but we will pro-
" vide, said he, that the *præmunire* shall never go off of your

" backs. In some late cases he heard the judges declare what
" the king might do against an act of parliament, and what
" danger they were in that meddled in such matters. These
" things being so fresh in his memory, he thought he might
" write what he did to the lords of the council." But by this
it appears, that no sort of men is so much for the king's prerogative, but, when it becomes in any instance uneasy to them,
they will shelter themselves under the law. He continued afterwards, by many letters to the protector, to complain of his
[Ibid. p. 69.] ill usage : " that he had been then seven weeks in the Fleet
" without servants, a chaplain, or a physician ; that, though he
" he had his writ of summons, he was not suffered to come to
" the parliament, which might be a ground afterwards of ques-
" tioning their proceedings. He advised the protector not to
" make himself a party in these matters ; and used all the in-
" sinuations of decent flattery that he could invent, with many
" sharp reflections on Cranmer, and stood much on the force
" of laws, that they could not be repealed by the king's will ;
" concerning which he mentions a passage that fell out between
" Cromwell and himself before the late king. Cromwell said,
" that the king might make or repeal laws as the Roman em-
[Ibid. p. 65.] " perors did, and asked his opinion about it, whether the
" king's will was not a law ? To which he answered facetiously,
" that he thought it was much better for the king to make the
" law his will, than to make his will a law." But, notwithstanding all his letters, (which are printed in the second
[Fox, lib. ix. p. 53, sqq.] volume of Acts and Monuments, edit. 1641.) yet he continued
a prisoner till the parliament was over, and then by the act of
pardon he was set a liberty. This was much censured as an
invasion of liberty ; and it was said, these at court durst not
suffer him to come to the house, lest he had confounded them
in all they did. And the explaining justification with so much
nicety, in homilies that were to be read to the people, was 39
thought a needless subtilty. But the former abuses of trusting
to the acts of charity that men did, by which they fancied
they bought heaven, made Cranmer judge it necessary to express the matter so nicely ; though the expounding those
places of St. Paul was, as many thought, rather according to
the strain of the Germans, than to the meaning of these
Epistles. And, upon the whole matter, they knew Gardiner's

haughty temper, and that it was necessary to mortify him a little; though the pretence on which they did it seemed too slight for such severities. But it is ordinary, when a thing is once resolved on, to make use of the first occasion that offers for effecting it. The party that opposed the reformation, finding these attempts so unsuccessful, engaged the lady Mary to appear for them. She therefore wrote to the protector, that she thought all changes in religion, till the king came to be of age, were very much contrary to the respect they owed the memory of her father, if they went about to shake what he had settled; and against their duty to their young master to hazard the peace of his kingdom, and engage his authority in such points before he was capable of judging them. I gather this to have been the substance of her letter, from the answer which the protector wrote, which is in the Collection. In it he wrote, "that he believed her letter flowed not immediately " from herself, but from the instigation of some malicious per- " sons. He protests they had no other design but the glory " of God, and the honour and safety of the king; and that " what they had done was so well considered, that all good " subjects ought rather to rejoice at it than find fault with it. " And whereas she had said, that her father had brought reli- " gion to a godly order and quietness, to which both spiritu- " alty and temporalty did without compulsion give their " assent; he remembers her what opposition the stiff-necked " papists gave him, and what rebellions they raised against " him, which he wonders how she came so soon to forget; " adding, that death had prevented him before he had finished " these godly orders which he had designed; and that no " kind of religion was perfected at his death, but all was left " so uncertain, that it must inevitably bring on great disorders, " if God did not help them; and that himself and many others " could witness what regret their late master had, when he " saw he must die before he had finished what he intended. " He wondered that she, who had been well bred, and was " learned, should esteem true religion and the knowledge of the " scriptures *newfangledness* or *fantasy*. He desired she " would turn the leaf, and look on the other side, and would " with an humble spirit, and by the assistance of the grace of " God, consider the matter better."

[sidenotes:] The lady Mary dissatisfied with the reformation. The protector writ to her. Collect. Numb. 15.

The parliament meets.
[Journals of Lords, p. 293.]
Nov. 3.
Rot. Pat. 1.
reg. part 7.
[ap. Rymer, xv. 164.]

Nov. 10.
[Journals of Lords, p. 296.]
Nov. 10.

Nov. 19.

Dec. 24.

An act repealing former severe laws. [cap. 12. Statutes, iv. p. 18.]

[Ibid. p. 19]

Thus things went on till the parliament met, which was summoned to meet the fourth of November. The day before it met, the protector gave too public an instance how much his prosperous success had lifted him up. For, by a patent under the great seal, he was warranted to sit in parliament on the right hand of the throne, under the cloth of state,[23] and was to have all the honours and privileges that at any time any of the uncles of the kings of England, whether by the father's or mother's side, had enjoyed; with a *non obstante* to the statute of precedence. The lord Rich had been made lord chancellor[24] on the twenty-fourth of October; but whether the protector, or he, opened the parliament by any speech,[25] does not appear from 40 the Journal of the lords' house. On the tenth of December[26] a bill was brought in for the repealing several statutes. It was read the second time on the twelfth, and the third time on the sixteenth day. On the nineteenth some provisos were added to it, and it was sent down to the commons, who sent it up the twenty-third[27] of December, to which the royal assent was given. The commons had formed a new bill for repealing these statutes, which upon some conferences they were willing to let fall; only some provisos were added to the old one; upon which the bishops of London, Durham, Ely, Hereford, and Chichester, dissented. The preamble of it sets forth, " That " nothing made a government happier, than when the prince " governed with much clemency, and the subjects obeyed out " of love. Yet the late king and some of his progenitors, being " provoked by the unruliness of some of their people, had made " severe laws; but they, judging it necessary now to recom- " mend the king's government to the affections of the people, " repealed all laws that made any thing to be treason, but " what was in the act of 25 Edward the Third; as also two of " the statutes about Lollardies, together with the act of the six

---

[23] Cloth of state not mentioned. [S.]

[24] Ric. Riche Miles, Dominus Riche constitutus Cancellarius Angliæ 30 Nov. Pat. 1 Edw. 6. p. 3. m. 14. Dugdale, Orig. Jurid. [p. 86.] [B.]

[25] The lord Rich made the speech mentioned, though not inserted in the Lords' Journals. [S] [See Journals of Lords p. 293.]

[26] For December read November. [S]

[27] For twenty-third read twenty-fourth. [S.] [It was read the third time on Tuesday the 15th, and the fourth time on the 16th. See Journals of Lords pp. 296, 297.]

" articles, and the other acts that followed in explanation of
" that. All acts in king Henry the Eighth's time, declaring any
" thing to be felony that was not so declared before, were also
" repealed, together with the acts that made the king's procla-
" mations of equal authority with acts of parliament. It was
" also enacted, that all who denied the king's supremacy, or
" asserted the pope's in words, should for the first offence forfeit [Ibid. p.
" their goods and chattels, and suffer imprisonment during 20.]
" pleasure ; for the second offence should incur the pain of
" *præmunire;* and for the third offence be attainted of treason.
" But if any did in writing, printing, or by any overt act or deed,
" endeavour to deprive the king of his estate or titles, particu-
" larly of his supremacy, or to confer them on any other, after
" the first of March next, he was to be adjudged guilty of high
" treason : and if any of the heirs of the crown should usurp
" upon another, or did endeavour to break the succession of the
" crown, it was declared high treason in them, their aiders and
" abettors. And all were to enjoy the benefit of clergy, and the
" privilege of sanctuary, as they had it before king Henry the
" Eighth's reign, excepting only such as were guilty of murder,
" poisoning, burglary, robbing on the highway, the stealing of
" cattle, or stealing out of churches or chapels : poisoners [Ibid. p.
" were to suffer as other murderers. None were to be accused 22.]
" of words, but within a month after they were spoken. And
" those who called the French king by the title of king of
" France, were not to be esteemed guilty of the pains of trans-
" lating the king's authority or titles on any other." This act In Cor. Ch.
was occasioned by a speech that archbishop Cranmer had made Coll. Camb.
in convocation, in which he exhorted the clergy to give them- among Par-
selves much to the study of the scripture, and to consider ker's papers. [?]
seriously what things were in the church that needed reformation, that so they might throw out all the popish trash that was
not yet cast out. Upon this some intimated to him, that, as
long as the six articles stood in force, it was not safe for them
to deliver their opinions. This he reported to the council, upon
which they ordered this act of repeal. By it the subjects were
delivered from many fears they were under, and had good
hopes of a mild government, when, instead of procuring new
41 severe laws, the old ones were let fall. The council did also
free the nation of the jealousies they might have of them by

such an abridgment of their own power. But others judged it had been more for the interest of the government to have kept up these laws still in force, but to have restrained the execution of them. This repeal drew on another, which was sent from the commons on the twentieth of December, and was agreed to by the lords on the twenty-first. It was of an act in the twenty-eighth year of the last king, by which all laws made while his son was under twenty-four years of age, might be by his letters patents, after he attained that age, annulled as if they had never been. Which they altered thus: that the king, after that age, might by his letters patents void any act of parliament for the future; but could not so void it from the beginning, as to annul all things done upon it between the making and annulling of it, which were still to be lawful deeds.

[Cap. 17.
Statutes
vol. iii. p.
673.]

[Cap. ii.
ibid. vol. iv.
p. 7.]

The next bill of a public nature was concerning the sacrament, which was brought in, and read the first time, on the twelfth of November; the second time on the fifteenth, and was twice read on the seventeenth. And on the twenty-fourth [29] a bill was brought in for the communion to be received in both kinds; on the third of December it was read the second time, and given to the protector; on the fifth read again, and given to two judges; on the seventh it was read again and joined to the other bill about the sacrament. And on the tenth the whole bill was agreed to by all the peers, except the bishops of London, Hereford, Norwich, Worcester and Chichester; and sent down to the commons. On the seventeenth a *proviso* was sent after it, but was rejected by the commons, since the lords had not agreed to it. On the twentieth it was sent up agreed to, and had afterwards the royal assent. " By it, " first, the value of the holy sacrament, commonly called *the* " *sacrament of the altar*, and in the scripture the *supper* and " *table of the Lord*, was set forth; together with its first insti- " tution: but it having been of late marvellously abused, some " had been thereby brought to a contempt of it, which they had " expressed in sermons, discourses, and songs, in words not fit " to be repeated; therefore whosoever should so offend, after " the first of May next, was to suffer fine and imprisonment " at the king's pleasure; and the justices of the peace were to

Act about
the commu-
nion.
[cap. 1.
Statutes, iv.
p. 2.]
[Journals
of Lords,
pp. 296,
297.
[Ibid. p.
303.]
[Ibid. p.
305.]

[Ibid. p.
306.]

[Ibid. p.
309.]

[Ibid. p.
310.]

---

[29] [This was on Saturday the twenty-sixth of November. Journals of Lords, p. 301.]

"take information, and make presentments of persons so offend-
"ing, within three months after the offences so committed,
"allowing them witnesses for their own purgation. And it [Cap. 1,
"being more agreeable to Christ's first institution, and the Statutes,
"practice of the church for five hundred years after Christ, 3.]
"that the sacrament should be given in both the kinds of bread
"and wine, rather than in one kind only; therefore it was
"enacted, that it should be commonly given in both kinds,
"except necessity did otherwise require it. And it being also
"more agreeable to the first institution, and the primitive
"practice, that the people should receive with the priest, than
"that the priest should receive it alone; therefore, the day
"before every sacrament, an exhortation was to be made to
"the people to prepare themselves for it, in which the benefits
"and danger of worthy and unworthy receiving were to be
"expressed: and the priests were not without a lawful cause to
"deny it to any who humbly asked it."

This was an act of great consequence, since it reformed two Commu-
abuses that had crept into the church. The one was, the deny- nion ap-
42 ing the cup to the laity; the other was, the priest's communi- both kinds.
cating alone. In the first institution it is plain, that, as Christ
bade all drink of the cup, and his disciples all drank of it, so
St. Paul directed every one *to examine himself, that he might* [1 Cor. xi.
eat of that bread and drink of that cup. From thence the 28.]
church for many ages continued this practice; and the superstition of some, who received only in one kind, was severely
censured; and such were appointed either to receive the whole
sacrament, or to abstain wholly. It continued thus till the
belief of the corporal presence of Christ was set up; and then
the keeping and carrying about the cup in processions not
being so easily done, some began to lay it aside. For a great
while the bread was given dipped in the cup, to represent a
bleeding Christ, as it is in the Greek church to this day. In
other places the laity had the cup given them, but they were to
suck it through pipes, that nothing of it should fall to the
ground. But since they believed that Christ was in every
crumb of bread, it was thought needless to give the sacrament
in both kinds: so in the council of Constance the cup was
ordered to be denied the laity, though they acknowledged it to
have been instituted and practised otherwise. To this the

Bohemians would never submit; though to compel them to it much blood was shed in this quarrel. And now in the reformation this was every where one of the first things with which the people were possessed, the opposition of the Roman church herein to the institution of Christ being so manifest.

And all private masses put down.

At first this sacrament was also understood to be a communion of the body and blood of Christ, of which many were to be partakers: while the fervour of devotion lasted, it was thought a scandalous and censurable thing if any had come unto the Christian assemblies, and had not stayed to receive these holy mysteries; and the denying to give any one the sacrament was accounted a very great punishment: so sensible were the Christians of their ill condition when they were hindered to participate of it. But afterwards, the former devotion slackening, the good bishops in the fourth and fifth centuries complained oft of it, that so few came to receive; yet the custom being to make oblations before the sacrament, out of which the clergy had been maintained during the poverty of the church, the priests had a great mind to keep up the constant use of these oblations, and so persuaded the laity to continue them, and to come to the sacrament, though they did not receive it: and in process of time they were made to believe, that the priest received in behalf of the whole people. And whereas this sacrament was the commemoration of Christ's sacrifice on the cross, and so, by a phrase of speech, was called a *sacrifice*; they came afterwards to fancy that the priest's consecrating and consuming the sacrament was an action of itself expiatory, and that both for the dead and the living. And there rose an infinite number of several sorts of masses; some were for commemorating the saints, and those were called the masses of such saints; others for a particular blessing, for rain, health, &c. and indeed for all the accidents of human life, where the addition or variation of a collect made the difference: so that all that trade of massing was now removed. An intimation was also made of exhortations to be read in it, which they intended next to set about. These abuses in the mass gave great advantages to those who intended to change it into a communion. But many, instead of managing them prudently, made unseemly jests about them; and were carried by a lightness of temper to make songs and plays of the mass: for now the press went quick, and many books were printed this year about matters of religion, the greatest number of them being concerning the mass; which were not written in so decent and grave a style as the matter required. Against this act only five bishops protested. Many of that order were absent from the parliament, so the opposition made to it was not considerable.

The next bill brought into the house of lords was concerning the admission of bishops to their sees by the king's letters patents. Which being read, was committed to the archbishop of Canterbury's care on the fifth of November, and was read the second time on the tenth, and committed to some of the judges; and was read the third time on the twenty-eighth of November, and sent down to the commons on the fifth of December[30]. There was also another bill brought in, concerning the ecclesiastical jurisdiction in the bishops' courts, on the seventeenth of November, and passed, and sent down on the thirteenth of December. But both these bills were put in one, and sent up by the commons on the twentieth of that month, and assented to by the king. By this act it was set forth " that the way of choosing bishops by *congé d'élire* was tedious " and expenseful; that there was only a shadow of election in " it, and that therefore bishops should thereafter be made by " the king's letters patents, upon which they were to be conse- " crated : and whereas the bishops did exercise their authority, " and carry on processes, in their own names, as they were " wont to do in the time of popery ; and since all jurisdiction, " both spiritual and temporal, was derived from the king, that " therefore their courts, and all processes, should be from " henceforth carried on in the king's name, and be sealed by the " king's seal, as it was in the other courts of common law, after " the first of July next; excepting only the archbishop of " Canterbury's courts, and all collations, presentations[31], or

An act about the admission of bishops. [Cap. 2. Statutes iv. p. 3.] [Nov. 15] [Nov. 16.]

[Ibid. p. 4.]

---

[30] [This was read the first time on Tuesday Nov. 15, the second time on the 16th, and committed to the Bishops of Durham and Ely, the Chief Baron, and the King's attorney. It was read the third time Nov. 28, again Dec. 3, and with a provision annexed on Dec. 5, and sent to the Commons. Journals of the Lords pp. 297, 298, 302, 304.]

[31] The archbishop might only use his own name and seal for faculties and disputations; being in all other cases as much restrained as other bishops. [G.]

The archbishop of Canterbury might use his own name in all faculties and dispensations. [S.]

" letters of orders, which were to pass under the bishops'
" proper seals as formerly." Upon this act great advantages
were taken to disparage the reformation, as subjecting the
bishops wholly to the pleasure of the court.

The an-
cient ways
of electing
bishops.

At first bishops were chosen and ordained by the other
bishops in the countries where they lived. The apostles, by
that spirit of discerning, which was one of the extraordinary
gifts they were endued with, did ordain the first fruits of their
labours ; and never left the election of pastors to the discretion
of the people : indeed, when they were to ordain deacons, who
were to be trusted with the distribution of the public alms, they
appointed such as the people made choice of ; but when St.
Paul gave directions to Timothy and Titus about the choice of
pastors, all that depended on the people by them was, that

[1 Tim. iii.
2. Tit. i. 6.]

they should be *blameless and of good report*. But afterwards,
the poverty of the church being such, that churchmen lived
only by the free bounty of the people, it was necessary to consider them much ; so that in many places the choice began
among the people ; and in all places it was done by their
approbation and good liking. But great disorders followed
upon this, as soon as, by the emperors turning Christians, the
wealth of church-benefices made the pastoral charge more
desirable ; and the vast numbers of those who turned Christians with the tide, brought in great multitudes to have their
votes in these elections. The inconvenience of this was felt
early in Phrygia, where the council of Laodicea made a canon 44
against these popular elections. Yet in other parts of Asia,
and at Rome, there were great and often contests about it.
In some of these many men were killed. In many places the
inferior clergy chose their bishops ; but in most places the
bishops of the province made the choice, yet so as to obtain the
consent of the clergy and people. The emperors by their laws
made it necessary, that it should be confirmed by the metropolitans : they reserved the elections of the great sees to themselves, or at least the confirmation of them. Thus it continued
till Charles the Great's time. But then the nature of church-
employments came to be much altered : for though the church
had predial lands with the other rights that belonged to them
by the Roman law, yet he first gave bishops and abbots great
territories, with some branches of royal jurisdiction in them,

who held these lands of him, according to the feudal laws. This, as it carried churchmen off from the humility and abstraction from the world, which became their function; so it subjected them much to the humours and interests of those princes, on whom they had their dependence. The popes, who had made themselves heads of the hierarchy, could not but be glad to see churchmen grow rich and powerful in the world; but they were not so well pleased to see them made so much the more dependent on their princes: and no doubt by some of those princes, that were thus become patrons of churches, the bishoprics were either given for money, or charged with reserved pensions. Upon this the popes filled the world with the complaints of simony, and of enslaving churchmen to court interests; and so would not suffer them to accept of investitures from their princes; but set up for free elections, as they called them, which they said were to be confirmed by the see apostolic. So the canons secular or regular in cathedral churches were to choose the bishops, and their election was to be confirmed at Rome. Yet princes in most places got some hold of those elections, so that still they went as they had a mind they should: which was oft complained of as a great slavery on the church; and would have been more universally condemned, if the world had not been convinced that the matter would not be much the better if there should have been set up either the popular or synodical elections, in which faction was like to sway all. King Henry had continued the old way of the elections by the clergy, but so as that it seemed to be little more than a mockery; but now it was thought a more ingenuous way of proceeding, to have the thing done directly by the king, rather than under the thin covert of an involuntary election.

For the other branch about ecclesiastical courts, the causes before them concerning wills and marriages, being matters of a mixed nature, and which only belong to these by the laws of the land, and being no parts of the sacred functions, it was thought no invasion of the sacred offices to have these tried in the king's name. But the collation of benefices and giving of orders, which are the chief parts of the episcopal function, were to be performed still by the bishops in their own names. Only excommunication by a fatal neglect, continued to be the punishment for contempts of these courts; which belonging only to the spiritual cognizance, ought to have been reserved for the bishop, with the assistance of his clergy. But the canonists had so confounded all the ancient rules about the government 45 of the church, that the reformers being called away by considerations that were more obvious and pressing, there was not that care taken in this that the thing required. And these errors or oversights in the first concoction have by a continuance grown since into so formed a strength, that it is easier to see what is amiss, than to know how to rectify it.

[Nov. 30, Journals of Lords, p. 302.]
An act against vagabonds.
[Cap. 3, Statutes, vol. iv. p. 5.]

On the twenty-ninth of November[32] the bill against vagabonds was brought in. By this it was enacted, "That all that " should any where loiter without work, or without offering " themselves to work three days together ; or that should run " away from work, and resolve to live idly, should be seized on; " and whosoever should present them to a justice of peace, was " to have them adjudged to be his slaves for two years, and " they were to be marked with the letter V. imprinted with a " hot iron on their breast." A great many provisos follow concerning clerks so convict; which shew that this act was chiefly levelled at the idle monks and friars, who went about the country, and would betake themselves to no employment ; but, finding the people apt to have compassion on them, they continued in that course of life : which was of very ill consequence to the state ; for these vagrants did every where alienate the people's minds from the government, and persuaded them, that things would never be well settled till they were again restored to their houses. Some of these came often to London, on pretence of suing for their pensions, but really to practise up and down through the country: to prevent this, there was a proclamation set out, on the eighteenth of September, requiring them to stay in the places where they lived, and to send up a certificate where they were to the court of augmentations, who should thereupon give order for their constant payment. Some thought this law against vagabonds was too severe, and contrary to that common liberty, of which the English nation has been always very sensible, both in their own and their neighbours' particulars. Yet it could not be denied, but extreme diseases required extreme remedies ;

[32] [The house was adjourned from Monday the 28th, to Wednesday. Journals of Lords, p. 302.]

and perhaps there is no punishment too severe for persons that
are in health, and yet prefer a loitering course of life to an
honest employment. There followed in the act many excellent
rules for providing for the truly poor and indigent in the
several places where they were born and had their abode. Of
which this can only be said, that as no nation has laid down
more effectual rules for the supplying the poor than England,
so that indeed none can be in absolute want; so the neglect of
these laws is a just and great reproach on those who are
charged with the execution of them, when such numbers of poor
vagabonds swarm every where, without the due restraints that
the laws have appointed.

On the sixth of December, the bill for giving the chantries **An act,**
to the king was brought into the house of lords. It was read **giving the chantries**
the second time on the twelfth, the third time on the thirteenth, **to the king.**
and the fourth time on the fourteenth of that month [33]. It was **[Cap. 14. Statutes,**
much opposed, both by Cranmer on the one hand, and the po- **vol. iv. p. 24.]**
pish bishops on the other. The late king's executors saw they
could not pay his debts, nor satisfy themselves in their own
pretensions, formerly mentioned, out of the king's revenue; and
so intended to have these to be divided among them. Cranmer
opposed it long; for the clergy being much impoverished by
the sale of the impropriated tithes, that ought in all reason to
46 have returned into the church, but upon the dissolution of the
abbeys were all sold among the laity; he saw no probable way
remaining for their supply, but to save these endowments till
the king were of age, being confident he was so piously-dis-
posed, that they should easily persuade him to convert them
all to the bettering of the condition of the poor clergy, that
were now brought into extreme misery. And therefore he was
for reforming and preserving these foundations till the king's
full age. The popish bishops liked these endowments so well,
that, upon far different motives, they were for continuing them
in the state they were in. But those who were to gain by it
were so many, that the act passed; the archbishop of Canter- **[Journals**
bury, the bishops of London, Durham, Ely, Norwich, Hereford, **of lords, p. 308.]**
Worcester, and Chichester dissenting. So it being sent down
to the house of commons, was there much opposed by some

[33] [It was read the third time on   15th. Journals of Lords, pp. 307,
the 14th, and the fourth time on the   308.]

burgesses; who represented, that the boroughs, for which they served, could not maintain their churches, and other public works of the guilds and fraternities, if the rents belonging to them were given to the king; for these were likewise in the act. This was chiefly done by the burgesses of Lynn and Coventry, who were so active, that the whole house was much set against that part of the bill for the guild-lands: therefore those who managed that house for the court took these off by an assurance, that their guild-lands should be restored to them, and so they desisted from their opposition, and the bill passed on the promise given to them, which was afterwards made good by the protector. In the preamble of the act it is set forth, " that the great superstition of Christians, rising out of their " ignorance of the true way of salvation by the death of Christ, " instead of which they had set up the vain conceits of purga- " tory, and masses satisfactory, was much supported by tren- " tals and chantries. And since the converting these to godly " uses, such as the endowing of schools, provisions for the poor, " and the augmenting of places in the universities, could not " be done by parliament, they therefore committed it to the " care of the king. And then, reciting the act made in the

[Statutes, vol. iv. p. 25.]

" thirty-seventh year of his father's reign, they give the king " all such chantries, colleges, and chapels, as were not possessed " by the late king, and all that had been in being any time " these five years last passed; as also all revenues belonging to " any church for anniversaries, obits, and lights, together with " all guild-lands which any fraternity of men enjoyed for obits, " or the like; and appoint these to be converted to the main- " tenance of grammar-schools, or preachers, and for the in- " crease of vicarages." After this followed the act, giving the

[Cap. 13. ibid. p. 22.]

king the customs known by the name of tonnage and poundage, besides some other laws of matters that are not needful to be

[Cap. 15. ibid. p. 33.]

remembered in this History. Last of all came the king's general pardon, with the common exceptions, among which, one was of those who were then prisoners in the Tower of London, in which the duke of Norfolk was included. So, all business

[Journals of Lords, p. 313.]

being ended, the parliament was prorogued from the twenty-fourth of December to the twentieth of April following.

Acts that were proposed, but not carried.

But, having given this account of these bills that were passed, I shall not esteem it an unfruitful piece of history to shew what other bills were designed.   There were put into the house of lords two bills that were stifled: the one was, for the use of the scriptures, which came not to a second reading ; the other 47 was, a bill for erecting a new court of chancery for ecclesiastical and civil causes; which was committed to some bishops and temporal lords, but never more mentioned.   The commons sent up also some bills which the lords did not agree to.   One was about benefices, with cure and residence; it was committed, but never reported.   Another was, for the reformation of divers laws, and of the courts of common law ; and a third was, that married men might be priests, and have benefices.   To this the commons did so readily agree, that, it being put in on the nineteenth of December, and read then for the first time, it was read twice the next day, and sent up to the lords on the twenty-first.   But, being read there once, it was like to have raised such debates, that, it being resolved to end the session before Christmas, the lords laid it aside.

But, while the parliament was sitting, they were not idle in the convocation ; though the popish party was yet so prevalent in both houses, that Cranmer had no hopes of doing any thing till they were freed of the trouble which some of the great bishops gave them.   The most important thing they did was, the carrying up four petitions to the bishops, which will be found in the Collection.   First, that, according to the statute made in the reign of the late king, there might be persons empowered for reforming the ecclesiastical laws.   The second, that, according to the ancient custom of the nation, and the tenor of the bishops' writ to the parliament, the inferior clergy might be permitted again to sit in the house of commons, or that no acts concerning matters of religion might pass without the sight and assent of the clergy.   The third, that, since divers prelates, and other divines, had been in the late king's time appointed to alter the service of the church, and had made some progress in it, that this might be brought to its full perfection.   The fourth, that some consideration might be had for the maintenance of the clergy the first year they came into their livings, in which they were charged with the first-fruits; to which they added a desire to know, whether they might safely speak their minds about religion, without the danger of any law.   For the first of these four petitions, an account of it

[Nov. 15.
Journals of
Lords, p.
297.]
[Nov. 23.
ibid. p.
300.]

[Nov. 21.
ibid. p.
299.]
[Dec. 5.
Journals of
Commons,
p. 2.]

[Journals
of Lords,
p. 311.]

The convocation
meets.
[Nov. 5.
Wilkins,
Conc. iv.
15.]
The lower
house
made some
petitions.
Numb. 16.

shall be given hereafter. As to the second, it was a thing of great consequence, and deserves to be further considered in this place.

The inferior clergy desire to be admitted to have representatives in the house of commons.

Anciently, all the free men of England, or at least those that held of the crown in chief, came to parliament: and then the inferior clergy had writs as well as the superior; and the first of the three estates of the kingdom were the bishops, the other prelates, and the inferior clergy. But when the parliament was divided into two houses, then the clergy made likewise a body of their own, and sat in convocation, which was the third estate. But the bishops having a double capacity, the one of ecclesiastical prelature, the other of being the king's barons, they had a right to sit with the lords as a part of their estate, as well as in the convocation. And though, by parity of reason, it might seem that the rest of the clergy, being freeholders as well as clerks, had an equal right to choose or be chosen into the house of commons; yet, whether they were ever in possession of it, or whether, according to the clause *præmonentes* in the bishops' writ, they were ever a part of the house of commons, is a just doubt. For, besides this assertion in the petition that was mentioned, and a more large one in the second petition which they presented to the same purpose, which

Numb. 17. is likewise in the Collection, I have never met with any good 48 reason to satisfy me in it. There was a general tradition in queen Elizabeth's reign, that the inferior clergy departed from their right of being in the house of commons, when they were all brought into the *præmunire* upon cardinal Wolsey's legatine power, and made their submission to the king. But that is not credible; for as there is no footstep of it, which, in a time of so much writing and printing, must have remained, if so great a change had been then made; so it cannot be thought, that those who made this address but seventeen years after, that submission, (many being alive in this who were of that convocation, Polydore Vergil in particular, a curious observer, since he was maintained here to write the history of England,) none of them should have remembered a thing that was so fresh, but have appealed to writs and ancient practices. But though this design of bringing the inferior clergy into the house of commons did not take at this time, yet it was again set on foot in the end of queen Elizabeth's reign, and reasons were offered to

persuade her to set it forward; which not being then successful, these same reasons were again offered to king James, to
induce him to endeavour it. The paper that discovers this was
communicated to me by Dr. Borlace, the worthy author of the
History of the Irish Rebellion[34]. It is corrected in many places
by the hand of bishop Ravis, then bishop of London[35], a man
of great worth. This, for the affinity of the matter, and the
curiosity of the thing, I have put into the Collection, with a Numb. 18.
large marginal note, as it was designed to be transcribed for
king James. But whether this matter was ever much considered, or lightly laid aside, as a thing unfit and unpracticable,
does not appear; certain it is, that it came to nothing. Upon
the whole matter, it is not certain what was the power or right
of these proctors of the clergy in former times. Some are of Coke iv.
opinion, that they were only assistants to the bishops, but had Inst. 3, 4.
no voice in either house of parliament. This is much confirmed
by an act passed in the parliament of Ireland, in the twenty-
eighth year of the former reign, which sets forth in the preamble, "that though the proctors of the clergy were always
" summoned to parliament, yet they were no part of it, nor had
" they any right to vote in it, but were only assistants in case
" matters of controversy or learning came before them, as the
" convocation was in England: which had been determined by
" the judges of England, after much inquiry made about it.
" But the proctors were then pretending to so high an au-
" thority, that nothing could pass without their consents; and
" it was presumed they were set on to it by the bishops, whose
" chaplains they were for the most part. Therefore they were
" by that act declared to have no right to vote."

From this, some infer they were no other in England, and
that they were only the bishops' assistants and council. But as
the clause *præmonentes* in the writ seems to make them a part [Rymer
of the parliament, so these petitions suppose that they sat in xiv. p.
the house of commons anciently; where it cannot be imagined 563.]
they could sit, if they came only to be assistants to the bishops;

---

[34] [Borlace, (Edmond). The history of the execrable Irish rebellion,
traced from many preceding acts, to
the grand eruption in 1641, and
thence pursued to the act of settle-

ment in 1661. Lond. 1680. fol.]
[35] [Thomas Ravis, bishop of Gloucester, translated to London, May
18, 1607, died Dec. 14, 1609.]

for then they must have sat in the house of lords rather as the
judges, the masters of chancery, and the king's council do. Nor
is it reasonable to think they had no voice; for then their sitting
in parliament had been so insignificant a thing, that it is not
likely they would have used such endeavours to be restored to
it; since their coming to parliament upon such an account must 49
have been only a charge to them.

[Statutes, vol. ii. p. 98.]
There is against this opinion an objection of great force from
the acts passed in the twenty-first year of Richard the Second's
reign. In the second act of that parliament it is said, "that it
" was first prayed by the commons; and that the lords spiritual,
" and the proctors of the clergy, did assent to it; upon which
" the king, by the assent of all the lords and commons, did
" enact it." The twelfth act of that parliament was a repeal
of the whole parliament that was held in the eleventh year of
[Ibid. p. 102.]
that reign; and concerning it, it is expressed, "that the lords
" spiritual and temporal, the proctors of the clergy, and the
" commons, being severally examined, did all agree to it."
From hence it appears, that these proctors were then not only
a part of the parliament, but were a distinct body of men, that
did severally from all the rest deliver their opinions. It may
seem strange, that, if they were then considered as a part of
either house of parliament, this should be the only time in
which they should be mentioned as bearing their share in the
legislative power. In a matter that is so perplexed and dark,
I shall presume to offer a conjecture, which will not appear
perhaps improbable. In page 129 of the former part, I gave
the reasons that made me think the lower house of convocation
consisted at the first only of the proctors of the clergy[36]. So
that by the proctors of the clergy, both in the statute of Ireland,

---

[36] [See part i. p. 113, where Pole,
dean of Exeter, is spoken of as being
of the lower house of convocation;
and p. 129, for the conjecture that
abbots, deans, and archdeacons, sat
in the upper house. This opinion
the author admits (part iii. p. 81.)
to have been adopted without any
good ground. The author, at the
time of writing the first part of his
history, probably had not seen the
document inserted in the addenda
to the Records, where the names of
the clergy are signed, the bishops,
abbots, and priors, as belonging to
the upper house; the deans, archdeacons and proctors, as of the lower
house. It is a remarkable instance of
carelessness that the mistake should
have been repeated in this second part,
the whole of which was composed after
the publication of the first part of
the history. See Harmer's Specimen
of Errors, pp. 28–35, and 72–77.]

and in those made by Richard the Second ,is perhaps to be
understood, the lower house of convocation : and it is not unreasonable to think, that, upon so great an occasion as the annulling a whole parliament, to make it pass the better, in an
age in which the people paid so blind a submission to the clergy,
the concurrence of the whole representative of the church might
have been thought necessary. It is generally believed, that
the whole parliament sat together in one house before Edward
the Third's time, and then the inferior clergy were a part of
that body without question. But when the lords and commons
sat apart, the clergy likewise sat in two houses, and granted
subsidies as well as the temporalty. It may pass for no unlikely conjecture, that the clause *præmonentes* was first put in
the bishops' writ for the summoning of the lower house of convocation, consisting of these proctors; and afterwards, though
there was a special writ for the convocation, yet this might at
first have been continued in the bishops' writ by the neglect of
a clerk, and from thence be still used. So that it seems to me
most probable, that the proctors of the clergy were, both in
England and Ireland, the lower house of convocation. Now
before the submission which the clergy made to king Henry, as
the convocation gave the king great subsidies, so the whole
business of religion lay within their sphere. But after the submission, they were cut off from meddling with it, except as
they were authorized by the king : so that, having now so
little power left them, it is no wonder they desired to be put
in the state they had been in before the convocation was separated from the parliament; or at least that matters of religion
should not be determined till they had been consulted, and had
reported their opinions and reasons. The extreme of raising
the ecclesiastical power too high in the times of popery, had
now produced another, of depressing it too much. For seldom
50 is the counterpoise so justly balanced, that extremes are reduced
to a well-tempered mediocrity.

For the third petition, it was resolved that many bishops and
divines should be sent to Windsor to labour in the matter of
the church service. But that required so much consideration,
that they could not enter on it during a session of parliament.
And for the fourth, what answer was given to it, doth not
appear.

[Nov. 30.
C.C.C.C.
No. cxxi.
p. 5 a.]

On the twenty-ninth of November a declaration was sent down from the bishops concerning the sacraments being to be received in both kinds; to which John Tyler[37], the prolocutor, and several others, set their hands: and being again brought before them, it was agreed to by all without a contradictory vote; sixty-four being present, among whom I find

[Wilkins,
Conc. iv.
16.]

Polydore Vergil was one. And on the seventeenth of December the proposition concerning the marriage of the clergy was also sent to them, and subscribed by thirty-five affirmatively, and by fourteen negatively[38]; so it was ordered, that a bill should be drawn concerning it. I shall not here digress to give an account of what was alleged for or against this, reserving that to its proper place, when the thing was finally settled.

And this is all the account I could recover of this convocation. I have chiefly gathered it from some notes and other papers of the then Dr. Parker, (afterwards archbishop of Canterbury,) which are carefully preserved with his other MSS. in Corpus Christi college library at Cambridge. To which library I had free access by the favour of the most learned master, Dr. Spencer, with the other worthy fellows of that house; and from thence I collected many remarkable things in this history.

The parliament being brought to so good a conclusion, the protector took out a new commission; in which all the addition that is made to that authority he formerly had, is, that in his absence he is empowered to substitute another, to whom he might delegate his power.

The state
of affairs
in Germany.

And thus this year ended in England. But as they were carrying on the reformation here, it was declining apace in Germany. The duke of Saxe and the landgrave were this year to command their armies apart. The duke of Saxe kept within his own country; but having there unfortunately divided his forces, the emperor overtook him near the Elbe at Muhlberg, where the emperor's soldiers crossing the river, and pursuing him with great fury, after some resistance, in which he himself performed all that could be expected from so great a captain, was taken prisoner, and his country all possessed by Maurice, who was now to be invested with the

Apr. 24,
1547. duke
of Saxe
taken.

[37] For Tyler read Taylour. [S.]
[38] [Cui propositioni multi sub- scripserunt affirmantes 53, negantes 22. Wilkins, Conc. iv. 16.]

electoral dignity. He bore his misfortunes with a greatness [Sleidan,
and equality of mind that is scarce to be paralleled in history. fol. 307.]
Neither could the insolence with which the emperor treated
him, nor the fears of death, to which he adjudged him, nor
that tedious imprisonment which he suffered so long, ever
shake or disorder a mind that was raised so far above the
inconstancies of human affairs. And though he was forced
to submit to the hardest conditions possible, of renouncing his
dignity and dominions, some few places being only reserved for
his family; yet no entreaties nor fears could ever bring him to
yield any thing in matters of religion. He made the Bible his
chief companion and comfort in his sharp afflictions; which he
51 bore so, as if he had been raised up to that end, to let the
world see how much he was above it. It seemed inimitable;
and therefore engaged Thuanus, with the other excellent [Thuanus,
writers of that age, to set it out with all the advantages that lib. iv.
cap. 11]
so unusual a temper of mind deserved. Yet had those writers
lived in our age, and seen a great king, not overpowered by a
superior prince, but by the meanest of his own people, and
treated with equal degrees of malice and scorn, and at last put
to death openly, with the pageantry of justice; and bearing
all this with such invincible patience, heroical courage, and
most Christian submission to God, they had yet found a nobler
subject for their eloquent pens: but he saved the world the
labour of giving a just representation of his behaviour in his
sufferings, having left his own portraiture drawn by himself in
such lively and lasting colours[39].

The landgrave of Hesse saw he could not long withstand
the emperor's army, now so lifted up with success; and therefore was willing to submit to him on the best terms that his
sons-in law, the elector of Brandenburg and Maurice of Saxe,
could obtain for him. Which were very hard : only he was to
enjoy his liberty, without any imprisonment, and to preserve
his dominions. But the emperor's ministers dealt most unfaith-
fully with him in this : for in the German language there was
but one letter's difference, and that only inverted, between perpetual imprisonment, and any imprisonment, (ewig for emig[40] ;) [Thuanus,
lib. iv. cap.
13.]

[39] [Published in the reign of   [40] [The story, which has no ab-
Charles II. The allusion is to the   solutely contemporary authority, is
celebrated Icon Basilike.]   taken from De Thou, where the two

so, by this base artifice, he was, when he came and submitted
to the emperor, detained a prisoner. He had not the duke of
Saxe's temper, but was out of measure impatient, and did
exclaim of his ill usage ; but there was no remedy, for the
emperor was now absolute. All the towns of Germany, Magdeburg and Bremen only excepted, submitted to him, and
redeemed his favour by great sums of money, and many pieces
of ordnance. And the Bohemians were also forced to implore
his brother's mercy, who, before he would receive them into
his hands, got his revenue to be raised vastly. And now the
empire was wholly at the emperor's mercy. Nothing could
withstand him, who had in one year turned out two electors.

Apr. 16,
1546,
Herman
excommu-
nicated at
Rome.
[Sleidan,
fol. 270,
and 302.]

For Herman bishop of Cologne, as he was before condemned
by the pope, so was also degraded from that dignity by the
emperor ; and Adolph, whom he had procured to be made
his coadjutor, was declared elector. Many of his subjects and
neighbour princes offered their service, if he would stand to his
own defence ; but he was very old, and of so meek a temper,
that he would suffer no blood to be shed on his account ; and
therefore withdrew peaceably to a retirement [41], in which he

Nov. 4.
Herman
resigned.

lived four years, till his death. His brother, that was bishop
of Munster, and dean of Bonn, who had gone along with him

[Ibid. fol.
302.]

in his reformation, was also turned out ; and Gropper was
made dean, who was esteemed one of the learnedest and best
men of the clergy at this time. He is said to have expressed a
generous contempt of the highest dignity the see of Rome
could bestow on him, for he refused a cardinal's hat when
it was offered him ; yet in this matter he had not behaved
himself as became so good a man and so learned a divine : for
he had consented to the changes which had been made, and
was in a correspondence with Martin Bucer, whom Herman
brought to Cologne ; (as will appear by an excellent letter of

Collect.
Numb. 19.

Bucer's to him, which will be found in the Collection, concerning that matter ;) by which it is plain, he went along with
them from the beginning. But it seems he did it covertly and 52

phrases are given at length, written
in the Roman character. 'Nicht
ein einig tag gefangen sein, et Nicht
ein ewig tag gefangen sein.' The
author appears to have been ignorant
of German and to have read *in* as *m*,
a mistake which has been per-
petuated in subsequent editions.]

41 [The resignation of Herman
and succession of Adolph is placed
by Sleidan in 1547, January 25.]

fearfully, and was afterwards drawn off, either by the love
of the world, or the fears of the cross : of which it appears
Bucer had then some apprehensions, though he expressed them
very modestly. Gropper's memory being in such high esteem,
and this letter being found among Bucer's papers, I thought
the publishing of it would not be unacceptable, though it be of
a foreign matter.

Germany being thus under the power and dread of the [Hist. of
emperor, a diet was summoned to Augsburg ; where the chief Council of
church was taken from the protestants, and put into the car- Trent,
dinal of Augsburg's hands, to have the mass set up again in it ; p. 256.]
though the town was so much protestant, that they could find
none that would come to it, but some poor people who were
hired.   The emperor, among other propositions he put into
the diet, pressed this, that all differences in religion, which
had so distracted Germany, might be removed.   The ecclesiastical princes answered, that the only way to effect that was,
to submit to the general council that was at Trent.   Those
that were for the Augsburg Confession said, they could submit
to no council where the pope presided, and where the bishops
were sworn to obey him ; but would submit to it, if that oath
was dispensed with, and their divines admitted to defend their
opinions, and all the decrees that had been made were again
considered.   In this difference of opinion, the emperor thought,
that, if the whole matter should be left to his discretion, to
which all should be bound to submit, he would then be able to
determine it as he pleased.   So he dealt privately with the
electors Palatine and Saxe ; and, as they published it afterwards, gave them secret assurances about the freedom of their
religion, and that he only desired this to put him in a capacity
of dealing on other terms with the pope.   Upon which they
consented to a decree, referring the matter of religion wholly
to his care.   But the deputies from the cities, who looked
on this as a giving up of their religion, could not be wrought
to do it without conditions, which they put into another writing,
as explanatory of the submission : but the emperor took no
notice of that, and only thanked them for their confidence in
him ; and so the decree was published.   All this was in some
sort necessary for the emperor, who was then in very ill terms
with the pope about the business of Piacenza.   For the pope's

Sept. 10.
1547,
Petrus
Aloisius
killed.
[Sleidan,
fol. 315.]

natural son, Petrus Aloisius, being killed by a conspiracy, the governor of Milan had seized on Piacenza, which made the pope believe the emperor was accessary to it; for which the reader is referred to the Italian historians. The pope saw the emperor in one summer delivered of a war, which he had hoped would have entangled him his whole life; and though in decency he could not but seem to rejoice, and did so, no doubt, at the ruin of those whom he called heretics, yet he was not a little grieved to see the emperor so much exalted.

The pro-
ceedings at
Trent.

At Trent the legates had been oft threatened and affronted by the emperor's ambassadors and bishops, who were much set on reforming abuses, and lessening the power of the see of Rome. So they had a mind to break up the council: but that would have been so scandalous a thing, and so resented by the emperor, that they resolved rather on a translation into some town of the pope's, to which it was not likely the imperialists would follow them; and so at least the council would be suspended, if not dissolved. For this remove, they laid hold

April 21.
The first
session of
Bologna.

on the first colour they could find. One dying of a malignant fever, it was given out, and certified by physicians, that he died of the plague; so in all haste they translated the council to Bologna. The imperialists protested against it, but in vain; for thither they went. The emperor was hereby quite disappointed of his chief design, which was, to force the Germans to submit to a council held in Germany; and therefore no plague appearing at Trent, he pressed the return of the council

[Hist. of
Council of
Trent,
p. 260.]

thither. But the pope said, it was the council's act, and not his; and that their honour was to be kept up; that therefore such as stayed at Trent were to go first to Bologna, and acknowledge the council, and they should then consider what was to be done. So that now all the hope the Germans had was, that this difference between the pope and emperor might give them some breathing; and time might bring them out of these extremities, into which they were then driven. Upon these disorders the foreign reformers, who generally made Germany their sanctuary, were now forced to seek it

[Sleidan,
fol. 319.]

elsewhere. So Peter Martyr, in the end of November this year, was brought over to England, by the invitation which the archbishop of Canterbury sent him in the king's name. He was born in Florence, where he had been an Augustinian

monk. He was learned in the Greek and the Hebrew, which
drew on him the envy of the rest of his order, whose manners
he inveighed oft against. So he left them, and went to Naples,
where he gathered an assembly of those who loved to worship
God more purely. This being made known, he was forced
to leave that place, and went next to Lucca, where he lived in
society with Tremellius and Zanchius. But being also in
danger there, he went to Zurich with Bernardinus Ochinus,
that had been one of the most celebrated preachers of Italy,
and now forsook his former superstitions. From Zurich he
went to Basle; and from thence, by Martin Bucer's means, he
was brought to Strasburg, where Cranmer's letters found both
him and Ochinus. The latter was made a canon of Canterbury, [May 9,
with a dispensation of residence : and, by other letters patents, 1548.]
forty marks were given yearly to him, and as much to Peter
Martyr.

There had been this year some differences between the Eng- The French
lish and French concerning the fortifications about Boulogne. quarrel
The English were raising a great fort by the harbour there. logne.
This being signified to king Henry by Gaspard Coligny, afterwards the famous admiral of France, then governor of the
neighbouring parts to Boulogne; it was complained of at the
court of England. It was answered, that this was only to make
the harbour more secure ; and so the works were ordered to
be vigorously carried on. But this could not satisfy the
French, who plainly saw it was of another sort than to be
intended only for the sea. The king of France came and
viewed the country himself, and ordered Coligny to raise a
fort on a high ground near it, which was called the Chastilian
fort, and commanded both the English fort and the harbour.
But the protector had no mind to give the French a colour for
breaking with the English ; so there was a truce and further
cessation agreed on in the end of September. These are all the
considerable foreign transactions of this year in which England
was concerned. But there was a secret contrivance laid at
home of a high nature, which though it broke not out till the
next year, yet the beginnings of it did now appear.

54　　The protector's brother, Thomas Seymour, was brought to The breach
such a share in his fortunes, that he was made a baron and lord between
admiral. But this not satisfying his ambition, he endeavoured tor and

the admi-
ral.
[Aug. 30.
Rymer xv.
p. 157.]

to have linked himself into a nearer relation with the crown,
by marrying the king's sister, the lady Elizabeth. But, finding
he could not compass that, he made his addresses to the queen
dowager, who, enjoying now the honour and wealth the late king
had left her, resolved to satisfy herself in her next choice, and
entertained him a little too early; for they were married so
soon after the king's death, that it was charged afterwards on
the admiral, that, if she had brought a child as soon as might
have been after the marriage, it had given cause to doubt whether it had not been by the late king, which might have raised
great disturbance afterwards; but, being thus married to the
queen, he concealed it for some time, till he procured a letter
from the king, recommending him to her for a husband; upon
which they declared their marriage, with which the protector
was much offended. Being thus possessed of great wealth, and
being husband to the queen dowager, he studied to engage all
that were about the king to be his friends; and he corrupted
some of them by his presents, and forced one on sir John Cheke.
That which he designed was, that whereas in former times the
infant kings of England had had governors of their persons,
distinct from the protectors of their realms, which trusts were
divided between their uncles, it being judged too much to join
both in one person, who was thereby too great; whereas a governor of the king's person might be a check on the protector:
he would therefore himself be made governor of the king's
person; alleging, that, since he was the king's uncle, as well
as his brother, he ought to have a proportioned share with
him in the government. About Easter this year he first set
about this design, and corrupted some about the king, who
should bring him sometimes privately through the gallery to
the queen's lodgings; and he desired they would let him know
when the king had occasion for money, and that they should
not always trouble the treasury, for he would be ready to furnish him: and he thought a young king might be taken with
this. So it happened, that the first time Latimer preached at
court, the king sent to him to know what present he should
make him: Seymour sent him 40*l.*; but said, he thought 20*l.*
enough to give Latimer, and the king might dispose of the rest
as he pleased. Thus he gained ground with the king, whose
sweet nature exposed him to be easily won by such artifices.

It is generally said, that all this difference between the brothers was begun by their wives, and that the protector's lady, being offended that the younger brother's wife had the precedence of her, which she thought belonged to herself, did thereupon raise and inflame the differences. But in all the letters that I have seen concerning this breach, I could never find any such thing once mentioned ; nor is it reasonable to imagine that the duchess of Somerset should be so foolish as to think that she ought to have the precedence of the queen[42] dowager ; therefore I look upon this story as a mere fiction : though it is probable enough there might, upon some other accounts, have been some animosities between the two high-spirited ladies, which might have afterwards been thought to have occasioned their husbands' quarrel.

55   It is plain in the whole thread of this affair, that the protector was at first very easy to be reconciled to his brother, and was only assaulted by him ; but bore the trouble he gave him with much patience for a great while ; though in the end, seeing his factious temper was incurable, he laid off nature too much when he consented to his execution. Yet all along till then, he had rather too much encouraged his brother to go on, by his readiness to be, after every breach, reconciled to him. When the protector was in Scotland, the admiral then began to act more avowedly, and was making a party for himself, of which Paget took notice, and charged him with it in plain terms. He asked him, why he would go about to reverse that which himself and others had consented to under their hands ? Their family was now so great, that nothing but their mutual quarrelling could do them any prejudice : but there would not be wanting officious men to inflame them, if they once divided among themselves ; and the breaches among near friends commonly turned to the most irreconcilable quarrels. Yet all was ineffectual ; for the admiral was resolved to go on, and either get himself advanced higher, or to perish in the attempt. It was the knowledge of this which forced the protector to return

---

[42] She is acknowledged to have been an insolent woman, p. 194, and to have had a great power over her husband, where it is assigned as a chief cause of procuring an act of parliament for the disinheriting and excludiug from his honours his children by his former wife. [G.]

from Scotland so abruptly, and disadvantageously for the securing of his interest with the king, on whom his brother's artifices had made some impression.   Whether there was any reconciliation made between them before the parliament met, is not certain : but, during the session, the admiral got the king to write with his own hand a message to the house of commons, for the making of him the governor of his person ; and he intended to have gone with it to the house, and had a party there, by whose means he was confident to have carried his business : he dealt also with many of the lords and counsellors to assist him in it.   When this was known, before he had gone with it to the house, some were sent to him in his brother's name, to see if they could prevail with him to proceed no further.   He refused to hearken to them, and said, that if he were crossed in his attempt, he would make this the blackest parliament that ever was in England.   Upon that he was sent for by order from the council, but refused to come : then they threatened him severely, and told him, the king's writing was nothing in law, but that he, who had procured it, was punishable for doing an act of such a nature, to the disturbance of the government, and for engaging the young king in it.   So they resolved to have sent him to the Tower, and to have turned him out of all his offices ; but he submitted himself to the protector and council ; and his brother and he seemed to be perfectly reconciled.   Yet, as the protector had reason to have a watchful eye over him, so it was too soon visible, that he had not laid down, but only put off, his high projects till a fitter conjuncture ; for he began the next Christmas to deal money again among the king's servants, and was on all occasions infusing into the king a dislike of every thing that was done, and did often persuade him to assume the government himself. But the sequel of this quarrel proved fatal to him, as shall be told in its proper place.   And thus ended the year 1547.

1548.
Jan. 8.
[Council
Book, p.
265.]
On the eighth of January next year Gardiner was brought before the council, where it was told him, that his former offences being included in the king's general pardon, he was thereupon discharged.   A grave admonition was given him to 56 carry himself reverently and obediently, and he was desired to declare whether he would receive the Injunctions and Homilies, and the doctrine to be set forth from time to time by the king

and clergy of the realm. He answered, he would conform himself as the other bishops did, and only excepted to the homily of Justification, and desired four or five days to consider of it. What he did at the end of that time does not appear from the council-book, no further mention being made of this matter; for the clerks of council did not then enter every thing with that exactness that is since used[43]. He went home to his diocese, where there still appeared in his whole behaviour great malignity to Cranmer, and to all motions for reformation; yet he gave such outward compliance, that it was not easy to find any advantage against him, especially now since the council's great power was so much abridged.

In the end of January the council made an order concerning the marquis of Northampton, which will oblige me to look back a little for the clear account of it. This lord, who was brother to the queen dowager, had married Anne Bourchier, daughter to the earl of Essex, the last of that name; but she being convicted of adultery, he was divorced from her, which, according to the law of the ecclesiastical courts, was only a separation from bed and board. Upon which divorce it was proposed in king Henry's time to consider what might be done in favour of the innocent person, when the other was convicted of adultery. So, in the beginning of king Edward's reign, on the seventh of May, a commission was granted to the archbishop of Canterbury, the bishops of Durham and Rochester, (this was Holbeche, who was not then translated to Lincoln,) to Dr. Ridley, and six more, ten in all, of whom six were a quorum, to try

The marquis of Northampton sues a divorce for adultery. [Jan. 28. Council Book, p. 275.]

---

[43] [" It had been more cautious in the historian to have said that he could not find such exact entries made by them. For I find an order of Council made 1550, April 19th, and entered in the beginning of a large original book, containing the acts of council for the last four years of King Edward 6th, that there shall be a clerk attendant upon the said Council, to write, enter, and register all such decrees, determinations, and other things as he should be appointed to enter in a book to remain always as a ledger as well for the discharge of the said Counsellors, touching such things as they shall pass from time to time, as also for a memorial unto them of their own proceedings. Unto which office William Thomas was appointed by the King's highness with the advice of his aforesaid Council and in presence of the same Council sworn. Accordingly all the acts of Council are therein entered largely and with great exactness, the original hands of the privy counsellors then present being added to the acts and orders of every several day." Harmer's Specimen of Errors, p. 77.]

whether the lady Anne was not by the word of God so lawfully divorced, that she was no more his wife, and whether thereupon he might not marry another wife. This being a new case, and of great importance, Cranmer resolved to examine it with his ordinary diligence, and searched into the opinions of the fathers and doctors so copiously that his collections about it grew into a large book, (the original whereof I have perused;) the greatest part of it being either written or marked, and interlined with his own hand[44]. This required a longer time than the marquis of Northampton could stay; and therefore, presuming on his great power, without waiting for judgment, he solemnly married Elizabeth, daughter to Brooke, lord Cobham. On the twenty-eighth of January information was brought to the council of this, which gave great scandal, since his first marriage stood yet firm in law. So he, being put to answer

Ex MSS.
D. Stilling-
fleet,
[Lambeth,
No. 1108,
fol. 144—
161.]

[44] [This paper has been very erroneously described by the author, and imperfectly by subsequent readers and editors. The whole subject, including the paper here alluded to as well as the other paper mentioned further on, p. 58, occupies the last 48 folios of the Lambeth MSS. No. 1108. The important passages, whichever way they seem to incline, are underlined in red ink, and it seems doubtful if the author's reading extended much beyond these passages; for his description is throughout extremely careless and in many cases entirely wrong. The tract begins at fol. 144, which is marked *De Divortio*, and on the back is the quotation from Hermas; next comes the opinion of Origen; that of Euaristus which is on the second page of fol. 146, as well as those of Cyprian, Lactantius, and Hilary, on the back of fol. 148, are taken no notice of by the author. The first page of fol. 152 is vacant; on the back is the reference to S. Basil, where the grossest misrepresentation on the part of the author occurs. The reference to S. Jerome occurs in the middle of fol. 153, that to Chromatius on the back of fol. 154, but it does not bear out what the author says. Quotations from SS. Chrysostom and Augustine are given from fol. 155 to 157. Fol. 158 is entirely blank, with the exception that it contains the name of Rupertus. Fol. 159 contains the texts of scripture, and fol. 160 the reference to popes and councils. This folio is endorsed twice *De Divortio*, as if it were the end of the book, and yet there can be no doubt that fol. 161, which contains the reference to the councils of Arles, Elvira, and Milevi, forms part of the same book, for it is half of the same sheet of which fol. 144 is the other half. The whole volume is so loosely and carelessly put together that it is conjectured that fol. 159 may have originally formèd, as the author's description seems to imply, the commencement of the tract. Strype and Baker had both seen this volume, of which Baker truly observes, that the quotations are put down without any reflections; but neither of these writers could have carefully read through the whole document, or they would certainly have commented upon Burnet's inaccuracies.]

for himself, said he thought that by the word of God he was
discharged of his tie to his former wife; and the making marriages indissoluble was but a part of the popish law, by which
it was reckoned a sacrament; and yet the popes, knowing that
the world would not easily come under such a yoke, had, by
the help of the canonists, invented such distinctions, that it was
no uneasy thing to make a marriage void among them: and
that the condition of this church was very hard, if upon
adulteries the innocent must either live with the guilty, or be
exposed to temptations to the like sins, if a separation was only
allowed, but the bond of the marriage continued undissolved.
But, since he had proceeded so far before the delegates had
given sentence, it was ordered, that he and his new wife should
57 be parted; and that she should be put into his sister the queen
dowager's keeping, till the matter were tried, whether it was
according to the word of God, or not; and that then further
order should be given in it. Upon this the delegates made
haste, and gathered their arguments together, of which I shall
give an abstract, both for the clearing of this matter, (concerning which not many years ago there were great debates in
parliament,) and also to shew the exactness of the proceedings in
that time.

Christ condemned all marriages upon divorces, *except in the*
case of adultery ; which seemed manifestly to allow them in
that case. And though this is not mentioned by St. Mark and
St. Luke, yet it is enough that St. Matthew has it. Christ
also defined the state of marriage to be, that in which *two are*
one flesh; so that, when either of the two hath broken that
union, by becoming one with another person, then the marriage
is dissolved. And it is oft repeated in the gospel, that married
persons have *power over one another's bodies,* and that they
are to give *due benevolence* to each other; which is plainly
contrary to this way of separation without dissolving the bond.
St. Paul, putting the case of an unbeliever departing from the
partner in marriage, says, *the believing party, whether brother*
or sister, is not under bondage in such a case; which seems a
discharge of the bond in case of desertion: and certainly adultery is yet of a higher nature. But against this was alleged,
on the other side, that our Saviour's allowing divorce in the
case of adultery was only for the Jews, to whom it was spoken,

The grounds on which he suffered to marry again.

to mitigate the cruelty of their law, by which the adulteress
was to be put to death; and therefore he yielded divorce in
that case to mitigate the severity of the other law. But the
apostle, writing to the Gentile Christians at Rome and Corinth,
said, the wife was *tied by the law to the husband as long as
he lived;* and that other general rule, *Whom God has joined
together, let no man put asunder,* seems against the dissolving
the bond. To this it was answered, that it is against separating as well as dissolving; that the wife is *tied to her husband;*
but if he ceaseth to be her husband, that tie is at an end: that
our Saviour left the wife at liberty to divorce her husband for
adultery, though the law of Moses had only provided, that the
adulterous wife, and he who defiled her, were to die; but the
husband who committed adultery was not so punishable; therefore our Saviour had by that provision declared the marriage
to be clearly dissolved by adultery.

From hence they went to examine the authorities of the
fathers. Hermas was for putting away the adulteress, but so
as to receive her again upon repentance. Origen thought the
wife could not marry again after divorce. Tertullian allowed
divorce, and thought it dissolved the marriage as much as
death did. Epiphanius did also allow it. And Ambrose in one
place allows the husband to marry after divorce for adultery,
though he condemns it always in the wife. Basil allowed it on
either side upon adultery. Jerome, who condemns the wife's
marrying, though her husband were guilty of adultery; and
who disliked the husband's marrying again, though he allowed
him to divorce upon adultery, or the suspicion of it; yet, when
his friend Fabiola had married after a divorce, he excuses it,
saying, it was better for her to marry than to burn. Chromatius allowed of second marriages after divorce. And so
did Chrysostom, though he condemned them in women so 58
divorcing. St. Austin was sometimes for a divorce, but
against marriage upon it; yet in his Retractations he writ
doubtfully of his former opinion. In the civil law, the
Christian emperors allowed the power of divorcing both to
husband and wife, with the right of marrying afterwards. Nor
did they restrain the grounds of divorce only to adultery, but
permitted it in many other cases; as, if the wife were guilty of
treason, had treated for another husband, had procured an

[Lambeth, No. 1108, fol. 159.]

[Ibid. fol. 144.]

[Ibid. fol. 147.]

[Ibid. fol. 149.]

[Ibid. fol. 152.]

[Ibid. fol. 154.]

[Ibid. fol. 155.]

[Ibid. fol. 156.]

abortion, had been whole nights abroad, or had gone to see the
public plays without leave from her husband; besides many
other particulars : against which none of the fathers had
writ, nor endeavoured to get them repealed. All these laws
were confirmed by Justinian, when he gathered the laws into
a body, and added to it where they were defective. In the
canon law it is provided, that he whose wife is defiled must not
be denied lawful marriage. Pope Gregory denied a second [Ibid. fol.
marriage to the guilty person, but allowed it to the innocent ¹⁶⁰.]
after divorce. Pope Zachary allowed the wife of an incestuous
adulterer to be married, if she could not contain. In the canon-
law, the council of Tribur is cited for allowing the like privilege
to the husbands. By the council of Elvira, a man that finds that
his wife intends to kill him may put her away, and marry
another; but she must never marry. The council of Arles [Ibid. fol.
recommended it to husbands whose wives were found in adul- ¹⁶¹.]
tery not to marry during their lives. And that of Elvira
denied the sacrament to a wife who left an adulterous husband,
and married another; but she might have the communion when
her first husband died : so the second marriage was accounted
good, but only indecent. But the council of Milevi forbids
both man and wife to marry after a divorce. All these were
collected by Cranmer, with several very important reflections on
most of the quotations out of the fathers, With these, there is
another paper⁴⁵, given in by one who was against the dissolving [Ibid. fol.
                                                                162—168.]

⁴⁵ The fathers and canons cited
in that paper are Hermas, Tertullian, Origen, Basil, Ambrose, Jerome
Augustine, Chrysostom: the councils of Arles, Elvira and Milevi. If
any modern authorities are cited, I
have not noted them. [B.]

[This document also has been
so imperfectly described that it is
thought better to give some account
of it, especially as no reader seems
to have discovered that the leaves
are put together in the wrong order.
It occupies the remaining leaves of
the volume, part of which is described in note ⁴⁴, from fol. 162 to
fol. 182. Fol. 162 to 168 is a distinct paper, headed, *Quod non liceat
post divortium viveute priore conjuge*

secundas nuptias contrahere. It is
rightly described by Baker, and the
reference to S. Chrysostom ends at
fol. 167, the next leaf being vacant.
Fol. 169 begins a new paper, being
part of the same leaf with fol. 170,
which is vacant. It contains the
eight answers printed in No. 20 of the
Collection without the Questions.
On the back is given *Autoritates
doctorum admittentium repudium
propter adulterium, et post, ob eam
causam factum repudium, novas etiam
priore conjuge superstite nuptias.*
The authorities quoted are Augustine, Tertullian, Hilary, and for
others reference is made to Erasmus'
Commentary on 1 Cor. vii.
From 171 to the end of fol. 182

the bond, in which there are many quotations brought, both from the canon law and the fathers, for the contrary opinion. But most of the fathers there cited are of the latter ages; in which the state of celibate had been so exalted by the monks, that, in all doubtful cases, they were resolved still to prefer that opinion which denied liberty for further marriages. In conclusion, this whole question was divided into eight queries, which were put to some learned men; (who these were does not appear;) and they returned their answer in favour of the second marriage, which will be found in the Collection. In the end, sentence was given, allowing the second marriage in that case, and by consequence confirming the marquis of Northampton's marriage to his second wife, who upon that was suffered to cohabit with him. Yet, four years after, he was advised to have a special act of parliament for confirming this sentence; of which mention shall be made in its due time and place.

Collect. Numb. 20.

The next thing that came under consideration was, the great contradiction that was in most of the sermons over England. Some were very earnest to justify and maintain all the old rites that yet remained; and others were no less hot to have them laid aside. So that, in London especially, the people were wonderfully distracted by this variety among their teachers. The ceremonies of Candlemas, and their observance of Lent, 59 with the rites used on Palm-Sunday, Good-Friday, and Easter,

Some further advance in the reformation. [Fox, lib. ix. p. 7.]

is certainly a separate book with the insertion of a single leaf, fol. 180, which is distinct and does not belong to it, as it contains the questions printed at the beginning of No. 20 of the Collection of Records. Fol. 171 begins with *Quod non liceat a divortio facto repudii gratiâ, novum inire conjugium.* This is divided into 19 paragraphs, the numbers being marked in red ink, which are written on fol. 171, 172, and are continued on fol. 179 and fol. 181, which are the other halves respectively of 172 and 171. Fol. 173 is an insertion on which are answered seriatim the 19 paragraphs of fol. 171, and it is continued on fol. 178. Fol. 174 is another paper, headed, *Quod liceat post divortium secundum inire conjugium.* This contains a few lines of preface and then five paragraphs all on the same folio, of which the remaining half, viz. fol. 177, is vacant. Fol. 175 and 176 are a separate paper containing replies to the five paragraphs of the previous paper. At the end of the whole on the back of 181 is written *Collectiones de divortio.* The book is so loosely put together that the leaves might easily be taken apart and arranged in their proper order. The editor believes that attention has never before been drawn to the fact of their being displaced.]

were now approaching. Those that were against them condemned them as superstitious additions to the worship of God,
invented in the dark ages, when an outward pageantry had
been the chief thing that was looked after. But others set out
the good use that might be made of these things; and taught
that, till they were abolished by the king's authority, they
ought to be still observed. In a visitation that had been made,
(when I cannot learn, only it seems to have been about the end
of king Henry's reign,) it had been declared, that fasting
in Lent was only a positive law. Several directions were also
given about the use of the ceremonies, and some hints, as
if they were not to be long continued; and all wakes and
Plough-Mondays were suppressed, since they drew great
assemblies of people together, which ended in drinking and
quarrelling. These I have also inserted in the Collection; Collect.
having had a copy of the articles, left at the visitation of Numb. 21.
the deanery of Doncaster, communicated to me by the favour
of a most learned physician, and curious antiquary, Dr. Na-
thaniel Johnston, who sent me this, with several other papers
out of his generous zeal for contributing every thing in his
power to the perfecting of this work.

The country people generally loved all these shows, processions, and assemblies, as things of diversion; and judged it
a dull business only to come to church for divine worship, and
the hearing of sermons: therefore they were much delighted
with the gaiety and cheerfulness of those rites. But others,
observing that they kept up all these things, just as the heathens did their plays and festivities for their gods, judged them
contrary to the gravity and simplicity of the Christian religion,
and therefore were earnest to have them removed. This was [Wilkins,
so effectually represented to the council by Cranmer, that an Conc. iv.
order was sent to him about it. He sent it to Bonner, who, [Jan. 27.]
being dean of the college of bishops in the province of Canterbury, was to transmit all such orders over the whole province. By it, the carrying of candles on Candlemas-day, of
ashes on Ash-Wednesday, and palms on Palm-Sunday, were
forbidden to be used any longer. And this was signified by [Jan. 28.
Bonner to Thirlby, bishop of Westminster, on the twenty- Bonner's
eighth of June, as appears by the register. fol. 110.]

After this, on the sixth of February, a proclamation was A proclamation

issued out against such as should on the other hand rashly innovate, or persuade the people from the old accustomed rites, under the pains of imprisonment, and other punishments, at the king's pleasure ; excepting only the formerly-mentioned rites : to which are added, the creeping to the cross on Good-Friday, taking holy bread and water, and any other, that should be afterwards at any time certified by the archbishop of Canterbury to the other bishops, in the king's name, to be laid aside. And, for preventing the mischiefs occasioned by rash preachers, none were to preach without license from the king or his visitors, the archbishop of Canterbury, or the bishop of the diocese where they lived ; excepting only incumbents preaching in their own parishes. Those who preached otherwise were to be imprisoned till order were given for their punishment; and the inferior magistrates were required to see to the execution of these orders. This proclamation, which is

in the Collection, was necessary for giving authority to the archbishop of Canterbury's letters, which were censured as a **60** great presumption for him, without any public order, to appoint changes in sacred rites. Some observed, that the council went on making proclamations, with arbitrary punishments, though the act was repealed that had formerly given so great authority to them. To this it was answered, that the king by his supremacy might still in matters of religion make new orders, and add punishments upon the transgressors ; yet this was much questioned, though universally submitted to.

[Feb. 21.
Wilkins'
Conc. iv.
22.]
The ge-
neral tak-
ing away of
all images.
Numb. 23.
On the eleventh [45] of February there was a letter sent from the council to the archbishop, for a more considerable change. There were every where great heats about the removing of images, which had been abused to superstition : some affirming, and others denying, that their images had been so abused. There were in the churches some images of so strange a nature, that it could not be denied that they had been abused. Such was the image of the blessed Trinity, which was to be censed,

on the day of the Innocents, by him that was made the bishop of the children : this shews it was used on other days, in which it is like it was censed by the bishop where he was present.

---

[45] [This is a mistake, probably copied from Fox, lib. ix. p. 8, for February 21, which is the date assigned in the Records and in Cranmer's Register, fol. 32 a.]

How this image was made, can only be gathered from the prints that were of it at that time: in which the Father is represented sitting on the one hand as an old man with a triple crown and rays about him, the Son on the other hand as a young man with a crown and rays, and the blessed Virgin between them, and the emblem of the Holy Ghost a dove spread over her head. So it is represented in a fair book of the hours according to the use of Sarum, printed anno 1526[46]. The impiety of this did raise horror in most men's minds, when that inconceivable mystery was so grossly expressed. Besides, the taking of the Virgin into it was done in pursuance to what had been said by some blasphemous friars, of her being assumed into the Trinity. In another edition of these, it is represented by three faces formed in one head. These things had not been set up by any public warrant; but, having been so long in practice, they stood upon the general plea that was for keeping the traditions of the church; for it was said, that the promises made to the church were the same in all ages, and that therefore every age of the church had an equal right to them. But for the other images, it was urged against them, that they had been all consecrated with such rites and prayers, that it was certain they were every one of them superstitious: since it was prayed, that they might be so blessed and consecrated, that whosoever worshipped them might, by the saints' prayers and aid, whom they represented, obtain every thing that he desired. So they resolved on an entire removal of all images. And the protector, with the council, wrote to Cranmer, that, for putting an end to all these contests, and that the living images of Christ might not quarrel about the dead ones, it was concluded they should all of them be taken down; and he was to give order to see this executed in his own diocese, and to transmit it to the other bishops, to be in like manner executed by them. There were also orders given, that all rich shrines, with all the plate belonging to them, should be brought in to the king's use, and that the clothes that covered them should be converted to the use of the poor. This gave Gardiner, and those of his party, a new

[46] [Horæ beatæ Mariæ Virginis secundum usum Sarum, Parisiis, per Franciscum Regnault 1526. 4to.]

affliction: for in his diocese he had been always on their side that were for keeping up the images. But they all submitted; and so the churches were emptied of all these pictures and 61 statues, which had been for divers ages the chief objects of the people's worship.

Some re-
straints put
on preach-
ers, May 13.
Numb. 24.

And now, the greatest care of the reformers was, to find the best men they could, who should be licensed by the king's authority to preach. To whom the council sent a letter in the beginning of May, intimating, that, by the restraint put on preaching, they only intended to put an end to the rash contentions of indiscreet men, and not to extinguish the lively preaching of the pure word of God, made after such sort as the Holy Ghost should for the time put in the preacher's mind: they are therefore charged to preach sincerely, and with that caution and moderation, that the time and place shall require; and particularly, that they should not set on the people to make innovations, or to run before those whom they should obey; but should persuade them to amend their lives, and keep the commandments of God, and to forsake all their old superstitions. And for the things not yet changed, they ought to wait patiently, and to conclude, that the prince did either allow or suffer them: and in delivering things to the people, they were ordered to have a special regard to what they could bear.

But this temper was not observed. Some plainly condemned it as a political patching, and said, Why should not all these superstitions be swept away at once? To this it was answered by others, that, as Christ forbade the pulling up of the tares, lest with them they should pull up good wheat; so, if they went too forwardly to the changing of things, they might in that haste change much for the worse: and great care was to be had not to provoke the people too much, lest in the infancy of the king, or in some ill conjuncture of affairs, they might be disposed to make commotions. And the compliances that both Christ and his apostles gave to the Jews, when they were to abrogate the Mosaical law, were often insisted on. It was said, if they who were clothed with a power of miracles, for the more effectual conviction of the world, condescended so far; it was much more reasonable for them, who had not that authority over men's consciences, and had no immediate signs to shew from heaven, to persuade the people rather by degrees to forsake their old mistakes, and not to precipitate things by an overhaste.

This winter there was a committee of selected bishops and divines appointed for examining all the offices of the church, and for reforming them. Some had been in king's Henry's time employed in the same business, in which they had made a good progress, which was now to be brought to a full perfection. Therefore, the archbishops of Canterbury and York; the bishops of London, Durham, Worcester, Norwich, St. Asaph, Salisbury, Coventry and Lichfield, Carlisle, Bristol, St. David's, Ely, Lincoln, Chichester, Hereford, Westminster, and Rochester; with doctors Cox, May, Taylor, Haynes, Robertson, and Redmayn; were appointed to examine all the offices of the church, and to consider how far any of them needed amendment. Bishops and divines examine the offices of the church.

The thing they first examined was, the sacrament of the eucharist; which being the chief symbol of Christian communion, was thought to deserve their chief care. And here they managed their inquiries in the same manner that was used in the former reign; in which, when any thing was considered in order to a change, it was put into several queries, to which every one in commission was to give his answer in writing. It is no wonder if the confusions that followed in queen Mary's reign have deprived us of most of these papers; yet there is one set of them preserved relating to some questions about the priest's single communicating; Whether one man's receiving it can be useful to another? What was the oblation or sacrifice that was made of Christ in the mass? Wherein the mass consisted? When the priest's receiving alone began? Whether it was convenient to retain that, and continue masses satisfactory for departed souls? Whether the gospel ought to be taught at the time of the mass? Whether it were convenient to have it all in a known tongue or not? And when the reserving or hanging up of the sacrament first began? To these the bishops made their several answers. Some answered them all; others answered only a few of them; it is like, suspending their opinions about those which they

62

answered not. The bishops of London, Worcester, Chichester, and Hereford, gave in their answers once in one paper together[47]; but afterwards they joined with the bishops of Norwich and St. Asaph, and all those six gave a joint answer in one paper. Those are not all subscribed, as those which I inserted in the former volume were; or at least the papers I have are not the originals. But Cranmer's hand is over every one of them[48], marking the name of the bishop to whom they belonged; and Dr. Cox hath set his hand and seal to his

Numb. 25.   answer[49]. By these, which are in the Collection, the reader will perceive how generally the bishops were addicted to the old superstition, and how few did agree in all things with Cranmer[50]. It may be thought, that these questions were given

[47] The bishops of London, Worcester, Chichester, and Hereford's answers related to another set of questions. [B.]

[48] Cranmer's hand is not over Richard Cox, nor W. Menevens. nor John Taylor's, who have subscribed their own names. [B.]

[49] I can assure your lordship there is no mystery in this. Cox had sent in his paper folded and closed with wax: the foldings yet remain, according to which foldings the paper had been sealed, which is now torn where it had been sealed, and some of the paper left upon the wax. [B.]

[50] [This paper has also been very imperfectly described. It begins at fol. 6, No. 1108, of the Lambeth MSS. The first leaf contains the questions written on the left hand side of the page, with the answers opposite to them on the same page, written in a very small hand and in very bad spelling, and headed *Lincolnien*. The next leaf is vacant. Fol. 8 is headed *Cantuarien*. fol. 10 *Roffen*. and they contain respectively the answers of the archbishop of Canterbury and the bishop of Rochester. Fol. 11 is signed at the bottom of the first page as well as on

the back, *Ric. Cox*. He begins with the fifth question and gives the questions with the answers, numbering them from 1 to 7, not from 5 to 11. The questions are repeated also on fol. 13 which is signed at the end of the first page, *By me, John Taylor*. The back of it and fol. 14 are vacant. Fol. 15 begins with four questions, after which comes *The answer of Richard bishop of Coventre and Lichfelde to the articles above written*. Fol. 16 is vacant. Fol. 17 contains four questions, after which *An answer to the questions* signed by *W. Meneven*. Fol. 18 also contains four questions after which come the four answers signed, *Ric. Cox*, with a broken seal. The bishops of Durham, Salisbury, and Bristol, give their answers on fols. 19, 23, 25 respectively. There is a distinct paper which begins at fol. 40 of the same volume and which appears to have been originally described as *The answers of the bishops of Worcester of Hareford and of Chichestre;* the names of the bishops of London, Norwich and S. Asaph having been apparently added afterwards. The author has taken no notice of fol. 43, which begins with the questions written in a good hand,

out before the act of parliament passed, in which the priest's single communicating is turned into a communion of more: yet by that act it was only provided, that all who came to receive should be admitted; but priests were not forbid to consecrate, if none were to communicate, which was the thing now inquired into.

It is certain there was no part of worship more corrupted than this sacrament was. The first institution was so plain and simple, that, except in the words, *This is my body*, there is nothing which could give a colour to the corruptions that were afterwards brought in. The heathens had their mysteries, which the priests concealed with hard and dark words, and dressed up with much pomp, and thereby supported their own esteem with the people, since they looked on these to be of so high a nature, that all those who had the ordering of them were accounted sacred persons. The primitive Christians retained the first simplicity of divine institutions for some ages. But afterwards, as their number increased, they made use of some things not unlike those the heathens had practised, to draw the Gentiles more easily into their belief, since external shows make deep impressions in the vulgar. And those that were thus brought over might afterwards come to like these things for their own sakes, which were at first made use of only to gain the world. Others, finding some advantage in such services, that were easy, and yet appeared véry pompous, that they might cover great faults by countenancing and complying with the follies that were in vogue, contributed liberally to the improvement of them. And after the Roman emperors turned Christian, much of that vast wealth, of which they and their people were masters, was brought into the church, and applied to these superstitions. Yet it became not so universally corrupted, till, by the invasion of the Goths, Vandals, and other barbarous nations, the Roman empire was broken and divided into many kingdoms. These new conquerors were rude and ignorant, wholly given to sensible things; and learning

The corruptions in the office of the communion examined.

perhaps Cranmer's, the seven occupying the first page, nor of fol. 44 which contains questions meant to break down the answers previously given. These have been printed in the edition of Strype's Cranmer, published by the Ecclesiastical History Society, vol. ii, p. 478. Fol. 46 belongs to another subject.]

being universally extinguished, gross superstition took place;
for more refined superstitions would not serve the turn of darker
ages: but as they grew in ignorance, they continued in the
belief and practice of more absurd things.

The high opinion they justly had of this sacrament being
much raised by the belief of the corporal presence of Christ in
it, which came in afterwards, then the dull wits of the priests,
and the wealth of the people, were employed to magnify it
with all the pomp possible. All the vessels and garments
belonging to it were consecrated and anointed with much
devotion; the whole office was in an unknown tongue. A
great part of it was to be secretly whispered, to make it appear
the more wonderful charm. But chiefly the words of consecration were by no means to be heard by the people; it being
fabled, that, when the words were spoken aloud, some shepherds had repeated them over their bread, which was thereupon
presently turned into flesh. Besides that, it was but suitable,
that a change, which was not to be seen, should be made by
words not to be heard. The priest was not to approach it but after
so many bowings, crossings, and kissings of the altar; and, all
the while he went through with the office, the people were only
now and then blessed by a short blessing, *The Lord be with
you*, and even that in Latin. Then, after consecration, the
bread was lifted up, and all the people worshipped it as if
Christ had appeared in the clouds. It was oft exposed on the
altar, and carried about in processions, with the ceremonies of
carrying flambeaux before it, which the greatest persons accounted it an honour to do; the priest that carried it all the
while going pompously under a rich canopy.

This was also thought most effectual for all the accidents of
life. And whereas it was at first only intended to be a commemoration and communion of the death of Christ; that seemed
almost forgotten, but it was applied to all other ends imaginable.
That which brought in most custom was trentals, which was a
method of delivering souls out of purgatory by saying thirty
masses a year for them. And whereas it was observed, that
men, on the anniversaries of their birthdays, wedding, or other
happy accidents of their lives, were commonly in better humour,
so that favours were more easily obtained; they seemed to have

had the same opinion of God and Christ; so they ordered it, that three of these should be said on Christmas-Day, three on Epiphany, three on the purification of the blessed Virgin, three on the Annunciation, three on the Resurrection, three on the Ascension, three on Whit-Sunday, three on Trinity-Sunday, three on the Assumption of the blessed Virgin, and three on her birthday; hoping that these days would be the *mollia tempora*, when God and Christ, or the blessed Virgin, would be of easier access, and more ready to grant their desires. Yet the most unaccountable part of all was, the masses on the saints' days; praying that the intercession of the saint might make the sacrafice acceptable; that the saint for whose honour these oblations were solemnly offered, would by his merits procure them to

64 be accepted, and that the sacrifice might bring to them a greater indulgence, being offered up by the suffrages of the saint. If the sacrifice was of Jesus Christ, and was of its own nature expiatory, how this should be done in honour to a saint, and become of greater virtue by his intercession, was a thing very hard to be understood. There were many pieces of ridiculous pageantry also used in it, as the laying the host in the sepulchre they made for Christ on Good-Friday; and that, not only the candles that were to burn at the Easter celebration, but the very fire that was to kindle them, was particularly consecrated on Easter-Eve. Some masses were believed to have a peculiar virtue in them: for, in the mass-book printed at London, anno 1500[50], there is a mass for avoiding sudden death, which pope Clement made in the college, with all his cardinals, and granted to all who heard it two hundred and seventy days of indulgence, charging them, that they should hold in their hand a burning candle all the while it was saying, and for five days after should likewise hold a candle, kneeling during the whole mass; and to those that did so, sudden death should do no harm. And it is added, that this was certain and approved in Avignon, and all the neighbouring places. All this I have opened the more largely, to let the reader plainly understand what things were then in this sacrament that required reformamation: and I have gathered these things out of the mass-book then most used in England, and best known by the name of the *Missal after the use of Sarum.*

[50] [Missale ad usum Ecclesiæ Sarum. Lond. R. Pynson, 1500. fol.]

A new of-
fice for the
commu-
nion set
out.
The first step these deputed bishops and divines made was, to reform this. But they did not at once mend every thing that required it, but left the office of the mass as it was, only adding to it that which made it a communion. It began first with an exhortation, to be used the day before, which differs not much from that now used; only, after the advice given concerning confession, it is added, that such as desired to make auricular confession should not censure those who were satisfied with a general confession to God; and that those who used only confession to God and to the church should not be offended with those who used auricular confession to a priest; but that all should keep the rule of charity, every man being satisfied to follow his own conscience, and not judging another man's in things not appointed by God. After the priest had received the sacrament, he was to turn to the people, and read an exhortation to them; the same we now use, only a little varied in words. After that followed a denunciation against sinners, requiring them who were such, and had not repented, to withdraw, lest the Devil should enter into them, as he did into Judas. Then, after a little pause, to see if any would withdraw, there was to follow a short exhortation, with a confession of sins, and absolution, the very same which we do yet retain. Then those texts of scripture were read which we yet read, followed with the prayer, *We do not presume,* &c. After this, the sacrament was to be given in both kinds; first to the ministers then present, and then to all the people, with these words: *The body of our Lord Jesus Christ, which was given for thee, preserve thy body unto everlasting life;* and, *The blood of our Lord Jesus Christ, which was shed for thee, preserve thy soul unto everlasting life.* When all was done, the congregation was to be dismissed with a blessing. The bread was to be such as had been formerly used, and every one of the breads so consecrated was to be broken in two or more pieces; and the people were to be taught that there was no 65 difference in the quantity they received, whether it were small or great, but that in each of them they received the whole body of Christ. If the wine that was at first consecrated did not serve, the priest was to consecrate more; but all to be without any elevation. This office being thus finished, was set forth with a proclamation, reciting, that whereas the parliament

had enacted, that the communion should be given in both kinds
to all the king's subjects; it was now ordered to be given in
the form here set forth: and all were required to receive it
with due reverence and Christian behaviour, and with such
uniformity as might encourage the king to go on in the setting
forth godly orders for reformation, which he intended most
earnestly to bring to effect by the help of God; willing his subjects
not to run before his direction, and so by their rashness to hinder
such things; assuring them of the earnest zeal he had to set
them forth, hoping they would quietly and reverently tarry for it.

This was published on the eighth [51] of March; and on the
thirteenth, books were sent to all the bishops of England,
requiring them to send them to every parish in their diocese,
that the curates might have time both to instruct themselves
about it, and to acquaint their people with it; so that by the
next Easter it might be universally received in all the churches
of the nation. This was variously censured. Those that were
for the old superstition were much troubled to have confes- It is vari-
sion thus left indifferent, and a general confession of sins ously censured.
to be used, with which they apprehended the people would sured.
for the most part content themselves. In the scripture Chiefly,
there was a power of binding and loosing sins given to the that auricular con-
apostles. And St. James exhorted those to whom he wrote, to fession was
confess their faults *to one another*. Afterwards penitents came laid down.
to be reconciled to the church, when they had given public
scandal either by their apostasy or ill life, by an open confession
of their sins; and, after some time of separation from the other
pure Christians in worship, and an abstention from the sacrament,
they were admitted again to their share of all the privileges that
were given in common to Christians. But, according to the
nature of their sins, they were, besides the public confession,
put under such rules as might be most proper for curing these
ill inclinations in them; and, according to the several ranks of
sins, the time and degrees of this penitence was proportioned.
And the councils that met in the fourth and fifth centuries made
the regulating these penitentiary canons the chief subject of

---

[51] [The order of the Communion.
Imprinted at London the eight daie
of Marche, in the second yere of the
reigne of our souereigne lorde Kyng
Edward the VI. By Rychard Grafton, printer to his moste royall Maiestie. In the yere of our Lorde
M.D.XLVIII. Cum priuilegio ad
imprimendum solum.]

their consultations. In many churches there were penitentiary priests, who were more expert in the knowledge of these rules, and gave directions about them, which were taken away in Constantinople, upon the indiscretion of which one of them had been guilty. For secret sins there was no obligation to confess, since all the canons were about public scandals; yet for these, the devout people generally went to their priests for their counsel, but were not obliged to it; and so went to them for the distempers of their minds, as they did to physicians for the diseases of their bodies.

About the end of the fifth century they began in some places to have secret penances, either within monasteries, or other places which the priests had appointed; and, upon a secret confession, and performing the penance imposed, absolution was also given secretly; whereas in former times confession and absolution had been performed openly in the church. In 66 the seventh century it was every where practised, that there should be secret penance for secret sins, which Theodore, archbishop of Canterbury, did first bring into a method and under rules. But, about the end of the eighth century, the commutation of penance, and exchanging it for money, or other services to the church, came to be practised: and then began pilgrimages to holy places, and afterwards the going to the holy war; and all the severities of penance were dispensed with to such as undertook these. This brought on a great relaxation of all ecclesiastical discipline. Afterwards crusades came in use, against such princes as were deposed by popes; and to these was likewise added, to encourage all to enter into them, that all rules of penitence were dispensed with to such as put on that cross. But penitence being now no more public, but only private, the priests managed it as they pleased; and so by confession entered into all men's secrets, and by absolution had their consciences so entirely in their power, that the people were generally governed by them. Yet because the secular priests were commonly very ignorant, and were not put under such an association as was needful to manage those designs, for which this was thought an excellent engine; therefore the friars were employed every where to hear confessions, and to give absolutions. And, to bring in customers to them, two new things were invented. The one was, a reserving of certain cases, in which such as were guilty of them could not be absolved but by the popes, or those deputed by them; and the friars had faculties in the pope's name to absolve in these cases. The other was, on some occasion the use of certain new secrets, by which men were to obtain great indulgences; either by saying such prayers, or performing such impositions : and these were all trusted to the friars, who were to trade with them, and bring all the money they could gather by that means to Rome. They being bred up to a voluntary poverty, and expecting great rewards for their industry, sold those secrets with as much cunning as mountebanks use in selling their tricks: only here was the difference, that the ineffectualness of the mountebanks' medicines was soon discovered, so their trade must be but short in one place ; whereas the other could not be so easily found out ; the chief piece of the religion of those ages being to believe all that their priests taught them. Of this sort the reader will find in the Collection an essay of indulgences as they were printed in the Collect. Numb. 26. Hours after the use of Sarum[52], which were set down in English, though the prayers be all Latin, that so all the people might know the value of such ware. Those had been all by degrees brought from Rome, and put into people's hands, and afterwards laid together in their offices. By them, indulgences of many years, hundreds, thousands, and millions of years, and of all sins whatsoever, were granted to such as devoutly said such collects ; but it was always understood, that they must confess and be absolved, which is the meaning of those expressions concerning their being in *a state of grace.* And so the whole business was a cheat.

And now all this trade was laid aside, and confession of secret sins was left to all men's free choice ; since it was certain that the confession to a priest was no where enjoined in the scriptures. It was a reasonable objection, that, as secret confession and private penance had worn out the primitive practice 67 of the public censuring of scandalous persons, so it had been well if the reviving of that discipline had driven out these later abuses ; but to let that lie unrestored, and yet to let con-

---

[52] [Horæ Beatæ Mariæ Virginis in usum Ecclesiæ Sarisburiensis. Paris. Regnault, 4to. et 8vo, 1526.]

fession wear out, was to discharge the world of all outward restraints, and to leave them to their full liberty, and so to throw up that power of binding and loosing, which ought to take place chiefly in admitting them to the sacrament. This was confessed to be a great defect, and effectual endeavours were used to retrieve it, though without success: and it was openly declared to be a thing which they would study to repair: but the total disuse of all public censure had made the nation so unacquainted with it, that, without the effectual concurrence of the civil authority, they could not compass it. And though it was acknowledged to be a great disorder in the church, yet, as they could not keep up the necessity of private confession, since it was not commanded in the gospel; so the generality of the clergy being superstitious men, whose chief influence on the people was by those secret practices in confession, they judged it necessary to leave that free to all people, and to represent it as a thing to which they were not obliged, and in the place of that ordered the general confession to be made in the church, with the absolution added to it. For the power of binding and loosing, it was by many thought to be only declarative; and so to be exercised, when the gospel was preached, and a general absolution granted, according to the ancient forms. In which forms, the absolution was a prayer that God would absolve; and so it had been still used in the absolution which was given on Maundy-Thursday; but the formal absolution given by the priest in his own name, *I absolve thee*, was a late invention to raise their authority higher, and signified nothing distinct from those other forms that were anciently used in the church.

Others censured the words in distributing the two kinds in the Lord's supper; the *body* being given for the preserving the *body*, and the *blood* of Christ for preserving the *soul*. This was thought done on design to possess the people with an high value of the chalice, as that which preserved their *souls;* whereas the bread was only for the preservation of their *bodies*. But Cranmer, being ready to change any thing for which he saw good reason, did afterwards so alter it, that in both it was said, *Preserve thy body and soul:* and yet it stands so in the prayer, *We do not presume,* &c. On all this I have digressed so long, because of the importance of the matter, and for satisfying the scruples that many still have upon the laying aside of confession in our reformation.

Comnissions were next given to examine the state of the chantries and guildable lands. The instruction about them will be found in the Collection; of which I need give no abstract here, for they were only about the methods of inquiring into their value, and how they were possessed, or what alienations had been made of them. Collect. Numb. 27.

The protector and council were now in much trouble. The war with Scotland they found was like to grow chargeable, since they saw it was supported from France. There was a rebellion also broke out in Ireland; and the king was much indebted: nor could they expect any subsidies from the parliament; in which it had been said, that they gave the chantry-lands, that they might be delivered from all subsidies: therefore the parliament was prorogued till winter. Upon this the whole council did on the seventeenth of April unanimously resolve, that it was necessary to sell five thousand pounds a year of chantry-lands for raising such a sum as the king's occasions required; and sir Henry Mildmay was appointed to treat about the sale of them.

68

The new communion-book was received over England without any opposition. Only complaints were brought of Gardiner, that he did secretly detract from the king's proceedings. Upon which the council took occasion to reflect on all his former behaviour. And here it was remembered, how at first, upon his refusing to receive the king's injunctions, he had been put in the Fleet, where he had been as well used as if it had been his own house; (which is far contrary to his letters to the protector, of which mention has been already made;) and that he, upon promise of conformity, had been discharged. But when he was come home, being forgetful of his promises, he had raised much strife and contention, and had caused all his servants to be secretly armed and harnessed, and had put public affronts on those whom the council sent down to preach in his diocese; for in some places, to disgrace them, he went into the pulpit before them, and warned the people to beware of such teachers, and to receive no other doctrine but what he had taught them. Upon this he had been sent

Gardiner falls into new troubles. [Council Book, p. 356.]

[Ibid. p. 357.]

[Ibid. p. 359.]

for a second time; but again, upon his promise of conformity, was discharged, and ordered to stay at his own house in London. That there he had continued still to meddle in public matters; of which being again admonished, he desired that he might be suffered to clear himself of all misrepresentations that had been made of him, in a sermon which he should preach before the king, in which he should openly declare how well he was satisfied with his proceedings: yet it is added, that in his sermon, where there was a wonderful audience, he did most arrogantly meddle with some matters that were contrary to an express command given him, both by word of mouth, and by letters; and in other matters used such words as had almost raised a great tumult in the very time, and had spoken very seditiously concerning the policy of the kingdom. So they saw that clemency wrought no good effect on him; and it seeming necessary to terrify others by their proceedings with him, he was sent to the Tower, and the door of his closet was sealed up. Thus it is entered in the council-book, signed, *E. Somerset, T. Cant., W. St. John, J. Russell,* and *T. Cheyne.* Yet it seems this order was not signed when it was made, but some years after: for the lord Russell signed first *Bedford;* but, remembering that at the time when this order was made he had not that title, therefore he dashed it out, (but so as it still appears,) and signed, *J. Russell.*

[Ibid. p. 360.]

[Ibid. p. 361.]

Fox's Acts and Monuments.
[lib. ix. p. 74]
The account that Gardiner himself gives of this business is, that, being discharged upon the act of pardon, he was desired to promise that he would set forth the Homilies; and a form was given him, to which he should set his hand: but he, considering of it a fortnight, returned, and said, he could not subscribe it; so he was confined to his house. Then Ridley and Mr. Cecil (afterwards the great lord Burleigh, lord treasurer to queen Elizabeth, at that time secretary to the protector) were sent to him, and so prevailed, that he did set his hand to it. But, upon some complaints that were made of him, he was sent for after Whit-Sunday, and accused, that he had carried palms, had crept to the cross, and had a sepulchre on Good-Friday, which was contrary to the king's proclamations: all which he denied, and said, he had and would still give obedience to what the king should command. That of affronting the king's preachers was objected to him; to which

he answered, telling matter of fact how it was done, but he does not in his writing set it down. Then it was complained, that in a sermon he had said, The apostles came away rejoicing from *the council, the council, the council;* repeating it thus, to make it seem applicable to himself. This he denied. Then it was objected, that he preached the *real presence* in the sacrament, the word *real* not being in scripture ; and so it was not the setting forth the pure word of God : he said, he had not used the word *real*, only he had asserted the presence of Christ in such words as he had heard the archbishop of Canterbury dispute for it against Lambert, that had been burnt. He was commanded to tarry in London ; but he desired, that, since he was not an offender, he might be at his liberty. He complained much of the songs made of him, and of the books written against him, and particularly of one Philpot in Westminster, whom he accounted a madman.

Then he relates, that Cecil came to him, and proposed to [Ibid. p. him to preach before the king, and that he should write his 75.] sermon; and also brought him some notes, which he wished him to put in his sermon: he said, he was willing to preach, but would not write it, for that was to preach as an offender ; nor would he make use of notes prepared by other men. Then he was privately brought to the protector, none but the lord [Ibid. p. St. John being present, who shewed him a paper, containing 76.] the opinion of some lawyers of the king's power, and of a bishop's authority, and of the punishment of disobeying the king : but he desired to speak with those lawyers, and said, no subscription of theirs should oblige him to preach otherwise than as he was convinced. The protector said, he should either do that or do worse. Secretary Smith came to him to press him further in some points; but what they were is not mentioned. Yet by the other papers in that business it appears, [Ibid. p. they related to the king's authority when under age, and 75.] for justifying the king's proceedings in what had been done about the ceremonies ; and that auricular confession was indifferent. So the contest between him and the protector ended, and there was no writing required of him ; but he left the whole matter to him, so that he should treat plainly of those things mentioned to him by Cecil. He chose St. Peter's day, [June 29.] because the gospel agreed to his purpose. Cecil shewed him some notes, written with the king's hand, of the sermons preached before him, especially what was said of the duty of a king; and warned him, that, whenever he named the king, he should add, *and his council.* To this he made no answer; for though he thought it wisely done of a king to use his council, yet, being to speak of the king's power according to scripture, he did not think it necessary to add any thing of his council; and hearing, by a confused report, some secret matter, he resolved not to meddle with it. Two days before he preached, the protector sent him a message not to meddle with those questions about the sacrament that were yet in controversy among learned men; and that therefore he was resolved there should be no public determination made of them beforehand in the pulpit. He said, he could not forbear to speak of the mass, for he looked on it as the chief foundation 70 of Christian religion; but he doubted not that he should so speak of it, as to give them all content. So the day following the protector writ to him, (as will be found in the Collection,) requiring him, in the king's name, not to meddle with these points, but to preach concerning the articles given him, and about obedience and good life, which would afford him matter enough for a long sermon; since the other points were to be reserved to a public consultation. The protector added, that he held it a great part of his duty, under the king, not to suffer wilful persons to dissuade the people from receiving such truths as should be set forth by others. But Gardiner pretended that there was no controversy about the presence of Christ. And so the next day he took his text out of the gospel for the day, *Thou art Christ,* &c. In his sermon (of which I have seen large notes) he expressed himself very fully concerning the pope's supremacy as justly abolished, and the suppression of monasteries and chantries; he approved of the king's proceedings; he thought images might have been well used, but yet they might be well taken away. He approved of the sacrament in both kinds, and the taking away that great number of masses satisfactory, and liked well the new order for the communion. But he asserted largely the presence of Christ's flesh and blood in the sacrament: upon which many of the assembly, that were indiscreetly hot on both sides, cried out, some approving, and others disliking it.

[Ibid: p. 76.]

[Ibid. p. 77.]

[June 28.]
Numb. 28.

Parker's MSS. ex C. Ch. Col. Cant. [cxxvii. 5. p. 15.] He preached before the king.

Of the king's authority under age, and of the power of the council in that case, he said not a word; and upon that he was imprisoned.

The occasion of this was, the popish clergy began generally to have it spread among them, that, though they had acknowledged the king's supremacy, yet they had never owned the council's supremacy. That the council could only see to the execution of the laws and orders that had been made, but could not make new ones; and that therefore the supremacy could not be exercised, till the king, in whose person it was vested, came to be of age to consider of matters himself. Upon this the lawyers were consulted; who did unanimously resolve, that the supremacy, being annexed to the regal dignity, was the same in a king under age, when it was executed by the council, that it was in a king at full age; and therefore things ordered by the council now had the same authority in law that they could have when the king did act himself. But this did not satisfy the greater part of the clergy: some of whom, by the high flatteries that had been given to kings in king Henry's time, seemed to fancy that there were degrees of divine illumination derived unto princes by the anointing them at the coronation; and these not exerting themselves till a king attained to a ripeness of understanding, they thought the supremacy was to lie dormant while he was so young. The protector and council endeavoured to have got Gardiner to declare against this, but he would not meddle in it. How far he might set forward the other opinion, I do not know. These proceedings against him were thought too severe, and without law; but he being generally hated, they were not so much censured as they had been if they had fallen on a more acceptable man.

And thus were the orders made by the council generally obeyed; many being terrified with the usage Gardiner met with, from which others inferred what they might look for, if they were refractory, when so great a bishop was so treated.

71   The next thing Cranmer set about was, the compiling of a Catechism [53], or large instruction of young persons in the

Cranmer sets out a Catechism.

---

[53] This Catechism was first made in Latin by another, but translated by Cranmer's order, and it was reviewed by him. [S.]

[Wharton observes, (Specimen of Errors, p. 78,) " In truth Cranmer

grounds of the Christian religion. In it he reckons the two first commandments but one, though he says many of the ancients divided them in two. But the division was of no great consequence, so no part of the Decalogue were suppressed by the church. He shewed, that the excuses the papists had for images were no other than what the heathens brought for their idolatry; who also said, they did not worship the image, but that only which was represented by it. He particularly takes notice of the image of the Trinity. He shews how St. Peter would not suffer Cornelius, and the angel would not suffer St. John, to worship them. The believing that there is a virtue in one image more than in another, he accounts plain idolatry. Hezekiah broke the brasen serpent when abused, though it was a type or image of Christ, made by God's command, to which a miraculous virtue had been once given. So now there was good reason to break images, when they had been so abused to superstition and idolatry; and when they gave such scandal to Jews and Mahometans, who generally accounted the Christians idolaters on that account. He asserts, besides the two sacraments of baptism and the Lord's supper, the power of reconciling sinners to God, as a third; and fully owns the divine institution of bishops and priests; and wishes that the canons and rites of public penitence were again restored; and exhorts much to confession, and the people's dealing with their pastors about their consciences, that so they might upon knowledge bind and loose according to the gospel. Having finished this easy, but most useful work, he dedicated it to the king: and, in his epistle to him, complains of the great neglect, that had been in former times, of catechising;

only translated this Catechism out of Dutch, at least translated it from the Latin translation of Justus Jonas, who had translated the Dutch Catechism, as both the title and the preface of it might have informed the historian. The title saith it was overseen and corrected by the archbishop; and Cranmer himself, in another book, speaketh of this Catechism in these words: 'A Catechism by me translated and set forth.' He added indeed a large discourse of his own to the exposition of the second commandment, and inserted some few sentences elsewhere." The title is, 'Catechismus, that is to say, a shorte Instruction into Christian Religion for the synguler commoditie and profyte of children and yong people.' Lond. by Nycolas Hyll, for Gwalter Lynne, 1548, 16mo. It was reprinted in 8vo. Lond. without date, about 1552.]

and that confirmation had not been rightly administered, since
it ought to be given only to those of age, who understood the
principles of the Christian doctrine, and did upon knowledge,
and with sincere minds, renew their baptismal vow. From this
it will appear, that, from the beginning of this reformation, the
practice of the Roman church in the matter of images was
held idolatrous. Cranmer's zeal for restoring the penitentiary
canons is also clear : and it is plain, that he had now quite laid
aside those singular opinions which he formerly held of the
ecclesiastical functions ; for now, in a work which was wholly
his own, without the concurrence of any others, he fully sets
forth their divine institution.

All these things made way for a greater work, which these A general
selected bishops and divines, who had laboured in the setting reformation of all
forth of the office of the communion, were now preparing ; the offices
which was, the entire reformation of the whole service of the of the
church. In order to this, they brought together all the offices is set about.
used in England. In the southern parts, those after the use of
Sarum were universally received, which were believed to have
been compiled by Osmund bishop of Sarum. In the north of
England, they had other offices after the use of York. In
South Wales, they had them after the use of Hereford. In
North Wales, after the use of Bangor. And in Lincoln, another
sort of an office proper to that see.

In the primitive church, when the extraordinary gifts ceased,
the bishops of the several churches put their offices and prayers
72 into such a method as was nearest to what they had heard or
remembered from the apostles. And these liturgies were
called by the apostles' names, from whose forms they had been
composed ; as that at Jerusalem carried the name of St. James,
and that of Alexandria the name of St. Mark ; though those
books that we have now under these names are certainly so
interpolated, that they are of no great authority : but in the
fourth century we have these liturgies first mentioned. The
council of Laodicea appointed the same office of prayers to be [366 A.D.]
used in the mornings and evenings. The bishops continued to
draw up new additions, and to put old forms into other methods.
But this was left to every bishop's care : nor was it made the
subject of any public consultation till St. Austin's time ; when,
in their dealings with heretics, they found they took advantages

from some of the prayers that were in some churches.   Upon
this, he tells us, it was ordered, that there should be no prayers
used in the church but upon common advice; after that the
liturgies came to be more carefully considered.   Formerly, the
worship of God was a pure and simple thing; and so it continued till superstition had so infected the church, that those
forms were thought too naked, unless they were put under
more artificial rules, and dressed up with much ceremony.
Gregory the Great was the first that took much care to make
the church-music very regular; and he did also put the liturgies
in another method than had been formerly used.   Yet he
had no such fondness of his own composures, but left it to
Austin the monk, whom he sent over into England when he
consulted him in it, either to use the Roman or French rituals,
or any other, as he should find they were most likely to edify
the people.   After this, in most sees there were great variations;
for as any prelate came to be canonized, or held in high esteem
by the people, some private collects or particular forms that he
had used were practised in his, or perhaps, as his fame spread,
in the neighbouring dioceses.   In every age there were notable
additions made: and all the writers almost, in the eighth and
ninth centuries, employed their fancies to find out mystical sig-
nifications for every rite that was then used; and so, as a new
rite was added, it was no hard matter to add some mystery to
it.   This had made the offices swell out of measure, and there
was a great variety of them; missals, breviaries, rituals, ponti-
ficals, portoises, pies, graduals, antiphonals, psalteries, hours,
and a great many more.   Every religious order had likewise
their peculiar rites, with the saints' days that belonged to their
order, and services for them; and the understanding how to
officiate was become so hard a piece of the trade, that it was
not easy to learn it exactly, without a long practice in it.   So
now it was resolved to correct and examine these.

It was re-
solved
there
should
be a new
liturgy.

I do not find it was ever brought under consideration,
whether they should compose a form for all the parts of divine
worship, or leave it to the sudden and extemporary heats of
those who were to officiate, which some have have called since
that time, the worshipping *by the Spirit*: of this way of serving
God they did not then dream; much less that the appointing
of forms of prayer was encroaching on the kingly office of

Christ; but thought, whatever *praying in the Spirit* might
have been in the apostles' time, (where yet every man brought
his psalms, which are a sort of prayers as well as praises, and
73 these look like some written composures, as St. Paul expresses
it,) that now, to pray with warm affection and sincere devotion
was spiritual worship; and that, where it was the same thing
that was to be daily asked of God, the using the same expressions was the sign of a steady devotion, that was fixed on the
thing prayed for; whereas the heat that new words raised,
looked rather like a warmth in the fancy. Nor could it agree
with the principles of a reformation, that was to divest the
churchmen of that unlimited authority which they had formerly
exercised over men's consciences, to leave them at liberty to
make the people pray after them as they pleased; this being
as great a resignation of the people, when their devotion
depended on the sudden heats of their pastors, as the former
superstition had made of their faith and conscience to them.
So, it being resolved to bring the whole worship of God under
set forms, they set one general rule to themselves, (which they
afterwards declared,) of changing nothing for novelty's sake,
or merely because it had been formerly used. They resolved
to retain such things as the primitive church had practised,
cutting off such abuses as the later ages had grafted on them;
and to continue the use of such other things, which, though
they had been brought in not so early, yet were of good use to
beget devotion; and were so much recommended to the people
by the practice of them, that the laying these aside would
perhaps have alienated them from the other changes they made.
And therefore they resolved to make no change without very
good and weighty reasons; in which they considered the practice of our Saviour, who did not only comply with the rites of
Judaism himself, but even the prayer he gave to his disciples
was framed according to their forms; and his two great institutions of baptism and the eucharist did consist of rites that
had been used among the Jews. And since he who was delivering a new religion, and was authorized in the highest manner
that ever any was, did yet so far comply with received practices, as from them to take those which he sanctified for the use
of his church, it seemed much fitter for those, who had no such
extraordinary warrant to give them authority in what they did,

when they were reforming abuses, to let the world see they did it not from the wanton desire of change, or any affectation of novelty : and with those resolutions they entered on their work.

In the search of the former offices, they found an infinite deal of superstition, in the consecrations of water, salt, bread, incense, candles, fire, bells, churches, images, altars, crosses, vessels, garments, palms, flowers; all looked like the rites of heathenism, and seemed to spring from the same fountain. When the water or salt were blessed, it was expressed to be to this end, that they might be health both to soul and body; and devils (who might well laugh at these tricks which they had taught them) were adjured not to come to any place where they were sprinkled; and the holy bread was blessed to be a defence against all diseases and snares of the Devil; and the holy incense, that devils might not come near the smoke of it, but that all who smelled at it might perceive the virtue of the Holy Ghost; and the ashes were blessed so, that all who were covered with them might deserve to obtain the remission of their sins. All those things had drawn the people to such confidence in them, that they generally thought, that, without those harder terms of true holiness they might upon such superstitious observances be sure of heaven. So all these they 74 resolved to cast out, as things which had no warrant in scripture, and were vain devices to draw men away from a lively application to God through Christ, according to the method of the gospel. Then the many rites in sacramental actions were considered, all which had swelled up to an infinite heap. And as some of these, which had no foundation in scripture, were thrown out, so the others were brought back to a greater simplicity. In no part of religion was the corruption of the former offices more remarkable, than in the priests' granting absolution to the living and the dead. To such as confessed, the absolution was thus granted: *I absolve thee in the name of the Father, the Son, and the Holy Ghost.* To which this was added: *And I grant to thee, that all the indulgences given, or to be given thee, by any prelate, with the blessings of them, all the sprinklings of holy water, all the devout beatings of thy breast, the contritions of thy heart, this confession, and all thy other devout confessions, all thy fastings, abstinences, almsgivings, watchings, disciplines, prayers, and pilgrimages,*

[Fox, vol. iii. p. 10.]

*and all the good thou hast done or shall do, and all the evils
thou hast suffered or shall suffer for God; the passions of
our Lord Jesus Christ, the merits of the glorious and blessed
Virgin Mary, and of all other saints, and the suffrages of all
the holy catholic church, turn to thee for the remission of
these and all other thy sins, the increase of thy merits, and
the attainment of everlasting rewards.* When extreme unction
was given to dying persons, they applied it to the ears, lips,
nose, and other parts with this prayer: *By this holy unction,
and his own most tender mercy, and by the intercession of the
blessed Virgin, and all the saints, may God pardon thee whatever thou hast sinned, by thy hearing, speaking, or smelling;*
and so in the other parts. And when the dead body was laid
in the grave, this absolution was said over it; *The Lord Jesus
Christ, who gave to St. Peter and his other disciples power to
bind and loose, absolve thee from all the guilt of thy sins;
and in so far as is committed to my weakness, be thou absolved
before the tribunal of our Lord, and may thou have eternal
life, and live for evermore.* This was thought the highest
abuse possible; when, in giving the hopes of heaven, and the
pardon of sins, which were of all the other parts of religion
the most important, there were such mixtures: and that which
the scriptures had taught could be only attained by Jesus
Christ, and that upon the sincere belief and obedience of his
gospel, was now ascribed to so many other procuring causes.
These things had possessed the world with that conceit, that
there was a trick for saving souls, besides that plain method
which Christ had taught, and that the priests had the secret of
it in their hands; so that those who would not come under the
yoke of Christ, and be saved that way, needed only to apply
themselves to priests, and purchase their favour, and the
business would be done.

There were two other changes, which run through the whole
offices. The one was, the translating them into a vulgar tongue.
The Jewish worship was either in Hebrew, or, after the cap-
tivity, in the Syriac, and vulgar tongues of Palestine. The
apostles always officiated in the tongues that were best understood; so that St. Paul did copiously censure those who in
prayers or psalms used any language that was not understood.
And Origen, Basil, with all the fathers that had occasion to

mention this, took notice, that every one in their own tongue 75 worshipped God. After the rending of the Roman empire by the Goths and other barbarous nations, the Roman tongue did slowly mix with their tongues, till it was much changed and altered from itself by degrees; yet it was so long a doing that, that it was not thought necessary to translate the liturgy into their languages. But in the ninth century, when the Slavons were converted, it being desired that they might have divine offices in their own language, while some opposed it, a voice was said to be heard, *Let every tongue praise God*: upon which pope John the Eighth writ to Methodius, their bishop, that it might be granted; and founded it on St. Paul's Epistle to the Corinthians, and on these words of David, *Let every tongue praise the Lord*. And in the fourth council of Lateran it was decreed, that bishops, who lived in places where they were mixed with Greeks, should provide fit priests for performing divine offices, according to the rites and language of those to whom they ministered. But the Roman church, though so merciful to the Greeks and Slavons, was more cruel to the rest of Europe; and since only Hebrew, Greek, and Latin, had been written on the cross of Christ by Pilate, they argued, that these languages were thereby consecrated; though it is not easy to apprehend what holiness could be derived into these tongues by Pilate, who ordered these inscriptions. It was also pretended, that it was a part of the communion of saints, that every where the worship should be in the same tongue. But the truth was, they had a mind to raise the value of the priestly function, by keeping all divine offices in a tongue not understood; which in people otherwise well seasoned with superstition, might have that effect; but it did very much alienate the rest of the world from them. There was also a vast number of holydays formerly observed, with so many prayers and hymns belonging to them, and so many lessons that were to be read; which were many of them such impudent forgeries, that, the whole breviary and missal being full of these, a great deal was to be left out. There is in the whole breviary scarce one saint, but the lessons concerning him contain some ridiculous legend, such as indeed could not be well read in a vulgar tongue, without the scorn and laughter of the hearers; and for most part the prayers and hymns do relate to these lying stories. Many of the prayers and hymns were also in such a style, that the pardon of sin, grace, and heaven, were immediately desired from the saints; as if these things had come from their bounty, or by their merits, or were given by them only; of which the reader shall have a little taste in the Collection, in some of the addresses made to them. Collect. Numb. 29.

The reformers, having thus considered the corruptions of the former offices, were thereby better prepared to frame new ones. But the priests had officiated in some garments which were appropriated to that use, as surplices, copes, and other vestments; and it was long under consideration whether these should continue. It was objected, that these garments had been parts of the train of the mass, and had been superstitiously abused only to set it off with the more pomp. On the other hand it was argued, that, as white was anciently the colour of the priests' garments in the Mosaical dispensation, so it was used in the African churches in the fourth century; and it was thought a natural expression of the purity and decency 76 that became priests : besides, the clergy were then generally extreme poor, so that they could scarce afford themselves decent clothes; the people also, running from the other extreme of submitting too much to the clergy, were now as much inclined to despise them, and to make light of the holy function; so that, if they should officiate in their own mean garments, it might make the divine offices grow also into contempt. And therefore it was resolved to continue the use of them; and it was said, that their being blessed and used superstitiously, gave as strong an argument against the use of churches and bells; but that St. Paul had said, *That every creature of God was good;* and even the meat of the sacrifice offered to an idol, than which there could be no greater abuse, might lawfully be eaten ; therefore they saw no necessity, because of a former abuse, to throw away habits that had so much decency in them, and had been formerly in use.

In the compiling the offices, they began with morning and evening prayer. These were put in the same form they are now, only there was no confession nor absolution; the office beginning with the Lord's Prayer. In the Communion Service the Ten Commandments were not said as they are now, but in other things it was very near what it is now. All that had been in the order of the communion formerly mentioned was

put into it. The offertory was to be made of bread, and wine
mixed with water. Then was said the prayer for the state of
Christ's church, in which they gave thanks to God for his
wonderful grace declared in his saints, in the blessed Virgin,
the patriarchs, apostles, prophets, and martyrs ; and they
commended the saints departed to God's mercy and peace,
that, at the day of the resurrection, we with them might be
set on Christ's right hand. To this, the consecratory prayer
which we now use was joined as a part of it, only with these
words, that are since left out ; *With thy Holy Spirit vouchsafe
to bless and sanctify these thy gifts and creatures of bread
and wine, that they may be unto us the body and blood of thy
most dearly beloved Son,* &c. To the consecration was also
joined the prayer of thanksgiving now used. After the consecration, all elevation was forbidden, which had been first used
as a rite expressing how Christ was lifted up on the cross ; but
was, after the belief of the corporal presence, made use of to
shew the sacrament, that the people might all fall down and
worship it. And it was ordered, that the whole office of the
communion, except the consecratory prayer, should be used on
all holydays, when there was no communion, to put people in
mind of it, and of the sufferings of Christ. The bread was to
be unleavened, round, but no print on it, and somewhat thicker
than it was formerly. And though it was anciently put in the
people's hands, yet, because some might carry it away, and
apply it to superstitious uses, it was ordered to be put by the
priest into their mouths. It is clear, that Christ delivered it
into the hands of the apostles, and it so continued for many
ages ; as appears by several remarkable stories of holy men
carrying it with them in their journeys. In the Greek church,
where the bread and wine were mingled together, some began
to think it more decent to receive it in little spoons of gold,
than in their hands ; but that was condemned by the council in
Trullo : yet soon after they began in the Latin church to appoint men to receive it with their hands, but women to take it
in a linen cloth, which was called their *dominical.* But when 77
the belief of the corporal presence was received, then a new
way of receiving was invented, among other things, to support
it : the people were now no more to touch that which was conceived to be the flesh of their Saviour, and therefore the priest's
thumb and fingers were particularly anointed, as a necessary

disposition for so holy a contact; and so it was by them put into the mouths of the people. A litany was also gathered, consisting of many short petitions, interrupted by suffrages between them; and was the same that we still use, only they had one suffrage that we have not, to be delivered from the tyranny of the bishop of Rome, and all his detestable enormities.

In baptism, there was, besides the forms which we still retain, a cross at first made on the child's forehead and breast, with an adjuration of the Devil to go out of him, and come at him no more. Then the priest was to take the child by the right hand, and to place him within the font; there he was to be dipped thrice, once on the right side, once on the left, and once on the breast; which was to be discreetly done: but if the child were weak, it was sufficient to sprinkle water on his face. Then was the priest to put a white vestment or chrysome on him, for a token of innocence, and to anoint him on the head, with a prayer for the unction of the Holy Ghost. In confirmation, those that came were to be catechised; which having in it a formal engagement to make good the baptismal vow, was all that was asked: (the Catechism then was the same that is now, only there is since added an explanation of the sacraments.) ·This being said, the bishop was to sign them with the cross, and to lay his hands on them, and say, *I sign thee with the sign of the cross, and lay my hands on thee, in the name of the Father,* &c. The sick, who desired to be anointed, might have the unction on their forehead, or their breast only; with a prayer, that, as their body was outwardly anointed with oil, so they might receive the Holy Ghost, with health, and victory over sin and death. At funerals, they recommended the soul departed to God's mercy, and prayed that his sins might be pardoned, that he might be delivered from hell, and carried to heaven, and that his body might be raised at the last day.

They also took care that those who could not come, or be brought to church, should not therefore be deprived of the use of the sacraments. The church of Rome had raised the belief of the indispensable necessity of the sacraments so high, that they taught they did *ex opere operato*, by the very action itself, without inward acts, justify and confer grace, unless there were a bar put to it by the receiver: and the first rise of the questions about justification seems to have come from this; for that church teaching that men were justified by sacramental actions, the reformers opposed this, and thought men were justified by the internal acts of the mind: if they had held at this, the controversy might have been managed with much greater advantages; which they lost in a great measure by descending to some minuter subtilties. In the church of Rome, pursuant to their belief concerning the necessity of the sacraments, women were allowed in extreme cases to baptize; and the midwives commonly did it; which might be the beginning of their being licensed by bishops to exercise that calling. And they also believed that a simple attrition with the sacraments was sufficient for salvation in those who were grown up; and 78 upon these grounds the sacraments were administered to the sick.

In the primitive church they sent portions of the sacrament to those who were sick, or in prison: and did it not only without pomp or processions, but sent it often by the hands of boys, and other laics, as appears from the famed story of Serapion; which as it shews they did not then believe it was the very flesh and blood of Christ; so, when that doctrine was received, it was a natural effect of that belief, to have the sacrament carried by the priest himself with some pomp and adoration. The ancients thought it more decent, and suitable to the communion of saints, to consecrate the elements only in the church, and to send portions to the sick, thereby expressing their communion with the rest. The reformers considering these things, steered a middle course: they judged the sacraments necessary, where they could be had, as appointments instituted by Christ; and though they thought it more expedient to have all baptisms done in the church at the fonts, than in private houses, thereby signifying that the baptized were admitted to the fellowship of that church; yet, since our Saviour had said, *That where two or three are gathered together, he will be in the midst of them;* they thought it savoured too much of a superstition to the walls or fonts of churches, to tie this action so to these, that where children, either through infirmity, or the sharpness of weather, could not be without danger carried to church, they should be denied baptism. But still they thought public baptism more expressive of the communion of the saints; so that they recommended it much, and only permitted the other in cases of necessity. This has since grown to a great abuse; many thinking it a piece of state to have their children baptized in their houses; and so bringing their pride with them even into the most sacred performances. There may be also a fault in the ministers, who are too easily brought to do it. But it is now become so universal, that all the endeavours of some of our bishops have not been able to bring it back to the first design of not baptizing in private houses, excepting only where there was some visible danger in carrying the children to church.

As for the other sacrament, it was thought by our reformers, that, according to the mind of the primitive church, none should be denied it in their extremities; it never being more necessary than at that time to use all means that might strengthen the faith, and quicken the devotion, of dying persons; it being also most expedient that they should then profess their dying in the faith, and with a good conscience, and in charity with all men : therefore they ordered the communion to be given to the sick ; and that, before it was so given, the priest should examine their consciences, and upon the sincere profession of their faith, and the confession of such sins as oppressed their consciences, with the doing of all that was then in their power for the completing of their repentance, as the forgiving injuries, and dealing justly with all people, he should give them the peace of the church in a formal absolution, and the holy eucharist. But, that they might avoid the pomp of vain processions on the one hand, and the indecencies of sending the sacrament by common hands on the other, they thought it better to gather a congregation about the sick person, and 79 there to consecrate and give the sacrament to that small assembly; where, as Christ's promise, *of being in the midst of two or three that were gathered together in his name,* should have put an end to the weak exceptions some have made to these private communions; so on the other hand it is to be feared, that the greater part retain still too much of the superstition of popery : as if the priest's absolution, with the sacrament, and some slight sorrow for sin, would be a sure passport for their admittance to heaven; which it is certain can only be had upon so true a faith, as carries a sincere repentance, with a change of heart and life, along with it; for to such only the mercies of God, through the merits of Jesus Christ, are applied in all ordinary cases.

The preface to the Book of Common Prayer.

To all this they prefixed a preface concerning ceremonies, the same that is still before the Common Prayer Book. In which preface they make a difference between those ceremonies that were brought in with a good intent, and were afterwards abused; and others, that had been brought in out of vanity and superstition at first, and grew to be more abused: the one they had quite rejected, the other they had reformed and retained for decency and edification. Some were so set on their old forms, that they thought it a great matter to depart from any of them; others were desirous to innovate in every thing: between both which they had kept a mean. The burden of ceremonies in St. Austin's days was such, that he complained of them then as intolerable, by which the state of Christians was worse than that of the Jews; but these were swelled to a far greater number since his days, which did indeed darken religion, and had brought Christians under a heavy yoke: therefore they had only reserved such as were decent, and apt to stir up men's minds with some good signification. Many ceremonies had been so abused by superstition and avarice, that it was necessary to take them quite away: but since it was fit to retain some for decency and order, it seemed better to keep those which were old than to seek new ones. But these that were kept were not thought equal with God's law, and so were upon just causes to be altered: they were also plain and easy to be understood, and not very subject to be abused. Nor did they, in retaining these, condemn other nations, or prescribe to any but their own people. And thus was this book made ready against the next meeting of parliament.

Reflections made on the new liturgy.

In it the use of the cross was retained, since it had been used by the ancient Christians as a public declaration that they were not ashamed of the cross of Christ: though they acknowledged this had been strangely abused in the later ages, in which the bare use of the cross was thought to have some magical virtue in it; and this had gone so far, that in the Roman Pontifical it was declared, that the crosier-staff was to be worshipped with that supreme degree of adoration called *Latria*. But it was thought fit to retain it in some

parts of worship; and the rather, because it was made use of among the people to defame the reformers, that they had no veneration for the cross of Christ.   And therefore, as an outward expression of that in the sacrament of baptism, and in the office of confirmation, and in the consecration of the sacramental elements, it was ordered to be retained, but with this difference; that the sign of the cross was not made with the opinion of any virtue or efficacy in it to drive away evil spirits,
80 or to preserve one out of dangers, which were thought virtues that followed the use of it in the Roman church: for in baptism, as they used the sign of the cross, they added an adjuration to the *evil spirit not to violate it;* and in the making it said, *Receive the sign of the cross both in thy forehead and in thy heart, and take the faith of the heavenly precepts.* Thus a sacramental virtue was pretended to be affixed to it, which the reformers thought could not be done without a warrant from a divine institution, of which it is plain there was none in scripture.   But they thought the use of it only as an expression of the belief of the church, and as a badge of Christianity, with such words added to it as could import no more, was liable to no exception.   This seems more necessary to be well explained, by reason of the scruples that many have since raised against significant ceremonies, as if it were too great a presumption in any church to appoint such, since these seem to be of the nature of sacraments.   Ceremonies that signify the conveyance of a divine grace and virtue are indeed sacraments, and ought not to be used without an express institution in scripture; but ceremonies that only signify the sense we have, which is sometimes expressed as significantly in dumb shows as in words, are of another kind: and it is as much within the power of the church to appoint such to be used, as it is to order collects or prayers; words and signs being but different ways of expressing our thoughts.   The belief of Christ's corporal presence was yet under consideration: and they, observing wisely how the Germans had broken by their running too soon into contests about that, resolved to keep up still the old general expressions of the sacraments being the whole and true body of Christ, without coming to a more particular explanation of it.   The use of oil on so many occasions was taken from the ancient Christians, who, as Theophilus

says, began early to be anointed; and understood those words of St. Paul, of God's *anointing* and *sealing,* literally.   It was also anciently applied to the receiving of penitents.   But it was not used about the sick, from the apostles' times, till about the tenth century: and then, from what St. James writ to those in the dispersion, of sending for the elders to come to such as were sick, who should anoint them with oil, and their sins should be forgiven them, and they should recover; they came to give it to those that were dying, but not while there was any hope of life left in them: though it is clear, that what St. James writ related to that extraordinary gift of healing, by imposition of hands, and anointing with oil, which yet continued in the church when he writ that Epistle.   And it is plain, that this passage in St. James was not so understood by the ancients, as it is now in the Roman church; since the ancients, though they used oil on many other occasions, yet applied it not at all to the sick till after so many ages, that gross superstition had so disposed the world to new rites, that there could be no discovery or invention more acceptable than the addition of a new ceremony, though they were then much oppressed with the old ones.

The changes that were made, and those that were designed to be made, occasioned great heats every where.   And the pulpits generally contending with one another; to restrain that clashing, the power of granting licenses to preach was taken from the bishops of each diocese, so that none might give them but the king and the archbishop of Canterbury. 81

All preach-
ing was for
a time re-
strained.
[Wilkins,
Conc. iv.
30.]
Yet that not proving an effectual restraint, on the twenty-third of September a proclamation is said to have come out, setting forth, that whereas according to former proclamations none was to preach but such as had obtained licenses from the king or the archbishop; yet some of those that were so licensed had abused that permission, and had carried themselves irreverently, contrary to the instructions that were sent them: therefore the king, intending to have shortly an uniform order over all the kingdom, and to put an end to all controversies in religion, about which some bishops and other learned men were then assembled; and though many of the preachers so licensed had carried themselves wisely, to the honour of God, and the king's great contentation; yet, till the order now preparing

should be set forth, he did inhibit all manner of persons to preach in any public audience, to the intent that the clergy might apply themselves to prayer for a blessing on what the king was then about to do; not doubting but the people would be employed likewise in prayer, and hearing the Homilies read in their churches, and be ready to receive that uniform order that was to be set forth; and the inferior magistrates were required to see to the execution of this. I never met with any footstep of this proclamation [54], neither in records, nor in letters, nor in any book written at that time. But Mr. Fuller has printed it, and Dr. Heylyn has given an abstract of it [Fuller, lib. vii. p. 388. Heylyn, p. 64.] from him. If Fuller had told how he came by it, it might have been further examined. But we know not whether he saw the printed proclamation, or only a copy of it. And if he saw but a copy, we have reason to doubt of it; for that might have been only the essay of some projecting man's pen. But, because I found it in those authors, I thought best to set it down as it is, and leave the reader to judge of it.

Having thus given an account of the progress of the refor- [The affairs in Scotland this year.] mation this summer, I shall now turn to transactions of state, and shall first look towards Scotland. The Scots, gaining time [Thuanus, lib. v. cap. 15. p. 189.] the last winter, and being in daily expectation of succours from France, were resolved to carry on the war. The governor began the year with the siege of Broughty Castle, a little below Dundee. But the English that were in it defended themselves so well, that, after they had been besieged three months, the siege was raised, and only so many were left about it as might cover the country from their excursions. The English on the other side had taken and fortified Haddington, and were at work also at Lauder to make it strong. The former of these lying in a plain, and in one of the most fruitful counties of Scotland, within twelve miles of Edinburgh, was a [Buchanan, lib. xv. p. 306.] very fit place to be kept as a curb upon the country. About the end of May six thousand men were sent from France under the command of d'Essé: three thousand of these were Germans, commanded by the Rhinegrave; two thousand of them were French, and a thousand were of other nations [55]; they

---

[54] This proclamation was printed by Grafton among king Edward's proclamations. [S.]

[55] [Ac mille diversi generis equites duce Francisco Anglurio Etaugio. Thuanus, v. 15. p. 189.]

landed at Leith; and the governor having gathered eight thousand Scots to join with them, they sat down before Haddington; and here the Scottish nobility entered into a long consultation about their affairs.

[Thuanus,
p. 190.]
The protector had sent a proposition to them, that there might be a truce for ten years. (But whether he offered to remove the garrisons, does not appear.) This he was forced to upon many accounts. He saw the war was like to last long, and to draw on great expense, and would certainly end in another war with France; he durst not any more go from court, and march himself at the head of the army, and leave 82 the king to the practices of his brother. There were also great discontents in England; many were offended with the changes made in religion; the commons complained generally of oppression, and of the enclosing of grounds, of which the sad effects broke out next year: he began to labour under the envy of the nobility; the clergy were almost all displeased with him; and the state of affairs in Germany made it necessary to join with the king of France against the emperor. All this made him very desirous of such a peace with Scotland as might at least preserve the queen from being disposed of for ten years. In that time, by treaty and pensions, they might hope to gain their ends more certainly than by a war, which only inflamed the Scots against them, according to the witty saying of one of the Scots, who, being asked what he thought of the match with England, said he knew not how he should like the marriage, but he was sure he did not like the way of wooing. On the other hand, the French pressed the Scots to send their young queen into France in the ships that had brought over their forces, who should be married to the dauphin, and then they might depend on the protection of
[Buchanan,
p. 300.]
France. Many were for accepting the propositions from England, (particularly all those who secretly favoured the reformation;) they thought it would give them present quiet, and free them from all the distractions which they either felt, or might apprehend, from a lasting war with so powerful an enemy; whereas the sending away of their queen would put them out of a capacity of obtaining a peace, if the war this year proved as unsuccessful as it was the last; and the defence they had from France was almost as bad as the invasions of

the English, for the French were very insolent, and committed great disorders. But all the clergy were so apprehensive of their ruin by the marriage with England, that they never judged themselves safe till the thing was out of their power by the sending their queen into France. And it was said, that when once the English saw the hopes of the marriage irrecoverably lost, they would soon grow weary of the war; for then the king of France would engage in the defence of Scotland with his whole force, so that nothing would keep up the war so much as having their queen still among them. To this many of the nobility yielded, being corrupted by money from France; and the governor consented to it, for which he was to be made duke of Chastelherault in France, and to have an estate of twelve thousand livres a year. And so it was agreed to send their queen away. This being gained, the French ships set sail to sea, as if they had been to return to France, but sailed round Scotland by the isles of Orkney, and came into Dumbarton Frith, near to which the queen was kept, in Dumbarton castle; and, receiving her from thence with an honourable convoy that was sent to attend on her, they carried her over to Bretagne in France, and so by easy journeys she was brought to court, where her uncles received her with great joy, hoping by her means to raise and establish their fortunes in France. _{The Scottish queen is sent to France.}

In the mean time the siege of Haddington was carried on with great valour on both sides. The French were astonished at the courage, the nimbleness, and labours of the Scotch Highlanders, who were half naked, but capable of great hardships, and used to run on with marvellous swiftness. In one sally which the besieged made, one of those got an Englishman on his shoulders, and carried him away with that quickness, that nothing could stop him; and though the Englishman bit him so in the neck, that, as soon as he had brought him into camp, he himself fell down as dead, yet he carried him off, for which he was nobly rewarded by d'Essé. The English defended themselves no less courageously; and though a recruit of about one thousand foot, and three hundred horse, that was sent from Berwick, led by sir Robert Bowes and sir Thomas Palmer, was so fatally intercepted, that they were almost all to a man killed, yet they lost no heart. Another

The siege of Haddington. Thuanus, [p. 190.]

[Ibid. p. 191.]

[Buchanan, p. 301.]
party of about three hundred escaped the ambush laid for them, and got into the town, with a great deal of ammunition and provisions, of which the besieged were come to be in want. But at the same both Home-castle and Fast-castle were lost.

[Ibid. p. 300.]
The former was taken by treachery; for some coming in as deserters, seeming to be very zealous for the English quarrel, and being too much trusted by the governor, and going often out to bring intelligence, gave the lord Home notice, that on that side where the rock was, the English kept no good watches, trusting to the steepness of the place: so they agreed, that some should come and climb the rock, to whom they should give assistance; which was accordingly done, and so it was surprised in the night. The governor of Fast-castle had summoned the country people to bring him in provisions; upon which (by a common stratagem) soldiers, coming as country-men, threw down their carriages at the gates, and fell on the sentinels; and so, the signal being given, some, that lay concealed near at hand, came in time to assist them, and took the castle.

A fleet sent against Scotland.
The protector, till the army was gathered together, sent a fleet of ships to disturb the Scots, by the descents they should make in divers places; and his brother being admiral, he commanded him to go to his charge. He landed first in Fife, at St. Monan; but there the queen's natural brother, James, afterwards earl of Murray, and regent of Scotland, gathered the country people together, and made head against them. The English were twelve hundred, and had brought their cannon to land; but the Scots charged them so home, that they forced them to their ships: many were drowned, and many killed; the Scots reckoned the number of the slain to be six hundred,

[Ibid. p. 301.] But was not successful. [Thuanus, p. 192.]
and a hundred prisoners taken. The next descent they made was no more prosperous to them: for, landing in the night at Mountross, Erskine of Dun gathered the country together, and divided them in three bodies, ordering one to appear soon after the former had engaged; the enemy, seeing a second and a third body come against them, apprehending greater numbers, ran back to their ships; but with so much loss, that, of eight hundred who had landed, the third man got not safe to the ships again. So the admiral returned, having got nothing but loss and disgrace by the expedition.

But now the English army came into Scotland commanded
by the earl of Shrewsbury : though both the Scotch writers
and Thuanus say, the earl of Lennox had the chief command ; [Thuanus,
but he only came with the earl of Shrewsbury, as knowing the P. 191.]
country and people best, and so being the fitter both to get
intelligence, and to negotiate, if there was room for it. The
Scots were by this time gone home for the most part ; and the
84 nobility, with d'Essé, agreed, that it was not fit to put all to
hazard, and therefore raised the siege of Haddington, and Aug. 20.
marched back to Edinburgh. The lord Grey, with a great the siege of
part of the English army, followed him in the rear, but did ton raised.
Haddington part of the English army, followed him in the rear, but did
not engage him into any great action ; by which a good opportunity was lost, for the French were in great disorder. The
English army came into Haddington. They consisted of about
seventeen thousand men ; of which number seven thousand
were horse[56], and three thousand of the foot were German
lanceknights, whom the protector had entertained in his service. These Germans were some of the broken troops of the
protestant army, who, seeing the state of their own country
desperate, offered their service to the protector. He too easily
entertained them ; reckoning, that, being protestants, they
would be sure to him, and would depend wholly on himself.
But this proved a fatal counsel to him ; the English having
been always jealous of a standing, but much more of a foreign
force about their prince : so there was great occasion given by
this to those who traded in sowing jealousies among the people.
The English, having victualled Haddington, and repaired the
fortifications, returned back into their own country : but had
they gone on to Edinburgh, they had found things there in
great confusion. For d'Essé, when he got thither, having lost
five hundred of his men in the retreat, went to quarter his
soldiers in the town ; but the provost (so is the chief magistrate there called) opposed it. The French broke in with
force, and killed him and his son, with all they found in the
streets, men, women, and children : and, as a spy, whom the
English had in Edinburgh, gave them notice, the Scots were
now more alienated from the French than from the English.

---

[56] [Igitur Levinius qui Anglorum   lium peditum, septingentorum equi-
partes tunc sequebatur, terrestribus   tum erat. Thuanus, lib. v. cap. 15.
copiis præficitur ; eæ octodecim mil-   p. 191.]

The French had carried it very gently, till the queen was sent away; but reckoned Scotland now a conquered country, and a province to France: so the Scots began, though too late, to repent the sending away of the queen. But it seems the English had orders not to venture too far; for the hopes of the marriage were now gone, and the protector had no mind to engage in a war with France. These things happened in the beginning of October. D'Essé, apprehending that at Haddington they were now secure, the siege being so lately raised, resolved to try if he could carry the place by surprise. The English from thence had made excursions as far as Edinburgh; in one of which the French fell on them, pursued them, and killed about two hundred, and took sixscore prisoners, almost within their works. Soon after, d'Essé marched in the night, and surprised one of their outworks, and was come to the gates: where the place had been certainly lost, if it had not been for a French deserter, who knew, if he were taken, what he was to expect. He therefore fired one of the great cannon, which, being discharged among the thickest of the French, killed so many, and put the rest in such disorder, that d'Essé was forced to quit the attempt. From thence he went and fortified Leith, which was then but a mean village; but the situation of the place being recommended by the security it now had, it soon came to be one of the best peopled towns in Scotland. From thence he intended to have gone on to take Broughty Castle, and to recover Dundee, which were then in the hands of the English; but he was ordered by the queen regent to make an inroad into England. There, after some slight engagements, in which the English had the worst, the Scotch and French came in as far as Newcastle, and returned loaded with spoil: which the French divided among themselves, allowing the Scots no share of it. An English priest was taken, who bore that disgrace of his country so heavily, that he threw himself on the ground, and would not eat, nor so much as open his eyes, but lay thus prostrate till he died: this the French, who seldom let their misfortunes afflict them, looked on with much astonishment. But at that time the English had fortified Inch-keith, an island in the Frith, and put eight hundred men in it. Seventeen days after that, d'Essé brought his forces from Leith, and recovered it; having

85

[Thuanus, p. 194.]

[Ibid. p. 195.]

killed four hundred English, and forced the rest to surrender.

Thus ended this year, and with it d'Essé's power in Scot- Discontents in Scotland.
land. For the queen mother and the governor had made great
complaints of him at the court of France, that he put the nation
to vast charge to little purpose ; so that he was more uneasy
to his friends than his enemies : and his last disorder at Edinburgh had on the one hand so raised the insolence of the
French soldiers, and on the other hand so alienated and inflamed the people, that, unless another were sent to command,
who should govern more mildly, there might be great danger
of a defection of a whole kingdom. For now the seeds of their
distaste of the French government were so sown, that men
came generally to condemn their sending the queen away, and
to hate the governor for consenting to it ; but chiefly to abhor
the clergy, who had wrought it for their own ends.

Monsieur de Thermes was sent over to command ; and Mon- Monluc sent thither to be lord chancellor ; [Thuanus, p. 195.]
luc, bishop of Valence, came with him to govern the counsels,
and be chancellor of the kingdom. He had lately returned
from his embassy at Constantinople. He was one of the wisest
men of that time, and was always for moderate counsels in
matters of religion ; which made him be sometime suspected of
heresy.   And indeed the whole sequel of his life declared him
to be one of the greatest men of that age ; only his being so
long and so firmly united to queen Catharine Medici's interest,
takes off a great deal of the high character which the rest of
his life has given of him.   But he was at this time unknown, But was not well received.
and ill represented, in Scotland ; where they, that looked for
advantages from their alliance with France, took it ill to see a
Frenchman sent over to enjoy the best office in the kingdom.
The queen mother herself was afraid of him : so, to avoid new
grounds of discontent, he left the kingdom, and returned into
France.

Thus ended the war between Scotland and England this
year, in almost an equal mixture of good and bad success. The
English had preserved Haddington, which was the chief matter
of this year's action.   But they had been at great charge in
the war, in which they were only on the defensive : they had
lost other places, and been unsuccessful at sea ; and, which was
worst of all, they had now lost all hopes of the marriage, and

were almost engaged in a war with France, which was like to fall on the king when his affairs were in an ill condition, his people being divided and discontented at home, and his treasure much exhausted by this war.

The affairs of Germany. [Sleidan, fol. 329.] The state of Germany was at this time most deplorable: the pope and emperor continued their quarrelling about the translation of the council. Mendoza at Rome, and Velasco at Bologna, declared, in the emperor's name, that a council being called by his great and long endeavours for the quieting of 86 Germany, and he being engaged in a war to get it to be received; and having procured a submission of the empire to the council, it was, upon frivolous and feigned causes, removed out of Germany to one of the pope's towns: by which the Germans thought themselves disengaged of their promise, which was, to submit to a council in Germany: and therefore that he protested against it as an unlawful meeting, to whose decrees he would not submit; and that, if they did not return to Trent, he would take care of settling religion some other way. But the pope, being encouraged by the French king,

The emperor, being displeased with the translation of the council, orders the Interim to be drawn. [Thuanus, p. 171. Sleidan, fol. 330.] was not ill pleased to see the emperor anew embroil himself with the Germans; and therefore intended the council should be continued at Bologna. Upon this the emperor ordered three divines, Julius Pflugius, bishop of Naumburg, Michael Sidonius, and Islebius Agricola, to draw a form of religion. The two former had been always papists, and the latter was formerly a protestant, but was believed to be now corrupted by the emperor, that the name of one of the Augsburg Confession might make what they were to set out, pass the more easily. They drew up all the points of religion in a book, which was best known by the name of the Interim, because it was to last during that interval, till a general council should meet in Germany. In it all the points of the Romish doctrine were set forth in the smoothest terms possible: only, married

[Sleidan, fol. 333. Thuanus, p. 172.] Feb. Diet at Augsburg. men might officiate as priests, and the communion was to be given in both kinds. The book being thus prepared, a diet was summoned to Augsburg in February, where the first thing done was, the solemn investiture of Maurice in the electorate of Saxony. He had been declared elector last year by the emperor before Wittenberg: but now it was performed with

Feb. 24. Maurice great ceremony on the twenty-fourth of February, which was

the emperor's birthday; John Frederick looking on with his made elector of Saxony.
usual constancy of mind. All he said was, " Now they triumph
" in that dignity, of which they have against justice and equity [Thuanus, p. 176.
" spoiled me: God grant they may enjoy it peaceably and Sleidan,
" happily, and may never need any assistance from me or my p. 332.]
" posterity." And, without expressing any further concern
about it, he went to his studies, which were almost wholly
employed in the scriptures.

The book of the Interim being prepared, the elector of
Brandenburg sent for Martin Bucer, who was both a learned
and moderate divine, and shewed it him. Bucer, having read
it, plainly told him, that it was nothing but downright popery,
only a little disguised: at which the elector was much offended,
for he was pleased with it : and Bucer, not without great
danger, returned back to Strasburg. On the fifteenth of May 15.
March [57] the book was proposed to the diet ; and the elector The Interim received in the diet.
of Mentz, without any order, did in all the princes' names give
the emperor thanks for it : which he interpreted as the assent [Sleidan,
of the whole diet; and after that would not hear any that fol. 334.]
came to him to stop it, but published it as agreed to by the
diet.

At Rome and Bologna it was much condemned, as an high The papists offended at it, as well as the protestants.
attempt in the emperor to meddle with points of religion ; such
as dispensing with the marriage of priests, and the communion
in both kinds. Wherefore some of that church writ against it.
And matters went so high, that wise men of that side began to
fear the breach between the emperor and them might, before
87 they were aware, be past reconciling : for they had not forgot
that the last pope's stiffness had lost England, and they were
not a little afraid they might now lose the emperor. But if the
pope were offended for the concessions in these two particulars,
the protestants thought they had much greater cause to dislike
it ; since in all other controverted points it was against them :
so that several of that side writ likewise against it. But the
emperor was now so much exalted with his success, that he resolved to go through with it, little regarding the opposition of
either hand. The new elector of Saxony went home, and
offered it to his subjects. But they refused to receive it, and

[57] [Sleidan, p. 334, says, Cæsar igitur idibus Maii convocat omnes or-
dines &c.]

Cott. lib.
Titus B. ii.
[fol. 76,
dated July
17, 1548.]
said, (as sir Philip Hobby, then ambassador from England at the emperor's court, writ over,) that they had it under the emperor's hand and seal, that he should not meddle with matters of religion, but only with reforming the common-wealth : and that, if their prince would not protect them in this matter, they should find another, who would defend them from such oppression. An exhortation for the receiving of it was read at Augsburg ; but they also refused it. Many towns sent their addresses to the emperor, desiring him not to op-press their consciences. But none was of such a nature as that from Linda, a little town near Constance, which had declared for the emperor in the former war. They returned answer, that they could not agree to the Interim without incurring eternal damnation : but, to shew their submission to him in all other things, they should not shut their gates, nor make resist-ance against any he should send, though it were to spoil and destroy their town. This let the emperor and his council see how difficult a work it would be to subdue the consciences of the Germans. But his chancellor, Granvelle, pressed him to extreme counsels, and to make an example of that town, who had so peremptorily refused to obey his commands. Yet he had little reason to hope he should prevail on those who were at liberty, when he could work so little on his prisoner, the duke of Saxe : for he had endeavoured, by great offers, to persuade him to agree to it ; but all was in vain ; for he always told them that kept him, that his person was in their power, but his conscience was in his own ; and that he would not on any terms depart from the Augsburg Confession. Upon this he was severely used ; his chaplain was put from him, with most of his servants ; but he continued still unmoved, and as cheerful as in his greatest prosperity. The Lutheran divines entered into great disputes, how far they might comply. Me-lancthon thought, that the ceremonies of popery might be used, since they were of their own nature indifferent. Others, as Amstorfius, Illiricus, with the greatest part of the Lutherans, thought the receiving the ceremonies would make way for all the errors of popery ; and though they were of their own nature indifferent, yet they ceased to be so when they were enjoined as things necessary to salvation. But the emperor going on resolutely, many divines were driven away ; some

concealed themselves in Germany, others fled into Switzerland, and some came over into England.

When the news of the changes that were made here in England were carried beyond sea, and, after Peter Martyr's being with Cranmer, were more copiously written by him to his friends; Calvin and M. Bucer, who began to think the reformation almost oppressed in Germany, now turned their eyes more upon England. Calvin writ to the protector, on the twenty-ninth of October[58], encouraging him to go on notwith-
88 standing the wars; as Hezekiah had done in his reformation. He lamented the heats of some that professed the gospel; but complained, that he heard there were few lively sermons preached in England; and that the preachers recited their discourses coldly. He much approves a set form of prayers, whereby the consent of all the churches did more manifestly appear. But he advises a more complete reformation. He taxed the *prayers for the dead*, the *use of chrism* and *extreme unction*, since they were no where recommended in scripture. He had heard, that the reason why they went no further was, because the times could not bear it: but this was to do the work of God by political maxims; which, though they ought to take place in other things, yet should not be followed in matters in which the salvation of souls was concerned. But above all things he complained of the great impieties and vices that were so common in England; as *swearing, drinking*, and *uncleanness*; and prayed him earnestly, that these things might be looked after.

Martin Bucer writ also a discourse, congratulating the changes then made in England; which was translated into English by sir Philip Hobby's brother. In it he answered the book that Gardiner had written against him; which he had formerly delayed to do, because king Henry had desired he would let it alone, till the English and Germans had conferred about religion. That book did chiefly relate to the marriage of the clergy. Bucer shewed from many fathers that they thought every man had not the gift of chastity:

Calvin writ to the protector. [Oct. 22.]

Bucer writ against Gardiner.

[58] [This letter is dated from Geneva October 22. A Latin version of it appears in Calvin's Works, vol. IX. pt. ii. p. 39, and a contemporary English translation may be seen in vol. IV. of the Domestic Papers in the State Paper Office.]

which Gardiner thought every one might have that pleased. He taxed the open lewdness of the Romish clergy, who, being much set against marriage, which was God's ordinance, did gently pass over the impurities which the forbidding it had occasioned among themselves. He particularly taxed Gardiner himself, that he had his rents paid him out of stews. He taxed him also for his state, and pompous way of living ; and shewed, how indecent it was for a churchman to be sent in embassies : and that St. Ambrose, though sent to make peace, was ashamed of it, and thought it unbecoming the priesthood. Both Fagius and he being forced to leave Germany upon the business of the Interim, Cranmer invited them over to England, and sent them to Cambridge, as he had done Peter Martyr to Oxford. But Fagius, not agreeing with this air, died soon [59] after ; a man greatly learned in the oriental tongues, and a good expounder of the scripture.

[Nov. 12. Thuanus, vi. 5. p. 206.]

Nov. 24. parliament sits.

This being the state of affairs both abroad and at home, a session of parliament was held in England on the 24th of November, to which day it had been prorogued from the 15th of October, by reason of the plague then in London. The first bill that was finished was that about the marriage of the priests. It was brought into the house of commons the 3rd of December, read the second time on the 5th, and the third time the 6th. But this bill being only that married men might be made priests, a new bill was framed, that, besides the former provision, priests might marry. This was read the first time the 7th, the second time the 10th, and was fully argued on the 11th, and agreed on the 12th, and sent up to the lords on the 13th of December. In that house it stuck as long, as it had been soon despatched by the commons. It lay on the table till the 9th of February. Then it was read the first time, and the 11th the second time : on the 16th it was committed to the bishops of Ely and Westminster, the lord chief justice, and the attorney-general : and on the 19th of February it was agreed to ; the bishops of London, Durham, Norwich, Carlisle, Hereford, Worcester, Bristol, Chichester, and Llandaff, and the lords Morley, Dacres, Windsor, and Wharton, dissenting. It

89

[59] This your lordship seems to place in the year 1548 ; whereas they did not leave Germany till April 1549, and Fagius died in November following. I have his will, proved Jan. 12, 1549[50]. [B.]

had the royal assent, and so became a law. The preamble sets
forth, " that it were better for priests, and other ministers of An act
" the church, to live chaste, and without marriage ; whereby about the marriage of
" they might better attend to the ministry of the gospel, and the clergy.
" be less distracted with secular cares, so that it were much to [Cap. 21,. Statutes,
" be wished that they would of themselves abstain. But great vol. iv. p.
" filthiness of living, with other inconveniences, had followed 67.]
" on the laws that compelled chastity, and prohibited marriage ;
" so that it was better they should be suffered to marry, than
" be so restrained. Therefore all laws and canons that had
" been made against it, being only made by human authority,
" are repealed. So that all spiritual persons, of what degree
" soever, might lawfully marry, providing they married accord-
" ing to the order of the church. But a proviso was added, that,
" because many divorces of priests had been made after the six
" articles were enacted, and that the women might have there-
" upon married again ; all these divorces, with every thing
" that had followed on them, should be confirmed." There
was no law that passed in this reign with more contradiction
and censure than this ; and therefore the reader may expect
the larger account of this matter.

The unmarried state of the clergy had so much to be said Which was much in-quired into.
for it, as being a course of life that was more disengaged from
secular cares and pleasures, that it was cast on the reformers
every where as a foul reproach, that they could not restrain
their appetites, but engaged in a life that drew after it domestic
cares, with many other distractions. This was an objection so
easy to be apprehended, that the people had been more preju-
diced against the marriage of the clergy, if they had not felt
greater inconveniences by the debaucheries of priests ; who,
being restrained from marriage, had defiled the beds, and de-
floured the daughters, of their neighbours, into whose houses
they had free and unsuspected access ; and whom, under the
cloak of receiving confessions, they could more easily entice.
This made them, that they were not so much wrought on by
the noise of chastity, (when they saw so much and so plainly
to the contrary,) as otherwise they would have been, by a
thing that sounded so well. But, on the other hand, there
was no argument which the reformers had more considered.
There were two things upon which the question turned : the

one was, the obligation that priesthood brought with it to live unmarried; the other was, the tie they might be under by any vow they had made. For the former, they considered, that God, having ordained a race of men to be priests under Moses' law, who should offer up expiatory sacrifices for the sins of the Jews, did not only not forbid marriage, but made it necessary; for that office was to descend by inheritance, so that priesthood was not inconsistent with that state. In the New Testament, some of the qualifications of a bishop and deacon are, their being *the husband of one wife;* and their having well ordered their house, and brought up their children. St. Peter, and other apostles, were married: it was thought St. Paul was so likewise. Aquila was certainly married to Priscilla, and carried her about with him. Our Saviour, speaking of the help that an unmarried state was to the kingdom of God, recommended 90 it equally to all ranks of men, as they could bear it. St. Paul said, *Let every man have his own wife: It is better to marry than to burn;* and, *Marriage is honourable in all :* and the *forbidding to marry* is reckoned by him a mark of the apostasy of the latter times; so that the matter seemed clear from the scriptures.

Arguments for it from scripture;

And from the fathers. In the first ages, Saturninus, Basilides, Montanus, Novatus, and the Encratites, condemned marriage, as a state of liberty, more than was fit for Christians. Against those was asserted, by the primitive fathers, the lawfulness of marriage to all Christians, without discrimination : and they, who, entering into holy orders, forsook their wives, were severely condemned by the apostolical canons, and by the council of Gangra, in the beginning of the fourth, and the council in Trullo in the fifth [60] age. Many great bishops in these times lived still with their wives, and had children by them; as namely, both Nazianzen's and Basil's fathers. And Hilary of Poictiers, when banished to Phrygia, and very old, writing to his own daughter Abra, bid her ask her mother the meaning of those things which she, by reason of her age, understood not : by which it appears, that his daughter was then very young, and by consequence, born to him after he was a bishop. In the council of Nice, it being proposed that clergymen should depart from their wives;

[60] In the latter end of the seventh, or rather in the beginning of the eighth. [G.]

Paphnutius, though himself unmarried, opposed it as an unreasonable yoke. And Heliodorus, bishop of Tricca, the author of the first of those love-fables, now known by the name of romances, being suspected of too much lasciviousness, and concerned to clear himself of that charge, did first move, that clergymen should be obliged to live single : which, the historian says, they were not tied to before ; but bishops, as they pleased, lived still with their wives. The fathers in those times extolled a single life very high ; and yet they all thought a man once married might be a bishop, though his wife were yet living. They did not allow it indeed to him that had married twice : but for this they had a distinction ; that if a man had been once married before his baptism, and again after his baptism, he was to be understood to be in the state of a single marriage. So that Jerome, who writ warmly enough against second marriages, yet says, (*ad Oceanum,*) that the bishops in his age, who were but once married in that sense, were not to be numbered ; and that more of these could be reckoned than were at the council of Ariminum, who are said to have been eight hundred bishops. It is true, that in that age they began to make canons against the marriage of those who were in orders, especially in the Roman and African churches ; but those were only positive laws of the church ; and the frequent repeating of those canons shews that even there they were not generally obeyed. Of Synesius we read, that, when he was ordained priest, he declared that he would not live secretly with his wife, as some did ; but that he would dwell publicly with her, and wished that he might have many children by her. In the eastern church, all their clergy, below the order of bishops, are usually married before they be ordained ; and afterward live with their wives, and have children by them, without any kind of prohibition. In the western church, the married clergy are taken notice of in many of the Spanish and Gallican synods, and the bishops' and priests' wives are called *episcopæ* and *presbyteræ.* In most of the cathedrals of England the clergy were married in the Saxon times ; but, as was shown, p. 22. 91 of the first Part, because they would not quit their wives, they were put out, not of sacred orders, but only out of the seats they were then in, and those were given to the monks. When pope Nicolas had pressed the celibate of the clergy, in the ninth century, there was great opposition made to it, chiefly by Huldericus, bishop of Augsburg, who was held a saint, notwithstanding this opposition. Restitutus, bishop of London, lived openly with his wife. Nor was the celibate of the clergy generally imposed till pope Gregory the Seventh's time, in the eleventh century; who, projecting to have the clergy depend wholly on himself, and so to separate them from the interests of those princes, in whose dominions they lived, considered, that, by having wives and children, they gave pledges to the state where they lived; and reckoned, that, if they were free from this incumbrance, then, their persons being sacred, there would be nothing to hinder, but that they might do as they pleased, in obedience to the pope's, and opposition to their own prince's orders. The writers near Gregory the Seventh's time called this a new thing, against the mind of the holy fathers, and full of rashness in him, thus to turn out married priests. Lanfranc, archbishop of Canterbury, did not impose celibate on the clergy in the villages, but only on those that lived in towns, and on prebendaries[61]. But Anselm carried it further, and simply imposed it on all the clergy: yet himself laments, that sodomy was become then very common, and even public; which was also the complaint of Petrus Damiani, in pope Gregory's time. Bernard said, that that sin was frequent among the bishops in his time; and that this, with many other abominations, was the natural effect of prohibiting marriage. This made abbot Panormitan wish that it were left to men's liberty to marry if they pleased. And Pius the Second said, there might have been good reasons

[61] [" This mistake is wholly the historian's own. Our reformers understood the history of the English church too well to lead the way in such an error. Lanfranc imposed celibacy on prebendaries; but allowed to the clergy living in towns and villages the use of their marriage already contracted. His constitution was conceived in these words; Nullus Canonicus uxorem habeat. Sacerdotum vero in castellis et in vicis habitantium habentes uxores non cogantur ut dimittant, non habentes interdicantur ut habeant. Our reformers who wrote of the marriage of the clergy represented this constitution aright. So archbishop Parker, (p. 279,) who having related his prohibition of marriage to prebendaries, adds, ' But yet he moderated so the matter that he made a decree that such priests as dwelt in towns and villages, being married, should not be separated, but continue with their wives in their ministrations ecclesiastical.' " Harmer, Specimen of Errors, p. 86.]

for imposing celibate on the clergy, but he believed there were far better reasons for taking away these laws that imposed it. Yet, even since those laws had been made, Petrarch had a license to marry, and keep his preferments still. Boniface archbishop of Canterbury, Richard bishop of Chichester, and Geofrey bishop of Ely, are said to have had wives; and though there were not so many instances of priests marrying after orders, yet, if there were any thing in the nature of priesthood inconsistent by the law of God with marriage, then it was as unlawful for them to continue in their former marriages as to contract a new one. Some few instances were also gathered out of church history, of bishops and priests marrying after orders; but as these were few, so there was just reason to controvert them.

Upon the whole matter it was clear, that the celibate of the clergy flowed from no law of God, nor from any general law of the church; but the contrary, of clergymen's living with their wives, was universally received for many ages. As for vows, it was much questioned how far they did bind in such cases. It seemed a great sin to impose such on any, when they were yet young, and did not well know their own dispositions. Nor was it in a man's power to keep them: for, continence being none of those graces that are promised by God to all that ask it, as it was not in a man's power, without extreme severities on himself, to govern his own constitution of body, so he had no reason to expect God should interpose when he had provided another remedy for such cases. Besides, the promise made by clergymen, according to the rites of the Roman Pontifical, did not oblige them to celibate. The words were, *Wilt thou follow chastity and sobriety?* To which the sub-deacon answered, *I will.* By *chastity* was not to be understood a total abstinence from all, but only from unlawful embraces; since a man might live chaste in a state of marriage as well as out of it. But whatever might be in this, the English clergy were not concerned in it; for there was no such question nor answer made in the forms of their ordination: so they were not by any vow precluded from marriage. And for the expediency of it, nothing was more evident, than that these laws had brought in much uncleanness into the church; and those who pressed them most had been signally noted for

The vows and other reasons against it examined.

92

these vices. No prince in the English history lewder than Edgar, that had so promoted it. The legate, that in king Henry the Second's time got that severe decree made, that put all the married clergy from their livings, was found the very night after (for the credit of celibate) in bed with a whore[62]. On this subject many indecent stories were gathered, especially by Bale[63], who was a learned man, but did not write with that temper and discretion that became a divine. He gathered all the lewd stories that could be raked together to this purpose; and the many abominable things found in the monasteries were then fresh in all men's memories. It was also observed, that the unmarried clergy had been, as much as the married could be, intent upon the raising families, and the enriching of their nephews and kindred, (and sometimes of their bastards; witness the present pope Paul the Third, and, not long before him, Alexander the Sixth;) so that the married clergy could not be tempted to more covetousness than had appeared in the unmarried. And for the distraction of domestic affairs, the clergy had formerly given themselves up to such a secular course of life, that it was thought nothing could increase it: but if the married clergy should set themselves to raise more than a decent maintenance for their children, such as might fit them for letters or callings, and should neglect hospitality, become covetous, and accumulate livings and preferments, to make estates for their children; this might be justly curbed by new laws, or rather the renewing of the ancient canons, by which clergymen were declared to be only intrusted with the goods of the church for public ends, and

---

62 [" This mistake also is altogether owing to the historian. Our reformers, consonantly to the testimony of all our ancient histories, relate this misfortune to have happened to Johannes de Crema the pope's legate in the year 1125 in the reign of king Henry the first. And the Annals of Winchester, lately published, (Anglia Sacra, vol. i. p. 298,) relate another like miscarriage of the same legate in the same year." Harmer, Specimen of Errors, p. 86.]

63 [Comedy concernynge the Lawes of Nature, Moses and Christ, corrupted by the Sodomytes, Pharisees and Papystes most wycked. MDXXXVIII and lately inprented per Nicolaum Bamburgensem, 8vo. Also Actes of Englysh Votaryes, comprehendynge their vnchast Practyses and Examples by all Ages, from the Worldes Begynnynge to thys present Yeare, collected out of their owne Legendes and Chronycles. Wesel, 1546, 8vo.]

were not to apply them to their own private uses, nor to leave them to their children and friends.

Thus had this matter been argued in many books that were written on this subject by Poynet[64] and Parker[65]; the one afterwards bishop of Winchester, and the other archbishop of Canterbury; also by Bale, bishop of Ossory, with many more. Dr. Ridley, Dr. Taylor, (afterwards bishop of Lincoln,) Dr. Benson, and Dr. Redmayn, appeared more confidently in it than many others; being men that were resolved never to marry themselves, who yet thought it necessary, and therefore pleaded, (according to the pattern that Paphnutius had set them,) that all should be left to their liberty in this matter.

The debate about it was brought into the convocation, where Dr. Redmayn's authority went a great way. He was a man of great learning and probity, and of so much greater weight, because he did not in all points agree with the reformers; but being at this time sick, his opinion was brought under his 93 hand, which will be found in the Collection, copied from the original. It was to this purpose; "that though the scriptures "exhorted priests to live chaste, and out of the cares of the "world, yet the laws forbidding them marriage were only "canons and constitutions of the church, not founded on the "word of God; and therefore he thought that a man once "married might be a priest; and he did not find the priests "in the church of England had made any vow against mar- "riage; and therefore he thought that the king, and the "higher powers of the church, might take away the clog of "perpetual continence from the priests, and grant that such "as could not or would not contain, might marry once, and "not be put from their holy ministration." It was opposed by many in both houses, but carried at last by the major vote. All this I gather from what is printed concerning it: for I

Collect.
Numb. 30.

---

[64] [A defence for Mariage of Priestes, by Scripture and aunciente Wryters. Made by John Ponet, Doctoure of Divinitee. Lond. in the House of Reynolde Wolfe, *anno Domini* MDLIX.]

[65] [A defence of Priestes Mariages, stablysshed by the imperiall Lawes of the Realme of England, against a Civilian namyng himself, Thomas Martin, doctour of the Ciuile lawes. London, by I. Kingston, without date.]

Parker's book was not wrote till the reign of queen Mary, *ad leniendum suum in illâ Marianâ persecutione mœrorem*—as said in his life; nor published till the reign of queen Elizabeth, and could have no relation to this reign. [B.]

have seen no remains of this, or of any of the other convocations that came afterwards in this reign; the registers of them being destroyed in the fire of London. This act seemed rather a connivance, and permission of the clergy to marry, than any direct allowance of it. So the enemies of that state of life continued to reproach the married clergy still; and this was much heightened by many indecent marriages, and other light behaviour of some priests[66]. But these things made way for a more full act concerning this matter about three years after.

An act confirming the liturgy. [Cap. i. Statutes, vol. iv. p. 37.]

The next act that passed in this parliament was about the public service, which was put into the house of commons on the ninth of December, and the next day was also put into the house of lords: it lay long before them, and was not agreed to till the fifteenth of January; the earl of Derby, the bishops of London, Durham, Norwich, Carlisle, Hereford, Worcester, Westminster, and Chichester, and the lords Dacres and Windsor, protesting. The preamble of the act sets forth, "that "there had been several forms of service, and that of late "there had been great difference in the administration of the "sacraments, and other parts of divine worship; and that the "most effectual endeavours could not stop the inclinations of "many to depart from the former customs, which the king "had not punished, believing they flowed from a good zeal. "But, that there might be an uniform way over all the king- "dom, the king, by the advice of the lord protector and his "council, had appointed the archbishop of Canterbury, with "other learned and discreet bishops and divines, to draw an "order of divine worship, having respect to the pure religion "of Christ taught in the scripture, and to the practice of the "primitive church; which they, by the aid of the Holy Ghost, "had with one uniform agreement concluded on: wherefore "the parliament having considered the book, and the things "that were altered or retained in it, they gave their most "humble thanks to the king for his care about it; and did "pray, that all who had formerly offended in these matters, "except such as were in the Tower of London, or the prison "of the Fleet, should be pardoned. And did enact, that, from

---

66 [For a notice of several of the author's mistakes in this account of the marriage of the clergy, see Harmer's Specimen of Errors, pp. 78–87.]

" the feast of Whitsunday next, all divine offices should be
" performed according to it; and that such of the clergy as
" should refuse to do it, or continue to officiate in any other
" manner, should, upon the first conviction, be imprisoned six
" months, and forfeit a year's profit of their benefice; for the
" second offence, forfeit all their church-preferments, and suf-
" fer a year's imprisonment; and for the third offence, should
94 " be imprisoned during life. And all that should write, or
" put out things in print against it, or threaten any clergymen
" for using it, were to be fined in 10l. for the first offence;
" 20l. for the second; and to forfeit all their goods, and be
" imprisoned for life, upon a third offence. Only at the uni- [Ibid. p. 38.]
" versities they might use it in Latin and Greek, excepting
" the office of the communion. It was also lawful to use other
" psalms or prayers, taken out of the Bible, so these in the
" book were not omitted." This act was variously censured *The cen-*
by those who disliked it. Some thought it too much that it *sures pass-*
ed upon it.
was said, the book was drawn by *the aid of the Holy Ghost.*
But others said, this was not to be so understood, as if they
had been inspired by extraordinary assistance; for then there
had been no room for any correction of what was now done:
and therefore it was only to be understood in that sense, as all
good motions and consultations are directed, or assisted, by
the secret influences of God's holy Spirit; which do oft help
good men, even in their imperfect actions, where the good
that is done is justly ascribed to the grace of God. Others
censured it because it was said to be done by uniform agreement; though four of the bishops that were employed in the
drawing of it protested against it. These were, the bishops of
Norwich[67], Hereford, Chichester, and Westminster; but these
had agreed in the main parts of the work, though in some few
particulars they were not satisfied, which made them dissent
from the whole.

The proviso for the psalms and prayers, taken out of the *Singing of*
Bible, was for the singing-psalms, which were translated into *psalms*
brought in.
verse, and much sung by all who loved the reformation, and
were in many places used in churches. In the ancient church,
the Christians were much exercised in repeating the Psalms of

---

[67] Rugg, bishop of Norwich, was not employed in compiling the book.
The other three were. [S.]

David : many had them all by heart, and used to be reciting them when they went about their work : and those who retired into a monastical course of life, spent many of their hours in repeating the Psalter. Apollinaris put them in verse, as being easier for the memory. Other devout hymns came to be also in use. Nazianzen among the Greeks, and Prudentius among the Latins, laboured on that argument with the greatest success. There were other hymns that were not put in verse ; the chief of which were, that most ancient hymn, which we use now after the sacrament ; and the celebrated Ambrosian hymn, that begins *Te Deum laudamus*. But as, when the worship of the departed saints came to be dressed up with much pomp, hymns were also made for their honour ; and the Latin tongue, as well as prosody, being then much decayed, these came to be cast into rhymes, and were written generally in a fantastical affected style : so now, at the reformation, some poets, such as the times afforded, translated David's Psalms into verse[68] ; and it was a sign, by which men's affections to that work were every where measured, whether they used to sing these, or not. But as the poetry then was low, and not raised to that justness to which it is since brought ; so this work, which then might pass for a tolerable composure, has not been since that time so reviewed or changed as perhaps the thing required. Hence it is, that this piece of divine worship, by the meanness of the verse, has not maintained its due esteem. Another thing, that some thought deserved to be considered in such a work, was, that many of the Psalms, being such as related more specially to David's victories, and contained passages in them not easily understood ; it seemed better to leave out these, which it was not so easy to sing with 95 devotion, because the meaning of them either lay hid, or did not at all concern Christians.

1549.
[Dec. 21.]
[Jan. 8.
Journals of
Commons,
p. 6.]

The parliament was adjourned from the twenty-second of December to the second of January. On the seventh of January the commons sent an address to the protector to restore Latimer to the bishopric of Worcester : but this took no effect ;

[68] [Thomas Sternhold died in 1549, having printed 51 Psalms, which were published with the title, ' All such Psalms of David as

Thomas Sternholde did in his lyfe drawe into Englyshe Metre.' Lond. 1549. 8vo.]

for that good old man did choose rather to go about and preach, than to engage in a matter of government, being now very ancient. A bill was put in by the lords for appointing of parks, and agreed to, the earl of Arundel only dissenting; but being sent down to the commons, it was upon the second reading thrown out; yet not so unanimously but that the house was divided about it. _{Journal}

Journal
Procer.
[p. 337.]

On the fourth of February a bill was put in against eating flesh in Lent, and on fasting-days: it was committed to the archbishop of Canterbury, the bishops of Ely, Worcester, and Chichester, and sent to the commons on the sixteenth; who sent it up on the seventh of March, with a proviso, to which the lords agreed. In the preamble it is said; "that though "it is clear, by the word of God, that there is no day, nor "kind of meat, purer than another, but that all are in them- "selves alike; yet many, out of sensuality, had contemned "such abstinence as had been formerly used: and since due "abstinence was a mean to virtue, and to subdue men's bodies "to their soul and spirit, and was also necessary to encourage "the trade of fishing, and for saving of flesh; therefore all "former laws about fasting and abstinence were to be after "the first of May repealed: and it was enacted, that from the "first of May none should eat flesh on Fridays, Saturdays, "Ember-days, in Lent, or any other days that should be de- "clared fish-days, under several penalties. A proviso was "added for excepting such as should obtain the king's license, "or were sick, or weak, and that none should be indicted but "within three months after the offence."

[Ibid.]

[Ibid. p. 349.]
An act a-
bout fasts.
[Cap. 19.
Statutes,
vol. iv. p.
65.]

Christ had told his disciples, that, when he should *be taken from them, then they should fast*. Accordingly the primitive Christians used to fast oft, more particularly before the anniversary of the passion of Christ, which ended in a high festivity at Easter. Yet this was differently observed, as to the number of days. Some abstained forty days, in imitation of Christ's fast; others, only that week; and others had only an entire fast, from the time of Christ's death till his resurrection. On these fasts they eat nothing till the evening, and then they eat most commonly herbs and roots. Afterwards, the Fridays were kept as fasts, because on that day Christ suffered. Saturdays were also added in the Roman church, but not without contradiction. Ember-weeks came in afterwards, being some days before those Sundays in which orders were given. And a general rule being laid down, that every Christian festival should be preceded by a fast[69], thereupon the vigils of holy-days came, though not so soon, into the number. But this, with the other good institutions of the primitive times, became degenerate, even in St. Austin's time; religion came to be placed in these observances, and anxious rules were made about them. Afterwards, in the church of Rome, they were turned into a mockery; for as on fast-days they dined, which the ancients did not, so the use of the most delicious fish, dressed in the most exquisite manner, with the richest wines that could be had, was allowed; which made it ridiculous. So now they resolved to take off the severities of the former laws, and yet to keep up such laws about fasting and abstinence as might be agreeable to its true end; which is, to subdue the flesh to the spirit, and not to gratify it by a change of one sort of diet into another, which may be both more delicate and more inflaming. So fond a thing is superstition, that it will help men to deceive themselves by the slightest pretences that can be imagined.

It was much lamented then, and there is as much cause for it still, that, carnal men have taken advantages, from the abuses that were formerly practised, to throw off good and profitable institutions; since the frequent use of fasting, with prayer and true devotion joined to it, is perhaps one of the greatest helps that can be devised to advance one to a spiritual temper of mind, and to promote a holy course of life: and the mockery, that is discernible in the way of some men's fasting, is a very slight excuse for any to lay aside the use of that which the scriptures have so much recommended.

Some bills were rejected.
[Journals of Lords, pp. 335, 6.]
There were other bills put into both houses, but did not pass. One was for declaring it treason to marry the king's sisters without consent of the king and his council: but it was thought that king Henry's will disabling them from the succession, in that case would be a stronger restraint; and so it was laid aside. Another bill was put in for ecclesiastical juris-

---

[69] The festivals between Easter and the Ascension day were not so, on the pretended reason that the Bridegroom was with them; as also Michaelmas. [G.]

diction. Great complaints were made of the abounding of vices and immoralities, which the clergy could neither restrain nor punish; and so they had nothing left but to preach against them, which was done by many with great freedom. In some of these sermons, the preachers expressed their apprehensions of signal and speedy judgments from Heaven if the people did not repent; but their sermons had no great effect, for the nation grew very corrupt, and this brought on them severe punishments. The temporal lords were so jealous of putting power in churchmen's hands, especially to correct those vices of which themselves perhaps were most guilty, that the bill was laid aside. The pretence of opposing it was, that the greatest part of the bishops and clergy were still papists in their hearts: so that, if power were put into such men's hands, it was reasonable to expect they would employ it chiefly against those who favoured the reformation, and would vex them on that score, though with pretences fetched from other things.

There was also put into the house of commons a bill for reforming of processes at common law, which was sent up by the commons to the lords; but it fell in that house. I have seen a large discourse written then upon that argument, in which it is set forth, that the law of England was a barbarous kind of study, and did not lead men into a finer sort of learning, which made the common lawyers to be generally so ignorant of foreign matters, and so unable to negotiate in them; therefore it was proposed, that the common and statute laws should be, in imitation of the Roman law, digested into a body under titles and heads, and put in good Latin. But this was too great a design to be set on, or finished, under an infant king. If it was then necessary, it will be readily acknowledged to be much more so now, the volume of our statutes being so much swelled since that time; besides the vast number 97 of reports, and cases, and the pleadings growing much longer than formerly: yet whether this is a thing to be much expected or desired, I refer it to the learned and wise men of that robe.

A design for digesting the common law into a body. [Feb. 15. Journals of Commons, p. 8.]

The only act that remains of this session of parliament, about which I shall inform the reader, is the attainder of the admiral. The queen dowager, that had married him, died in September last, not without suspicion of poison. She was a good and virtuous lady, and in her whole life had done nothing

The admiral's attainder. [cap. 18. Statutes, vol. iv. p. 61.]

unseemly, but the marrying him so indecently, and so soon after the king's death. There was found among her papers a discourse written by her concerning herself, entitled, The Lamentation of a Sinner [69], which was published by Cecil, who writ a preface to it. In it she with great sincerity acknowledges the sinful course of her life for many years; in which she, relying on external performances, such as fasts and pilgrimages, was all that while a stranger to the internal and true power of religion, which she came afterwards to feel by the study of the scripture, and the calling upon God for his Holy Spirit. She explains clearly the notion she had of justification by faith, so that holiness necessarily followed upon it; but lamented the great scandal given by many gospellers: so were all those called who were given to the reading of the scriptures.

The queen dowager dying, he courted the lady Elizabeth.

She being thus dead, the admiral renewed his addresses to the lady Elizabeth, but in vain: for as he could not expect that his brother and the council would consent to it, so, if he had married her without that, the possibility of succeeding to the crown was cut off by king Henry's will. And this attempt of his occasioned that act to be put in which was formerly mentioned, for declaring the marrying the king's sisters, without consent of council, to be treason. Seeing he could not compass that design, he resolved to carry away the king to his house of Holt in the country; and so to displace his brother, and to take the government into his own hands. For this end he had laid in magazines of arms, and listed about ten thousand men in several places; and openly complained, that his brother intended to enslave the nation, and make himself master of all; and had therefore brought over those German soldiers. He had also entered into treaty with several of the nobility, that envied his brother's greatness, and were not ill pleased to see a breach between them, and that grown to be irreconcilable. To these he promised, that they should be of the council, and that he would dispose of the king in marriage to one of their daughters. The person is not named. The protector had often told him of these things, and warned him of the danger into which he would throw himself by such ways: but he per-

---

[69] [' The lamentacion of a Synner: Made by the moste vertuouse Lady, Quene Caterine, bewailynge the Ignorance of her blind Life.' London, 1548. 8vo.]

sisted still in his designs, though he denied and excused them
as long as was possible. Now his restless ambition seeming
incurable, he was on the nineteenth[70] of January sent to the
Tower. The original warrant, signed by all the privy-council,
is in the council-book formerly mentioned ; where the earl of
Southampton signs with the rest; who was now, in outward
appearance, reconciled to the protector. On the day following
the admiral's seal of his office was sent for, and put into secretary Smith's hands. And now many things broke out against
him ; and particularly a conspiracy of his with sir W. Sharing-
ton, vice-treasurer of the mint at Bristol, who was to have
furnished him with ten thousand pounds, and had already coined
about twelve thousand pounds[71] false money, and had clipped
a great deal more, to the value of forty thousand pounds in all ;
for which he was attainted by a process at common-law, and that
was confirmed in parliament. Fowler also, that waited in the
privy-chamber, with some few others, were sent to the Tower.
Many complaints being usually brought against a sinking man,
the lord Russell, the earl of Southampton, and secretary Petre,
were ordered to receive their examinations. And thus the
business was let alone till the twenty-eighth[72] of February, in
which time his brother did again try if it were possible to
bring him to a better temper : and as he had, since their first
breach, granted him eight hundred pounds a year in land to
gain his friendship, so means were now used to persuade him
to submit himself, and to withdraw from court, and from all
employment. But it appeared, that nothing could be done to
him that could cure his ambition, or the hatred he carried to
his brother. And therefore, on the twenty-second of February,
a full report was made to the council of all the things that were
informed against him ; consisting not only of the particulars
formerly mentioned, but of many foul misdemeanours in the
discharge of the admiralty : several pirates being entertained
by him, who gave him a share of their robberies, and whom he
had protected, notwithstanding the complaints made by other

Margin notes:

Jan. 17.
the admiral
sent to the
Tower.
[Council
Book, p.
451.]
[Ibid. p.
454.]
[Ibid. p.
455.]

98

[Feb. 22.]

[Council
Book, p.
471.]

---

[70] [The entry in the Council
Book is headed, ' At Westminster
on Thursday the 17th of January,
1548.']

[71] For twelve thousand read ten
thousand. [S.]

[72] [This is a mistake for Feb. 22,
as appears from the Council Book,
p. 471.]

princes ; by which the king was in danger of a war from the
princes so complaining. The whole charge consists of thirty-
three articles, which will be found in the Collection. The
particulars, as it is entered in the council-book, were so manifestly proved, not only by witnesses, but by letters under his
own hand, that it did not seem possible to deny them. Yet he
had been sent to, and examined by some of the council, but
refused to make a direct answer to them, or to sign those
answers that he had made. So it was ordered, that the next
day all the privy-council, except the archbishop of Canterbury,
and sir John Baker, speaker to the house of commons, who
was engaged to attend in the house, should go to the Tower
and examine him. On the twenty-third the lord chancellor,
with the other counsellors, went to him, and read the articles
of his charge, and earnestly desired him to make plain answers
to them, excusing himself where he could, and submitting himself in other things : and that he would shew no obstinacy of
mind. He answered them, that he expected an open trial, and
his accusers to be brought face to face. All the counsellors
endeavoured to persuade him to be more tractable ; but to no
purpose. At last the lord chancellor required him on his allegiance to make his answer. He desired they would leave the
articles with him, and he would consider of them ; otherwise he
would make no answer to them. But the counsellors resolved
not to leave them with him on those terms. On the twenty-
fourth of February it was resolved in council, that the whole
board should after dinner acquaint the king with the state of
that affair, and desire to know of him whether he would have
the law to take place ; and since the thing had been before the
parliament, whether he would leave it to their determination ;
so tender they were of their young king in a case that concerned his uncle's life. But the king had begun to discern his
seditious temper, and was now much alienated from him.

When the counsellors waited on him, the lord chancellor
opened the matter to the king, and delivered his opinion for
leaving it to the parliament. Then every counsellor by himself spoke his mind, all to the same purpose. Last of all the
protector spoke : he protested this was a most sorrowful busi- 99
ness to him ; that he had used all the means in his power to
keep it from coming to this extremity ; but were it son or

brother, he must prefer his majesty's safety to them, for he
weighed his allegiance more than his blood : and that therefore
he was not against the request that the other lords had made ;
and said, if he himself were guilty of such offences, he should
not think he were worthy of life ; and the rather, because he
was of all men the most bound to his majesty, and therefore he
could not refuse justice.   The king answerd them in these
words : " We perceive that there are[73] great things objected
" and laid to my lord admiral my[74] uncle, and they tend to trea-
" son ; and we perceive that you require but justice to be done.
" We think it reasonable, and we will[75], that you proceed ac-
" cording to your request."   Which words (as it is marked in
the council-book) coming so suddenly from his grace's mouth,
of his own motion, as the lords might well perceive, they were
marvellously rejoiced, and gave the king most hearty praise
and thanks ; yet resolved that some of both houses should be
sent to the admiral, before the bill should be put in against
him, to see what he could, or would say.   All this was done, to
try if he could be brought to a submission.   So the lord chancellor, the earls of Shrewsbury, Warwick, and Southampton,
and sir John Baker, sir Thomas Cheney, and sir Anthony
Denny, were sent to him.   He was long obstinate, but after
much persuasion was brought to give an answer to the first
three articles, which will be found in the Collection at the end
of the articles ; and then on a sudden he stopped, and bade
them be content, for he would go no further : and no entreaties
would work on him, either to answer the rest, or to set his
hand to the answers he had made.

    On the twenty-fifth of February the bill was put in for at-
tainting him, and the peers had been so accustomed to agree to
such bills in king Henry's time, that they did easily pass it.
All the judges, and the king's council, delivered their opinions,
that the articles were treason.   Then the evidence was brought :
many lords gave it so fully, that all the rest with one voice
consented to the bill ; only the protector, *for natural pity's
sake*, as is in the council-book, desired leave to withdraw.   On
the twenty-seventh the bill was sent down to the commons,
with a message, that if they desired to proceed as the lords

Side notes:
Who con-
sented to it.

[Ibid. p.
487.]

[Ibid. p.
488.]

[Ibid. p.
489.]

[Ibid. p.
491.]

[Journals
of Lords,
p. 345.]

The bill
passed in
both
houses.

[Ibid. p.
346.]

---

    [73] ['There is great things which be objected]   [74] [mine]
              [75] [we will well]

had done, those lords that had given their evidence in their own house should come down and declare it to the commons. But there was more opposition made in the house of commons. Many argued against attainders in absence, and thought it an odd way that some peers should rise up in their places in their own house, and relate somewhat to the slander of another, and that he should be thereupon attainted : therefore it was pressed, that it might be done by a trial, and that the admiral should

[Journals of Commons, p. 9.] be brought to the bar, and be heard plead for himself. But on the fourth of March a message was sent from the king, that he thought it was not necessary to send for the admiral: and that the lords should come down and renew before them the evidence they had given in their own house. This was done ; and so the bill was agreed to by the commons in a full house, judged about four hundred; and there were not above ten or twelve

[Council Book, p. 492.] that voted in the negative. The royal assent was given on the fifth of March. On the tenth of March, the council resolved to press the king that justice might be done on the admiral; and since the case was so heavy and lamentable to the pro- 100 tector, (so it is in the council-book,) though it was also sorrowful to them all, they resolved to proceed in it, so that neither

[Ibid. p. 493.] the king nor he should be further troubled with it. After dinner they went to the king, the protector being with them. The king said, he had well observed their proceedings, and thanked them for their great care of his safety, and commanded them to proceed in it without further molesting him or

[Ibid. p. 494.]
[15 Mar.] the protector ; and ended, *I pray you, my lords, do so*[76]. Upon this they ordered the bishop of Ely to go to the admiral, and to instruct him in the things that related to another life ; and to prepare him to take patiently his deserved execution.

[Ibid. p. 495.] And on the seventeenth of March, he having made report to them of his attendance on the admiral, the council signed a

Collect. Numb. 32. warrant for his execution, which will be found in the Collection, to which both the lord protector, and the archbishop of Can-

March 20, the admiral beheaded. terbury, set their hands. And on the twentieth his head was cut off. What his behaviour was on the scaffold I do not find[77].

---

[76] [And I pray you my lords so do.]

[77] There is a pretty remarkable account of his death and behaviour in bishop Latimer's fourth sermon, ed. I. p. 56, (left out of the follow-

Thus fell Thomas lord Seymour, lord high admiral of England, a man of high thoughts, of great violence of temper, and ambitious out of measure. The protector was much censured Censures for giving way to his execution, by those who looked only at passed upon it; that relation between them, which they thought should have made him still preserve him. But others, who knew the whole series of the affair, saw it was scarce possible for him to do more for the gaining his brother than he had done. Yet the other being a popular notion, that it was against nature for one brother to destroy another, was more easily entertained by the multitude, who could not penetrate into the mysteries of state. But the way of proceeding was much condemned; since to attaint a man without bringing him to make his own defence, or to object what he could say to the witnesses that were brought against him, was so illegal and unjust, that it could not be defended. Only this was to be said for it, that it was a little more regular than *parliamentary attainders* had been formerly; for here the evidence upon which it was founded was given before both houses.

One particular seemed a little odd, that Cranmer signed the And on warrant for his execution; which, being in a *cause of blood*, Cranmer's signing the was contrary to the canon-law. In the primitive times, church- warrant men had only the cure of souls lying on them, together with for his execution. the reconciling of such differences as might otherwise end in suits of law before the civil courts, which were made up of infidels. When the empire became Christian, these judgments, which they gave originally on so charitable an account, were by the imperial laws made to have great authority; but further than these, or the care of widows and orphans, they were forbid, both by the council of Chalcedon, and other lesser councils, to meddle in secular matters. Among the endowments made to some churches, there were lands given, where the slaves, according to the Roman law, came within the patrimony of these churches; and by that law masters had power of life and death over their slaves.

In some churches this power had been severely exercised, Laws against

ing editions,) where amongst other things he says, ' He (the admiral) died very dangerously, irksomely, horribly.' And surely, so he did, if the letter referred to by him on the scaffold were genuine, which Latimer says he saw. [B.]

church-
men's med-
dling in
matters of
blood.
even to maiming and death, which seemed very indecent in a churchman. Besides, there was an apprehension that some severe churchmen, who were but masters for life, might be more profuse of the lives of such slaves than those that were to transmit them to their families. Therefore, to prevent the 101 waste that should be made in the church's patrimony, it was agreed on, that churchmen should not proceed capitally against any of their vassals or slaves. And, in the confusions that were in Spain, the princes that prevailed had appointed priests to be judges, to give the greater reputation to their courts. This being found much to the prejudice of the church, it was decreed in the fourth council of Toledo, that priests, who were chosen by Christ to the ministry of salvation, should not judge in capital matters, unless the prince should swear to them that he would remit the punishment; and such as did otherwise, were held guilty of blood-shedding, and were to lose their degree in the church. This was soon received over all the western church; and arguments were found out afterwards by the canonists to prove the necessity of continuing it: from David's not being suffered to build the temple, since he was *a man of blood;* and from the qualification required by St. Paul in a bishop, *that he should be no striker;* since he seemed to strike, that did it either in person, or by one whom he deputed to do it. But when afterwards Charles the Great, and all the Christian princes in the west, gave their bishops great lands and dominions, they obliged them to be in all their councils, and to do them such services as they required of them by virtue of their tenures. The popes, designing to set up a spiritual empire, and to bring all church-lands within it, required the bishops to separate themselves from a dependence on their princes as much as it was possible: and these laws formerly made about cases of blood were judged a colour good enough why they should not meddle in such trials; so they procured these cases to be excepted. But it seems Cranmer thought his conscience was under no tie from those canons, and so judged it not contrary to his function to sign that order.

[Journals
of Lords, p.
353.]
The parliament was on the fourteenth of March prorogued to the fourth of November; the clergy having granted the king a subsidy of six shillings in the pound, to be paid in three years. In the preamble of the bill of subsidy they acknow-

ledged the great quietness they enjoyed under him, having no
let nor impediment in the service of God. But the laity set
out their subsidy with a much fuller preamble, of the great
happiness they had by the true religion of Christ; declaring,
that they were ready to forsake all things rather than Christ;
as also to assist the king in the conquest of Scotland, which
they call a part of his dominion: therefore they give twelve-
pence in the pound of all men's personal estates, to be paid in
three years.

Subsidies
granted by
the clergy
and laity.
[Cap. 35,
Statutes,
vol. iv. p.
74.]
[Cap. 36.
ibid. p. 78.]

But now to look into matters of religion: there was, immediately after the act of uniformity passed, a new visitation,
which it is probable went in the same method that was observed in the former. There were two things much complained of: the one was, that the priests read the prayers
generally with the same tone of voice that they had used formerly in the Latin service; so that it was said, the people did
not understand it much better than they had done the Latin
formerly. This I have seen represented in many letters; and
it was very seriously laid before Cranmer by Martin Bucer.
The course taken in it was, that in all parish churches the service should be read in a plain audible voice; but that the former way should remain in cathedrals, where there were great
quires, who were well acquainted with that tone, and where it
agreed better with the music that was used in the anthems.
102 Yet even there, many thought it no proper way in the Litany,
where the greatest gravity was more agreeable to such humble
addresses, than such a modulation of the voice, which, to those
unacquainted with it, seemed light; and for others, that were
more accustomed to it, it seemed to be rather use that had reconciled them to it, than the natural decency of the thing, or
any fitness in it to advance the devotion of their prayers. But
this was a thing judged of less importance. It was said, that
those who had been accustomed to read in that voice, could
not easily alter it: but as those dropped off and died, others
would be put in their places, who would officiate in a plainer
voice. Other abuses were more important. Some used in the
communion-service many of the old rites; such as kissing the
altar, crossing themselves, lifting the book from one place to
another, breathing on the bread, shewing it openly before the
distribution, with some other of the old ceremonies. The peo-

A new visi-
tation.

Some of
the old
abuses con-
tinued in
the new
service.

ple did also continue the use of their praying by beads; which was called an innovation of Peter the Hermit, in the twelfth century. By it ten Aves went for one Pater-Noster; and the reciting these so oft in Latin had come to be almost all the devotion of the vulgar: and therefore the people were ordered to leave that unreasonable way of praying; it seeming a most unaccountable thing, that the reciting the Angel's salutation to the blessed Virgin should be such a high piece of divine worship. And that this should be done ten times for one prayer to God, looked so like *preferring the creature to the Creator,* that it was not easy to defend it from an appearance of idolatry. The priests were also ordered to exhort the people to give to the poor. The curates were required to preach and declare the Catechism, at least every sixth week. And some priests continuing secretly the use of soul-masses; in which, for avoiding the censure of the law, they had one to communicate with them, but had many of these in one day; it was ordered, that there should be no selling of the communion in trentals, and that there should be but one communion in one church, except on Easter-day and Christmas; in which the people coming to the sacrament in greater numbers, there should be one sacrament in the morning, and another near noon. And there being great abuses in churches and church-yards, in which, in the times of popery, markets had been held, and bargains made; that was forbid, chiefly in the time of divine service or sermon.

Collect.
Numb. 33.

These instructions, which the reader will find in the Collection, were given in charge to the visitors. Cranmer had also a visitation about the same time; in which the articles he gave out are all drawn according to the king's injunctions. By some questions in them, they seem to have been sent out before the parliament, because the book of service is not mentioned:

[Wilkins,
Conc. iv.
p. 26.]

but the last question save one being of such as contemned married priests, and refused to receive the sacrament at their hands, I conceive that these were compiled after the act concerning their marriage was passed, but before the feast of Whitsunday following; for till then the Common-Prayer-Book

[Fox, lib.
ix. p. 10.]

was not to be received. There were also orders sent by the council to the bishop of London, to see that there should be no special masses in St. Paul's church; which being the mother-

church in the chief city of the kingdom, would be an example
to all the rest ; and that therefore there should be only one
communion at the great altar, and that at the time when the
103 high mass was wont to be celebrated, unless some desired a
sacrament in the morning, and then it was to be celebrated at
the high altar. Bonner, who resolved to comply in every
thing, sent the council's letter to the dean and residentiaries
of St. Paul's, to see it obeyed. And indeed, all England over
the book was so universally received, that the visitors did
return no complaint from any corner of the whole kingdom.
Only the lady Mary continued to have mass said in her house ; All receiv-
of which the council being advertised, writ to her to conform ed the new
herself to the laws, and not to cast a reproach on the king's cept the
government : for the nearer she was to him in blood, she was lady Mary.
to give the better example to others ; and her disobedience 44.]
might encourage others to follow her in that contempt of the
king's authority. So they desired her to send to them her
comptroller, and Dr. Hopton, her chaplain ; by whom she
should be more fully advertised of the king and council's
pleasure. Upon this, she sent one to the emperor to interpose
for her, that she might not be forced to any thing against her
conscience.

At this time there was a complaint made at the emperor's The ambas-
court of the English ambassador, sir Philip Hobby, for using sador at the
the new Common-Prayer-Book there : to which he answered, court not
he was to be obedient to the laws of his own prince and country : suffered to
and as the emperor's ambassador had mass at his chapel at use it.
London without disturbance, though it was contrary to the law
of England ; so he had the same reason to expect the like
liberty. But the emperor espousing the interest of the lady
Mary, both Paget (who was sent over ambassador extraordinary
to him, upon his coming into Flanders) and Hobby promised in
the king's name, that he should dispense with her for some
time, as they afterwards declared upon their honours, when the
thing was further questioned ; though the emperor and his
ministers pretended, that without any qualification it was promised, that she should enjoy the free exercise of her religion.
The emperor was now grown so high with his success in Germany, and that at a time when a war was coming on with
France, that it was not thought advisable to give him any

A treaty of
marriage
for the
lady Mary.
Cot. Lib.
Galba, B.
xii. [fol.
42.] offence.   There was likewise a proposition sent over by him to the protector and council, for the lady Mary to be married to Alphonso, brother to the king of Portugal.   The council entertained it ; and though the late king had left his daughters but 10,000*l.* a-piece, yet they offered to give with her 100,000 crowns in money, and 20,000 crowns worth of jewels.   The infant of Portugal was about her own age, and offered 20,000 crowns jointure.   But this proposition fell ; on what hand I do

She writ to
the council
concerning
the new
service ;
[Fox,
lib. ix.
p. 44.] not know.   The lady Mary writ on the twenty-second of June to the council, that she could not obey their late laws ; and that she did not esteem them laws, as made when the king was not of age, and contrary to those made by her father, which they were all bound by oath to maintain.   She excused the not sending her comptroller, Mr. Arundel, and her priest : the one did all her business, so that she could not well be without him ; the other was then so ill, that he could not travel.   Upon this the council sent a peremptory command to these, requiring them to come up and receive their orders.   The lady Mary

wrote a second letter to them on the twenty-seventh of June, in which she expostulated the matter with the council.   She said she was subject to none of them, and would obey none of the laws they made ; but protested great obedience and subjection to the king.   When her officers came to court, they were commanded to declare to the lady Mary, that, though the king was young in person, yet his authority was now as great as ever : that those who have his authority, and act in

his name, are to be obeyed : and though they, as single persons, were her humble servants ; yet, when they met in council, they acted in the king's name, and so were to be considered by all the king's subjects as if they were the king himself. They had indeed sworn to obey the late king's laws, but that could bind them no longer than they were in force ; and, being now repealed, they were no more laws, other laws being made in their room.   There was no exception in the laws ; all the king's subjects were included in them : and for a reformation of religion made when a king was under age, one of the most perfect that was recorded in scripture was so carried on when Josiah was much younger than their king was ; therefore they gave them in charge to persuade her grace (for that was her title) to be a good example of obedience, and not to encourage

104

peevish and obstinate persons by her stiffness.   But this business was for some time laid aside.

And now the reformation was to be carried on to the establishing of a form of doctrine, which should contain the chief
points of religion.   In order to which, there was this year
great inquiry made into many particular opinions, and chiefly
concerning the presence of Christ in the sacrament.   There *The man-*
was no opinion for which the priests contended more igno- *ner of*
Christ's
rantly and eagerly, and that the people generally believed *presence in*
more blindly and firmly, as if a strong belief were nothing else *the sacra-*
ment ex-
but winking very hard.   The priests, because they accounted *amined.*
it the chief support now left of their falling dominion, which
being kept up might in time retrieve all the rest: for while it
was believed that their character qualified them for so strange
and mighty a performance, they must needs be held in great
reverence.   The people, because they thought they received
the very flesh of Christ; and so (notwithstanding our Saviour's
express declaration to the contrary, that *the flesh profiteth
nothing*) looked on those who went about to persuade them
otherwise, as men that intended to rob them of the greatest
privilege they had.   And therefore it was thought necessary
to open this fully, before there should be any change made in
the doctrine of the church.

The Lutherans seemed to agree with that which had been
the doctrine of the Greek church, that in the sacrament there
was both the substance of bread and wine, and Christ's body
likewise : only many of them defended it by an opinion that
was thought akin to the Eutychian heresy, that his human
nature, by virtue of the union of the Godhead, was every
where; though even in this way it did not appear that there
was any special presence in the sacrament more than in other
things.   Those of Switzerland had on the other hand taught,
that the sacrament was only an institution to commemorate the
sufferings of Christ.   This, because it was intelligible, was
thought by many too low and mean a thing, and not equal to
the high expressions that are in the scripture, of its being *the
communion of the body and blood of Christ*.   The princes of
Germany saw what mischief was like to follow on the diversity
of opinions in explaining the sacrament ; and as Luther, being
impatient in his temper, and too much given to dictate, took it

very ill to see his doctrine so rejected; so, by the indecent way of writing in matters of controversy, to which the Germans are too much inclined, this difference turned to a direct breach 105 among them. The landgrave of Hesse had laboured much to have these diversities of opinion laid asleep, since nothing gave their common enemies such advantage as their quarrelling among themselves. Martin Bucer was of a moderate temper, and had found a middle opinion in this matter, though not so easy to be understood. He thought there was more than a *remembrance*, to wit, a *communication* of the body and blood of Christ in the sacrament; that in general a *real presence* ought to be asserted, and that the way of explaining it ought not to be anxiously inquired into ; and with him Calvin agreed, that it was truly the *body and blood of Christ*, not *figuratively*, but *really* present. The advantage of these general expressions was, that thereby they hoped to have silenced the debates between the German and Helvetian divines, whose doctrine came likewise to be received by many of the cities of the empire, and by the elector palatine. And, among Martin Bucer's papers, I met with an original paper of Luther's[78],

Collect.
Numb. 34.

(which will be found in the Collection,) in which he was willing to have that difference thus settled : " Those of the Augsburg " Confession should declare, that in the sacrament there was " truly bread and wine ; and those of the Helvetian Confession " should declare, that Christ's body was truly present : and so, " without any further curiosities in the way of explaining it, in " which divines might use their liberty, the difference should " end."   But how this came to take no effect, I do not understand. It was also thought that this way of expressing the doctrine would give least offence, for the people were scarce able to bear the opinion of the sacrament's being only a figure; but wherein this *real presence* consisted, was not so easy to be made out. Some explained it more intelligibly in a sense of law, that in the sacrament there was a real application of the merit of Christ's death, to those who received it worthily ; so that Christ as crucified was really present : and these had this to say for themselves, that the words of the institution do not call the elements simply Christ's *body* and *blood*, but his *body broken* and his *blood shed*, and that therefore Christ was *really* present as he was crucified, so that the importance of *really*

[78] [See Part iii. p. 175.]

was *effectually*.   Others thought all ways of explaining the
manner of the presence were needless curiosities, and apt to
beget differences : that therefore the doctrine was to be established in general words ; and, to save the labour both of explaining and understanding it, it was to be esteemed a mystery.
This seems to have been Bucer's opinion ; but Peter Martyr
inclined more to the Helvetians.

 There were public disputations held this year both at Oxford
and Cambridge upon this matter.   At Oxford the popish party
did so encourage themselves by the indulgence of the government, and the gentleness of Cranmer's temper, that they became upon this head insolent out of measure.   Peter Martyr
had read in the chair concerning the presence of Christ in the
sacrament, which he explained according to the doctrine of
the Helvetian churches.   Dr. Smith did upon this resolve to
contradict him openly in the schools, and challenge him to dispute on these points ; and had brought many thither, who
should by their clamours and applauses run him down : yet
this was not so secretly laid, but a friend of Peter Martyr's
brought him word of it before he had come from his house,
and persuaded him not to go to the schools that day, and so
disappoint Smith.   But he looked on that as so mean a thing,
that he would by no means comply with it.   So he went to
the divinity-schools.   On his way, one brought him a challenge
from Smith to dispute with him concerning the eucharist.   He
went on and took his place in the chair, where he behaved
himself with an equal measure of courage and discretion.   He
gravely checked Smith's presumption, and said, he did not
decline a dispute, but was resolved to have his reading that
day, nor would he engage in a public dispute without leave
from the king's council : upon this a tumult was like to rise,
so the vice-chancellor sent for them before him : Peter Martyr
said, he was ready to defend every thing that he had read in
the chair in a dispute ; but he would manage it only in scrip-
ture-terms, and not in the terms of the schools.

 This was the beating the popish doctors out of that which
was their chief strength ; for they had little other learning
but a sleight of tossing some arguments from hand to hand,
with a gibberish kind of language, that sounded like somewhat
that was sublime ; but had really nothing under it.   By con-

Margin notes:
Public dis-
putations
about it.

[Wood,]
Antiq.
Oxon.
[p. 267.]

06

stant practice they were very nimble at this sort of legerde-
main, of which both Erasmus and sir Thomas More, with the
other learned men of that age, had made such sport, that it
was become sufficiently ridiculous: and the protestants laid
hold on that advantage which such great authorities gave them
to disparage it.   They set up another way of disputing from
the original text of the scripture in Greek and Hebrew, which
seemed a more proper thing, in matters of divinity, than the
metaphysical language of the schoolmen.

This whole matter being referred to the privy-council, they
appointed some delegates to hear and preside in the disputation : but Dr. Smith being brought into some trouble, either
for this tumult, or upon some other account, was forced to put
in sureties for his good behaviour. He, desiring that he might
be discharged of any further prosecution, made the most
humble submission to Cranmer that was possible; and being
thereupon set at liberty, he fled out of the kingdom : it is said
he went first to Scotland, and from thence to Flanders.   But,
[May 28.] not long after this, Peter Martyr had a disputation before the
commissioners sent by the king, who were, the bishop of Lincoln, Dr. Cox, then chancellor of the university, and some
[May 29.] others ; in which Tresham, Chadsey, and Morgan, disputed
[May 30.] against those three propositions : 1. *In the sacrament of
thanksgiving there is no transubstantiation of bread and
wine in the body and blood of Christ. 2. The body or blood
of Christ is not carnally or corporally in the bread and wine ;
nor, as others use to say, under the bread and wine. 3. The
body and blood of Christ are united to the bread and wine
[Fuller, sacramentally.* Ridley was sent also to Cambridge, with
Hist. Univ. some others of the king's commissioners ; where, on the 20th,
Camb. p. 24th, and 27th of June, there were public disputations on these
127.] two positions :

" Transubstantiation cannot be proved by the plain and
" manifest words of scripture ; nor can it be necessarily col-
" lected from it ; nor yet confirmed by the consent of the
" ancient fathers.

" In the Lord's supper there is none other oblation and
" sacrifice than of a remembrance of Christ's death and of
" thanksgiving."

[June 20.   Dr. Madew defended these ; and Glyn, Langdale, Sedgwick,

and Young, disputed against them the first day: and the Fox, lib. ix.
07 second day Glyn defended the contrary propositions; and p. 104.]
Pern, Grindal, Guest, and Pilkington, disputed against them.
On the third day the dispute went on, and was summed up in [June 25.]
[Ibid. p.
a learned determination by Ridley against the corporal pre- 120.]
sence.   There had been also a long disputation in the parliament on the same subject; but of this we have nothing remaining, but what king Edward writ in his Journal.   Ridley had,
by reading Bertram's book of the body and blood of Christ,
been first set on to examine well the old opinion concerning
the presence of Christ's very flesh and blood in the sacrament:
and, wondering to find that in the ninth century that opinion
was so much controverted, and so learnedly writ against by
one of the most esteemed men of that age, began to conclude,
that it was none of the ancient doctrines of the church, but
lately brought in, and not fully received, till after Bertram's
age.   He communicated the matter with Cranmer, and they
set themselves to examine it with more than ordinary care.
Cranmer afterwards gathered all the arguments about it into
the book which he writ on that subject; to which Gardiner
set out an answer, under the disguised name of Marcus Constantius: and Cranmer replied to it.   I shall offer the reader
in short the substance of what was in these books, and of the
arguments used in the disputations; and in many other books
which were at that time written on this subject.

Christ in the institution took bread, and gave it: so that The manner of the
his words, *This is my body*, could only be meant of the bread. presence
Now the bread could not be his body literally.   He himself explained
according
also calls the cup, *The fruit of the vine*.   St. Paul calls it, *The* to the
bread that we break, and *the cup that we bless;* and, speak- scripture.
ing of it after it was blessed, calls it, *That bread, and that* [Cranmer's
Works, i.
cup.   For the reason of that expression, *This is my body;* it p. 29 sqq.]
was considered, that the disciples, to whom Christ spoke thus,
were Jews; and that they, being accustomed to the Mosaical
rites, must needs have understood his words in the same sense
they did Moses' words concerning the paschal lamb, which is
called *the Lord's passover*.   It was not that literally, for *the
Lord's passover* was the angel's passing by the Israelites,
when he smote the first-born of the Egyptians; so the lamb
was only *the Lord's passover*, as it was the memorial of it:

and thus Christ, substituting the eucharist to the paschal lamb, used such an expression, calling it *his body*, in the same manner of speaking as the lamb was called *the Lord's passover*. This was plain enough; for his disciples could not well understand him in any other sense than that to which they had been formerly accustomed. In the scripture many such figurative expressions occur frequently. In baptism, the other sacrament instituted by Christ, he is said to baptize *with the Holy Ghost and with fire:* and such as are baptized are said to *put on Christ;* which were figurative expressions. As also, in the sacrament of the Lord's supper, the cup is called *the new testament in Christ's blood*, which is an expression full of figure. Further, it was observed, that that sacrament was instituted for a remembrance of Christ, and of his death; which implied, that he was to be absent at the time when he was to be remembered. Nor was it simply said, that the elements were his body and blood; but that they were his *body broken*, and his *blood shed;* that is, they were these, as suffering on the cross: which as they could not be understood literally, for Christ did institute this sacrament before he had suffered on the cross; so now Christ must be present in the sacrament, not as glorified in heaven, but as suffering on his cross. From those places where it is said, that Christ is in heaven, and that he is to continue there; they argued, that he was not to be any more upon earth. And those words in the sixth of St. John, of *eating Christ's flesh*, and *drinking his blood*, they said were to be understood not of the sacrament; since many receive the sacrament unworthily, and of them it cannot be said that *they have eternal life in them:* but Christ there said of them that received him in the sense that was meant in that chapter, that *all that did so eat his flesh had eternal life in them;* therefore these words can only be understood figuratively of receiving him *by faith*, as himself there explains it. And so, in the end of that discourse, finding some were startled at that way of expressing himself, he gave a key to the whole, when he said, *his words were spirit and life;* and, *that the flesh profited nothing, it was the spirit that quickened.* It was ordinary for him to teach in parables; and *the receiving of any doctrine* being oft expressed by the prophets by the figure of *eating and drinking,* he, upon the occasion of the

people's coming to him after he had fed them with a few
loaves, did discourse of their believing in these dark expressions ; which did not seem to relate to the sacrament, since it
was not then instituted.   They also argued, from Christ's ap-
pealing to the senses of his hearers in his miracles, and especially in his discourses upon his resurrection, that the testimony
of sense was to be received where the object was duly applied,
and the sense not vitiated.   They also alleged natural reasons
against a body's being in more places than one, or being in a
place in the manner of a spirit, so that the substance of a complete body could be in a crumb of bread, or drop of wine ;
and argued, that, since the elements after consecration would
nourish, might putrefy, or could be poisoned, these things
clearly evinced, that the substance of bread and wine remained
in the sacrament.

From this they went to examine the ancient fathers.   Some
of them called it *bread and wine;* others said, it *nourished
the body,* as Justin Martyr ; others, *that it was digested in
the stomach,* and *went into the draught,* as Origen.   Some
called it a *figure* of Christ's body ; so Tertullian, and St. Austin : others called the elements *types* and *signs;* so almost all
the ancient Liturgies, and the Greek fathers generally.   In
the creeds of the church it was professed, that Christ still sat
on the right hand of God ; the fathers argued from thence,
that he was in heaven, and not on earth.   And the Marcion-
ites, and other heretics, denying that Christ had a true body,
or did really suffer ; the fathers appealed in that to the testimony of sense, as infallible.   And St. Austin giving rules concerning figurative speeches in scripture ; one is this, that they
must be taken figuratively, where in the literal sense the thing
were a crime ; which he applies to these words of *eating
Christ's flesh, and drinking his blood.*   But that on which
they put the stress of the whole cause, as to the doctrine of
the fathers, was the reasoning that they used against the
Eutychians, who said, that Christ's body and human nature
was swallowed up by his divinity.   The Eutychians, arguing
from the eucharist's being called Christ's body and blood,
in which they said Christ's presence did convert the substance of the bread and wine into his own flesh and blood ;
so in like manner, said they, his Godhead had converted the
manhood into itself.   Against this, Gelasius bishop of Rome,

And from
the fathers.
[Cranmer's
Works, i.
p. 264.]

[Ibid. p.
119.]

[Ibid. pp.
115, 137.]

[Ibid. pp.
289, 299.]

109

and Theodoret, one of the learnedest fathers of his age, argue in plain words, that the substance of the bread and wine remained, as it was formerly, in its own nature and form; and from their opinion of the presence of Christ's body in it, without converting the elements, they turned the argument to show how the divine and human nature can be together in Christ, without the one's being changed by the other. Peter Martyr had brought over with him the copy of a letter of St. Chrysostome's, which he found in a MS. at Florence, written to the same purpose, and on the same argument; which was the more remarkable, because that Chrysostom had said higher things in his sermons and commentaries, concerning Christ's being present in the sacrament, than any of all the fathers: but it appeared by this letter, that those high expressions were no other than rhetorical figures of speech, to beget a great reverence to this institution; and from hence it was reasonable to judge, that such were the like expressions in other fathers, and that they were nevertheless of Chrysostom's mind touching the presence of Christ in the sacrament. That epistle of his does lie still unpublished, though a very learned man, now in France, has procured a copy of it; but those of that church know the consequence that the printing of it would have, and so it seems are resolved to suppress it if they can. From all these things it was plain, that though the fathers believed there was an extraordinary virtue in the sacrament, and an unaccountable presence of Christ in it, yet they thought not of transubstantiation, nor any thing like it. But when darkness and ignorance crept into the church, the people were apt to believe any thing that was incredible; and were willing enough to support such opinions as turned religion into external pageantry. The priests also, knowing little of the scriptures, and being only or chiefly conversant in those writings of the ancients that had highly extolled the sacrament, came generally to take up the opinion of the corporal presence; and, being soon apprehensive of the great esteem it would bring to them, cherished it much. In the ninth century, Bertram, Rabanus Maurus, Amalarius, Alcuinus, and Joannes Scotus, all writ against it; nor were any of them censured or condemned for these opinions. It was plainly and strongly contradicted by some homilies that were in the Saxon tongue, in which not a few of Bertram's words occur;

[Cranmer's Works, i. p. 287.]

[Ibid. p. 173.]

particularly in that which was to be read in the churches on
Easter-day. But in the eleventh or twelfth century it came
to be universally received; as indeed any thing would have
been that much advanced the dignity of priesthood. And it [Ibid. p.
was further advanced by pope Innocent the Third, and so ²⁴⁰·]
established in the fourth council of Lateran; that same council
in which the rooting out of heretics, and the pope's power of
deposing heretical princes, and giving their dominions to others
were also decreed.

But there was another curious remark made of the progress
of this opinion. When the doctrine of the corporal presence
was first received in the western church, they believed that
the whole loaf was turned into one entire body of Jesus Christ:
so that in the distribution one had an eye, a nose, or an ear;
another a tooth, a finger, or a toe; a third a collop, or a piece
of tripe: and this was supported by pretended miracles suited
110 to that opinion; for sometimes the host was said to bleed,
parts of it were also said to be turned to pieces of flesh. This
continued to be the doctrine of the church of Rome for near
three hundred years. It appears clearly in the renunciation [Ibid.p.46.]
which they made Berengarius swear. But when the school-
men began to form the tenets of that church by more artificial
and subtle rules; as they thought it an ungentle way of treating Christ to be thus mangling his body, and eating it up in
gobbets, so the maxims they set up about the extension of
matter, and of the manner of spirit's filling a space, made them
think of a more decent way of explaining this prodigious mystery. They taught, that Christ was so in the host and chalice,
that there was one entire body in every crumb and drop: so
that the body was no more broken; but, upon every breaking
of the host, a new whole body flew off from the other parts,
which yet remained an entire body, notwithstanding that diminution. And then the former miracles, being contrary to this
conceit, were laid aside, and new ones invented, fitted for this
explanation; by which Christ's body was believed present
after the manner of a spirit. It was given out, that he sometimes appeared as a child all in rays upon the host, sometimes
with angels about him, or sometimes in his mother's arms:
and, that the senses might give as little contradiction as was
possible, instead of a loaf they blessed then only wafers, which

are such a shadow of bread as might more easily agree with
their doctrine of the accidents of bread being only present;
and, lest a larger measure of wine might have encouraged the
people to have thought it was wine still, by the sensible effects
of it, that came also to be denied them.

This was the substance of the arguments that were in those
writings. But an opinion, that had been so generally received,
was not of a sudden to be altered: therefore they went on
slowly in discussing it, and thereby did the better dispose the
people to receive what they intended afterwards to establish
concerning it. And this was the state of religion for this year.

Proceed·
ingsagainst
anabap-
tists:

At this time there were many anabaptists in several parts
of England. They were generally Germans, whom the revolutions there had forced to change their seats. Upon Luther's
first preaching in Germany, there arose many, who, building
on some of his principles, carried things much further than he
did. The chief foundation he laid down was, that the scripture was to be the only rule of Christians. Upon this, many
argued, that the mysteries of the Trinity, and Christ's incarnation and sufferings, of the fall of man, and the aids of grace,
were indeed philosophical subtilties, and only pretended to be
deduced from scripture, as almost all opinions of religion were;
and therefore they rejected them. Among these, the baptism
of infants was one. They held that to be no baptism, and so
were rebaptized: but from this, which was most taken notice
of, as being a visible thing, they carried all the general name

Of whom
there were
two sorts.

of anabaptists. Of these, there were two sorts most remarkable. The one was, of those who only thought that baptism
ought not to be given but to those who were of an age capable
of instruction, and who did earnestly desire it. This opinion
they grounded on the silence of the New Testament about the
baptism of children. They observed, that our Saviour, com-
manding the apostles to baptize, did join teaching with it: and
they said, the great decay of Christianity flowed from this 111
way of making children Christians, before they understood
what they did. These were called the gentle, or moderate
anabaptists. But others, who carried that name, denied almost
all the principles of the Christian doctrine, and were men of
fierce and barbarous tempers. They had broke out into a
general revolt over Germany, and raised the war, called *the*

rustic war; and, possessing themselves of Munster, made one
of their teachers, John of Leyden, their king, under the title
of *The King of the New Jerusalem.* Some of them set up a
fantastical, unintelligible way of talking of religion, which they
turned all into allegories: these, being joined in the common
name of anabaptists with the other, brought them also under
an ill character.

On the twelfth of April there was a complaint brought to
the council, that, with the strangers that were come into England, some of that persuasion had come over, and were disse-
minating their errors, and making proselytes: so a commission Rot. Pat.
Par. 6.
was ordered for the archbishop of Canterbury, the bishops of 3. regn.
Ely, Worcester, Westminster, Chichester, Lincoln, and Ro- [ap.Rymer,
xv. p. 181.]
chester, sir William Petre, sir Thomas Smith, Dr. Cox, Dr.
May, and some others, (three of them being a *quorum*,) to
examine and search after all anabaptists, heretics, or contemners
of the Common Prayer. They were to endeavour to reclaim
them, to enjoin them penance, and give them absolution: or,
if they were obstinate, to excommunicate and imprison them,
and to deliver them over to the secular power, to be further
proceeded against. Some tradesmen in London were brought
before these commissioners in May, and were persuaded to
abjure their former opinions: which were, "that a man re-
" generate could not sin; that though the outward man sinned,
" the inward man sinned not; that there was no Trinity of
" Persons; that Christ was only a holy prophet, and not at
" all God; that all we had by Christ was, that he taught us
" the way to heaven; that he took no flesh of the Virgin;
" and that the baptism of infants was not profitable." One of
those, who thus abjured, was commanded to carry a fagot
next Sunday at St. Paul's; where there should be a sermon,
setting forth his heresy. But there was another of these extreme obstinate; Joan Bocher, commonly called Joan of Kent.
" She denied that Christ was truly incarnate of the Virgin, [Wilkins,
" whose flesh being sinful, he could take none of it: but the Conc. iv.
43.]
" Word, by the consent of the inward man in the Virgin, took
" flesh of her." These were her words. They took much
pains about her, and had many conferences with her; but she
was so extravagantly conceited of her own notions, that she
rejected all they said with scorn: whereupon she was adjudged

an obstinate heretic, and so left to the secular power. The

Collect.
Numb. 35.

sentence against her will be found in the Collection. This being returned to the council, the good king was moved to sign a warrant for burning her, but could not be prevailed on to do it : he thought it a piece of cruelty, too like that which they had condemned in papists, to burn any for their consciences. And, in a long discourse he had with sir J. Cheke, he seemed much confirmed in that opinion. Cranmer was employed to persuade him to sign the warrant. He argued from the law of Moses, by which blasphemers were to be stoned. He told the king, he made a great difference between errors in other points of divinity, and those which were directly against the Apostles' Creed: that these were impieties against God, which a prince, as being God's deputy, ought to punish ; as the king's deputies were obliged to punish offences against 112 the king's person. These reasons did rather silence, than satisfy the young king ; who still thought it a hard thing (as in truth it was) to proceed so severely in such cases : so he set his hand to the warrant, with tears in his eyes ; saying to Cranmer, that if he did wrong, since it was in submission to his authority, he should answer for it to God. This struck the archbishop with much horror, so that he was very unwilling to have the sentence executed. And both he and Ridley took the woman then in custody to their houses, to see if they could persuade her : but she continued, by jeers and other insolences, to carry herself so contemptuously, that at last the sentence was executed on her, the second of May the next

Ananabaptist burnt.

year, bishop Scory preaching at her burning. She carried herself then, as she had done in the former parts of her process, very indecently, and in the end was burnt.

This action was much censured, as being contrary to the clemency of the gospel ; and was made oft use of by the papists, who said, it was plain, that the reformers were only against burning when they were in fear of it themselves. The woman's carriage made her be looked on as a frantic person, fitter for Bedlam than a stake. People had generally believed, that all the statutes for burning heretics had been repealed : but now, when the thing was better considered, it was found, that the burning of heretics was done by the common law ; so that the statutes made about it were only for making the con-

viction more easy; and the repealing the statutes did not take
away that which was grounded on a writ at common law. To
end all this matter at once: two years after this, one George
Van Pare, a Dutchman, being accused for saying that God
the Father was only God, and that Christ was not very God,
he was dealt with long to abjure, but would not: so, on the
sixth of April, 1551, he was condemned in the same manner
that Joan of Kent was; and on the twenty-fifth of April was
burnt in Smithfield.   He suffered with great constancy of
mind, and kissed the stake, and fagots that were to burn him.
Of this Pare, I find a popish writer saying, that he was a man
of most wonderful strict life; that he used not to eat above
once in two days; and, before he did eat, would lie some time
in his devotion prostrate on the ground.   All this they made
use of to lessen the credit of those who had suffered formerly;
for it was said, they saw now that men of harmless lives might
be put to death for heresy, by the confession of the reformers
themselves.   And in all the books published in queen Mary's
days, justifying her severity against the protestants, these instances were always made use of; and no part of Cranmer's
life exposed him more than this did.   It was said, he had consented both to Lambert's and Anne Askew's death, in the former reign, who both suffered for opinions which he himself
held now : and he had now procured the death of these two
persons ; and, when he was brought to suffer himself afterwards, it was called a just retaliation on him.   One thing was
certain, that what he did in this matter flowed from no cruelty
of temper in him, no man being further from that black disposition of mind ; but it was truly the effect of those principles
by which he governed himself.

   For the other sort of anabaptists, who only denied infants
baptism, I find no severities used to them : but several books
were written against them, to which they wrote some answers.
113 It was said that Christ allowed little children to be brought to
him, and said, of *such was the kingdom of heaven,* and blessed
them.   Now if they were capable of the *kingdom of heaven,*
they must be regenerated ; for Christ said, none but such as
were *born of water and of the Spirit* could enter into it.   St.
Paul had also called the children of believing parents *holy ;*
which seemed to relate to such a consecration of them as was

[Wilkins,
Conc. iv.
44.]

Another
burnt.
[April 24.
Stow, p.
605.]

This was
much cen-
sured.

Disputes
concerning
the bap-
tism of in-
fants.

made in baptism. And baptism being the seal of Christians, in the room of circumcision among the Jews, it was thought the one was as applicable to children as the other. And one thing was observed, that the whole world in that age having been baptized in their infancy, if that baptism was nothing, then there were none truly baptized in being; but all were in the state of mere nature. Now it did not seem reasonable that men who were not baptized themselves should go and baptize others: and therefore the first heads of that sect, not being rightly baptized themselves, seemed not to act with any authority when they went to baptize others. The practice of the church, so early begun, and continued without dispute for so many ages, was at least a certain confirmation of a thing which had (to speak moderately) so good foundations in scripture for the lawfulness, though not any peremptory, but only probable proof for the practice of it.

The doctrine of predestination much abused.

These are all the errors in opinion that I find were taken notice of at this time. There was another sort of people, of whom all the good men in that age made great complaints. Some there were called gospellers, or readers of the gospel, who were a scandal to the doctrine they professed. In many sermons I have oft met with severe expostulations with these, and heavy denunciations of judgments against them: but I do not find any thing objected to them, as to their belief, save only that the doctrine of predestination having been generally taught by the reformers, many of this sect began to make strange inferences from it; reckoning, that since every thing was decreed, and the decrees of God could not be frustrated, therefore men were to leave themselves to be carried by these decrees. This drew some into great impiety of life, and others into desperation. The Germans soon saw the ill effects of this doctrine. Luther changed his mind about it, and Melancthon openly writ against it. And since that time the whole stream of the Lutheran churches has run the other way. But both Calvin and Bucer were still for maintaining the doctrine of these decrees; only they warned the people not to think much of them, since they were secrets which men could not penetrate into; but they did not so clearly shew how these consequences did not flow from such opinions. Hooper, and many other good writers, did often dehort people from entering into these curiosities; and a caveat to that same purpose was put afterwards into the article of the church about predestination.

One ill effect of the dissoluteness of people's manners broke out violently this summer, occasioned by the inclosing of lands[79]. While the monasteries stood, there were great numbers of people maintained about these houses; their lands were easily let out, and many were relieved by them. But now the numbers of the people increased much, marriage being universally allowed: they also had more time than formerly, by the abrogation of many holydays, and the putting down of processions 114 and pilgrimages: so that, as the numbers increased, they had more time than they knew how to bestow. Those who bought in the church lands, as they every where raised their rents, of which old Latimer made great complaints in one of his court-sermons, so they resolved to inclose their grounds, and turn them to pasture: for trade was then rising fast, and corn brought not in so much money as wool did. Their flocks also being kept by few persons in grounds so inclosed, the landlords themselves enjoyed the profit which formerly the tenants made out of their estates: and so they intended to force them to serve about them at any such rates as they would allow. By this means the commons of England saw they were like to be reduced to great misery. This was much complained of, and several little books were written about it. Some proposed a sort of Agrarian law, that none might have farms above a set value, or flocks above a set number of two thousand sheep; which proposal I find the young king was much taken with, as will appear in one of the discourses he wrote with his own hand. It was also represented, that there was no care taken of the educating of youth, except of those who were bred for learning; and many things were proposed to correct this: but in the mean time the commons saw the gentry were like to reduce them to a very low condition.

The protector seemed much concerned for the commons[80], and oft spoke against the oppression of landlords. He was naturally just and compassionate, and so did heartily espouse the cause of the poor people, which made the nobility and gentry hate him much. The former year, the commons about Hampton-Court petitioned the protector and council, complaining,

Tumults in England.

[79] [See Part iii. p. 189.]　　　[80] [Ibid. Part iii. p. 190.]

that whereas the late king in his sickness had inclosed a park there, to divert himself with private easy game, the deer of that park did overlay the country, and it was a great burden to them; and therefore they desired that it might be disparked. The council, considering that it was so near Windsor, and was not useful to the king, but a charge rather, ordered it to be disparked, and the deer to be carried to Windsor; but with this proviso, that if the king, when he came of age, desired to have a park there, what they did should be no prejudice to him. There was also a commission issued out to inquire about inclosures and farms; and whether those who had purchased the abbey-lands kept hospitality, to which they were bound by the grants they had of them; and whether they encouraged husbandry. But I find no effect of this. And indeed there seemed to have been a general design among the nobility and gentry to bring the inferior sort to that low and servile state to which the peasants in many other kingdoms are reduced.

[Journals of Lords, p. 337.]

In the parliament an act was carried in the house of lords for imparking grounds, but was cast out by the commons; yet gentlemen went on every where taking their lands into their own hands, and inclosing them.

Many are easily quieted. [Hayward, p. 292.]

In May the commons did rise first in Wiltshire; where sir William Herbert gathered some resolute men about him, and dispersed them, and slew some of them. Soon after that, they rose in Sussex, Hampshire, Kent, Gloucestershire, Suffolk, Warwickshire, Essex, Hertfordshire, Leicestershire, Worcestershire, and Rutlandshire; but by fair persuasions the fury of the people was a little stopped, till the matter should be represented to the council. The protector said, he did not wonder the commons were in such distempers, they being so oppressed, that it was easier to die once than to perish for want; and therefore he set out a proclamation, contrary to the mind of the whole council, against all new inclosures; with another, indemnifying the people for what was past, so they carried themselves obediently for the future. Commissions were also sent every where, with an unlimited power to the commissioners, to hear and determine all causes about inclosures, highways, and cottages. The vast power these commissioners assumed was much complained of; the landlords said, it was an invasion of their property to subject them thus to the pleasure of those who were sent to examine the matters, without proceeding in the ordinary courts according to law. The commons, being encouraged by the favour they heard the protector bore them, and not able to govern their heat, or stay for a more peaceable issue, did rise again, but were anew quieted. Yet the protector being opposed much by the council, he was not able to redress this grievance so fully as the people hoped. So in Oxfordshire and Devonshire they rose again, and also in Norfolk and Yorkshire. Those in Oxfordshire were dissipated by a force of fifteen hundred men, led against them by the lord Grey. Some of them were taken and hanged by martial law, as being in a state of war; the greatest part ran home to their dwellings.

In Devonshire the insurrection grew to be better formed; But those for that country was not only far from the court, but it was of Devonshire grew generally inclined to the former superstition, and many of the formidable. old priests ran in among them. They came together on the tenth of June, being Whit-Sunday [81]; and in a short time they [June 9.] grew to be ten thousand strong. At court it was hoped this might be as easily dispersed as the other risings were. But the protector was against running into extremities, and so did not move so speedily as the thing required. He, after some days, at last sent the lord Russell with a small force to stop their proceedings. And that lord, remembering well how the duke of Norfolk had with a very small army broken a formidable rebellion in the former reign, hoped that time would likewise weaken and disunite these; and therefore he kept at some distance, and offered to receive their complaints, and to send them to the council. But these delays gave advantage and strength to the rebels, who were now led on by some gentlemen; Arundel of Cornwall being in chief command among them: and, in answer to the lord Russell, they agreed on fifteen articles [82], the substance of which was as follows:

1. " That all the general councils, and the decrees of their Their de " forefathers, should be observed. mands.

2. " That the act of the six articles should be again in force.

3. " That the mass should be in Latin, and that the priests " alone should receive.

[81] [The mistake is from Fuller, they drew up their demands in seven vii. 393.] articles.' [S.]
[82] After articles add, 'Before this

4. " That the sacrament should be hanged up, and worshipped; and those who refused to do it should suffer as heretics.

5. " That the sacrament should only be given to the people at Easter in one kind.

6. " That baptism should be done at all times.

7. " That holy bread, holy water, and palms be again used; and that images be set up, with all the other ancient ceremonies.

8. " That the new service should be laid aside, since it was 116 like a Christmas game; and the old service again should be used, with the procession in Latin.

9. " That all preachers in their sermons, and priests in the mass, should pray for the souls in purgatory.

10. " That the Bible should be called in, since otherwise the clergy could not easily confound the heretics.

11. " That Dr. Moreman and Crispin should be sent to them, and put in their livings.

12. " That cardinal Pole should be restored, and made of the king's council.

13. " That every gentleman might have only one servant for every hundred marks of yearly rent that belonged to him.

14. " That the half of the abbey and church lands should be taken back, and restored to two of the chief abbeys in every county; and all the church boxes for seven years should be given to such houses, that so devout persons might live in them, who should pray for the king and the commonwealth.

15. " And that for their particular grievances, they should be redressed, as Humphrey Arundel and the mayor of Bodmin should inform the king; for whom they desired a safe-conduct."

Cranmer
drew an
answer to
them.
Ex MS.
Coll. C. C.
Cant. [cii.
p. 337.
printed in
Strype's
Cranmer,
App. N°.
40.]

These articles being sent to the council, the archbishop of Canterbury was ordered to draw an answer to them, which I have seen, corrected with his own hand. The substance of it was, that their demands were insolent, such as were dictated to them by some seditious priests: they did not know what general councils had decreed; nor was there any thing in the church of England contrary to them, though many things had been formerly received which were so. And for the decrees, they were framed by the popes to enslave the world, of which he gave several instances.

For the six articles, he says, they had not been carried in parliament, if the late king had not gone thither in person, and procured that act; and yet of his own accord he slackened the execution of it.

To the third, it was strange that they did not desire to know in what terms they worshipped God. And for the mass, the ancient canons required the people to communicate in it; and the prayers in the office of the mass did still imply that they were to do it.

For the hanging up and adoring the host, it was but lately set up by pope Innocent and Honorius, and in some places it had never been received.

For the fifth; The ancient church received that sacrament frequently, and in both kinds.

To the sixth; Baptism, in cases of necessity, was to be administered at any time; but out of these cases, it was fit to do it solemnly: and in the ancient church it was chiefly done on the eves of Easter and Whit-Sunday; of which usage some footsteps remained still in the old offices.

To the seventh; These were late superstitious devices: images were contrary to the scriptures, first set up for remembrance, but soon after made objects of worship.

17 To the eighth: The old service had many ludicrous things in it; the new was simple and grave: if it appeared ridiculous to them, it was as the gospel was long ago, *foolishness* to the Greeks.

To the ninth: The scriptures say nothing of it: it was a superstitious invention, derogatory to Christ's death.

To the tenth: The scriptures are the word of God, and the readiest way to confound that which is heresy indeed.

To the eleventh: These were ignorant, superstitious, and deceitful persons.

To the twelfth: Pole had been attainted in parliament for his spiteful writings and doings against the late king.

To the thirteenth: It was foolish and unreasonable. One servant could not do a man's business; and by this many servants would want employment.

To the fourteenth: This was to rob the king, and those who

P 2

had these lands of him; and would be a means to make so foul a rebellion be remembered in their prayers.

To the fifteenth: These were notorious traitors, to whom the king's council was not to submit themselves.

They make new demands; [Hayward, p. 293.]

After this, they grew more moderate, and sent eight articles: 1. Concerning baptism. 2. About confirmation. 3. Of the mass. 4. For reserving the host. 5. For holy bread and water. 6. For the old service. 7. For the single lives of priests[83]. 8. For the six articles. And concluded, *God save the king*; for they were *his, both body and goods.* To this

Which were also rejected. [Holinshed, p. 1005.]

there was an answer sent, in the king's name, on the eighth of July[84], (so long did the treaty with them hold,) in which, after expressions of the king's affection to his people, he taxes their rising in arms against him their king, as contrary to the laws of God. He tells them, that they are abused by their priests, as in the instance of baptism; which (according to the book) might, necessity requiring it, be done at all times: that the changes that had been set out were made after long and great consultation; and the worship of this church, by the advice of many bishops and learned men, was reformed as near to what Christ and his apostles had taught and done as could be; and all things had been settled in parliament. But the most specious thing that misled them being that of the king's age, it was shewed them, that his blood, and not his years, gave him the crown. And the state of government requires, that at all times there should be the same authority in princes, and the same obedience in the people. It was all penned in a high threatening style; and concluded with an earnest invitation of them to submit to the king's mercy, as others that had risen had also done; to whom he had not only shewed mercy, but granted redress of their just grievances; otherwise they might expect the utmost severity that traitors deserved.

But nothing prevailed on this enraged multitude; whom the priests inflamed with all the artifices they could imagine; and among whom the host was carried about by a priest on a cart,

---

83 That the service might be said or sung in the choir. [S.]

84 [An answer with this date has been printed from the original in the State Paper Office, in Tytler's Original Letters, vol. i. p. 178. It does not correspond very exactly to the description in the text, which has been abridged from Fox, lib. ix. p. 14.]

that all might see it. But when this commotion was thus grown to a head, the men of Norfolk rose the sixth of July, being led by one Kett, a tanner. These pretended nothing of religion, but only to suppress and destroy the gentry, and to raise the 8 commons, and to put new counsellors about the king. They increased mightily, and became twenty thousand strong; but had no order nor discipline, and committed many horrid outrages. The sheriff of the county came boldly to them, and required them, in the king's name, to disperse, and go home: but had he not been well mounted, they had put him cruelly to death. They came to Moushold-Hill, above Norwich, and were much favoured by many in that city. Parker, afterwards archbishop of Canterbury, came among them, and preached very freely to them of their ill lives, their rebellion against the king, and the robberies they daily committed; by which he was in great danger of his life. Kett assumed to himself the power of judicature; and under an old oak, called from thence *the oak of reformation,* did such justice as might be expected from such a judge, and in such a camp. The marquis of Northampton was sent against them, but with orders to keep at a distance from them, and to cut off their provisions: for so it was hoped, that, without the shedding much blood, they might come to themselves again. When the news of this rising came into Yorkshire, the commons there rose also, being further encouraged by a prophecy, that there should be no king nor nobility in England: that the kingdom should be ruled by four governors, chosen by the commons, who should hold a parliament, in commotion, to begin at the south and north seas. This they applied to the Devonshire men on the south seas, and themselves on the north seas. They, at their first rising, fired beacons, and so gathered the country, as if it had been for the defence of the coast: and meeting two gentlemen, with two others with them, they, without any provocation, murdered them, and left their naked bodies unburied. At the same time that England was in this commotion, the news came that the French king had sent a great army into the territory of Boulogne; so that the government was put to most extraordinary straits.

There was a fast proclaimed in and about London. Cranmer preached on the fast-day at court: I have seen the greatest

Side notes:

The rebellion in Norfolk headed by Kett, a tanner. [Holinshed, p. 1028.]

[Hayward, p. 297.]

A rising in Yorkshire. [Ibid. p. 300.]

The French fall into the Boulognois.

A fast at court, where

Cranmer
preached.
Ex MS.
C. C. C.
Cantab.
[cii. p. 409,
printed in
Cranmer's
Remains,
p. 190.]
part of his sermon, under his own hand; and it is the only sermon of his I ever saw. It is a very plain, inartificial discourse; no shows of learning, or conceits of wit in it: but he severely expostulated, in the name of God, with his hearers for their ill lives, their blasphemies, adulteries, mutual hatred, oppression, and contempt of the gospel; and complained of the slackness in punishing these sins, by which the government became, in some sort, guilty of them. He set many passages of the Jewish story before them, of the judgments such sins drew on, and of God's mercy in the unexpected deliverances they met with upon their true repentance. But he chiefly lamented the scandal given by many who pretended a zeal for religion, but used that for a cloak to disguise their other vices. He set before them the fresh example of Germany; where people generally loved to hear the gospel, but had not amended their lives upon it; for which God had now, after many years' forbearance, brought them under a severe scourge: and intimated his apprehensions of some signal stroke from Heaven upon the nation, if they did not repent.

The rebels in Devonshire went and besieged Exeter, where the citizens resisted them with great courage. They set fire to the gates of the city; which those within fed with much fuel, for hindering their entry, till they had raised a rampart within the gates; and when the rebels came to enter, the fire being spent, they killed many of them. The rebels also wrought a mine; but the citizens countermined, and poured in so much water, as spoiled their powder. So, finding they could do nothing by force, they resolved to lie about the town, reckoning that the want of provision would make it soon yield. The lord Russell, having but a small force with him, stayed a while for some supplies, which sir William Herbert was to bring him from Bristol: but, being afraid that the rebels should inclose him, he marched back from Honiton, where he lay; and finding they had taken a bridge behind him, he beat them from it, killing six hundred of them, without any loss on his side. By this he understood their strength, and saw they could not stand a brisk charge, nor rally when once in disorder. So the lord Grey, and Spinola, that commanded some Germans, joining him, he returned to raise the siege of Exeter, which was much straitened for want of victuals. The rebels

119

had now shut up the city twelve days : they within had eat their horses, and endured extreme famine, but resolved to perish rather than fall into the hands of those savages ; for the rebels were indeed no better. They had blocked up the ways, and left two thousand men to keep a bridge, which the king's forces were to pass. But the lord Russell broke through them, and killed about one thousand of them : upon that, the rebels raised the siege, and retired to Lanceston. The lord Russell gave the citizens of Exeter great thanks in the king's name for their fidelity and courage ; and pursued the rebels, who were now going off in parties, and were killed in great numbers. Some of their heads, as Arundel, and the mayor of Bodmin, Tempson and Barret, two priests, with six or seven more, were taken and hanged. And so this rebellion was happily subdued in the west about the beginning of August, to the great honour of the lord Russell ; who, with a very small force, had saved Exeter, and dispersed the rebels' army, with little or no loss at all.

But is relieved, and the rebels defeated by the lord Russell.

[Fox, lib. ix. p. 17.] [Aug. 6, Holinshed, p. 1025.]

But the marquis of Northampton was not so successful in Norfolk. He carried about eleven hundred men [85] with him, but did not observe the orders given him, and so marched on to Norwich. The rebels were glad of an occasion to engage with him, and fell in upon him the next day with great fury ; and the town not being strong, he was forced to quit it, but lost one hundred of his men in that action, among whom was the lord Sheffield, who was much lamented. The rebels took about thirty prisoners, with which they were much lifted up. This being understood at court, the earl of Warwick was sent against them with six thousand foot, and fifteen hundred horse, that were prepared for an expedition to Scotland. He came to Norwich, but was scarce able to defend it ; for the rebels fell often in upon him, neither was he well assured of the town. But he cut off their provisions ; so that the rebels, having wasted all the country about them, were forced to remove : and then he followed them with his horse. They turned upon him ; but he quickly routed them, and killed two thousand of them, and took Kett their captain, with his brother, and a great many more. Kett was hanged in chains at Norwich next January.

Warwick disperses the rebels at Norfolk.

The rebels in Yorkshire had not become very numerous,

[85] [Holinshed (p. 1033) says 1500. So also Hayward, p. 297.]

not being above three thousand in all; but, hearing of the defeating of those in other parts, they accepted of the offer of pardon that was sent them: only some few of the chief ring- 120 leaders continued to make new stirs, and were taken, and hanged in York the September following.

When these commotions were thus over, the protector pressed that there might be a general and free pardon speedily proclaimed, for quieting the country, and giving their affairs a reputation abroad. This was much opposed by many of the council; who thought it better to accomplish their several ends, by keeping the people under the lash, than by so profuse a mercy. But the protector was resolved on it, judging *A general* the state of affairs required it. So he gave out a general *pardon.* pardon of all that had been done before the twenty-first of August; excepting only those few whom they had in their hands, and resolved to make public examples. Thus was England delivered from one of the most threatening storms that at any time had broke out in it; in which deliverance the great prudence and temper of the protector seems to have had no small share. Of this whole matter advertisement was given *Collect.* to the foreign ministers in a letter, which will be found in the *Numb. 36.* Collection.

A visita- There was this year a visitation of the university of Cam-
tion at bridge. Ridley was appointed to be one of the visitors, and
Cambridge. to preach at the opening of it: he thereupon writ to May, dean of St. Paul's, to let him know what was to be done at it, that so his sermon might be adjusted to their business. He received answer, that it was only to remove some superstitious practices and rites, and to make such statutes as should be found needful. But when he went to Cambridge, he saw the instructions went further. They were required to procure a resignation of some colleges, and to unite them with others; and to convert some fellowships, appointed for encouraging the study of divinity, to the study of the civil law. In particular, Clare Hall [86] was to be suppressed. But the master and fellows would not resign; and after two days labouring to per-

---

[86] There were no other colleges to be suppressed besides Clare Hall, in order to found a new college of civilians, either by uniting it to Trinity Hall, or by augmenting the number of Trinity Hall to twenty fellows; as appears by king Edward's Statutes, drawn up before the visitors came down, compared with his injunctions (all upon the Black book) drawn up after.

Indeed Trinity Hall was to be

suade them to it, they absolutely refused to do it.   Upon this
Ridley said, he could not, with a good conscience, go on any
further in that matter: the church was already so robbed and
stripped, that it seemed there was a design laid down by some,
to drive out all civility, learning, and religion out of the nation:
therefore he declared, he would not concur in such things;
and desired leave to be gone.   The other visitors complained
of him to the protector, that he had so troubled them with his
barking, (so indecently did they express that strictness of conscience in him,) that they could not go on in the king's service.
And because Clare Hall was then full of northern people, they
imputed his unwillingness to suppress that house to his partial
affection to his countrymen ; for he was born in the bishopric
of Durham.   Upon this, the protector writ a chiding letter to
him.   To it he writ an answer, so suitable to what became a
bishop, who would put all things to hazard rather than do any
thing against his conscience, that I thought it might do no
small right to his memory to put it, with the answer which the
protector writ to him, in the Collection.   These, with many
more, I found among his majesty's papers of state, in that re-
pository of them commonly called the Paper-office : to which
I had a free access, by a warrant which was procured to me
from the king by the right honourable the earl of Sunderland,
one of the principal secretaries of state ; who very cheerfully
and generously expressed his readiness to assist me in any
thing that might complete the history of our reformation.
121 That office was first set up by the care of the earl of Salisbury,
when he was secretary of state in king James' time : which
though it is a copious and certain repertory for those that are
to write our history ever since the papers of state were laid up
there, yet for the former times it contains only such papers as

*Collect.
Numb. 59,
60.*

---

surrendered in order to the union
or new foundation, wherein Gardiner, bishop of Winchester, then
master, did good service : who refused to surrender, and that I suppose partly upon politic reasons.
For had he parted with his old
house, he would never have been
made master of the new law-college,
though he were doctor both of the
canon, and civil law. [B.]

The two colleges of Clare Hall
and Trinity Hall could not be
brought to surrender, in order to
the uniting them.   Some visitors
were for doing it by the king's absolute power.   To this Ridley would
not agree, and for this he was complained of. [S.]

that great minister could then gather together; so that it is
not so complete in the transactions that fall within the time of
which I writ.

A contest
about pro-
nouncing
the Greek.
There was also a settlement made of the controversy concerning the Greek tongue.　There had been in king Henry's
time a great contest raised concerning the pronunciation of
the Greek vowels.　That tongue was but lately come to any
perfection in England, and so no wonder the Greek was pronounced like English, with the same sound and apertures of
the mouth: to this Mr. Cheke, then reader of that tongue in
Cambridge, opposed himself, and taught other rules of pronunciation.　Gardiner was, it seems, so afraid of every innovation,
though ever so much in the right, that he contended stiffly to
have the old pronunciation retained; and Cheke persisting in
his opinion, was either put from the chair, or willingly left it,
to avoid the indignation of so great and so spiteful a man as
Gardiner was, who was then chancellor [87] of the university.
Cheke wrote a book [88] in vindication of his way of pronouncing
Greek; of which this must be said, that it is very strange to
see how he could write with so much learning and judgment
on so bare a subject.　Redmayn, Poynet, and other learned
men, were of his side, yet more covertly: but sir Thomas
Smith, now secretary of state, writ three books on the same
argument, and did so evidently confirm Cheke's opinion, that
the dispute was now laid aside, and the true way of pronouncing the Greek took place; the rather because Gardiner was in
disgrace, and Cheke and Smith were in such power and authority: so great an influence had the interests of men in supporting the most speculative and indifferent things.

Bonner
falls into
trouble.
Soon after this, Bonner fell into new troubles; he continued
to oppose every thing as long as it was safe for him to do it,
while it was under debate, and so kept his interest with the
papists: but he complied so obediently with all the laws and
orders of council, that it was not easy to find any matter
against him.　He executed every order that was sent him so

---

[87] Cheke was not put from the
chair nor did he part with it, till
after he was sent for by the king
to instruct the prince, as appears
from the account of the life of his

successor. Nicholas Carr, p. 59 and
otherwise. [B.]

[88] [Disputatio de Pronunciatione
linguæ Græcæ.　Basil. 1555, 12mo.]

readily, that there was not so much as ground for any complaint; yet it was known he was in his heart against every thing they did, and that he cherished all that were of a contrary mind. The council being informed, that, upon the com- [Wilkins, motions that were in England, many in London withdrew from Conc. iv. 35.] the service and communion, and frequented masses, which was laid to his charge, as being negligent in the execution of the king's laws and injunctions; they writ to him, on the twenty-third of July, to see to the correcting of these things, and that he should give good example himself. Upon which, on the [Ibid. p. twenty-sixth following, he sent about a charge to execute the 36.] order in this letter, which he said he was most willing and desirous to do. Yet it was still observed, that, whatsoever obedience he gave, it was against his heart. And therefore he was called before the council on the eleventh of August. [Fox, lib. There a writing was delivered to him, complaining of his re- ix. p. 12.] missness; and particularly, that whereas he was wont formerly, tions are on all high festivals, to officiate himself, yet he had seldom or given him. never done it since the new service was set out: as also, that
122 adultery was openly practised in his diocese, which he took no care, according to his pastoral office, to restrain or punish; therefore he was strictly charged to see these things reformed. He was also ordered to preach on Sunday come three weeks at St. Paul's Cross; and that he should preach there once a [Ibid. p. quarter for the future, and be present at every sermon made 13.] there, except he were sick: that he should officiate at St. Paul's at every high festival, such as were formerly called *majus duplex*, and give the communion: that he should proceed against all who did not frequent the common-prayer, nor receive the sacrament once a year; or did go to mass: that he should search out and punish adulterers: that he should take care of the reparation of churches, and paying tithes, in his diocese, and should keep his residence in his house in London. As to his sermon, he was required to preach against rebellion, setting out the heinousness of it; he was also to shew what was true religion; and that external ceremonies were nothing in themselves, but that in the use of them men ought to obey the magistrate, and join true devotion to them; and that the king was no less king, and the people no less bound to obey, when he was in minority, than when he was of full age.

In his sermon he did not set forth the king's power under age, as he had been required to do.

On the first of September, being the day appointed for him to preach, there was a great assembly gathered to hear him. He touched upon the points that were enjoined him, excepting that about the king's age, of which he said not one word. But since the manner of Christ's presence in the sacrament was a thing which he might yet safely speak of, he spent most of his sermon on the asserting the corporal presence; which he did with many sharp reflections on those who were of another mind. There were present, among others, William Latimer, and John Hooper, soon after bishop of Gloucester, who came and informed against him, that, as he had wholly omitted that about the king's age, so he had touched the other points but slightly, and did say many other things which tended to stir up disorder and dissension. Upon this there was a commission issued out to Cranmer and Ridley, with the two secretaries of state, and Dr. May, dean of St. Paul's, to examine that matter. They or any three of them had full power by this commission to suspend, imprison, or deprive him, as they should see cause. They were to proceed in the summary way, called in their courts *de plano*.

[Sept. 8.]

Rot. Pat. 11. par. 3. reg. [ap. Rymer, xv. p. 191.]

He is proceeded against.

On the tenth of September Bonner was summoned to appear before them at Lambeth. As he came into the place where they sat, he carried himself as if he had not seen them, till one pulled him by the sleeve to put off his cap to the king's commissioners: upon which he protested he had not seen them; which none of them could believe. He spake slightingly to them of the whole matter, and turned the discourse off to the mass, which he wished were had in more reverence. When the witnesses were brought against him, he jeered them very indecently, and said, the one talked *like a goose*, and the other *like a woodcock;* and denied all they said. The archbishop asked him, Whether he would refer the matter in proof to the people that heard him? and so asked, whether any there present had heard him speak of the king's authority when under age? Many answered, No, no. Bonner looked about and laughed, saying, *Will you believe this fond people?* Some he called *dunces,* and others *fools,* and behaved himself more like a madman than a bishop. The next day he was again brought before them. Then the commission was read. The archbishop opened the matter, and desired Bonner to 123

[Fox, lib. ix. p. 22, but not in] Regist. Bonner, [fol. 222, sqq.]

His insolent behaviour.

answer for himself. He read a protestation which he had prepared, setting forth, that, since he had not seen the commission, he reserved to himself power to except, either to his judges, or to any other branch of the commission, as he should afterwards see cause. In this he called it a pretended commission, and them pretended judges, which was taxed as irreverent : but he excused it, alleging, that these were terms of law, which he must use, and so not be precluded from any objections he might afterwards make use of. The bill of complaint was next read, and the two informers appeared with their witnesses to make it good. But Bonner objected against them, that they were notorious heretics; and that the ill will they bore him was, because he had asserted the true presence of Christ in the sacrament of the altar. That Hooper in par- [Ibid. p. ticular had, in his sermon that very day on which he had 23.] preached, denied it; and had refuted and misrecited his sayings, *like an ass*, as he was *an ass indeed :* so ill did he govern his tongue. Upon this Cranmer asked him, Whether he thought Christ was in the sacrament with face, mouth, eyes, nose, and the other lineaments of his body ? and there passed some words between them on that head : but Cranmer told him, that was not a time and place to dispute; they were come to execute the king's commission. So Bonner desired to see both it and the denunciation ; which were given him : and the court adjourned till the thirteenth.

Secretary Smith sat with them at their next meeting, which [Sept. 13.] he had not done the former day, though his name was in the commission. Upon this Bonner protested, that, according to [Ibid. the canon law, none could act in a commission but those who p. 24.] were present the first day in which it was read. But to this it was alleged, that the constant practice of the kingdom had been to the contrary: that all, whose names were in any commission, might sit and judge, though they had not been present at the first opening of it. This protestation being rejected, he read his answer in writing to the accusation. He first ob- His de- jected to his accusers, that they were heretics in the matter fence. of the sacrament; and so were, according to the laws of the catholic church, under excommunication, and therefore ought not to be admitted into any Christian company. Then he denied that the injunctions given to him had been signed,

either with the king's hand or signet, or by any of his council.
[Ibid. p. 27.]
But, upon the whole matter, he said, he had in his sermon
condemned the late rebellion in Cornwall, Devonshire, and
Norfolk, and had set forth the sin of rebellion according to
several texts of scripture: he had also preached for obedience
to the king's commands; and that no ceremonies that were
contrary to them ought to be used: in particular he had exhorted the people to come to prayers, and to the communion
as it was appointed by the king, and wondered to see them so
slack in coming to it; which he believed flowed from a false
opinion they had of it. And therefore he taught, according
to that which he conceived to be the duty of a faithful pastor,
the true presence of Christ's body and blood in the sacrament;
which was the true motive of his accusers in their prosecuting
him thus. But though he had forgot to speak of the king's
power under age, yet he had said that which necessarily inferred it; for he had condemned the late rebels for rising
against their lawful king, and had applied many texts of scripture to them, which clearly implied, that the king's power was 124
then entire, otherwise they could not be rebels.

These are rejected.
But to all this it was answered, that it was of no great consequence who were the informers, if the witnesses were such
that he could not except against them. Besides, they were
empowered by their commission to proceed *ex officio;* so that
it was not necessary for them to have any to accuse. He was
told, that the injunctions were read to him in council by one
of the secretaries, and then were given to him by the protector himself; that afterwards they were called for, and that
article concerning the king's power before he came to be of
age being added, they were given him again by secretary
Smith; and he promised to execute them. He was also told,
that it was no just excuse for him to say he had forgot that
about the king's power; since it was the chief thing pretended by the late rebels, and was mainly intended by the
council in their injunctions; so that it was a poor shift for
him to pretend he had forgot it, or had spoken of it by a consequence.

[Ibid. p. 28.]
The court adjourned to the sixteenth day: and then Latimer
and Hooper offered to purge themselves of the charge of
heresy, since they had never spoken nor written of the sacra-

ment but according to the scripture. And whereas Bonner
had charged them, that on the first of September they had
entered into consultation and confederacy against him; they
protested they had not seen each other that day, nor been
known to one another till some days after. Bonner upon
this read some passages of the sacrament out of a book of
Hooper's, whom he called, *that varlet*. But Cranmer cut
off the discourse, and said, it was not their business to determine that point; and said to the people, that the bishop
of London was not accused for any thing he had said about
the sacrament. Then Bonner, turning to speak to the people,
was interrupted by one of the delegates, who told him, he was
to speak to them, and not to the people : at which some laughing, he turned about in great fury, and said, *Ah woodcocks !
woodcocks !* But to the chief point he said he had prepared
notes of what he intended to say about the king's power in his [Ibid. p.
minority, from the instances in scripture of Ahaz and Uzziah, 29.]
who were kings at ten; of Solomon and Manasseh, who reigned
at twelve; and of Josiah, Jehoiachin, and Joash, who began to
reign when they were but eight years old. He had also
gathered out of the English history, that Henry the Third,
Edward the Third, Richard the Second, Henry the Sixth, and
Edward the Fifth, were all under age; and even their late
king was but eighteen when he came to the crown: and yet
all these were obeyed as much before, as after they were of
full age. But these things had escaped his memory, he not
having been much used to preach. There had been also a
long bill sent him from the council to be read, of the defeat of
the rebels, which he said had disordered him; and the book
in which he had laid his notes fell out of his hands when he
was in the pulpit : for this he appealed to his two chaplains,
Bourn and Harpsfield, whom he had desired to gather for him
the names of those kings who reigned before they were of age.
For the other injunctions, he had taken care to execute them, [Ibid. p.
and had sent orders to his archdeacons to see to them; and, 30.]
as far as he understood, there were no masses, nor service in
Latin, within his diocese, except at the lady Mary's, or in the
chapels of ambassadors. But the delegates required him posi-
125 tively to answer, whether he had obeyed that injunction about
the king's authority, or not; otherwise they would hold him

as guilty. And if he denied it, they would proceed to the examination of the witnesses. He refusing to answer otherwise than he had done, they called the witnesses, who were, sir John Cheke, and four more, who had their oaths given them: and Bonner desiring a time to prepare his interrogatories, it was granted. So he drew a long paper of twenty interrogatories, every one of them containing many branches in it, full of all the niceties of the canon law; a taste of which may be had from the third in number, which is indeed the most material of all. The interrogatory was, " Whether they, or " any of them, were present at his sermon; where they stood, " and near whom; when they came to it, and at what part of " his sermon; how long they tarried; at what part they were " offended; what were the formal words, or substance of it; " who with them did hear it; where the other witnesses stood, " and how long they tarried, or when they departed?"

[Ibid. p. 31.]

The court adjourned to the eighteenth of September: and then there was read a declaration from the king, explaining their former commission, chiefly in the point of the denunciation, that that they might proceed either that way, or *ex officio*, as they saw cause; giving them also power finally to determine the matter, cutting off all superfluous delays. Bonner gave in also some other reasons why he should not be obliged to make a more direct answer to the articles objected against him: the chief of which was, that the article about the king's age was not in the paper given him by the protector, but afterwards added by secretary Smith of his own head. Cranmer admonished him of his irreverence, since he called them always his *pretended* judges. Smith added, that though proctors did so in common matters for their clients, yet it was not to be endured in such a case, when he saw they acted by a special commission from the king. New articles were given him, more explicit and plain than the former, but to the same purpose. And five witnesses were sworn upon these, who were all the clerks of the council, to prove that the article about the king's age was ordered by the whole council, and only put in writing by secretary Smith, at their command. He was appointed to come next day, and make his answer. But on the nineteenth two of his servants came, and told the delegates, that he was sick, and could not attend. It was therefore ordered, that the

[Wilkins, Conc. iv. 37.]

[Fox, lib. ix. p. 33.]

knight-marshal should go to him, and, if he were sick, let him alone; but if it were not so, should bring him before them next day. On the twentieth, Bonner appearing, answered as [Ibid. p. he had done formerly; only he protested, that it was his 35.] opinion, that the king was as much a king, and the people as much bound to obey him, before he was of age, as after it: and after that, secretary Smith having taken him up more sharply than the other delegates, he protested against him as He pro- no competent judge, since he had expressed much passion tests a- gainst against him, and had not heard him patiently, but had com- secretary pared him to thieves and traitors, and had threatened to send Smith. him to the Tower, to sit with Kett and Arundel: and that he had added some things to the injunctions given him by the protector, for which he was now accused, and did also proceed to judge him, notwithstanding his protestation, grounded on his not being present when the commission was first opened 126 and received by the court. But this protestation also was re- jected by the delegates: and Smith told him, that whereas he took exception at his saying, that he acted as thieves and traitors do; it was plainly visible in his doings: upon which Bonner, being much inflamed, said to him, that, as he was [Ibid. p. secretary of state, and a privy counsellor, he honoured him; 36.] but as he was sir Thomas Smith, he told him, he lied, and that he defied him. At this the archbishop chid him, and said, he deserved to be sent to prison for such irreverent carriage. He answered, he did not care whither they sent him, so they sent him not to the Devil, for thither he would not go. He had a few goods, a poor carcase, and a soul; the two former were in their power, but the last was in his own. After this, being made to withdraw, he, when called in again, put in an appeal from them to the king, and read an instrument of it, which he had prepared at his own house that morning; and so would make no other answer, unless the secretary should remove. For this contempt he was sent to the prison of the Marshalsea; and as he was led away he broke out in great passion, both against Smith and also at Cranmer, for suffering heretics to infect the people; which he required him to abstain from, as he would answer for it to God and the king.

On the twenty-third he was again brought before them; [Ibid. p. where, by a second instrument, he adhered to his former 38.]

appeal. But the delegates said, they would go on and judge him, unless there came a *supersedeas* from the king; and so required him to answer those articles which he had not yet answered, otherwise they would proceed against him as *contumax*, and hold him as *confessing*: but he adhered to his appeal, and so would answer no more. New matter was also brought, of his going out of St. Paul's in the midst of the sermon on the fifteenth of the month, and so giving a public disturbance and scandal; and of his writing next day to the lord mayor, not to suffer such preachers to sow their ill doctrine. This was occasioned by the preacher's speaking against the corporal presence of Christ in the sacrament. But he would give the court no account of that matter; so they adjourned to the twenty-seventh, and from that to the first of October. In that time great endeavours were used to persuade him to submit, and to behave himself better for the future; and upon that condition he was assured he should be gently used: but he would yield to nothing. So on the first of October, when he was brought before them, the archbishop told him, they had delayed so long, being unwilling to proceed to extremities with him; and therefore wished him to submit. But he read another writing, by which he protested, that he was brought before them by force; and that otherwise he would not have come, since, that having appealed from them, he looked on them as his judges no more. He said, that he had also written a petition to the lord chancellor, complaining of the delegates, and desiring that his appeal might be admitted; and said, by that appeal it was plain, that he esteemed the king to be clothed with his full royal power now that he was under age, since he thus appealed to him. Upon which the archbishop, the bishop of Rochester, secretary Smith, and the dean of St. Paul's, gave sentence against him; that since he had not declared the king's power while under age in his sermon, as he was commanded by the protector and council, therefore the archbishop, with the consent and assent of his colleagues, did deprive him of the bishopric of London. Sentence being thus given, he appealed again by word of mouth. The court did also order him to be carried to prison till the king should consider further of it. This account of his trial is drawn from the register of London, where all these particulars

[Ibid. p. 39.]

[Ibid. p. 40.]

He is deprived from his bishopric.

Sen- 127

[Oct. 4. ibid. p. 41.]

are inserted. From thence it was that Fox printed them. For Bonner, though he was afterwards commissioned by the queen to deface any records that made against the catholic cause, yet did not care to alter any thing in this register, after his re-admission in queen Mary's time. It seems he was not displeased with what he found recorded of himself in this matter.

Thus was Bonner deprived of his bishopric of London. This judgment, as all such things are, was much censured. It was said, it was not canonical, since it was by a commission from the king, and since secular men were mixed with clergymen in the censure of a bishop. To this it was answered, that the sentence being only of deprivation from the see of London, it was not so entirely an ecclesiastical censure, but was of a mixed nature, so that laymen might join in it. And since he had taken a commission from the king for his bishopric, by which he held it only during the king's pleasure, he could not complain of this deprivation, which was done by the king's authority. Others, who looked further back, remembered that Constantine the emperor had appointed secular men to inquire into some things objected to bishops, who were called *cognitores,* or *triers :* and such had examined the business of Cecilian bishop of Carthage, even upon an appeal, after it had been tried in several synods, and given judgment against Donatus and his party. The same Constantine had also by his authority put Eustathius out of Antioch, Athanasius out of Alexandria, and Paul out of Constantinople : and though the orthodox bishops complained of these particulars, as done unjustly, at the false suggestion of the Arians, yet they did not deny the emperor's authority in such cases. Afterwards, the emperors used to have some bishops attending on them in their *comitatus,* or court, to whose judgment they left most causes, who acted only by commission from the emperor. So Epiphanius was brought to condemn Chrysostom at Constantinople, who had no authority to judge him by the canons. Others objected, that it was too severe to deprive Bonner for a defect in his memory ; and that therefore they should have given him a new trial in that point, and not have proceeded to censure him on such an omission, since he protested it was not on design, but a pure forgetfulness : and all people perceived clearly, it had been beforehand resolved to lay him aside ; and

Censures passed upon it.

that therefore they now took him on this disadvantage, and so deprived him. But it was also well known, that all the papists infused this notion into the people, of the king's having no power till he came to be of age: and he being certainly one of them, there was reason to conclude, that what he said for his defence was only a pretence; and that it was of design that he had omitted the mentioning the king's power when under age. The adding of imprisonment to his deprivation was thought by some to be an extreme accumulation of punishments: but that was no more than what he drew upon himself by his rude and contemptuous behaviour. However, it seems that some of these objections wrought on secretary Petre; for he never sat with the delegates after the first day, and he was now turning about to another party.

On the other hand, Bonner was little pitied by most that 128 knew him. He was a cruel and fierce man: he understood little of divinity, his learning being chiefly in the canon law. Besides, he was looked on generally as a man of no principles. All the obedience he gave, either to the laws or the king's injunctions, was thought a compliance against his conscience, extorted by fear. And his indecent carriage during his process had much exposed him to the people; so that it was not thought to be hard dealing, though the proceedings against him were summary and severe. Nor did his carriage afterwards, during his imprisonment, discover much of a bishop or a Christian: for he was more concerned to have puddings and pears sent him, than for any thing else. This I gather from some original letters of his to Richard Lechmore, esq. in Worcestershire, (which were communicated to me by his heir lineally descended from him, the worshipful Mr. Lechmore, now the senior bencher of the Middle Temple;) of which I tran-
Collect.
Numb. 37. scribed the latter part of one, that will be found in the Collection. In it he desires a large quantity of pears and puddings to be sent him; otherwise he gives those to whom he writes an odd sort of benediction, very unlike what became a man of his character: he gives them *to the Devil, to the Devil,* and *to all the devils,* if they did not furnish him well with pears and puddings. It may perhaps be thought indecent to print such letters, being the privacies of friendship, which ought not to be made public: but I confess Bonner was so brutish, and so

bloody a man, that I was not ill pleased to meet with any thing that might set him forth in his natural colours to the world.

Thus did the affairs of England go on this summer within the kingdom : but it will be now necessary to consider the state of our affairs in foreign parts. The king of France, finding it was very chargeable to carry on the war wholly in Scotland, resolved this year to lessen that expense, and to make war directly with England, both at sea and land. So he came in person with a great army, and fell into the country of Boulogne, where he took many little castles about the town ; as Sellacque, Blackness, Ambleteuse, Newhaven, and some lesser ones. The English writers say those were ill provided, which made them be so easily lost : but Thuanus says, they were all very well stored. In the night they assaulted Boulognebourg, but were beat off : then they designed to burn the ships that were in the harbour, and had prepared wildfire, with other combustible matter, but were driven away by the English. At the same time, the French fleet met the English fleet at Jersey ; but, as king Edward writes in his diary, they were beat off with the loss of one thousand men ; though Thuanus puts the loss wholly on the English side. The French king sat down before Boulogne in September, hoping that the disorders then in England would make that place be ill supplied, and easily yielded. The English, finding Boulognebourg was not tenable, razed it, and retired into the town ; but the plague broke into the French camp, so the king left it under the command of Châtillon. He endeavoured chiefly to take the pier, and so to cut off the town from the sea, and from all communication with England ; and, after a long battery, he gave the assault upon it, but was beat off. There followed many skirmishes between him and the garrison, and he made many attempts to close up the channel, and thought to have sunk a galley full of stones 129 and gravel in it ; but in all these he was still unsuccessful. And therefore, winter coming on, the siege was raised ; only the forts about the town, which the French had taken, were strongly garrisoned ; so that Boulogne was in danger of being lost the next year.

In Scotland also the English affairs declined much this year. Thermes, before the winter was ended, had taken Broughty Castle, and destroyed almost the whole garrison. In the

Marginal notes:
Foreign affairs.

The French take many places about Boulogne.

[Thuanus, vi. 5. p. 206.]

The English unsuccessful in Scotland.

southern parts there was a change made of the lords wardens of the English marches. Sir Robert Bowes was complained of as negligent in relieving Haddington the former year; so the lord Dacres was put in his room. And the lord Grey, who lost the great advantage he had when the French raised the siege of Haddington, was removed, and the earl of Rutland was sent to command. The earl made an inroad into Scotland, and supplied Haddington plentifully with all sorts of provisions necessary for a siege. He had some Germans and Spaniards with him: but a party of Scotch horse surprised the Germans' baggage; and Romero, with the Spanish troop, was also fallen on and taken, and almost all his men were cut off. The earl of Warwick was to have marched with a more considerable army this summer into Scotland, had not the disorders in England diverted him, as it has been already shown. Thermes did not much more this year. He intended once to have renewed the siege of Haddington; but, when he understood how well they were furnished, he gave it over. But the English council, finding how great a charge the keeping of it was, and the country all about it being destroyed, so that no provisions could be had but what were brought from England, from which it was twenty-eight miles distant, resolved to withdraw their garrison, and quit it, which was done on the first of October; so that the English having now no garrison within Scotland but Lauder, Thermes sat down before that, and pressed it so, that, had not the peace been made up with France, it had fallen into his hands.

Things being in this disorder both at home and abroad, the protector had nothing to depend on but the emperor's aid; and he was so ill satisfied with the changes that had been made in religion, that much was not to be expected from him. The confusions this year occasioned that change to be made in the office of the daily prayers; where the answer to the petition, *Give peace in our time, O Lord*, which was formerly, and is still continued, was now made, *Because there is none other that fighteth for us, but only thou, O God*[83]. For now the emperor, having reduced all the princes, and most of the cities of Germany, to his obedience, none but Magdeburg and Bre-

[83] This, my lord, I do not well understand; for this petition and answer stand in the first liturgy of Edward the Sixth, fol. 4. [B.]

men standing out, did by a mistake incident to great conquerors neglect those advantages which were then in his hands,
and did not prosecute his victories; but, leaving Germany,
came this summer into the Netherlands, whither he had ordered his son prince Philip to come from Spain to him, through
Italy and Germany, that he might put him into possession of
these provinces, and make them swear homage to him. Whether
at this time the emperor was beginning to form the design of
retiring, or whether he did this only to prevent the mutinies
and revolts that might fall out upon his death, if his son were
not in actual possession of them, is not so certain.   One thing
is memorable in that transaction, that was called the *lætus
introitus*, or the terms upon which he was received prince of
130 Brabant, to which the other provinces had been formerly
united into one principality : after many rules and limitations
of government, in the matter of taxes and public assemblies,
the not keeping up of forces, and governing them not by
strangers, but by natives, it was added, " that, if he broke Cott. Lib.
" these conditions, it should be free for them not to obey him, Galba B.
" or acknowledge him any longer, till he returned to govern 46-72.]
" according to their laws."   This was afterwards the chief
ground on which they justified their shaking off the Spanish
yoke; all these conditions being publicly violated.

At this time there were great jealousies in the emperor's Jealousies
family.   For as he intended to have had his brother resign arise in the
his election to be king of the Romans, that it might be trans- emperor's
ferred on his own son; so there were designs in Flanders, family.
which the French cherished much, to have Maximilian, Ferdinand's son, the most accomplished and virtuous prince that had
been for many ages, to be made their prince.   The Flemings
were much disgusted with the queen regent's government,
who, when there was need of money, sent to Bruges and Antwerp, ordering deputies to be sent her from Flanders and
Brabant : and when they were come, she told them what
money must be raised; and if they made any objections, she
used to bid them give over merchandising with the emperor,
for he must and would have the money he asked; so that nothing remained to them, but to see how to raise what was thus
demanded of them, rather than desired from them.   This, as
the English ambassador writ from Bruges, seemed to be the

reason that moved the emperor to make his son swear to such
rules of government; which the sequel of his life shewed he
meant to observe in the same manner that his father had done
before him. At the same time, in May this year, I find a
secret advertisement was sent over from France to the English
court, that there was a private treaty set on foot between that
king and the princes of Germany for restoring the liberty of
the empire; but that the king of France was resolved to have
Boulogne in his hands before he entered on new projects.
Therefore it was proposed to the protector, to consider whether
it were not best to deliver it up by a treaty, and so to leave
the king of France free to the defence of their friends in the
empire; for I find the consideration of the protestant religion
was the chief measure of our councils all this reign.

A great
faction
against the
protector. Upon this there was great distraction in the councils at
home. The protector was inclined to deliver up Boulogne for
a sum of money, and to make peace both with the French and
Scots. The king's treasure was exhausted, affairs at home
were in great confusion, the defence of Boulogne was a great
charge, and a war with France was a thing of that consequence, that, in that state of affairs, it was not to be adventured on. But, on the other hand, those who hated the protector, and measured counsels more by the bravery than the
solidity of them, said it would be a reproach to the nation to
deliver up a place of that consequence, which their late king,
in the declining of his days, had gained with so much loss of
men and treasure; and to sell this for a little money was accounted so sordid, that the protector durst not adventure on it.

Paget's ad-
vice about
foreign af-
fairs. Upon this occasion I find sir William Paget (being made comptroller of the king's household, which was then thought an
advancement from the office of a secretary of state) made a
long discourse, and put it in writing: the substance of it was,

Cott. Lib.
Titus, B.
[ii. fol. 91.] to balance the dangers in which England was at that time. 131
The business of Scotland and Boulogne drew France into a
quarrel against it. On the account of religion, it had no reason
to expect much from the emperor. The interest of England
was then to preserve the protestants of Germany, and therefore to unite with France; which would be easily engaged in
that quarrel against the emperor. He proposed a firm alliance
with the Venetians, who were then jealous of the emperor's

progress in Italy, and would be ready to join against him, if
he were thoroughly engaged in Germany ; and by their means
England was to make up an agreement with France.   On the
other hand, William Thomas, then a clerk of the council, writ Thomas's
a long discourse of other expedients.   He agreed with Paget advice differs from
as to the ill state of England, having many enemies, and no this.
friends.   The north of England was wasted by the incursion of MSS.Vesp.
the Scots.   Ireland was also in an ill condition ; for the natives D. xviii.
[fol. 35.]
there did generally join with the Scots, being addicted to the
old superstition.   The emperor was so set on reducing all to
one religion, that they could expect no great aid from him,
unless they gave him some hope of returning to the Roman
religion.   But the continuance of the war would undo the
nation : for if the war went on, the people would take advantage from it to break out into new disorders ; it would be also
very dishonourable to deliver up, or rather to sell, the late conquests in France.   Therefore he proposed, that, to gain time,
they should treat with the emperor, and even give him hopes
of re-examining what had been done in religion ; though there
was danger even in that of disheartening those of Magdeburg, [Ibid. fol.
and a few remaining protestants in Germany ; as also they 40.]
might expect the emperor would be highly enraged when he
should come to find that he had been deluded : but the gaining
of time was then so necessary, that the preservation of the
nation depended on it.   For Scotland, he proposed, that the [Ibid. fol.
governor of that kingdom should be pressed to pretend to the 41.]
crown, since their queen was gone into a strange country : by
this means Scotland would be for that whole age separated
from the interests of France, and obliged to depend on England.   And the French were now so hated in Scotland, that
any who would set up against them would have an easy work,
especially being assisted by the nearness of England.   And for
Ireland, he proposed, that the chief heads of families should be
drawn over, and kept at court : and that England thus being
respited from foreign war, the nation should be armed and exercised, the coin reformed, treasure laid up, and things in the
government at home, that were uneasy, should be corrected.

Thus I have opened the counsels at that time, as I found
them laid before me in these authentic papers, from which I
drew them.   The result of their consultation was, to send over

Paget sent
over to
treat with
the em-
peror.
Collect.
Numb. 38.
sir William Paget to join with sir Philip Hobby, then resident at the emperor's court. His instructions will be found in the Collection. The substance of them was, that the treaty between the emperor and the late king should be renewed with this king, and confirmed by the prince and the states of Flanders; that some ambiguous passages in it should be cleared; that the emperor would comprehend Boulogne within the league defensive, and so protect it, England being ready to offer any thing reciprocal in the room of it. He was also to show their readiness to agree to the emperor concerning the lady Mary's mar- 132 riage; to adjust some differences occasioned by the complaints made of the admiralty, and about trade; to shew the reason of the messages that passed between them and France; and to engage, that, if the emperor would heartily assist them, they would never agree with France. Paget was also to propose, as of himself, that Boulogne should be put into the emperor's hands, upon a reasonable recompense. Thus was Paget instructed, and sent over in June this year. But the emperor put him off with many delays, and said, the carrying of his son about the towns in Flanders and Brabant, with the many ceremonies and entertainments that followed it, made it not easy for him to consider of matters that required such deep consultation. He put him off from Brussels to Ghent, and from Ghent to Bruges. But Paget growing impatient of such delays, since the French were marched into the Boulognois, the bishop of Arras, (son to Granvelle, that had been long the emperor's chief minister,) who was now like to succeed in his father's room, that was old and infirm, and the two presidents of the emperor's councils, St. Maurice and Viglius, came to sir William Paget, and had a long communication with him and Hobby; an account whereof will be found in the Collection, in a despatch from them to the protector.

Collect.
Numb. 39.

He meets
with the
emperor's
ministers.
They first treated of an explanation of some ambiguous words in the treaty, to which the emperor's ministers promised to bring them an answer. Then they talked long of the matters of the admiralty; the emperor's ministers said, no justice was done in England upon the merchants' complaints. Paget said, every mariner came to the protector, and if he would not solicit their business, they ran away with a complaint that there was no justice; whereas he thought, that, as

they meddled with no private matters, so the protector ought
to turn all these over upon the courts, that were the competent
judges. But the bishop of Arras said, there was no justice to
be had in the admiralty courts, who were indeed parties in all
these matters. Paget said, there was as much justice in the
English admiralty courts as was in theirs; and the bishop
confessed there were great corruptions in all these courts. So
Paget proposed, that the emperor should appoint two of his
council to hear and determine all such complaints in a summary way, and the king should do the like in England. For
the confirmation of the treaty, the bishop said, the emperor
was willing his son should confirm it; but that he would never
sue to his subjects to confirm his treaties: and he said, when it
was objected that the treaty with France was confirmed by the
three estates, that the prerogative of the French crown was so
restrained that the king could alienate nothing of his patrimony
without the parliament of Paris, and his three estates. He believed the king of England had a greater prerogative: he was
sure the emperor was not so bound up: he had fifteen or sixteen several parliaments, and what work must he be at, if all
these must descant on his transactions? When this general
discourse was over, the two presidents went away, but the
bishop of Arras stayed with him in private. Paget proposed
the business of Boulogne: but the bishop, having given him
many good words in the general, excepted much to it, as dishonourable to the emperor, since Boulogne was not taken
when the league was concluded between the emperor and
133 England; so that if he should now include it in the league, it
would be a breach of faith and treaties with France: and he
stood much on the honour and conscience of observing these
treaties inviolably. So this conversation ended: in which the
most remarkable passage is that concerning the limitations on
the French crown, and the freedoms of the English; for at that
time the king's prerogative in England was judged of that extent, that I find, in a letter written from Scotland, one of the
main objections made to the marrying their queen to the king
of England was, that an union with England would much alter
the constitution of their government, the prerogatives of the
kings of England being of a far larger extent than those in
Scotland.

Two or three days after the former conversation, the emperor's ministers returned to Paget's lodging, with answer to
the propositions which the English ambassador had made: of
Collect.
Numb. 40. which a full account will be found in the Collection, in the
letter which the ambassadors writ upon it into England. The
emperor gave a good answer to some of the particulars, which
were ambiguous in former treaties. For the confirmation of
the treaty, he offered that the prince should join in it; but
since the king of England was under age, he thought it more
necessary that the parliament of England should confirm it.
To which Paget answered, that their kings, as to the regal
power, were the same in all the conditions of life: and therefore, when the great seal was put to any agreement, the king
was absolutely bound by it. If his ministers engaged him in
ill treaties, they were to answer for it at their perils; but howsoever, the king was tied by it. They discoursed long about
the administration of justice, but ended in nothing. And as
for the main business about Boulogne, the emperor stood on
his treaties with the French, which he could not break: upon
which Paget said to the bishop, that his father had told him,
they had so many grounds to quarrel with France, that he had
his sleeve full of them, to produce when there should be occasion to make use of them. But, finding the bishop's answers
were cold, and that he only gave good words, he told him,
that England would then see to their own security: and so he
took that for the emperor's final answer, and thereupon resolved to take his leave, which he did soon after, and came
back into England. But at home the councils were much divided, of which the sad effects broke out soon afterward.

Debates in
council
concerning
peace.

It was proposed in council, that the war with Scotland should
be ended. For it having been begun, and carried on, only on
design to obtain the marriage, since the hopes of that were
now so far gone, that it was not in the power of the Scots
themselves to retrieve them, it was a vain and needless expense
both of blood and money to keep it up. And since Boulogne
was by the treaty after a few more years to be delivered up to
the French, it seemed a very unreasonable thing, in the low
state to which the king's affairs were driven, to enter on a
war, in which they had little reason to doubt but they should
lose Boulogne, after a new expense of a siege, and another

year's war. The protector had now many enemies, who laid hold on this conjuncture to throw him out of the government. The earl of Southampton was brought into the council, but had not laid down his secret hatred of the protector, and did all he could to make a party against him. The earl of War-

134 wick was the fittest man to work on : him therefore he gained over to his side; and, having formed a confidence in him, he shewed him that he had really got all these victories, for which the protector triumphed : he had won the field of Pinkey near Musselburgh, and had subdued the rebels of Norfolk; and as he had before defeated the French, so, if he were sent over thither, new triumphs would follow him : but it was below him to be second to any. So he engaged him to quarrel in every thing with the protector, all whose wary motions were ascribed to fear or dulness. To others he said, What friendship could any expect from a man who had no pity on his own brother ? But that which provoked the nobility most was, the partiality the protector had for the commons in the insurrections that had been this summer. He had also given great grounds of jealousy, by entertaining foreign troops in the king's wars; which, though it was not objected to him, because the council had consented to it, yet it was whispered about, that he had extorted that consent : but the noble palace he was raising in the Strand, (which yet carries his name,) out of the ruins of some bishops' houses and churches, drew as public an envy on him as any thing he had done. It was said, that when the king was engaged in such wars, and when London was much disordered by the plague that had been in it for some months, he was then bringing architects from Italy, and designing such a palace as had not been seen in England. It was also said, that many bishops and cathedrals had resigned many manors to him for obtaining his favour. Though this was not done without leave obtained from the king; for in a grant of some lands made to him by the king on the eleventh of July, in the second year of his reign, it is said, that these lands were given him as a reward of his services in Scotland, for which he was offered greater rewards; but that he, refusing to accept of such grants as might too much impoverish the crown, had taken a license to the bishop of Bath and Wells for his alienating some of the lands of that bishopric to him : he is in that

Complaints against the protector.

Rot. Pat. 4. par. 2. reg.

patent called by the *grace of God* duke of Somerset, which
had not of late years been ascribed to any but sovereign
princes.   It was also said, that many of the chantry lands had
been sold to his friends at easy rates, for which they concluded
he had great presents ; and a course of unusual greatness had
raised him up too high, so that he did not carry himself towards the nobility with that equality that they expected from
him.

All these things concurred to beget him many enemies;
and he had very few friends, for none stuck firmly to him, but
Paget and secretary Smith, and especially Cranmer, who never
forsook his friend.   All that favoured the old superstition were
his enemies ; and, seeing the earl of Southampton heading the
party against him, they all ran in to it.   And of the bishops
that were for the reformation, Goodrich of Ely likewise joined
to them : he had attended on the admiral in his preparations
for death, from whom, it seems, he drank in ill impressions of
the protector.   All his enemies saw, and he likewise saw it
himself, that the continuance of the war must needs destroy
him ; and that a peace would confirm him in his power, and
give him time and leisure to break through the faction that
was now so strong against him, that it was not probable he
could master it without the help of some time.   So in the
council his adversaries delivered their opinions against all mo- 135
tions for peace ; and though, upon Paget's return from Flanders, it appeared to be very unreasonable to carry on the war,
yet they said, Paget had secret instructions to procure such
an answer, that it might give a colour to so base a project.
The officers, that came over from these places that the French
had taken, pretended, as is common for all men in such circumstances, that they wanted things necessary for a siege ;
[Thuanus, and though in truth it was quite contrary, (as we read in
vi. 5. p.
216.] Thuanus,) yet their complaints were cherished and spread
about among the people.   The protector had also, against the
mind of the council, ordered the garrison to be drawn out of
Haddington, and was going, notwithstanding all their opposition, to make peace with France, and did in many things act
by his own authority, without asking their advice, and often
against it.   This was the assuming a regal power, and seemed
not to be endured by those who thought they were in all

points his equals. It was also said, that when, contrary to
the late king's will, he was chosen protector, it was with that
special condition, that he should do nothing without their consent; and though, by the patent he had for his office, his [Rymer,
power was more enlarged, (which was of greater force in law xv. p. 174.]
than a private agreement at the council-table,) yet even that
was objected to him as an high presumption in him to pretend
to such a vast power. Thus all the month of September there
were great heats among them : several persons interposed to
mediate, but to no effect; for the faction against him was now
so strong, that they resolved to strip him of his exorbitant
power, and reduce him to an equality with themselves. The
king was then at Hampton-Court, where also the protector
was, with some of his own retainers and servants about him,
which increased the jealousies; for it was given out, that he
intended to carry away the king. So on the sixth of October Most of the
some of the council met at Ely-house; the lord St. John, pre- council separate from
sident; the earls of Warwick, Arundel, and Southampton; sir him.
Edward North, sir Richard Southwell, sir Edmund Peckham, Book, p. 1.]
[Council
sir Edward Wotton, and Dr. Wotton; and secretary Petre
being sent to them, in the king's name, to ask what they met
for, joined himself likewise to them. They sat as the king's
council, and entered their proceedings in the council-book,
from whence I draw the account of this transaction.

These being met together, and considering the disorders
that had been lately in England, the losses in Scotland and
France, laid the blame of all on the protector, who, they said,
was given up to other counsels so obstinately, that he would
not hearken to the advices they had given him, both at the
board and in private : and they declared, that, having intended
that day to have gone to Hampton-Court, for a friendly communication with him, he had raised many of the commons to
have destroyed them, and had made the king set his hand to
the letters he had sent for raising men, and had also dispersed
seditious bills against them; therefore they intended to see to
the safety of the king and the kingdom. So they sent for the [Ibid. p. 2.]
lord mayor and aldermen of London, and required them to
obey no letters sent them by the protector, but only such as
came from themselves. They also writ many letters to the [Ibid. p. 3.]
nobility and gentry over England, giving them an account of

their designs and motives, and requiring their assistance. They
also sent for the lieutenant of the Tower, and he submitted to
their orders. Next day, the lord chancellor, the marquis of 136
Northampton, the earl of Shrewsbury, sir Thomas Cheyney, sir
John Gage, sir Ralph Sadler, and the lord chief-justice Montague, joined with them. Then they wrote to the king a
letter, (which is in the Collection,) full of expressions of their
duty and care of his person, complaining of the duke of Somerset's not listening to their counsels, and of his gathering a
force about him for maintaining his wilful doings; they owned
that they had caused secretary Petre to stay with them, and
in it they endeavoured to persuade the king, that they were
careful of nothing so much as of his preservation. They also
wrote to the archbishop of Canterbury, and to sir William
Paget, to see to the king's person, and that his own servants
should attend on him, and not those that belonged to the duke
of Somerset. But the protector, hearing of this disorder, had
removed the king to Windsor in all haste; and had taken
down all the armour that was either there, or at Hampton-
Court, and had armed such as he could gather about him for
his preservation.

The council at London complained much of this, that the
king should be carried to a place where there were no provisions fit for him: so they ordered all things that he might
need, to be sent to him from London. And on the eighth of
October they went to Guildhall, where they gave an account
of their proceedings to the common-council of the city; and
assured them, they had no thoughts of altering the religion,
as was given out by their enemies, but intended only the safety
of the king, and the peace of the kingdom: and for these ends
desired their assistance. The whole common-council with one
voice declared, they thanked God for the good intentions
they had expressed, and assured them they would stand by
them with their lives and goods. At Windsor, when the protector understood that not only the city, but the lieutenant of
the Tower, of whom he had held himself assured, had forsaken
him, he resolved to struggle no longer; and though it is not
improbable that he, who was chiefly accused for his protecting
the commons, might have easily gathered a great body of men
for his own preservation; yet he resolved rather to give way

Marginal notes:

[Oct. 7.
Ibid. p. 4.]

Collect.
Numb. 41.

[Oct. 7.
Ibid. p. 6.]

[Ibid. p. 8.]

[Ibid. p. 7.]

The city
of London
joins with
them.

to the tide that was now against him. So he protested before
the king, and the few counsellors then about him, that he had
no design against any of the lords; and that the force he had
gathered was only to preserve himself from any violent attempt that might be made on his person. He declared, that
he was willing to submit himself; and therefore proposed, that
two of those lords should be sent from London, and they, with
two of those that were yet about the king, should consider
what might be done; in whose determination he would acquiesce: and desired, that whatsoever was agreed on should
be confirmed in parliament. Hereupon there was sent to
London a warrant under the king's hand, for any two of the
lords of the council that were there, to come to Windsor, with
twenty servants apiece, who had the king's faith for their
safety in coming and going: and Cranmer, Paget, and Smith
wrote to them to dispose them to end the matter peaceably,
and not follow cruel counsels, nor to be misled by them who
meant otherwise than they professed, of which they knew
more than they would then mention. This seemed to point at
the earl of Southampton.

The protector offers to treat and submit. Collect. Numb. 42.

137 On the ninth of October the council at London increased by
the accession of the lord Russell, the lord Wentworth, sir
Anthony Browne, sir Anthony Wingfield, and sir John Baker,
the speaker of the house of commons. For now, those who
had stood off a while, seeing the protector was resolved to
yield, came and united themselves with the prevailing party;
so that they were in all two and twenty. They were informed
that the protector had said, that, if they intended to put him
to death, the king should die first; and if they would famish
him, they should famish the king first: and that he had armed
his own men, and set them next to the king's person, and was
designing to carry him out of Windsor, and, as some reported,
out of the kingdom: upon which they concluded, that he was
no more fit to be protector. But of those words no proofs
being mentioned in the council-books, they look like the forgeries of his enemies to make him odious to the people. The
council ordered a proclamation of their proceedings to be
printed; and writ to the lady Mary and the lady Elizabeth,
acquainting them with what they had done. They also wrote
to the king, (as will be found in the Collection,) acknowledg-

[Ibid. p. 8.]

[Ibid. p. 12.]

[Ibid.]

Collect. Numb. 43.

ing the many bonds that lay on them in gratitude, both for
his father's goodness to them, and his own, to take care of
him. They desired he would consider they were his whole
council, except one or two, and were those whom his father
had trusted with the government; that the protector was not
raised to that power by his father's will, but by their choice,
with that condition, that he should do all things by their advice; which he had not observed, so that they now judged
him most unworthy of these honours: therefore they earnestly
desired they might be admitted to the king's presence, to do
their duties about him; and that the forces gathered about
his person might be sent away, and the duke of Somerset
might submit himself to the order of council. They also wrote
Collect.
Numb. 44. to the archbishop and sir William Paget, (which is in the Collection,) charging them, as they would answer it, that the
king's person might be well looked to, that he should not be
removed from Windsor, and that he should be no longer
guarded by the duke of Somerset's men, (as they said he had
been, of which they complained severely,) but by his own
sworn servants; and they required them to concur in advancing the desire they had signified by their letter to the king,
protesting that they would do with the duke of Somerset as
they would desire to be done by, and with as much moderation and favour as in honour they could; so that there was no
reason to apprehend from them such cruelty as they had mentioned in their letters. These were sent by sir Philip Hobby,
who was returned from Flanders, and had been sent by the
[Ibid. p.
13.] king to London on the day before. Upon this, Cranmer and
Paget (as is entered in the council-book) persuaded both the
king and the protector to grant their desire. The protector's
servants were dismissed, and the king's were set about his person. And Cranmer, Paget, and Smith wrote to the council
at London, that all they had proposed should be granted:
they desired to know whether the king should be brought to
London, or stay at Windsor; and that three of the lords might
be sent thither, who should see all things done according to
their minds; and for other things they referred them to Hob-
Collect.
Numb. 45. by, that carried the letter, (which is in the Collection.) Upon
this the council sent sir Anthony Wingfield, sir Anthony St.
Leger, and sir John Williams, to Windsor, with a charge to

138 see that the duke of Somerset should not withdraw before they arrived: and that sir Thomas Smith the secretary, sir Michael Stanhope, sir John Thynne, Edward Wolf, and William Cecil, should be restrained to their chambers till they examined them. On the twelfth of October the whole council went to Windsor; and, coming to the king, they protested that all they had done was out of the zeal and affection they had to his person and service. The king received them kindly, and thanked them for their care of him; and assured them, that he took all they had done in good part. On the thirteenth day they sat in council, and sent for those who were ordered to be kept in their chambers; only Cecil was let go. They charged them, that they had been the chief instruments about the duke of Somerset in all his wilful proceedings: therefore they turned Smith out of his place of secretary, and sent him, with the rest, to the Tower of London. On the day following[84], the protector was called before them, and articles of misdemeanours and high treason were laid to his charge; (which will be found in the Collection.) The substance of them was, that, being made protector on condition that he should do nothing without the consent of the other executors, he had not observed that condition, but had treated with ambassadors, made bishops and lord lieutenants, by his own authority; and that he had held a court of requests in his own house, and had done many things contrary to law; had embased the coin; had in the matter of enclosures set out proclamations, and given commissions, against the mind of the whole council; that he had not taken care to suppress the late insurrections, but had justified and encouraged them; that he had neglected the places the king had in France, by which means they were lost; that he had persuaded the king, that the lords who met at London intended to destroy him, and had desired him never to forget it, but to revenge it, and had required some young lords to keep it in his remembrance; and had caused those lords to be proclaimed traitors; that he had said, if he should die, the king should die too; that he had carried the king so suddenly to Windsor, that he was not only

[Ibid. p. 14.]

[Ibid. p. 15.]

He is accused, and sent to the Tower.

Collect. Numb. 46.

---

[84] [This is entered in the Council Book as Monday the 13th of October, but it should be the 14th, the days of the month being for several successive days wrongly dated.]

put in great fear, but cast into a dangerous disease; that he had gathered the people, and armed them for war, and had armed his friends and servants, and left the king's servants unarmed; and that he intended to fly to Jersey or Guernsey. So he was sent to the Tower, being conducted thither by the earls of Sussex and Huntingdon. That day the king was carried back again to Hampton-Court; and an order was made, that six lords should be the governors of his person; who were, the marquis of Northampton, the earls of Warwick and Arundel, the lords St. John, Russell, and Wentworth. Two of those were in their course to attend constantly on the king.

[Ibid. p. 15.]

[Ibid. p. 16.]

Censures passed upon him.

And thus fell the duke of Somerset from his high offices and great trust. The articles objected to him seem to say as much for his justification as the answers could do, if they were in my power. He is not accused of rapine, cruelty, or bribery; but only of such things as are incident to all men that are of a sudden exalted to a high and disproportioned greatness. What he did about the coin was not for his own advantage, but was done by a common mistake of many governors, who, in the necessity of their affairs, fly to this, as their last shift, to draw out their business as long as is possible; but it ever rebounds on the government, to its great prejudice and loss. 13 He bore his fall more equally than he had done his prosperity; and set himself in his imprisonment to study and reading: and falling on a book[85] that treated of patience, both from the principles of moral philosophy and of Christianity, he was so much taken with it, that he ordered it to be translated into English, and writ a preface to it himself, mentioning the great comfort he had found in reading it, which had induced him to take care that others might reap the like benefit from it. Peter Martyr writ him also a long consolatory letter, which was printed both in Latin, and in an English translation[86]: and all the reformed, both in England and abroad, looked on

---

[85] [Wermylierus (Otho), A spirituall and most precyous Pearle, teachyng all Men to loue and embrace the Crosse. Sett forth by the Duke hys Grace of Somerset, as appeareth by hys Epistle set before the same. London, for Gwalter Lynne, 1550. 16mo. It has been several times reprinted.]

[86] [A copy in MS. is in the royal collection, 17 C. v. An epistle written by D. Peter Martir to the Duke of Somerset, translated by Thomas Norton. Lond. 1550. 16mo.]

his fall as a public loss to that whole interest, which he had so steadily set forward.

But, on the other hand, the popish party were much lifted up at his fall; and the rather, because they knew the earl of Southampton, who they hoped should have directed all affairs, was entirely theirs. It was also believed, that the earl of Warwick had given them secret assurances; so it was understood at the court of France, as Thuanus writes. They had also, among the first things they did, gone about to discharge the duke of Norfolk of his long imprisonment, in consideration of his great age, his former services, and the extremity of the proceedings against him, which were said to have flowed chiefly from the ill offices the duke of Somerset had done him. But this was soon laid aside. So now the papists made their addresses to the earl of Warwick. The bishop of Winchester wrote to him a hearty congratulation, rejoicing that the late tyranny (so he called the duke of Somerset's administration) was now at an end: he wished him all prosperity; and desired, that, when he had leisure from the great affairs, that were in so unsettled a condition, some regard might be had of him. The bishop of London, being also in good hopes, since the protector and Smith, whom he esteemed his chief enemies, were now in disgrace, and Cranmer was in cold if not in ill terms with the earl of Warwick, sent a petition that his appeal might be received, and his process reviewed. Many also began to fall off from going to the English service, or the communion, hoping that all would be quickly undone that had been settled by the duke of Somerset. But the earl of Warwick, finding the king so zealously addicted to the carrying on of the reformation, that nothing could recommend any one so much to him, as the promoting it further would do, soon forsook the popish party, and was seemingly the most earnest on a further reformation that was possible. I do not find that he did write any answer to the bishop of Winchester: he continued still a prisoner. And for Bonner's matter, there was a new court of delegates appointed to review his appeal, consisting of four civilians, and four common lawyers; who, having examined it, reported, that the process had been legally carried on, and the sentence justly given, and that there was no good reason why the

The papists much lifted up.

[Thuanus, vi. 13. p. 218.]

But their hopes soon vanish.

appeal should be received: and therefore they rejected it. This being reported to the council, they sent for Bonner in the beginning of February, and declared to him, that his appeal was rejected, and that the sentence against him was in full force still.

Ambassa-
dors sent to
the empe-
ror.
But the business of Boulogne was that which pressed them most. They misdoubting, as was formerly shewn, that Paget had not managed that matter dextrously and earnestly with 140 the emperor, sent on the 18th of October, sir Thomas Cheyney and sir Philip Hobby to him, to entreat him to take Boulogne into his protection; they also sent over the earl·of Huntingdon to command it, with the addition of a thousand men for the garrison. When the ambassadors came to the emperor, they desired leave to raise two thousand horse and three thousand
Cott. libr.
Galb.B.xii.
[fol. 11
and 119.]
foot in his dominions for the preservation of Boulogne. The emperor gave them very good words, but insisted much on his league with France, and referred them to the bishop of Arras, who told them plainly, the thing could not be done. So sir Thomas Cheyney took his leave of the emperor, who, at parting, desired him to represent to the king's council, how necessary it was to consider matters of religion again, that so they might be all of one mind; for, to deal plainly with them, till that were done, he could not assist them so effectually as otherwise he desired to do. And now the council saw clearly they had not been deceived by Paget in that particular, and there-
The earl of
Southamp-
ton leaves
the court.
fore resolved to apply themselves to France for a peace. But now the earl of Warwick falling off wholly from the popish party, the earl of Southampton left the court in great discontent. He was neither restored to his office of chancellor, nor made lord treasurer; (that place, which was vacant by the
[Feb. 3.]
[Jan. 19.]
duke of Somerset's fall, being now given to the lord St. John, who soon after was made earl of Wiltshire;) nor was he made one of those who had charge of the king's person. So he began to lay a train against the earl of Warwick; but he was too quick for him, and discovered it: upon which he left the court in the night, and it was said he poisoned himself, or pined away with discontent: for he died in July after.

A new of-
fice for or-
dinations.
So now the reformation was ordered to be carried on; and there being one part of the divine offices not yet reformed,

that is, concerning the giving orders, some bishops and divines, brought now together by a session of parliament, were appointed to prepare a book of ordination.

But now I turn to the parliament, which sat down on the fourth of November. In it a severe law was made against unlawful assemblies: that if any, to the number of twelve, should meet together unlawfully for any matter of state, and, being required by any lawful magistrate, should not disperse themselves, it should be treason; and if any broke hedges, or violently pulled up pales about enclosures, without lawful authority, it should be felony. It was also made felony to gather the people together without warrant by ringing of bells, or sound of drums and trumpets, or the firing of beacons. There was also a law made against prophecies concerning the king or his council, since by these the people were disposed to sedition: for the first offence it was to be punished by imprisonment for a year, and 10*l.* fine; for the second it was imprisonment during life, with the forfeiture of goods and chattels. All this was on the account of the tumults the former year, and not with any regard to the duke of Somerset's security, as some have without any reason fancied; for he had now no interest in the parliament, nor was he in a condition any more to apprehend tumults against himself, being stripped of his so much envied greatness. Another law was made against vagabonds; relating, That the former statute made in this reign being too severe, was by that means not executed; so it was repealed, and the law made in king Henry the Eighth's reign put in force. Provisions were laid down for relieving the sick and impotent, and setting the poor that were able to work: that once a month there should be every where a visitation of the poor by those in office, who should send away such as did not belong to that place; and those were to be carried from constable to constable, till they were brought to such places as were bound to see to them. There was a bill brought in for the repealing of a branch of the act of uniformity; but it went no further than one reading.

On the 14th of November the bishops made a heavy complaint to the lords, of the abounding of vice and disorder, and that their power was so abridged that they could punish no sin, nor oblige any to appear before them, or to observe the

Marginal notes:

A session of parliament.

An act against tumultuary assemblies; [Cap. 5, Statutes, vol. iv. p. 104.]

[Cap. 15. ibid. p. 114.]

And against vagabonds. [Cap. 16. ibid. p. 115.]

The bishops move for a reviving of ecclesiastical censures.

Line number: 141

[Journal of
Lords, p.
359.]
[Ibid. p.
360.]
orders of the church. This was heard by all the lords with
great regret, and they ordered a bill to be drawn about it.
On the 18th of November, a bill was brought in, but rejected
at first reading, because it seemed to give the bishops too
much power. So a second bill was appointed to be drawn by
a committee of the house. It was agreed to, and sent down to
[Nov. 23.] the commons, who laid it aside after the second reading. They
thought it better to renew the design that was in the former
reign, of two and thirty persons being authorized to compile
the body·of ecclesiastical laws ; and when that was prepared,
it seemed more proper, by confirming it, to establish ecclesiastical jurisdiction, than to give the bishops any power, while the
rules of their courts were so little determined or regulated.
[Cap. 11.
Statutes,
vol. iv. p.
111.]
So an act passed, empowering the king to name sixteen persons
of the spiritualty, of whom four should be bishops ; and sixteen
of the temporalty, of whom four should be common lawyers,
who, within three years, should compile a body of ecclesiastical
laws : and those, being nothing contrary to the common and
statute laws of the land, should be published by the king's
warrant under the great seal, and have the force of laws in the
ecclesiastical courts. Thus they took care that this should not
be turned over to an uncertain period, as it had been done in
the former reign, but designed that it should be quickly finished. The bishops of that time were generally so backward
in every step to a reformation, that a small number of them
was made necessary to be of this commission. The effect that
it had shall be afterwards opened.

[Dec. 5.
Journal of
Commons,
p. 13.]
There was a bill brought into the house of commons, That
the preaching and holding of some opinions should be declared
felony : it passed with them, but was laid aside by the lords.
An act
about the
forms of
giving
orders.
A bill for the form of ordaining ministers was brought into the
house of lords, and was agreed to ; the bishops of Durham,
Carlisle, Worcester, Chichester, and Westminster, protesting
against it. The substance of it was, That such forms of ordain-
[Cap. 12,
Statutes,
vol. iv. p.
112.]
ing ministers as should be set forth by the advice of six prelates
and six divines, to be named by the king, and authorized by a
warrant under the great seal, should be used after April next,
An act
about the
duke of
Somerset.
and no other. On the second of January a bill was put in
against the duke of Somerset, of the articles formerly mentioned, with a confession of them signed by his hand. This he

was prevailed with to do, upon assurances given that he should [Journal of Lords, p. 374.] be gently dealt with, if he would freely confess, and submit himself to the king's mercy. But it was said by some of the lords, that they did not know whether that confession was not 142 drawn from him by force; and that it might be an ill precedent to pass acts upon such papers, without examining the party, whether he had subscribed them freely and uncompelled: so they sent four temporal lords, and four bishops, to examine [Ibid. p. 375.] him concerning it. And the day following the bishop of Coventry and Lichfield made the report, that he thanked them for that kind message, but that he had freely subscribed the confession that lay before them. He had made it on his knees before the king and council, and had signed it on the 13th of December. He protested his offences had flowed from rashness and indiscretion, rather than malice, and that he had no treasonable design against the king or his realms. So he was fined by act of parliament in 2000l. a year of land; and he lost all his goods and offices. Upon this he wrote to the council, acknowledging their favour in bringing off his matter by a fine; he confessed that he had fallen into the frailties that often attend on great places, but what he had done amiss was rather for want of true judgment, than from any malicious meaning: he humbly desired they would interpose with the king for a moderation of his fine, and that he might be pardoned, and restored to favour; assuring them, that for the future he should carry himself so humbly and obediently, that he should thereby make amends for his former follies. This was much censured by many as a sign of an abject spirit; others thought it was wisely done in him, once to get out of prison on any terms, since the greatness of his former condition gave such jealousy to his enemies, that, urless he had his pardon, he would be in continual danger, as long as he was in their hands. So on the sixth of February he was set at liberty, [Council Book, p. 78.] giving bond of 10,000l. for his good behaviour; and being [Ibid. p. 79.] limited that he should stay at the king's house of Shene, or his own of Sion, and should not go four miles from them, nor come to the king or the council, unless he were called. He had his pardon on the sixteenth of February, and carried himself after that so humbly, that his behaviour, with the king's great kindness to him, did so far prevail, that, on the tenth of April after, he [Ibid. p. 141.]

was restored into favour, and sworn of the privy-council. And so this storm went over him much more gently than was expected; but his carriage in it was thought to have so little of the hero, that he was not much considered after this.

The reformation is set on vigorously.

But to go on with the business of the parliament. Reports had been spread, that the old service would be again set up; and these were much cherished by those who still loved the former superstition, who gave out, that a change was to be expected, since the new service had been only the act of the duke of Somerset. Upon this the council wrote on Christmas-day a letter to all the bishops of England, to this effect; "That " whereas the English service had been devised by learned " men, according to the scripture, and the use of the primitive " church; therefore, for putting away those vain expectations, " all clergymen were required to deliver to such as should be " appointed by the king to receive them, all antiphonals, mis- " sals, grayles, processionals, manuals, legends, pies, portuasses, " journals, and ordinals, after the use of Sarum, Lincoln, York, " or any other private use: requiring them also to see to the " observing one uniform order in the service set forth by the " common consent of the realm, and particularly to take care " that there should be every where provision made of bread " and wine for the communion on Sunday." This will be found in the Collection. But, to give a more public declaration of their zeal, an act was brought into parliament about it, and was agreed to by all the lords, except the earl of Derby, the bishops of Durham, Coventry and Lichfield, Carlisle, Worcester, Westminster, and Chichester, and the lords Morley, Stourton, Windsor, and Wharton. By it, not only all the books formerly mentioned were to be destroyed; but all that had any image, that had belonged to any church or chapel, were required to deface it before the last of June; and in all the Primers set out by the late king, the prayers to the saints were to be dashed out. There was also an act for a subsidy, to be paid in one year, for which there was a release granted of a branch of the subsidy formerly given. Last of all came the king's general pardon, out of which those in the Tower, or other prisons, on the account of the state, as also all anabaptists, were excepted.

Thus were all matters ended; and on the first of February

Collect.
Numb. 47.

[Cap. 10.
Statutes,
vol. iv. p.
110.]

[Ibid. p.
111.]

143

the parliament was prorogued : only in the house of commons there was a debate that deserves to be remembered. It seems that before this time the eldest sons of peers were not members of the house of commons: and sir Francis Russell becoming, by the death of his elder brother, heir apparent to the lord Russell; it was, on the twenty-first of January, carried upon a debate, *That he should abide in the house as he was before.* So it is entered in the original journal of the house of commons ; which was communicated to me by Mr. Surle and Mr. Clark, in whose hands it is now, and is the first journal that ever was taken in that house. [Journal of Commons, p. 15.]

But it may be expected that I should next give an account of the forms of ordination now agreed on. Twelve were appointed by the council to prepare the book, among whom Heath, bishop of Worcester, was one ; but he would not consent to the reformations that were proposed in it: so on the eighth of February he was called before the council, and required to agree to that which all the rest had consented to. But he could not be prevailed with to do it: wherefore, on the fourth of March, he was committed to the Fleet, because (as it is entered in the council-books) that he obstinately denied to subscribe the book for the making of bishops and priests. He had hitherto opposed every thing done towards reformation in parliament, though he had given an entire obedience to it when it was enacted : he was a man of a gentle temper and great prudence, that understood affairs of state better than matters of religion. But now it was resolved to rid the church of those compliers, who submitted out of fear, or interest, to save their benefices ; but were still ready, upon any favourable conjuncture, to return back to the old superstition. [Heath, bishop of Worcester, put in prison for not agreeing with the others appointed to draw the book for ordinations. [Council Book, p. 109.]

As for the forms of ordination, they found that the scripture mentioned only the imposition of hands, and prayer. In the Apostolical Constitutions, in the fourth council of Carthage, and in the pretended works of Denis the Areopagite, there was no more used. Therefore all those additions of anointing, and giving them consecrated vestments, were later inventions : but most of all, the conceit, which from the time of the council of Florence was generally received, that the rites by which a priest was ordained were, the delivering him the vessels for consecrating the eucharist, with a power to offer sacrifice to

God for the dead and the living. This was a vain novelty, 144 only set up to support the belief of transubstantiation ; and had no ground in the scriptures, nor the primitive practice. So they agreed on a form of ordaining deacons, priests, and bishops ; which is the same we yet use, except in some few words that have been added since in the ordination of a priest or bishop : for there was then no express mention made in the words of ordaining them, that it was for the one or the other office ; in both it was said, *Receive thou the Holy Ghost, in the name of the Father, &c.* But that having been since made use of to prove both functions the same, it was of late years altered, as it is now.   Nor were these words, being the same in giving both orders, any ground to infer that the church esteemed them one order ; the rest of the office shewing the contrary very plainly.   Another difference between the ordination-book set out at that time, and that we now use, was, that the bishop was to lay his one hand on the priest's head, and with his other to give him a Bible, with a chalice and bread in it, saying the words now said at the delivery of the Bible. In the consecration of a bishop there was nothing more than what is yet in use, save that a staff was put into his hand, with this blessing, *Be to the flock of Christ a shepherd.* By the rule of this ordinal, a deacon was not to be ordained before he was twenty-one, a priest before he was twenty-four, nor a bishop before he was thirty years of age.

The additions brought into the church of Rome in giving orders.

In this ritual all those superadded rites were cut off, which the later ages had brought in to dress up these performances with the more pomp ; whereof we have since a more perfect account than it was possible for them then to have. For in our age Morinus, a learned priest of the Oratorian order, has published the most ancient rituals he could find ; by which it appears, how these offices swelled in every age by some new addition. About the middle of the sixth century, they anointed and blessed the priest's hands in some parts of France ; though the Greek church never used anointing, nor was it in the Roman church two ages after that ; for pope Nicolas the First plainly says, it was never used in the church of Rome. In the eighth century, the priest's garments were given with a special benediction for the priest's *offering expiatory sacrifices;* it was no ancienter that that phrase was used in ordinations :

and in that same age there was a special benediction of the
priest's hands used before they were anointed ; and then his
head was anointed.   This was taken partly from the Levitical
law, and partly because the people believed that their kings derived the sacredness of their persons from their being anointed:
so the priests, having a mind to have their persons secured and
exempted from all secular power, were willing enough to use
this rite in their ordinations.   And in the tenth century, when
the belief of transubstantiation was received, the delivering of
the vessels for the eucharist, with the power of offering sacrifices, was brought in, besides a great many other rites.   So
that the church did never tie itself to one certain form of ordinations ; nor did it always make them with the same prayers :
for what was accounted anciently the form of ordination, was
in the later ages but a preparatory prayer to it.

The most considerable addition that was made in the book
of ordinations was, the putting questions to the persons to be
145 ordained ; who, by answering these, make solemn declarations
of sponsions and vows to God.   The first question, when one is
presented to orders, is, *Do you trust that you are inwardly
moved by the Holy Ghost to take upon you this office and ministration, to serve God, for the promoting his glory, and for
the edifying of his people ?*   To which he is to answer, *He
trusts he is.*   It has been oft lamented, that many come to
receive orders before ever they have seriously read over these
questions, and examined themselves whether they could, with
a good conscience, make the answers there prescribed : since it
is scarce credible, that men of common honesty would lie in the
presence of God on so great an occasion ; and yet it is too visible, that many have not any such inward vocation, nor have
ever considered seriously what it is.   If it were well apprehended, that heat that many have to get into orders would
soon abate ; who perhaps have nothing in their eye but some
place of profit, or benefice, to which way must be made by that
preceding ceremony : and so enter into orders, as others are
associated into fraternities and corporations, with little previous
sense of that holy character they are to receive, when they
thus dedicate their lives and labours to the service of God in
the gospel.   In the primitive church the apprehension of this
made even good and holy men afraid to enter under such

Interroga-
tions and
sponsions
in the new
book.

bonds; and therefore they were often to be dragged almost by force, or catched at unawares, and be so initiated : as appears in the lives of those two Greek fathers, Nazianzen and Chrysostom. If men make their first step to the holy altar by such a lie, (as is their pretending to a motion of the Holy Ghost, concerning which they know little, but that they have nothing at all of it,) they have no reason to expect that blessing which otherwise attends on such dedications. And it had been happy for the church, if all those that are authorized to confer orders had stood on this more critically ; and not been contented with a bare putting these questions to those who come to be ordained, but had used a due strictness beforehand, suitable to that grave admonition of St. Paul's to Timothy, *Lay hands suddenly on no man, and be not partaker of other men's sins.*

In the sponsions made by the priests, they bind themselves to *teach the people committed to their charge, to banish away all erroneous doctrines, and to use both public and private monitions and exhortations, as well to the sick as the whole, within their cures, as need shall require, and as occasion shall be given.* Such as remember that they have plighted their faith for this to God, will feel the pastoral care to be a load indeed, and so be far enough from relinquishing it, or hiring it out perhaps to a loose or ignorant mercenary. These are the blemishes and scandals that lie on our church, brought on it partly by the corruption of some simoniacal patrons, but chiefly by the negligence of some, and the faultiness of other clergymen ; which could never have lost so much ground in the nation upon such trifling accounts as are the contests since raised about ceremonies, if it were not that the people, by such palpable faults in the persons and behaviour of some churchmen, have been possessed with prejudices, first against them, and then, upon their account, against the whole church : so that these corrupt churchmen are not only to answer to God for all those souls within their charge that have perished through their neglect, but in a great degree for all the mischief of the schism among us, to the nourishing whereof they have given so great and palpable occasion. The importance of 146 those things made me judge they deserved this digression, from which I now turn to other affairs.

The business of Boulogne lay heavy on the council. The
French had stopped all communication between Calais and it;
so that it was not easy to supply it from thence. The council,
to rid the nation of the foreigners, sent them all to Calais, with
3000 English; and resolved to force a way through, if it came
to extremities: but at this time both the French and English
were well disposed to a peace. The king of France knew the
emperor intended to go into Germany next summer; so he
longed to be at liberty to wait on his motions. The English
council, that opposed the delivery of Boulogne chiefly to throw
off the duke of Somerset, that being done, were all convinced
that it was not worth the cost and danger of a war: only they
stood on the indecency of yielding it; especially they having
raised such clamours against the protector, when he went
about the delivering it up. So they made great shows of preparations to defend it; but at the same time were not unwilling
to listen to propositions of peace. One Guidotti, a Florentine,
that lived in England, was employed by the constable of France,
Montmorency, to set on a treaty; yet he was to do it without
owning he had any orders from that king. He went often to
and again between Paris and London; and at last it was resolved on both sides that there should be a treaty. But at
this time there was a great change of affairs in Italy. Pope
Paul the Third, having held that see fifteen years, died the
tenth of November, in the eighty-second year of his age; much
broken in mind at the calamity of his family, the killing of his
son, the loss of Piacenza, and the ingratitude of his grandchild.
Upon his death, all the cardinals, being gathered from Bologna, Trent, and other neighbouring places, entered the conclave, where one that is to have such a share in the following
part of this work was so much concerned, that it will be no impertinent digression to give an account of it. There were
great animosities between the imperialists and the French;
cardinal Farnese had also many votes that followed him: so
that these three factions were either of them strong enough to
exclude any that was unacceptable to them. Cardinal Pole
was set up by Farnese as a moderate imperialist, who had
carried it so well at Trent, that he saw he would not blindly
follow the emperor. He had lived many years at Viterbo,
where he was made legate, after he had given over his prac-

*It is re-
solved to
deliver
Boulogne
to the
French.*

*Pope Paul
III. dies.
[Thuanus,
p. 212.]*

*Cardinal
Pole was
elected
pope.*

tices against England. There he gave himself wholly to the study of divinity, not without some imputations of favouring heresy : for one Antonio Flaminio, that was also suspected of Lutheranism, lived with him ; Tremellius, that learned Jew, who had been baptized in his house, was also known to incline that way ; and many, who left their monasteries, and went to Germany, used to stay some time with him on their way, and were well received by him ; nor would he proceed against any suspected of heresy. There was cause enough to raise suspicion in a less jealous people than Italians. Yet the vast zeal that he had shewn for the exaltation of the papacy made all those things be overlooked. He was sent one of the pope's legates to Trent, where he asserted the German doctrine of justification by faith ; but upon the emperor's setting out the Interim, he wrote freely against it. He was indeed a man of an easy and generous temper, but much in the power of those whom he 147 loved and trusted. Farnese therefore, looking on him as one that would be governed by him, and that was acceptable to the imperialists, and not much hated by the French, the cardinal of Guise being his friend, resolved to promote him ; and, by the scrutiny they made, it was found that they were

[Thuanus, p. 213.]

within two of the number that was requisite. But he seemed so little concerned at it himself, that he desired them not to make too much haste in a thing of that nature; for that dignity was rather to be undertaken with fear than to be ambitiously desired. The cardinals, who had heard of such things among the ancient Romans, but had seen few such modern instances, and who valued men by nothing more than their ambitious aspiring, imputed this either to dulness or hypocrisy. He himself seemed nothing affected with it, and did not change his behaviour, and carried it with an equality of mind, that became one who had divided his time between philosophy and divinity. Caraffa, that hated him, did all he could to alienate the conclave from him ; he objected to him, not only heresy, but also the suspicion of incontinence, since he bred up a nun who was believed to be his daughter. Of these things he coldly purged himself: he shewed, that he had suffered so much on the account of religion in his own country, that he was beyond the suspicion of heresy ; and he proved, that the girl whom he maintained among the nuns was an

Englishman's daughter, to whom he had assigned an allowance.
Caraffa prevailed little, and the next night the number was
complete, so that the cardinals came to adore him, and make [Ibid. p.
him pope: but he, receiving that with his usual coldness, said, 214.]
it was night, and God loved light better than darkness; therefore he desired to delay it till day came.   The Italians, who,
whatever judges they may be about the qualifications of such a
pope as is necessary for their affairs, understood not this temper of mind, which in better times would have recommended
one with the highest advantages, shrunk all from him : and,
after some intrigues usual on such occasions, chose the cardinal [Feb. 8.
De Monte, afterwards pope Julius the Third ; who gave a Thuanus,
strange omen of what advancements he intended to make, p. 215.]
when he gave his own hat, according to the custom of the
popes, who bestow their hats before they go out of the conclave, on a mean servant of his, who had the charge of a mon-
key that he kept : and being asked what he observed in him
to make him a cardinal, he answered, as much as the cardinals
had seen in him to make him pope.   But it was commonly
said, that the secret of this promotion was an unnatural affection to him.   Upon this occasion I shall refer the reader to a
letter, which I have put in the Collection, written by cardinal Collect.
Wolsey, upon the death of pope Adrian the Sixth, to get him- Numb. 48.
self chosen pope : it sets out so naturally the intrigues of that
court on such occasions, that, though it belongs to the former
volume, yet, having fallen upon it since I published it, I
thought it would be no unacceptable thing to insert in this
volume, though it does not belong to it.   It will demonstrate
how likely it is that a bishop chosen by such arts should be
the infallible judge of controversies, and the head of the
church.

    And now to return to England.   It was resolved to send A treaty
ambassadors to France ; who were, the lord Russell, Paget, between
now made a lord, secretary Petre, and sir John Mason. Their lish and
instructions will be found in the Collection.   The substance of Collect.
148 them was ; they were not to stick about the place of treaty, Numb. 49.
but to have it at Calais or Boulogne, if it might be : they were tions given
to agree to the delivery up of Boulogne ; but to demand, that to the Eng-
the Scotch queen should be sent back for perfecting the mar- bassadors.
riage formerly agreed on : that the fortifications of Newhaven

and Blackness should be ruinated: that the perpetual pension agreed to king Henry should still be paid, together with all arrears that were due before the wars: they were only to insist on the last, if they saw the former could not be obtained: they were to agree the time and manner of the delivery of Boulogne to be as honourable as might be. For Scotland, they being also in war with the emperor, the king of England could not make peace with them, unless the emperor, his ally, who had made war on them upon his account, were also satisfied: all places there were to be offered up, except Roxburgh and Aymouth. If the French spoke any thing of the king's marrying their king's daughter Elizabeth, they were to put it off, since the king was yet so young. They were also at first to agree to no more but a cessation. So they went over on the 21st of January. The French commissioners appointed to treat with them were, Rochepot, Châtillon, Mortier, and De Sacy; who desired the meeting might be near Boulogne, though the English endeavoured to have brought it to Guisnes. Upon the English laying out their demands, the French answered them roundly, that, for delivering up the queen of Scots, they would not treat about it, nor about a perpetual pension; since, as the king was resolved to marry the Scotch queen to the dauphin, so he would give no perpetual pension, which was in effect to become a tributary prince; but for a sum of money they were ready to treat about it. As to Scotland, they demanded that all the places that had been taken should be restored, as well as Roxburgh and Aymouth, as Lauder and Dunglass. The latter two were soon yielded to, but the commissioners were limited as to the former. There was also some discourse of razing the fortifications of Alderney and Serk, two small islands in the channel, that belonged to England: the latter was in the hands of the French, who were willing to yield it up; so the fortifications both in it and Alderney were razed. Upon this there were second instructions sent over from the council, (which are in the Collection,) that they should so far insist on the keeping of Roxburgh and Aymouth, as to break up their conference upon it: but if that did not work on the French, they should yield it rather than give over the treaty. They were also instructed to require hostages from the French till the money were all paid, and to

Collect.
Numb. 50.

offer hostages on the part of England till Boulogne was delivered; and to struggle in the matter of the isles all they
could, but not to break about it.   Between the giving the first [Rymer xv.
and second instructions, the lord St. John was created earl of P. 217.]
Wiltshire, as appears by his subscriptions.   The commissioners
finished their treaty about the end of February, on these arti- Articles of
cles, on condition that all claims of either side should be re- the treaty.
served as they were at the beginning of the war.   This was a [Rymer
temper between the English demand, of all the arrears of king xv. p. 211.]
Henry's pension, and the French denial of it; for thus the
king reserved all the right he had before the war.   Boulogne
was to be delivered within six months[87], with all the places
49 about it, and the ordnance, except what the English had cast
since they had it; for which surrender the French were to [Ibid. p.
pay 400,000 crowns, (then of equal value with the English 213.]
noble;) the one half three days after the town was in their
hands, and the other in the August after.   There was to be a [Aug. 15.]
peace with Scotland; and Roxburgh and Aymouth, Lauder
and Dunglass, were to be razed; and there was to be a free
trade between England, France, and Scotland.   Six hostages [Ibid. p.
were to be given on either side; all the English were to be 214.]
sent back upon the delivery of the town; and three of the
French on the first, and the rest on the second payment.   The
French hostages were, the duke of Enghien; the marquis de
Mayenne, son to the duke of Guise; Montmorency, son to the
constable; the duke of Tremouille; the vicedam of Chartres;
and Hunaudaye, son to Annebaut, the admiral.   On the English side were, the duke of Suffolk; the earl of Hertford; the
earl of Shrewsbury; the earl of Arundel's son, the lord Strange;
and the lord Matravers.   So was the peace concluded; all the
articles in it were duly performed, and the hostages delivered
back.   It was proclaimed in London on the 29th of March,
being confirmed by both the kings.   Only it was much observed, that, when it was to be confirmed in England, the earl
of Warwick, on pretence of sickness, was absent.   Those who

---

[87] [This is a mistake for six weeks.
The words of the treaty are, 'Item
conventum concordatum et conclu-
sum est, quod urbs Bolloniæ et por-
tus ejusdem.... ante sex septimanas

a die datæ præsentis tractatûs resti-
tuentur in manus et potestatem
Christianissimi Regis, &c.' Rymer,
xv. p. 213.]

began to conceive great jealousies of him thought this was to make a show to the people that he abhorred so dishonourable a thing, as himself had oft called it during the duke of Somerset's administration; and that therefore he would not by his presence seem to consent to it, though he had signed all the orders for it.

And now was the king entering in the fourth year of his reign, free from all wars, which had hitherto much distracted his government. So the council was more at leisure to settle the affairs at home. But the earl of Warwick, beginning to form great designs, resolved first to make himself popular, by calling all that had meddled in the king's affairs to a strict account; and either to make them compound for great sums, by which the king's debts should be paid, or to keep them under the lash till he made them subservient to his ends. He began with the earl of Arundel, to whose charge many things being laid, he submitted himself to a fine of 12,000*l.* to be paid in twelve years. This was the more taken notice of, because Southampton, Arundel, and he, with sir Richard Southwell, master of the rolls, had been the chief contrivers of the duke of Somerset's fall: Southampton was driven away, Arundel fined, and Southwell was soon after put in the Fleet for dispersing some seditious bills This wrought much on the vulgar, who imputed it to a secret curse on those who had conspired against the duke of Somerset; and the delivery of Boulogne made it yet more plain that the charge against him was chiefly grounded on malice. After Arundel's disgrace, all the duke of Somerset's friends made their compositions, and were discharged: sir Thomas Smith, sir Michael Stanhope, Thomas Fisher, and William Gray, each of them acknowledged they owed the king 3000*l.* and sir John Thynne submitted to 6000*l.* fine.

The earl of Warwick governs the councils.

But I shall next prosecute the narration of what concerned the church. It was now resolved to fill the see of London: Ridley, being esteemed both the most learned and most thoroughly zealous for the reformation, was pitched on to be the man. So on the 21st of February he was writ for, and on the 24th he was declared bishop of London and Westminster, and was to have 1000*l.* a year of the rents of the bishopric; 150 and, for his further supply, was dispensed with to hold a pre-

Ridley made bishop of London.

bendary of Canterbury and Westminster. It was thought
needless to have two bishoprics so near one another; and
some, gaping after the lands of both, procured this union.
But I do not see any reason to think, that at any time in this
reign the suppression of the deaneries and prebends in cathedrals was designed. For neither in the suppression of the
bishoprics of Westminster, Gloucester, or Durham, was there
any attempt made to put down the deaneries or prebendaries
in these places; so that I look on this as a groundless conceit,
among many others that pass concerning this reign. For
Thirlby of Westminster, there was no cause given to throw
him out, for he obeyed all the laws and injunctions when they
came out, though he generally opposed them when they were
making. So, to make way for him, William Repps, the bishop
of Norwich, was prevailed with to resign, and he was pro- [Jan. 31.]
moted to that see, vacant (as his patent has it) by the free resignation of William the former bishop. And the same day,
being the first of April, Ridley was made bishop of London [Rymer,
and Westminster. Both were, according to the common form, ^xv. p. 222.]
to be bishops *durante vitâ naturali*, during life.

The see of Winchester had been two years as good as vacant Proceed-
ingsagainst
by the long imprisonment of Gardiner, who had been now Gardiner.
above two years in the Tower [88]. When the Book of Common
Prayer was set out, the lord St. John and secretary Petre
were sent with it to him, to know of him whether he would
conform himself to it or not; and they gave him great hopes,
that, if he would submit, the protector would sue to the king
for mercy to him. He answered, that he did not know himself
guilty of any thing that needed mercy; so he desired to be
tried for what had been objected to him according to law.
For the book, he did not think, that, while he was a prisoner,
he was bound to give his opinion about such things; it might
be thought he did it against his conscience, to obtain his
liberty: but if he were out of prison, he should either obey it,
or be liable to punishment according to law. Upon the duke
of Somerset's [89] fall, the lord treasurer, the earl of Warwick,
sir William Herbert, and secretary Petre were sent to him:

---

[88] [See Part iii. p. 193.]

[89] The duke of Somerset was not
then fallen. It was between his two

falls. The proceedings in council
are signed by him. [S.]

[Fox, lib.
ix. p. 81.]
(Fox says[90], this was on the ninth of July : but there must be
an error in that; for Gardiner in his answer says, that, upon
the duke of Somerset's coming to the Tower, he looked to
have been let out within two days, and had made his farewell
feast : but when these were with him, a month or thereabout
had passed : so it must have been in November the former
year.) They brought him a paper, to which they desired he
would set his hand. It contained, first, a preface, which was
an acknowledgment of former faults, for which he had been
justly punished : there were also divers articles contained in it,
which were, touching the king's supremacy ; his power of appointing or dispensing with holydays and fasts ; that the Book
of Common Prayer set out by the king and parliament was a
most Christian and godly book, to be allowed of by all bishops
and pastors in England, and that he should both in sermons
and discourses commend it to be observed ; that the king's
power was complete now when under age, and that all owed
obedience to him now, as much as if he were thirty or
forty years old ; that the six articles were justly abrogated ;
and that the king had full authority to correct and reform
what was amiss in the church, both in England and Ireland. 151
He only excepted to the preface ; and offered to sign all the
articles, but would have had the preface left out. They bid
him rather write on the margin his exceptions to it : so he
writ, that he could not with a good conscience agree to the
preface ; and with that exception he set his hand to the whole
paper. The lords used him with great kindness, and gave
him hope that his troubles should be quickly ended. Herbert
and Petre came to him some time after that, but how soon is
not so clear, and pressed him to make the acknowledgment
without exception : he refused it, and said, he would never
defame himself ; for when he had done it, he was not sure
but it might be made use of against him as a confession. Two
or three days after that, Ridley was sent to him, together with
the other two, and they brought him new articles. In this
paper the acknowledgment was more general than in the former : it was said here in the preface, that he had been suspected of not approving the king's proceedings ; and, being

Some arti-
cles are
sent to
him.

Which he
signed,
with some
exceptions.

90 Fox says it. It is so in king Edward's Journal. [S.]

appointed to preach, had not done it as he ought to have done, and so deserved the king's displeasure, for which he was sorry. The articles related to the pope's supremacy, the suppression of abbeys and chantries, pilgrimages, masses, images, the ador- ing the sacrament, the communion in both kinds, the abolish- ing the old books, and bringing in the new book of service, and that for ordaining of priests and bishops, the completeness of the scripture, and the use of it in the vulgar tongue, the lawfulness of clergymen's marriage, and to Erasmus' Para- phrase, that it had been on good considerations ordered to be set up in churches. He read all these, and said, he desired first to be discharged of his imprisonment, and then he would freely answer them all, so as to stand by it, and suffer if he did amiss : but he would trouble himself with no more articles while he remained in prison ; since he desired not to be de- livered out of his troubles in the way of mercy, but of justice. After that, he was brought before the council ; and the lords told him, they sat by a special commission to judge him, and so required him to subscribe the articles that had been sent to him. He prayed them earnestly to put him to a trial for the grounds of his imprisonment, and when that was over, he would clearly answer them in all other things : but he did not think he could subscribe all the articles after one sort ; some of them being about laws already made, which he could not qualify ; others of them being matters of learning, in which he might use more freedom : in conclusion, he desired leave to take them with him, and he would consider how to answer them. But they required him to subscribe them all, without any qualification ; which he refused to do. Upon this the fruits of his bishopric were sequestered ; and he was required to conform himself to their orders within three months, upon pain of deprivation : and the liberty he had of walking in some open galleries, when the duke of Norfolk was not in them, was taken from him, and he was again shut up in his chamber.

All this was much censured, as being contrary to the liber- ties of Englishmen, and the forms of all legal proceedings. It was thought very hard to put a man in prison upon a com- plaint against him ; and without any further inquiry into it, after two years durance, to put articles to him : and they which

New arti-
cles sent
to him.

[Ibid. p. 82.]

[Ibid. p. 83.]

But he, re-
fusing to
sign them,
was hardly
used.

spoke freely said, it savoured too much of the inquisition. But 152
the canon law not being rectified, and the king being in the
pope's room, there were some things gathered from the canon
law, and the way of proceeding *ex officio,* which rather excused than justified this hard measure he met with. The sequel
of this business shall be related in its proper place.

Latimer's
advice to
the king
concerning
his mar-
riage.

This Lent old Latimer preached before the king. The
discourse of the king's marrying a daughter of France had
alarmed all the reformers, who rather inclined to a daughter
of Ferdinand, king of the Romans. (To a marriage with her
it is no wonder they all wished well; for both Ferdinand and
his son Maximilian were looked upon as princes that in their
hearts loved the reformation, and the son was not only the
best prince, but accounted one of the best men of the age.)
But Latimer in his sermon advised the king to marry in the
Lord; and to take care that marriages might not be made
only as bargains, which was a thing too frequently done, and
occasioned so much whoredom and divorcing in the nation.
He ran out in a sad lamentation of the vices of the time, the
vanity of women, the luxury and irregularity of men : he complained, that many were gospellers for love of the abbey and
chantry lands: he pressed, that the discipline of the church,
and the excommunicating of scandalous persons, might be
again set up : he advised the king to beware of seeking his
pleasure too much, and to keep none about him who would
serve him in it : he said, he was so old, that he believed he
would never appear there more, and therefore he discharged
his conscience freely : he complained the king's debts were
not paid, and yet his officers lived high, made great purchases,
and built palaces : he prayed them all to be good to the king,
and not to defraud the poor tradesmen that wrought for his
stores, who were ill paid. This I set down, not so much to
give an account of that sermon, as of the state of the court
and nation, which he so freely discoursed of.

Hooper is
made bi-
shop of
Glouces-
ter :

Wakeman, that had been abbot of Tewkesbury, and was
after made bishop of Gloucester, died in December last year;
and on the third[91] of July this year, Hooper was by letters

---

[91] [Harmer observes (Specimen
of Error, p. 92), that ' The council

book saith, on the 15th of May Mr.
Hooper was constituted bishop of

patents appointed to be his successor.   Upon which there fol- [Rymer xv. p. 240.]
lowed a contest[92] that has since had such fatal consequences,
that of it we may say with St. James, *How great a matter
hath a little fire kindled!* It has been already shewn, that
the vestments used in divine service were appointed to be re-
tained in this church; but Hooper refused to be consecrated But refuses to wear the episcopal vestments.
in the episcopal vestments.   The grounds he went on were,
that they were human inventions, brought in by tradition or
custom, not suitable to the simplicity of the Christian religion;
that all such ceremonies were condemned by St. Paul as beg-
garly elements: that these vestments had been invented chiefly
for celebrating the mass with much pomp, and had been consecrated for that effect; therefore he desired to be excused
from the use of them.   Cranmer and Ridley, on the other
hand, alleged, that traditions in matters of faith were justly
rejected; but in matters of rites and ceremonies, custom was
oft a good argument for the continuance of that which had
been long used.   Those places of St. Paul did only relate to Upon this a great dispute rises.
the observance of the Jewish ceremonies, which some in the
apostles' time pleaded were still to be retained, upon the authority of their first institution by Moses: so this implying that
153 the Messias was not yet come, in whom all these had their
accomplishment, the apostles did condemn the use of them on
any such account; though when the bare observing them,
without the opinion of any such necessity in them, was likely
to gain the Jews, they both used circumcision, and purified
themselves in the temple.   If then they, who had such absolute
authority in those matters, did condescend so far to the weakness of the Jews, it was much more becoming subjects to give
obedience to laws in things indifferent.   And the abuse that
had been formerly was no better reason to take away the use
of these vestments, than it was to throw down churches, and
take away the bells, because the one had been consecrated,
and the other baptized, with many superstitious ceremonies.
Therefore they required Hooper to conform himself to the law.
Cranmer, who, to his other excellent qualities, had joined a [Cranmer's Remains, p. 428.]
singular modesty and distrust of himself, writ about this dif-

Gloucester: king Edward's Journal   relate to his nomination, the second
saith, July 20th Hooper was made   to the signing of his patent.]
bishop of Gloucester: the first may   [92] [See Part iii. p. 199.]

ference to Bucer, reducing it to these two plain questions: *Whether it was lawful, and free from any sin against God, for the ministers of the church of England to use those garments in which they did then officiate; since they were required to do it by the magistrate's command? And whether he that affirmed that it was unlawful, or on that account refused, to use those vestments, did not sin against God; calling that unclean which God had sanctified, and the magistrate required; since he thereby disturbed the public order of the kingdom?* To this Bucer writ a large answer on

Bucer's opinion concerning them. [Bucer, Scripta Anglicana, p. 681.]

the eighth of December this year. He thought that those who used these garments ought to declare they did not retain them as parts of Moses' law, but as things commanded by the law of the land. He thought every creature of God was good, and no former abuse could make it so ill, that it might not be retained; and since these garments had been used by the ancient fathers before popery, and might still be of good use to the weak when well understood, and help to maintain the ministerial dignity, and to shew that the church did not of any lightness change old customs, he thought the retaining them was expedient: that so the people might, by seeing these vestments, consider of the candour and purity that became them: and in this sense he thought, *to the pure all things were pure;* and so the apostles complied in many things with the Jews. Upon the whole matter, he thought they sinned who refused to obey the laws in that particular. But he added, that since these garments were abused by some to superstition, and by others to be matter of contention, he wished they were taken away, and a more complete reformation established. He also prayed that a stop might be put to the spoiling of churches, and that ecclesiastical discipline against offenders might be set up; for, said he, unless these manifest and horrid sacrileges be put down, and the complete kingdom of Christ be received, so that we all submit to his yoke, how intolerably shall the wrath of God break out on this kingdom! The scripture sets many such examples before our eyes, and Germany offers a most dreadful prospect of what England might look for.

[Ibid. p. 705.]

He writ also to Hooper upon the same argument. He wished the garments were removed by law; but argued fully for the use of them till then: he lamented the great corruptions that were among the clergy, and wished that all good men would unite their strength against these; and then lesser abuses would be more easily redressed: he also answered 154 Hooper's objections on the principles formerly laid down. Peter Martyr was also writ to; and, as he writ to Bucer, he was fully of his mind, and approved of all he had writ about it. And he added these words, which I shall set down in his own terms, copied from the original letter: *Quæ de Hopero ad me scribis, non potuerunt non videri mira; certe illis auditis obstupui. Sed bene habet, quod episcopi literas meas viderunt; unde invidiâ ego quidem sum liberatus. Ecce illius causa sic jacet, ut melioribus et piis nequaquam probetur. Dolet, dolet, idque mihi gravissime, talia inter evangelii professores contingere. Ille toto hoc tempore, cum illi sit interdicta concio, non videtur posse quiescere: suæ fidei confessionem edidit, quâ rursus multorum animos exacerbavit: deinde queritur de consiliariis, et fortasse, quod mihi non refert, de nobis: Deus felicem catastrophen non lætis actibus imponat.* In English: "What you wrote to me about Hooper "could not but seem wonderful to me: when I heard it, I was "struck with it. It was well that the bishops saw my letters, "by which I am freed from their displeasure. His business is "now at that pass, that the best and most pious disapprove of "it. I am grieved, and sadly grieved, that such things should "fall out among the professors of the gospel. All this while "in which he is suspended from preaching, he cannot be at "rest: he has set out a profession of his faith, by which he "has provoked many: he complains of the privy counsellors; "and perhaps of us too, of which he says nothing to me. God "give an happy issue to these uncomfortable beginnings." This I set down more fully, that it may appear how far either of these divines were from cherishing such stiffness in Hooper. He had been chaplain to the duke of Somerset, as appeared by his defence of himself in Bonner's process; yet he obtained so much favour of the earl of Warwick, that he writ earnestly in his behalf to the archbishop to dispense with the use of the garments, and the oath of canonical obedience at his consecration[93]. Cranmer wrote back, that he could not do it without

(marginal note:) And Peter Martyr's.

---

[93] The oath of canonical obedience, as printed in the form of con-

incurring a *præmunire :* so the king was moved to write to him, warranting him to do it, without any danger which the law could bring on him for such an omission. But though this was done on the fourth of August, yet he was not consecrated

[March 8.] till March next year ; and in the mean while it appears by Peter Martyr's letters that he was suspended from preaching.

A congregation of Germans in London. [Rymer,xv. p. 242.]

This summer John A Lasco[94], with a congregation of Germans, that fled from their country upon the persecution raised there for not receiving the interim, was allowed to hold his assembly at St. Austin's in London.   The congregation was erected into a corporation.   John A Lasco was to be superintendent, and there were four other ministers associated with him.   For the curiosity of the thing, I have put the patents in

Collect. Numb. 51.

the Collection. There were also 380 of the congregation made denizens of England, as appears by the records of their patents. But A Lasco did not carry himself with that decency that became a stranger who was so kindly received ; for he wrote against the orders of this church, both in the matter of the habits, and about the posture in the sacrament, being for sitting rather than kneeling.

Polydore Vergil leaves England.

This year Polydore Vergil, who had been now almost forty years in England, growing old, desired leave to go nearer the sun.   It was granted him on the second of June[95] ; and, in

secration, an. 1549, is so unexceptionable, that there seems to be no ground for scruple ; being only a promise of all due reverence and obedience to the archbishop, &c. It seems to have been the oath of supremacy, which at that time contained expressions more liable to exception, being a kind of *et cetera* oath requiring obedience to acts and statutes made or to be made, and concluding with, So help me God, all saints, &c.

Fuller, who was once of opinion that it was the oath of canonical obedience that Hooper scrupled, yet altered his opinion (Worthies in Somersetshire, p. 22) upon these or such like reasons. If Parsons' authority were of any weight, he expressly says, it was the oath of supremacy. De tribus convers. par. 3.

chap. 6. sect. 68. [B.]

[94] They were most of them Netherlanders, or French, only a few Germans, and consequently not concerned with the Interim ; and the language they officiated in was the Low-German and French, &c. Utenhov. Narrat. de institut. et dissipat. Belgarum, &c., p. 12, 28, &c. Those that went off with A Lasco were Low-Germans, French, English, or Scots. Ib. p. 22.   This seems confirmed by what is said, p. 250 of this volume, of their being of the Helvetian Confession, and of their reception in Denmark. However, I am not positive further than Utenhovius' account will bear me out, which I have not by me. [B.]

[95] The passport was signed in March 1554, to go with four servants, and three horses. [S.]

consideration of the public service he was thought to have done
155 the nation by his History, he was permitted to hold his arch- Rot. Pat. 4.
deaconry of Wells, and his prebend of Nonnington, notwith- Ed. VI.
part. 2.
standing his absence out of the kingdom.   On the 26th [96] of [ap. Rymer,
xv. p. 234.]
June Poynet was declared bishop of Rochester, and Coverdale
was made coadjutor to Veysey, bishop of Exeter.

About the end of this year, or the beginning of the next, A review of
the Com-
monPrayer
Book.
[Jan. 18,
1552, Ry-
mer, xv.
p. 250.]
there was a review made of the Common Prayer Book.   Seve-
ral things had been continued in it, either to draw in some of
the bishops, who by such yielding might be prevailed on to
concur in it; or in compliance with the people, who were fond
of their old superstitions.   So now a review of it was set about.
Martin Bucer was consulted in it; and Alesse, the Scotch
divine mentioned in the former [97] part, translated it into Latin
for his use.   Upon which Bucer writ his opinion, which he Bucer's ad-
vice con-
cerning it.
finished the fifth of January in the year following.   The sub-
stance of it was, that he found all things in the common service and daily prayers were clearly according to the scriptures.
He advised, that in cathedrals the quire might not be too far
separated from the congregation, since in some places the people could not hear them read prayers.   He wished there were
a strict discipline to exclude scandalous livers from the sacrament.   He wished the old habits might be laid aside, since
some used them superstitiously, and others contended much
about them.   He did not like the half office of communion or
second service to be said at the altar, when there was no sacrament.   He was offended with the requiring the people to
receive at least once a year, and would have them pressed to
it much more frequently.   He disliked that the priests generally read prayers with no devotion, and in such a voice that
the people understood not what they said.   He would have the
sacrament delivered into the hands, and not put into the
mouths of the people.   He censured praying for the dead, of
which no mention is made in the scripture, nor by Justin Martyr, an age after.   He thought that the prayer, that the elements might be to us the body and blood of Christ, favoured
transubstantiation too much ; a small variation might bring it

[96] [The letters patent are dated
June 6. Vide Rymer, Fœd. xv.
p. 237.   He was consecrated June

29th.   King Edward's Journal says
that he did homage June 30th.]
[97] [See part I. p. 308.]

nearer to a scripture form. He complained that baptism was generally in houses, which, being the receiving infants into the church, ought to be done more publicly. The hallowing of the water, the chrism, and the white garment, he censured as being too scenical. He excepted to the exorcising the Devil, and would have it turned to a prayer to God; that authoritative way of saying, *I adjure,* not being so decent. He thought the godfathers answering in the child's name not so well as to answer in their own, that they should take care in these things all they could. He would not have confirmation given upon a bare recital of the Catechism; but would have it delayed till the persons did really desire to renew the baptismal vow. He would have catechising every holyday, and not every sixth Sunday : and that people should be still catechised, after they were confirmed, to preserve them from ignorance. He would have all marriages to be made in the full congregation. He would have the giving unction to the sick, and praying for the dead, to be quite laid aside : as also the offering the chrisoms at the churching of women. He advised, that the communion should be celebrated four times a year. He sadly lamented the want of faithful teachers; and entreated the archbishop to see to the mending of this, and to think on some stricter ways of examining those who were to be ordained, than barely the 156 putting of some questions to them. All this I have gathered out the more largely, that it may appear how carefully things were then considered : and that almost in every particular the most material things which Bucer excepted to were corrected afterwards.

But at the same time, the king having taken such care of him, that, hearing he had suffered in his health last winter by the want of a stove, such as is used in Germany, he had sent him 20*l.* to have one made for him. He was told that the king would expect a new year's gift from him, of a book made for his own use : so, upon that occasion, he writ a book entitled, *Concerning the Kingdom of Christ* [98]. He sets out in it the miseries of Germany, which, he says, were brought on them by their sins; for they would bear no discipline; nor were the ministers so earnest in it as was fitting : though in Hungary it

Bucer writ a book for the king's use.

[98] [De Regno Christi libri duo. Bas. 1557.]

was otherwise. He writes largely of ecclesiastical discipline ; which was intended chiefly for separating ill men from the sacrament, and to make good men avoid their company, whereby they might be ashamed. He presses much the sanctification of the Lord's day, and of the other holydays, and that there might be many days of fasting : but he thought Lent had been so abused, that other times for it might be more expedient. He complains much of pluralities and nonresidence, as a remainder of•popery, so hurtful to the church, that in many places there were but one or two, or few more sermons in a whole year : but he thought that much was not to be expected from the greatest part of the clergy, unless the king would set himself vigorously to reform these things. Lastly, he would have a complete exposition of the doctrine of the church digested, and set out : and he proposed divers laws to the king's consideration ; as,

1. For catechising children.

2. For sanctifying holydays.

3. For preserving churches for God's service, not to be made places for walking, or for commerce.

4. To have the pastoral function entirely restored to what it ought to be ; that bishops, throwing off all secular cares, should give themselves to their spiritual employments : he advises that coadjutors might be given to some, and a council of presbyters be appointed for them all. It was plain, that many of them complied with the laws against their minds ; these he would have deprived. He advises rural bishops to be set over twenty or thirty parishes, who should gather their clergy often together, and inspect them closely : and that a provincial synod should meet twice a year, where a secular man, in the king's name, should be appointed to observe their proceedings.

5. For restoring church lands, that all who served the church might be well provided : if any lived in luxury upon their high revenues, it was reasonable to make them use them better ; but not to blame or rob the church for their fault.

6. For the maintenance of the poor, for whom anciently a fourth part of the church's goods was assigned.

The 7th was about marriage. That the prohibited degrees might be well settled ; marriage without consent of parents annulled; and that a second marriage might be lawful after a divorce, which he thought might be made for adultery, and some other reasons.

8. For the education of youth.

157

9. For restraining the excess of some people's living.

10. For reforming and explaining the laws of the land, which his father had begun.

11. To place good magistrates; that no office should be sold, and that inferior magistrates should often give an account to the superior, of the administration of their offices.

12. To consider well who were made judges.

13. To give order that none should be put in prison upon slight offences.

The 14th was for moderating of some punishments: chiefly, the putting of thieves to death, which was too severe; whereas adultery was too slightly passed over: though adultery be a greater wrong to the suffering party than any theft, and so was punished with death by Moses' law.

The king thinks of reforming many abuses.

Col. K. Ed. Remains, Numb. 2.

This book was sent to the young king. And he having received it, set himself to write a general discourse about a reformation of the nation, which is the second among the discourses written by him, that follow the Journal of his reign. In it he takes notice of the corrections of the book of the Liturgy which were then under consideration; as also, that it was necessary there should be a rule of church discipline, for the censure of ill livers; but he thought that power was not to be put into the hands of all the bishops at that time. From thence he goes on to discourse of the ill state of the nation, and of the remedies that seemed proper for it. The first he proposes was the education of youth; next, the correction of some laws; and there either broke it off, or the rest of it is lost. In which, as there is a great discovery of a marvellous probity of mind, so there are strange hints, to come from one not yet fourteen years of age. And yet it is all written with his own hand, and in such a manner, that any who shall look on the original will clearly see it was his own work: the style is simple, and suitable to a child. Few men can make such composures, but somewhat above a child will appear in their style; which makes me conclude it was all a device of his own.

This year the king began to write his Journal himself. The He writes a journal of all proceedings during his reign.
first three years of his reign are set down in a short way of
recapitulating matters: but this year he set down what was
done every day, that was of any moment, together with the
foreign news that were sent over. And oftentimes he called
to mind passages some days after they were done; and sometime, after the middle of a month, he tells what was done in
the beginning of it: which shews clearly it was his own work;
for if it had been drawn for him by any that were about him,
and given him only to copy out for his memory, it would have
been more exact: so that there remains no doubt with me but
that it was his own originally. And therefore, since all who
have writ of that time have drawn their informations from
that Journal; and though they have printed some of the letters
he wrote when a child, which are indeed the meanest things
that ever fell from him; yet, except one little fragment,
nothing of it has been yet published: I have copied it out
entirely, and set it before my Collection. I have added to it Collect. King Edward's Remains, Numb. 1.
some other papers that were also writ by him. The first of
158 these is in French; it is a collection of many passages out of
the Old Testament against idolatry and the worshipping of
images, which he dedicated to his uncle, being then protector;
the original under his own hand lies in Trinity college in Cambridge, from whence I copied the preface and the conclusion,
which are printed in the Collection after his Journal.

There was nothing else done of moment this year, in rela- Ridley visits his diocese. [Ridley's Register, fol. 305.]
tion to the church, save the visitation made of the diocese of
London by Ridley, their new bishop. But the exact time of
it is not set down in the register. It was, according to king
Edward's Journal, some time before the 26th of June: for he
writes, that on that day, sir John Gates, the high sheriff of
Essex, was sent down with letters to see the bishop of London's
injunctions performed, which touched the plucking down of
superaltaries, altars, and such like ceremonies and abuses: so
that the visitation must have been about the beginning of June.
The articles of it are in bishop Sparrow's Collection. They
are concerning the doctrines, and lives, and labours, and charities of the clergy; viz. Whether they spake in favour of the
bishop of Rome, or against the use of the scripture, or against
the Book of Common Prayer? Whether they stirred up

sedition, or sold the communion, or trentals, or used private masses any where? Whether any anabaptists or others used private conventicles, with different opinions and forms from these established? Whether there were any that said the wickedness of the minister took away the effect of the sacraments, or denied repentance to such as sinned after baptism? Other questions were about baptisms and marriages. Whether the curates did visit the sick, and bury the dead, and expound the Catechism, at least some part of it, once in six weeks? Whether any observed abrogated holydays, or the rites that were now put down?

Collect.
Numb. 52.

To these he added some injunctions, which are in the Collection. Most of them relate to the old superstitions, which some of the priests were still inclinable to practise, and for which they had been gently, if at all, reproved by Bonner. Such were, washing their hands at the altar, holding up the bread, licking the chalice, blessing their eyes with the paten or sudary, and many other relics of the mass. The ministers were also required to charge the people oft to give alms, and to come oft to the communion, and to carry themselves reverently at church. But that which was most new was, that there having been great contests about the form of the Lord's board, whether it should be made as an altar, or as a table;

He orders all altars to be turned to tables for the communion.

therefore, since the form of a table was more like to turn the people from the superstition of the popish mass, and to the right use of the Lord's supper, he exhorted the curates and churchwardens to have it in the fashion of a table, decently covered; and to place it in such part of the quire or chancel as should be most meet, so that the ministers and communicants should be separated from the rest of the people: and that they should put down all by-altars.

There are many passages among ancient writers, that shew their communion tables were of wood; and that they were so made as tables, that those who fled into churches for sanctuary did hide themselves under them. The name *altar* came to be given to these generally, because they accounted the eucharist a sacrifice of praise, as also a commemorative sacrifice of the oblation which Christ made of himself on the cross. From 159 hence it was, that the communion table was called also an altar. But now it came to be considered, whether, as these terms had

been on good reason brought into the church, when there was
no thought of the corruptions that followed; so if it was not
fit, since they did still support the belief of an expiatory sacrifice in the mass, and the opinion of transubstantiation, and
were always but figurative forms of speech, to change them:
and to do that more effectually, to change the form and place
of them. Some have fondly thought, that Ridley gave this
injunction after the letter which the council writ to him in the
end of November following. But as there was no fit time to
begin a visitation after that time this year, so the style of the
injunctions shews that they were given before the letter. The
injunction only *exhorts* the curates to do it, which Ridley could
not have done in such soft words, after the council had *required and commanded* him to do it: so it appears, that the
injunctions were given only by his episcopal power. And that
afterwards, the same matter being brought before the council,
who were informed, that in many places there had been contests about it, some being for keeping to their old custom, and
others being set on a change, the council thought fit to send
their letter concerning it to Ridley in the beginning [96] of November following. The letter sets out, that altars were taken
away, in divers places, upon good and godly considerations,
but still continued in other places; by which there rose much
contention among the king's subjects; therefore, for avoiding
that, they did charge and command him to give substantial
order through all his diocese for removing all altars, and setting up tables every where for the communion to be administered in some convenient part of the chancel: and, that these
orders might be the better received, there were reasons sent
with the letters, which he was to cause discreet preachers to
declare, in such places as he thought fit, and that himself
should set them out in his own cathedral, if conveniently he
could.

The reasons [97] were, to remove the people from the superstitious opinions of the popish mass; and because *a table* was a
more proper name than *an altar*, for that on which the sacrament was laid. And whereas in the Book of Common Prayer
these terms are promiscuously used, it is done without prescrib-

[96] For beginning say the 24th. [S.]
[97] These reasons were drawn up by Ridley. [S.]

ing any thing about the form of them, so that the changing the one into the other did not alter any part of the Liturgy. It was observed, that altars were erected for the sacrifices under the law; which ceasing, they were also to cease: and that Christ had instituted the sacrament not at an altar, but at a table. And it had been ordered by the preface to the Book of Common Prayer, that, if any doubt arose about any part of it, the determining of it should be referred to the bishop of the diocese. Upon these reasons therefore was this change ordered to be made all over England, which was universally executed this year.

Sermons on working-days forbidden.

There began this year a practice, which might seem in itself not only innocent, but good, of preaching sermons and lectures on the week-days, to which there was great running from neighbouring parishes. This, as it begat emulation in the clergy, so it was made use of as a pretence for many to leave their labour, and gad idly about. Upon complaint therefore made of it, Ridley had a letter sent to him from the council against all preaching on working-days, on which there should only be prayers. How this was submitted to then, is not clear. But it cannot be denied, that there have been since that time excesses on all hands in this matter: while some have, with great sincerity and devotion, kept up these in market-towns; but others have carried them on with too much faction, and a design to detract from such as were not so eminent in their way of preaching. Upon these abuses, while some rulers have studied to put all such performances down, rather than to correct the abuses in them, great contradiction has followed on it; and the people have been possessed with unjust prejudices against them, as hinderers of the word of God: and that opposition has kept up the zeal for these lectures; which nevertheless, since they have been more freely preached, have of late years produced none of the ill effects that did follow them formerly, when they were endeavoured to be suppressed.

And thus I end the transactions about religion this year. The rest of the affairs at home were chiefly for the regulating of many abuses, that had grown up and been nourished by a long continuance of war. All the foreign soldiers were dismissed: and though the duke of Lunenberg had offered the king ten thousand men to his assistance, and desired to enter

into a treaty of marriage for the lady Mary, they only thanked
him for the offer of his soldiers, of which they, being now at
peace with all their neighbours, had no need ; and since the
proposition for marrying the lady Mary to the infant of Portugal was yet in dependence, they could not treat in that kind
with any other prince till that overture was some way ended.
There were endeavours also for encouraging trade, and reforming the coin.   And at the court things began to put on a new
visage : for there was no more any faction ; the duke of Somerset and the earl of Warwick being now joined into a near
alliance ; the earl's eldest son, the lord Lisle, marrying the
duke's daughter : so that there was a good prospect of happy
times.

In Scotland, the peace being proclaimed, the government
was now more entirely in the hands of the duke of Châtelherault, who gave himself up wholly to the counsels of his base
brother, who was archbishop of St. Andrew's.   And he was so
abandoned to his pleasures, that there was nothing so bad that
he was ashamed of.   He kept another man's wife openly for
his concubine.   There were also many excesses in the government.   Which things, as they alienated all people's minds from
the clergy, so they disposed them to receive the new doctrines,
which many teachers were bringing from England, and prepared them for the changes that followed afterwards.   The
queen-mother went over into France in September, pretending
it was to see her daughter, and the rest of her kindred there :
where she laid down the method for the wresting of the government of Scotland out of the governor's hands, and taking
it into her own.

The emperor appointed a diet of the empire to meet in the
end of July [98], and required all to appear personally at it, except such as were hindered by sickness, of which they were to
make faith upon oath.   And at the same time he proscribed
the town of Magdeburg.   But the magistrates of that town set
out a large manifesto for their own vindication, as they had
done the former year.   They said, " They were ready to give
" him all the obedience that they were bound to by the laws of
" the empire.   They were very apprehensive of the mischiefs

The affairs of Scotland ; [Thuanus, p. 219.]

And of Germany. [June 26, Thuanus, p. 228.]

61

---

[98] [Cæsar ... significabat ... de-
crevisse conventus Imperii habere
Augustæ Vindelicorum ad vi. Kal.
Quintil. quibus ut omnes intersint
et rogat et jubet &c. Thuanus, vi.
17. p. 228.]

" of a civil war. They were not so blind as to think they were
" able to resist the emperor's great armies, lifted up with so
" many victories, if they trusted only to their own strength.
" They had hitherto done no act of hostility to any, but what
" they were forced to for their own defence. It was visible,
" the true ground of the war of Germany was religion, to ex-
" tinguish the light of the gospel, and to subdue them again to
" the papal tyranny : for the artifices that were formerly used
" to disguise it did now appear too manifestly ; so that it was
" not any more denied. But it would be too late to see it,
" when Germany was quite oppressed. In civil matters, they
" said, they would yield to the miseries of the time : but St.
" Peter had taught them, that it was better to obey God than
" man ; and therefore they were resolved to put all things to
" hazard, rather than to make shipwreck of faith and a good
" conscience." There were tumults raised in Strasburg, and
divers other towns, against those who set up the mass among
them ; and, generally, all Germany was disposed to a revolt, if
they had had but a head to lead them.

[Ibid. p. 229.]
 The emperor had also set out a very severe edict in Flanders, when he left it, against all that favoured the new doctrines, as they were called. But the execution of this was
stopped at the intercession of the town of Antwerp, when they
perceived the English were resolved to remove from thence,
[July 26.] and carry their trade to some other place. When the diet was
opened, the emperor pressed them to submit to the council,
which the new pope had removed back to Trent. Maurice of
Saxe answered, he could not submit to it, unless all that had
[Ibid. p. 230.] been done formerly in it should be reviewed, and the divines of
the Augsburg Confession were both heard and admitted to a
suffrage ; and the pope should subject himself to their decrees,
and dispense with the oath which the bishops had sworn to
him : on these terms he would submit to it, and not otherwise.
This was refused to be entered into the registers of the diet by
the elector of Mentz ; but there was no haste, for the council
was not to sit till the next year. The emperor complained
much that the Interim was not generally received : to which it
was answered by the princes, that it was necessary to give the
people time to overcome their former prejudices. All seemed
to comply with him : and Maurice did so insinuate himself into
him, that the siege of Magdeburg being now formed, and a

great many princes having gathered forces against it, among
whom the duke of Brunswick and the duke of Mecklenburg
were the most forward : yet he got himself declared by the
diet general of the empire, for the reduction of that place ;
and he had 100,000 crowns for undertaking it, and 60,000 [Ibid.
crowns a month were appointed for the expense of the war. p. 233.]
He saw well, that, if Magdeburg were closely pressed, it would
soon be taken, and then all Germany would be brought to the
emperor's devotion : and so the war would end in a slavery.
But he hoped so to manage this small remainder of the war, as
to draw great effects from it. This was a fatal step to the
emperor, thus to trust a prince who was of a different religion,
and had a deep resentment of the injury he had done him, in
detaining his father-in-law, the landgrave of Hesse, prisoner,
against the faith he had given him. But the emperor reck-
162 oned, that, as long as he had John duke of Saxe in his hands,
Maurice durst not depart from his interests ; since it seemed
an easy thing for him to repossess the other of his dominions
and dignity. Thus was the crafty emperor deluded ; and now
put that, upon which the completing of his great designs depended, into the hands of one that proved too hard for him at
that in which he was such a master, *cunning* and *dissimulation*.

In these consultations did this year end. In the beginning 1551.
of the next year there was a great complaint brought against The com-
Dr. Oglethorp, afterwards bishop of Carlisle under queen Mary, the popish
and now president of Magdalen college in Oxford. But he, to clergy.
secure himself from that part of the complaint that related to
religion, being accused as one that was against the new book of
service, and the king's other proceedings, signed a paper,
(which will be found in the Collection,) in which he declared, Collect.
" that he had never taught any thing openly against those, Numb. 53.
" but that he thought them good, if well used : and that he
" thought the order of religion now set forth to be better and
" much nearer the use of the apostolical and primitive church
" than that which was formerly : and that, in particular, he
" did approve of the communion in both kinds ; the people's
" communicating always with the priest, the service in English,
" and the Homilies that had been set forth : and that he did
" reject the lately received doctrine of transubstantiation, as

" being not agreeable to the scriptures, or to ancient writers :
" but he thought there was an inconceivable presence of Christ's
" body in the sacrament, and that therefore it should be re-
" ceived not without great examination beforehand." So compliant was he now, though he became of another mind in queen
Mary's time ; yet then he was more moderate than the greatest part of those who did now comply most servilely. In particular, Dr. Smith had written a book for the celibate of priests[99],
and had opposed all the changes that had been made. He was
brought to London upon the complaints that were sent up
against him from Oxford : but, after a while's imprisonment,
he was set at liberty, giving surety for his good behaviour ;
and carried himself so obediently after it, that Cranmer[1] got
his sureties to be discharged : upon which he writ him a letter
as full of acknowledgment as was possible ; which is in the

Collect.
Numb. 54. Collection. " He protested he should retain the sense of it as
" long as he lived : he wished that he had never written his
" book of the celibate of priests, which had been printed against
" his will: he found he was mistaken in that which was the
" foundation of it all, that the priests of England had taken a
" vow against marriage : he desired to see some of the collec-
" tions Cranmer had made against it." (It seems Cranmer was
inquiring after a MS. of Ignatius' Epistles ; for he tells him,
" they were in Magdalen college library.") " He acknow-
" ledged the archbishop's great gentleness toward all those
" who had been complained of for religion in that university ;
" and protested, that, for his own part, if ever he could serve
" his basest servant, he would do it ; wishing that he might
" perish if he thought otherwise than he said ; and wished
" him long life for the propagation and advancement of the
" Christian doctrine." Soon after, he writ another letter to
Cranmer[2], in which he cited some passages out of Austin concerning his retractations ; and professes he would not be
ashamed to make the like, and to set forth Christ's true re-

99 [Defensio cœlibatûs sacerdotum contra Petrum Martyrem. Lov.
1550, 8vo., with Confutatio quorun-
dam articulorum de votis monasticis
Pet. Martyris Itali.]

1 This was not before Cranmer,
but long after, before archbishop
Parker. [S.]

2 These letters I have seen. I
can assure your lordship they are
wrote to Parker, not to Cranmer.
And if your lordship has any doubt
of it, I can make it very evident.
[B.]

163 ligion; and called, in St. Paul's words, *God to be a witness against his soul if he lied.* He had also, in the beginning of this reign, made a recantation sermon of some opinions he had held concerning the mass; but what these were, king Edward's Journal (from whence I gather it) does not inform us [3]. Day, bishop of Chichester, did also now so far comply as to preach a sermon at court against transubstantiation, though he had refused to set his hand to the Book of Common Prayer, before it was enacted by law. For the principle that generally ran among the popish party was, that though they would not consent to the making of such alterations in religion, yet, being made, they would give obedience to them, which Gardiner plainly professed; and it appeared in the practice of all the rest. This was certainly a gross sort of compliance in those who retained the old opinions, and yet did now declare against them; and, in the worship they offered up to God, acted contrary to them: which was the highest degree of prevarication, both with God and man, that was possible. But Cranmer was always gentle and moderate: he left their private consciences to God; but thought, that, if they gave an external obedience, the people would be brought to receive the changes more easily; whereas the proceeding severely against them might have raised more opposition. He was also naturally a man of bowels and compassion, and did not love to drive things to extremities. He considered, that men who had grown old in some errors could not easily lay them down, and so were by degrees to be worn out of them. Only in the proceedings against Gardiner and Bonner, he was carried beyond his ordinary temper. But Gardiner he knew to be so inveterate a papist, and so deep a dissembler, that he was for throwing him out, not so much for the particulars objected to him, as upon the ill character he had of him. Bonner had also deceived

[3] The particulars were: 1. concerning submission to governors in church and state; 2. concerning unwritten traditions; 3. concerning the sacrifice of the mass, &c.; as may be seen in his retractation, printed at London, an. 1547 *cum priv.* entitled, 'A godly and faithful retractation made and published at Paul's cross in London Anno 1547, 15 Mary: by Master Richard Smith, D. D. and reader of the King's Majesty's lecture in Oxford; revoking therein certain errors and faults by him committed in some of his books. It was repeated at Oxford, July the 24th, the same year. [B.]

him so formerly, and had been so cruel a persecutor upon the statute of the six articles, and was become so brutal and luxurious, that he judged it necessary to purge the church of him: and the sees of London and Winchester were of such consequence, that he was induced, for having these well supplied, to stretch a little in these proceedings against those dissembling bishops.

Bucer's death.

In the end of February he lost his friend Martin Bucer, on whose assistance he had depended much, in what remained yet to be done.   Bucer died of the stone, and griping of the guts, on the 28th of February [4].   He lay ill almost all that month, and expressed great desire to die.   Bradford, who will be mentioned in the next book with much honour, waited most on him in his sickness.   He lamented much the desolate state of Germany, and expressed his apprehensions of some such stroke coming upon England, by reason of the great dissoluteness of the people's manners, of the want of ecclesiastical discipline, and the general neglect of the pastoral charge.   He was very patient in all his pain, which grew violent on him: he lay oft silent; only, after long intervals, cried out sometimes, *Chastise me, Lord, but throw me not off in my old age.*   He was, by order from Cranmer and sir John Cheke, buried with the highest solemnities that could be devised, to express the value the university had for him.   The vice-chancellor, and all the graduates, and the mayor, with all the town, accompanied his funeral to St. Mary's; where, after prayers, Haddon, the university orator, made such a speech concerning him, and pronounced it with that affection, that almost the whole assembly 164 shed tears.   Next, Dr. Parker, that had been his most intimate friend, made an English sermon in his praise, and concerning the sorrowing for our departed friends.   And the day following Dr. Redmayn, then master of Trinity college, made another sermon concerning death; and in it gave a full account of Bucer's life and death.   He particularly commended

[4] It is not very material whether he died this day or the day after. But he died the 1st of March, if Parker and Haddon's account may be taken, who were present, and bore a part at his funeral, and were executors of his will.

Nicholas Carr, likewise present, says *Calendis Martiis* in his letter to Cheke. These I suppose are the best authorities. [B.]

the great sweetness of his temper to all, but remarkably to
those who differed from him. Redmayn and 'he had differed
in many things, both concerning justification, and the influences of the divine grace. But he said, as Bucer had satisfied
him in some things, so he believed, if he had lived, he had
satisfied him in more; and that, he being dead, he knew none
alive from whom he could learn so much. This character given
him by so grave and learned a man, who was in many points
of a different persuasion from him, was a great commendation
to them both. And Redmayn was indeed an extraordinary
person. All in the university, that were eminent either in
Greek or Latin poetry, did adorn his coffin with epitaphs; in
which they expressed a very extraordinary sense of their loss:
about which one Carr[5] writ a copious and passionate letter to
sir John Cheke. But Peter Martyr bore his death with the
most sensible sorrow that could be imagined; having in him
lost a father, and the only intimate friend he had in England.
He was a very learned, judicious, pious, and moderate person. His charac-
Perhaps he was inferior to none of all the reformers for learn- ter.
ing; but for zeal, for true piety, and a most tender care of
preserving unity among the foreign churches, Melancthon and
he, without any injury done the rest, may be ranked apart by
themselves. He was much opposed by the popish party at
Cambridge; who, though they complied with the law, and so
kept their places, yet, either in the way of argument, as it had
been for dispute's sake, or in such points as were not determined, set themselves much to lessen his esteem. Nor was he
furnished naturally with the quickness that is necessary for
a dispute, from which they studied to draw advantages; and
therefore Peter Martyr writ to him to avoid all public disputes
with them: for they did not deal candidly on these occasions.
They often kept up their questions till the hour of the dispute,
that so the extemporary faculty of him who was to preside
might be the more exposed; and, right or wrong, they used
to make exclamations, and run away with a triumph. In one
of his letters to Bucer, he particularly mentions Dr. Smith for
an instance of this. It was that Smith, he said, who writ
against the marriage of priests, and yet was believed to live in

[5] Nicholas Carr, Regius Professor   and a great restorer of learning in
of the Greek tongue in Cambridge,   that University. [G.]

adultery with his man's wife. This letter was occasioned by
the disputes that were in August the former year, between
Bucer and Sedgwick, Young and Pern, about the authority of
the scripture and the church. Which disputes Bucer intending
to publish, caused them to be writ out, and sent the copy to
them to be corrected; offering them, that, if any thing was
omitted that they had said, or if they had any thing else to
say which was forgot in the dispute, they might add it: but
they sent back the papers to him without vouchsafing to read
them. At Ratisbon he had a conference with Gardiner, who
was then king Henry's ambassador; in which Gardiner broke
out into such a violent passion, that, as he spared no reproachful words, so the company thought he would have fallen on
Bucer and beat him. He was in such disorder, that the little
vein between his thumb and fore-finger did swell and palpi- 165
tate; which, Bucer said, he had never before that observed in
any person in his life.

Gardiner is
deprived.

[Fox, lib.
ix. p. 84.]

But as Bucer was taken away by death, so Gardiner was
soon after[6] put out, which was a kind of death; though he had
afterwards a resurrection fatal to very many. There was a
commission issued out to the archbishop; the bishops of London, Ely, and Lincoln; secretary Petre; judge Hales; Griffith, and Leyson, two civilians[7], and Goodrick, and Gosnold,
two masters of chancery, to proceed against Gardiner for his
contempt in the matters formerly objected to him. He put in
a compurgation, by which he endeavoured to shew there was
malice borne to him and conspiracies against him, as appeared
by the business of sir Henry Knyvet, mentioned in the former
part, and the leaving him out of the late king's will, which he
said was procured by his enemies. He complained of his long
imprisonment without any trial, and that articles of one sort
after another were brought to him: so that it was plain he
was not detained for any crime, but to try if such usage could
force him to do any thing that should be imposed on him.
He declared, that what order soever were set out by the
king's council, he should never speak against it, but to the
council themselves: and that though he could not give con-

6 Soon after—*read* sometime before. It was on the 14th of February. [S.]

7 Griffith Leyson was only one
civilian: the other was John Oliver,
LL.D. [B.]

sent to the changes before they were made, he was now well satisfied to obey them; but he would never make any acknowledgment of any fault. The things chiefly laid against him were, that, being required, he refused to preach concerning the king's power when he was under age; and that he had affronted preachers sent by the king into his diocese, and had been negligent in obeying the king's injunctions; and continued, after all, so obstinate, that he would not confess his fault, nor ask the king mercy. His crimes were aggravated by this, that his timely asserting the king's power under age might have been a great mean for preventing the rebellion and effusion of blood, which had afterwards happened, chiefly on that pretence, to which his obstinacy had given no small occasion. Upon this, many witnesses were examined; chiefly the duke of Somerset, the earls of Wiltshire and Bedford, who deposed against him. But to this he answered, that he was not required to do it by any order of council, but only in a private discourse, to which he did not think himself bound to give obedience. Other witnesses were also examined on the other particulars. But he appealed from the delegates to the king in person. Yet his judges, on the 18th of April [8], gave sentence against him; by which, for his disobedience and contempt, they deprived him of his bishopric. Upon that he renewed his protestation and appeal: and so his process ended, and he was sent back to the Tower, where he lay till queen Mary discharged him.

The same censures, with the same justifications, belong both to this and Bonner's business: so I shall repeat nothing that was formerly said. He had taken a commission, as well as Bonner, to hold his bishopric only during the king's pleasure; so they both had the less reason to complain, which way soever the royal pleasure was signified to them. Eight days after [9], on the 26th of April, Poynet was translated from Rochester to

[8] [His successor had been previously appointed, as appears by the following extract from the Council Book:

'At Westminster the 8 Day of March an. 1550. This day, by the King's Majesty's own appointment, Doctor Poynete Bishop of Rochester, was appointed and admitted Bishop of Winchester.' Archæologia, vol. xviii. p. 153.]

[9] [The letters patent are dated March 23, 1550-1. Vide Rymer, Fœd. xv. p. 253.] See also Harmer, Specimen of Errors, p. 99.

Winchester; and had two thousand marks a year in lands assigned him out of that wealthy bishopric for his subsistence.

[April 6.]
[Rymer,
xv. p. 282.]

Dr. Story [10] was made bishop of Rochester. Vesey, bishop of Exeter, did also resign, pretending extreme old age; but he **166** had reserved 485*l.* a year in pension for himself during life, out of the lands of the bishopric; and almost all the rest he had basely alienated, taking care only of himself, and ruining

[Aug. 4,
ibid. p.
283.]
Hooper
is conse-
crated
upon his
conform-
ity.
[March 8.]

his successors. Miles Coverdale was made bishop of Exeter. So that now the bishoprics were generally filled with men well affected to the reformation [11]. The business of Hooper was now also settled: he was to be attired in the vestments that were prescribed when he was consecrated, and when he preached before the king, or in his cathedral, or in any public place; but he was dispensed with upon other occasions. On these conditions he was consecrated in March; for the writ for doing it bears date the 7th of that month. So now, the bishops being generally addicted to the purity of religion, most of this year was spent in preparing acticles, which should contain the doctrine of the church of England.

Many thought they should have begun first of all with those. But Cranmer, upon good reasons, was of another mind, though much pressed by Bucer about it. Till the order of bishops was brought to such a model, that the far greater part of them would agree to it, it was much fitter to let that design go on slowly, than to set out a profession of their belief, to which so great a part of the chief pastors might be obstinately averse. The corruptions that were most important were those in the worship, by which men, in their immediate addresses to God, were necessarily involved in unlawful compliances; and these seemed to require a more speedy reformation. But for speculative points there was not so pressing a necessity to have them all explained, since in these men might with less prejudice be left to a freedom in their opinions. It seemed also advisable to open and ventilate matters in public disputations and books, written about them for some years, before they should go too hastily to determine them; lest, if they went too fast in that

---

[10] For Dr. Scory. [G.] [Probably the author spelt the name as he found it in the Letters Patent, where it is written as in the text.]

[11] The greater part of the bishops were enemies to the reformation. [S.]

affair, it would not be so decent to make alterations afterwards; nor could the clergy be of a sudden brought to change
their old opinions. Therefore, upon all these considerations,
that work was delayed till this year; in which they set about
it, and finished it, before the convocation met in the next
February. In what method they proceeded for the compiling
of these articles; whether they were given out to several
bishops and divines to deliver their opinions concerning them,
as was done formerly, or not, it is not certain. I have found
it often said, that they were framed by Cranmer and Ridley;
which I think more probable; and that they were by them
sent about to others, to correct or add to them as they saw
cause. They are in the Collection, with the differences be- Collect.
tween these and those set out in queen Elizabeth's time marked Numb. 55.
on the margin.

They began with the assertion of the blessed Trinity, the The Arti-
incarnation of the eternal Word, and Christ's descent into hell; cles of Re-
grounding this last on these words of St. Peter, of his *preach-* ligion are
ing to the spirits that were in prison. The next article was prepared.
about Christ's resurrection. The fifth, about the scriptures
containing all things necessary to salvation: so that nothing
was to be held an article of faith that could not be proved
from thence. The sixth, That the Old Testament was to be
kept still.

167　The 7th, For the receiving the three Creeds; the Apostles',
the Nicene, and Athanasius' Creed: in which they went according to the received opinion, that Athanasius was the author
of that Creed, which is now found not to have been compiled
till near three ages after him.

The 8th makes original sin to be the corruption of the nature of all men descending from Adam; by which they had
fallen from original righteousness, and were by nature given
to evil: but they defined nothing about the derivation of guilt
from Adam's sin.

The 9th; For the necessity of prevailing grace, without
which we have no freewill to do things acceptable to God.

The 10th; About divine grace, which changeth a man, and
yet puts no force on his will.

The 11th; That men are justified by faith only; as was declared in the homily.

The 12th; That works done before grace are not without sin.

The 13th; Against all works of supererogation.

The 14th; That all men, Christ only excepted, are guilty of sin.

The 15th; That men who have received grace may sin afterwards, and rise again by repentance.

The 16th; That the blaspheming against the Holy Ghost is, when men out of malice and obstinately rail against God's word, though they are convinced of it, yet persecuting it; which is unpardonable.

The 17th; That predestination is God's free election of those whom he afterwards justifies; which though it be matter of great comfort to such as consider it aright, yet it is a dangerous thing for curious and carnal men to pry into: and, it being a secret, men are to be governed by God's revealed will. They added not a word of reprobation.

The 18th; That only the name of Christ, and not the law or light of nature, can save men.

The 19th; That all men are bound to keep the moral law.

The 20th; That the church is a congregation of faithful men, who have the word of God preached, and the sacraments rightly administered: and that the church of Rome, as well as other particular churches, have erred in matters of faith.

The 21st; That the church is only the witness and keeper of the word of God: but cannot appoint any thing contrary to it, nor declare any articles of faith without warrant from it.

The 22nd; That general councils may not be gathered without the consent of princes; that they may err, and have erred, in matters of faith: and that their decrees in matters of salvation have strength only as they are taken out of the scriptures.

The 23rd; That the doctrines of purgatory, pardons, worshipping of images and relics, and invocation of saints, are without any warrant, and contrary to the scriptures.

The 24th; That none may preach or minister the sacraments, without he be lawfully called by men who have lawful authority.

The 25th; That all things should be spoken in the church in a vulgar tongue.

The 26th; That there are two sacraments, which are not

bare tokens of our profession, but effectual signs of God's good-
68 will to us; which strengthen our faith, yet not by virtue only
of the work wrought, but in those who receive them worthily.

The 27th; That the virtue of these does not depend on the
minister of them.

The 28th; That by baptism we are the adopted sons of
God; and that infant baptism is to be commended, and in any
ways to be retained.

The 29th; That the Lord's supper is not a bare token of
love among Christians, but is the communion of the body and
blood of Christ; that the doctrine of transubstantiation is contrary to scripture, and hath given occasion to much superstition: that a body being only in one place, and Christ's body
being in heaven, therefore there cannot be a real and bodily
presence of his flesh and blood in it: and that this sacrament
is not to be kept, carried about, lifted up, nor worshipped.

The 30th; That there is no other propitiatory sacrifice, but
that which Christ offered on the cross.

The 31st; That the clergy are not by God's command
obliged to abstain from marriage.

The 32nd; That persons rightly excommunicated are to be
looked on as heathens, till they are by penance reconciled, and
received by a judge competent.

The 33rd; It is not necessary that ceremonies should be the
same at all times; but such as refuse to obey lawful ceremonies ought to be openly reproved as offending against law and
order, giving scandal to the weak.

The 34th; That the Homilies are godly and wholesome, and
ought to be read.

The 35th; That the Book of Common Prayer is not re-
pugnant, but agreeable to the gospel, and ought to be received
by all.

The 36th; That the king is supreme head under Christ:
that the bishop of Rome hath no jurisdiction in England: that
the civil magistrate is to be obeyed for conscience sake: that
men may be put to death for great offences: and that it is
lawful for Christians to make war.

The 37th; That there is not to be a community of all men's
goods; but yet every man ought to give to the poor according
to his ability.

The 38th; That though rash swearing is condemned, yet such as are required by the magistrate may take-an oath.

The 39th; That the resurrection is not already past, but at the last day men shall rise with the same bodies they now have.

The 40th; That departed souls do not die, nor sleep with their bodies, and continue without sense till the last day.

The 41st; That the fable of the Millenaries is contrary to scripture, and a Jewish dotage.

The last condemned those who believed that the damned, after some time of suffering, shall be saved.

Thus was the doctrine of the church cast into a short and plain form: in which they took care both to establish the positive articles of religion, and to cut off the errors formerly introduced in the time of popery, or of late broached by the ana- 16⁹ baptists and enthusiasts of Germany; avoiding the niceties of schoolmen, or the peremptoriness of the writers of controversy; leaving, in matters that are more justly controvertible, a liberty to divines to follow their private opinions, without thereby disturbing the peace of the church.

There was in the ancient church a great simplicity in their creeds, and the exposition of the doctrine. But afterwards, upon the breaking out of the Arian and other heresies concerning the person of Jesus Christ, as the orthodox fathers were put to find out new terms to drive the heretics out of the equivocal use of these formerly received, so they too soon grew to love niceties, and to explain mysteries with similes, and other subtleties, which they invented: and councils afterwards were very liberal in their anathematisms against any who did not agree in all points to their terms or ways of explanation. And though the council of Ephesus decreed that there should be no additions made to the creed, they understood that not of the whole belief of Christians, but only of the creed itself; and did also load the Christian doctrine with many curiosities. But though they had exceeded much, yet the schoolmen getting the management of the doctrine, spun their thread much finer; and did easily procure condemnations, either by papal bulls, or the decrees of such councils as met in these times, of all that differed from them in the least matter. Upon the progress of the reformation, the German writers, particularly Osiander,

Illyricus, and Amstorfius, grew too peremptory, and not only condemned the Helvetian churches for differing from them in the manner of Christ's presence in the sacrament, but were severe to one another for lesser punctilios; and were at this time exercising the patience of the great and learned Melancthon, because he thought, that, in things of their own nature indifferent, they ought to have complied with the emperor. This made those in England resolve on composing these articles with great temper in many such points. Only one notion, that has been since taken up by some, seems not to have been then thought of; which is, that these were rather articles of peace than of belief: so that the subscribing was rather a compromise not to teach any doctrine contrary to them, than a declaration that they believed according to them. There appears no reason for this conceit, no such thing being then declared; so that those who subscribed did either believe them to be true, or else they did grossly prevaricate.

The next business in which the reformers were employed this year was, the correcting the Common Prayer Book, and the making some additions, with the changing of such particulars, as had been retained only for a time.[11] The most considerable additions were, that in the daily service they prepared a short, but most simple and grave, form of a general confession of sins; in the use of which they intended, that those who made this confession should not content themselves with a bare recital of the words, but should join with them in their hearts a particular confession of their private sins to God. To this was added, a general absolution, or pronouncing, in the name of God, the pardon of sin to all those who did truly repent, and unfeignedly believe the gospel. For they judged, that if the people did seriously practise this, it would keep up in their thoughts frequent reflections on their sins; and it was thought, that the pronouncing a pardon upon these conditions might have a better effect on the people, than that absolute and unqualified pardon which their priests were wont to give in confession: by which absolution, in times of popery, the people were made to believe that their sins were thereupon certainly forgiven; than which nothing could be invented that would harden them into a more fatal security, when they thought a

Some corrections made in the Common Prayer Book.

170

[11 See Part iii. p. 210.]

full pardon could be so readily purchased. But now they heard the terms, on which they could only expect it, every day promulgated to them. The other addition was also made, upon good consideration, in the office of the communion, to which the people were observed to come without due seriousness or preparation : therefore, for awakening their consciences more feelingly, it was ordered, that the office of the communion should begin with a solemn pronouncing of the Ten Commandments, all the congregation being on their knees, as if they were hearing that law anew; and a stop to be made at every Commandment, for the people's devotion, of imploring mercy for their past offences, and grace to observe it for the time to come. This seemed as effectual a means as they could devise, till church-penitence were again set up, to beget in men deep reflections on their sins, and to prepare them thereby to receive that holy sacrament worthily. The other changes were, the removing of some rites which had been retained in the former book : such as the use of oil in confirmation, and extreme unction; the prayers for souls departed, both in the communion service and in the office of burial; the leaving out some passages in the consecration of the eucharist, that seemed to favour the belief of the corporal presence, with the use of the cross in it, and in confirmation; with some smaller variations. And, indeed, they brought the whole Liturgy to the same form in which it is now, except some inconsiderable variations that have been since made for the clearing of some ambiguities.

An account of kneeling in the communion.

In the office of the communion, they added a rubric concerning the posture of kneeling, which was appointed to be still the gesture of communicants. It was hereby declared, that that gesture was kept up, as a most reverent and humble way of expressing our great sense of the mercies of God in the death of Christ there communicated to us; but that thereby there was no adoration intended to the bread and wine, which was gross idolatry : nor did they think the very flesh and blood of Christ were there present; since his body, according to the nature of all other bodies, could be only in one place at once: and so he, being now in heaven, could not be corporally present in the sacrament. This was by queen Elizabeth ordered to be left out of the Common Prayer Book ; since it might have given offence to some, otherwise inclinable to the communion of the church, who yet retained the belief of the corporal presence. But, since his[12] present majesty's restoration, many having excepted to the posture, as apprehending something like idolatry or superstition might lie under it, if it were not rightly explained; that explication which was given in King Edward's time was again inserted in the Common Prayer Book.

For the posture, it is most likely that the first institution was in the table-gesture, which was lying along on one side. But it was apparent, in our Saviour's practice, that the Jewish church had changed the posture of that institution of the passover, in whose room the eucharist came. For though Moses had appointed the Jews to eat their paschal lamb standing, with their loins girt, with staves in their hands, and shoes on their feet; yet the Jews did afterwards change this into the common table-posture: of which change, though there is no mention in the Old Testament, yet we see it was so in our Saviour's time; and since he complied with the common custom, we are sure that change was not criminal. It seemed reasonable to allow the Christian church the like power in such things with the Jewish; and as the Jews thought their coming into the promised land might be a warrant to lay aside the posture appointed by Moses, which became travellers best; so Christ being now exalted it seemed fit to receive this sacrament with higher marks of outward respect than had been proper in the first institution, when he was in the state of humiliation, and his divine glory not yet so fully revealed. Therefore in the primitive church they received standing and bending their body, in a posture of adoration: but how soon that gesture of kneeling came in, is not so exactly observed, nor is it needful to know. But surely there is a great want of ingenuity in them that are pleased to apply these orders of some later popes for kneeling at the elevation, to our kneeling: when ours is not at one such part, which might be more liable to exception, but during the whole office; by which it is one continued act of worship, and the communicants kneel all the while. But of this no more needs to be said than is expressed in the rubric, which occasioned this digression.

Thus were the reformations both of doctrine and worship

Some orders given

[12] [This was written and published in the reign of King Charles II.]

to the
king's
chaplains.
prepared: to which all I can add of this year is, that there were six eminent preachers chosen out to be the king's chaplains in ordinary : two of those were always to attend at court; and four to be sent over England to preach and instruct the people. In the first year, two of these were to go into Wales, and the other two into Lancashire ; the next year, two into the marches of Scotland, and two into Yorkshire ; the third year, two into Devonshire, and two into Hampshire ; and the fourth year, two into Norfolk, and two into Kent and Sussex : these were, Bill, Harle [13], Pern, Grindal, Bradford ; the name of the sixth [14] is so dashed in the king's Journal, that it cannot be read. These, it seems, were accounted the most zealous and readiest preachers of that time ; who were thus sent about as itinerants to supply the defects of the greatest part of the clergy, who were generally very faulty.

The lady
Mary con-
tinued to
have mass
said in her
chapel.
The business of the lady Mary was now taken up with more heat than formerly. The emperor's earnest suit, that she might have mass in her house, was long rejected: for it was said, that as the king did not interpose in the matters of the emperor's government, so there was no reason for the emperor to meddle in his affairs. Yet the state of England making his friendship at that time necessary to the king, and he refusing to continue in his league, unless his kinswoman obtained that favour, it was promised, that for some time, in hope she would reform, there should be a forbearance granted. The emperor's ambassadors pressed to have a license for it under the great seal : it was answered, that, being against law, it could not be done. Then they desired to have it certified under the king's hand in a letter to the emperor ; but even that was refused: so that they only gave a promise for some time by word of 172 mouth ; and Paget and Hobby, who had been the ambassadors with the emperor, declared they had spoke of it to him with the same limitations. But the emperor, who was accustomed to take for absolute what was promised only under conditions, writ to the lady Mary, that he had an absolute promise for the free exercise of her religion : and so she pretended this, when she was at any time questioned about it. The two grounds

---

[13] For Harley afterward bp. of Hereford. [G.]
[14] The name of the sixth was Knox. [S.]

she went on were, that she would follow the ancient and universal way of worship, and not a new invention that lay within
the four seas : and that she would continue in that religion in
which her father had instructed her. To this the king sent an
answer, telling her, that she was a part of this church and na- [Jan. 24,
tion, and so must conform herself to the laws of it; that the 1551. Fox
way of worship now set up was no other than what was clearly p. 46.]
consonant to the pure word of God ; and the king's being young
was not to be pretended by her, lest she might seem to agree
with the late rebels. After this she was sent for to court, and
pains were taken to instruct her better: but she refused to
hear anything, or to enter into any reasonings; but said, she
would still do as she had done. And she claimed the promise
that was said to be made to the emperor: but it was told her,
that it was but temporary and conditional. Whereupon the
last summer she was designing to fly out of England ; and the [Ibid.
king of France gave sir John Mason, the English resident, no- p. 48.]
tice, that the regent of Flanders had hired one Scipperus, who
should land on the coast of Essex, as if it had been to victual
his ship, and was to have conveyed her away. Upon this information, order was given to see well to the coast ; so the design
being discovered, nothing could be effected. It was certainly
a strange advice to carry her away ; and no less strange in the
king's ministers to hinder it, if there was at that time any design formed to put by her succession: for if she had been beyond sea at the king's death, it is not probable that she could
have easily come to the crown. The emperor's ambassador
solicited for her violently, and said, he would presently take
leave, and protest, that they had broken their faith to his master: who would resent the usage of the lady Mary as highly
as if it were done immediately to himself The counsellors
having no mind to draw a new war on their heads, especially
from so victorious a prince, were all inclined to let the matter
fall. There was also a year's cloth lately sent over to Antwerp ;
and 1500 quintals of powder, with a great deal of armour, bought
there for the king's use, was not come over. So it was thought
by no means advisable to provoke the emperor, while they
had such effects in his ports ; nor were they very willing to give
higher provocations to the next heir of the crown. Therefore
they all advised the king not to do more in that matter at pre-

sent, but to leave the lady Mary to her discretion; who would certainly be made more cautious by what she had met with, and would give as little scandal as was possible by her mass.

The king is very earnest against it.

[March 22. Hayward, p. 316.]

But the king could not be induced to give way to it; for he thought the mass was impious and idolatrous: so he would not consent to the continuance of such a sin. Upon this the council ordered Cranmer, Ridley and Poynet to discourse about it with him. They told him, that it was always a sin in a prince to permit any sin: but to give a connivance, that is, not to punish, was not always a sin; since sometimes a lesser evil connived at might prevent a greater. He was overcome by this; yet not so easily, but that he burst forth in tears, lamenting his sister's 178 obstinacy, and that he must suffer her to continue in so abominable a way of worship, as he esteemed the mass. So he answered the emperor's agents, that he should send over an ambassador to clear that matter. And Dr. Wotton was despatched about it; who carried over attestations from all the council, concerning the qualifications of the promise that had been made: and was instructed to press the emperor not to trouble the king in his affairs at home in his own kingdom. If the lady Mary was his kinswoman, she was the king's sister and subject. He was also to offer, that the king would grant as much liberty for the mass in his dominions, as the emperor would grant for the English service in his dominions. But the emperor pretended, that when her mother died, she left her to his protection, which he had granted her, and so must take care of her. And the emperor was so exalted with his successes, that he did not easily bear any contradiction. But the council being further offended with her for the project of going beyond sea, and being now less in fear of the emperor, since they had made peace with France, resolved to look more nearly to her. And finding that Dr. Mallet and Barkley,

[Fox, lib. ix. p. 47.]

[Dec. 4, 1550.]

[Ibid. p. 48.]

her chaplains, had said mass in one of her houses, when she was not in it, they ordered them to be proceeded against. Upon which, in December the last year, she writ earnestly to the council to let it fall. By her letter it appears that Mallet used to be sometimes at his benefice, where it is certain he could officiate no other way but in that prescribed by law: so, it seems, his conscience was not very scrupulous. The council writ a long answer, which, being in the style of a churchman, seems to have been penned either The council writ to her of it [Dec. 25. by Cranmer or Ridley.   In which letter they fully cleared the matter of the promise: then they shewed how express the law was, with which they could not dispense; and how ill grounded Ibid. p. 48.] her faith, as she called it, was.   They asked her what warrant [Ibid. p. 49.] there was in scripture, that the prayers should be in an unknown tongue; that images should be in the church; or, that the sacrament should be offered up for the dead.   They told her, that, in all questions about religion, St. Austin, and the other ancient doctors, appealed to the scripture; and if she would look into these, she would soon see the errors of the old superstition, which were supported by false miracles and lying stories, and not by scripture, or good authority.   They expressed themselves in terms full of submission to her; but said, they were trusted with the execution of the king's laws, in which they must proceed equally.   So they required her, [Ibid. p. 50.] if the chaplains were in her house, to send them to the sheriff of Essex.   But, it seems, they kept out of the way, and so the matter slept till the beginning of May this year, that Mallet was found, and put in the Tower, and convicted of his offence. Upon this there passed many letters between the council and [Ibid. p. 50. sqq.] her; she earnestly desiring to have him set at liberty, and they as positively refusing to do it.

In July the council sent for Rochester, Englefield, and Wal- [Ibid. p. 52.] grave, three of her chief officers; and gave them instructions to signify the king's express pleasure to her, to have the new service in her family; and to give the like charge to her chaplains, and all her servants; and to return with an answer.   In August they came back, and said, she was much indisposed, and received the message very grievously.   She said, she would obey the king in all things, except where her conscience was 174 touched: but she charged them to deliver none of their message to the rest of her family; in which they being her servants could not disobey her, especially when they thought it might prejudice her health.   Upon this, they were sent to the Tower. The lord chancellor, sir Anthony Wingfield, and sir William And sent some to her. Petre, were next sent to her, with a letter from the king, and instructions from the council, for the charge they were to give to her and her servants.   They came to her house of Copthall [Aug. 28.] in Essex.   The lord chancellor gave her the king's letter, which she received on her knees; and said, she paid that respect to the king's hand, and not to the matter of the letter, which she knew proceeded from the council: and when she read it, she said, *Ah! Mr. Cecil took much pains here* [15] : (he was then secretary of state in Dr. Wotton's room.) So she turned to the counsellors, and bid them deliver their message to her. She wished them to be short, for she was not well at ease; and would give them a short answer, having writ her mind plainly to the king with her own hand. The lord chancellor told her, that all the council were of one mind, that she must be no longer suffered to have private mass, or a form of religion different from what was established by law. He went to read the names of those who were of that mind; but she desired him to spare his pains; she knew they were all of a sort. They next told her, they had order to require her chaplains to use no other service, and her servants to be present at no other, than

But she was intractable.

what was according to law. She answered, she was the king's most obedient subject, and sister; and would obey him in every thing, but where her conscience held her, and would willingly suffer death to do him service: but she would lay her head on a block rather than use any other form of service than what had been at her father's death: only she thought she was not worthy to suffer death on so good an account. When the king came to be of age, so that he could order these things himself, she would obey his commands in religion: for although he,

[Archæologia, xviii. p. 163.]

good sweet king, (these were her words,) had more knowledge than any of his years, yet he was not a fit judge in these matters: for if ships were to be set to sea, or any matter of policy to be determined, they would not think him fit for it, much less could he be able to resolve points of divinity. As for her chaplains, if they would say no mass, she could hear none; and for her servants, she knew they all desired to hear mass: her chaplains might do what they would, it was but a while's imprisonment: but for the new service, it should never be said in her house; and if any were forced to say it, she would stay no longer in the house. When the counsellors spake of Rochester, Englefield, and Walgrave, who had not fully executed

---

[15] ["Ah! good Mr. Cicill tooke muche pains here." For the whole account of this transaction, extracted from the Council Book, see Archæologia, vol. xviii. pp. 154–166.]

their charge; she said, it was not the wisest counsel to order
her servants to control her in her own house; and they were
the honester men not to do such a thing against their consciences. She insisted on the promise made to the emperor,
which she had under his hand, whom she believed better than
them all: they ought to use her better for her father's sake,
who had raised them almost out of nothing. But though the
emperor were dead, or would bid her obey them, she would
not change her mind; and she would let his ambassador know
how they used her. To this they answered, clearing the mis-
175 take about the promise, to which she gave little heed. They
told her, they had brought one down to serve as her comptroller in Rochester's room: she said, she would choose her [Ibid. p.
own servants; and if they went to impose any on her, she ¹⁶⁴·]
would leave the house. She was sick, but would do all she
could to live; but if she died, she would protest they were the
causes of it: they gave her good words, but their deeds were
evil. Then she took a ring from her finger, and on her knees
gave it to the lord chancellor, to give to the king as a token
from her, with her humble commendations; and protested
much of her duty to him; but she said, this will never be told
him. The counsellors went from her to her chaplains, and delivered their message to them, who promised they would obey.
Then they charged the rest of the servants in like manner,
and also commanded them to give notice if those orders were
broken: and so they went to go away. But as they were in
the court, the lady Mary called to them from her window, to
send her comptroller to her; for she said, that now she herself
received the accounts of her house, and knew how many loaves
were made of a bushel of meal, to which she had never been
bred, and so was weary of that office; but if they would needs
send him to prison, she said, I beshrew him if he go not to it
merrily and with a good-will; and concluded, I pray God to
send you to do well in your souls and bodies, for some of you
have but weak bodies. This is the substance of the report
these counsellors gave when they returned back to the court
on the 29th of August ¹⁶. By which they were now out of all [Ibid. p.
hopes of prevailing with her by persuasions or authority: so ¹⁶¹·]

¹⁶ [This report is in the 13th volume of the Domestic Papers in the

it was next considered, whether it was fit to go to further extremities with her. How the matter was determined, I do not clearly find: it is certain the lady Mary would never admit of the new service, and so I believe she continued to keep her priests, and have mass; but so secretly, that there was no ground for any public complaint. For I find no further mention of that matter than what is made by Ridley, of a passage that befel him in September next year.

[Sept. 8, 1552.]
Nor would she hear bishop Ridley preach.
[Fox, lib. ix. p. 131.]

He went to wait on her, she living then at Hunsden: where she received him at first civilly, and told him, she remembered of him in her father's time; and at dinner sent him to dine with her officers. After dinner he told her, he came not only to do his duty to her, but to offer to preach before her next Sunday: she blushed, and once or twice desired him to make the answer to that himself. But when he pressed her further, she said, the parish church would be open to him, if he had a mind to preach in it; but neither she, nor any of her family, should hear him. He said, he hoped she would not refuse to hear God's word: she said, she did not know what they called God's word; but she was sure that was not now God's word that was called so in her father's days. He said, God's word was the same at all times. She answered, she was sure he durst not for his ears have avowed these things in her father's time, which he did now: and for their books, as, she thanked God, she never had, so she never would read them. She also used many reproachful words to him, and asked him, if he was of the council. He said not. She replied, he might well enough be, as the council goes nowadays; and so dismissed him, thanking him for coming to see her, but not at all for offering to preach before her. Sir Thomas Wharton, one of her officers, carried him to a place where he desired him to drink; which Ridley did: but, reflecting on it, said, he had 176 done amiss, to drink in a place where God's word was rejected; for if he had remembered his duty, he should upon that refusal have shaken the dust off his feet for a testimony against the house, and have departed immediately. These words he was observed to pronounce with an extraordinary concern, and

State Paper Office, Nᵒ. 35, and, together with the letters on the subject which passed between the king and the princess Mary, is in the Council Book, pp. 360–381.]

went away much troubled in his mind. And this is all I find
of the lady Mary during this reign. For the lady Elizabeth,
she had been always bred up to like the reformation; and
Dr. Parker, who had been her mother's chaplain, received a
strict charge from her mother, a little before her death, to
look well to the instructing her daughter in the principles of
true religion: so that there is no doubt to be made of her
cheerful receiving all the changes that had been established
by law.

And this is all that concerns religion that falls within this *The de-*
year. But now a design came to be laid, which, though it *signs of the*
earl of
broke not out for some time, yet it was believed to have had a *Warwick.*
great influence on the fall of the duke of Somerset. The earl
of Warwick began to form great projects for himself, and
thought to bring the crown into his family. The king was
now much alienated from the lady Mary; the privy-council
had also embroiled themselves so with her, that he imagined
it would be no hard matter to exclude her from the succession.
There was but one reason that could be pretended for it, which
was, that she stood illegitimated by law; and that therefore
the next heirs in blood could not be barred their right by her:
since it would be a great blot on the honour of the English crown
to let it devolve on a bastard. This was as strong against the
lady Elizabeth, since she was also illegitimated by a sentence
in the spiritual court, and that confirmed in parliament: so if
their jealousy of the elder sister's religion, and the fear of her
revenge, moved them to be willing to cut her off from the succession, the same reason that was to be used in law against
her was also to take place against her sister. So he reckoned
that these two were to be passed over, as being put both in
the act of succession, and in the late king's will, by one error.
The next in the will were the heirs of the French queen by
Charles Brandon; who were, the duchess of Suffolk, and her
sister: though I have seen it often said, in many letters and
writings of that time, that all that issue by Charles Brandon
was illegitimated, since he was certainly married to one Mortimer before he married the queen of France, which Mortimer
lived long after his marriage to that queen [17]; so that all her

17 Charles Brandon first married   John Nevil, marquis Mountague,
Margaret, one of the daughters of   widow of sir John Mortimer; se-

children were bastards. Some say he was divorced from his marriage to Mortimer, but that is not clear to me.

This year the sweating sickness, that had been formerly both in Henry the Seventh and the late king's reign, broke out with that violence in England, that many were swept away by it. Such as were taken with it died certainly if they slept, to which they had a violent desire; but if it took them not off in twenty-four hours, they did sweat out the venom of the distemper: which raged so in London, that in one week eight hundred died of it. It did also spread into the country, and the two sons of Charles Brandon by his last wife, both dukes of Suffolk, died within a day one of another [18]. So that title was fallen. Their sister by the half blood was married to Grey, lord marquis of Dorset: so she being the eldest daughter to the French queen, the earl of Warwick resolved to link himself to that family, and to procure the honour of the dukedom of 177 Suffolk to be given the marquis of Dorset, who was a weak man, and easily governed. He had three daughters: the eldest was Jane, a lady of as excellent qualities as any of that age; of great parts, bred to learning, and much conversant in scripture; and of so rare a temper of mind, that she charmed all who knew her: in particular the young king, about whom she was bred, and who had always lived with her in the familiarities of a brother. The earl of Warwick designed to marry her to Guilford, his fourth son then living, his three elder being already married; and so to get the crown to descend on them, if the king should die, of which it is thought he resolved to take care. But apprehending some danger from the lady Elizabeth's title, he intended to send her away: so an ambassador was despatched to Denmark, to treat a marriage for her with that king's eldest son.

To amuse the king himself, a most splendid embassy was

condly Anne, daughter of sir Anthony Browne, by whom he had issue, after marriage, Mary, wedded to Thomas Stanley, lord Monteagle; thirdly Mary, queen of France, as sir William Dugdale hath it in the text, though in the scheme adjoined by him, the order is inverted. 1st Anne, 2nd Margaret, but *repudiata*,

3rd Mary. [G.]

[18] And both lie buried in the chancel of Bugden church, they dying at the bishop's house. [S.] [This paragraph was added in the text of the folio edition of 1715, with the exception that for the words *chancel of Bugden church* were substituted *church of Brandon*.

sent to France, to propose a marriage for the king to that *the French king's daughter Elizabeth, afterwards married to Philip of* *king for a marriage* Spain. The marquis of Northampton was sent with this pro- *with his daughter.* position, and with the order of the garter. With him went the *[May 21.* earls of Worcester, Rutland, and Ormond; 'the lords Lisle, *Hayward, p. 318.]* Fitzwater, Bray, Abergavenny, and Evers; and the bishop of Ely, who was to be their mouth: with them went many gentlemen of quality, who, with their train, made up near five hundred. King Henry received the garter with great expressions of esteem for the king. The bishop of Ely told him, [June 20.] They were come to desire a more close tie between these crowns by marriage, and to have the league made firmer between them in other particulars. To which the cardinal of Lorraine made answer in his way of speaking, which was always vain, and full of ostentation. A commission was given to that cardinal, the constable, the duke of Guise, and others, to treat about it.

The English began first, for form's sake, to desire the queen of Scots, but that being rejected, they moved for the daughter of France, which was entertained; but so that neither party should be bound in honour and conscience till the lady were twelve years of age. Yet this never taking effect, it is needless to enlarge further about it; of which the reader will find all the particulars in king Edward's Journal. The king of *[Hayward, France sent another very noble embassy into England, with* *p. 319.]* the order of St. Michael to the king, and a very kind message, that he had no less love to him than a father could bear to his own son. He desired the king would not listen to the vain rumours, which some malicious persons might raise to break their friendship; and wished there might be such a regulation on their frontiers, that all differences might be amicably removed. To this the young king made answer himself, " That " he thanked his good brother for his order, and for the assur- " ances of his love, which he would always requite. For ru- " mours, they were not always to be credited, nor always to " be rejected; it being no less vain to fear all things, than it " was dangerous to doubt of nothing: and for any differences " that might arise, he should be always ready to determine " them by reason rather than force, so far as his honour should " not be thereby diminished." Whether this answer was prepared beforehand, or not, I cannot tell; I rather think it was: otherwise it was extraordinary for one of fourteen to talk thus on the sudden.

A conspiracy against the duke of Somerset.

But while all this was carrying on, there was a design laid 178 to destroy the duke of Somerset. He had such access to the king, and such freedoms with him, that the earl of Warwick had a mind to be rid of him, lest he should spoil all his projects. The duke of Somerset seemed also to have designed in April this year to have got the king again in his power: and dealt with the lord Strange, that was much in his favour, to persuade him to marry his daughter Jane; and that he would advertise him of all that passed about the king. But the earl of Warwick, to raise himself and all his friends higher, procured a great creation of new honours. Grey was made duke of Suffolk, and himself duke of Northumberland; for Henry Percy, the last earl of Northumberland, dying without issue, his next heirs were the sons of Thomas Percy, that had been attainted in the last reign for the Yorkshire rebellion. Paulet, then lord treasurer, and earl of Wiltshire, was made marquis of Winchester; and sir William Herbert, that had married the marquis of Northampton's sister, was made earl of Pembroke. The lord Russell had been made earl of Bedford last year, upon his return from making the peace with the French; sir Thomas Darcy had also been made lord Darcy. The new duke of Northumberland could no longer bear such a rival in his greatness as the duke of Somerset was, who was the only person that he thought could take the king out of his hands. So on the 17th of October the duke was apprehended, and sent to the Tower; and with him the lord Grey; sir Ralph Vane, who had escaped over the river, but was taken in a stable in Lambeth, hid under the straw: sir Thomas Palmer, and sir Thomas Arundel, were also taken; yet not sent at first to the Tower, but kept under guards in their chambers. Some of his followers, Hammond, Newdigate, and two of the Seymours, were sent to prison. The day after, the duchess of Somerset was also sent to the Tower, with one Crane and his wife, that had been much about her, and two of her chamber-women. After these, sir Thomas Holcroft, sir Miles Partridge, sir Michael Stanhope, Wingfield, Banister, and Vaughan, were all made prisoners. The evidence against the duke was, that he

[Oct. 11. Holinshed, p. 1066. State Papers, Domestic, vol. xiii. 56.]

[Oct. 16. Holinshed, p. 1066.]

[Hayward, p. 321.]

had made a party for getting himself declared protector in
the next parliament: which the earl of Rutland did positively
affirm; and the duke did so answer it, that it is probable it
was true. But though this might well inflame his enemies, yet
it was no crime. But sir Thomas Palmer, though imprisoned
with him as a complice, was the person that ruined him. He
had been before that brought secretly to the king, and had
told him, that on the last St. George's day, the duke, apprehending there was mischief designed against him, thought to
have raised the people, had not sir William Herbert assured
him he should receive no harm : that lately he intended to
have the duke of Northumberland, the marquis of Northampton, and the earl of Pembroke, invited to dinner at the
lord Paget's; and either to have set on them by the way, or
to have killed them at dinner; that sir Ralph Vane had two
thousand men ready, that sir Thomas Arundel had assured the
Tower, and that all the gendarmerie were to be killed. The
duke of Somerset, hearing Palmer had been with the king,
challenged him of it; but he denied all. He sent also for
secretary Cecil, and told him, he suspected there was an ill
design against him: to which the secretary answered, if he
were not in fault, he might trust to his innocency; but if he
were, he had nothing to say but to lament him.

79   All this was told the king with such circumstances, that he
was induced to believe it; and the probity of his disposition
wrought in him a great aversion to his uncle, when he looked
on him as a conspirator against the lives of the other counsellors: and so he resolved to leave him to the law. Palmer,
being a second time examined, said, that sir Ralph Vane was
to have brought two thousand men, who, with the duke of
Somerset's one hundred horse, were on a muster-day to have
set on the gendarmerie: that being done, the duke resolved
to have gone through the city, and proclaimed Liberty, liberty!
and if his attempt did not succeed, to have fled to the Isle of
Wight, or to Poole. Crane confirmed all that Palmer had said:
to which he added, that the earl of Arundel was privy to the
conspiracy; and that the thing had been executed, but that
the greatness of the enterprise had caused delays, and sometimes diversity of advice; and that the duke, being once given
out to be sick, had gone privately to London, to see what

The king is
possessed
against
him.

friends he could make.   Hammond, being examined, confessed nothing, but that the duke's chamber at Greenwich had been guarded in the night by many armed men.   Upon this evidence both the earl of Arundel and the lord Paget were sent to the Tower.   The earl had been one of the chief of those who had joined with the earl of Warwick to pull down the protector; and being, as he thought, ill rewarded by him, was become his enemy: so this part of the information seemed very credible.   The thing lay in suspense till the first of December,

He is
brought to
his trial.
[Dec. 2.
Holinshed,
p. 1067.]
[Hayward,
p. 322.]

that the duke of Somerset was brought to his trial; where the marquis of Winchester was lord steward.   The peers that judged him were twenty-seven in number: the dukes of Suffolk and Northumberland; the marquis of Northampton; the earls of Derby, Bedford, Huntingdon, Rutland, Bath, Sussex, Worcester, Pembroke; and the viscount of Hereford; the lords Abergavenny, Audley, Wharton, Evers, Latimer, Borough, Zouch, Stafford, Wentworth, Darcy, Stourton, Windsor, Cromwell, Cobham, and Bray.   The crimes laid against him were cast into five several indictments, as the king has it in his Journal: but the record mentions only three: whether indictments or articles is not so clear.   That he had designed to have seized on the king's person, and, so have governed all affairs; and that he, with one hundred others, intended to have imprisoned the earl of Warwick, afterwards duke of Northumberland; and that he had designed to have raised an insurrection

[Cap. 5.
Statutes,
vol. iv.
p. 104.]

in the city of London.   Now, by the act that passed in the last parliament, if twelve persons should have assembled together to have killed any privy counsellor, and upon proclamation they had not dispersed themselves, it was treason: or if such twelve had been by any malicious artifice brought together for any riot, and being warned did not disperse themselves, it was felony, without benefit of clergy or sanctuary.

[Ibid. p.
105.]

It seemed very strange that the three peers, Northumberland, Northampton, and Pembroke, who were his professed enemies, and against the first of whom it was pretended in the indictment that he had conspired, should sit his judges; for though by the law no peer can be challenged in a trial, yet the law of nations, that is superior to all other laws, makes, that a man cannot be judge in his own cause: and, which was very unusual, the lord chancellor, though then a peer, was left out of the

number; but it is like the reconciliation between the duke of
Somerset and him was then suspected, which made him not be
called to be one of his judges.

30   The duke of Somerset being, it seems, little acquainted with
law, did not desire counsel to plead or assist him in point of
law; but only answered to matters of fact. He prefaced, that
he desired no advantage might be taken against him for any
idle or angry word that might have at any time fallen from
him. He protested he never intended to have raised the
northern parts; but had only, upon some reports, sent to sir
William Herbert to be his friend: that he had never determined to have killed the duke of Northumberland, or any
other person; but had only talked of it, without any intention
of doing it: that for the design of destroying the gendarmerie,
it was ridiculous to think that he with a small troop could
destroy so strong a body of men, consisting of nine hundred;
in which though he had succeeded, it could have signified
nothing: that he never designed to raise any stirs in London,
but had always looked on it as a place where he was most safe:
that his having men about him in Greenwich was with no ill
design, since, when he could have done mischief with them, he
had not done it, but upon his attachment rendered himself a
prisoner without any resistance. He objected also many things
against the witnesses, and desired they might be brought face
to face: he particularly spake much against sir Thomas Palmer, the chief witness: but the witnesses were not brought,
only their examinations were read. Upon this the king's council pleaded against him, that to levy war was certainly treason;
that to gather men with intention to kill privy councillors was
also treason; that to have men about him to resist the attachment was felony; and to assault the lords, or contrive their
deaths, was felony. Whether he made any defence in law, or
not, does not appear: for the material defence is not mentioned in all the accounts I have seen of it; which was, that
these conspiracies, and gatherings of the king's subjects, were
only treasonable and felonious after they had been required to
disperse themselves, and had refused to give obedience: and in
all this matter, that is never so much as alleged, no, not in the
indictment itself, to have been done. It is plain it was not
done; for if any such proclamation or charge had been sent

him, it is probable he would either have obeyed it, or gone
.into London, or to the country, and tried what he could have
done by force; but to have refused such a command, and so to
have come within the guilt of treason, and yet not to stir from
his house, are not things consistent.

When the peers withdrew, it seems the proofs about his design of raising the north, or the city, or of the killing the
gendarmes, did not satisfy them: for all these had been without question treasonable. So they only held to that point, of
conspiring to imprison the duke of Northumberland. If he,
with twelve men about him, had conspired to do that, and had
continued together after proclamation, it was certainly felony:
but that not being pretended, it seems there was no proclamation made. The duke of Suffolk was of opinion, that no contention among private subjects should be on any account
screwed up to be treason. The duke of Northumberland said,
he would never consent that any practice against him should
be reputed treason. After a great difference of opinion, they
all acquitted him of treason: but the greater number found
him guilty of felony. When they returned him not guilty of
treason, all the people, who were much concerned for his pre- 1
servation, shouted for joy so loud and so long, that they were
heard at Charing-Cross. But the joy lasted not long, when
they heard that he was condemned of felony, and sentence was
thereupon given that he should die as a felon.

And is acquitted of treason, but found guilty of felony. [Hayward, p. 323.]

The duke had carried himself all the while of the trial with
great temper and patience: and though the king's council had,
in their usual way of pleading, been very bitter against him,
perhaps the rather, that thereby they might recommend themselves to the duke of Northumberland; yet he never took notice of these reflections, nor seemed much affected with them.
When sentence was given, he thanked the lords for their
favour, and asked pardon of the duke of Northumberland,
Northampton, and Pembroke, for his ill intentions against
them; and made suit for his life, and for his wife and children.
From thence he was carried back to the Tower. Whether this
asking the lords' pardon had in it a full confession of the crime
charged on him, or was only a compliment to them, that they
might not obstruct his pardon, is but a matter of conjecture.
He confessed he had spoken of killing them, and this made it

reasonable enough for him to ask their pardon; so that it does not imply a confession of the crime. All people thought, that being acquitted of treason, and there being no felonious action done by him, but only an intention of one, and that only of imprisoning a peer, proved; that one so nearly joined to the king in blood would never be put to death on such an occasion. But, to possess the king much against him, a story was brought him, and put by him in his Journal, that, at the duke's coming to the Tower, he had confessed, that he had hired one Barteville to kill the lords; and that Barteville himself acknowledged it; and that Hammond knew of it. But whether this was devised to alienate the king wholly from him, or whether it was true, I can give no assurance. But though it was true, it was felony in Barteville, if he were the king's servant; but not in the duke, who was a peer. Yet no doubt this gave the king a very ill opinion of his uncle, and so made him more easily consent to his execution: since all such conspiracies are things of that inhuman and barbarous cruelty, that it is scarce possible to punish them too severely. But it is certain, that there was no evidence at all of any design to kill the duke of Northumberland; otherwise the indictment had not been laid against him, only for designing to seize on and imprison him, as it was; the conspiring to kill him not being so much as mentioned in the indictment: but it was maliciously given out to possess the world, and chiefly the king, against him.

See the indictment. Coke's Entries, fol. 482.

The king also, in his letter to Barnaby Fitz-Patrick, who was like to be his favourite, and was then sent over for his breeding into France, writ, that the duke seemed to have acknowledged the felony; and that after sentence he had confessed it, though he had formerly vehemently sworn the contrary: from whence it is plain, that the king was persuaded of his being guilty. Sir Michael Stanhope, sir Thomas Arundel, sir Ralph Vane, and sir Miles Partridge, were next brought to their trials. The first and the last of these were little pitied. For as all great men have people about them, who make use of their greatness only for their own ends, without regarding their master's honour or true interest, so they were the persons upon whom the ill things which had been done by the duke of Somerset were chiefly cast. But sir Thomas Arundel was much pitied, and had hard measure in his trial, which

[Fuller, vii. 409.]

Some of his friends also condemned.

[Hayward, P. 326.]

began at seven o'clock in the morning, and continued till noon : then the jury went aside, and they did not agree on their verdict till next morning, when those who thought him not guilty, yet, for preserving their own lives, were willing to yield to the fierceness of those who were resolved to have him found guilty. Sir Ralph Vane was the most lamented of them all. He had done great services in the wars, and was esteemed one of the bravest gentlemen of the nation. He pleaded for himself, that he had done his country considerable service during the wars; though now, in time of peace, the coward and the courageous were equally esteemed. He scorned to make any submissions for life. But this height of mind in him did certainly set forward his condemnation : and, to add more infamy to him in the manner of his death, he and Partridge were hanged, whereas the other two were beheaded.

[Jan. 26, 1552. Holinshed, p. 1081.]

The duke of Somerset was using means to have the king better informed and disposed towards him, and engaged the lord chancellor to be his friend : who thereupon sent him an advertisement of somewhat designed against him by the council, and, being in haste, writ only on the back of his letter, *To the duke;* and bid one of his servants carry it to the Tower, without giving him particular directions to the duke of Somerset. But his servant, having known of the familiarities between his master and the duke of Norfolk, who was still in the Tower, and knowing none between him and the other duke, carried the letter to the duke of Norfolk. When the lord chancellor found the mistake at night, he knew the duke of Norfolk, to make Northumberland his friend, would certainly discover him; so he went in all haste to the king, and desired to be discharged of his office, and thereby prevented the malice of his enemies: and upon this he fell[17] sick, either pretending he was ill, that it might raise the more pity for him, or perhaps the fright in which he was did really cast him into sickness. So the seal was sent for by the marquis of Winchester, the duke of Northumberland, and the lord Darcy, on the 21st of December, and put into the hands of the bishop of Ely, who was made keeper during pleasure; and when the session of parliament came on, he was made lord chancellor.

The seals are taken from the lord Rich : [Fuller, vii. 408.]

And given to the bishop of Ely.

[17] He was sick before; for a commission was granted to some to do the business of the Chancery. [S.]

But this was much censured: when the reformation was first preached in England, Tyndale, Barnes, and Latimer took an occasion, from the great pomp and luxury of cardinal Wolsey, and the secular employments of the other bishops and clergymen, to represent them as a sort of men that had wholly neglected the care of souls, and those spiritual studies and exercises that disposed men to such functions; and only carried the names of bishops and churchmen to be a colour to serve their ambition and covetousness. And this had raised great prejudices in the minds of the people against those who were called their pastors, when they saw them fill their heads with cares that were at least impertinent to their callings, if not inconsistent with the duties that belonged to them. So now, [Jan. 19.] upon Goodrich's being made lord chancellor, that was a reformed bishop, it was said by their adversaries, these men only condemned secular employments in the hands of churchmen, because their enemies had them; but changed their mind as soon as any of their own party came to be advanced to them. But as Goodrich was raised by the popish interest, in opposition to the duke of Somerset, and to Cranmer, that was his firm friend: so it appeared, in the beginning of queen Mary's reign, that he was ready to turn with every tide: and that, whether he joined in the reformation only in compliance to the time, or was persuaded in his mind concerning it; yet he had not that sense of it that became a bishop, and was one of these who resolved to make as much advantage by it as he could, but would suffer nothing for it. So his practice in this matter is neither a precedent to justify the like in others, nor can it cast a scandal on those to whom he joined himself. Christ, being spoke to to divide an inheritance between two brethren, said, *Who made me a judge, or a divider?* St. Paul, speaking of churchmen, says, *No man that warreth entangleth himself with the affairs of this life:* which was understood by St. Cyprian as a perpetual rule against the secular employments of the clergy. There are three of the apostolical canons against it: and Cyprian, reckoning up the sins of his time, that had provoked God to send a persecution on the church, names this; that many bishops, forsaking their sees, undertook secular cares. In which he was so strict, that he thought the being tutor to orphans was a distraction unsuitable to their

character: so that one priest leaving another tutor to his
children, because by the Roman law he to whom this was left
was obliged to undergo it, the priest's name who made that
testament was appointed to be struck out of the list of those
churchmen who had died in the faith, and were remembered
in the daily offices.   Samosatenus is represented as one of the
first eminent churchmen that involved himself much in secular
cares.   Upon the emperors' turning Christian, it was a natural
effect of their conversion for them to cherish the bishops much:
and many of the bishops became so much in love with the
court and public employments, that canons were made against
their going to court, unless they were called; and the *canalis*,
or road to the court, was kept by the bishop of Rome, so that
none might go without his warrant.   Their meddling in secular
matters was also condemned in many provincial councils, but
most copiously and amply by the general council at Chalcedon.
It is true, the bishops had their courts for the arbitration of
civil differences; which were first begun upon St. Paul's Epistle
to the Corinthians, against their going to law before unbe-
lievers, and for submitting their suits to some among themselves.   The reasons of this ceased when the judges in the
civil courts were become Christians; yet these episcopal audi-
ences were still continued after Constantine's time, and their
jurisdiction was sometimes enlarged, and sometimes abridged,
as there was occasion given.   St. Austin, and many other holy
bishops, grew weary even of that, and found that the hearing
causes, as it took up much of their time, so filled their heads
with thoughts of another nature than what properly belonged
to them.

The bishops of Rome and Alexandria, taking advantage from
the greatness and wealth of their sees, began first to establish
a secular principality of the church: and the confusions that
fell out in Italy after the fifth century gave the bishops of
Rome great opportunities for it, which they improved to the
utmost advantage.   The revolutions in Spain gave a rise to the
Spanish bishops meddling much in all civil matters.   And
when Charles the Great and his son had given great territories and large jurisdictions to many sees and monasteries,
bishops and abbots came after that not only to have a share 184
in all the public councils of most of the states of Europe, to

which their lands gave them a right, but to be chiefly employed in all affairs and offices of state. The ignorance of
these ages made this in a manner necessary: and church preferments were given as rewards to men who had served in the
state in embassies, or in their princes' courts of justice. So
that it was no wonder, if men advanced upon that merit continued in their former method and course of life. Thus the
bishops became, for the greatest part, only a sort of men who
went in peculiar habits, and upon some high festivities performed a few offices: but for the pastoral care, and all the
duties incumbent on them, they were universally neglected;
and that seriousness, that abstraction from the world, that
application to study and religious exercises, and chiefly the
care of souls, which became their function, seemed inconsistent
with that course of life which secular cares brought on men
who pursued them. Nor was it easy to persuade the world,
that their pastors did very much aspire to heaven, when they
were thrusting themselves so indecently into the courts of
princes, or ambitiously pretending to the administration of
matters of state: and it was always observed, that churchmen
who assumed to themselves employments, and an authority
that was eccentric to their callings, suffered so much in that
esteem, and lost so much of that authority, which of right belonged to their character and office.

But to go on with the series of affairs. There was all possible care taken to divert and entertain the king's mind with
pleasing sights, as will appear by his Journal: which, it seems,
had the effect that was desired; for he was not much concerned
in his uncle's preservation.

An order was sent for beheading the duke of Somerset
on the 22nd of January, on which day he was brought to
the place of execution on Tower-hill. His whole deportment
was very composed, and no way changed from what it had ordinarily been: he first kneeled down, and prayed; and then he
spake to the people in these words: [Holinshed, p. 1067.]

    "Dearly beloved friends, I am brought here to suffer death,
"albeit that I never offended against the king neither by word
"nor deed; and have been always as faithful and true to this
"realm, as any man hath been. But for so much as I am by
"law condemned to die, I do acknowledge myself, as well as

The duke of Somerset's speech at his execution. [Fox, lib.ix. p. 98.]

" others, to be subject thereto. Wherefore, to testify my
" obedience which I owe unto the laws, I am come hither to
" suffer death; whereunto I willingly offer myself, with most
" hearty thanks to God, that hath given me this time of repent-
" ance; who might through sudden death have taken away
" my life, that neither I should have acknowledged him, nor
" myself. Moreover there is yet somewhat that I must put
" you in mind of, as touching Christian religion; which, so
" long as I was in authority, I always diligently set forth, and
" furthered to my power: neither repent I me of my doings,
" but rejoice therein, sith that now the state of Christian reli-
" gion cometh most near unto the form and order of the
" primitive church; which thing I esteem as a great benefit
" given of God both to you and me; most heartily exhorting
" you all, that this, which is most purely set forth to you, you
" will with like thankfulness accept and embrace, and set out
" the same in your living: which thing if you do not, without
" doubt greater mischief and calamity will follow."

[Holin-
shed,
p. 1068.]

When he had gone so far, there was an extraordinary noise 185
heard, as if some house had been blown up with gunpowder;
which frighted all the people, so that many ran away, they
knew not for what: and the relator, who tarried still, says, it
brought into his remembrance the astonishment that the band
was in that came to take our Saviour, who thereupon fell back-

[Hayward,
p. 324.]

wards to the ground. At the same time sir Anthony Browne
came riding towards the scaffold, and they all hoped he had
brought a pardon; upon which there was a general shouting,
Pardon, pardon, God save the king; many throwing up their
caps; by which the duke might well perceive how dear he was
to the people. But as soon as these disorders were over, he
made a sign to them with his hand to compose themselves, and
then went on in his speech thus:

[Holin-
shed,
p. 1068.]

" Dearly beloved friends, there is no such matter here in
" hand, as you vainly hope or believe. It seemeth thus good
" unto Almighty God, whose ordinance it is meet and neces-
" sary that we all be obedient to. Wherefore I pray you all
" to be quiet, and to be contented with my death; which I am
" most willing to suffer. And let us now join in prayer to the
" Lord for the preservation of the king's majesty, unto whom
" hitherto I have always shewed myself a most faithful and

" firm subject. I have always been most diligent about his
" majesty, in his affairs both at home and abroad; and no less
" diligent in seeking the common commodity of the whole
" realm; (upon this the people cried out, *it was most true;*)
" unto whose majesty I wish continual health, with all felicity,
" and all prosperous success. Moreover, I do wish unto all his
" counsellors the grace and favour of God, whereby they may
" rule in all things uprightly with justice: unto whom I ex-
" hort you all in the Lord to shew yourselves obedient, as it is
" your bounden duty, under the pain of condemnation; and
" also most profitable for the preservation and safeguard of the [Holin-
" king's majesty. Moreover, for as much as heretofore I have shed,
" had affairs with divers men, and hard it is to please every p. 1069.]
" man, therefore, if there have been any that have been of-
" fended or injured by me, I most humbly require and ask him
" forgiveness; but especially Almighty God, whom, throughout
" all my life, I have most grievously offended: and all other
" whatsoever they be that have offended me, I do with my
" whole heart forgive them." Then he desired them to be
quiet, lest their tumults might trouble him; and said, " Albeit
" the spirit be willing and ready, the flesh is frail and waver-
" ing; and through your quietness I shall be much more
" quieter. Moreover, I desire you all to bear me witness, that
" I die here in the faith of Jesus Christ, desiring you to help
" me with your prayers, that I may persevere constant in the
" same to my life's end."

Then Dr. Cox, who was with him on the scaffold, put a paper His death.
in his hand, which was a prayer he had prepared for him. He
read it on his knees; then he took leave of all about him, and
undressed himself to be fitted for the axe. In all which there
appeared no change in him, only his face was a little ruddier
than ordinary: he continued calling, *Lord Jesus, save me*, till
the executioner severed his head from his body.

Thus fell the duke of Somerset[18]: a person of great virtues, And cha-
eminent for piety, humble and affable in his greatness, sincere racter.
and candid in all his transactions. He was a better captain
than a counsellor; had been oft successful in his undertakings,
186 was always careful of the poor and oppressed; and, in a word,

[18] [See Part iii. p. 209.]

had as many virtues, and as few faults, as most great men, especially when they were so unexpectedly advanced, have ever had.   It was generally believed, that all this pretended conspiracy, upon which he was condemned, was only a forgery: for both Palmer and Crane, the chief witnesses, were soon after discharged: as were also Barteville and Hammond, with all the rest that had been made prisoners on the pretence of this plot.   And the duke of Northumberland continued after that in so close a friendship with Palmer, that it was generally believed he had been corrupted to betray him.   And indeed the not bringing the witnesses into the court, but only the depositions, and the parties sitting judges, gave great occasion to condemn the proceedings against him: for it was generally thought, that all was an artifice of Palmer's, who had put the duke of Somerset in fears of his life, and so got him to gather men about him for his own preservation; and that he afterwards, being taken with him, seemed through fear to acknowledge all that which he had before contrived.   This was more confirmed by the death of the other four formerly mentioned, who were [Fox,lib.ix. executed on the 26th of February, and did all protest they had p. 99.] never been guilty of any design, either against the king, or to kill the lords.   Vane added, that his blood would make Northumberland's pillow uneasy to him.   The people were generally much affected with this execution; and many threw handkerchiefs into the duke of Somerset's blood, to preserve it in remembrance of him.   One lady, that met the duke of Northumberland when he was led through the city in queen Mary's reign, shaking one of these bloody handkerchiefs, said, " Behold the blood of that worthy man, that good uncle of " that excellent king, which was shed by thy malicious prac-. " tice, doth now begin apparently to revenge itself on thee." Sure it is, that Northumberland, as having maliciously contrived this, was ever after hated by the people.

But, on the other hand, great notice was taken that the duke of Norfolk (who, with his son the earl of Surrey, were believed to have fallen in all their misery by the duke of Somerset's means) did now outlive him, and saw him fall by a conspiracy of his own servants, as himself and his son had done. The proceeding against his brother was also remembered, for which many thought the judgments of God had overtaken him.

Others blamed him for being too apt to convert things sacred
to his own use, and because a great part of his estate was raised
out of the spoils of many churches; and some late writers have
made an inference from this, upon his not claiming the benefit
of clergy, that he was thus left of God not to plead that benefit,
since he had so much invaded the rights and revenues of the
church.   But in this they shewed their ignorance : for by the
statute, that felony of which he was found guilty was not to be
purged by clergy.   Those who pleased themselves in com- [Fox,
paring the events in their own times with the transactions of $\substack{\text{lib. ix.} \\ \text{p. 99.}}$
the former ages, found out many things to make a parallel be-
tween the duke of Somerset, and Humphrey the good duke of
Gloucester in Henry the Sixth's time; but I shall leave the
reader in that to his own observation.

Now was the duke of Northumberland absolute at court, all
offices being filled with those that were his associates.   But
here I stop to give a general view of affairs beyond sea this
187 year, though I have a little transgressed the bounds of it, to
give an account of the duke of Somerset's fall all together.   The
siege of Magdeburg went on in Germany.   But it was coldly The affairs
followed by Maurice, who had now other designs.   He had of Ger-
                                                                  many.
agreed with the French king, who was both to give him assistance, and to make war on the emperor at the same time when
he should begin.   Ferdinand was also not unwilling to see his
brother's greatness lessened; for he was pressing him, not
without threatenings, to lay down his dignity as king of the
Romans, and thought to have established it on his son.   All
the other princes of Germany were also oppressed by him, so
that they were disposed to enter into any alliance for the
shaking off of that yoke.   Maurice did also send over to try
the inclinations of England; if they would join with him, and
contribute 400,000 dollars towards the expense of a war for
the preservation of the protestant religion, and recovering
the liberty of Germany.   The ambassadors were only sent to
try the king's mind, but were not empowered to conclude any
thing.   They were sent back with a good answer, that the
king would most willingly join in alliance with them that were
of the same religion with himself; but he desired, that the
matter of religion might be plainly set down, lest, under the
pretence of that, war should be made for other quarrels.   He

desired them also to communicate their designs with the other princes, and then to send over others more fully empowered. Maurice, seeing such assistances ready for him, resolved both to break the emperor's designs, and, by leading on a new league against him, to make himself more acceptable to the empire, and thereby to secure the electoral dignity in his family. So, after Magdeburg had endured a long siege, he, giving a secret intimation to some men in whom they confided,

[Nov. 17. Thuanus, p. 278.]

persuaded them about the end of November to surrender to him; and then broke up his army: but they fell into the dominions of several of the popish princes, and put them under very heavy contributions. This alarmed all the empire; only the emperor himself, by a fatal security, did not apprehend it till it came so near him, that he was almost ruined before he dreamed of any danger.

Proceedings at Trent.

This year the transactions of Trent were remarkable. The pope had called the council to meet there, and the first of May this year there was a session held. There was a war now broken out between the pope and the king of France on this occasion. The pope had a mind to have Parma in his own hands; but that prince, fearing that he would keep it, as the emperor did Piacenza, and so he should be ruined between them, implored the protection of France, and received a French garrison for his safety. Upon this, the pope cited him to Rome, declaring him a traitor if he appeared not: and this engaged the pope in a war with France. At first he sent a threatening message to that king, that, if he would not restore Parma to him, he would take France from him. Upon this the king of France protested against the council of Trent, and threatened that he would call a national council in France. The council was adjourned to the tenth of September. In the mean while the emperor pressed the Germans to go to it. So Maurice, and the other princes of the Augsburg Confession, ordered their divines to consider of the matters which they would propose to the council. The electors of Mentz and Trier went to Trent. But the king of France sent the abbot of Bellosana 188

[History of Council of Trent, p. 300.]

thither, to make a protestation, that, by reason of the war that the pope had raised, he could not send his bishops to the council; and that therefore he would not observe their decrees: (for they had declared in France, that absent churches were not

bound to obey the decrees of a council; for which many authorities were cited from the primitive time.)   But at Trent
they proceeded for all this, and appointed the articles about
the eucharist to be first examined: and the presidents recommended to the divines to handle them according to scripture, tradition, and ancient authors, and to avoid unprofitable curiosities.   The Italian divines did not like this: for [Ibid. p.
they said, to argue so was but an act of the memory, and was ³⁰⁵·]
an old and insufficient way, and would give great advantage to
the Lutherans, who were skilled in the tongues; but the school
learning was a mystical and sublime way, in which it was easier
to set off or conceal matters, as was expedient.   But this was
done to please the Germans: and, at the suit of the emperor,
the matter of communicating in both kinds was postponed till
the German divines could be heard.   A safe conduct was desired by the Germans, not only from the emperor, but from
the council.   For at Constance, John Huss and Jerome of
Prague were burnt upon this pretence, that they had not the
council's safe conduct; and therefore, when the council of Basle
called for the Bohemians, they sent them a safe conduct, besides that which the emperor gave them.   So the princes desired one in the same form that was granted by those of Basle.
One was granted by the council, which in many things differed
from that of Basle; particularly in one clause, that all things
should be determined according to the scriptures, which was in
that safe conduct of Basle, but was now left out.   In October
an ambassador from the elector of Brandenburg came to Trent,
who was endeavouring to get his son settled in the archbishop- [Ibid. p.
ric of Magdeburg, which made him more compliant.   In his ³²²·]
first address to the council he spake of the respect this master
had to the fathers in it, without a word of submitting to their
decrees: but in the answer that was made in the name of the
council, it was said, they were glad he did submit to them, and
would obey their decrees.   This being afterwards complained
of, it was said, that they answered him according to what he
should have said, and not according to what he had said.   But
in the meanwhile the council published their decrees about the
eucharist; in the first part of which they defined, that the way
of the presence could hardly be expressed, and yet they called
transubstantiation a fit term for it.   But this might be well

enough defended, since that was a thing as hard to be either
expressed or understood as any thing they could have thought
on. They went on next to examine confession and penitence.
And now, as the divines handled the matter, they found the gathering proofs out of scripture grew endless and trifling; for
there was not a place in scripture where *I confess* was to be
found, but they drew it in to prove auricular confession. From
that they went on to extreme unction. But then came the ambassadors of the duke of Wittenberg, another prince of the
Augsburg Confession, and shewed their mandate to the emperor's ambassadors; who desired them to carry it to the presidents: but they refused to do that, since it was contrary to
the protestation which the princes of their Confession had made
against a council in which the pope should preside. On the 189
25th of November they published the decree of the necessity
of auricular confession, that so the priest might thereby know
how to proportion the penance to the sin. It was much censured, to see it defined that Christ had instituted confession to
a priest, and not shewed where or how it was instituted. And
the reason for it, about the proportioning the penance, was
laughed at, since it was known what slight penances were universally enjoined to expiate the greatest sins. But the ambassadors of Wittenberg moving that they might have a safe conduct for their divines to come and propose their doctrine; the
legate answered, that they would not upon any terms enter
into any disputation with them; but if their divines had any
scruple, in which they desired satisfaction, with a humble and
obedient mind, they should be heard. And for a safe conduct,
he thought it was a distrusting the council to ask any other
than what was already granted. Soon after this, there arrived
ambassadors from Strasburg and from other five cities; and
those sent from the duke of Saxe were on their journey: so
the emperor ordered his ambassadors to study to gain time till
they came; and then an effectual course must be taken for
compassing that about which he had laboured so long in vain
to bring it to a happy conclusion. And thus this year ended.

A session of parliament. The parliament was opened on the 23rd[19] of January, and

[Ibid. p. 325.]

[Ibid. p. 330.]

[Ibid. p. 334.]

[Ibid. p. 335.]

[Ibid. p. 338.]

[Ibid. p. 339.]

---

[19] [In the statutes of the realm
this session is said to have com-
menced on the thirtieth of January.
A note is added, stating that old

sat till the 15th of April. So I shall begin this year with the account of the proceedings in it. The first act that was put into the house of lords was for an order to bring men to divine service; which was agreed to on the 26th, and sent down to the commons, who kept it long before they sent it back. On the 6th of April, when it was agreed to, the earl of Derby, the bishops of Carlisle and Norwich, and the lords Stourton and Windsor, dissented. The lords afterwards brought in another bill for authorizing a new Common Prayer Book, according to the alterations which had been agreed on the former year. This the commons joined to the former, and so put both in one act. By it was first set forth, "that, an order of divine sei . e " being published, many did wilfully abstain from it, and re- " fused to come to their parish churches; therefore all are " required, after the feast of All-hallows next, to come every " Sunday and holyday to common prayers, under pain of the " censures of the church. And the king, the lords temporal, " and the commons, did in God's name require all archbishops, " bishops, and other ordinaries, to endeavour the due execu- " tion of that act, as they would answer before God for such " evils and plagues, with which he might justly punish them .or " neglecting that good and wholesome law: and they were i lly " authorized to execute the censures of the church on all that " should offend against this law. To which is added, that " there had been divers doubts raised about the manner of the " ministration of the service, rather by the curiosity of the " ministers and mistakers, than of any other worthy cause; " and that, for the better explanation of that, and for the " greater perfection of the service, in some places where it was " fit to make the prayer and fashion of service more earnest " and fit, to stir Christian people to the true honouring of " Almighty God; therefore it had been by the command of " the king and parliament perused, explained, and made more 190 " perfect. They also annexed to it the form of making bishops, " priests, and deacons; and so appointed this new book of " service to be every where received after the feast of All-

[Journal of Lords, p. 421.]

An act au-thorizing the new Common Prayer Book.

[Cap. 1. Statutes, vol. iv. p. 130.]

printed copies assign its commence-ment to the twenty-third, which accounts for this cession being cited as the 5th and 6th years of the King's reign, the latter beginning on the twenty-eighth day of Janu-ary.]

" Saints next, under the same penalties that had been enacted
" three years before, when the former book was set out."

Which was
much cen-
sured.
It was upon this act said by the papists, that the reformation
was like to change as oft as the fashion did : since they seemed
never to be at a point in any thing, but new models were thus
continually framing.   To which it was answered, that it was no
wonder that the corruptions, which they had been introducing
for above a thousand years, were not all discovered or thrown
out at once ; but now the business was brought to a fuller perfection, and they were not like to see any more material changes.
Besides, any that would take the pains to compare the offices
that had been among the papists, would clearly perceive, that
in every age there was such an increase of additional rites and
ceremonies, that, though the old ones were still retained, yet it
seemed there would be no end of new improvements and additions.   Others wondered why the execution of this law was put
off so long as till the end of the year.   All the account I can
give of this is, that it was expected that by that time the new
body of the ecclesiastical laws, which was now preparing, should
be finished ; and therefore, since this act was to be executed by
the clergy, the day in which it was to be in force, was so long
delayed, till that reformation of their laws were concluded.

An act con-
cerning
treasons.
[Feb. 18.
Journal of
Lords, pp.
402, 403.]
On the eighth of February a bill of treasons was put in, and
agreed to by all the lords, except the lord Wentworth.   It was
sent down to the commons, where it was long disputed.   And
many sharp things were said of those who now bore the sway :
that whereas they who governed in the beginning of this reign
had put in a bill for lessening the number of such offences ; now
they saw the change of councils, when severer laws were proposed.   The commons at last rejected the bill, and then drew
[Cap. 2.
Statutes,
vol. iv. p.
144.]
a new one, which was passed.   By it they enacted, " that if
" any should call the king or any of his heirs named in the
" statute of the 35th of his father's reign, heretic, schismatic,
" tyrant, infidel, or usurper of the crown ; for the first offence
" they should forfeit their goods and chattels, and be im-
" prisoned during pleasure ; for the second, should be in a
" præmunire; for the third, should be attainted of treason :
" but any who should advisedly set that out in printing, or
" writing, was for the first offence to be held a traitor.   And
" that those who should keep any of the king's castles, artillery,

" or ships, six days after they were lawfully required to deliver
" them up, should be guilty of treason: that men might be
" proceeded against for treasons committed out of the kingdom
" as well as in it.   They added a proviso, that none should be
" attainted of treason on this act, unless two witnesses should
" come, and to their face aver the fact for which they were to
" be tried; except such as without any violence should confess
" it: and that none should be questioned for any thing said or
" written but within three months after it was done."

This proviso seems clearly to have been made with relation
to the proceeding against the duke of Somerset, in which the
witnesses were not brought to aver the evidence to his face;
and by that means he was deprived of all the benefit and advantage which he might have had by cross-examining them.
It is certain, that, though some false witnesses have practised
the trade so much, that they seemed to have laid off all shame,
and have a brow that cannot be daunted; yet for the greatest
part a bright serenity and cheerfulness attends innocence, and
a lowering dejection betrays the guilty, when the innocent and
they are confronted together.

On the third of March a bill was brought in to the lords for An act
holydays and fasting-days, and sent down to the commons on about fasts
and holy-
the 15th of March; by whom it was passed, and had the royal days.
assent.   In the preamble it is set forth, "That men are not [Cap. 3.
Statutes,
" at all times so set on the performance of religious duties as vol. iv. p.
" they ought to be; which made it necessary that there should 132.]
" be set times, in which labour was to cease, that men might on
" these days wholly serve God: which days were not to be
" accounted holy of their own nature, but were so called,
" because of the holy duties then to be set about; so that the
" sanctification of them (was not any magical virtue in that
" time, but) consisted in the dedicating them to God's service:
" that no day was dedicated to any saint; but only to God, in
" remembrance of such saints: that the scripture had not de-
" termined the number of holydays, but that these were left to
" the liberty of the church.   Therefore they enact, that all
" Sundays, with the days marked in the Calendar and Liturgy,
" should be kept as holydays: and the bishops were to proceed
" by the censures of the church against the disobedient."   A
proviso was added for the observation of St. George's feast

by the knights of the garter: and another, that labourers or fishermen might, if need so required, work on those days, either in or out of harvest. The eves before holydays were to be kept as fasts; and in Lent, and on Fridays and Saturdays, abstinence from flesh was enacted: but if a holyday fell to be on a Monday, the eve for it was to be kept on Saturday, since Sunday was never to be a fasting-day. But it was generally observed, that, in this and all such acts, the people were ready enough to lay hold on any relaxation made by it; but did very slightly observe the stricter parts of it; so that the liberty left to tradesmen to work in cases of necessity was carried further than it was intended, to a too public profanation of the time so sanctified; and the other parts of it, directing the people to a conscientious observing of such times, was little minded.

[Journal of Lords, p. 408.] On the fifth of March a bill concerning the relief of the poor was put into the house of lords. The form of passing it has given occasion to some to take notice, that, though it is a bill for taxing the subjects, yet it had its first birth in the lords' house, and was agreed to by the commons. By it the churchwardens were empowered to gather charitable collections for the poor; and, if any did refuse to contribute, or did dissuade others from it, the bishop of the diocese was to proceed against them.

[Ibid. p. 409.] On the ninth of March the bishops put in a bill for the security of the clergy from some ambiguous words that were in the submission, which the convocation had made to king Henry in the 21st year of his reign: by which they were under a *præmunire* if they did any things in their courts contrary to the king's prerogative; which was thought hard, since some through ignorance might transgress. Therefore it was desired, that no prelate should be brought under a *præmunire* unless they had proceeded in any thing after they were prohibited by the king's writ. To this the lords consented; but it was let fall by the commons.

An act for the marriage of the clergy. [Feb. 10. Ibid. p. 401.]

[Cap. 12. Statutes, vol. iv. p. 146.] There was another act brought in for the marriage of the clergy, which was agreed to by the lords; the earls of Shrewsbury, Derby, Rutland, and Bath, and the lords Abergavenny, Stourton, Monteagle, Sandes, Windsor, and Wharton, protesting against it. The commons also passed it, and it was assented to by the king. By it was set forth, "that many took occasion, "from words in the act formerly made about this matter, to

"say, that it was only permitted, as usury and other unlawful
"things were, for the avoiding greater evils; who thereupon
"spake slanderously of such marriages, and accounted the
"children begotten in them to be bastards, to the high dis-
"honour of the king and parliament, and the learned clergy of
"the realm; who had determined, that the laws against priests'
"marriages were most unlawful by the law of God, to which
"they had not only given their assent in the convocation, but
"signed it with all their hands.   These slanders did also occa-
"sion, that the word of God was not heard with due reverence:
"whereupon it was enacted, that such marriages, made accord-
"ing to the rules prescribed in the book of service, should be
"esteemed good and valid; and that the children begot in
"them should be inheritable according to law."

The marquis of Northampton did also put in a bill for con- [March 9.
firming his marriage, which was passed; only the earl of Derby, Journal
the bishops of Carlisle and Norwich, and the lord Stourton, dis- of Lords, p. 409.]
sented.   By it, "the marriage is declared lawful, as by the law
"of God indeed it was; any decretal, canon, ecclesiastical law,
"or usage to the contrary notwithstanding."   This occasioned
another act, that no man might put away his wife, and marry [March 19.
another, unless he were formerly divorced; to which the bishop Ibid. p. 413.]
of Norwich dissented, because he was of opinion, that a divorce did not break the marriage bond.   But this bill fell in
the house of commons, being thought not necessary; for the
laws were already severe enough against such double marriages.

By another act, the bishopric of Westminster was quite sup- [Ibid. p.
pressed, and reunited to the see of London: but the collegiate 407.]
church, with its exempted jurisdiction, was still continued.
Another bill was put in against usury; which was sent from An act
the lords to the commons, and passed by both, and assented to. against
By it an act, passed in parliament in the 37th year of the late [Cap. 20.
king's reign, "that none might take above twenty *per cent.* for Statutes,
"money lent, was repealed; which, they say, was not intended 155.]
"for the allowing of usury, but for preventing further incon-
"veniences.   And since usury was by the word of God for-
"bidden, and set out in divers places of scripture as a most
"odious and detestable vice; which yet many continue to
"practise, for the filthy gain they made by it: therefore, from

" the first of May, all usury or gain for money lent was to
" cease; and whosoever continued to practise to the contrary
" were to suffer imprisonment, and to be fined at the king's
" pleasure."

This act has been since repealed, and the gain for money
lent has been at several times brought to several regulations.
It was much questioned, whether these prohibitions of usury
by Moses were not judicial laws, which did only bind the nation
of the Jews; whose land being equally divided among the 19
families by lot, the making gain by lending money was forbid
to them of that nation: yet it did not seem to be a thing of its
nature sinful, since they might take increase of a stranger.
The not lending money on use was more convenient for that
nation; which abounding in people, and being shut up in a
narrow country, they were necessarily to apply themselves to
all the ways of industry for their subsistence: so that every
one was, by that law of not lending upon use, forced to employ
his money in the way of trade or manufacture, for which they
were sure to have vent, since they lay near Tyre and Sidon,
that were then the chief places of traffic and navigation of the
world; and without such industry the soil of Judæa could not
possibly have fed such vast numbers as lived on it; so that it
seemed clear that this law in the Old Testament properly
belonged to that policy. Yet it came to be looked on by many
Christians as a law of perpetual obligation. It came also to be
made a part of the canon law; and absolution could not be given
to the breakers of it, without a special faculty from Rome.
But, for avoiding the severity of the law, the invention of mort-
gages was fallen on; which at first were only purchases made,
and let back to the owner, for such rent as the use of the
money came to: so that the use was taken as the rent of the
land thus bought. And those who had no land to sell thus, fell
upon another way: the borrower bought their goods, to be paid
within a year, (for instance 110*l.*) and sold them back for a
sum to be presently laid down as they should agree; (it may
be 100*l.*) by this means the one had 100*l.* in hand, and the
other was to have 10*l.* or more at a year's end. But this,
being in the way of sale, was not called usury. This law was
looked on as impossible to be observed in a country like England: and it could not easily appear where the immorality lay

of lending money upon moderate gain, such as held proportion
to the value of land, provided that the perpetual rule of Christian
equity and charity were observed; which is, not to exact above
the proportion duly limited by the law, and to be merciful in
not exacting severely of persons who by inevitable accidents
have been disabled from making payment. This digression I
thought the more necessary, because of the scruples that many
good and strict persons have still in that matter.

Another act passed both houses against all simoniacal pac- A bill
tions, the reservation of pensions out of benefices, and the against si-
granting advowsons while the incumbent was yet alive. It was [Journal
agreed to by the lords, the earls of Derby, Rutland, and Sussex, of Lords,
the viscount Hereford, and the lords Monteagle, Sandes, Whar- p. 420.]
ton[20], and Evers, dissenting. But, upon what reason I do not
know, the bill was not assented to by the king; who being
then sick, there was a collection made of the titles of the bills
which were to have the royal assent, and those the king signed,
and gave commission to some lords to pass them in his name.
These abuses have been oft complained of, but there have been
still new contrivances found out to elude all laws against simony;
either bargains being made by the friends of the parties concerned without their express knowledge, or bonds of resignation given, by which incumbents lie at the mercy of their
patrons; and in these the faultiness of some clergymen is made
the colour of imposing such hard terms upon others, and of
robbing the church oftentimes by that means.

194   There was a private bill put in about the duke of Somerset's A repeal of
estate, which had been by act of parliament entailed on his the entail
son in the 23rd year of the last king's reign. On the third of of Somer-
March it was sent to the house of commons, signed by the [Journal of
king; it was for the repeal of that act. Whether the king Commons,
was so alienated from his uncle, that this extraordinary thing p. 19.]
was done by him for the utter ruin of his family, or not, I cannot determine: but I rather incline to think it was done in
hatred to the duchess of Somerset and her issue. For the
estate was entailed on them by that act of parliament, in prejudice of the issue of the former marriage, of whom are descended the Seymours of Devonshire: who were disinherited
and excluded from the duke of Somerset's honours by his pa-

[20 This is a mistake for *Windsor*, as appears from the Journal, p. 420.]

tents, and from his estate by act of parliament; partly upon some jealousies he had of his former wife, but chiefly by the power his second wife had over him. This bill of repeal was much opposed in the house, though sent to them in so unusual

[Journal of Commons, p: 19.]

a way by the king himself. And though there was on the eighth of March a message sent from the lords, that they should make haste towards an end of the parliament, yet still they stuck long upon it; looking on the breaking of entails, that were made by act of parliament, as a thing of such consequence, that it dissolved the greatest security that the law of England gives for property. It was long argued by the commons, and was fifteen several days brought in. At last a new bill was devised, and that was much altered too: it was not quite ended till the day before the parliament was dissolved. But, near the end of the session, a proviso was sent from the lords to be added to the bill, confirming the attainder of the duke and his complices. It seems his enemies would not try this at first, till they had by other things measured their strength in that house; and finding their interest grew there, they adventured on it: but they mistook their measures, for the commons would not agree to it. In conclusion, the bill of repeal was agreed to. But whereas there had been some writings for a marriage between the earl of Oxford's daughter and the duke of Somerset's son, and a bill was put in for voiding

[Ibid.p.21.]

these; upon a division of the house the 28th of March, there were sixty-eight that agreed, and sixty-nine that rejected it: so this bill was cast out. By this we see what a thin house of commons there was at that time, the whole being but 137 members. But this was a natural effect of a long parliament; many of those who were at first chosen being infirm, and others not willing to put themselves to the charge and trouble of such constant and long attendance. It is also from hence clear, how great an interest the duke of Somerset had in the affections of the parliament.

The commons refuse to attaint the bishop of Durham by bill. [Journal of Commons, p. 21.]

Another bill gave a more evident discovery how hateful the duke of Northumberland was to them. The bishop of Durham was, upon some complaint brought against him of misprision of treason, put into the Tower about the end of December last year. What the particulars were, I do not find; but it was visible that the secret reason was, that he being attainted, the

duke of Northumberland intended to have had the dignities and jurisdiction of that principality conferred on himself: so that he should have been made count palatine of Durham. Tunstall had in all points given obedience to every law, and to all the injunctions that had been made: but had always in
195 parliament protested against the changes in religion; which he thought he might with a good conscience submit to and obey, though he could not consent to them: only in the matter of the corporal presence he was still of the old persuasion, and writ about it [22]. But the Latin style of his book is much better than the divinity and reasonings in it. So what he would have done, if he had been required to subscribe the articles that were now agreed on, did not appear; for he was all this while prisoner. There was a constant good correspondence between Cranmer and him; though in many things they differed in opinion: yet Tunstall was both a man of candour and of great moderation, which agreed so well with Cranmer's temper, that no wonder they lived always in good terms. So when the bill for attainting him as guilty of misprision of treason was passed in the house of lords on the 31st of March, being put in on the 28th, Cranmer spake so freely against it, that the duke of Northumberland and he were never after that in friendship together. What his arguments were, I could not recover: but, when he could do no more, he protested against it, being seconded only by the lord Stourton. How it came to pass that the other popish lords and bishops, that protested against the other acts of this parliament, did not join in this, I cannot imagine; unless it was, that they were the less concerned for Tunstall, because Cranmer had appeared to be so much his friend, or were awed by their fear of offending the duke of Northumberland. But when the bill was carried down to the commons, with the evidences against him, which were some depositions that had been taken, and brought to the lords; they who were resolved to condemn that practice for the future, would not proceed upon it now. So on the fifth of April they ordered the privy-counsellors of their house to move the lords, that his accusers and he might be heard face to face; and that not being done, they went no further in the bill.

[Journal of Lords, pp. 416, 418.]

[April 4. Journal of Commons, p. 21.]

[[22] Cuthberti Tonstalli de Veritate Corporis et Sanguinis Domini in Eucharistia, lib. 2. Lutet. ap. Vascosan. 1554, 4to.]

By these indications the duke of Northumberland saw how little kindness the house of commons had for him. The parliament had now sat almost five years; and, being called by the duke of Somerset, his friends had been generally chose to be of it. So that it was no wonder, if upon his fall they were not easy to those who had destroyed him: nor was there any motion made for their giving the king a supply. Therefore the duke of Northumberland thought it necessary for his interest to call a new parliament: and accordingly, on the 15th **The parliament is dissolved.** of April, the parliament was dissolved; and it was resolved to spend this summer in making friends all over England, and to have a new parliament in the opening of the next year.

The convocation at this time agreed to the articles of religion that were prepared the last year: which, though they have been often printed, yet since they are but short, and of so great consequence to this history, I have put them into the Collection, as was formerly told.

Thus the reformation of doctrine and worship were brought to their perfection; and were not after this in a tittle mended or altered in this reign, nor much afterwards; only some of the articles were put in more general words under queen Elizabeth.

A reformation of ecclesiastical courts considered. Another part of the reformation was yet unfinished, and it was the chief work of this year; that was, the giving rules to the ecclesiastical courts, and for all things relating to the government of the church, and the exercise of the several 196 functions in it. In the former volume it was told, that an act had passed for this effect; yet it had not taken effect, but a commission was made upon it, and those appointed by king Henry had met and consulted about it, and had made some progress in it, as appears by an original letter of Cranmer's to that king in the year 1545, in which he speaks of it as a thing then almost forgotten, and quite laid aside: for from the time of the six articles till then the design of the reformation had been going backward. At that time the king began to reassume the thoughts of it; and was resolved to remove some ceremonies, such as the creeping to the cross, the ringing of bells on St. Andrew's eve, with other superstitious practices: **[Cranmer's Remains, p. 414.]** for which Cranmer sent him the draught of a letter to be written in the king's name to the two archbishops, and to be by them communicated to the rest of the clergy. In the postscript of his letter he complains much of the sacrilegious waste [Ibid. p. of the cathedral church of Canterbury, where the dean and prebendaries had been made to alienate many of their manors upon letters obtained by courtiers from the king, as if the lands had been desired for the king's use; upon which they had surrendered those lands, which were thereupon disposed of to the courtiers that had an eye upon them. This letter should have come in in the former volume, but I had not seen it then; so I took hold on this occasion to direct the reader to it in the Collection.

It was also formerly told, that an act had passed in this reign to empower thirty-two persons, who should be named by the king, to make a reformation of the ecclesiastical laws, which was to be finished within three years. But the revolutions of affairs, and the other more pressing things that were still uncompleted, had kept them hitherto from setting to that work. On the first[23] of November last year a commission was given to eight persons to prepare the matter for the review of the two and thirty, that so it might be more easily compiled, being in a few hands, than could well be done if so many had been to set about it. These eight were, the archbishop of Canterbury and the bishop of Ely; Dr. Cox and Peter Martyr, two divines; Dr. May and Dr. Taylor, two doctors of the law; and John Lucas and Richard Goodrick, two common lawyers. But on the 14th of November the commission was renewed; and the bishop of London was named in the room of the bishop of Ely, one Traheron[24] in the room of May, and Gosnald in Goodrick's room. These, it seems, desiring more time than one year to finish it in, for two of the years were now lapsed, in the last session of the parliament they had three years more time offered them. But it seems the work was believed to be in such a forwardness, that this

[Ibid. p. 416.]

Collect. Numb. 61.

---

[23] For first, read eleventh. [S.]

[24] Bartholomew Traheron, afterward made lecturer of Divinity at Frankfort in the new moulding of the congregation there, in queen Mary's days; and dean of Chichester in queen Elizabeth's. [G.]

[This is a mistake. He was dean of Chichester in 1553 in the reign of Edward. This preferment he vacated in the same year after Mary's accession, and was not restored to it in the reign of Elizabeth. The mistake probably originated in an erroneous assertion in Wood's Ath. Oxon. 1st edit., which was omitted in the second edition.]

continuation was not judged necessary; for the royal assent was not given to that act. After the parliament was ended, they made haste with it. But I find it said in the preface to the book, as it was printed in queen Elizabeth's reign, that Cranmer did the whole work almost himself [25] : which will justify the character some give of him, that he was the greatest canonist then in England. Dr. Haddon [26], that was University Orator in Cambridge, and sir John Cheke, were employed to put it in Latin. And they did so imitate the style of the Roman laws, that any who reads the book will fancy himself to be reading a work of the purer ages of that state; when their language was not yet corrupted with these barbarous terms 197 which the mixture of other nations brought in, and made it no where more nauseously rude than in the canon law.

The work was digested and cast into fifty-one titles, to bring it near the number of the books of the Pandects, into which Justinian had digested the Roman law. It was prepared by February this year, and a commission was granted to thirty-two persons, of whom the former eight were a part: consisting of eight bishops, eight divines, among whom John a Lasco was one, eight civilians, and eight common lawyers. They were to revise, correct, and perfect the work, and so to present it to the king. They divided themselves into four classes, eight to a classis; and every one of these were to prepare their corrections, and so to communicate them to the rest. And thus was the work carried on and finished; but, before it received the royal confirmation, the king died, and this fell with him: nor do I find it was ever since that time taken up or prosecuted with the care that a thing of such consequence deserved; and therefore I shall not think it improper for me, having before shewed what was done, in the next place to give an account of what was then intended to be done; and is now very fit to be well considered.

[25] All that I find in that preface is, that these thirty-two were divided into four classes, and that what was concluded in one class was to be communicated to the rest; and that summæ negotii præfuit Tho. Cranmerus, Archiep. Cant.; as it was fit he should preside. [B.] Cranmer's part is thus expressed,

summæ negotii præfuit. [S.]

[26] Haddon never was University-orator at Cambridge; as appears from a very exact catalogue upon the Orator's book, and otherwise. [B.]

Haddon was the king's professor of civil law, and not the University Orator. [S.]

The first title was of the Trinity, and the catholic faith; The chief
in which those who denied the Christian religion were to suffer heads of it.
death, and the loss of their goods.   The books of scripture
were numbered, those called apocryphal being left out of the
canon; which, though they were read in the church, it was
only for the edification of the people, but not for the proof of
the doctrine.   The power of the church was subjected to the
scriptures : the four general councils were received ; but all
councils were to be examined by the scripture ; as were also
the writings of the fathers, who were to be much reverenced,
but, according to what themselves have written, they were
only to be submitted to when they agreed with the scriptures.

The second title contains an enumeration of many heresies,
viz. against the Trinity, Jesus Christ, the scriptures, about
original sin, justification, the mass, purgatory; and censured
those who denied magistracy to be lawful, or asserted the
community of goods, or wives; or who denied the pastoral
office, and thought any might assume it at pleasure; or who
thought the sacraments naked signs, who denied the baptism
of infants, or thought none could possibly be saved that were
not baptized; or who asserted transubstantiation, or denied
the lawfulness of marriage, particularly in the clergy; or who
asserted the pope's power; or such as excused their ill lives
by the pretence of predestination, as many wicked men did:
from which and other heresies all are dissuaded, and earnestly
exhorted to endeavour the extirpation of them.

The third was about the judgments of heresy before the
bishop of the diocese, even in exempted places.   They were to
proceed by witnesses; but the party, upon fame, might be
required to purge himself: if he repented, he was to make
public profession of it in those places where he had spread it;
and to renounce his heresy, swearing never to return to it any
more : but obstinate heretics were to be declared infamous,
incapable of public trust, or to be witnesses in any court, or to
have power to make a testament, and were not to have the
198 benefit of the law.   Clergymen falling into heresy were not to
return to their benefices, unless the circumstances were such
that they required it; and thus all capital proceedings for
heresy were laid down.

The fourth was about blasphemy, flowing from hatred or

rage against God, which was to be punished as obstinate heresy was.

The fifth was about the sacraments of baptism and the Lord's supper. To which is added, that imposition of hands is to be retained in the ordination of pastors ; that marriages are to be solemnly made ; that those who renew their baptismal vow be confirmed by the bishop ; and that the sick should be visited by their pastors.

The sixth was about idolatry, magic, witchcraft, or consulting with conjurers ; who were to be arbitrarily punished, if they submitted : otherwise to be excommunicated.

The seventh was about preachers ; whom the bishops were to examine carefully before they licensed them : and were once a year to gather together all those who were licensed in their dioceses, to know of them the true state of their flock ; what vices abounded, and what remedies were most proper. Those who refused to hear sermons, or did make disturbance in them, were to be separated from the communion. It seems it was designed, that there should be in every diocese some who should go round a precinct, and preach like evangelists, as some then called them.

The eighth was about marriage ; which was to be after asking banns three Sundays, or holydays. Those who were married in any other form than that in the book of service, were not to be esteemed lawfully married : those who corrupted virgins were to be excommunicated, if they did not marry them ; or if that could not be done, they were to give them the third part of their goods, besides other arbitrary punishments. Marriages made without the consent of parents or guardians were declared null. Then follow the things that may void marriages ; they are left free to all. Polygamy is forbid ; marriages made by force are declared void ; mothers are required to suckle their children.

The ninth is about the degrees of marriage. All those in the Levitical law, or those that are reciprocal to them, are forbidden. But spiritual kindred was not to hinder marriage, since there was nothing in scripture about it, nor was there any good reason for it.

The tenth was about adultery. A clergyman guilty of it was to forfeit all his goods and estate to his wife and children ;

or if he had none, to the poor, or some pious use; and to lose
his benefice, and be either banished, or imprisoned during life.
A layman was to restore his wife's portion, and to give her the
half of his goods, and be imprisoned, or banished, during life.
Wives that were guilty were to be in like manner punished.
But the innocent party might marry again: yet such were
rather exhorted, if they saw hope of amendment, to be reconciled to the offending party.   No marriage was to be dissolved
without a sentence of divorce. Desertion, long absence, capital
enmities, where either party was in hazard of their life, or the
constant perverseness or fierceness of a husband against his
wife, might induce a divorce. But little quarrels might not do
199 it; nor a perpetual disease, relief in such a misery being one
of the ends of marriage. But all separation from bed and
board, except during a trial, was to be taken away.

The eleventh was about admission to ecclesiastical benefices.
Patrons were to consider, the choice of the person was trusted
to them, but was not to be abused to any sacrilegious or base
ends: if they did otherwise, they were to lose their right for
that time.   Benefices were not to be given or promised before
they were void; nor let lie destitute above six months, otherwise they were to devolve to the bishop. Clergymen before
their ordination were to be examined by the archdeacons, with
such other triers as the bishop should appoint to be assistant
to them: and the bishop himself was to try them, since this
was one of the chief things, upon which the happiness of the
church depended. The candidate was to give an oath to answer
sincerely, upon which he was to be examined about his doctrine, chiefly of the whole points of the Catechism, if he understood them aright; and what knowledge he had of the scriptures: they were to search him well, whether he held heretical
opinions.   None was to be admitted to more cures than one;
and all privileges for pluralities were for ever to cease: nor
was any to be absent from his cure, except for a time, and a
just cause, of which he was to satisfy his ordinary.   The bishops were to take great care to allow no absence longer than
was necessary: every one was to enter upon his cure within
two months after he was instituted by the bishop. Prebendaries, who had no particular cure, were to preach in the churches
adjacent to them. Bastards might not be admitted to orders,

unless they had eminent qualities. But the bastards of patrons were upon no account to be received, if presented by them. Other bodily defects, unless such as did much disable them, or made them very contemptible, were not to be a bar to any. Beside the sponsions in the office of ordination, they were to swear that they had made no agreement to obtain the benefice to which they were presented; and that if they come to know of any made by others on their account, they should signify it to the bishop; and that they should not do any thing to the prejudice of their church.

The 12th and 13th were about the renouncing or changing of benefices.

The 14th was about purgation upon common fame, or when one was accused for any crime, which was proved incompletely, and only by presumptions. The ecclesiastical courts might not reexamine any thing that was proved in any civil court; but upon a high scandal a bishop might require a man to purge himself, otherwise to separate him from holy things. The form of a purgation was, to swear himself innocent; and he was also to have four compurgators of his own rank, who were to swear, that they believed he swore true: upon which the judge was to restore him to his fame. Any that were under suspicion of a crime might by the judge be required to avoid all the occasions from which the suspicion had risen: but all superstitious purgations were to be rejected.

The 15th, 16th, 17th, and 18th, were about dilapidations, the letting of the goods of the church, the confirming the former rules of election in cathedrals or colleges, and the collation of benefices. And there was to be a purgation of simony, 200 as there should be occasion for it.

The 19th was about divine offices. In the morning on holydays, the Common Prayer was to be used, with the communion service joined to it. In cathedrals, there was to be communion every Sunday and holyday; where the bishop, the dean, and the prebendaries, and all maintained by that church, were to be present. There was no sermon to be in cathedrals in the morning, lest that might draw any from the parish churches; but only in the afternoons. In the anthems, all figured music, by which the hearers could not understand what they sung, was to be taken away. In parish churches there were only to be sermons in the morning; but none in the afternoon, except in great parishes. All who were to receive the sacrament were to come the day before, and inform the minister of it; who was to examine their consciences, and their belief. On holydays in the afternoon the Catechism was to be explained for an hour. After the evening prayers, the poor were to be looked to; and such as had given open scandal were to be examined, and public penitence was to be enjoined them: and the minister, with some of the ancients of the parish, were to commune together about the state of the people in it; that if any carried themselves indecently, they might be first charitably admonished; and, if that did not prevail, subjected to severer censures; but none were to be excommunicated without the bishop were first informed, and had consented to it. Divine offices were not to be performed in chapels, or private houses, lest the churches should under that pretence be neglected, and errors more easily disseminated; excepting only the houses of peers and persons of great quality, who had numerous families; but in these, all things were to be done according to the Book of Common Prayer.

The 20th was about those that bore office in the church; sextons, churchwardens, deacons, priests, and rural deans. This last was to be a yearly office; he that was named to it by the bishop, being to watch over the manners of the clergy and people in his precinct, was to signify the bishop's pleasure to them, and to give the bishop an account of his precinct every sixth month. The archdeacons were to be general visitors over the rural deans. In every cathedral, one of the prebendaries, or one procured by them, was thrice a week to expound some part of the scriptures. The bishops were to be over all, and to remember that their authority was given to them for that end, that many might be brought to Christ, and that such as had gone astray might be restored by repentance. To the bishop all were to give obedience according to the word of God. The bishop was to preach often in his church; was to ordain none for rewards, or rashly; was to provide good pastors, and to deprive bad ones: he was to visit his diocese every third year, or oftener, as he saw cause; but then he was to do it at his own charge: he was to have yearly synods, and to confirm such as were well instructed. His family was to consist of clergymen, whom he should bring up to the service of the church; (so was St. Austin's, and other ancient bishops' families constituted:) this being a great means to supply the great want of good and faithful ministers. Their wives and children were also to avoid all levity or vain dressing. They were never to be absent from their dioceses, but upon a 20 public and urgent cause: and when they grew sick or infirm, they were to have coadjutors. If they became scandalous or heretical, they were to be deprived by the king's authority. The archbishops were to exercise the episcopal function in their diocese; and were once to visit their whole province, and to oversee the bishops, to admonish them for what was amiss, and to receive and judge appeals, to call provincial synods upon any great occasion, having obtained warrant from the king for it. Every bishop was to have a synod of his clergy some time in Lent, so that they might all return home before Palm-Sunday. They were to begin with the Litany, a sermon, and a communion; then all were to withdraw into some private place, where they were to give the bishop an account of the state of the diocese, and to consult of what required advice: every priest was to deliver his opinion, and the bishop was to deliver his sentence, and to bring matters to as speedy a conclusion as might be; and all were to submit to him, or to appeal to the archbishop.

The 21st, 22nd, 23rd, 24th, 25th, 26th, 27th, 28th, and 29th titles are about churchwardens, universities, tithes, visitations, testaments, ecclesiastical censures, suspension, sequestration, deprivation.

The 30th is about excommunication; of which, as being the chief ecclesiastical censure, I shall set down their scheme the more fully.

Their design concerning the use of excommunication.

Excommunication they reckon an authority given of God to the church, for removing scandalous or corrupt persons from the use of the sacraments, or fellowship of Christians, till they give clear signs of their repentance, and submit to such spiritual punishments, by which the flesh may be subdued, and the spirit saved. This was trusted to churchmen, but chiefly to archbishops, bishops, archdeacons, deans, and any other appointed for it by the church. None ought to be excommunicated but for their obstinacy in great faults; but it was never

to be gone about rashly ; and therefore the judge who was to
give it was to have a justice of peace with him, and the minister of the parish where the party lived, with two or three
learned presbyters, in whose presence the matter was to be
examined, and sentence pronounced, which was to be put in
writing.   It was to be intimated in the parish where the party
lived, and in the neighbouring parishes, that all persons might
be warned to avoid the company of him that was under excommunication; and the minister was to declare what the nature
and consequences of excommunication were, the person so censured being cut off from the body of Christ : after that, none
was to eat, or drink, or keep company with him, but those of
his own family : whosoever did otherwise, if being admonished
they continued in it, were also to be excommunicated.   If the
person censured continued forty days without expressing any
repentance, it was to be certified into the chancery, and a writ
was to issue for taking and keeping him in prison till he should
become sensible of his offences : and when he did confess these,
and submitted to such punishments as should be enjoined, the
sentence was to be taken off, and the person publicly reconciled to the church.   And this was to take place against those,
who, being condemned for capital offences, obtained the king's
pardon, but were notwithstanding to be subject to church
censures.

202   Then follows the office of receiving penitents.   They were
first to stand without the church, and desire to be again received into it, and so to be brought in : the minister was to
declare to the people the heinousness of sin, and the mercies
of God in the gospel, in a long discourse, of which the form is
there prescribed : then he was to shew the people, that, as
they were to abhor hardened sinners, so they were to receive,
with the bowels of true charity, all sincere penitents; he was
next to warn the person, not to mock God, and deceive the
people, by a feigned confession; he was thereupon to repeat,
first a general confession, and then more particularly to name
his sin, and to pray to God for mercy to himself, and that
none by his ill example might be defiled; and finally to beseech them all to forgive him, and to receive him again into
their fellowship.   Then the minister was to ask the people
whether they would grant his desires; who were to answer,

they would : then the pastor was to lay his hand on his head, and to absolve him from the punishment of his offences, and the bond of excommunication; and so to restore him to his place in the church of God. Then he was to lead him to the communion table, and there to offer up a prayer of thanksgiving to God for reclaiming that sinner. For the other titles, they relate to the other parts of the law of those courts, for which I refer the reader to the book itself.

How far any of those things, chiefly the last about excommunication, may be yet brought into the church, I leave to the consultations of the governors of it, and of the two houses of parliament. It cannot be denied, that vice and immorality, together with much impiety, have overrun the nation: and though the charge of this is commonly cast on the clergy, who certainly have been in too many places wanting to their duty ; yet, on the other hand, they have so little power, or none at all by law, to censure even the most public sins, that the blame of this great defect ought to lie more universally on the whole body of the nation, that have not made effectual provision for the restraining of vice, the making illmen ashamed of their ways, and the driving them from the holy mysteries, till they change their course of life.

A project for relieving the clergy reduced to great poverty.

There was another thing proposed this year for the correcting the great disorders of clergymen, which were occasioned by the extreme misery and poverty to which they were reduced. There were some motions made about it in parliament, but they took not effect: so one writ a book concerning it, which he dedicated to the lord chancellor, then the bishop of Ely. He shewed, that, without rewards or encouragements, few would apply themselves to the pastoral function, and that those in it, if they could not subsist by it, must turn to other employments; so that at that time many clergymen were carpenters and tailors, and some kept alehouses. It was a reproach on the nation, that there had been so profuse a zeal for superstition, and so much coldness in true religion. He complains of many of the clergy who did not maintain students at the universities according to the king's injunctions; and that in schools and colleges the poor scholars' places were generally filled with the sons of the rich; and that livings were most scandalously sold; and the greatest part of the country clergy were so ignorant, that they could do little more than read.   But there was no hope of doing any thing effectually for redressing so great a calamity, till the king should be of age himself to set forward such laws as might again recover a competent maintenance for the clergy.

This year, both Heath of Worcester, and Day bishop of Chichester, were put out of their bishoprics.   For Heath, it has been already said, that he was put in prison for refusing to consent to the book of ordinations.   But for Day, whether he refused to submit to the new book, or fell into other transgressions, I do not know.   Both these were afterwards deprived, not by any court consisting of churchmen, but by secular delegates, of whom three were civilians, and three common lawyers, as king Edward's Journal informs us.   Day's sentence is something ambiguously expressed in the patent that Scory bishop of Rochester had to succeed him; which bears date the 24th of May, and mentions his being put there in the room of George late bishop of that see, who had been deprived or[25] removed from it.   In June following, upon Holbeche bishop of Lincoln's death, Taylor, that had been dean of Lincoln, was made bishop.   This year the bishopric of Gloucester was quite suppressed, and converted into an exempted archdeaconry; and Hooper was made bishop of Worcester.   In the December before, Worcester and Gloucester had been united, by reason of their vicinage, and their great poverty, and that they were not very populous: so they were to be for ever after one bishopric with two titles, as Coventry and Lichfield, and Bath and Wells were; and Hooper was made bishop of Worcester and Gloucester.   But now they were put into another method, and the bishop was to be called only bishop of Worcester.   In all the vacancies of sees, there were a great many of their best lands taken from them: and the sees that before had been profusely enriched, were now brought to so low a condition, that it was scarce possible for the bishops to subsist: and yet, if what was so taken from them had been converted to good uses, to the bettering the condition of the poor clergy over England, it had been some mitigation of so heinous a

Side notes:

Heath and Day turned out of their bishoprics. [Oct. 10, 1551.]

[Rymer xv. p. 303.]

[Aug. 2, 1551.] [June 26.] [May 20.]

---

25 [The letters patent are dated May 23. They use the words *deprivationis seu remotionis*, whereas *per deprivationem* is used in case of Heath, bishop of Worcester.]

robbery; but these lands were snatched up by every hungry courtier, who found this to be the easiest way to be satisfied in their pretensions: and the world had been so possessed with the opinion of their excessive wealth, that it was thought they never could be made poor enough.

The affairs of Ireland.   This year a passage fell out relating to Ireland, which will give me occasion to look over to the affairs of that kingdom. The kings of England had formerly contented themselves with the title of lords of Ireland: which king Henry the Eighth, in the thirty-third year of his reign, had, in a parliament there, changed into the title of a kingdom. But no special crown or coronation was appointed, since it was to follow the crown of England. The popes and the emperors have pretended, that the conferring titles of sovereign dignity belonged to them. The pope derived his claim from what our Saviour said, *that all power in heaven and in earth was given to him,* and by consequence to his vicar. The emperors, as being a dead shadow of the Roman empire, which title, with the designation of Cæsar, they still continued to use, and pretended, that, as the Roman emperors did anciently make kings, so they had still the same right: though, because those emperors made kings in the countries which were theirs by conquest, it was an odd stretch to infer, that those, who retained nothing of their empire but the name, should therefore make kings in 204 countries that belonged not to them; and it is certain, that every entire or independent crown or state may make for or within itself what titles they please. But the authority the crown of England had in Ireland was not then so entire, as, by the many rebellions that have fallen out since, it is now become. The heads of the clans and names had the conduct of all their several tribes, who were led on by them to what designs they pleased; and though, within the English pale, the king was obeyed, and his laws executed almost as in England, yet the native Irish were an uncivilized and barbarous nation, and not yet brought under the yoke; and for the greatest part of Ulster, they were united to the Scots, and followed their interests.

There had been a rebellion in the second year of this reign: but sir Anthony St. Leger, then deputy, being recalled, and sir Edward Bellinghame sent in his room, he subdued O'Canor

and O'More, that were the chief authors of it; and, not being
willing to put things to extremities, when England was otherwise distracted with wars, he persuaded them to accept of
pensions of 100*l.* a-piece, and so they came in and lived in the
English pale.   But the winter after, there was another rebellion designed in Ulster by O'Neal, O'Donnel, O'Docart, and
the heads of some other tribes; who sent to the queen dowager
of Scotland to procure them assistance from France, and they
would keep up the disorders in Ireland.   The bishop of Valence, being then in Scotland, was sent by her to observe their
strength, that he might accordingly persuade the king of
France to assist them.   He crossed the seas, and met with
them, and with Wauchop, a Scotchman, who was the bishop
of Armagh of the pope's making, and who, though he was
blind[26], was yet esteemed one of the best at riding post in the
world.   They set out all their greatness to the French bishop,
to engage him to be their friend at the court of France : but
he seemed not so well satisfied of their ability to do any great
matter, and so nothing followed on this.   One passage fell out [Melville's
here, which will a little discover the temper of that bishop. Memoirs,
When he was in O'Docart's house, he saw a fair daughter of his, p. 10.]
whom he endeavoured to have corrupted, but she avoided him
carefully.   Two English grey friars, that had fled out of
England for their religion, and were there at that time, observing the bishop's inclinations, brought him an English
whore, whom he kept for some time.   She one night looking
among his things, found a glass full of somewhat that was
very odoriferous, and poured it all down her throat; which the
bishop perceiving too late, fell into a most violent passion; for
it had been presented to him by Soliman the Magnificent, at
his leaving that court, as the richest balm in Egypt, and was
valued at two thousand crowns.   The bishop was in such a
rage, that all the house was disturbed with it; whereby he
discovered both his lewdness and passion at once.   This is related by one that was then with him, and was carried over by
him to be a page to the Scotch queen; sir James Melville, who
lived long in that court, under the constable of France, and

26 He was not blind, only short-   questa virtu, di correr alla posta
sighted : Il quale huomo di bre-   meglio d'huomo del mondo. Hist.
vissima vista era commendato di   del Conc. Trid. l. 2. p. 144. [B.]

was afterwards much employed by the prince elector palatine in many negotiations; and coming home to his own country, was sent on many occasions to the court of England, where he lived in great esteem. He in his old age writ a narrative of all the affairs that himself had been concerned in, which is one 205 of the best and perfectest pieces of that nature that I have seen. The original is yet extant under his own hand in Scotland: a copy of it was shewed me by one descended from him, from which I shall discover many considerable passages, though the affairs in which he was most employed were something later than the time of which I am to write. But to return to Ireland. Upon the peace made with France and Scotland, things were quieted there, and sir Anthony St. Leger was in August 1550 again sent over to be deputy there. For the reformation, it made but a small progress in that kingdom. It was received among the English, but I do not find any endeavours were used to bring it in among the Irish. This year Bale was sent into Ireland. He had been a busy writer upon all occasions, and had a great deal of learning, but wanted temper, and did not write with the decency that became a divine, or was suitable to such matters; which it seems made those who recommended men to preferment in this church not think him so fit a person to be employed here in England. But the bishopric of Ossory being void, the king proposed him to be sent thither. So in August this year Dr. Goodacre was sent over to be bishop of Armagh, and Bale to be bishop of Ossory. There were also two other, who were Irishmen, to be promoted. When they came thither, the archbishop of Dublin intended to have consecrated them according to the old pontifical; for the new book of ordination had not been yet used among them. Goodacre and the two others were easily persuaded to it, but Bale absolutely refused to consent to it; who being assisted by the lord chancellor, it was carried, that they should be ordained according to the new book. When Bale went into his diocese, he found all things there in dark popery; but before he could make any reformation there, king Edward's death put an end to his and all such designs.

A change made in the order of the garter.

In England nothing else that had any relation to the reformation passed this year, unless what belongs to the change made in the order of the garter may be thought to relate to it. On

the 23rd of April the former year, being St. George's day, a
proposition was made to consider the order and statutes, since
there was thought to be a great deal of superstition in them;
and the story upon which the order was founded, concerning
St. George's fighting with the dragon, looked like a legend
formed in the darker ages to support the humour of chivalry,
that was then very high in the world. And as the story had
no great credibility in itself, so it was delivered by no ancient
author. Nor was it found that there had been any such saint:
there being among ancient writers none mentioned of that
name, but George of Alexandria, the Arian bishop, that was put
in when Athanasius was banished. Upon this motion in the
former year, the duke of Somerset, the marquis of Northampton, and the earls of Wiltshire and Warwick, were appointed
to review the statutes of the order. So this year the whole
order was changed; and the earl of Westmorland and sir
Andrew Dudley, who were now to be installed, were the first
that were received according to the new model; (which the
reader will find in the Collection, as it was translated into Latin King Ed-
out of the English, by the king himself, written all with his ward's
Remains,
own hand, and it is the third paper after his Journal.) The Numb. 3.
preamble of it sets forth the noble design of the order, to
animate great men to gallant actions, and to associate them into
206 a fraternity, for their better encouragement and assistance;
but says, it had been much corrupted by superstition, therefore
the statutes of it were hereafter to be these :

It was no more to be called the order of St. George, nor was
he to be esteemed the patron of it; but it was to be called the
order of the garter. The knights of this order were to
wear the blue riband or garter as formerly; but at the
collar instead of a George, there was to be on one side
of the jewel a knight carrying a book upon a sword point,
on the sword to be written *Protectio*, on the book *Verbun
Dei;* on the reverse, a shield, on which should be written
Fides; to express their resolution, both with offensive and defensive weapons, to maintain the word of God. For the rest of
the statutes I shall refer the reader to the paper I mentioned.
But this was repealed by queen Mary, and so the old rules took
place again, and do so still. This design seems to have been
chiefly intended, that none but those of the reformed religion

might be capable of it; since the adhering to and standing for the scriptures was then taken to be the distinguishing character between the papists and the reformers.

This is the sum of what was either done or designed this year with relation to religion. As for the state, there was a strict inquiry made of all who had cheated the king in the suppression of chantries, or in any other thing that related to churches; from which the visitors were believed to have embezzled much to their own uses; and there were many suits in the star-chamber about it. Most of all these persons had been the friends or creatures of the duke of Somerset: and the inquiry after these things seems to have been more out of hatred to him, than out of any design to make the king the richer by what should be recovered for his use. But on none did the storm break more severely than on the lord Paget. He had been chancellor of the duchy of Lancaster, and was charged with many misdemeanours in that office, for which he was fined in 6000*l.* But that which was most severe was, that on St. George's eve he was degraded from the order of the garter for divers offences: but chiefly, because he was no gentleman, neither by father's side nor mother's side. His chief offence was his greatest virtue. He had been on all occasions a constant friend to the duke of Somerset; for which the duke of Northumberland hated him mortally, and so got him to be degraded to make way for his own son. This was much censured as a barbarous action, that a man who had so long served the crown in such public negotiations, and was now of no meaner blood than he was when king Henry first gave him the order, should be so dishonoured, being guilty of no other fault but what is common to most courtiers, of enriching himself at his master's cost; for which his fine was severe enough for the expiation. But the duke of Northumberland was a person so given up to violence and revenge, that an ordinary disgrace did not satisfy his hatred.

Sir Anthony St. Leger, another knight of the order, was at the same time accused, upon complaint sent from the archbishop of Dublin in Ireland, for some high words that he had used. But these being examined, he was cleared, and admitted to his place among the knights at the garter. Many others that were obnoxious came in, upon this violent prosecution, to

Marginal note: Paget degraded from being a knight of the garter.

207 purchase the favour of Northumberland, who was much set on
framing a parliament to his mind, and so took those methods
which he thought likeliest to work his ends : it being ordinary
for men of insolent and boisterous tempers, who are generally
as abject when they are low, as they are puffed up with prosperity, to measure other people by themselves; therefore,
knowing that the methods of reason and kindness would have
no operation on themselves, and that height and severity are
the only ways to subdue them, they use that same way of
gaining others which they find most effectual with themselves.

This year the king went on in paying his debts, reforming
the coin, and other ways that might make the nation great and
wealthy.　And one great project was undertaken, which has
been the chief beginning and foundation of the great riches,
and strength of shipping, to which this nation has attained
since that time.　From the days of king Henry the Third, the
free towns of Germany, who had assisted him in his wars, obtained great privileges in England; they were made a corporation, and lived together in the Stillyard near the bridge.
They had in Edward the Fourth's time been brought into
some trouble for carrying their privileges further than their
charter allowed them; and so judgment was given that they
had forfeited it : but they redeemed themselves out of that, by
a great present which they made to the king.　That which
chiefly supported them at court was, that they, trading in a
body, were not only able to take the trade out of all other
persons' hands, by underselling them, but they had always à
great stock of money; and so when the government was in a
strait, they were ready, upon a good security, to lend great
sums; and on lesser occasions could obtain the favour of a
statesman by the presents they made him.　But now trade
was raised much above what it had been; and courts becoming
more magnificent than formerly, there was a greater consump-
tion, particularly of cloth, than had ever been known.　The
discovery of the Indies had raised both trade and navigation,
so that there was a quicker circulation of the wealth of the
world than had been in former ages.

Antwerp and Hamburg, lying both conveniently, the one
in the mouth of the Elbe, and the other near the mouth of the

*The in-
crease of
trade.*

Rhine, which were the two greatest rivers that fell into those seas, the merchants of those two cities at that time had the chief trade of the world. The English began to look on those Easterlings with envy. All that was imported or exported came for the most part in their bottoms; all markets were in their hands, so that commodities of foreign growth were vented by them in England, and the product of the kingdom was bought up by them. And all the nation being then set much on pasture, they had much advanced their manufacture; insomuch that their own wool, which had been formerly wrought at Antwerp, was now made into cloth in England, which the Stillyard-men obtained leave to carry away. At first they shipped not above eight cloths in a year, after that 100, then 1000, then 6000; but this last year there was shipped in their name 44,000 cloths; and not above 1100 by all others that traded within England.

The merchant-adventurers found they could not hold out, unless this company was broke; so they put in their complaint against them in the beginning of this year; to which the Stillyard-men made answer, and they replied. Upon this the council made a decree, that the charter was broken, and so 208 dissolved the company. Those of Hamburg and Lubeck, and the regent of Flanders, solicited the council to have this redressed, but in vain; for the advantage the nation was to have by it was too visible to admit of any interposition. But the design of trade being thus set on foot, another project of a higher nature followed it. The war was now begun between the emperor and the king of France; and that, with the persecution raised in Flanders against all that leaned to the doctrine of the protestants, made many there think of changing their seats. It was therefore proposed here in England to open a free trade, and to appoint some mart-towns, that should have greater privileges and securities for encouraging merchants to live in them, and should be easier in their customs than they were any where else. Southampton for the cloth trade, and Hull for the northern trade, were thought the two fittest places: and for the advantages and disadvantages of this design, I find the young king had balanced the matter exactly; for there is a large paper, all written with his own hand, containing what was to be said on both sides. But his

death, and queen Mary's marrying the prince of Spain, put an
end to this project: though all the addresses her husband
made, seconding the desires of the Easterlings, could never
prevail to the setting up of that company again. If the reader
would understand this matter more perfectly, he may find a
great deal of it in the king's Journal, and in the fourth paper
that follows it, where the whole affair seems to be considered
on all hands: but men that know merchandise more perfectly,
will judge better of these things.

King Edward's Remains, Numb. 4.

This summer, Cardan, the great philosopher of that age,
passed through England. He was brought from Italy on the
account of Hamilton, archbishop of St. Andrew's, who was then
desperately sick of a dropsy. Cardan cured him of his disease;
but, being a man much conversant both in astrology and magic,
as himself professed, he told the archbishop, that, though he
had at present saved his life, yet he could not change his fate,
for he was to die on a gallows. In his going through England
he waited on king Edward, where he was so entertained by
him, and observed his extraordinary parts and virtues so narrowly, that on many occasions he writ afterwards of him, with
great astonishment, as being the most wonderful person he had
ever seen.

Cardan in England.

But the mention of the Scotch archbishop's sickness leads
me now to the affairs of Scotland. The queen had passed
through England from France to Scotland last year. In her
passage she was treated by the king with all that respect that
one crowned head could pay to another. The particulars are
in his Journal, and need not be recited here. When she came
home, she set herself much to persuade the governor to lay
down the government, that it might be put in her hands; to
which he, being a soft man, was the more easily induced, because his brother, who had great power over him, and was a
violent and ambitious man, was then so sick, that there was
no hope of his life. He had also received letters from France,
in such a style, that he saw he must either lay down the government, or not only lose the honour and pension he had
there, but be forced to struggle for what he had in his own
country. Whether the French understood any thing by their
209 spies in the court of England, that it had been proposed there
to persuade him to pretend to the crown, and were therefore

The affairs of Scotland.

the more earnest to have the government out of his hands, I
do not know; but, though I have seen many hundreds of
letters that passed in those times between England and Scotland, I could not find by any of them that he ever entered
into any treaty about it.

It seems his base brother had some thoughts of it; for
when he was so far recovered that he could inquire after
news, and heard what his brother had done, he flew out in a
passion, and called him *a beast for parting with the govern-*
ment, since there was none but a   lass between him and
the crown. I set down his own words; leaving a space void
for an epithet he used of the young queen, scarce decent
enough to be mentioned. There had been a great consultation
in France what to do with the queen of Scotland. Her uncles
pressed the king to marry her to the dauphin; for thereby
another kingdom would be added to France, which would be
a perpetual thorn in the side of England: she had also some
prospect of succeeding to the crown of England; so that on
all accounts it seemed the best match in Europe for the dauphin. But the wise constable had observed, that the Spaniards
lost by their dominions that lay so remote from the chief seat
of their government, though these were the richest countries
in Europe; namely, Sicily, Naples, Milan, and the Netherlands: and wisely apprehended, that France might suffer
much more by the accession of such a crown, which not only
was remote, but where also the country was poor, and the
people not easily governed. It would be a vast charge to them
to send navies, and to pay armies there. The nobility might,
when they would, by confederating with England, either shake
off the French government, or put them to a great expense to
keep it: so that, whereas Scotland had been hitherto, by a
pension, and sometimes by a little assistance, kept in a perpetual alliance with France, he apprehended by such an union it
might become their enemy, and a great weight on their government. This the constable pressed much, both out of his
care of his master's interest, and in opposition to the house of
Guise. He advised the king rather to marry her to some of
his subjects, of whom he was well assured, and to send her and
her husband home into Scotland; by which means the perpetual amity of that kingdom might be preserved on easy

[*skitteren*,
Melville's
Memoirs,
p. 73.]

terms. But the king was so possessed with the notion of the
union of that crown to France, that he gave no ear to this
wise advice, thinking it flowed chiefly from the hatred and
enmity which he knew the constable bore the family of Guise.
This the constable himself told Melville, from whose narrative
I have it. The queen mother of Scotland, being possessed of
the government, found two great factions in it. The head of
the one was the archbishop; who now recovering, and finding
himself neglected, and the queen governed by other counsels,
set himself much against her, and drew the clergy for the
most part into his interests. The other faction was of those
who hated him and them both, and inclined to the reformation. They set up the prior of St. Andrew's, who was their
young queen's natural brother, as their head, and by his means
offered their service to the queen, now made regent. They
210 offered that they would agree with her to send the matrimonial crown to the dauphin, and consent to the union of both
kingdoms; only they desired her protection from the violence
of the clergy, and that they might have secretly preachers in
their houses to instruct them in the points of religion. This
offer the queen readily accepted of; and so, by their assistance, carried things till near the end of her regency with great
moderation and discretion. And now the affairs of Scotland
were put in a channel, in which they held long steady and
quiet, till about six years after this, that, upon the peace with
the king of Spain, there were cruel counsels laid down in
France, and from thence sent over into Scotland, for extirpating heresy. But of that we shall discourse in its proper
place.

As for the affairs of Germany, there was this year a great
and sudden turn of things there; with which the emperor
was surprised by a strange supineness, that proved as fatal to
him as it was happy to the empire, though all the world besides saw it coming on him. Upon the delivery of Magdeburg, Maurice of Saxe's army, pretending there was an ar-
rear due to them, took up their winter quarters near Saxe, in
the dominions of some popish princes, where they were very
unwelcome guests. The sons of the landgrave, being required
by their father, pressed the duke of Saxe on his honour to
free their father, or to become their prisoner in his room,

The affair
of Ger-
many.

[Nov. 3,
1551. Slei-
dan, fol.
381.]

since they had his faith for his liberty : so he went to them,
and offered them his person; but though he did not trust
them with his whole design, yet he told them so much, that
they were willing to let him go back. The emperor's counsellors were alarmed with what they heard from all hands;
and the duke of Alva (well known afterwards by his cruelties
in the Netherlands) advised him to send for Maurice to come
and give an account of all those suspicious passages, to take
the army out of his hands, and to take such securities from
him, as might clear all the jealousies, for which his carriage
had given great cause. But the bishop of Arras was on the
other hand so assured of him, that he said, the giving him
any suspicion of the emperor's distrust might really engage
him into such designs; and that such deep projects as they
heard he was in were too fine conceits for Dutch drunken
heads. He also assured them, he had two of his secretaries
in pension, so that he was advertised of all his motions. But
the duke of Saxe came to know, that those his secretaries
were the emperor's pensioners; and dissembled it so well,
that he used them in all appearance with more confidence
than formerly : he held all his consultations in their presence,
and seemed to open his heart so to them, that they possessed
the bishop with a firm confidence of his sincerity and steadi-
ness to the emperor's interests. Yet his lingering so at the
town of Magdeburg, with the other dark passages concerning
him, made the emperor conceive at last a jealousy of him ;
and he writ for him to come and clear himself; then he re
fined it higher; for, having left orders with the officers whom
he had made sure to him, to follow with the army in all the
haste they could, he himself took post, with as small a train
as his dignity could admit of, and carried one of those corrupted secretaries with him : but on the way he complained
of pains in his side, so that he could not hold on his journey ;
but sent forward his secretary, who gave such an account of
him, that it, together with his coming so readily a great part
of his way in so secure a manner, made the emperor now lay
down all his former distrusts. The emperor writ to Trent,
and to many other places, that there was no cause of fear
from Maurice. And Maurice, to colour the matter more completely, had sent his ambassadors to Trent, and had ordered

Melancthon, and his other divines, to follow them slowly, that, as soon as the safe conduct was obtained, they might go on and defend their doctrine.

Upon their coming to Trent, and proposing their desires, that all might be again considered, the legates rejected the proposition with much scorn. The emperor's ambassadors and prelates pressed that they might be well received. The archbishop of Toledo showed how much Christ had borne with the scribes and pharisses; and that, in imitation of him, they ought to leave nothing undone that might gain upon them. So it was resolved, that the council should make a protestation, that the usage they gave them was out of charity, which is above all law; since it was against the decretals to have any treaty with professed heretics. At the same time the imperialists dealt no less earnestly with the ambassadors from the protestant princes, not to ask too much at once, but to go on by degrees; and assured them, they had a mind to lessen the pope's greatness as much as they had. The ambassador's first step was to be for obtaining a safe conduct. They excepted to that which the council had given, as different from that the council of Basle had sent to the Bohemians, in four material points. The first was, That their divines should have a decisive voice. 2. That all points should be determined according to the scriptures; and according to the fathers, as they were conformable to those. 3. That they should have the exercise of their religion within their own houses. 4. That nothing should be done in contempt of their doctrine. So they desired that the safe conduct might be word for word the same with that of Basle.

But the legates abhorred the name of that council, that had endeavoured so much to break the power of the popedom; and had consented to that extraordinary safe conduct only to unite Germany, and to gain them by such compliance to be of their side against the pope. Yet the legates promised to consider of it. The ambassadors were received in a congregation, which differed from a session of the council, just as a committee of a whole house of parliament differs from the house when set according to its forms. They began their speech with this salutation, *Most reverend and most mighty fathers and lords:* they added a cold compliment, and desired a safe conduct. At this

Marginal notes:
Procedings at Trent. [History of the Council of Trent, p. 344.]

[Ibid. p. 345.]

[Ibid. p. 346.]

time the pope, hearing that the emperor was resolved to bring
on the old designs of some councils for lessening his greatness,
[Ibid.
p. 349.]
and that the Spanish bishops were much set on it, united himself to France, and resolved to break the council as soon as it
was possible; and therefore he ordered the legates to proceed
in the decision of the doctrine, hoping that the protestants
would despair of obtaining any thing, and so go away. So
the safe conduct they had desired was not granted them; and
another was offered in its room, containing only full security 21
for their persons. Upon this security, such as it was, divines
[Ibid.
p. 352.]
came both from Wurtemberg and the town of Strasburg. But,
as they were going on to treat of matrimony, the war of Ger-
[Ibid.
p. 353.]
many broke out; and the bishops of the empire, with the other
ambassadors, immediately went home. The legates laid hold
on this so readily, that, though the session was to have been
[May 1.]
held on the second of May, they called an extraordinary
[Ibid.
p. 354.]
one on the 28th of April, and suspended the council for two
years.

An ac-
count of
the council
of Trent.
And being to have no other occasion to say any thing more
of this council, I shall only add, that there had been a great
expectation over Christendom of some considerable event of a
general council for many years. The bishops and princes had
much desired it, hoping it might have brought the differences
among divines to a happy composure; and have settled a reformation of those abuses which had been long complained of,
and were still kept up by the court of Rome, for the ends of
that principality that they had assumed in sacred things. The
popes for the same reasons were very apprehensive of it;
fearing that it might have lessened their prerogatives, and, by
cutting off abuses, that brought in a great revenue to them,
have abridged their profits. But it was, by the cunning of the
legates, the dissensions of princes, the great number of poor
Italian bishops, and the ignorance of the greatest part of the
other, so managed, that, instead of composing differences in
religion, things were so nicely defined, that they were made irreconcilable. All those abuses, for which there had been nothing
but practice, and that much questioned before, were now, by
the provisos and reservations, excepted for the privileges of the
Roman see, made warrantable. So that it had in all particulars
an issue quite contrary to what the several parties concerned

had expected from it ; and has put the world ever since out of the humour of desiring any more general councils, as they are accustomed to call them.   The history of that council was writ with as much life, and beauty, and authority, as had been ever seen in any human writing, by friar Paul of Venice, within half an age of the time in which it was ended ; when the thing was yet fresh in men's memories, and many were alive who had been present : and there was not one in that age that engaged to write against it.   But about forty years after, when father Paul, and all his friends, who knew from what vouchers he writ, were dead, Pallavicini, a Jesuit, who was made a cardinal for this service, undertook to answer him by another history of that council ;[27] which, in many matters of fact, contradicts father Paul, upon the credit (as he tells us) of some journals and memorials of such as were present, which he perused, and cites upon all occasions.   We see that Rome hath been in all ages so good at forging those things which might be of use to its interests, that we know not how to trust that shop of false wares in any one thing that comes out of it.   And therefore it is not easy to be assured of the truth and genuineness of any of the materials, out of which the Jesuit composed his work. But as for the main thread of the story, both his and father Paul's accounts do so agree, that whosoever compares them, will clearly see, that all things were managed by intrigues and secret practices ; so that it will not be easy for a man of common sense, after he has read over Pallavicini's history, to fancy that there was any extraordinary influence of the Holy Ghost hovering over and directing their counsels.   And the care they took for palliating all the corruptions then complained of was so apparent, that their historian had no other way by which to excuse it, but to set up a new hypothesis, which a French writer since has wittily called *the Cardinal's new Gospel;* "That there must be a temporal principality in the " church ; that all things which support that principality are " to be at least tolerated, though they be far contrary to the " primitive patterns, and to the first delivery of the gospel by " Christ and his apostles.   That which was then set up, he ac- " counts a state of infancy, to which milk was proper ; but the

And a judgment of the histories of it.

13

[27] [Pallavicini (Sforza,) Istoria del Concilio di Trento. Rom. 1664. 4º.]

" church being since grown to its full state and strength, other
" things are now necessary for the maintaining and preserving
" of it."

But to return to Maurice, he having possessed the emperor
with an entire confidence in him, gathered his army together,
took Augsburg, with many other imperial cities, and displaced
the magistrates which the emperor had put in them, and restored their old ones, with the banished ministers: so that
every thing began to put on a new face. Ferdinand king of
the Romans did mediate, both on his own account, for the
Turks were falling into Hungary ; and on the empire's, for the
king of France was come with a great army to the confines of
the empire: and the constable, pretending that he only desired
passage through the town of Metz, entered it, and possessed
himself of it. Toul and Verdun fell also into his hands; and
the French were endeavouring to be admitted into Strasburg.
The emperor was now in great disorder: he had no army
about him; those he had confided in were declared against
him; his own brother was not ill pleased at his misfortune;
the French were like to gain ground on his hereditary dominions. Being thus perplexed and irresolved, he did not send
a speedy answer to Maurice's demands, which he had sent by
his brother; for the setting of the landgrave at liberty, restoring the freedoms of the empire, and particularly in matters
of religion. But, to lose no time the mean while, Maurice
marched on to Inspruch, where the emperor lay; and surprised a pass to which he had trusted, so that he was within
two miles of him before he was aware of it. Upon this the emperor rose from supper in great haste, and by torchlight fled
away to make his escape into Italy. He gave the duke of
Saxe his liberty: but he generously resolved to follow him in
this his calamity; and perhaps he was not willing to owe his
liberty to his cousin Maurice. Thus all that design, which the
emperor had been laying so many years, was now broken off
on a sudden: he lost all the advantages he had of his former
victories, and was forced to set the prisoners at liberty, and to
call in the proscriptions; and in conclusion, the edict of Passau
was made, by which the several princes and towns were
secured in the free exercise of their religion.

I have made this digression, which I thought not disagree- 2

[Thuanus,
x. 5. p. 345.]

[Melville's
Memoirs,
p. 18.]

able to the matter of my history, to give account of the extreme danger in which religion was in Germany, and how strangely it was recovered; in which he who had been the chief instrument of the miseries it had groaned under, was now become its unlooked-for deliverer. 'I have enlarged on some passages that are in none of the printed histories, which I draw from Melville's Memoirs, who says he had them from [Ibid. the elector Palatine's own mouth.   p. 19.]

But the emperor's misfortunes redoubled on him: for, hav- The empe-
ing made peace in the empire, he would, against all reason, or $\substack{\text{ror is much} \\ \text{cast down.}}$
probability of success, sit down before Metz. But the duke of [Thuanus,
Guise defended the place so against him, and the time of the $\substack{\text{x. 6. p. 347} \\ \text{and xi. 11.}}$
year was so unseasonable, being in December, that, after a p. 394 sqq.]
great loss of men, and vast expense of treasure, he was forced
to raise his siege. From thence he retired into Flanders;
where his affliction seized so violently on him, that for some
time he admitted none to come near him: some said he was
frantic; others, that he was sullen and melancholy. The
English ambassadors at Brussels for many weeks could learn
nothing certain concerning him. Here, it is said, he began to
reflect on the vanity of the world; when he, who had but a
year before given law to Christendom, was now driven to so
low an ebb, that, as he had irrecoverably lost all his footing in
Germany, so in all other things his counsels were unlucky. It
was one of the notablest turns of fortune that had been in
many ages; and gave a great demonstration, both of an over-
ruling Providence, that disposes of all human affairs at pleasure, and of a particular care that God had of the reformation,
in thus recovering it when it seemed gone without hope in
Germany.

These reflections made deep impressions on his mind, and
were believed to have first possessed him with the design,
which not long after he put in execution, of laying down his
crowns, and retiring to a private course of life. In his retirement having time to consider things more impartially, he was
so much changed in his opinion of the protestant religion, that
he, who hitherto had been a most violent opposer of it, was
suspected of being turned to it before he died.

Thus ended this year; and now I come to the last and fatal A regula-
year of this young king's life and reign: The first thing done $\substack{\text{tion of the} \\ \text{privy-coun-} \\ \text{cil.}}$

in it was a regulation of the privy-council, which was divided
into so many committees, and every one of these had its proper
work, and days appointed for the receiving and despatching of
all affairs. In all these things a method was prescribed to
them, of which the reader will see a full account in the sixth
paper of those that follow king Edward's Journal: which
paper, though it is not all written with his hand, as the others
be, yet it is in so many places interlined by him, that he seems
to have considered it much, and been well pleased with it. His
second parliament was opened on the first of March. On the
sixth of March it was moved in the house of commons to give
the king two tenths and two fifteenths, with a subsidy for two
years: it was long argued at first, and at the passing the bill
it was again argued; but at last the commons agreed to it.
The preamble of it is a long accusation of the duke of Somerset for involving the king in wars, wasting his treasure, engaging him in much debt, embasing the coin, and having given
occasion to a most terrible rebellion. In fine, considering the
great debt the king was left in by his father, the loss he put
himself to in reforming the coin, and they finding his temper
to be set wholly on the good of his subjects, and not on enriching himself; therefore they give him two tenths, and two fifteenths, with one subsidy for two years. Whether the debate
in the house of commons was against the subsidies in this act,
or against the preamble, cannot be certainly known: but it is
probable the debate at the engrossing the bill was about the
preamble, which the duke of Northumberland and his party
were the more earnestly set on, to let the king see how acceptable they were, and how hateful the duke of Somerset
had been. The clergy did also, for an expression of their
affection and duty, give the king six shillings in the pound of
their benefices. There was also a bill sent down from the
lords, that none might hold any spiritual promotion, unless he
were either priest or deacon: but after the third reading it
was cast out. The reason of it was, because many noblemen
and gentlemen's sons had prebends given them on this pretence, that they intended to fit themselves by study for entering
into orders; but they kept these, and never advanced in their
studies: upon which the bishops prevailed to have the bill
agreed to by the lords, but could carry it no further.

215

[King Ed-
ward's
Remains,
Numb. 6.]

A new par-
liament.
[Journal of
Commons,
pp. 24, 25.]

[An act for
the grant
of a sub-
sidy, cap.
12. Sta-
tutes, vol.
iv. p. 176.]

[Ibid. p.
177.]

[Mar. 21.]

[Mar. 30.]

[Journal of
Lords,
p. 437.]

Another act passed for the suppressing the bishopric of
Durham, which is so strangely misrepresented by those who
never read more than the title of it, that I shall therefore give
a more full account of it. It is set forth in the preamble,
" that that bishopric being then void of a prelate, so that the
" gift thereof was in the king's pleasure; and the compass of
" it being so large, extending to so many shires so far distant,
" that it could not be sufficiently served by one bishop; and
" since the king, according to his godly disposition, was de-
" sirous to have God's holy word preached in these parts,
" which were wild and barbarous for lack of good preaching,
" and good learning; therefore he intended to have two bi-
" shoprics for that diocese; the one at Durham, which should
" have 2000 marks revenue; and another at Newcastle, which
" should have 1000 marks revenue: and also to found a ca-
" thedral church at Newcastle, with a deanery and chapter,
" out of the revenues of the bishopric; therefore the bishopric
" of Durham is utterly extinguished and dissolved, and au-
" thority is given for letters patents to erect the two new
" bishoprics, together with the deanery and chapter at New-
" castle; with a proviso that the rights of the deanery, chap-
" ter, and cathedral of Durham should suffer nothing by this
" act."

When this bill is considered, that dissolution that was designed by it will not appear to be so sacrilegious a thing as
some writers have represented it. For whosoever understands
the value of old rents, especially such as these were, near the
marches of an enemy, where the service of the tenants in the
war made their lands be set at very low rates, will know, that
3000 marks of rent being reserved, besides the endowing of
the cathedral, which could hardly be done under another
thousand marks, there could not be so great a prey of that
bishopric as has been imagined. Ridley, as himself writes in
one of his letters, was named to be bishop of Durham, being
one of the natives of that country; but the thing never took
effect. For in May, and no sooner, was the temporalty of the
bishopric turned into a county palatine, and given to the duke
of Northumberland. But the king's sickness, and soon after
his death, made that and all the rest of these designs prove
abortive.

How Tunstall was deprived, I cannot understand. It was for misprision of treason, and done by secular men: for Cranmer refused to meddle in it. I have seen the commission given by queen Mary to some delegates to examine it: in which it is said, that the sentence was given only by laymen; and that Tunstall, being kept prisoner long in the Tower, was brought to his trial, in which he had neither counsel assigned him, nor convenient time given him for clearing himself; and that, after divers protestations, they had, notwithstanding his appeal, deprived him of his bishopric. He was not only turned out, but kept prisoner, till queen Mary set him at liberty.

At the end of this parliament the king granted a free pardon; concerning which this is only remarkable, that whereas it goes for a maxim, that the acts of pardon must be passed without changing any thing in them, the commons, when they sent up this act of pardon to the lords, desired that some words might be amended in it; but it is not clear what was done, for that same day the acts were passed, and the parliament was dissolved.

In it the duke of Northumberland had carried this point, that the nation made a public declaration of their dislike of the duke of Somerset's proceedings; which was the more necessary, because the king had let fall words concerning his death, by which he seemed to reflect on it with some concern, and looked on it as Northumberland's deed. But the act had passed with such difficulty, that either the duke did not think the parliament well enough disposed for him, or else he resolved totally to vary from the measures of the duke of Somerset, who continued the same parliament long; whereas this, that was opened on the first, was dissolved on the last day of March.

Visitors were soon after appointed to examine what church plate, jewels, and other furniture, was in all cathedrals and churches; and to compare their account with the inventories made in former visitations; and to see what was embezzled, and how it was done. And because the king was resolved to have churches and chapels furnished with that that was comely and convenient for the administration of the sacraments; they were to give one or two chalices of silver, or more, to every 217 church, chapel, or cathedral, as their discretions should direct

Marginal notes:

[Rymer, xv. p. 334.]

[A free pardon granted, cap. 14. ibid. p. 193.]

[Journal of Lords, p. 444.]

A visitation for the plate in the churches.

them; and to distribute comely furniture for the communion
table, and for surplices; and to sell the rest of the linen, and
give it to the poor: and to sell copes, and altar-cloths, and
deliver all the rest of the plate and jewels to the king's treasurer, sir Edmund Pecham. This is spitefully urged by one of
our writers, who would have his reader infer from it, that the
king was ill principled as to the matters of the church, because, when this order was given by him, he was now in the
16th year of his age. But if all princes should be thus judged
by all instructions that pass under their hands, they would be
more severely censured than there is cause. And for the particular matter that is charged on the memory of this young
prince, which, as it was represented to him, was only a calling
for the superfluous plate and other goods that lay in churches
more for pomp than for use; though the applying of it to
common uses, except upon extreme necessities, is not a thing
that can be justified; yet it deserved not so severe a censure;
especially the instructions being signed by the king in his
sickness; in which it is not likely that he minded affairs of
that kind much, but set his hand easily to such papers as the
council prepared for him.

These instructions were directed, in the copy that I have Instruc-
perused, to the earl of Shrewsbury, lord president of the tions for
north: upon which occasion, I shall here make mention of that dent of the
which I know not certainly in what year to place, namely, the north.
instructions that were given to that earl when he was made
president of the north. And I mention them the rather, because there have been since that time some contests about that
office, and the court belonging to it. There was by his instructions a council to be assistant to him; whereof some of
the members were at large, and not brand to attendance,
others were not to leave him without licence from him: and
he was in all things to have a negative voice in it. For the
other particulars, I refer the reader to the copy, which he will
find in the Collection. One instruction among them belongs Collect.
to religion; that he and the other counsellors, when there was Numb. 56.
at any time assemblies of people before them, should persuade
them to be obedient chiefly to the laws about religion, and
especially concerning the service set forth in their own mother-
tongue. There was also a particular charge given them con-

cerning the abolished power of the bishop of Rome: whose abuses they were by continual inculcation so to beat into the minds of the people, that they might well apprehend them, and might see that those things were said to them from their hearts, and not from their tongues only for form's sake. They were also to satisfy them about the abrogation of many holydays appointed by the same bishop; who endeavoured to persuade the world that he could make saints at his pleasure: which, by leading the people to idleness, gave occasion to many vices and inconveniencies. These instructions were given after the peace was made with Scotland; otherwise there must have been a great deal in them relating to that war: but the critical time of them I do not know.

[May 26.]
[Mar. 30.]

This year Harley was made bishop of Hereford, instead of 218 Skip, who died the last year. And he being the last of those who were made so by letters patents, I shall give the reader some satisfaction concerning that way of making bishops. The patents began with the mention of the vacancy of the see, by death or removal: upon which the king being informed of the good qualifications of such a one, appoints him to be bishop during his natural life, or so long as he shall behave himself well; giving him power to ordain and deprive ministers, to confer benefices, judge about wills, name officials and commissaries, exercise ecclesiastical jurisdiction, visit the clergy, inflict censures, and punish scandalous persons, and to do all the other parts of the episcopal function that were found by the word of God to be committed to bishops; all which they were to execute and do in the king's name and authority. After that, in the same patent, follows the restitution of the temporalities. The day after, a certificate in a writ called a *significavit* was to be made of this, under the great seal, to the archbishop, with a charge to consecrate him.

The form of the bishops' letters patents.

[Rymer, xv. p. 169.]

The first that had his bishopric by the king's patents was Barlow, that was removed from St. David's to Bath and Wells. They bear date the third of February, in the second year of the king's reign: and so Ferrar, bishop of St. David's, was not the first, as some have imagined; for he was made bishop the first of August that year. This Ferrar was a rash indiscreet man, and drew upon himself the dislike of the prebendaries of St. David's. He was made bishop upon the duke of

[July 31. Rymer, xv. p. 173.]

Somerset's favour to him. But last year many articles were
objected to him : some, as if he had incurred a *præmunire* for
acting in his courts, not in the king's, but his own name, and
some for neglecting his charge ; and some little indecencies
were objected to him, as, going strangely habited, travelling on
foot, whistling impertinently, with many other things, which, if
true, shewed in him much weakness and folly. The heaviest articles he denied : yet he was kept in prison, and commissioners
were sent into Wales to examine witnesses, who took many depositions against him. He lay in prison till queen Mary's time ;
and then he was kept in on the account of his belief. But his
suffering afterwards for his conscience, when Morgan, who had
been his chief accuser before on those other articles, being then
made his judge, condemned him for heresy, and made room for
himself to be bishop by burning him, did much turn the
people's censures from him upon his successor.

By these letters patents it is clear, that the episcopal function was acknowledged to be of divine appointment, and that
the person was no other way named by the king than as lay
patrons present to livings ; only the bishop was legally authorized, in such a part of the king's dominions, to execute that
function which was to be derived to him by imposition of hands.
Therefore here was no pretence for denying that such persons
were true bishops, and for saying, as some have done, that
they were not from Christ, but from the king.

Upon this occasion it will not be improper to represent to
the reader how this matter stands according to the law at this
219 day ; which is the more necessary, because some superficial
writers have either misunderstood or misrepresented it. The
act that authorized those letters patents, and required the
bishops to hold their courts in the king's name, was repealed [Statutes,
both by the 1 Mar. chap. 2. and 1 and 2 Phil. and Mary, chap. 8. vol. iv. pp.
The latter of these, that repealed only a part of it, was re- 202, 246.]
pealed by the 1 Eliz. chap. 1. and the former by the 1 Jac. [Ibid. pp.
chap. 25. So some have argued, that since those statutes, 350, 1052.]
which repealed this act of Edward the Sixth, 1 par. chap, 2.
are since repealed, that it stands now in full force. This seems
to have some colour in it, and so it was brought in question in
parliament in the fourth year of king James. And great debate being made about it, the king appointed the two chief
justices to search into the matter : they upon a slight inquiry

agreed, that the statute of Edward the Sixth was in force by that repeal; but the chief baron, and the other judges, searching the matter more carefully, found, that the statute had been in effect repealed by the 1st of Eliz. ch. 1, where the act of the 25 Hen. VIII. concerning the election and jurisdiction of bishops, as formerly they had exercised it, was revived: so that being in full force, the act of Edward the Sixth, that repealed it, was thereby repealed. To this all the learned men of the law did then agree: so that it was not thought so much as necessary to make an explanatory law about it, the thing being indeed so clear, that it did not admit of any ambiguity.

Coke 2. Inst. p. 684. 685. [lib. 2. cap. 11. sect. 201.]

In May this year the king by his letters patents authorized all schoolmasters to teach a new and fuller Catechism, compiled as is believed by Poynet.[28]

These are all the passages in which the church is concerned this year. The foreign negotiations were important. For now the balance began to turn to the French side; therefore the council resolved to mediate a peace between the French and the emperor. The emperor had sent over an ambassador in September last year, to desire the king would consider the danger in which Flanders was now, by the French king's having Metz, with the other towns in Lorraine, which did in a great measure divide it from the assistance of the empire: and therefore moved, that, according to the ancient league between England and the house of Burgundy, they would enter into a new league with him. Upon this occasion the reader will find how the secretaries of state bred the king to the understanding of business, with relation to the studies he was then about: for secretary Cecil set down all the arguments for and against that league, with little notes on the margin, relating to such topics from whence he brought them; by which it seems the king was then learning logic. It is the fifth of those papers after his Journal.

King Edward's Remains, Numb. 5.

It was resolved on to send sir Richard [29] Morison with instructions to compliment the emperor upon his coming into Flanders, and to make an offer of the king's assistance against the Turks,

A treaty with the emperor.

[28] Instead of Poynet, undoubtedly by Alexander Nowel. [S.] [See Dibdin's Ames, iii. 19, and Collier, ii. 336. and Strype, Memorials, ii. 367. See also Part iii. p. 214.]

[29] John, read Richard. [S.] [This note refers to the first edition of 1681. *John* had been altered into *Richard* in the second folio of 1683.]

who had made great depredations that year both in Hungary, Italy, and Sicily. If the emperor should upon that complain of the French king, and say, that he had brought in the Turks, and should have asked assistance against him; he was to move 220 the emperor to send over an ambassador to treat about it; since he that was then resident in England was not very acceptable. These instructions (which are in the Collection) were signed in September, but not made use of till January this year: and then new orders were sent to propose the king to be a mediator between France and the emperor. Upon which, the bishop of Norwich and sir Philip Hobby were sent over to join with sir Richard Morison: and sir William Pickering and sir Thomas Chaloner were sent into France. In May the emperor fell sick, and the English ambassadors could learn nothing certainly concerning him: but then the queen of Hungary and the bishop of Arras treated with them. The bishop of Arras complained, that the French had begun the war, had taken the emperor's ships at Barcelona, had robbed his subjects at sea, had stirred up the princes of Germany against him, had taken some of the towns of the empire from him; while the French ambassadors were all the while swearing to the emperor, that their master intended nothing so much as to preserve the peace: so that now, although the French were making several overtures for peace, they could give no credit to any thing that came from them. In fine, the queen and bishop of Arras promised the English ambassadors to let the emperor know of the king's offering himself to mediate; and afterwards told them, that the emperor delayed giving answer till he were well enough to do it himself

On the 26th of May the ambassadors writ over, that there was a project sent them out of Germany of an alliance between the emperor, Ferdinand king of the Romans, the king of England, and the princes of the empire. They did not desire that the king should offer to come into it of his own accord; but John Frederick of Saxe would move Ferdinand to invite the king into it. This way they thought would give least jealousy. They hoped the emperor would easily agree to the conditions that related to the peace of Germany, since he was now out of all hopes of making himself master of it. The princes neither loved nor trusted him; but loved his brother,

*Collect.
Numb. 57.*

and relied much on England. But the emperor having proposed, that the Netherlands should be included in the perpetual league of the empire, they would not agree to that, unless the quotas of their contribution were much changed: for these provinces were like to be the seats of wars, therefore they would not engage for their defence but upon reciprocal advantages and easy terms.

When the English ambassadors in the court of France desired to know on what terms a peace might be mediated, they found they were much exalted with their success: so that (as they writ over on the first of May) they demanded the restitution of Milan, and the kingdoms of Sicily, Naples, and Navarre, the sovereignty of Flanders, Artois, and the town of Tournay; they would also have Siena to be restored to its liberty, and Metz, Toul, and Verdun to continue under the protection of France. These terms the council thought so unreasonable, that, though they writ them over as news to their ambassadors in Flanders, yet they charged them not to propose them. But 221 the queen of Hungary asked them what propositions they had for a peace, knowing already what they were; and from thence studied to inflame the ambassadors, since it appeared how little the French regarded their mediation, or the peace of Christendom, when they asked such high and extravagant things upon a little success.

On the ninth of June the emperor ordered the ambassadors to be brought into his bedchamber, whither they were carried by the queen of Hungary. He looked pale and lean; but his eyes were lively, and his speech clear. They made him a compliment upon his sickness, which he returned with another for their long attendance. Upon the matter of their embassy, he said, the king of France had begun the war, and must likewise begin the propositions of peace: but he accepted of the king's offer very kindly, and said, they should always find in him great inclinations to a just peace. On the first of July the council writ to their ambassadors. First, assuring them that the king was still alive, and they hoped he should recover; they told them, they did not find that the French would offer any other terms than those formerly made: and they continued still in that mind, that they could not be offered by them as mediators; yet they ordered them to impart them unto the emperor

as news, and carefully to observe his looks and behaviour upon
their opening of every one of them.

But now the king's death broke off this negotiation, together   The king's
with all his other affairs. He had last year, first the measles,   sickness.
and then the smallpox, of which he was perfectly recovered:
in his progress, he had been sometimes violent in his exercises,
which had cast him into great colds; but these went off, and
he seemed to be well after it. But in the beginning of January
this year he was seized with a deep cough; and all medicines
that were used did rather increase than lessen it; upon which
a suspicion was taken up, and spread over all the world, (so that
it is mentioned by most of the historians of that age,) that some
lingering poison had been given him: but more than rumours,
and some ill-favoured circumstances, I could never discover
concerning this. He was so ill when the parliament met, that
he was not able to go to Westminster; but ordered their first
meeting and the sermon to be at Whitehall. In the time of
his sickness, bishop Ridley preached before him, and took occasion to run out much on works of charity; and the obligation
that lay on men of high condition to be eminent in good
works. This touched the king to the quick: so that presently   His care of
after sermon he sent for the bishop. And after he had com-   the relief of
the poor.
manded him to sit down by him, and be covered, he resumed   [Holin-
most of the heads of the sermon, and said, he looked on him-   shed,
p. 1081.]
self as chiefly touched by it: he desired him, as he had already
given him the exhortation in general, so to direct him how to
do his duty in that particular. The bishop, astonished at this
tenderness in so young a prince, burst forth in tears, expressing how much he was overjoyed to see such inclinations in
him: but told him, he must take time to think on it, and   [Ibid.
craved leave to consult with the lord mayor and court of   p. 1082.]
222 aldermen. So the king writ by him to them to consult speedily
how the poor should be relieved. They considered there were
three sorts of poor: such as were so by natural infirmity or
folly, as impotent persons, and madmen, or idiots; such as
were so by accident, as sick, or maimed persons; and such as
by their idleness did cast themselves into poverty. So the
king ordered the Grey-Friars' church near Newgate, with the
revenues belonging to it, to be a house for orphans; St. Bartholomew's near Smithfield to be an hospital; and gave his

own house of Bridewell to be a place of correction and work for such as were wilfully idle. He also confirmed and enlarged the grant for the hospital of St. Thomas in Southwark, which he had erected and endowed in August last. And when he set his hand to these foundations, which was not done before the 26th of June this year, he thanked God, that had prolonged his life till he had finished that design. So he was the first founder of those houses, which, by many great additions since that time, have risen to be among the noblest in Europe.

He expressed in the whole course of his sickness great submission to the will of God, and seemed glad at the approaches of death: only the consideration of religion and the church touched him much; and upon that account, he said, he was

Several
marriages.

desirous of life. About the end of May, or beginning of June, the duke of Suffolk's three daughters were married; the eldest, lady Jane, to the lord Guilford Dudley, the fourth son of the duke of Northumberland, (who was the only son whom he had yet unmarried;) the second, the lady Catharine, to the earl of Pembroke's eldest son, the lord Herbert; the third, the lady Mary, who was crooked, to the king's groom-porter Martyn Keys. The duke of Northumberland married his two daughters, the eldest to sir Henry Sidney, son to sir William Sidney, that had been steward to the king when he was prince; the other was married to the lord Hastings, son to the earl of Huntingdon. The people were mightily inflamed against this insolent duke; for it was generally given out, that he was sacrificing the king to his own extravagant ambition. He seemed little to regard their censures, but attended on the king most constantly, and expressed all the care and concern about him that was possible. And finding that nothing went so near his heart as the ruin of religion, which he apprehended would follow upon his death, when his sister Mary should

He is persuaded to leave the crown to the lady, Jane;

come to the crown; upon that, he and his party took advantage to propose to him to settle the crown by his letters patents on the lady Jane Grey. How they prevailed with him to pass by his sister Elizabeth, who had been always much in his favour, I do not so well understand. But the king being wrought over to this, the duchess of Suffolk, who was next in king Henry's will, was ready to devolve her right on her daughter, even though she should come afterwards to have sons. So on the eleventh of June, Montague, that was chief justice of the common pleas, and Baker and Bromley, two judges, with the king's attorney and solicitor, were commanded to come to council. There they found the king with some privy counsellors about him. The king told them, he did now 223 apprehend the danger the kingdom might be in, if upon his death his sister Mary should succeed; who might marry a stranger, and so change the laws and the religion of the realm. So he ordered some articles to be read to them, of the way in which he would have the crown to descend. They objected, that the act of succession, being an act of parliament, could not be taken away by any such device: yet the king required them to take the articles, and draw a book according to them. They asked a little time to consider of it. So, having examined the statute of the first year of this reign concerning treasons, they found that it was treason, not only after the king's death, but even in his life, to change the succession. Secretary Petre in the mean while pressed them to make haste. When they came again to the council, they declared, they could not do any such thing, for it was treason; and all the lords should be guilty of treason if they went on in it. Upon which the duke of Northumberland, who was not then in the council-chamber, being advertised of this, came in great fury, calling Montague a traitor, and threatened all the judges; so that they thought he would have beaten them. But the judges stood to their opinion. They were again sent for, and came, with Gosnald added to them, on the 15th of June. The king was present, and he somewhat sharply asked them, Why they had not prepared the book as he had ordered them? They answered, That whatever they did would be of no force without a parliament. The king said, he intended to have one shortly. Then Montague proposed, that it might be delayed till the parliament met. But the king said, he would have it first done, and then ratified in parliament: and therefore he required them on their allegiance to go about it: and some counsellors told them, if they refused to obey that, they were traitors. This put them in a great consternation; and old Montague, thinking it could not be treason whatever they did in this matter while the king lived, and at worst, that

Which the judges at first opposed;

[Fuller, lib. viii. p. 2.]

[Ibid. p. 3.]

[Ibid. p. 4.]

a pardon under the great seal would secure him, consented to set about it, if he might have a commission requiring him to do it, and a pardon under the great seal when it was done.

But through fear all yielded except judge Hales.

Both these being granted him, he was satisfied. The other judges, being asked if they would concur, did all agree, being overcome with fear; except Gosnald, who still refused to do it. But he also, being sorely threatened, both by the duke of Northumberland and the earl of Shrewsbury, consented to it the next day. So they put the entail of the crown in form of law, and brought it to the lord chancellor to put the seal to it. They were all required to set their hands to it, but both Gosnald and Hales refused. Yet the former was wrought on to do it; but the latter, though a most steady and zealous man for the reformation, would upon no consideration yield to it: after that, the lord chancellor, for his security, desired that all the counsellors might set their hands to it; which was done on the 21st of June by thirty-three of them; it is like, including the judges in the number. But Cranmer, as he came

[ap. Strype, Mem. Eccles. ii. 480.]

seldom to council[30] after the duke of Somerset's fall, so he was that day absent on design. Cecil, in a relation which he made one write of this transaction, for clearing himself afterwards, says, that, when he had heard Gosnald and Hales declare how much it was against law, he refused to set his hand to it as a counsellor, and that he only signed as a witness to the king's subscription. But Cranmer still refused to do it after they had all signed it[31], and said, he would never consent to the disinheriting of the daughters of his late master. Many con-

Cranmer was very hardly brought to consent to it.

sultations were had to persuade him to it. But he could not be prevailed on, till the king himself set on him; who used many arguments, from the danger religion would otherwise be in, together with other persuasions; so that, by his reasons, or rather importunities, at last he brought him to it. But whether he also used that distinction of Cecil's, that he did it as a witness, and not as a counsellor, I do not know: but it seems probable, that if that liberty was allowed the one, it would not be denied the other.

The king's sickness becomes desperate.

But though the settling this business gave the king great content in his mind, yet his distemper rather increased than abated; so that the physicians had no hope of his recovery.

[30] [See Part iii. p. 215.]   [31] Cranmer came at this time oft to council. [S.]

Upon which, a confident woman came, and undertook his cure, if
he might be put into her hands. This was done, and the physi- [Hayward,
cians were put from him, upon this pretence, that they having p. 327.]
no hopes of his recovery, in a desperate case desperate remedies were to be used. This was said to be the duke of Northumberland's advice in particular: and it increased the people's
jealousy of him, when they saw the king grow very sensibly
worse every day after he came under the woman's care; which
becoming so plain, she was put from him, and the physicians
were again sent for, and took him into their charge. But if
they had small hopes before, they had none at all now. Death
thus hastening on him, the duke of Northumberland, who
knew he had done but half his work, except he had the king's
sisters in his hands, got the council to write to them in the
king's name, inviting them to come and keep him company in
his sickness. But as they were on the way, on the sixth of
July, his spirits and body were so sunk, that he found death
approaching; and so he composed himself to die in a most
devout manner. His whole exercise was in short prayers and
ejaculations. The last that he was heard to use was in these
words: *Lord God, deliver me out of this miserable and* His last
wretched life, and take me among thy chosen: howbeit not prayer.
[Fox, lib.
my will but thine be done: Lord, I commit my spirit to thee. ix. p. 130.]
O Lord, thou knowest how happy it were for me to be with
thee: yet for thy chosen's sake send me life and health, that I
may truly serve thee. O my Lord God, bless my people,
and save thine inheritance; O Lord God, save thy chosen
people of England; O Lord God, defend this realm from
papistry, and maintain thy true religion, that I and my
people may praise thy holy name, for Jesus Christ his sake.
Seeing some about him, he seemed troubled that they were so
near, and had heard him; but with a pleasant countenance he
said, he had been praying to God. And soon after, the pangs
of death coming on him, he said to sir Henry Sidney, who
was holding him in his arms, *I am faint, Lord have mercy on*
me, and receive my spirit; and so he breathed out his innocent soul. The duke of Northumberland, according to Cecil's
relation, intended to have concealed his death for a fortnight,
but it could not be done.   His death
and cha-
Thus died king Edward the Sixth, that incomparable racter.

young prince. He was then in the sixteenth year of his age,
and was counted the wonder of that time. He was not only
learned in the tongues, and other liberal sciences, but knew 225
well the state of his kingdom. He kept a book, in which he
writ the characters that were given him of all the chief men of
the nation, all the judges, lord lieutenants, and justices of the
peace over England; in it he had marked down their way of
living, and their zeal for religion. He had studied the matter
of the mint, with the exchange, and value of money; so that
he understood it well, as appears by his Journal. He also
understood fortification, and designed well. He knew all the
harbours and ports, both of his own dominions, and of France,
and Scotland: and how much water they had, and what was
the way of coming in to them. He had acquired great knowledge in foreign affairs; so that he talked with the ambassadors about them in such a manner, that they filled all the
world with the highest opinion of him that was possible;
which appears in most of the histories of that age. He had
great quickness of apprehension; and, being mistrustful of his
memory, used to take notes of almost every thing he heard:
he writ these first in Greek characters, that those about him
might not understand them; and afterwards writ them out in
his Journal. He had a copy brought him of every thing that
passed in council, which he put in a chest, and kept the key of
that always himself.

In a word, the natural and acquired perfections of his mind
were wonderful; but his virtues and true piety were yet more
extraordinary. He was such a friend to justice, that, though
he loved his uncle the duke of Somerset much, yet when he
was possessed of a belief of his designing to murder his fellow-
counsellors, he was alienated from him; and being then but
fourteen, it was no wonder if that was too easily infused in
him. His chief favourite was Barnaby Fitz-Patrick, to whom
he writ many letters and instructions when he sent him to be
bred in France. In one of his letters to him he writ, that he
must not think to live like an ambassador, but like a private
gentleman, who was to be advanced as he should deserve it.
He allowed him to keep but four servants: he charged him to
follow the company of gentlemen, rather than of ladies: that
he should not be superfluous in his apparel: that he should

[Fuller,
lib. vii.
p. 411.]

go to the campagne, and observe well the conduct of armies, and the fortification of strong places : and let the king know always when he needed money, and he would supply him. All these, with many other directions, the king writ with his own hand : and at his return, to let him see he intended to raise him by degrees, he gave him a pension only of 150*l*. This Fitz-Patrick did afterwards fully answer the opinion this young king had of him. He was bred up with him in his learning ; and, as it is said, had been his whipping-boy, who, according to the rule of educating our princes, was always to be whipped for the king's faults. He was afterwards made by queen Elizabeth baron of Upper Ossory in Ireland, which was his native country.

King Edward was tender and compassionate in a high measure : so that he was much against the taking away the lives of heretics ; and therefore said to Cranmer, when he persuaded him to sign the warrant for the burning of Joan of Kent, that he was not willing to do it, because he thought that was to send her quick to hell. He expressed great tenderness to the miseries of the poor in his sickness, as hath been already 226 shown. He took particular care of the suits of all poor persons ; and gave Dr. Cox special charge to see that their petitions were speedily answered, and used oft to consult with him how to get their matters set forward. He was an exact keeper of his word ; and therefore, as appears by his Journal, was most careful to pay his debts, and to keep his credit : knowing that to be the chief nerve of government ; since a prince that breaks his faith, and loses his credit, has thrown up that which he can never recover, and made himself liable to perpetual distrusts and extreme contempt.

He had above all things a great regard to religion. He took notes of such things as he heard in sermons, which more specially concerned himself ; and made his measures of all men by their zeal in that matter. This made him so set on bringing over his sister Mary to the same persuasions with himself, that, when he was pressed to give way to her having mass, he said, that he would not only hazard the loss of the emperor's friendship, but of his life, and all he had in the world, rather than consent to what he knew was a sin : and he cited some passages of scripture, that obliged kings to root out idolatry :

[Fox, vol.
ii. pt. 2.
p. 2.]

by which, he said, he was bound in conscience not to consent
to her mass; since he believed it was idolatry: and did argue
the matter so learnedly with the bishops, that they left him,
being amazed at his knowledge in divinity. So that Cranmer
took Cheke by the hand upon it, and said, he had reason all
the days of his life to rejoice that God had honoured him to
breed such a scholar. All men who saw and observed these
qualities in him, looked on him as one raised by God for most
extraordinary ends: and when he died, concluded that the
sins of England must needs be very great, that had provoked
God to take from them a prince, under whose government
they were like to have seen such blessed times. He was so
affable and sweet natured, that all had free access to him at all
times; by which he came to be most universally beloved: and
all the high things that could be devised were said by the
people to express their esteem of him. The fable of the phœnix
pleased most; so they made his mother one phœnix, and him
another, rising out of her ashes. But graver men compared
him to Josiah; and, long after his death, I find both in letters
and printed books they commonly named him Our Josias;
others called him Edward the Saint.

A prince of such qualities, so much esteemed and loved,
could not but be much lamented at his death; and this made
those of the reformation abhor the duke of Northumberland,
who they suspected had hastened him to such an untimely end:
which contributed, as much as any thing, to the establishing
of queen Mary on the throne; for the people reckoned none
could be so unworthy to govern, as those who had poisoned so
worthy a prince, and so kind a master. I find nothing of opening his body for giving satisfaction about that which brought
him to his end; though his lying unburied till the eighth of
August makes it probable that he was opened.

But indeed the sins of England did at this time call down
from Heaven heavy curses on the land. They are sadly expressed in a discourse that Ridley writ soon after, under the
title of the Lamentation of England[32]: he says, lechery, op-

[30] [A pituous Lamentation of the
miserable Estate of the Churche of
Christ in Englande: whereunto are
also annexed certayne Letters (3) of
John Careles, written in the time
of his Imprisonment. London, by
Willyam Powell. 1566. 16mo.]

227 pression, pride, covetousness, and a hatred and scorn of religion, were generally spread among all people; chiefly those of
the higher rank.　Cranmer and he had been much disliked:
the former for delivering his conscience so freely on the duke
of Somerset's death; and both of them for opposing so much
the rapine and spoil of the goods of the church, which was
done without law or order.　Nor could they engage any to
take care of relieving the poor, except only Dobbs, who was
then lord mayor of London.　These sins were openly preached
against by Latimer, Lever, Bradford, and Knox, who did it
more severely; and by others, who did it plainly, though more
softly.　One of the main causes Ridley gives of all these evils
was, that many of the bishops, and most of the clergy, being
all the while papists in heart, who had only complied to preserve their benefices, took no care of their parishes, and were
rather well pleased that things were ill managed.　And of this
that good bishop had been long very apprehensive when he
considered the sins then prevailing, and the judgments which
they had reason to look for; as will appear by an excellent
letter, which he sent about to his clergy to set them on to such
duties as so sad a prospect required: it will be found in the
Collection, and though it belongs to the former year, yet I Collect.
choose rather to bring it in on this occasion.　These things Numb. 58.
having been fully laid open in the former parts of this work, I
shall not insist on them here, having mentioned them only for
this cause, that the reader may from hence gather, what we
may still expect, if we continue guilty of the same or worse
sins, after all that illumination and knowledge with which we
have been so long blessed in these kingdoms.

THE END OF THE FIRST BOOK.

THE HISTORY

OF

THE REFORMATION

OF

THE CHURCH OF ENGLAND.

Of the life and reign of Queen Mary.

Queen
Mary suc-
ceeds; but
is in great
danger,

UPON the death of king Edward, the crown devolved, according to king Henry's will, and the act of parliament made in the thirty-fifth year of his reign, on his eldest sister, the now queen Mary. She was on her way to London, in obedience to the letters that had been writ to her, to come and comfort her brother in his sickness; and was come within half a day's journey of the court, when she received an advertisement from the earl of Arundel, that her brother was dead, together with an account of what was done about the succession. The earl also informed her, that the king's death was concealed on design to entrap her before she knew of it: and therefore he advised her to retire. Upon this, she, knowing that the duke of Northumberland was much hated in Norfolk, for the great slaughter he had made of the rebels, when he subdued them in the third year of the last reign; therefore chose to go that way to the castle of Framlingham in Suffolk: which place being near the sea, she might, if her designs should miscarry,

And retires
to Suffolk.
[Godwin, p.
329.]

have an opportunity from thence to fly over to the emperor, that was then in Flanders.

At London, it seems, the whole business of setting up the lady Jane had been carried very secretly; since if queen Mary had heard any hint of it, she had certainly kept out of the way, and not adventured to have come so near the town. It was an unaccountable error in the party for the lady Jane, that they had not, immediately after the seal was put to the letters patents, or, at furthest, presently after the king's death, sent some to make sure of the king's sisters: instead of which they thus lingered, hoping they would have come into their toils in an easier and less violent way. On the eighth[1] of July they writ to the English ambassadors at Brussels the news of the king's death, but said nothing of the succession. On the ninth of July[2] they perceived the king's death was known; for queen Mary writ to them from Kenning-hall, that she understood the king her brother was dead: which how sorrowful it was to her, God only knew, to whose will she did humbly submit her will. The provision of the crown to her after his death, she said, was well known to them all; but she thought it strange, that he being three days dead, she had not been advertised of it by them. She knew what consultations were against her, and what engagements they had entered into; but was willing to take all their doings in good part: and therefore did give pardon[3] for all that was past to such as would accept of it, and required them to proclaim her title to the crown in London.

She writes to the council: [Holinshed, p. 1085.]

Upon this letter they saw the death of the king could no longer be concealed: so the duke of Suffolk and the duke of Northumberland went to Durham-house, where the lady Jane lay, to give her notice of her being to succeed to the crown in the room of the deceased king. She received the news with great sorrow for king Edward's death; which was not at all

Who declare for the lady Jane.

---

[1] On the 8th of July also, they sent for the mayor and certain aldermen, and told them of the king's death, and of the succession, but bade them keep it secret. [S.]

[2] [This letter is printed from Fox, iii. 11. in Tierney's edition of Dodd's Church History, vol. ii.

App. p. lxxxvii. There is another letter from her, dated July 8. in Lansdowne MSS. 1236 fol. 29]

[3] Read, she wrote 'she was ready to remit and pardon; and that she would take their doings in good part.' [S.]

lessened, but rather increased, by that other part of their message concerning her being to succeed him.

Lady Jane's character.

She was a lady that seemed indeed born for a great fortune; for as she was a beautiful and graceful person, so she had
great parts, and greater virtues. Her tutor was Dr. Aylmer,

[Fox, vol. iii. p. 11.]

believed to be the same that was afterwards made bishop of
London by queen Elizabeth. She had learned from him the
Latin and Greek tongues to great perfection; so that, being of
the same age with the late king, she seemed superior to him in
those languages. And having acquired the helps of knowledge, she spent her time much in the study of it. Roger Ascham, tutor to the lady Elizabeth, coming once to wait on her
at her father's house in Leicestershire, found her reading
Plato's works in Greek, when all the rest of the family were
hunting in the park. He asked her, how she could be absent
from such pleasant diversions? She answered, the pastimes in
the park were but a shadow to the delight she had in reading
Plato's Phædon, which then lay open before her: and added,
that she esteemed it one of the greatest blessings that God
ever gave her, that she had sharp parents, and a gentle school-
master; which made her take delight in nothing so much as in
her study. She read the scriptures much, and had attained
great knowledge in divinity. But with all these advantages of
birth and parts, she was so humble, so gentle and pious, that
all people both admired and loved her; and none more than
the late king. She had a mind wonderfully raised above the
world; and at the age wherein others are but imbibing the notions of philosophy, she had attained to the practice of the
highest precepts of it. She was neither lifted up with the
hope of a crown, nor cast down when she saw her palace made 235
afterwards her prison; but carried herself with an equal temper of mind in those great inequalities of fortune that so suddenly exalted and depressed her. All the passion she expressed in it was that which is of the noblest sort, and is the
indication of tender and generous natures, being much affected
with the troubles her father and husband fell in on her account.

Her unwill-
ingness to
accept of
the crown.

The mention of the crown, when her father, with her father-
in-law, saluted her queen, did rather heighten her disorder
upon the king's death. She said, she knew, by the laws of the

kingdom, and by natural right, the crown was to go to the
king's sisters: so that she was afraid of burdening her conscience by assuming that which belonged to them; and that
she was unwilling to enrich herself by the spoils of others.
But they told her, all that had been done was according to
the law, to which all the judges and counsellors had set their
hands. This, joined with their persuasions, and the importunities of her husband, who had more of his father's temper than
of her philosophy in him, at length prevailed with her to submit to it: of which her father-in-law did afterwards say in
council, she was rather, by enticement of the counsellors, and
force, made to accept of the crown, than came to it by her own
seeking and request.

Upon this, order was given for proclaiming her queen the
next day: and an answer was writ to queen Mary, signed by
the archbishop of Canterbury, the lord chancellor, the dukes
of Suffolk and Northumberland, the marquises of Winchester
and Northampton, the earls of Arundel, Shrewsbury, Huntingdon, Bedford, and Pembroke, the lords Cobham and Darcy,
sir Thomas Cheyney, sir Robert[4] Cotton, sir William Petre, sir
William Cecil, sir John Cheke, sir John Mason, sir Edward
North, and sir Robert Bowes; in all, one and twenty[5]: letting
her know, "That queen Jane was now their sovereign, ac-
"cording to the ancient laws of the land, and the late king's
"letters patents; to whom they were now bound by their alle-
"giance. They told her, that the marriage between her
"father and mother was dissolved by the ecclesiastical courts,
"according to the laws of God and of the land; that many
"noble universities in Christendom had consented to it; that
"the sentence had been confirmed in parliaments, and she had
"been declared illegitimate and uninheritable to the crown.
"They therefore required her to give over her pretences, and
"not to disturb the government: and promised, that, if she

Council writes to queen Mary. [July 9. Holinshed p. 1085.]

[4] For Robert read Richard. [S.]
[5] [This letter is printed from Fox, iii. 12. in Tierney's edition of Dodd's Church History, vol. ii. App. p. lxxxix. It is signed by 23 persons. The name of sir John Gates has been omitted by the author after that of sir Richard Cotton, and that of R. Rich after the earl of Pembroke. Lord Cobham's name has been accidentally omitted in Dodd, between the names of Pembroke and Rich.]

" shewed herself obedient, she should find them all ready to do
" her any service which in duty they could."

The day following they proclaimed queen Jane. The proclamation will be found in the Collection. It sets forth, " That
" the late king had, by his letters patents, limited the crown,
" that it should not descend to his two sisters, since they were
" both illegitimated by sentences in the spiritual courts, and
" acts of parliament; and were only his sisters by the half-
" blood, who (though it were granted they had been legitimate)
" are not inheritable by the law of England. It was added,
" that there was also great cause to fear that the king's sisters
" might marry strangers, and so change the laws of the king-
" dom, and subject it to the tyranny of the bishops of Rome, 236
" and other foreign laws. For these reasons they were ex-
" cluded from the succession : and the lady Frances, duchess
" of Suffolk, being next the crown, it was provided, that, if she
" had no sons at the death of the king, the crown should de-
" volve immediately on her eldest daughter Jane, and after
" her, and her issue, to her sisters; since she was born within
" the kingdom, and already married in it. Therefore she was
" proclaimed queen, promising to be most benign and gracious
" to all her people, to maintain God's holy word, and the laws
" of the land; requiring all the subjects to obey and acknow-
" ledge her." When this was proclaimed, great multitudes
were gathered to hear it; but there were very few that shouted
with the acclamations ordinary on such occasions. And whereas
a vintner's boy did some way express his scorn at that which
was done, it was ordered, that he should be made an example
the next day, by being set on a pillory, and having his ears.
nailed to it, and cut off from his head; which was accordingly
done, a herald in his coat reading to the multitude, that was
called together by sound of trumpet, the nature of his offence.

Upon this all people were in great distraction; the proclamation, opening the new queen's title, came to be variously
descanted on. Some, who thought the crown descended by
right of blood, and that it could not be limited by parliament,
argued, that the king having his power from God, it was only
to descend in the natural way of inheritance; therefore they
thought the next heir was to succeed. And whereas the king's

two sisters were both by several sentences and acts of parliament declared bastards; and whether that was well judged, or not, they were to be reputed such as the law declared them to be, so long as it stood in force; therefore they held that the queen of Scotland was to succeed: who, though she pretended this upon queen Mary's death, yet did not claim now, because by the papal law the sentence against queen Mary was declared null. Others argued, that though a prince were named by an immediate appointment from Heaven, yet he might change the course of succession; as David did, preferring Solomon before Adonijah. But this, it was said, did not belong to the kings of England, whose right to the crown, with the extent of their prerogative, did not come from any divine designation, but from a long possession, and the laws of the land: and that therefore the king might by law limit the succession, as well as he and other kings had in some points limited the prerogative; (which was clearly sir Thomas More's opinion;) and that therefore the act of parliament for the succession of the king's sisters was still strong in law. It was also said, that if the king's sisters were to be excluded for bastardy, all Charles Brandon's issue were in the same predicament; since he was not lawfully married to the French queen, his former wife Mortimer being then alive, and his marriage with her was never dissolved: (for though some English writers say they were divorced, yet those who wrote for the queen of Scots' title in the next reign denied it.) But in this the difference was great between them; since the king's sisters were declared bastards in law, whereas this against Charles Brandon's issue was only a surmise. Others objected, that if the blood gave an indefeasible title, how came it that the lady Jane's mother did not reign? It is 237 true, Maud the empress, and Margaret, countess of Richmond, were satisfied that their sons, Henry the Second, and Henry the Seventh, should reign in their rights; but it had never been heard of, that a mother had resigned to her daughter, especially when she was yet under age. But this was imputed to the duke of Suffolk's weakness, and the ambition of the duke of Northumberland. That objection concerning the half-blood, being a rule of common law in the families of subjects, to cut off from stepmothers the inclinations and advantages of destroying their husbands' children, was not thought applicable to the crown: nor was that of one's being born out of the kingdom, which was hinted at to exclude the queen of Scotland, thought pertinent to this case, since there was an exception made in the law for the king's children, which was thought to extend to all their issue. But all people agreed in this, that though, by act of parliament, king Henry was empowered to provide or limit the crown by his letters patents, yet that was a grant particularly to him, and did not descend to his heirs; so that the letters patents made by king Edward could have no force to settle the crown, and much less when they did expressly contradict an act of parliament. The proceeding so severely against the vintner's boy was imputed to the violent temper of the duke of Northumberland. And though, when a government is firm, and factions are weak, the making some public examples may intimidate a faction otherwise disheartened; yet severities in such a juncture as this, when the council had no other support but the assistance of the people, seemed very unadvised; and all thought it was a great error to punish him in that manner.

The duke of Northumberland much hated.

This made them reflect on the rest of Northumberland's cruelties: his bringing the duke of Somerset, with those gentlemen that suffered with him, to their end by a foul conspiracy; but above all things, the suspicions that lay on him of being the author of the late king's untimely death enraged the people so much against him, that, without considering what they might suffer under queen Mary, they generally inclined to set her up.

Many declare for queen Mary.

[Fox, vol. iii. p. 12.]

The lady Jane was proclaimed in many towns near London, yet the people were generally running to queen Mary; many from Norfolk came to her, and a great body of Suffolk men gathered about her, who were all for the reformation. They desired to know of her, whether she would alter the religion set up in king Edward's days: to whom she gave full assurances, that she would never make any innovation or change, but be contented with the private exercise of her own religion. Upon this they were all possessed with such a belief of her sincerity, that it made them resolve to hazard their lives and estates in her quarrel. The earls of Bath and Sussex [6] raised

[6] For Suffolk read Sussex. [S.] Suffolk had been altered into Sussex [This note refers to the first edition; in the second edition of 1683.]

forces, and joined with her; so did the sons of the lord Wharton and Mordaunt, with many more.

Upon this the council resolved to gather forces for the dispersing of theirs, and sent the earl of Huntingdon's brother to raise Buckinghamshire, and others to other parts, ordering them to meet the forces that should come from London at Newmarket. It was at first proposed to send the duke of Suffolk to command them: but the lady Jane was so much concerned in her father's preservation, that she urged he might not be sent; and he, being but a soft man, was easily excused. 238 So it fell next on the duke of Northumberland, who was now much distracted in his mind. He was afraid, if he went away, the city might declare for queen Mary; nor was he well assured of the council, who seemed all to comply with him rather out of fear than good-will. Cecil would not officiate as secretary, as himself relates; the judges would do nothing; and the duke plainly saw, that, if he had not (according to the custom of our princes on their first coming to the crown) gone with the lady Jane and the council into the Tower, whereby he kept them as prisoners, the council were inclined to desert him. This divided him much in his thoughts. The whole success of his design depended on the dispersing of the queen's forces: and it was no less necessary to have a man of courage continue still in the Tower. There was none there whom he could entirely trust, but the duke of Suffolk; and he was so mean spirited, that he did not depend much on him. But the progress the queen's forces made pressed him to go, and make head against her. So he laid all the heavy charges he could on the council to look to queen Jane, and to stand firmly to her interests; and left London on the 14th of July, marching out with 2000 horse and 6000 foot. But as he rode through Bishopsgate-street and Shoreditch, though there were great crowds looking on, none cried out to wish him success; which gave a sad indication how ill they were affected to him.

The council writ to the emperor by one Shelley, whom they sent to give notice of the lady Jane's succession, complaining that the lady Mary was making stirs, and that his ambassador had officiously meddled in their affairs; but that they had given orders for reducing the lady Mary to her duty. They also desired the continuance of his friendship, and that he would

[Side notes:]
The council orders forces to be sent against her.

[July 13, Godwin, p. 330.]

And write to the emperor. [July 11, Cotton. MSS. Galba, B. xii. 250, ap. Ellis, 3. iii. 309.]

command his resident to carry himself as became an ambassador. Sir Philip Hobby was continued ambassador there; the others were ordered to stay and prosecute the mediation of the peace. But the emperor would not receive those letters; and in a few days there went over others from queen Mary.

Ridley preaches for the lady Jane's title.
[July 16. Holinshed, p. 1087.]

Ridley was appointed to set out queen Jane's title in a sermon at Paul's; and to warn the people of the dangers they would be in, if queen Mary should reign: which he did, and gave an account in his sermon of what had passed between him and her, when he went and offered to preach to her. At the same time the duke of Northumberland, at Cambridge, where himself was both chancellor of the university and steward of the town, made the vice-chancellor preach to the same purpose. But he held in more general terms, and managed it so, that there was no great offence taken on either hand.

[Godwin, p. 332.]

[July 12.] Queen Mary's party grows strong:

But now the queen had made her title be proclaimed at Norwich; and sent letters all over England, requiring the peers, and others of great quality, to come to her assistance. Some ships had been sent about, to lie on that coast for intercepting her, if she should fly away: but those who commanded them were so dealt with, that, instead of acting against her, they declared for her. Sir Edward Hastings, having raised 4000 men in Buckinghamshire, instead of joining with the duke of Northumberland, went over with them into her service. Many were also from all places every day running to her, and in several counties of England she was proclaimed 239 queen. But none came in to the duke of Northumberland: so he writ earnestly to the lords at London to send him more supplies.

[Godwin, p. 331.]

And the council turn to her.

They understanding, from all the corners of England, that the tide grew every where strong for the queen, entered into consultations how to redeem their past faults, and to reconcile themselves to her. The earl of Arundel hated Northumberland on many accounts. The marquis of Winchester was famous for his dexterity in shifting sides, always to his own advantage. To them joined the earl of Pembroke, the more closely linked to the interests of the lady Jane, since his son had married her sister; which made him the more careful to disentangle himself in time. To those sir Thomas Cheyney, warden of the cinque ports, and sir John Mason, with the two secretaries, came over. It was said, that the French and Spanish ambassadors had desired an audience in some place in the city: and it was proposed to give it in the earl of Pembroke's house; who being the least suspected, it was agreed to by the duke of Suffolk, that they should be suffered to go from the Tower thither. They also pretended, that, since the duke of Northumberland had writ so earnestly for new forces, they must go and treat with my lord mayor and the city of London about it. But as soon as they were got out, the earl of Arundel pressed them to declare for queen Mary: and, to persuade them to it, he laid open all the cruelty of Northumberland, under whose tyranny they must resolve to be enslaved, if they would not now shake it off. The other consenting readily to it, they sent for the lord mayor, with the recorder, and the aldermen; and having declared their resolutions to them, they rode together into Cheapside, and there proclaimed queen Mary on the 19th of July: from thence they went to St. Paul's, where Te Deum was sung. An order was sent to the Tower, to require the duke of Suffolk to deliver up that place, and to acknowledge queen Mary; and that the lady Jane should lay down the title of queen. To this, as her father submitted tamely, so she expressed no sort of concern in losing that imaginary glory, which now had for nine days been rather a burden than any matter of joy to her. They also sent orders to the duke of Northumberland to disband his forces, and to carry himself as became an obedient subject to the queen. And the earl of Arundel, with the lord Paget, were sent to give her an account of it, who continued still at Framlingham in Suffolk.

And proclaimed her queen.

The duke of Northumberland had retired back to Cambridge, to stay for new men from London; but hearing how matters went there, before ever the council's orders came to him, he dismissed his forces, and went to the market-place, and proclaimed the queen, flinging up his own hat for joy, and crying, *God save queen Mary!* But the earl of Arundel being sent by the queen to apprehend him, it is said, that, when he saw him, he fell abjectly at his feet to beg his favour. This was like him; it being not more unusual for such insolent persons to be most basely sunk with their misfortunes, than to be out of measure blown up with success. He was, on the 25th of

The duke of Northumberland submits, and is taken,

With many more pri-

soners;
who were
sent to the
Tower of
London.
[Stow, p.
612.]

July, sent to the Tower, with the earl of Warwick, his eldest
son, Ambrose and Henry, two of his other sons. Some other
of his friends were made prisoners, among whom was sir Thomas Palmer, the wicked instrument of the duke of Somerset's 240
fall, who was become his most intimate confidant; and Dr. Sandys, the vice-chancellor of Cambridge.

Now did all people go to the queen to implore her mercy.
She received them all very favourably, except the marquis of
Northampton, Dr. Ridley, and lord Robert Dudley. The first

[Holin-
shed, p.
1089.]

of these had been a submissive fawner on the duke of Northumberland; the second had incurred her displeasure by his
sermon, and she gladly laid hold on any colour to be more severe to him, that way might be made for bringing Bonner to
London[4] again; the third had followed his father's fortunes.

[Stow, p.
613.]

On the 27th, the lords chief justices Cholmeley and Montague
were sent to the Tower; and the day after, the duke of Suffolk
and sir John Cheke went after them, the lady Jane and her
husband being still detained in the Tower. Three days after
an order came to set the duke of Suffolk at liberty, upon engagement to return to prison when the queen required it: for it was
generally known that he had been driven on by Dudley; and
as it was believed that he had not been faulty out of malice, so
his great weakness made them little apprehensive of any dangers from him: and therefore the queen being willing to express a signal act of clemency at her first coming to the crown,
it was thought best to let it fall on him.

The queen
enters
London.

Now did the queen come towards London, being met on the
way by her sister Elizabeth, with a thousand horse, who had
gathered about her to show their zeal to maintain both their
titles, which in this late contest had been linked together. She
made her entry to London on the third of August with great
solemnity and pomp. When she came to the Tower[5], the duke
of Norfolk, who had been almost seven years in it; Gardiner,
the bishop of Winchester, that had been five years there; the

---

[4] There needed no colours; he
had given too just offence. In a
MS. C.C.C. Miscel. P. this account
is given 'Sunday, July 16, Dr. Ridley, bishop of London, preached at
Paul's Cross; where he declared in
his sermon .... the lady Mary and

Elizabeth to be illegitimate, and not
lawfully begotten, &c. according to
God's law; .... and so found both
by the clergy and acts of parliament,
in Henry the 8th's time; which the
people murmured at.' [B.]

[5] [See Part iii. p. 220.]

duchess of Somerset, that had been kept there near two years; and the lord Courtenay, (whom she made afterwards earl of Devonshire,) that was son to the marquis of Exeter, and had been kept there ever since his father was attainted; had their liberty granted them. So now she was peaceably settled in the throne without any effusion of blood, having broke through a confederacy against her, which seemed to be so strong, that, if he that was the head of it had not been universally odious to the nation, it could not have been so easily dissipated. She was naturally pious and devout, even to superstition; had a generous disposition of mind, but much corrupted by melancholy, which was partly natural in her, but much increased by the cross accidents of her life, both before and after her advancement; so that she was very peevish and splenetic towards the end of her life. When the differences became irreconcilable between her father and mother, she followed her mother's interests, they being indeed her own, and for a great while could not be persuaded to submit to the king; who, being impatient of contradiction from any, but especially from his own child, was resolved to strike a terror in all his people, by putting her openly to death: which her mother coming to know, writ her a letter of a very devout strain, which will be found in the Collections. In which, "she encouraged her to " suffer cheerfully, to trust to God, and keep her heart clean. " She charged her in all things to obey the king's commands, " except in the matters of religion. She sent her two Latin 1 " books, the one of the Life of Christ, (which was perhaps the " famous book of Thomas à Kempis;) and the other, St. Je- " rome's Letter. She bid her divert herself at the virginals or " lute; but above all things to keep herself pure, and to enter " into no treaty of marriage, till these ill times should pass " over; of which her mother seemed to retain still good hopes." This letter should have been in my former volume, if I had then seen it; but it is no improper place to mention it here. At court, many were afraid to move the king for her; both the duke of Norfolk and Gardiner looked on, and were unwilling to hazard their own interests to preserve her. But (as it was now printed, and both these appealed to) Cranmer was the only person that would adventure on it. In his gentle way he told the king, that she was young and indiscreet, and there-

She had been in danger in her father's time;

Collect. Numb. 2.

And was preserved by Cranmer's means.

c c 2

fore it was no wonder if she obstinately adhered to that which her mother, and all about her, had been infusing into her for many years; but that it would appear strange if he should for this cause so far forget he was a father, as to proceed to extremities with his own child: that if she were separated from her mother, and her people, in a little time there might be ground gained on her; but to take away her life would raise horror through all Europe against him. By these means he preserved her at that time.

She submitted to her father. After her mother's death, in June following, she changed her note; for, besides the declaration she then signed, which was inserted in the former part of this work, she writ letters of such submission, as show how expert she was at dissembling. Three of these to her father, and one to Cromwell, Collect. Numb. 3, 4, 5, 6. I have put in the Collection; "in which she, with the most " studied expressions, declaring her sorrow for her past stub- " bornness and disobedience to his most just and virtuous laws, " implores his pardon, as lying prostrate at his feet: and, con- " sidering his great learning and knowledge, she puts her soul " in his hand, resolving that he should for ever thereafter di- " rect her conscience; from which she vows she would never " vary." This she repeats in such tender words, that it shews she could command herself to say any thing that she thought fit for her ends. And when Cromwell writ to her, to know " what her opinion was about pilgrimages, purgatory and relics, " she assures him, she had no opinion at all, but such as she " should receive from the king, who had her whole heart in " his keeping; and he should imprint upon it, in these and all " other matters, whatever his inestimable virtue, high wisdom, " and excellent learning, should think convenient for her." So perfectly had she learned that style that she knew was most acceptable to him. Having copied these from the originals, I thought it not unfit to insert them, that it may appear how far those of that religion can comply, when their interest leads them to it.

From that time this princess had been in all points most exactly compliant to every thing her father did; and after his death she never pretended to be of any other religion than that which was established by him: so that all that she pleaded for in her brother's reign was only the continuance of that way of worship that was in use at her father's death. But now, being come to the crown, that would not content her: yet, when she thought where to fix, she was distracted between two different schemes that were presented to her.

242　On the one hand, Gardiner and all that party were for bringing religion back to what it had been at king Henry's death; and afterward, by slow degrees, to raise it up to what it had been before his breach with the papacy. On the other hand, the queen, of her own inclination, was much disposed to return immediately to the union of the catholic church, as she called it: and it was necessary for her to do it, since it was only by the papal authority that her illegitimation was removed. To this it was answered, that all these acts and sentences that had passed against her might be annulled, without taking any notice of the pope. Gardiner, finding these things had not such weight with her as he desired, (for she looked on him as a crafty temporizing man,) sent over to the emperor, on whom she depended much, to assure him, that if he would persuade her to make him chancellor, and to put affairs into his hands, he should order them so, that every thing she had a mind to should be carried in time. But Gardiner understood she had sent for cardinal Pole: so he writ to the emperor, that he knew his zeal for the exaltation of the popedom would undo all; therefore he pressed him to write to the queen for moderating her heat, and to stop the cardinal's coming over. He said that Pole stood attainted by law, so that his coming into England would alarm the nation. He observed, that upon a double account they were averse to the papacy: the one was for the church lands, which they had generally bought from the crown on very easy terms; and they would ·not easily part with them. The other was, the fear they had of papal dominion and power, which had been now for about twenty-five years set out to the people as the most intolerable tyranny that ever was: therefore, he said, it was necessary to give them some time to wear out these prejudices; and the precipitating of counsels might ruin all. He gave the emperor also secret assurances of serving him in all his interests. All this Gardiner did the more warily, because he understood that cardinal Pole hated him as a false and deceitful man. Upon this the emperor writ to the

The designs for changing religion.

Gardiner's policy.

queen several letters with his own hand, which is so hardly legible, that it was not possible for me, or some others to whom I shewed them, to read them so well as to copy them out; and one that was written by his sister, the queen of Hungary, and signed by him, is no better: but, from many half sentences, I find, that all was with a design to temper her, that she should not make too much haste, nor be too much led by Italian counsels. Upon the return of this message, the seal, which had

July 20.] been taken from Goodrich, bishop of Ely, and put for some days in the keeping of Hare, master of the rolls, was on the

He is made 13th of August[6] given to Gardiner, who was declared lord chancellor. chancellor of England, and the conduct of affairs was chiefly put [Aug. 23.] in his hands. So that now the measure of the queen's counsels was to do everything slowly, and by such sure steps as might put them less in hazard.

The duke The first thing that was done was the bringing the duke of of North- Northumberland to his trial. The old duke of Norfolk was umberland made lord high steward; the queen thinking it fit to put the and others first character of honour on him, who had suffered so much for tried, being the head of the popish party. And here a subtle thing was started, which had been kept a great secret hitherto. It 248 was said, the duke of Norfolk had never been truly attainted; and that the act against him was not a true act of parliament: so that, without any pardon or restitution in blood, he was still duke of Norfolk[7]. This he had never mentioned all the last reign, lest that should have procured an act to confirm his attainder. So he came now in upon his former right, by which all the grants that had been given of his estate were to be de-

[Aug. 18.] clared void by common law. The duke of Northumberland, [Holin- with the marquis of Northampton and the earl of Warwick, shed, p. were brought to their trials. The duke desired two points 1089.] might be first answered by the judges in matter of law. The

[6] ['At Richemond the 23d day of August, anº 1553.

This daye the Queene's highnes made the Right Reverend Father in God Steeven Gardenere Bishope of Winchester, Lord Chauncelor of Englande.' Extract from Council Book, Harl. 643. See also Part iii. p. 220.]

[7] Yet in the second session of this parliament, a private act passed, to make void the duke of Norfolk's attainder. [S.]

one, Whether a man, acting by the authority of the great seal, and the order of the privy council, could become thereby guilty of treason? The other was, Whether those who had been equally guilty with him, and by whose direction and commands he had acted, could sit his judges? To these the judges made answer, that the great seal of one that was not lawful queen could give no authority nor indemnity to those that acted on such a warrant: and that any peer that was not, by an attainder upon record, convicted of such accession to his crime, might sit his judge, and was not to be challenged upon a surmise or report. So these points, by which only he could hope to have defended himself, being thus determined against him, he con- *And con-* fessed he was guilty, and submitted to the queen's mercy: so *demned.* did the marquis of Northampton, and the duke's son, the earl of Warwick, who (it seems by this trial) had a writ for sitting in the house of peers. They were all three found guilty. Judgment also passed next day, in a jury of commoners, against sir John Gates, and his brother sir Humphrey[8]; sir An- *[Aug. 19.]* drew Dudley, and sir Thomas Palmer, confessing their indictments. But of all these, it was resolved that only the duke of Northumberland, and sir John Gates and sir Thomas Palmer, should be made examples. Heath, bishop of Worcester, was employed to instruct the duke, and to prepare him for his death. Whether he had been always in heart what he then *At his death* professed, or whether he only pretended it, hoping that it *he professes he had been* might procure him favour, is variously reported; but certain it *always a pa-* is, that he said he had been always a catholic in his heart: yet *pist.* this could not save him. He was known to be a man of that temper, so given both to revenge and dissimulation, that his enemies saw it was necessary to put him out of the way, lest, if he had lived, he might have insinuated himself into the queen's favour, and then turned the danger upon them. So the earl of Arundel, now made lord steward of the household, with others, easily obtained that his head should be cut off, together with sir John Gates' and sir Thomas Palmer's.

On the 22nd of August he was carried to the place of exe- *[Stow, p.* cution. On the way there was some expostulation between *614.]* Gates and him; they, as is ordinary for complices in ill actions,

---

8 For Humphrey, read Henry. [S.]

laying the blame of their miseries on one another: yet they professed they did mutually forgive, and so died in charity together. It is said, that he made a long speech, accusing his former ill life, and confessing his treasons: but that part of it which concerned religion is only preserved. In it he exhorted the people to stand to the religion of their ancestors, and to reject that of later date, which had occasioned all the misery of the foregoing thirty years; and desired, as they would prevent the like for the future, that they would drive out of the nation 244 these trumpets of sedition, the new preachers: that for himself, whatever he had otherwise pretended, he believed no other religion than that of his forefathers; in which he appealed to his ghostly father, the bishop of Worcester, then present with him: but, being blinded with ambition, he had made wreck of his conscience by temporizing, for which he professed himself sincerely penitent. So did he, and the other two, end their days. Palmer was little pitied, as being believed a treacherous conspirator against his former master and friend, the duke of Somerset.

Thus died the ambitious duke of Northumberland. He had been, in the former parts of his life, a great captain, and had the reputation of a wise man: he was generally successful, and they that are so are always esteemed wise. He was an extra-ordinary man in a lower size, but had forgot himself much when he was raised higher, in which his mind seemed more exalted than his fortunes. But as he was transported by his rage and revenge out of measure, so he was as servile and mean in his submissions. Fox, it seems, was informed, that he had hopes given him of his life, if he should declare himself to be of the popish religion, even though his head were laid on the block: but which way soever he made that declaration, either to get his life by it, or that he had really been always what he now professed, it argued that he regarded religion very little, either in his life or at his death. But whether he did any thing to hasten the late king's death, I do not find it was at all inquired after: only those who considered how much guilt disorders all people, and that they have a black cloud over their minds, which appears, either in the violence of rage, or the abjectness of fear, did find so great a change in his deportment in these last passages of his life, from what was in

[Harl.
MSS. 284.
fol. 127,
printed in
Tytler, ii.
230.]

His cha-
racter.

[Fox, vol.
iii. p. 13.]

the former parts of it, that they could not but think there was some extraordinary thing within him from whence it flowed.

And for king Edward's death, those who had affairs now in their hands were so little careful of his memory, and indeed so glad of his death, that it is no wonder they made little search about it. It is rather strange that they allowed him such funeral rites: for the queen kept a solemn exequie, with all the other remembrances of the dead, and masses for him, used in the Roman church, at the Tower on the eighth of August, the same day that he was buried at Westminster; the lord treasurer, (who was the marquis of Winchester, still continued in that trust,) the earls of Shrewsbury and Pembroke, being the principal mourners. Day, that was now to be restored to his see of Chichester [9], was appointed to preach the funeral sermon: in which he commended and excused the king, but loaded his government severely; and extolled the queen much, under whom he promised the people happy days. It was intended that all the burial rites should have been according to the old forms that were before the reformation: but Cranmer opposed this vigorously; and insisted upon it, that, as the king himself had been a zealous promoter of that reformation, so the English service was then established by law. Upon this he stoutly hindered any other way of officiating, and himself performed all the offices of the burial [10]; to which he joined the solemnity of a communion. In these, it may be easily imagined, he did every thing with a very lively sorrow; 245 since, as he had loved the king beyond expression, so he could not but look on his funeral as the burial of the reformation, and in particular as a step to his own.

On the twelfth of August the queen made an open declara-

Marginal notes:
King Edward's funeral.

[Aug. 9, Stow, p. 613. Holinshed, p. 1089.]

The queen declares

---

[9] ['At Richemond the 4 day of September, anno 1553. A letter to the bishope of Cheechester, doinge him to understande that the Queenes Highnes hath specially appointed him to make a sermon on the coronation daye before her Grace at Westminstre.'—Extract from Council Book; Harl. 643. fol. 6.]

[10] It was highly improbable that he who was now under displeasure, about this time confined to his house, and soon after to the Tower, should be allowed to perform these offices in such manner. Godwin (an. 1533.) Annal., says, *Concionem habente Daio Cicestr. Episcopo qui etiam sacrum peregit, vernacula usus Anglicana et Eucharistiam praesentibus exhibuit, &c.* To the same purpose Holinshed, vol. ii. p. 1089. And I never could meet with any good authority for the contrary except your lordship's. [B.]

she will
force no
man's con-
science.

tion in council, that, although her conscience was staid in the matters of religion, yet she was resolved not to compel or strain others, otherwise than as God should put into their hearts a persuasion of that truth she was in; and this she hoped should be done by the opening his word to them, by godly, virtuous, and learned preachers. Now all the deprived bishops looked to be quickly placed in their sees again. Bonner went to St. Paul's on the 13th of August, being Sunday, where Bourne, that was his chaplain, preached before him. He spake honourably of Bonner, with sharp reflections on the proceedings against him in the time of king Edward. This did much provoke the whole audience, who, as they hated Bonner, so could not hear any thing said that seemed to detract from that king. Hereupon there was a great tumult in the church; some called to pull him down, others flung stones, and one threw a dagger towards the pulpit with that force that it stuck fast in the timber of it: Bourne, by stooping, saved himself from that danger; and Rogers and Bradford, two eminent preachers, and of great credit with the people, stood up, and gently quieted the heat: and they, to deliver Bourne out of their hands, conveyed him from the pulpit to a house near the church [11].

[Holin-
shed, p.
1089.]

A tumult
at Paul's
Cross.
[Fox, vol.
iii. p. 14.]

[Holin-
shed, p.
1089.]

This was such an accident as the papists would have desired; for it gave them a colour to proceed more severely, and to prohibit preaching, which was the first step they intended to make. There was a message sent to the lord mayor, to give a strict charge that every citizen should take care of all that belonged to him; and see that they went to their own parish church, and kept the peace: as also to acquaint them with what the queen had declared in council on the 13th of August. And on the 18th there was published an inhibition in the queen's name to this effect: "That she, considering the great "danger that had come to the realm by the differences in re-"ligion, did declare for herself, that she was of that religion "that she had professed from her infancy, and that she would "maintain it during her time, and be glad that all her sub-"jects would charitably receive it. Yet she did not intend to "compel any of her subjects to it, till public order should be "taken in it by common assent; requiring all, in the mean

An inhi-
bition of
all preach-
ing.
[Fox, vol.
iii. p. 14.]

11 [See Part iii. p. 220.]

" while, not to move sedition or unquietness till such order
" should be settled, and not to use the names of *papist* or
" *heretic*, but to live together in love, and in the fear of God:
" but if any made assemblies of the people, she would take
" care they should be severely punished. And she straitly
" charged them, that none should preach, or expound scrip-
" ture, or print any books, or plays, without her special li-
" cense. And required her subjects, that none of them should
" presume to punish any on pretence of the late rebellion, but
" as they should be authorized by her: yet she did not there-
" by restrain any from informing against such offenders. She
" would be most sorry to have cause to execute the severity of
" the law, but she was resolved not to suffer such rebellious
" doings to go unpunished; but hoped her subjects would not
" drive her to the extreme execution of the laws."

246   When this was published, which was the first thing that
was set out in her name since she had come to the crown [12], it
was much descanted on. The profession she made of her religion to be the same it had been from her infancy, shewed it
was not her father's religion, but entire popery that she intended to restore. It was also observed, that whereas before
she had said plainly she would compel none to be of it: now
that was qualified with this, till public order should be taken
in it; which was, till they could so frame a parliament, that it
should concur with the queen's design. The equal forbidding
of assemblies, or ill names, on both sides, was thought intended
to be a trap for the reformed, that they should be punished if
they offended; but the others were sure to be rather encouraged. The restraint of preaching without license was pretended to be copied from what had been done in king Edward's time: yet then there was a liberty left for a long time
to all to preach in their own churches, only they might preach
nowhere else without a license; and the power of licensing
was also lodged at first with the bishops in their several dioceses, and at last with the archbishop of Canterbury, as well as
with the king: whereas now, at one stroke, all the pulpits of
England that were in the hands of the reformed were brought

Censures passed upon it.

[12] It was not her first proclamation; for on the 19th of July, she
had by a proclamation taken on her
the imperial crown of the realm.
[S.]

under an interdict; for they were sure to obtain no licenses. But the cunningest part of these inhibitions was, the declaring that the queen would proceed with rigour against all that were guilty of the late rebellion, if they should provoke her. Many about London had some way or other expressed themselves for it; and these were the hottest among the reformed: so that here was a sharp threatening hanging over them, if they should express any more zeal about religion.

She requites the service of the men of Suffolk ill. [Fox, vol. iii. p. 13.]

When this was put out, the queen, understanding that in Suffolk those of that profession took a little more liberty than their neighbours, presuming on their great merit, and the queen's promises to them; there was a special letter sent to the bishop of Norwich's vicar, himself being at Brussels, to see to the execution of these injunctions, against any that should preach without license. Upon this, some came from Suffolk to put the queen in mind of her promise. This was thought insolent: and she returned them no other answer, but that they, being members, thought to rule her that was their head; but they should learn, that the members ought to obey the head, and not to think to bear rule over it. One of these had spoken of her promise with more confidence than the rest; his name was Dobbe; so he was ordered to stand three days in the pillory, as having said that which tended to the defamation of the queen. And from hence all saw what a severe government they were to come under, in which the claiming of former promises, that had been made by the queen when she needed their assistance, was to be accounted a crime. But there was yet a more unreasonable severity showed to Bradford and Rogers, who had appeased the tumult the Sunday before, and rescued the preacher from the rage of the people. It was said, that their appeasing it so easily shewed what interest they had with the people, and was a presumption that they had set it on; so, without any further proof, the one was put in the Tower, and the other confined to his house.

The popish bishops restored.

But now the deprived bishops, who were, Bonner of London, 247 Gardiner of Winchester, Tunstall of Durham, Heath of Worcester, and Day of Chichester, were to be restored to their sees. I have only seen the commission for restoring Bonner and Tunstall; but the rest were no doubt in the same strain, with a little variation. The commission for Bonner, bearing date the

22nd of August, was directed to some civilians, setting forth, that he had petitioned the queen to examine the appeal he had made from the delegates that had deprived him ; and that therefore, the sentence against him being unjust and illegal, he desired it might be declared to be of no effect. Upon which these did, without any great hesitation, return the sentences void, and the appeals good. So thus they were restored to their sees. But, because the bishopric of Durham was by act of parliament dissolved, and the regalities of it, which had been given to the duke of Northumberland, were now by his attainder fallen into the queen's hand, she granted Tunstall letters patents, erecting that bishopric again of new ; making mention, that some wicked men, to enrich themselves by it, had procured it to be dissolved.

On the 29th of August commission was granted to Gardiner to give licenses under the great seal to such grave, learned, and discreet persons as he should think meet and able to preach God's word. All who were so licensed were qualified to preach in any cathedral or parochial church, to which he should think it convenient to send them. By this, the reformers were not only out of hope to obtain any licenses, but likewise saw a way laid down for sending such men as Gardiner pleased into all their pulpits, to infect their people. Upon this they considered what to do. If there had been only a particular interdiction of some private persons, the considerations of peace and order being of a more public nature than the consequence of any one man's open preaching could be, they judged it was to be submitted to : but in such a case, when they saw this interdiction was general, and on design to stop their mouths till their enemies should seduce the people, they did not think they were bound in conscience to give obedience. Many of them therefore continued to preach openly : others, instead of preaching in churches, were contented to have only the prayers and other service there ; but, for instructing their people, had private conferences with them. The council hearing that their orders had been disobeyed by some in London, two in Coventry, and one in Amersham, they were sent for, and put in prison : and Coverdale bishop of Exeter, and Hooper of Gloucester, being cited to appear before the council, they came and presented themselves on the 29th and 30th of August ;

[Rymer, xv. p. 337.]

The consultations among the reformed doctors.

[Aug. 26 and 31,

Fox, vol.
iii. p. 15.]
and on the first of September Hooper was sent to the Fleet,
and Coverdale appointed to wait their pleasure.

At this time the popish party, growing now insolent over
England, began to be as forward in making changes before
the laws warranted them, as those of the reformation had been
in king Edward's time; so that in many places they set up
images, and the Latin service, with the old rites again. This
was plainly against law: but the council had no mind to hinder
it; but on the other hand encouraged it all they could. Upon
which judge Hales, who thought he might with the more assurance speak his mind, having appeared so steadily for the
queen, did, at the circuits [13] in Kent, give a charge to the
justices to see to the execution of king Edward's laws, which 248
were still in force and unrepealed. Upon this he was, without
any regard to his former zeal, put, first; into the Marshalsea [14]: from thence he was removed to the Counter, and after
that to the Fleet; where [15] the good old man was so disordered
with the cruelties that the warden told him were contriving
against all that would not change their [16] religion, that it turned
his brain, so that he endeavoured to have killed himself with a
penknife. He was after that, upon his submission, set at liberty; but never came to himself again: so he, not being well
looked to, drowned himself. This, with the usage of the Suffolk
men, was much censured; and from thence it was said, that
no merits or services could secure any from the cruelties of
that religion. And it appeared in another signal instance how
the actions of men were not so much considered as their religion. The lord chief justice Montague, who had very unwillingly drawn the letters patents for the lady Jane's succes-

The bar-
barous
usage of
judge
Hales.
[Fox, vol.
iii. p. 16.]

---

[13] Circuits, read the quarter-ses-
sions. [S.]

[14] Marshalsea, read the King's
Bench. [S.]

[15] The reason of the wounding
himself was the trouble of mind
that he felt for his compliance upon
bishop Day's communication with
him the day before. [S.]

[16] Speaking of judge Hales.
Judge Hales did change his reli-
gion. So Fox, vol. iii. p. 957. "Judge
Hales never fell into that incon-

venience before he had consented to
papistry." This probably was one
great occasion of his melancholy.
So Fox more expressly in the first
edition of his book, p. 1116, "He
was cast forthwith into a great repentance of the deed, and into a
terror of conscience." And Bradford (Letters of the Martyrs, p. 384)
proposes him as an example of one
that was fearfully left of God to our
admonition. [B.]

sion, was turned out of his place, kept six weeks in prison, fined in a thousand pounds, and some lands, that had been given him by king Edward, were taken from him; though he had sent his son with twenty men to declare for the queen, and had a great family of seventeen children, six sons and eleven daughters: whereas judge Bromley, that had concurred in framing the letters patents without any reluctancy, was made lord chief justice. The true reason was, Bromley was a papist in his heart, and Montague was for the reformation.

In many other places, where the people were popishly af- [Fox, vol.
fected, they drove away their pastors. At Oxford Peter Mar- iii. p. 15.]
tyr was so ill used, that he was forced to fly for safety to Lambeth; where he could not look for any long protection, since Cranmer himself was every day in expectation of being sent to prison. He kept himself quiet; and was contriving how to Cranmer
give some public and noble testimonies to the doctrine that he declared
had so long professed, and indeed had been the chief promoter against the
of in this church. But his quiet behaviour was laid hold on by mass.
his enemies; and it was given out, that he was resolved to comply with every thing the queen had a mind to. So I find Bonner's
Bonner wrote to his friend Mr. Lechmore, on the sixth of Sep- insolence.
tember, in that letter which is in the Collection: "He gives Collect.
" him notice, that the day before he had been restored to his Numb. 7.
" bishopric, and Ridley repulsed; for which he is very witty.
" Ridley had a steward for two manors of his, whose name was
" Shipside, his brother-in-law; upon which he plays as if he
" had been Sheepshead. He orders Lechmore to look to his
" estate, and he should take care at the next parliament that
" both the *sheepsheads* and the calvesheads should be used as
" they deserved. He adds, that Cranmer, whom in scorn he
" calls Mr. Canterbury, was become very humble, and ready to
" submit himself in all things: but that would not serve his
" turn; and it was expected that he should be sent to the
" Tower that very day." These reports being brought to Cranmer, some advised him to fly beyond seas: he said, he would not dissuade others from that course, now that they saw a persecution rising; but, considering the station he was in, and the hand he had in all the changes that were made, he thought it so indecent a thing for him to fly, that no entreaties should ever persuade him to it. So he, by Peter Martyr's ad-

Cranmers's
declar-
ation,
Collect.
Numb. 8.
[Fox, vol.
iii. p. 77.]

vice, drew up a writing, that I have put in the Collection; (in Latin, as it was at that time translated.) The substance of it was to this effect: "That as the devil had at all times set on 249 " his instruments by lies to defame the servants of God, so he " was now more than ordinarily busy. For whereas king " Henry had begun the correcting of the abuses of the mass, " which his son had brought to a further perfection; and so " the Lord's supper was restored to its first institution, and " was celebrated according to the pattern of the primitive " church: now the devil, intending to bring the mass again " into its room, as being his own invention, had stirred up " some to give out that it had been set up in Canterbury by " his the said Cranmer's order; and it was said, that he had " undertaken to sing mass to the queen's majesty, both at king " Edward's funeral, at Paul's, and other places: and though " for these twenty years he had despised all such vain and " false reports as were spread of him, yet now he thought " it not fit to lie under such misrepresentations. Therefore he " protested to all the world, that the mass was not set up at " Canterbury by his order; but that a fawning hypocritical " monk (this was Thornton, suffragan of Dover) [17] had done it " without his knowledge: and for what he was said to have " undertaken to the queen, her majesty knew well how false " that was; offering, if he might obtain her leave for it, to " maintain, that every thing in the communion service that " was set out by their most innocent and good king Edward " was according to Christ's institution, and the practice of the " apostles and the ancient church for many ages, to which the " mass was contrary, being full of errors and abuses. And al- " though Peter Martyr was by some called an ignorant man, " he, with him, or other four or five, such as he should choose, " would be ready to defend, not only their Book of Common " Prayer, and the other rites of their service, but the whole

---

[17] ['There was but one suffragan bishop in the diocese of Canterbury of the name of Thornton. He was suffragan to archbishop Warham in the year 1508, and had his title not from Dover, but *in partibus infidelium*, and died long before Cranmer's time. The suffragan under Cranmer and Pole was Richard Thornden, sometime monk, and afterwards, upon the suppression of the priory, first prebendary of the church of Canterbury. He died in the end of the year 1557, or rather in the beginning of 1558.' Specimen of Errors, p. 122.]

" doctrine and order of religion, set forth by the late king, as [Fox, vol.
" more pure and more agreeable to the word of God, than any iii. p. 77.]
" sort of religion that had been in England for a thousand
" years before it; provided that all things should be judged
" by the scriptures, and that the reasonings on both sides
" should be faithfully written down."

This he had drawn, with a resolution to have made a public *Published*
use of it: but Scory, who had been bishop of Chichester, *without his*
coming to him, he shewed him the paper, and bade him con- *ledge;*
sider of it. Scory indiscreetly gave copies of it; and one of
these was publicly read in Cheapside on the fifth of September.
So, on the eighth of that month, he was called before the star-
chamber, and asked, whether he was the author of that seditious bill, that was given out in his name; and if so, whether
he was sorry for it. He answered, that the bill was truly his; *But owned*
but he was very sorry it had gone from him in such a manner: *by him be-*
for he had resolved to have enlarged it in many things, and to *council.*
have ordered it to be affixed to the doors of Paul's, and of the
other churches in London, with his hand and seal to it. He
was at that time, contrary to all men's expectation, dismissed.
Gardiner plainly saw he could not expect to succeed him, and
that the queen had designed that see for cardinal Pole; so he
resolved to protect and preserve Cranmer all he could. Some
moved that he should be only put from his bishopric, and have
a small pension assigned him, with a charge to keep within a
confinement, and not to meddle with matters of religion. He
was generally beloved for the gentleness of his temper; so it
250 was thought, that proceeding severely with him might alienate
some from them, and embroil their affairs in the next parliament. Others objected, that if he, who had been the chief
promoter of heresy, was used with such tenderness, it would
encourage the rest to be more obstinate: and the queen, who
had forgot the services he did her in her father's time, remembering rather that he had pronounced the sentence of divorce
against her mother, was easily induced to proceed severely.
So on the 13th of September both he and Latimer were called *He and La-*
before the council: Latimer was that day committed; but *timer sent*
Cranmer was respited till next day, and then he was sent to *Tower.*
the Tower, both for matters of treason against the queen, and [Fox, vol.
for dispersing of seditious bills. Tayler of Hadley and several iii. p. 15.]

other preachers were also put in prison ; and, upon an information brought against Horne, dean of Durham, he was sent for.

The foreigners[17] that were come over upon public faith and
encouragement, were better used; for Peter Martyr was preserved from the rage of his enemies, and suffered to go beyond
sea.　There was also an order sent to John a Lasco and his
congregation to be gone, their church being taken from them,
and their corporation dissolved; and an hundred seventy-five
of them went away in two ships to Denmark on the 17th of
September, with all their preachers, except two, who were left
to look to those few which stayed behind; and being engaged
in trade, resolved to live in England, and follow their consciences in the matters of religion in private, with the assistance
of those teachers.　But a Lasco, after a long and hard passage,
arriving at Denmark, was as ill received there as if it had been
a popish country, when they understood that he and his company were of the Helvetian confession : so that, though it was
December, and a very severe winter, they were required to be
gone within two days; and could not obtain so much as liberty
to leave their wives or children behind them, till they could
provide a place for them.　From thence they went, first, to
Lubeck, then to Wismar and Hamburg, where they found the
disputes about the manner of Christ's presence in the sacrament had raised such violent animosities, that, after much barbarous usage, they were banished out of all those towns, and
could find no place to settle in till about the end of March,
that they came to Friseland, where they were suffered to plant
themselves.[18]

[17] [See Wilkins' Concilia, tom.
iv. p. 93, for 'Queen Mary's proclamation for the driving out of the
realm, strangers and foreigners.']

[18] ['A most exact account of the
foundation and dissolution of this
German congregation in England,
with their subsequent removals, was
written by Utenhovius, one of the
ministers, at the desire of the congregation, and is printed at Basle,
1560, 8º. with this title, 'Simplex et
fidelis narratio de instituta et demum
dissipata, Belgarum aliorumque pe-
regrinorum in Anglia ecclesia, per

Johannem Utenhovium Gandavum,'
being approved by John a Lasco
and the rest as a true account.
From this narration it appears, that
although some of the company went
to Hamburg, Lubeck, Wismar, &c.
yet that a Lasco himself went not
thither with them. He left Denmark on the 19th of November,
passed through Holsatia, and arrived
at Embden the 4th of December. He
was accompanied with a servant of
the king of Denmark, by whom he
sent back a severe, or rather un-
mannerly letter to the king.　In this

Many in England, seeing the government was set on severe Many English fly beyond sea. courses so early, did infer, that this would soon grow up to an extreme persecution ; so that above a thousand persons fled beyond seas : most of them went in the company, and as the servants, of French protestants ; who, having come over in king Edward's time, were now required, as the Germans had been, to return into their own country. The council, understanding this, took care that no Englishman should escape out of their hands ; and therefore sent an order to the ports, that none should be suffered to go over as Frenchmen, but those who brought certificates from the French ambassador. Among those that had got over, some eminent divines went ; who, either having no cures, or being turned out of their benefices, were not under such ties to any flock : so that they judged themselves disengaged, and therefore did not, as hirelings, leave their flock to the persecution then imminent, but rather 251 went to look after those who had now left England. The chief of these that went at first were Cox, Sandys, Grindal, and Horne. Cox was without any good colour turned out both of his deanery of Christ-Church and his prebendary at Westminster[19] : he was put into the Marshalsea ; but on the 19th of August was discharged. Sandys was turned out for his sermon before the duke of Northumberland at Cambridge : on what account Grindal was turned out, I know not. Horne, soon

same relation of Utenhovius is printed at large the charters given by King Edward to John a Lasco and his congregation, which the historian had before mentioned and put it into his collection *for the curiosity of the thing,* as himself saith. It was also published by Mr. Prynn, in his trial of archbishop Laud. I will further add, that it is more correct in Utenhovius than in the transcript ; which is the case of all the instruments and memorials published by him which I have had occasion to compare, either with the originals or with other copies.'— Specimen of Errrors, p. 123.]

[19] [' Cox had no prebendary (the historian would have said prebend) at Westminster but besides his deanery of Christ-Church, Oxford,

was dean of Westminster, and prebendary of Windsor, of all which he was deprived about this time. The cause of his deprivation was probably supposed to have been that he had acted in favour of Queen Jane. For being a considerable person in king Edward's court at the time of his death, and having been much employed even in state affairs, he could not well avoid to be concerned in that matter if he were then present at court. He was married indeed at this time, but I do not think that was alleged as a cause of his deprivation. For they did not yet proceed to deprive the married clergy until some months after this.' Specimen of Errors, p. 124.]

after he got beyond sea, printed an apology for his leaving his country; he tells, that he heard there were some crimes against the state objected to him, which made him come up from Durham to clear himself. It was said, that three letters had been written to him in the queen's name, requiring him to come up; and intimating, that they were resolved to charge him with contempt, and other points of state. He protests that he had never received but one, which was given him on the road; but seeing how he was like to be used, he withdrew out of England: upon which he takes occasion in that discourse to vindicate the preachers in king Edward's time, against whom it was now objected, that they had neglected fasting and prayer, and had allowed the people all sorts of liberty. This, he said, was so false, that the ruling men in that time were much offended at the great freedom which the preachers then took, so that many of them would hear no more sermons: and he says for himself, that though Tunstall was now his great enemy, he had refused to accept of his bishopric[20], and was ill used and threatened for denying to take it.

The queen rewards those who had served her.

All these things tended much to inflame the people. Therefore great care was taken, first, to oblige all those noblemen who had assisted the queen at her coming to the crown; since a grateful acknowledgment of past services is the greatest encouragement, both to the same persons to renew them, and to others to undertake the like upon new occasions. The earl of Arundel was made lord steward; sir Edward Hastings was made master of the horse, and afterwards lord Hastings; sir John Gage, lord chamberlain; sir John Williams, who had proclaimed the queen in Oxfordshire, was made lord Williams; and sir Henry Jerningham, that first gathered the men of Norfolk about her, was made captain of her guard. But Ratcliff, earl of Sussex, had done the most considerable service of them all; for to him she had given the chief command of her army, and he had managed it with that prudence, that others were thereby encouraged to come in to her assistance: so an unusual honour was contrived for him, that he might

---

[20] As far as I understand his meaning, this was meant of the administration of episcopal power. For Horne having said, 'The bishop was not ashamed to lay to my charge .... that I had exercised his office in his bishopric;' answers.... 'I never meddled with his office; I was in danger of much displeasure .... because I would not take upon me his office,' &c. [B.]

cover his head in her presence ; which passed under the great
seal the second of October, he being the only peer of England
in whom this honour was ever conferred, as far as I know[21].
The like was granted to the lord Courcy, baron of Kingsale in
Ireland, whose posterity enjoy it to this day : but I am not so
well informed of that family, as to know by which of our kings
it was first granted. The queen having summoned a parliament to the tenth[22] of October, was crowned on the first
of that month by Gardiner ; who, with ten other bishops, all in
their mitres, copes, and crosiers, performed that ceremony with
great solemnity : Day preaching the coronation sermon; who,
it seems, was accounted the best preacher among them, since
he was ordered to preach both at the late king's funeral, and
now again at the coronation

[Stow, p. 616.]

But Gardiner had prepared a largess of an extraordinary
252 nature for the queen to distribute that[23] day among her people,
besides her general pardon : he caused a proclamation to be
published, which did set forth, " that whereas the good subjects
" of England had always exhibited aid to their princes, when
" the good of the public, and honour of the realm, required it ;
" and though the queen, since her coming to the crown, found
" the treasury was marvellously exhausted, by the evil govern-
" ment of late years, especially since the duke of Northumber-
" land bare rule ; though she found herself charged with
" divers great sums of her father and brother's debts, which
" for her own honour, and the honour of the realm, she deter-
" mined to pay in times convenient and reasonable ; yet having
" a special regard to the welfare of her subjects, and account-
" ing their loving hearts and prosperity the chiefest treasure
" which she desired, next to the favour and grace of God ;
" therefore, since in her brother's last parliament, two tenths,
" two fifteenths, and a subsidy both out of lands and goods were
" given to him for paying his debts, which were now due to her ;

The queen
is crowned,
and dis-
charges all
taxes.

---

[21] Dr. Fuller assures us in his
Church History, book ix. p. 167,
that he had seen a charter granted
by king Henry the 8th, the 16th of
July, in the 18th of his reign, and
confirmed by act of parliament, to
Francis Brown, a commoner; giving
him leave to put on his cap, in the
presence of the king and his heirs,
and not to put it off but for his own
ease and pleasure. [G.]

[22] The tenth, read the fifth. [S.]

[23] The day of her coronation, read,
a month before; for it was on the 1st
of September. [S.]

" she of her great clemency did fully pardon and discharge
" these subsidies; trusting her said good subjects will have
" loving consideration thereof for their parts, whom she
" heartily requires to bend themselves wholly to God, to serve
" him sincerely, and with continual prayer, for the honour
" and advancement of the queen and the commonwealth."

A parlia-
ment sum-
moned.
[Fox, vol.
iii. p. 15.
Oct. 5.
Journal of
Commons,
p. 26.]

[Machyn's
Diary, p.
46.]

Bishops
violently
thrust out
for not
worship-
ping the
mass.

And thus matters were prepared for the parliament: which
was opened the tenth [24] of October. In the writ of summons,
and all other writs, the queen retained still the title of *supreme
head*. Taylor bishop of Lincoln, and Harley bishop of Hereford, came thither, resolving to justify their doctrine. Most of
the other reformed bishops were now in prison; for, besides
these formerly mentioned, on the fourth of October the archbishop of York was put in the Tower, no cause being given,
but heinous offences only named in general. When the mass
begun, it is said that those two bishops withdrew, and were
upon that never suffered to come to their places again. But
one Beal [25], the clerk of the council in queen Elizabeth's time,
reports this otherwise, and more probably; that bishop Taylor
took his place in his robes, but, refusing to give any reverence
to the mass, was violently thrust out of the house. He says
nothing of Harley, so it is probable that he followed the other.

Great dis-
order in
elections.

The same writer also informs us, that, in many places of the
country, men were chosen by force and threats; in other
places those employed by the court did by violence hinder the
commons from coming to choose; in many places false returns
were made; and that some were violently turned out of the
house of commons; upon which reasons he concludes that it
was no parliament, since it was under a force, and so might be
annulled, as the parliament held at Coventry, in the 38th year
of king Henry the Sixth, was, upon evidence of the like force,
declared afterwards to be no parliament. The journals of the
house of lords in this parliament are lost; so there is no light
to be had of their proceedings, but from the imperfect journals
of the house of commons.

On the second day of the session, one moved in the house of
commons for a review of king Edward's laws. But that being

[24] The tenth, read the fifth. This
mistake is taken from Fabian and
Fox. [S.]

[25] This name in Fox is Hales.
vol. iii. p. 976. [B.]

a while argued, was at this time laid aside, and the bill for
tonnage and poundage was put in.   Then followed a debate
253 upon Dr. Nowell's being returned from Loo in Cornwall, whether he, being a prebendary of [26] Westminster, could sit in that
house? and the committee being appointed to search for precedents, it was reported, that he, being represented in the con- [Oct. 13.]
vocation house, could not be a member of that house; so he
was cast out.   The bill of tonnage and poundage was sent up [Oct. 12.]
to the lords, who sent it down to the commons to be reformed [Journal of
in two provisos that were not according to former precedents. Commons,
                                                               p. 28.]
How far this was contrary to the rights of the commons, who
now say, that the lords cannot alter a bill of money, I am not
able to determine.   The only public bill that passed in this An act for
short session was for a declaration of treasons and felonies; by moderat-
                                                                ing some
which it was ordained, that nothing should be judged treason, severe
but what was within the statute of treasons in the 25th of Ed- laws.
ward the Third; and nothing should be so judged felony, that [Cap. 1,
                                                               Statutes,
was not so before the first year of king Henry the Eighth, ex- vol. iv. p.
                                                               198.]
cepting from any benefit of this act all such as had been in [Journal of
prison [27] before the last of September; who were also excepted Commons,
                                                               p. 27.]
out of the queen's pardon at her coronation.   Two private bills [Ibid. p.
also passed; the one for the restoring of the wife of the late 28.]
marquis of Exeter, who had been attainted in the 32nd year
of king Henry's reign; and the other for her son Edward
Courtenay earl of Devonshire.   And so the parliament was
prorogued from the 21st to the 24th of October, that there
might be a session of parliament consisting only of acts of
mercy; though this repeal of additional treasons and felonies
was not more than what had passed in the beginning of king
Edward's reign, without the clog of so severe a proviso, by
which many were cut off from the favour designed by it.

   Some have thought, that since treasons had been reduced
by the second act of Edward the Sixth to the standard of the
25th of Edward the Third, that therefore there was somewhat
else designed by this act than barely the repealing some late
severe acts, which being done the first of Edward the Sixth,
needed not be now repealed, if it imported no more.   And
since this act, as it is worded, mentions, or rather excepts,

---

[26] Yet Tregonnell, a prebendary of   [27] For treason, petty treason, or
Westminster, sat in the house in the   misprision of treason, [was inserted
second session of this parliament. [S.]   here in the edition of 1715.]

those treasons that are declared and expressed in the 25th of
Edward the Third, they have inferred that the power of parliaments declaring of treasons *ex post facto,* which was reserved by that statute, is hereby taken away; and that nothing
is now to be held treason, but what is enumerated in that statute.   Yet this is still liable to debate; since the one may be
thought to be declared and expressed in general words, as well
as the other specialties are in more particular words; and is
also still in force.   So nothing seems comprehended within this
repeal, but the acts passed in king Edward's reign, declaring
other crimes to be treason; some are added in the same act,
and others in that of the 3rd and 4th of his reign, chap. 5.   Nor
is it likely, that if the parliament had intended to have delivered the subjects from the apprehensions of all acts of attainder, upon a declaration of new treasons, they would not have
expressed it more plainly; since it must have been very grateful to the nation, which had groaned heavily under arbitrary
attainders of late years.

The mar-
riage of
queen Ca-
tharine to
king Henry
confirmed.
[Journal of
Commons,
p. 29.]
When the parliament met again, the first bill the commons
entered on was that of tonnage and poundage, which they
passed in two days.   Then was the bill about king Henry's
marriage with the queen's mother sent down on the 26th by
the lords, and the commons passed it on the 28th; so strangely 254
was the stream turned, that a divorce that had been for seven
years much desired by the nation, was now repealed upon
[Cap. I.
Statutes,
vol. iv. p.
200.]
fewer days' consultation.   In the preamble it was said, " That
" truth, how much soever obscured and borne down, will in the
" end break out: and that therefore they declared, that king
" Henry the Eighth, being lawfully married to queen Catha-
" rine by the consent of both their parents, and the advice of
" the wisest men in the realm, and of the best and notablest
" men for learning in Christendom, did continue that state
" twenty years, in which God blessed them with her majesty
" and other issue, and a course of great happiness; but then
" a very few malicious persons did endeavour to break that
" happy agreement between them, and studied to possess the
" king with a scruple in his conscience about it: and, to sup-
" port that, caused the seals of some universities to be got
" against it, a few persons being corrupted with money for
" that end.   They had also by sinistrous ways, and secret

" threatenings, procured the seals of the universities of this
" kingdom; and, finally, Thomas Cranmer did most ungodlily,
" and against law, judge the divorce, upon his own unadvised
" understanding of the scriptures, upon the testimonies of the
" universities, and some bare and most untrue conjectures; [Ibid.
" and that was afterwards confirmed by two acts of parlia- p. 201.]
" ment, in which was contained the illegitimacy of her ma-
" jesty: but that marriage not being prohibited by the law of
" God, and lawfully made, could not be so broken; since what
" God hath joined together, no man could put asunder: all
" which they considering, together with the many miseries
" that had fallen on the kingdom since that time, which they
" did esteem plagues sent from God for it; therefore they de-
" clare that sentence given by Cranmer to be unlawful, and of
" no force from the beginning: and do also repeal the acts of
" parliament that had confirmed it."

By this act, Gardiner had performed his promise to the Which was
queen, of getting her illegitimation taken off, without any re- much cen-
lation to the pope's authority. But in the drawing of it, he sured.
shewed that he was past all shame; when he could frame such
an act, of a business which himself had so violently and servilely promoted. The falsehood of that pretence of corrupting
universities has been shewn in the former volume; but it was
all they had now to say. The laying it all upon Cranmer was
as high a pitch of malice and impudence as could be devised;
for, as Gardiner had been setting it on long before Cranmer
was known to king Henry, so he had been joined with him in
the commission, and had given his assent to the sentence which
Cranmer gave. Nor was the divorce grounded merely upon
Cranmer's understanding of the scriptures, but upon the fullest
and most studied arguments that had perhaps been in any age
brought together in one particular case; and both houses of
convocation had condemned the marriage before his sentence.
But because in the right of his see he was legate to the pope,
therefore, to make the sentence stronger, it went only in his
name, though he had but a small share in it, compared to what
Gardiner had.

By this act there was also a second illegitimation brought The queen
on the lady Elizabeth, to whom hitherto the queen had been severely to
very kind, using her on all occasions with the tenderness of a the lady
Elizabeth.

sister; but from this time forwards she handled her more severely. It was perhaps occasioned by this act, since before they stood both equally illegitimated; but now the act that legitimated the queen, making her most certainly a bastard in law, the queen might think it now too much to use her as she had done formerly. Others suggest a more secret reason of this distaste. The new earl of Devonshire was much in the queen's favour, so that it was thought she had some inclinations to marry him; but he, either not presuming so high, or really having an aversion to her, and an inclination to her sister, who, of that moderate share of beauty that was between them, had much the better of her, and was nineteen years younger, made his addresses with more than ordinary concern to the lady Elizabeth; and this did bring them both in trouble, as shall be afterwards shewn.

255

The laws made by king Edward repealed. [Journal of Commons, p. 29.] [Cap. 2. Statutes, vol. iv. p. 202.]

The next bill that was sent from the lords to the commons was for the repealing king Edward's laws about religion. It was sent down on the 31st of October, and argued six days in the house of commons; but in the end it was carried, and sent back to the lords. The preamble of it sets forth the great disorders that had fallen out in the nation by the changes that had been made in religion, from that which their forefathers had left them by the authority of the catholic church: thereupon all the laws that had been made in king Edward's time about religion were now repealed; and it was enacted, that, from the 20th of December next, there should be no other form of divine service but what had been used in the last year of king Henry the Eighth, leaving it free to all till that day to use either the books appointed by king Edward, or the old ones, at their pleasure.

An act against the affronting priests. [Cap. iii. ibid. p. 203.]

Another act was passed, which the commons sent up to the lords, against all those who by any overt act should molest or disquiet any preacher, because of his office, or for any sermon that he might have preached; or should any way disturb them when they were in any part of the divine offices, that either had been in the last year of king Henry, or should be afterwards set forth by the queen; or should break or abuse the holy sacrament, or break altars, crucifixes, or crosses: those that did any of these things should be presented to the justices of peace, and be by them put in prison, where they should lie

three months, or till they were penitent for their offences;
and if any rescued them, they should be liable to the same
punishment. But to this a proviso was added by the lords,
that this act should no way derogate from the authority of the
ecclesiastical laws and courts, who might likewise proceed upon
such offences; and a certificate from the ordinaries, that such
offenders were punished by them, being brought to the justices
of peace, they were to proceed no further : or if the justices
made a certificate that they had punished them according to
law, the ordinary might not punish them a second time. But [Journal of
the commons were now so heated, that they sent up another Commons, p. 32.]
bill to the lords against those who came not to church, nor to
sacraments, after the old service should be again set up; the
inflicting of the punishments in these cases being left to the
ecclesiastical courts. This fell in the house of lords, not so
much from any opposition that was made, as that they were
afraid of alarming the nation too much, by many severe laws
at once.

Another law was made for securing the public peace against An act
256 unlawful and rebellious assemblies; that if any to the number unlawful
of twelve or above should meet to alter any thing of religion assemblies.
established by law, and being required by any, having the ibid. p.
queen's authority, to disperse themselves, should continue after [211.]
that an hour together, it should be felony; or if that number
met to break hedges or parks, to destroy deer or fish, &c. and
did not disperse upon proclamation, it should be felony; or if
any, by ringing of bells, drums, or firing of beacons, gathered
the people together, and did the things before mentioned, it
was felony; if the wives or servants of persons so gathered,
carried meat, money, or weapons to them, it should be felony;
and if any above the number of two, and within twelve, should
meet for these ends, they should suffer a year's imprisonment;
empowering the sheriffs or justices to gather the country for
the resistance of persons so offending, with penalties on all,
between eighteen and sixty, that, being required to come out
against them, should refuse to do it. When this act was known,
the people then saw clearly how they had been deceived by
the former act, that seemed so favourable, repealing all acts of
new treasons and felonies; since there was so soon after it an

act passed that renewed one of the severest laws of the last reign, in which so many things, that might flow from sudden heats, were made felonies, and a great many new and severe provisos were added to it. The queen's discharge of the subsidy was confirmed by another act.

[Cap. 17. ibid. p. 218.]

There followed two private acts, which occasioned more debate than the public ones had done: the one was, the repeal of the act that had confirmed the marquis of Northampton's marriage; it was much argued in the house of commons, and on the 28th of November it was agreed to. It contains, that the act of confirming the divorce, and the second marriage, was procured more upon untrue surmises and private respects, than for any public good, and increase of virtue; and that it was an encouragement for sensual persons to practise by false allegations that they might be separated from their wives, rather than a precedent to induce people to live with their wives in a godly sort: thereupon the act was repealed, and declared void and of no effect. In this it seems the arguments that were against it in the house of commons had so moderated the style of it, that it was not repealed as an act sinful in itself, but it was only declared that in that particular case the divorce was unlawfully made; for it is reasonable to believe, that the bishops had put in the first draught of the bill a simple repeal of it, and of all such divorces, founded on the indissolubleness of the marriage bond.

The marquis of Northampton's second marriage is annulled. [Journal of Commons, p. 31.]

The other act was about the duke of Norfolk, for declaring his attainder void. The patentees that had purchased some parts of his estate from the crown, desired to be heard to plead against it. But the session of the parliament being near at an end, the duke came down himself to the house of commons on the fourth of December, and desired them earnestly to pass his bill; and said, that the difference between him and the patentees was referred to arbiters, and if they could not agree it, he would refer it to the queen. It was long argued after that, but in the end it was agreed to. It sets forth, that the act, by which he was attainted, had no special matter in it, but only treasons in general, and a pretence, that, out of the parliament's care for the king, and his son the prince, it was necessary to attaint him: that the reasons they pretended were, his using coats of arms, which he and his ancestors had and

And the duke of Norfolk's attainder. [Journal of Commons, p. 32.]

257

might lawfully use. It further says, that the king died the next night after the commission was given for passing the bill; and that it did not appear that the king had given his assent to it: that the commission was not signed by the king's hand, but only by his stamp; and that was put to the nether end, and not to the upper part of the bill, which shewed it was done in disorder; and that it did not appear that these commissioned for it had given the royal assent to it. Upon which considerations, that pretended act is declared void and null by the common laws of the land. And it is further declared, that the law was, and ever hath been, that the royal assent should be given, either by the king being present, or, in his absence, by a commission under the great seal, signed with his hand, and publicly notified to the lords and commons.

The last act of which I shall give an account, was the confirmation of the attainders that had been made. On the 3rd of November [28], archbishop Cranmer, the lord Guilford Dudley, and the lady Jane his wife, with two other sons of the duke of Northumberland, (which were all, except the lord Robert, who was reserved for greater fortunes,) were brought to their trial. These all confessed their indictments. Only Cranmer appealed to those that judged him, how unwillingly he had consented to the exclusion of the queen; that he had not done it till those whose profession it was to know the law had signed it: upon which he submitted himself to the queen's mercy. But they were all attainted of high treason, for levying war against the queen, and conspiring to set up another in her room. So these judgments, with those that had passed before, were now confirmed by act of parliament.

Cranmer and others attainted. [Holinshed, p. 1093.]

And now Cranmer was legally divested of his archbishopric, which was hereupon void in law, since a man that is attainted can have no right to any church benefice; his life was also at the queen's mercy. But it being now designed to restore the ecclesiastical exemption and dignity to what it had been anciently, it was resolved, that he should be still esteemed archbishop, till he were solemnly degraded, according to the canon law. The queen was also inclined to give him his life at this time, reckoning, that thereby she was acquitted of all the obligations she had to him; and was resolved to have him pro-

But the see of Canterbury is not declared void.

[28] For third of November, read the thirteenth. [S.]

ceeded against for heresy, that so it might appear she did not act out of revenge, or on any personal account. So all that followed on this against Cranmer was, a sequestration of all the fruits of his archbishopric; himself was still kept in prison [29]: nor were the other prisoners proceeded against at this time. The queen was desirous to seem willing to pardon injuries done

[29] ['This, if true, would be a matter of great moment, and make a considerable change in the history of our church. But really it is a mere fiction. For immediately after his attainture, the see of Canterbury was declared void, and the dean and chapter of Canterbury thereupon assumed the administration of the spiritual jurisdiction of the archbishopric, as in other cases of vacancy.

'The attainture was completed in the middle of November 1553, and on the sixteenth of December following the dean and chapter of Canterbury gave out commissions to several persons for the exercise of the archiepiscopal jurisdiction in their names and by their authorities. The chapter continued in possession of this jurisdiction till the publication of cardinal Pole's bulls of provision to the archbishopric, viz. till the beginning of the year 1556; and during that time gave commissions to the several officers and judges of the courts of the archbishopric, had the spiritual jurisdiction of all vacant bishoprics; gave institution to all benefices in them, and in the diocese of Canterbury; gave commissions for the consecration of bishops, &c.; of all which acts done, a peculiar register was made, entitled, *Vacatio sedis metropoliticæ Christi Cantuariensis post depositionem Thomæ Cranmer nuper archiepiscopi Cantuariensis primo de crimine læsæ majestatis authoritate Parliamenti convicti et deinde ob varias hæreses authoritate sedis apostolicæ depositi, degradati, seculari brachio traditi, et postremo in alma universitate Oxoniensi igne consumpti sub annis* *Domini* 1553, 1554 *et* 1555, *regnorum vero Philippi et Mariæ regum, &c.* During this time all acts and instruments begin with these words: *Nicholaus Wotton utriusque juris doctor decanus Ecclesiæ Cathedralis et Metropolitices Christi Cantuar. et ejusdem ecclesiæ capitulum ad quem et quos omnis et omnimoda jurisdictio spiritualis et ecclesiastica, quæ ad Archiepiscopum Cantuariensem, sede plena, pertinuit, ipsa sede jam per attincturam Thomæ Cranmer, ultimi Archiepiscopi ejusdem, de alta proditione attincti et adjudicati, vacante, notorie dinoscitur pertinere.* Thus in particular beginneth the first instrument of the register, dated 1553, December the sixteenth. Long before his degradation also, the pope had solemnly excommunicated and deposed Cranmer for heresy; for it did not concern him to take any notice of the pretence of high treason. In the bull of provision to Cardinal Pole to the archbishopric of Canterbury, dated 1555, December 11, Pope Paul saith that he had by a solemn sentence excommunicated and deposed from the see of Canterbury, *filium iniquitatis Thomam Cranmer olim archiepiscopum Cantuariensem, ob notorias hæreses.* This bull sufficiently disproveth the historian's relation. But that which is chiefly to be regarded herein, is the register of the vacancy before mentioned, which puts it beyond all doubt that the see of Canterbury became void immediately upon the attainture of Cranmer, and was at least in England so accounted.'—Specimen of Errors, p. 127.]

against herself, but was so heated in the matters of religion, that she was always inexorable on that head.

Having given this account of public transactions, I must relate next what were more secretly carried on; but, breaking out at this time, occasioned the sudden dissolution of the parliament.

Cardinal Dandino, that was then the pope's legate at the emperor's court, sent over Commendone (afterwards a cardinal) to bring him a certain account of the queen's intentions concerning religion : he gave him in charge, to endeavour to speak with her in private, and to persuade her to reconcile her king-258 dom to the apostolic see. This was to be managed with great secrecy, for they did not know whom to trust in so important a negotiation: it seems, they neither confided in Gardiner, nor in any of the other bishops. Commendone, being thus instructed, went to Newport, where he gave himself out to be the nephew of a merchant, that was lately dead at London; and hired two servants, to whom he was unknown, and so he came over unsuspected to London. There he was so much a stranger, that he did not know to whom he should address himself. By accident he met with one Lee, a servant of the queen's, that had fled beyond sea during the former reign, and had been then known to him; so he trusted him with the secret of his business in England. He procured him a secret audience of the queen, in which she freely owned to him her resolution of reconciling her kingdom to the see of Rome, and so of bringing all things back to the state in which they had been before the breach made by her father : but she said, it was absolutely necessary to manage that design with great prudence and secrecy, lest, in that confusion of affairs, the discovery of it might much disturb her government, and obstruct her design. She writ by him to the pope, giving him assurance of her filial obedience; and so sent Commendone to Rome. She also writ by him to cardinal Pole, and ordered Commendone to move the pope, that he might be sent over with a legatine power. Yet he that writ that cardinal's life insinuates, that the queen had another design in desiring that Pole might be sent over; for she asked him, whether the pope might not dispense with the cardinal to marry, since he was only in deacon's orders? Before Commendone left England, he saw the

The queen treats about a reconciliation with Rome.

[Fléchier, Vie du Cardinal Commendon, p. 50.]

duke of Northumberland executed, and soon after he made all
the haste that was possible to carry those acceptable tidings
to Rome; and by his dexterity in this negotiation, he laid the
foundation of those great fortunes to which he was afterwards
advanced. There was no small joy in the consistory, when the
pope and the cardinals understood that a kingdom, from which
they had drawn so much wealth in former times, was now to
become again tributary to them. So there was a public rejoicing for three days, in which the pope said mass himself, and
distributed his ordinary largess of indulgences, of which he was
the more bountiful, because he hoped they should come in
credit again, and be purchased at the rates at which they had
been formerly sold. Yet in the consistory Commendone did
not positively say he was sent by the queen, that being only
communicated to the pope : all he told the cardinals was, that
he understood, from very good hands, that the queen was very
well disposed to that see, and that she desired that a legate
might be sent over with full powers. Many of the cardinals
thought this was too bare a message ; and that it was below
the papal dignity to send a legate till the pope was earnestly
desired to do it by an express message, and an embassy sent
by the queen. But it was said, that Commendone had said
nothing but by the queen's express orders, who was yet in so
unsettled a condition, that, till she held a session of parliament,
it might much endanger her to appear openly in such a matter :
they were to remember, how England had been lost by too
much stiffness formerly ; and they were to imitate the shepherd
in the parable, who left his ninety-nine sheep, to seek the one
that was strayed. So it was granted, that Pole should go legate with a full power. But Gardiner coming to know this, 259
sent to the emperor to stop his journey ; assuring him, that
things were going well on, and that his coming over would
spoil all. At this time the emperor began to think of marrying
his son Philip to the queen, who, though she was above nine
years elder than he, yet, being but thirty-seven years old, was
not out of hopes of having children. The emperor saw, that if
England were united to the Spanish crown, it would raise that
monarchy to a great height : they should have all the trade of
the world in their hands, and so enclose France, that it seemed
as probable a step to the universal monarchy as that he had

But
stopped in
his journey
by the em-
peror.

lately lost in Germany. When this match was first proposed, I do not know; but I have read some parts of a letter concerning it, (for it is not all legible,) which was written by the queen of Hungary, and signed by the emperor, in the beginning of November: this, though it was not the first proposition, yet seems to have followed soon after it. The queen entertained the motion easily, not trusting to the affections of her people, nor thinking it possible to have the papal authority set up, nor the church lands restored, without a foreign force to assist her. It is said, and I have shewn some ground to believe, that she had some inclinations to cardinal Pole; and that the emperor fearing that might be an hindrance to his design, therefore the cardinal's coming over was stopped till the queen was married to his son Philip. But of this I find no certain footsteps. On the contrary, Gardiner, whose eye was chiefly upon the archbishopric of Canterbury, would rather have promoted Pole's pretensions to the queen; since her marrying a subject, and not a stranger, would have made the government much easier, and more acceptable to the people: and it would have been the best thing he could do for himself, if he could have persuaded her to marry him, who alone was like to stand between him and that dignity.

The true account of it is: the emperor pressed her, first, to settle the state, and consummate her marriage; and that would more easily make way for what was to follow: for Gardiner had assured him, the bringing in of the papal power, and making up the marriage, both at once, would be things of such ill digestion, that it would not be easy to carry them together; and therefore it was necessary to let a considerable interval go between. This being resolved on, it was apparent the marriage ought to go first, as that which would give them more strength to conclude the other. And this was the true reason of stopping cardinal Pole at Dillingen[30]; which the emperor at first did by his own authority, but afterwards got the queen to send one to him to the same purpose. She sent Goldwell (after- The queen wards bishop of St. Asaph) to him, with the two acts that were sent one to him.

---

[30] A town on the Danube. Cardinal Pole was stopped in his journey by Mendoza, sent post to him from the emperor, desiring him not to proceed on his journey; upon which, he went back to Dilling, a town belonging to the cardinal of Augsburg. [S.]

passed for the justifying of her mother's marriage, and for
bringing all things back to the state in which they were at her
father's death.   Thereby she let him see, that she was going
forward in the business for which he was sent : but withal she
told him, that the commons, in passing those acts, had expressed great aversion to the taking of the supremacy from the
crown, or the restoring of the pope's power, and that they were
much alarmed to hear he was coming over legate ; and it pre-
judiced her affairs, that the message she had sent by Commendone had been published in the consistory.   Therefore she desired him to keep out of England till he were further adver- 260
tised.   But, to let him see how much she depended on his
counsels, she desired he would send her a list of such persons
as should be made bishops ; for many were now to be turned
out.   To this (besides the answer which he might have writ to
herself, that I have not seen) he writ a copious answer, in a
tedious paper of instructions, which he gave to Goldwell ; the
conclusion of which, summing up his whole mind fully enough,

Collect.
Numb. 9.

I thought sufficient to put into the Collection, for the instructions are extreme long, and very full of words to little purpose.
They seem to be of his own handwriting, but of that I am not
well assured, having seen nothing else of his hand, except his
subscription.

The advice
he sent to
the queen.

The substance of it was this : " He rejoiced much at the two
" acts that were passed, but yet he censures them both, be-
" cause he observed some defects in them : in the act for con-
" firming her mother's marriage, he found fault that there was
" no mention made of the pope's bulls by the authority of
" which only it could be a lawful marriage.   In the other, he
" did not like it, that the worship of God, and the sacraments,
" were to be as they were in the end of her father's reign ; for
" then the people were yet in a state of schism, and schismatics
" have no right to the sacraments : the pope's interdict still lay
" on the nation, and, till that were taken off, none could with-
" out sin either administer or receive them.   He told her, that
" Commendone had said nothing in her name to the consistory,
" but had spoken to them only on the reports which, he said,
" he had heard of her from good hands ; and it was necessary
" to say somewhat, in order to the sending a legate : that
" many in the consistory had opposed the sending of him, be-

" cause there was no express desire sent about it; but it was
" carried, that he should come over with very full graces, and
" power to reconcile the kingdom on very easy terms.   He
" also told her, he was afraid, that, when the pope and cardinals
" should hear that he was stopped, they would repent their
" benignity, and take this as an affront, and recal him and his
" powers, and send another that would not be so tender of the
" nation, or bring with him such full powers : that, to prevent
" this, he had sent one to the pope and cardinals, to mitigate
" their displeasure, by letting them know, he was only stopped
" for a little while, till the act of attainder that stood against
" him was repealed ; and, to make a show of going forward, he
" had sent his household stuff, to Flanders : but would stay
" where he was, till he had further orders.   He said, he knew
" this flowed chiefly from the emperor, who was for using such
" political courses, as himself had followed in the business of
" the Interim,"and was earnest to have the state settled, be-
" fore she meddled with religion ; he had spoke with his con-
" fessor about it, and had convinced him of the impiety of such
" courses, and sent him to work on him.   He also told the
" queen, he was afraid carnal policy might govern her too
" much, and that she might thereby fall from her simplicity in
" Christ, in which she had hitherto lived.   He encouraged her
" therefore to put on a spirit of wisdom and courage, and to
" trust in God, who had preserved her so long, and had settled
" her on the throne in so unlooked for a manner.   He desired
" she would shew as much courage in rejecting the supremacy,
" as her father had done in acquiring it.   He confessed, he
261 " knew none in either house of parliament fit to propose that
" matter : the spiritualty had all complied so far, had written
" and declared for it so much, that it could not flow from them
" decently ; and the temporalty being possessed of the church
" lands, would not willingly move it ; therefore he thought it
" best for herself to go to the parliament, having beforehand
" acquainted some few both of· the spiritualty and temporalty
" with her design ; and that she should tell both houses, she
" was touched in her conscience, that she and her people were
" in a schism from the catholic church and the apostolic see :
" and that therefore she had desired a legate to come over to
" treat about it, and should thereupon propose, that the attainder

" might be taken off from him, that he might be capable
" to come on that message. And he protested, that he had
" never acted against the king or kingdom, but only with de-
" sign to reduce them to the unity of the church, neither be-
" fore nor after the attainder. And whereas some might ap-
" prehend a thraldom from the papacy, she might give them
" assurance, that they should see all things so well secured,
" that there should no danger come to the nation from it; and
" he assured them, that he, for his part, should take as much
" care of that as any of all the temporalty could desire."
What recommendation she sent for the sees that were to be
declared vacant, I do not know.

But Gardiner's methods are preferred to him. When this despatch of his was brought into England, Gardiner, by the assistance of the emperor, convinced the queen, that his method was impracticable, and that the marriage must be first despatched. And now Gardiner and he did declare open enmity to one another. Gardiner thought him a weak man, that might have some speculative knowledge of abstracted ideas, but understood not the world, nor the genius of the English nation. Pole, on the other hand, thought him a false man, that made conscience of nothing, and was better at intrigues and dissimulation than the government of the church. But the emperor saw Gardiner had so prudently managed this parliament, that he concluded his measures were rather to be followed than the cardinal's.

The house of commons displeased with the marriage with Spain. In the house of commons it was given out, that it was necessary to gain the queen to the interest of the nation, and to turn her from foreign counsels and aid, by being easy to her in the matter of religion; and therefore they were ready both to repeal the divorce and king Edward's laws. But when they saw the design of the marriage, and uniting with Rome, was still carried on, they were all much alarmed: so they sent their speaker, and twenty of their house with him, with an earnest and humble address to her not to marry a stranger. This had so inflamed the house, that the court saw more could not be expected from them, unless they were satisfied in that point: so on the sixth of December the parliament was dissolved. Upon that Gardiner sent to the emperor to let him know, that the marriage was like to meet with such opposition, that, unless extraordinary conditions were offered, which all

The parliament is dissolved. [Journal of Commons, p. 32.]

should see were much to the advantage of the English crown, it could not be carried without a general rebellion. He also assured him, that if great sums of money were not sent over to gratify the chief nobility and leading men in the country, both for obliging them to his interest, and enabling them to carry elections for the next parliament, the opposition would be such, that the queen must lay down all thoughts of marrying his 262 son. Upon this, the emperor and his son resolved to offer what conditions the English would demand: for Philip reckoned, if he once had the crown on his head, it would be easy for him, with the assistance which his other dominions might give him, to make all these signify little. And for money, the emperor borrowed twelve hundred thousand crowns, (which in English money was 400,000*l*. for the crown was then a noble,) and promised to send it over, to be distributed as Gardiner and his ambassadors should think fit: but made his son bind himself to repay him that sum, when he had once attained the crown of England. And this the emperor made so little a secret, that when, a year after, some towns in Germany, that had lent a part of this money, desired to be repaid; he answered them, that he had lent his son 1,200,000 crowns to marry him to the queen of England, and had yet received of him only 300,000 crowns; but he had good security for the rest, and the merchants were bound to pay him 100,000*l*. sterling: and therefore he demanded a little more time of them. All this was printed soon after at Strasburg, by the English there, in a book which they sent over to England; in which, both the address made by the commons in parliament, and this answer of the emperor's to the towns, is mentioned. And that whole discourse (which is in the form of an address to the queen, the nobility, and the commons) is written with such gravity and simplicity of style, that, as it is by much the best I have seen of this time, so in these public transactions there is no reason to think it untrue. For the things which it relates are credible of themselves; and though the sum there mentioned was very great, yet he that considers that England was to be bought with it, will not think it an extraordinary price. In that discourse it is further said, that as Gardiner corrupted many by bribes, so, in the court of Chancery, common justice was denied to all but those who came into these designs.

1,200,000 crowns sent into England to procure the consent of the nation to the marriage.

The proceedings of the convocation.
[Oct. 6. -
Wilkins'
Conc. iv.
p. 88.]

Having thus given an account of what was done in the parliament, I shall next shew how the convocation proceeded. Bonner, being to preside in it, as being the first bishop of the province of Canterbury, appointed John Harpsfield, his chaplain, to preach, who took his text out of the twentieth of the Acts, (ver. 20.) *Feed the flock*. He ran out in his bidding prayers most profusely on the queen's praises, comparing her to Deborah and Esther[31], with all the servilest flatteries he could invent; next he bid them pray for the lady Elizabeth: but when he came to mention the clergy, he enlarged in the praises of Bonner, Gardiner, Tunstall, Heath, and Day, so grossly, that it seems the strains of flattering churchmen at that time were very coarse; and he ran out so copiously in them, as if he had been to deliver a panegyric, and not to bid the beads. In his sermon he inveighed against the late preachers for not observing fasts, nor keeping Lent, and for their marriages, which he severely condemned.

Disputes
concerning
the sacrament.

Weston, dean of Westminster, was presented prolocutor by the lower house, and approved of by Bonner. Whether any of the bishops that had been made in king Edward's time sat among them, I do not know: but in the lower house there was great opposition made. There had been care taken that there should be none returned to the convocation but such as would comply in all points: but yet there came six non-compliers, who, being deans or archdeacons, had a right to sit in the con- 263

[Ibid.]

vocation. These were, Philpot, archdeacon of Winchester; Philips, dean of Rochester; Haddon, dean of Exeter[32]; Cheyney, archdeacon of Hereford; Aylmer, archdeacon of Stow;

[Fox, vol.
iii. p. 16.]

and Young, chanter of St. David's. Weston the prolocutor proposed to them on the 18th of October, that there had been a Catechism printed in the last year of king Edward's reign in the name of that synod, and, as he understood, it was done without their consents, which was a pestiferous book, and full of heresies; there was likewise a very abominable book of Common Prayer set out: it was therefore the queen's pleasure that they should prepare such laws about religion as she would ratify with her parliament. So he proposed, that they should begin

---

[31] After Esther, add Judith, Mary the sister of Martha, and the Virgin Mary. [S.]

[32] [He is so called both by Fox and Godwin, but his name is omitted by Le Neve in his catalogue of deans.]

with condemning those books, particularly the articles in them contrary to the sacrament of the altar : and he gave out two questions about it, Whether in the sacrament, upon the sanctification of the bread and wine, all their substance did not vanish, being changed into the body and blood of Christ ? and, Whether the natural body of Christ was not corporally present in the eucharist, either by the transubstantiation of the elements into his body and blood, or by the conjunction of concomitance, as some expressed it ? The house was adjourned till the 20th, on which day every man was appointed to give in his answer to these questions. All answered and subscribed in the affirmative, except the six before mentioned. Philpot said, whereas it was given out that the Catechism was not approved by the convocation, though it was printed in their name : it was a mistake ; for the convocation had authorized a number of persons to set forth ecclesiastical laws, to whom they had committed their synodal authority ; so that they might well set out such books in the name of the convocation. He also said, that it was against all order to move men to subscribe in such points before they were examined : and, since the number of these on the one side was so unequal to those on the other side, he desired that Dr. Ridley, Mr. Rogers, and two or three more, might be allowed to come to the convocation. This seemed very reasonable ; so the lower house proposed it to the bishops : they answered, that these persons being prisoners, they could not bring them ; but they should move the council about it. A message also was sent from some great lords, that they intended to hear the disputation : so the house adjourned till the 23rd.

There was then a great appearance of noblemen and others. The prolocutor began with a protestation, that by this dispute they did not intend to call the truth in doubt, to which they had all subscribed ; but they did it only to satisfy the objections of those few who refused to concur with them. But it was denied to let any prisoners, or others, assist them ; for it was said, that that being a dispute among those of the convocation, none but members were to be heard in it. Haddon and Aylmer, foreseeing they should be run down with clamour and noise, refused to dispute ; Young went away : Cheyney being next spoke to, did propose his objections ; that St. Paul calls [Fox, vol. iii. p.17.]

the sacrament *bread* after the consecration; that Origen said, it went into the excrement; and Theodoret said, the bread and wine did not in the sacrament depart from their former *substance, form*, and *shape*. Moreman was called on to answer him : he said, that St. Paul calling it bread was to be understood thus, *the sacrament or form of bread*. To Origen's authority he answered nothing : but to Theodoret he said, the word they render *substance* stood in a more general signification, and so might signify *accidental substance*. Upon this, Aylmer, who had resolved not to dispute, could not contain himself, but said, the Greek word, οὐσία, could not be so understood, for the following words of *form* and *shape* belonged to the accidents, but that only belonged to the substance of the elements. Upon this there followed a contest about the signification of that word. Then Philpot struck in, and said, the occasion of Theodoret's writing plainly shewed that was a vain cavil; for the dispute was with the Eutychians, whether the body and human nature of Christ had yet an existence distinct from the divine nature? The Eutychians said, it was swallowed up by his Godhead; and argued from some expressions used concerning the sacrament, as if the presence of Christ in it had swallowed up the elements : against which Theodoret, according to the orthodox doctrine, argued to prove, that there was in Christ a human nature not swallowed up; and said, that as in the sacrament, notwithstanding the union of Christ with the elements, they did not depart from their *substance, form*, and *shape*, so the human nature of Christ was not absorbed by its union to the Godhead. So it plainly appeared, this word *substance* stood for the nature of the elements. Moreman being straitened in answering this, Philpot said, if he had not an answer ready, he would desire him to think on one against their next meeting : upon this the prolocutor checked him, as if he were bragging too soon. He insisted on his argument, but was commanded to be silent. Haddon upon that proposed another argument from these words of our Saviour, *The poor you have always with you, but me you have not always;* that therefore his body was not in the sacrament. To this the prolocutor answered, that Christ was not to be always with us so as to receive our alms, which is all that was intended by that place : but Haddon brought a copious citation out of St. Austin,

264

applying that very place to prove, that Christ's natural presence was no more on earth after his ascension into heaven.
To this Dr. Watson opposed another place of St. Austin, and [Fox, vol.
some dispute was about those places. After that, Haddon read iii. p. 18.]
more authorities of fathers, asserting that Christ was in heaven,
and not on earth: the words of the institution did plainly express it, both because the sacrament was to be in *remembrance
of Christ, and because it was to continue until his coming
again.* But to this they said, he was not on earth in a bodily
manner: and they endeavoured to take away the force of the
argument from the words, *until his coming again,* by some
other acceptions of the word *until.* But Haddon asked them,
whether they thought Christ did eat his own natural body,
when he instituted and took the sacrament? They said, he
did. Upon that he answered, that that was so absurd, that he
thought it needless to argue more with those who could yield
it: and so he sat down. Philpot argued, that Christ could not
receive his own body in the sacrament, since it was given for
the remission of sins, of which he was not capable, having no
sin: Weston answered, he might receive it, as well as be baptized; but Philpot answered, he was baptized, as he said himself, to be an example to others. So ended this day's dispute.

On the 25th, Philpot, who was ordered to begin that day,
265 had prepared a long discourse in Latin: but Weston inter- [Ibid.
rupted him, and said, he must make no speech, he was only to p. 19.]
propose his arguments, and that in English; though it had
been before ordered that the dispute should be in Latin. Then
Philpot went to explain what sort of presence he would dispute against, and what he allowed. Here Weston again interrupted him, and bid him form his argument. Upon that he fell
down on his knees, and begged of the lords and privy counsellors that were present, that he might have leave to speak his
mind; which they granted him: so, he said, for their sacrifice
of the mass, he would prove that it was no sacrament at all,
and that Christ was no way present in it; which if he should
not do, before the queen and her council, against any six that
would maintain the contrary, he should be willing to be burnt
before the court gates. Upon this there was great outcrying that
he was mad, and talked idly; and Weston threatened to send
him to prison. But this noise being laid, and he claiming the

privilege of the house for the freedom of speech, was required to go on to an argument. Then he proved, that Christ was in heaven; for himself said, *I leave the world, and go to my Father:* and, to prove there was no ambiguity in these words, he observed, that his disciples said upon this, *Now thou speakest plainly, without any parable.* It was answered by Dr. Chedsey, that those words were only meant of his visible ascension, but did not exclude his invisible presence: and he cited some words of Chrysostom's, that Christ took his flesh with him, and also left his flesh behind him. Weston and the rest said, that authority was unanswerable; and for a while would not

[Fox, vol. iii. p. 20.]

hear his answer. But Philpot shewed him, that Chrysostom's words must be understood in a large sense, as believers are said to be flesh of his flesh; for that father applies that also to baptism from these words, *As many as are baptized into Christ have put on Christ:* so the flesh that Christ left on earth, according to him, is not the corporal presence in the sacrament. Upon this, Pye, dean of Chichester, whispered somewhat to the prolocutor; who thereupon said to Philpot, that he had disputed enough. He answered, that he had a dozen of arguments, and they were enjoining him silence before he had got through one of them. They threatened to send him to prison if he spoke more. He said, that was far from the promise they had made of hearing them fully; and from what was preached last Sunday at Paul's, that all things should be answered in this disputation. But Pye said, he should be answered another way. Philpot replied, there was a company of them now got together, who had heretofore dissembled with God and the world; and were now met to suppress God's truth, and to set forth false devices, which they were not able to maintain. After this Aylmer stood up, and brought many authorities out of Greek authors, to prove that οὐσία in Theodoret could only be understood of the *substance* of bread and wine: and Moreman desired a day's time to consider of them. Then Pern, though he had subscribed with the rest, brought some arguments against transubstantiation: for which the prolocutor chid him, since he had before subscribed. Aylmer answered, that it was against the freedom of the house for any to be so chid for

[Ibid. p. 21.]

delivering his conscience. It was now become late; so they adjourned to the 27th.

266   Then they again disputed about Theodoret's words, where
Haddon shewed, that he said the symbols retained the same
substance that they had before.   After that, Cheyney fell to
argue about those words: he acknowledged a real presence,
but denied transubstantiation, and pressed Theodoret's authority so close, that Watson said he was a Nestorian; and if
Theodoret, who was but one, was of their side, there was above
a hundred fathers against them.   Upon this Cheyney quoted
Irenæus, who had said, that our flesh was nourished by the
bread and wine in the sacrament.   He also cited Hesychius,
who said, that in the church of Jerusalem the symbols that
were not consumed in the communion were burnt afterwards:
he desired to know, whether the ashes were the body of Christ,
or what it was that was burnt?   To all this Harpsfield made a [Fox, vol.
long answer concerning God's omnipotence, and the weakness iii. p. 22.]
of men's understandings, that could not comprehend divine
mysteries.   But Cheyney still asked, what it was that was
burnt?   Harpsfield replied, it was either the substance of
bread, or the body of Christ; and afterwards said, it was a
miracle.   At that Cheyney smiled, and said, then he could say
no more.   Weston asked, whether there was not enough said
in answer to these men's objections?   Many of the clergy cried
out, *Yes, yes*: but the multitude with repeated cries said, *No,
no*.   Weston said, he spake to those of the house, and not to
the rude multitude.   Then he asked those divines, whether
they would now for three days answer the arguments that
should be put to them?   Haddon, Cheyney, and Aylmer said,
they would not: but Philpot offered to do it.   Weston said, he
was a madman, and fitter to be sent to Bedlam.   Philpot said,
he, that had carried himself with so much passion and so little
indifferency, deserved a room there much better.   Weston, neglecting him, turned to the assembly, and said, they might see
what sort of men these were, whom they had now answered
three days: but though they had promised it, and the order
of disputation did require it, that they should answer in their
turn three days, they now declined it.   Upon that Aylmer
stood up and answered, that they had made no such promise,
nor undertaken any such disputation; but being required to
give their reasons why they would not subscribe with the rest,
they had done it, but had received no answer to them, and

therefore would enter into no further disputation before such
judges, who had already determined and subscribed those questions. So the house was adjourned to the 30th; and then
Philpot appeared to answer, but desired first leave to prosecute
his former argument, and urged, that since Christ as man is
like us in all things without sin, therefore as we are restrained
to one place at a time, so is Christ but in one place, and that

[Fox, vol.
iii. p. 23.]
is heaven; for St. Peter says, *The heavens must contain him
till the restitution of all things.* To this it was answered, that
Christ being God, his omnipotence was above our understanding; and that to shut him in one place was to put him in prison. Philpot said, he was not speaking of his divine nature, but
that as he was man he was like us: and for their saying, that
Christ was not to be imprisoned in heaven, he left to all men
to judge whether that was a good answer or not. Much discourse following upon this, the prolocutor commanded him to

[Ibid.
p. 24.]
come no more into the house. He answered, he thought himself happy to be out of their company. Others suggesting to
the prolocutor, that it would be said the meeting was not free, 267
if men were put out of the house for speaking their minds; he
said to him, he might come, so he were decently habited, and
did not speak but when he commanded him. To this he answered, that he had rather be absent altogether. Weston concluded all by saying, You have the *word*, but we have the
sword; truly pointing out wherein the strength of both causes
lay.

Censures
passed up-
on it.
This was the issue of that disputation: which was soon after
printed in English; and in Latin by Valerandus Pollanus[32], and
is inserted at large in Fox's Acts and Monuments. What account the other side gave of it, I do not find. But, upon all
such occasions, the prevailing party, when the inequality was
so disproportioned, used to carry things with so much noise and
disorder, that it was no wonder the reformers had no mind to
engage in this dispute. And those who reflected on the way of
proceeding in king Edward's time, could not but confess things
had been managed with much more candour and equality. For

---

[32] [Pollanus (Valerandus,) Vera
Expositio disputationis institutæ
mandato D. Mariæ Reginæ Angliæ
et Hiberniæ in Synodo Ecclesias-
tlcâ, Londini in comitiis Regni ad
18 Octob. anno 1553. Romæ, 1554.
16mo.]

in this very point there had been, as was formerly shewn, disputes for a year together, before there was any determination made: so that all men were free at that time to deliver their opinions without any fear; and then the disputes were in the universities, where, as there were a great silence, and collection of books, so the auditors were more capable of being instructed by them: but here the point was first determined, and then disputed; and this was in the midst of the disorder of the town, where the privy-council gave all possible encouragement to the prevailing party.

The last thing I find done this year was, the restoring Veysey to be bishop of Exeter, which was done on the 28th of December[33]. In his warrant for it under the great seal it is [Rymer, said, that he, for some just troubles both in body and mind, had xv. p. 340.] resigned his bishopric to king Edward, to which the queen now restored him. And thus ended this year. Foreign affairs did not so much concern religion, as they had done in the former reign; which, as it made me give some account of them then, so it causes me now not to prosecute them so fully.

In the beginning of the next year the emperor sent over the 1554. count of Egmont, and some other ambassadors, to make the Ambassadors sent proposition and treaty of marriage betwixt his son and the from the queen. In the managing of this treaty Gardiner had the chief emperor for the hand; for he was now the oracle at the council-board: he had marriage. thirty years' experience in affairs, a great knowledge of the [Holinshed, p. courts of Christendom and of the state of England, and had 1093.] great sagacity, with a marvellous cunning, which was not always regulated by the rules of candour and honesty. He, in drawing the articles of the marriage, had a double design: the one was, to have them so framed that they might easily pass in parliament; and the other was, to exclude the Spaniards from having any share in the government of England, which he intended to hold in his own hands. So the terms on which it was agreed were these:

---

[33] ['The register of Canterbury before mentioned recordeth that Veysey was restored to his bishopric because he had been induced by fear to resign it in the time of King Edward. The author of Athenæ Oxonienses saith, that he was forced to resign *pro corporis metu* 1551 August 14, and was restored by the queen's patent bearing date 1553, September 28.' Specimen of Errors, p. 129. This is also the date in the Patent Roll as printed in Rymer.]

The articles
agreed.
[Rymer,
xv. p. 377.] The queen should have the whole government of England, with the giving of offices and benefices, in her own hands: so that though Philip was to be called king, and his name was to be on the coin, and the seals, and in writs, yet her hand was to give force to every thing without his. Spaniards should not be admitted into the government, nor to any offices at court. 268 The laws should not be altered, nor the pleadings put into any other tongue. The queen should not be made to go out of England, but upon her own desire. The children born in the marriage should not go out of England, but by the consent of the nobility. If the queen outlived the prince, she should have 60,000*l.* a year out of his estate, 40,000 out of Spain, and [Ibid.
p. 379.] 20,000 of it out of the Netherlands. If the queen had sons by him, they should succeed, both to her own crowns, and the Netherlands, and Burgundy: and if the archduke Charles, Philip's only son, died, they should succeed to all her and his dominions. If she had only daughters, they should succeed to her crowns, and the Netherlands, if they married by their brother's consent; or otherwise, they should have such portions as was ordinarily given to those of their rank: but if the queen had no issue, the king was not to pretend to any part of the government after her death; but the crown was to descend, [Ibid.
p. 381.] according to the laws of England, to her heirs. There was to be a perpetual league betwixt England and Spain; but this was not to be in prejudice of their league with France, which was still to continue in force.

These were the conditions agreed on, and afterwards confirmed in parliament: by which it appears, the Spaniards were resolved to have the marriage on any terms; reckoning, that if prince Philip were once in England, he could easily enlarge his authority, which was hereby so much restrained.

The match
generally
disliked.
[Stow,
p. 618.] It was now apparent, the queen was to marry the prince of Spain, which gave an universal discontent to the whole nation. All that loved the reformation saw, that not only their religion would be changed, but a Spanish government and inquisition would be set up in its stead. Those who considered the civil liberties of the kingdom, without great regard to religion, concluded, that England would become a province to Spain; and they saw how they governed the Netherlands, and heard how they ruled Milan, Naples, and Sicily: but above all, they heard

the most inhuman things, that ever any age produced, had been acted by them in their new conquest in the West Indies.

It was said, What might they expect, but to lie at the mercy of such tyrannical masters, who would not be long kept within the limits that were now prescribed? All the great conditions now talked of were but the gilding the pill; but its operation would be fatal, if they once swallowed it down. These things had influence on many; but the chief conspirators were, the duke of Suffolk, sir Thomas Wiat [33], and sir Peter Carew: the one was to raise the midland counties, the other to raise Cornwall, and Wiat was to raise Kent; hoping, by rising in such remote places so to distract the government, that they should be able to engage the commons, who were now as much distasted with the queen, as they had been formerly fond of her. Plots to oppose it. [Godwin, p. 340.]

But as Carew was carrying on his design in the west, it came to be discovered; and one that he had trusted much in it was taken: upon that Carew fled over into France. Wiat was in Kent when he heard this; but had not yet laid his business as he intended: therefore, fearing to be undone by the discovery that was made, he gathered some men about him, and on the 25th of January went to Maidstone. There he made proclamation, that he intended nothing but to preserve the liberty of the nation, and keep it from coming under the yoke of strangers; which, he said, all the council, one or two excepted, were against: and assured the people, that all the nobility and chief men of England would concur with them. He said nothing of religion, but in private assured those that were for the reformation, that he would declare for them. One Roper came, and declared him and his company traitors; but he took him, with some gentlemen that were gathering to oppose him. From thence he went to Ro..nester, and writ to the sheriff of Kent, desiring his assistance against the strangers; for there were already, as he said, an hundred armed Spaniards landed at Dover. The sheriff sent him word, that, if he and those with him had any suits, they were to make them to the queen on their knees, but not with swords in their hands; and required them to disperse under pain of treason. Wiat kept his men in good order, so that they did no hurt, but only took all the arms they could find. Are discovered. Wiat breaks out. [Holinshed, p. 1093.]

269

[33] [See Part iii. p. 224.]

[Jan. 27,
Holinshed,
p. 1094.]
At the same time one Isley and Knevet gathered people together about Tunbridge, and went to join with Wiat. The queen sent down a herald to him with a pardon, if he would disperse his company in twenty-four hours; but Wiat made him deliver his message at the end of Rochester-bridge, and so sent him away. The high sheriff gathered together as many as he could, and shewed them how they were abused by lies: there was no Spaniards landed at all; and those that were to come were to be their friends and confederates against their enemies. Those that he brought together went to Gravesend to meet the duke of Norfolk and sir Henry Jerningham, who were come thither with six hundred[34] men from London; and they, hearing that Knevet was in his way to Rochester, went, and intercepted, and routed him: sixty of his men were killed, the rest saved themselves in the woods.

The news of this disheartened Wiat much, who was seen to weep; and called for a coat, which he stuffed with angels, designing to have escaped. But the duke of Norfolk marching to Rochester with 200 horse and 600 foot, commanded by one Bret, they were wrought on by a pretended deserter, Harper, who seemed to come over from Wiat: he persuaded the Londoners, that it was only the preservation of the nation from the Spaniards that they designed; and it was certain none would suffer under that yoke more than they. This had such an effect on them, that they all cried out, *We are all Englishmen;* and went over to Wiat. So the duke of Norfolk was forced to march back. And now Kent was all open to Wiat, who thereupon sent one to the duke of Suffolk, pressing him to make haste and raise his country; but the bearer was intercepted. Upon that, the earl of Huntingdon was sent down with some horse to seize on him. The duke was at all times a mean-spirited man; but it never appeared more than now: for, after a faint endeavour to raise the country, he gave it over, and concealed himself in a private house; but was betrayed by him to whom he had trusted himself, into the hands of the earl of Huntingdon, and so was brought to the Tower.

The Londoners revolt.

Wiat's party increasing, they turned towards London. As they came to Deptford, sir Edward Hastings and sir Thomas

34 [Apparently a mistake of the author's for *five hundred.* The account seems taken from Holinshed, p. 1094.]

Cornwallis came to them, in the queen's name, to ask what
270 would content them? Wiat desired, that he might have the Wiat's de-
command of the Tower; that the queen might stay under his mands.
guard; and that the council might be changed.   Upon these
extravagant propositions there passed high words, and the
privy counsellors returned to the queen.   After this she went [Holinshed,
into Guildhall, and there gave an account of her message to p. 1096.]
Wiat, and his answer.   And for her marriage, she said, she did
nothing in it but by advice of her council; and spoke very
tenderly of the love she bore to her people, and to that city.
On the 31st Wiat was become 4000 strong, and came near
Southwark.   On the second of February he fell into South- He came to
wark.   Some of his company had a mind to have broken into [Feb. 3.
Winchester-house, and robbed it; but he threatened to hang Stow,
any that should do it.   He was put in hope, that, upon his p. 619.]
coming to Southwark, London would have declared for him;
but in that he was deceived: the bridge was fortified, so that
he found it was not possible to force it.   Here he held a council of war with his officers: some were for turning back into
Kent, to disperse a body of men that the lord Abergavenny
had gathered together; but he said, that was a small game:
the strength of their party was in London, and therefore it
was necessary for him to be there as soon as he could; for,
though they could not open the bridge to him, yet he was
assured, if he were on the other side, many would come out to
him.   Some were for crossing over to Essex, where they heard
the people were well affected to them; but they had not boats
enough, so he marched to get over at Kingston-bridge.

On the fourth they came to Kingston, where the queen had He crossed
ordered the bridge to be cut: but his men repairing it, he at King-
crossed the river that night; and, though he lost much time ston;
by the mending of one of his carriages that broke by the way, Holinshed,
he was at Hyde-park by nine of the clock next morning, it p. 1098.]
being Ash Wednesday.   [Feb. 7.]

The earl of Pembroke had gathered a good body of men to But is de-
have fallen on him, for his men were now in great disorder; feated,
but they looked on, to let him cast himself into their hands.
He did not march by Holborn, as some advised, but came down
to Charing Cross.   There the lord Clinton fell in between the
several bodies of his men, and dispersed them so, that he had

not 500 left about him : but, with those that remained, he passed through the Strand and Fleet-street to Ludgate, where he stopped, in hopes to have found the gates open to him. That hope failing, he returned back ; and, being now out of all heart, was taken at Temple-bar by a herald. All this while the queen shewed great courage ; she would not stir out of Whitehall, nor go by water to the Tower, as some advised her, but went with her women and priests to her devotions.

And taken.

This was a rebellion both raised and dispersed in as strange a manner as could have been imagined. Wiat was a popular and stout man, but had not a head for such an undertaking; otherwise the government was so feeble, that it had not been a difficult thing to have driven the queen to great straits. It was not at all raised upon pretence of religion ; which, according to the printed account set out by the queen's order, was not so much as once named. And yet some of our own writers say, that Poynet, the late bishop of Winchester, was in it[35]. But this is certainly false : for so many prisoners being taken, it is not to be imagined but this would have been found out, and published, to make that religion more odious; and we cannot think but Gardiner would have taken care that he should have been attainted in the following parliament.

[Stow, p. 620.]
Poynet was not in that rebellion.

271

Christopherson soon after writ a book [36] against rebellion, in which he studies to fasten this rising on the preachers of the new religion, as he calls it ; and gives some presumptions, that amount to no more but little flourishes of his wit, but never names this, which had been a decisive proof. So that it is but a groundless fiction, made by those who have either been the

---

[35] Poynet wrote a book to justify the resisting the Queen, which I have seen. [S.] [This book is entitled, 'A short treatise of Politic Power,' &c. The initials on the title page are D. J. P. B. R. W. It seems doubtful who was the author. That he was in the rebellion is asserted by Stow, who is followed by Heylyn. See Collier ii. 363.

The following extract from Machyn's Diary refers to Poynet. 'The 27 day of July was the nuw bisshope of W...... was devorsyd from the bucher wyff with

shame enogh,' p. 8.]

[36] [An exhortation to all menne to take hede and beware of rebellion : wherein are set forth the causes that commonly moue men to rebellion, and that no cause is there that ought to moue any man thereunto, with a discourse of the miserable effects that ensue thereof, and of the wretched ends that all rebelles come to, most necessary to be redde in this seditiouse and troublesome tyme; made by John Christoferson. London, 1554, 16mo.]

authors, or at least have laid down the principles of all the rebellions in the Christian world; and yet would cast that blame
on others, and exempt themselves from it, as if they were the
surest friends of princes, while they design to enslave them to
a foreign power, and will neither allow them to reign, nor to
live, but at the mercy of the head of that principality, to which
all other powers must bend, or break, if they meet with an age
that is so credulous and superstitious as to receive their dictates [37].

This raw and soon-broken rebellion was as lucky to Gardiner, and those who set on the marriage, as if they had projected it: for now the people were much disheartened, and
their own designs as much fortified; since, as some fevers are
critical, and cast out those latent distempers, which no medicines could effectually purge away, and yet, if they were not
removed, must in the end corrupt the whole mass of blood;
so in a weak government, to which the people are ill-affected,
ill-digested rebellions raise the prince higher, and add as much
spirit to his friends as they take from the faction against him,
and give a handle to do some things, for which otherwise it
were not easy, either to find colours or instruments.

One effect of this [38] was, the proceeding severely against the The lady
lady Jane, and her husband the lord Guilford, who both suf- Jane and
her hus-
fered on the twelfth of February. The lady Jane was not band exe-
much disordered at it: for she knew, upon the first jealousy, cuted.
she must be the sacrifice; and therefore had now lived six
months in the continual meditations of death. Feckenham, [Godwin,
afterwards abbot of Westminster, was sent to her by the queen, p. 342.]
three days before, to prepare her to die. He had a long conversation with her; but she answered him with that calmness
of mind, and clearness of reason, that it was an astonishing
thing to hear so young a person of her sex and quality look on
death, so near her, with so little disorder, and talk so sensibly,
both of faith and holiness, of the sacrament, the scriptures, and
the authority of the church. Feckenham left her, seeing he
could work nothing on her; but procured, as is said, the continuance of her life three days longer, and waited on her on

[37] [For a most minute and particular account of this rebellion, see
'The Chronicle of Queen Jane,'

published by the Camden Society,
1850.]
    [38] [See Part iii. p. 225.]

the scaffold. She writ to her father to moderate his grief for
her death; (which must needs have been great, since his folly
had occasioned it.) " She expressed her sense of her sin in
" assuming the royal dignity, though he knew how unwillingly
" she was drawn to it; and that, in her royal estate, her en-
" forced honour had never defiled her innocent heart. She
" rejoiced at her approaching end; since nothing could be to
" her more welcome, than to be delivered from that valley of
" misery, into that heavenly throne, to which she was to be
" advanced, where she prayed that they might meet at last."

There was one Harding [39] that had been her father's chap- 272
lain, and that was a zealous preacher in king Edward's days;
before whose death he had animated the people much to prepare for persecution, and never to depart from the truth of the
gospel: but he had now fallen away himself. To him she writ
a letter full of severe expostulations and threatenings for his
apostasy; but it had no effect on him. It is of an extraordinary
strain, full of life in the thoughts, and of zeal, if there is not
too much, in the expressions. The night before her execution
she sent her Greek Testament, which she had always used, to
her sister, with a letter in the same [40] language; in which, in
most pathetic expressions, she sets out the value that she had
of it, and recommended the study and practice of it earnestly
to her. She had also composed a very devout prayer for her
retirements; and thus had she spent the last moments of her
life. She expressed great tenderness, when she saw her husband led out first; but soon overcame it, when she considered
how closely she was to follow him. He had desired to take
leave of her before he died; but she declined it, since it would
be rather an increase of grief, than any addition of comfort to
them. She said, she hoped they would shortly meet, and be
united in a happier state; and with a settled countenance she
saw them bring back the beheaded body to the chapel, where

[39] Thomas Harding, afterwards
antagonist to Bishop Jewel. [G.]
[40] The letter I suppose must have
been wrote in English, as it stands
in Fox, vol. iii. p. 35, and as printed
amongst the letters of the martyrs,
p. 662. [B.] That lady, under her
picture, is said to have been *nata*

1537. According to Ascham, who
may be supposed to have given in
her age at lowest, she was aged fifteen in the year 1550; when he
found her reading Plato's Phædon in
Greek; which was very unusual at
that age, but would have been extraordinary indeed at thirteen. [B.]

it was to be buried. When she was brought to the scaffold, [Holin-
which was raised for her within the Tower, to prevent the shed, p.
compassion which her dying more publicly might have raised, 1099.]
she confessed she had sinned in taking the queen's honour,
when it was given her : she acknowledged the act was unlawful,
as was also her consenting to it; but, she said, it was neither
procured nor desired by her. She declared, that she died a
true Christian; and hoped to be saved only by the mercy of
God in the blood of Christ. She acknowledged that she had
too much neglected the word of God, and had loved herself
and the world too much, for which that punishment had come
justly to her from God: but she blessed him that had made it
a means to lead her to repentance. Then, having desired the
people's prayers, she kneeled down and repeated the 51st
Psalm. Then she undressed herself, and stretched out her
head on the block, and cried out, *Lord, into thy hands I recommend my spirit :* and so her head was cut off.

All people lamented her sad and untimely end, which was
not easily consented to, even by the queen herself. Her death [Fox, vol.
had a most violent operation on judge Morgan, that had pro- iii. p. 30.]
nounced the sentence : soon after, he fell mad; and, in all his
ravings, still called to take away the lady Jane from him. Indeed the blame of her death was generally cast on her father
rather than on the queen, since the rivalry of a crown is a
point of such niceness, that even those who bemoaned her death
most could not but excuse the queen, who seemed to be driven
to it, rather from considerations of state, than any resentment
of her own. On the 17th of February was the duke of Suffolk Her fa-
tried by his peers, and condemned : he suffered on the [41] 21st. ther's exe-
He would have died more pitied for his weakness, if his prac- cution.
tices had not brought his daughter to her end. Next, Wiat [Stow, p.
was brought to his trial; where, in most abject words, he 622.]
begged his life, and offered to promote the queen's marriage, if [April 11.
273 they would spare him : but for all that he was beheaded. Bret Stow, p.
was hanged in chains at Rochester. In all, fifty-eight were 623.]
executed in several places, whose attainders were confirmed by
an act of the following parliament; six hundred of the rabble
were appointed to come before the queen with halters about
their necks, and to beg their lives, which she granted them:

[41] For twenty-first, read twenty-third. [S.]

and so was this storm dissipated. Only the effusion of blood after it was thought too liberal; and this excess of punishment was generally cast on Gardiner, and made him become very hateful to the nation, which has been always much moved at a repetition of such sad spectacles.

The lady Elizabeth unjustly suspected for plotting.

The earl of Devonshire and the lady Elizabeth came to be suspected of the plot, as if the rising in the west had been set on by the earl, with design, if it had succeeded, to have married the lady Elizabeth, and put her in the queen's room. Wiat did at his death clear them of any occasion to his confederacies. Yet the queen, who was much alienated from her sister upon old scores, was not unwilling to find a pretence for using her

[March 17. Holinshed, p. 1101.]

ill; so she was made a prisoner. And the earl of Devonshire had, upon the account formerly mentioned, offended the queen, who thought her kindness ill requited, when she saw he neglected her, and preferred her sister; so he was again put into

Many severe proceedings.

prison. Sir Nicholas Throgmorton was also charged with that same guilt, and brought to his trial, which lasted ten hours; but was acquitted by the jury: upon which they were cast into prison, and severely fined, some in two thousand pounds, and some in a thousand marks. This was fatal to his brother sir John, who was cast by the jury upon the same evidence that his brother had been acquitted; but he protested his innocence to the last. Sir John Cheke[42] had got beyond sea, finding he was also suspected and sought after; and both sir Peter Carew and he, hoping that Philip would be glad at his first admission to the crown of England to shew acts of favour, went into Flanders; where, upon assurances given of pardon and mercy, they rendered themselves[43]: but, upon their coming into England, they were both put into the Tower. Carew made his escape, and was afterwards employed by queen Elizabeth in her affairs in Ireland. Cheke was at this time discharged; but, upon some new offence, he was taken again in Flanders, in May 1556, and was prevailed upon to renounce his religion, and then he was set at liberty: but was so sadly affected at the unworthiness of that action, that it was believed to have cast

[42] Cheke was sent to the Tower with the duke of Suffolk, and had license to travel. [S.]

[43] They did not render themselves, but were seized in their journey, bound and thrown into a cart, and sent prisoners to England. [S.]

him into a languishing, of which he soon after died.   There
was a base imposture set up at this time, of one that seeméd to
speak from a wall with a strange sort of voice.   Many seditious
things were uttered by that voice, which was judged of variously.   Some called it the *spirit of the wall.*   Some said it
was an angel that spake; and many marvellous things were
reported of it: but the matter being narrowly inquired into, it
was found to be one Elizabeth Crofts, a girl, who, from a private hole in the wall, with the help of a whistle, had uttered
those words.   She was made to do penance openly at Paul's
for it; but, by the account then printed of it, I do not find any
complices [44] were found, except one Drake, to whom no particular character is added.   So it seems it was a trick laid betwixt these two; for what purpose I cannot find.   Sure enough,
in those times, it was not laid to the charge of the preachers of
the reformation.   Which I the rather take notice of, because of
the malignity of one of our historians, who has laid this to the
274 charge of the Zuinglian gospellers, though all the proof he
offers for casting it on them is in these words; *For I cannot
consider this but as a plot of theirs;* and sets it up in opposition to the notorious imposture of the Maid of Kent, mentioned in the former volume, and says, *Let not the papists be
more charged with that, since these were now as faulty.*

The nation being now settled, the queen did next give instructions to the bishops to proceed to visit the clergy, according to some articles which she sent them, which will be found
in the Collections.   In those, after a long and invidious preamble of the disorders that had been in the time of king Edward,
she commanded them to execute all such ecclesiastical laws as
had been in force in her father's reign: that the bishops should
in their courts proceed no more in the queen's name: that the
oath of supremacy should be no more exacted of any of the
clergy: that none suspected of heresy should be admitted to
orders: that they should endeavour to repress heresy, and
punish heretics: that they should suppress all naughty books
and ballads: that they should remove all married clergymen,
and separate them from their wives; but for those that re-

Margin notes:
The impos-
ture of the
spirit in
the wall.
[Holin-
shed, p.
1117.]

[Stow, p.
624.]

The in-
structions
to the bi-
shops.
Collect.
Numb. 10.

---

[44] Seven persons were discovered
to be complices; the words spoken
from the wall were against the
queen, the prince of Spain, the mass,
and confession. [S.]

nqunced their wives, they might put them into some other cure, or reserve a pension out of their benefice for them: that no religious man who had professed chastity should be suffered to live with his wife: that care should be taken of vacant churches; that, till they were provided, the people should go to the neighbouring churches: that all the ceremonies, holydays, and fasts, used in king Henry's time, should be again observed: that those who were ordained by the new book in King Edward's time, not being ordained in very deed, the bishop, if they were otherwise sufficient, should supply what was wanting before, and so admit them to minister: that the bishops should set forth an uniform doctrine of homilies; and compel the people to come to church and hear divine service: that they should carefully look to all schoolmasters and teachers of children: and that the bishops should take care to set forth the premises, with all kind of virtue, godly living, and good example; and endeavour to keep down all sort of vice.

[Fox, vol. iii. p. 31.]
Proceedings against the bishops that adhered to the reformation.

These were signed on the 4th of March, and printed, and sent over the kingdom. But, to make the married bishops examples of the severity of their proceedings, the queen gave a special commission[45] to Gardiner, Tonstall, Bonner, Parfew bishop of St. Asaph, Day, and Kitchin of Llandaff, making mention, "that with great grief of heart she had heard, that "the archbishop of York, the bishops of St. David's, Chester, "and Bristol, had broken their vows, and defiled their func-"tion, by contracting marriage: therefore those, or any three "of them, are empowered to call them before them; and, if "the premises be found to be true, to deprive and turn them "out of their bishoprics." This I have put into the Collec-

Collect. Numb. 11. 12.

tion, with another commission to the same persons, "to call the "bishops of Lincoln, Gloucester, and Hereford before them; "in whose patents it was provided, that they should hold their

---

[45] [The dates of the deprivations are preserved in the diary of Henry Machyn, published by the Camden Society— 'The 16 day of Marche was deprevyd the archebysshope of Yorke and the bysshope of Lynkolne, doctur Tayller, and the bysshope of Chester, the bysshope of sant Davys. The 17 day of Marche was deprevyd the bysshope of Harfford and the bysshope of Glosetur; commyssyonars that dyd depreyffe them, my lord chansseler and my lord of Durram, my lord of Londun, my lord of Chechastur, and my lord of sant Asse.']

" bishoprics so long as they behaved themselves well: and
" since they, by preaching erroneous doctrine, and by inor-
" dinate life and conversation, as she credibly understood, had
" carried themselves contrary to the laws of God, and the
" practice of the universal church; these, or any two of them,
" should proceed against them, either according to ecclesiastical
" canons, or the laws of the land, and declare their bishoprics
275 " void, as they were indeed already void." Thus were seven
bishops all at a dash turned out. It was much censured,
that, there having been laws made allowing marriage to the
clergy, the queen should by her own authority, upon the repealing these laws, turn out bishops for things that had been so
well warranted by law: for the repeal was only an annulling of
the law for the future, but did not void it from the beginning:
so that however it might have justified proceedings against
them for the future, if they had lived with their wives, yet it
could not warrant the punishing them for what was past; and
even the severest popes, or their legates, who had pressed the
celibate most, had always, before they proceeded to deprive any
priests for marriage, left it to their choice, whether they would
quit their wives or their benefices; but had never summarily
turned them out for being married. And for the other bishops,
it was an unheard-of way of procedure, for the queen, before
any process was made, to empower delegates to declare their
sees void, as they were indeed already void. This was to give
sentence before hearing. And all this was done by virtue of
the queen's supremacy; for though she thought that a sinful
and schismatical power, yet she was easily persuaded to use it
against the reformed clergy, and to turn them out of their
benefices upon such unjust and illegal pretences. So that now
the proceedings against Gardiner and Bonner, in which were
the greatest stretches made that had been in the last reign,
were far outdone by those new delegates. For the archbishop
of York, though he was now turned out, yet he was still kept
prisoner; till king Philip, among the acts of grace he did at
his coming over, procured his liberty. But his see was not
filled till February next; for then Heath had his *congé d'élire*. [Feb. 19.
On or before [46] the 18th of March this year were those other ¹555.]

---

[46] ['The register of Canterbury, in
which all these deprivations are   recorded, testifieth that on the 20th
of March, 1554, the bishops of Win-

[March 19.
Rymer, xv.
p. 374.] sees declared vacant: for that day did the *congé d'élire* go out to the deans and chapters of St. David's, Lincoln, Hereford, Chester, Gloucester, and Bristol; for Morgan, White, Parfew, [May 10.] Cotes, Brookes, and Holyman.   Goodrich of Ely died in April this [47] year.   He seems to have complied with the time, as he had done often before; for he was not at all cast into any trouble, which it cannot be imagined he could have escaped, since he had put the great seal to the patents for the lady Jane, if he had not redeemed it by a ready consenting to the changes that were to be made.   He was a busy secular spirited man, and had given himself up wholly to factions and intrigues of state; so that, though his opinion had always leaned to the reformation, it is no wonder if a man so tempered would prefer the keeping of his bishopric before the discharge of his conscience.
[Oct. 28.] Thirlby of Norwich was translated to Ely, and Hopton was made bishop of Norwich [48].   But Scory, that had been bishop of Chichester, though, upon Day's being restored, he was turned out of his bishopric, did comply merely: he came before Bonner, and renounced his wife, and did penance for it, and had his absolution under his seal the 14th of July this year;

chester, London, Chichester, and Durham, by virtue of the Queen's commission directed to them, pronounced the sentence of deprivation upon John Taylor, Bp. of Lincoln, *ob nullitatem consecrationis ejus et defectum tituli sui quem habuit a Rege Edwardo Sexto per literas patentes cum hâc clausulâ dum bene se gesserit*, upon John Hooper, bishop of Worcester and Gloucester, *propter conjugium et alia mala merita et vitiosum titulum ut supra*, upon John Harlowe, bishop of Hereford, *propter conjugium, et heresin, et ut supra*, upon John Bird, bishop of Chester, *propter conjugium*.   No sentence of deprivation was pronounced at that time upon Bush, bishop of Bristol. Whether he evaded it by renouncing his marriage, or by any other submission, is uncertain.   But he was never deprived.   However, willingly or unwillingly he resigned his bishopric in June following.   For in the same register the dean and chapter of Canterbury assumed the spiritual jurisdiction of the see of Bristol, void *per spontaneam resignationem Pauli Bushe*. 1554. *Junii* 21.' Specimen of Errors, p. 133.]

[47] There is an institution upon his register by his authority, May 9th, 1554.   And in a catalogue of their bishops upon their black book it is said Decimo Maii, anno Domini 1554,—mortem obiit apud Somersham, &c.   This, I think, has been taken notice of; I only mention it because it is from unquestionable authority.   [B.]   [Harmer also says (Specimen of Errors, p. 134) 'he died in May, either on the ninth or tenth day of the month.']

[48] Hopton, by the register of Canterbury, was consecrated the 28th of October.   Anthony Harmer, p. 134, says it was the 25th of October. [S.]

which is in the Collection. But it seems this was out of fear; Numb. 13.
for he soon after fled out of England, and lived beyond sea until queen Elizabeth's days, and then he came over: but it was
judged indecent to restore him to his former see, where it is
likely this scandal he had given was known; and so he was
made bishop of Hereford. The bishop of Bath and Wells,
276 Barlow, was also made to resign, as appears by the *congé
d'élire* for Bourne to succeed him, dated the 19th of March.
Therein it is said, that the see was vacant by the resignation of
the former bishop; though, in the election that was made on
the 28th of March, it is said, the see was vacant by the removal or deprivation of their former bishop. But I incline to
believe it truer, that he did resign[49]; since he is not mentioned
in the commissions formerly spoken of. But that was not all;
for at this time a book was set out in his name[50], whether
written by him, or forged and laid on his name, I cannot judge,
in which he retracts his former errors, and speaks of Luther
and Œcolampadius, and many others, with whom, he says, he
had familiarly conversed, with great bitterness. He also ac-
cuses the gospellers in England of gluttony, hypocrisy, pride,
and ill nature: and indeed it is one of the most virulent invec-
tives against the reformation that was written at that time.
But it is not likely, if he had turned so heartily as the strain of
that book runs, that he would have been quite thrown out[51]:
especially since he had never married[52], so I rather look on it

[49] ['It is most certain that Barlow
did resign. For in the aforesaid
register is a commission granted to
certain persons, by the dean and
chapter of Canterbury, to act during
the vacancy of the see of Bath and
Wells, which is there said to be
void *per liberam et spontaneam resignationem Willielmi Barlowe ultimi episcopi et pastoris ejusdem,*
This Commission was given between 20th December, 1553, and
25th March, 1554.' Specimen of
Errors, p. 135.]

[50] [A dialogue describing the original ground of these Lutheran
factions, and many of their abuses,
Lond. 8vo. 1553.]

[51] [See the note to part I, p. 18.

where this passage is alluded to;—
The conclusion of that note appears to have been written by the
author, though printed in the folio
edition as if it had been sent to him
by his unknown correspondent.]

[52] Especially since he had never
married. Query,—whether he were
not at that time married? Sir John
Harington, in his Continuation
of bishop Godwin, and who by his
being of Somersetshire, was the
better capacitated to know, says, that
he had some sons, one whereof in
his time was a worthy member of the
church of Wells, and five daughters.
[G.] He was married, and had seven sons and five daughters. [S.]

as a forgery cast on his name, to disgrace the reformation. He
fled beyond sea, where he lived till the beginning of queen
Elizabeth's reign; and then it seems there was some offence
taken at his former behaviour, for he was not restored to Bath
and Wells, but put into Chichester, that was a much meaner [52]
bishopric. Thus I have given a clear account, and free of all
partiality or reservation, of the changes made in the most of the
sees in England. The two archbishops, Cranmer and Holgate; the bishops, Ridley, Poynet, Scory, Coverdale, Taylor,
Harvey [53], Bird, Bush, Hooper, Ferrar, and Barlow, were all
removed; Rochester was void, and Griffith was put into it
[April 1.] this April. Goodrich dying now, Thirlby succeeded him;
[Sept. 25.] and Sampson of Coventry and Lichfield dying soon after,
Bayne succeeded him. So here were sixteen new bishops
brought in, which made no small change in the church.

The mass   When this was done, the bishops went about the executing
every   of the queen's injunctions. The new service was every where
where set   cast out, and the old ceremonies and service were again set up.
up.   In this business none was so hot as Bonner; for the act that
repealed king Edward's laws being agreed to by the commons,
to whom the lords had sent it, he, without staying for the royal
assent, did that very night set up the old worship at Paul's on
St. Catharine's day; and it being the custom, that on some
holydays the quire went up to the steeple to sing the anthems,
that fell to be on that night; which was an antic way of beginning a form of worship, to which the people had been long
disused: and the next day, being St. Andrew's, he did officiate
himself, and had a solemn procession [54].

---

[52] Harvey, read Harley. [S.]
Bishop Harley is said to have been
deprived because married, by Fox
and Godwin, though no notice be
taken of it in the order. [G.]

[53] Wells had lately been much
impoverished by the alienations in
Barlow's time; the regret whereof
might probably make him less desirous of returning to it. Afterward
its profits were raised by the lead-
mines, about Bishop Stillingfleet's
time: however, it is valued in the

king's books but £535, whereas Chichester is £677. [G.]

[54] ['Bonner had restored the mass
in the church of St. Paul's, on the
27th August, 1553, as was before
related out of Stow and Grafton.
If St. Andrew's day be the next day
to St. Catharine, our English calendar indeed wants great reformation,
which placeth it five days after St.
Catharine. But it may be presumed that if the calendar can retain any friends to plead its cause,

The most eminent preachers in London were either put in prison, or under confinement; and as all their mouths had been stopped by the prohibiting of sermons, unless a license were obtained, so they were now to be fallen on for their marriages. Parker estimates it, that there were now about 16,000 clergymen in England; and of these 12,000 were turned out upon this account: some he says were deprived without conviction, upon common fame; some were never cited to appear, and yet turned out; many that were in prison were cited, and turned out for not appearing, though it was not in their power; 277 some were induced to submit, and quit their wives for their livings: they were all summarily deprived[55]. Nor was this

it may in this case get the better of the historian.' Specimen of Errors, p. 137.]

[55] ['The historian would have obliged us if he had pleased to acquaint us in what book or writing Parker hath delivered this account. The testimony of so grave and so worthy a person would have excluded all doubt. In the ' Defence of priests' marriages,' wrote by an unknown layman, and published by Parker, this passage may indeed be found, fol. 6. *Is thus the honour of the clergy preserved to drive out so many, twelve of sixteen thousand, (as some writer maketh his account,) to so great a peril of getting their livings, and this just at the point of harvest?* Here it may be easily observed, that this author will by no means vouch for the truth of this computation. It would in truth be a very extraordinary matter, if twelve thousand clergymen should have married between the end of the year 1548, and the middle of 1553. I cannot affirm of my own knowledge that the account is extravagantly false, but am very apt to believe it. And in this belief I am confirmed; for that having had the curiosity to compute how many clergymen were deprived for marriage in this reign in the diocese and peculiar of the

see of Canterbury, I found the proportion far short of this account. For whereas there are contained therein about 380 benefices and other ecclesiastical promotions, no more than 73 clergymen therein were deprived for marriage or any other cause; which far from the proportion of 12 to 16 scarce bears the proportion of 3 to 16. Yet, Thornden and Harpsfield were as vigorous in prosecuting the married clergy of that diocese as any zealots in any part of England. As for the severe and unjust proceedings against some of the married clergy related by the historian; the author before mentioned attesteth the same thing. But when the historian saith they were all summarily deprived, I fear this is an addition of his own. For this author, on the contrary, saith, that a year's time was allowed to the clergy to abjure their heresy and put away their wives: although in some places their enemies were so zealous that they dispossessed many of them before the year expired. The first deprivation which I find to have been made on this account was in the church of Canterbury, by Thornden, then Vice-dean: who on the 16th of March, 1554, deprived six prebendaries, one of them the arch-

all; but, after they were deprived, they were also forced to leave their wives, which piece of severity was grounded on the vow, that (as was pretended) they had made; though the falsehood of this charge was formerly demonstrated.

Books a-
gainst the
marriage
of the
clergy.

To justify this severity of procedure, many were set to write against the marriage of the clergy. Smith, of whom I made mention in the former book, that had then so humbly recanted and submitted, did now appear very boldly, and reprinted his book, with many additions. But the most studied work was set out by Martin, a doctor of the laws[56]. It was certainly, for most part, Gardiner's work; and I have seen the proof sheets of a great part of it, dashed and altered in many places by Gardiner's hand. This Martin had made his court to Cranmer in former times. He had studied the law at Bourges, where Francis Balduin, one of the celebrated lawyers of that time, had publicly noted him for his lewdness, as being not only overrun himself with the French pox, but as being a corrupter of all the university; which Balduin certified in a letter[57] to one in England, that took care to print it.

It was also printed, that Bonner had many bastards, and himself was believed to be the bastard of one Savage, a priest in Leicestershire, that had been bastard to sir John Savage of Cheshire. Which priest, by Elizabeth Frodsham, the wife of one Edmund Bonner, had this Edmund, now bishop of London; and it seems his mother did not soon give over those her lewd courses, for Wymmesley, archdeacon of London, was another of her bastards. That kennel of the uncleanness of the priests

bishop's brother, archdeacon also, six preachers, and two minor canons of that church. In the register of the vacancy may be found many processes against and deprivations of married clergymen; from whence it appears plainly, that the usual forms of proceeding were at least in many cases observed, and that all were not *summarily* deprived.' Specimen of Errors, p. 137.]

[56] [Martin (Thomas) LL. D. 'A traictyse declaryng and plainly proving, that the pretended marriage of priestes and professed persons is no marriage, but altogether

unlawful.' London by Robert Caly, 1554, 4to. Also 'A confutation of Dr. John Poynet's book, entitled, A defence for the Marriage of Priests,' &c., London, 1555, 4to.]

[57] This letter I have now by me, printed in Bale's Declaration of Bonner's Articles, fol. 47, 48, but it was not Martin, but his host, that was overrun with the French p-x; Habitabat in Acad. Biturigum, apud quendam nomine Boium, sacrificulum turpissimum,—toto corpore leprosum, et infami morbo Gallico infectum. Though Martin's character there is bad enough. [B.]

and religious houses was again on this occasion raked and exposed with too much indecency; for the married priests, being openly accused for the impurity and sensuality of their lives, thought it was a just piece of self-defence to turn these imputations back on those who pretended to chastity, and yet led most irregular lives, under that appearance of greater strictness.

This was the state in which things were, when the new parliament met on the second of April.   Gardiner had beforehand prepared the commons, by giving the most considerable of them pensions; some had 200*l*, and some 100*l*. a year, for giving their voices to the marriage.   The first act that passed seemed of an odd nature, and has a great secret under it. The speaker of the house of commons brought in a bill, declaring, that whereas the queen had of right succeeded to the crown; but, because all the laws of England had been made by kings, and declared the prerogatives to be in the king's person; from thence some might pretend, that the queen had no right to them: it was therefore declared to have been the law, that these prerogatives did belong to the crown, whether it were in the hands of male or female; and whatsoever the law did limit and appoint for the king, was of right also due to the queen, who is declared to have as much authority as any other her progenitors. *A new parliament.*

The regal power asserted to be in a queen, as well as a king. [Cap. 1. Statutes, vol. iv. p. 222.]

Many in the house of commons wondered what was the intention of such a law; and as people were at this time full of jealousy, one Skinner, a member of the house, (who in queen Elizabeth's time took orders, and was made dean of Durham,) said, he could not imagine why such a frivolous law was desired, since the thing was without dispute; and, that that which was pretended of satisfying the people, was too slight: he was afraid there was a trick in these words, that the queen had as great authority as any of her progenitors; on which perhaps it might be afterwards said, she had the same power that William the Conqueror exercised, in seizing the lands of the English, and giving them to strangers; which also Edward the First did upon the conquest of Wales.   He did not know what relation this might have to the intended marriage, therefore he warned the house to look well to it; so a committee being appointed to correct it, such words were added as *The secret reasons for that act.*

Ex MSS. D. Gul. Petyt.

278

brought the queen's prerogative under the same limitations, as well as it exalted it to the height of her progenitors. But one Fleetwood, afterwards recorder of London, told the earl of Leicester the secret of this, in queen Elizabeth's time, who writ down his discourse; and from thence I have copied it. There was one that had been Cromwell's servant, and much employed by him in the suppression of monasteries: he was a man of great notions, but very busy and factious; so, having been a great stickler for the lady Jane, he was put in the Fleet, upon the queen's first coming to the crown, yet within a month he was discharged; but upon the last rising, was again put up, and indicted of high treason: he had great friends, and made application to one of the emperor's ambassadors, that was then the chancellor of the duchy of Milan, and by his means he obtained his liberty. Being brought to him, he shewed him a new platform of government, which he had contrived for the queen. She was to declare herself a conqueror; or that she, having succeeded to the crown by common law, was not at all to be limited by the statute laws, since those were only restrictions upon the kings, but not on the queens of England; and that therefore all those limitations of the prerogative were only binding in the persons of kings, but she was free from them: upon this, he shewed how she might establish religion, set up the monasteries, raise her friends, and ruin her enemies, and rule according to her pleasure. The ambassador carried this to the queen, and seemed much pleased with it; but desired her to read it carefully, and keep it as a great secret.

As she read it, she disliked it, and judged it contrary to the oath she had made at her coronation: and thereupon sent for Gardiner, and charged him, as he would answer it before the judgment-seat of God, at the general day of the holy doom, that he would consider the book carefully, and bring her his opinion of it next day, which fell to be Maundy-Thursday. So, as the queen came from her Maundy, he waited on her into her closet, and said these words; *My good and most gracious lady, I intend not to pray your highness with any humble petitions, to name the devisers of this new invented platform: but here I say, that it is pity that so noble and virtuous a lady should be endangered with the pernicious devices of such lewd and subtle sycophants; for the book is naught, and*

most horrible to be thought on. Upon this, the queen thanked him, and threw the book into the fire; and charged the ambassador, that neither he, nor any of his company, should receive more such projects from any of her people. This made
279 Gardiner apprehend, that if the Spaniards began so soon to put such notions into the queen's head, they might afterwards, when she was in their hands, make somewhat of them; and therefore, to prevent such designs for the future, he drew the act; in which, though he seemed to do it as an advantage to the queen, for the putting of her title beyond dispute, yet he really intended nothing by it, but that she should be restrained by all those laws that the former kings of England had consented to: and because king Henry the VIIth, though his best right to the crown flowed from his marriage to the heir of the house of York, had yet taken the government wholly into his own hands; he, fearing lest the Spaniards should pretend to such a power by the authority which marriage gives the husband over the wife, got the articles of the marriage to be ratified in parliament; by which they not only confirmed those agreed on, but made a more full explanation of that part of them, which declared the entire government of the kingdom to belong only to the queen.

To this the Spaniards gave too great an occasion, by publishing king Philip's pedigree, whom they derived from John of Gaunt. They said, this was only done to conciliate the favour of the nation, by representing him not a stranger, but a native. But this gave great offence; concerning which I have seen a little book that was then printed: it was there said, that king Henry the VIIth came in, pretending only to marry the heir of the house of York; but he was no sooner on the throne, than he declared his own title, and kept it his whole life. So it was said, the Spaniard would call himself heir of the house of Lancaster, and upon that pretension would easily wrest the power out of the queen's hands, who seemed to mind nothing but her devotions. This made Gardiner [58] look the better to the securing of the liberties of the crown and nation; so that it must

[margin: Great jealousies of the Spanish power.]

---

[58] If John Bale be good authority, the English were forward enough, in setting forth genealogies from John à Gaunt; Gardiner, White, and Harpsfield maintaining the same—Bale's Declaration of Bonner's Articles, fol. 9. [B.]

be acknowledged, that the preserving of England out of the hands of the Spaniards at that time seems to be almost wholly owing to him.

The bishopric of Durham restored. [cap. 3. Statutes, vol. iv. p. 226.]

In this parliament, the marquis of Northampton was restored in blood. And the act for restoring the bishopric of Durham not having gone through the last parliament when it was dissolved, was now brought in again. The town of Newcastle opposed it much, when it came down to the commons. But the bishop of Durham came to them on the 18th of April, and gave them a long account of all his troubles from the duke of Northumberland, and desired that they would despatch his bill. There were many provisos put into it, for some that

[Ibid. p. 227.]

[April 19, Journal of Commons, p. 34.]

were concerned in Gateside; but it was carried in the house, that, instead of these provisos, they should send a desire to him, recommending those persons to his favour: so, upon a division, there were one hundred and twenty against it, and two hundred and one for it. After this, came the bill confirming the attainders of the duke of Suffolk, and fifty-eight [59] more, who were attainted for the late rebellion. The lords put in a

[April 28. ibid. p. 34.]

proviso, excepting entailed lands out of their forfeitures; but the commons rejected the proviso, and passed the bill. Then did the commons send up a bill for reviving the statutes made against Lollardy: which being read twice by the lords, was laid aside. The commons intended next to have revived [60] the statute of the six articles: but it did not agree with the design at court to take any notice of king Henry's acts; so this was 280 let fall. Then they brought in another bill to extirpate erroneous opinions and books; but that was at the third reading laid aside. After that they passed a particular bill against Lollardy in some points, as the eating of flesh in Lent; but that also being sent up to the lords, was at the third reading laid aside by the major part of the house; so forward were the commons to please the queen, or such operation had the Spanish gold on them, that they contrived four bills in one session for the prosecution of those they called heretics. But, to

---

[59] [The bill for confirmation of attainder of the late duke of Suffolk, Wyatt, and other, to the number of 52 persons, was read a second time, April 25. Journal of Commons, p. 35.]

[60] The bill was to avoid and not to revive the statute of the six articles. [S.]

give some content on the other hand, they passed a bill, that neither the bishop of Rome, nor any other, should have any power to convene, or trouble any, for possessing abbey-lands; this was sent up to the lords, but laid aside at that time, assurance being given that the owners of those lands should be fully secured.   The reason of laying it aside was, that since by law the bishop of Rome had no authority at all in England, it was needless to pass an act against his power in that particular, for that seemed to assert his power in other things : and since they were resolved to reconcile the nation to him, it was said, that it would be indecent to pass an act that should call him only bishop of Rome, which was the compellation given him during the schism ; and it was preposterous to begin with a limitation of his power, before they had acknowledged his authority.   So this was laid aside, and the parliament ended on the 25th of May.

[May 5. Journal of Commons, p. 36.]

But the matters of the convocation are next to be related. Those of the reformation complained every where, that the disputes of the last convocation had not been fairly carried; that the most eminent men of their persuasion were detained in prison, and not admitted to it ; that only a few of them, that had a right to be in the house, were admitted to speak, and that these were much interrupted.   So that it was now resolved to adjourn the convocation for some time, and to send the prolocutor, with some of their number, to Oxford, that the disputations might be in the presence of that whole university.   And since Cranmer and Ridley were esteemed the most learned men of that persuasion, they were, by a warrant from the queen, removed from the Tower of London, to the prisons at Oxford.   And though Latimer was never accounted very learned, and was then about eighty years of age, yet he having been a celebrated preacher, who had done the reformation no less service by his labours in the pulpit, than others had done by their abler pens, he was also sent thither to bear his share in the debates.

[April 3, Wilkins' Conc. iv. p. 94.]

[March 10.]

Those who were sent from the convocation came to Oxford on the 13th of April, being Friday.   They sent for those bishops on Saturday, and assigned them Monday, Tuesday, and Wednesday, every one of them his day, for the defending of their doctrine : but ordered them to be kept apart ; and

Some sent to Oxford to dispute with reformed bishops. [Fox, vol. iii. p. 36.]

that all books and notes should be taken from them.   Three
questions were to be disputed.

1. *Whether the natural body of Christ was really in the
sacrament?*

2. *Whether any other substance did remain, but the body
and blood of Christ?*

3. *Whether in the mass there was a propitiatory sacrifice
for the sins of the dead and living?*

When Cranmer was first brought before them, the prolocutor 281
made an exhortation to him to return to the unity of the church.
To which he answered with such gravity and modesty, that
many were observed to weep: he said, he was as much for
unity as any, but it must be an unity in Christ, and according
to the truth.   The articles being shewed him, he asked, whether by the body of Christ they meant an *organical body?*
They answering, it was the body that was born of the Virgin;
then he said, he would maintain the *negative* of these questions.

On the 16th, when the dispute with Cranmer was to begin,
Weston, that was prolocutor, made a stumble in the beginning
of his speech; for he said, *Ye are this day assembled to confound the detestable heresy of the verity of the body of Christ
in the sacrament.*   This mistake set the whole assembly a
laughing; but he recovered himself, and went on: he said, it
was not lawful to call these things in doubt, since Christ had
so expressly affirmed them, that to doubt of them was to deny
the truth and power of God.   Then Chedsey urged Cranmer
with the words, *This is my body:* to which he answered, that
the sacrament was effectually Christ's body as broken on the
cross; that is, his passion effectually applied.   For the explanation of this he offered a large paper containing his opinion:
of which I need say nothing, since it is a short abstract of what
he writ on that head formerly; and of that a full account was
given in the former book.   There followed a long debate about
these words.   Oglethorp, Weston, and others, urged him much,
that Christ, making his testament, must be supposed to speak
truth, and plain truth; and they ran out largely on that.
Cranmer answered, that figurative speeches are true; and when
the figures are clearly understood, they are then plain likewise.
Many of Chrysostom's high expressions about the sacrament

[Fox, vol.
iii. p. 37.]

Cranmer
disputes.

[Ibid. p.
38.]

[Ibid. p.
41.]

were also cited; which, Cranmer said, were to be understood
of the spiritual presence received by faith.　Upon this much
time was spent, the prolocutor carrying himself very undecently
towards him, calling him an *unlearned, unskilful,* and *impu-* [Fox, vol.
dent man:* there were also many in the assembly that often ^{iii. p. 43.]}
hissed him down, so that he could not be heard at all; which
he seemed to take no notice of, but went on as often as the noise
ceased.　Then they cited Tertullian's words, *The flesh is fed
by the body and blood of Christ, that so the soul may be
nourished by God.*　But he turned this against them, and said,
hereby it was plain, the body as well as the soul received food
in the sacrament; therefore the substance of bread and wine
must remain, since the body could not be fed by that spiritual
presence of the body of Christ.　Tresham put this argument to
him: Christ said, as he lived by the Father, so they that eat
his flesh should live by him; but he is by his substance united
to his Father, therefore Christians must be united to his substance.　To this Cranmer answered, that the similitude did not
import an equality, but a likeness of some sort: Christ is essen-
tially united to his Father, but believers are united to him by
grace; and that in baptism, as well as in the eucharist.　Then
they talked long of some words of Hilary's, Ambrose's, and
Justin's.　Then they charged him, as having mistranslated [Ibid. p.
some of the passages of the fathers in his book; from which he ^{49.]}
vindicated himself, saying, that he had all his life, in all manner of things, hated falsehood.

282　After the dispute had lasted from the morning till two of the [Ibid. p.
clock, it was broke up; and there was no small triumph, as if ^{50.]}
Cranmer had been confounded in the opinion of all the hearers,
which they had expressed by their laughter and hissing.　There
were notaries that took every thing that was said; from whose
books Fox did afterwards print the account of it that is in his
great volume.

　　The next day Ridley was brought out; and Smith, who was And Rid-
spoke of in the former book, was now very zealous to redeem ley.
the prejudice which that compliance was like to be to him in [April 17.]
his preferment: so he undertook to dispute this day.　Ridley [Ibid. p.
began with a protestation, declaring, that whereas he had been ^{51.]}
formerly of another mind from what he was then to maintain;
he had changed upon no worldly consideration, but merely for

love of the truth, which he had gathered out of the word of God, and the holy fathers: but because it was God's cause he was then to maintain, he protested that he might have leave afterwards to add, or to change, as upon better consideration he should see cause for it. He also desired he might have leave to speak his mind without interruption; which though it was promised him, yet he was often stopped, as he went on explaining his doctrine. He argued against the corporal presence, as being contrary to the scriptures that spoke of Christ's leaving the world; as being against the article of his sitting at the right hand of God; and against the nature of the sacrament, which is a remembrance: he shewed, that by it the wicked receive Christ no less than the godly; that it is against nature to swallow down a living man; that this doctrine introduced many extraordinary miracles, without any necessity; and must have given advantage to the heretics, who denied Christ had a real body, or a true human nature; and that it was contrary to the doctrine of the fathers: he acknowledged that it was truly the communion of his body, that is, of Christ's death, and of the heavenly life given by him; and did, in a strong nervous discourse, as any I ever saw on that subject, gather together the chief arguments for his opinion.

Smith argued, that, notwithstanding Christ's being at the right hand of God, he was seen on earth: Ridley said, he did not deny but he might come and appear on earth, but that was for a moment, to convince some, and comfort others, as St. Paul and St. Stephen; though, he said, it might be they saw him in heaven; but he could not be, at the same time, both in heaven and on earth. They returned oft to Chrysostom's words, and pressed him with some of Bernard's; but as he answered the sayings of the former, that they were rhetorical and figurative; so he excepted against the judgment of the latter, as living in an age when their opinion was generally received. The dispute held till Weston grew weary, and stopped all, saying, *You see the obstinate, vainglorious, crafty, and inconstant mind of this man; but you see also the force of truth cannot be shaken: therefore cry out with me, Truth has the victory.* This being echoed again by the audience, they went away with great triumph; and now they reckoned the hardest part of their work was over, since Latimer only remained.

[Fox, vol. iii. p. 65.]

283　Latimer being next day brought forth, told them, he had **And Lati-** not used Latin much these twenty years, and was not able to **mer.** dispute; but he would declare his faith, and then they might do as they pleased. He declared, that he thought the presence of Christ in the sacrament to be only spiritual, since it is that by which we obtain eternal life, which flows only from Christ's abiding in us by faith; therefore it is not a bare naked sign: but for the corporal presence, he looked on it as the root of all the other errors in their church. He enlarged much against the sacrifice of the mass, and lamented that they had changed the communion into a private mass; that they had taken the cup away from the people, and, instead of service in a known tongue, were bringing the nation to a worship that they did not understand. He perceived they laughed at him; but he told them, they were to consider his great age, and to think what they might be when they came to it. They pressed him much to answer their arguments: he said his memory was gone, but his faith was grounded on the word of God; he was fully convinced by the book which Dr. Cranmer had written on that subject.

In this whole disputation, as Ridley wrote of it, there was **Censures** great disorder, perpetual shoutings, tauntings, and reproaches; **passed upon it.** so that it looked liker a stage than a school of divines; and **[Fox, vol.** the noise and confusions, with which he had been much of- **iii. p. 74.]** fended when he was in the Sorbonne, were modest, compared to this.

On April 28, they were again brought to St. Mary's; where **[April20.]** Weston told them, they were overcome in the disputation, therefore he required them to subscribe with the rest. Cranmer objected against their way of disputing: he said, they would not hear any one argue against their errors, or defend the truth; that oftentimes four or five of them were speaking at once, so that it was impossible for any to hear, or to answer all these: in conclusion, he refused to subscribe. Ridley and Latimer made the same answers. So they were all judged heretics, and the fautors of heresy. Then they were asked, Whether they intended to turn? They answered, That they would not turn: so they were judged obstinate heretics, and declared to be no more members of the church.

Upon which Cranmer answered; " From this your judg- **[Ibid. p. 75.]**

" ment and sentence, I appeal to the just judgment of Almighty
"'God, trusting to be present with him in heaven, for whose
" presence on the altar I am thus condemned."

Ridley answered ; " Although I be not of your company,
" yet I doubt not but my name is written in another place,
" whither this sentence will send us sooner than we should by
" the course of nature have come."

Latimer answered ; " I thank God most heartily that he
" hath prolonged my life to this end, that I may in this case
" glorify God with this kind of death."

To them Weston answered ; " If you go to heaven with this
" faith, then I will never come thither, as I am thus per-
" suaded."

After this, there was a solemn procession in Oxford, the
host being carried by Weston the prolocutor, who had been
(as himself said in his disputation) six years in prison in king
Edward's time. This gave him now great repute, though he 284
was known to be a constant drunkard. Ridley wrote to him,
desiring to see what the notaries had written, and that he
might have leave to add in any part, as had been promised
him ; but he had no answer. On the 23rd of April, the commissioners sent from the convocation returned to London.
Cranmer sent a petition, sealed, by Weston, to be delivered to
the council; in which he earnestly begged their favour with
the queen, that he might be pardoned for his treason, since
they knew how unwillingly he consented to the patents for excluding her. He also complained of the disorder in the disputes lately had ; saying, that he was not heard nor suffered
to propose his arguments; but all was shuffled up in a day,
though he had matter on that subject for twenty days' work ;
that it looked like a design to shut up all things in haste, and
make a triumph, and so to condemn them of heresy : he left it
to their wisdom to consider, if this was an indifferent way of
handling such a matter. Weston carried this petition half
way ; and then opening it, and finding what it contained, he
sent it back, and said, he would deliver no such petition.
Cranmer was so kept, that though Ridley and Latimer could
send to one another, yet it was not easy for them to send to
[Fox, vol.   him, without giving money to their keepers. In one of Rid-
iii. p. 76.]   ley's letters to Cranmer, he said, he heard they intended to

carry down Rogers, Crome, and Bradford, to Cambridge, and to make such a triumph there, as he had lately made of them at Oxford: he trusted the day of their deliverance out of all their miseries, and of their entrance into perpetual rest, and perpetual joy and felicity, drew nigh: he prayed God to strengthen them with the mighty spirit of his grace. He desired Cranmer to pray for him, as he also did for Cranmer. As for the letters which these and the other prisoners writ in their imprisonment, Fox gathered the originals from all people that had them: and sir Walter Mildmay, the founder of Emmanuel college, procured them from him, and put them into the library of that college, where I saw them; but they are all printed by Fox[61], so that the reader, who desires to see them, may find them in his Acts and Monuments. Of them all, Ridley writ with the greatest connection and force, both in the matter, and in the way of expression.

This being now over, there was great boasting among all the popish party, as if the champions of the reformation had been foiled. The prisoners in London, hearing they intended to insult over them as they had done over those at Oxford, set out a paper, to which the late bishops of Exeter, St. David's, and Gloucester, with Taylor, Philpot, Bradford, Crome, Sanders, Rogers, and Lawrence, set their hands on the eighth of May. The prisoners in London set out in writing their reasons against disputing by word of mouth.

The substance of it was; "That they, being prisoners, nei-" ther as rebels, traitors, nor transgressors of any law, but " merely for their conscience to God and his truth, hearing it " was intended to carry them to Cambridge to dispute, de- [Fox, vol. iii. p. 82.]

---

[61] Most of these letters are printed by Fox; but your lordship knows, the letters of the Martyrs were published in a distinct volume, with a preface by Coverdale (probably the publisher), and printed by John Day, an. 1564; which I could have wished had been taken notice of by your lordship in this place. [B.]

[The volume referred to here is entitled, 'Certain most godly, fruitful and comfortable letters of such true Saintes and holy Martyrs of God as in the late bloodye persecu-

tion here within this realme gave their lyves for the defence of Christes holy Gospel written in the tyme of theyr affliction and cruell imprysonment. *Though they suffer payne amonge men, yet is their hope full of immortalitie,* Sap. 3. Imprinted at London by John Day, dwelling ouer Aldersgate, beneath Saint Martines, 1564. Cum gratia et priuilegio Regiæ Majestatis. 8vo.' The letters are arranged separately under the names of the writers, and not otherwise in chronological order.]

" clared they would not dispute, but in writing, except it were
" before the queen and her council, or before either of the
" houses of parliament; and that for these reasons:

1. " It was clear, that the determinations of the universities
" were already made: they were their open enemies, and had
" already condemned their cause before they had heard it; 285
" which was contrary both to the word of God, and the deter-
" minations they had made in king Edward's time.

2. " They saw the prelates and clergy were seeking neither
" to find out the truth, nor to do them good, otherwise they
" would have heard them when they might have declared
" their consciences without hazard; but that they sought only
" their destruction, and their own glory.

3. " They saw that those who were to be the judges of
" these disputes were their inveterate enemies; and, by what
" passed in the covocation-house last year, and lately at
" Oxford, they saw how they must expect to be used.

4. " They had been kept long prisoners, some nine or ten
" months, without books or papers, or convenient places of
" study.

5. " They knew they should not be heard to speak their
" minds fully, but should be stopped, as their judges pleased.

6. " They could not have the nomination of their notaries,
" who would be so chosen, that they would write and publish
" what their enemies had a mind to. Therefore they would
" not engage in public disputes, except by writing; but they
" would give a summary of their faith, for which they would
" be ready to offer up their lives to the halter, or the fire, as
" God should appoint.

" They declared, that they believed the scriptures to be the
" true word of God, and the judge of all controversies in the
" matters of religion; and that the church is to be obeyed, as
" long as she follows this word. That they believed the Apo-
" stles' Creed, and those creeds set out by the councils of Nice,
" Constantinople, Ephesus, and Chalcedon, and by the first
" and fourth councils of Toledo; and the symbols of Athana-
" sius, Irenæus, Tertullian, and Damasus. That they believed
" justification by faith; which faith was not only an opinion,
" but a certain persuasion wrought by the Holy Ghost, which
" did illuminate the mind, and suppled the heart to submit it-

" self unfeignedly to God. That they acknowledged an inhe-
" rent righteousness; yet justification, and the pardon of sins,
" they believed came only by Christ's righteousness imputed
" to them. They thought the worship of God ought to be in
" a tongue understood by the people; that Christ only, and
" not the saints, were to be prayed to; that immediately after
" death the souls pass either to the state of the blessed, or of
" the damned, without any purgatory between; that baptism
" and the Lord's supper are the sacraments of Christ, which
" ought to be administered according to his institution; and
" therefore they condemned the denying the chalice, transub-
" stantiation, the adoration, or the sacrifice of the mass, and
" asserted the lawfulness of marriage to every rank of men.
" These things they declared they were ready to defend, as
" they often had before offered; and concluded, charging all
" people to enter into no rebellion against the queen, but to
" obey her in all points, except where her commands were
" contrary to the law of God."

In the end of this month [62], the lady Elizabeth was taken [May 19. out of the Tower, and put into the custody of the lord Wil- Fox, vol. liams; who waited on her to Woodstock, and treated her with iii. p. 83.]
286 great civility, and all the respect due to her quality: but this not being so acceptable to those who governed, she was put under the charge of sir Henry Bedingfield, by whom she was more roughly handled.

On the 20th of July [63], prince Philip landed at Southampton. Prince Phi-
When he set foot to land first, he presently drew his sword, lip lands.
and carried it a good way naked in his hand. Whether this [Ibid.]
was one of the forms of his country, I know not; but it was interpreted as an omen, that he intended to rule England with the sword; though others said, it shewed he intended to draw his sword in defence of the nation. The mayor of Southampton brought him the keys of the town; an expression of duty always paid to our princes: he took them from him, and gave

[62] ['The 20 day of May my lade Elisabeth the quen's syster cam owt of the Towre, and toke her barge at Towre Warfe and so to Rychemond, and from thens unto Wyndsor, and so to Wodstoke.' Machyn's Diary, p.63.]
[63] [This date is given by Fox;

Stow, p. 624, says, it was on the 19th July: 'The lord admiral .... met with the said prince the nine-teenth of July about the Needles, and from thence accompanied him unto Southampton, where he ar-rived the morrow after, the twenti-eth of July.' Holinshed, p. 1118.]

them back without speaking a word, or expressing by any sign
that he was pleased with it.   His stiffness amazed the English,
who use to be treated by their kings with great sweetness on
such occasions ; and so much gravity in so young a man was
not understood, but was looked on as a sign of vast pride and
moroseness.   The queen met him at Winchester ; where, on
the 25th of July, Gardiner married them in the cathedral, the
king being then in the 27th, and the queen in the 38th year
of her age.   They were presented from the emperor by his
ambassador, with a resignation of his titular kingdom of Jerusalem, and his more valuable one of Naples, which were pledges
of that total resignation that followed not long after.

*And is
married to
the queen.*

[Aug. 1.]

So on the 27th of July [64] they were proclaimed by their new
titles : " Philip and Mary, King and Queen of England, France,
" Naples, Jerusalem, and Ireland ; Princes of Spain and Sicily,
" Defenders of the Faith ; Archdukes of Austria ; Dukes of
" Milan, Burgundy, and Brabant ; Counts of Hapsburg, Flan-
" ders and Tyrol :" Spain having always delighted in a long
enumeration of pompous titles.

It was observed, how happy marriages had been to the
Austrian family ; who, from no extraordinary beginnings, had
now, in eighty years time, been raised by two marriages ; first,
with the heir of Burgundy and the Netherlands, and then with
the heir of Spain, to be the greatest family in Christendom :
and the collateral family by the marriage of the heir of Bohemia and Hungary was now the greatest in the empire.   And
surely, if issue had followed this marriage, the most extraordinary success possible would have seemed to be entailed on
them.   But there was no great appearance of that : for as the
queen was now far advanced in years, so she was in no good
state of health ; a long course of discontent had corrupted both
the health of her body and the temper of her mind : nor did
the matter alter much by her marriage, except for the worse.

[64] [The proclamation was made
in London on the 1st of August,
as appears from the Grey Friars'
Chronicle, p. 91 : ' The furst day of
August was a proclamacion made in
London for the hole stylle both for
the kynge and the qwene and alle
ther domynyons of both.'   Their
titles had been announced in a sermon preached July 29 by Harpsfield, at Paul's Cross, as appears
from Machyn's Diary, p. 67 ; and
previously in Winchester cathedral
immediately after the marriage ceremony, as appears from Holinshed,
p. 1120.]

The king's wonderful gravity and silence gained nothing upon the English; but his magnificence and bounty was very acceptable. He brought after him a vast mass of wealth: seven and twenty chests of bullion, every chest being a yard and some inches long, which were drawn in twenty carts to the Tower; after which came ninety-nine horse, and two carts, loaded with coined gold and silver. This great wealth was perhaps the sum that was formerly mentioned, which was to be distributed among the English; for it is not improbable, that though he empowered his ambassadors, and Gardiner, to promise great sums to such as should promote his marriage, 287 yet that he would not part with so much money till it was made sure, and therefore he ordered this treasure to be brought after him. (I mention it here, yet it came not into England till October and January following.) He made his entry into London with great state.

He brings a great treasure with him to England.

At his first settling in England, he obtained of the queen that many prisoners should be set at liberty; among whom the chief were, the archbishop of York, and ten knights, with many other persons of quality. These, I suppose, had been committed either for Wiat's rebellion, or the business of the lady Jane; for I do not believe any were discharged that were imprisoned on the account of religion. As for this archbishop, though he went along in the reformation, yet I find nothing that gives any great character of him. I never saw any letter of his, nor do I remember to have seen any honourable mention made of him any where; so that he seems to have been a soft and weak man; and, except those little fragments of his opinions in some points about the mass, (which are in the Collection,) I know no remains of his pen. It seems he did at this time comply in matters of religion, for without that it is not probable that either Philip would have moved for him, or that the queen would have been easily entreated.

Act of favour done by him.

The intercessions that Philip made for the lady Elizabeth and the earl of Devonshire did gain him the hearts of the nation more than any thing else that he ever did. Gardiner was much set against them, and studied to bear down the declaration that Wiat had made of their innocency all that he could; but it was made so openly on the scaffold, that it was not possible to suppress it. Before, in his examinations, Wiat had ac-

He preserves the lady Elizabeth.

cused them, hoping to have saved himself by so base an action; but he redeemed it all he could at his death. This had broken Gardiner's design, who thought all they did about religion was but half work, unless the lady Elizabeth were destroyed: for he knew, that though she complied in many things, yet her education had been wholly under the reformed; and, which was more to him, who judged all people by their interest, he reckoned that interest must make her declare against the papacy (since otherwise she was a bastard) if ever she should outlive her sister.

Philip opposed this at first upon a generous account, to recommend himself, by obtaining such acts of favour to be done by the queen. But afterwards, when the hopes of issue failed him by his marriage, he preserved her out of interest of state; for if she had been put out of the way, the queen of Scotland (that was to be married to the dauphin) was to succeed; which would have made too great an accession to the French crown: and besides, as it afterwards appeared, he was not without hopes of persuading her to marry himself, if her sister should die without issue. For the earl of Devonshire, he more easily obtained his freedom, though not till some months had passed. That earl being set at liberty, finding he was to lie under perpetual distrusts, and that he might be, perhaps upon the first disorder, again put into the Tower, to which his stars seemed to condemn him, resolved to go beyond sea; but died within a year after, as some say, of poison.

All this I have laid together, (though it fell not out all at once,) that I might give a full account of all the acts of grace that Philip did in England: but for the rest of his behaviour, it was no way acceptable to the people; for as he engaged the nation in all his interests, so that henceforth, during this reign, England had no share in the consultations of Europe, but was blindly led by him, which proved fatal to them in the conclusion by the ignominious loss of Calais; so his temper and way of deportment seemed most ridiculous, and extravagantly formal to the English genius, which naturally loves the mean between the excessive jollity and talkativeness of the French, and the sullen staidness of the Spaniard; rather inclining more to the briskness of the one than the superciliousness of the other. And indeed his carriage was such here, that the acting him

288 *(margin)*

He was little beloved by the English. *(margin)*

and his Spaniards was one of the great diversions of queen Elizabeth's court. The hall of the court was almost continually shut all his time, and none could have access, unless it were first demanded with as much formality as ambassadors use in asking audience: so that most of the nobility left the court, few staying but the officers of the household.

Gardiner had now the government put entirely in his hands: and he, to make his court the better with the new king, preached at St. Paul's the 30th of September [65]; where, after he had inveighed long against the preachers in king Edward's time, which was the common subject of all their sermons, he ran out much in commendation of the king, affirming him to be as wise, sober, gentle, and temperate, as any prince that ever was in England; and if he did not prove so, he was content that all his hearers should esteem him an impudent liar. The state of the court continued in this posture till the next parliament.

Gardiner magnifies him much in a sermon. [Fox, vol. iii. p. 85.]

But great discontents did now appear every where. The severe executions after the last rising, the marriage with Spain, and the overturning of religion, concurred to alienate the nation from the government. This appeared no where more confidently than in Norfolk; where the people, reflecting on their services, thought they might have the more leave to speak.

There were some malicious rumours spread, that the queen was with child [66] before the king came over. This was so much resented at court, that the queen writ a letter to the justices there (which is in the Collection) to inquire into those false reports, and to look to all that spread false news in the county. The earl of Sussex, upon this, examined a great many; but could make nothing out of it. It flowed from the officiousness of Hopton, the new bishop of Norwich; who thought to express his zeal to the queen, whose chaplain he had long been, by sending up the tales of the country to the council table; not considering how much it was below the dignity of the government to look after all vain reports.

Collect. Numb. 14.

This summer the bishops went their visitations, to see every

---

[65] ['The 30 day of September dyd pryche at Powlles Crosse my lord chansseler the bysshope of Wynchester, and he mad a goodly sermon; and ther wher as grett a audyensse as ever I saw in my lyff.' Machyn's Diary, p. 69.]

[66] [See Part iii. p. 223.]

Bonner's
carriage in
his visita-
tion.
[Fox, vol.
iii p. 86.]
thing executed according to the queen's injunctions. Bonner
went his with the rest. He had ordered his chaplains to draw
a book of Homilies, with an exposition of the Christian religion.
He says, in his preface to it, that he and his chaplains had compiled it; but it is likely he had only the name of it, and that
his chaplains composed it. Yet the greatest, and indeed the
best part of it, was made to their hands; for it was taken out 289
of the Institution of a Christian Man, set out by king Henry,
only varied in those points in which it differed from what
they were now about to set up: so that concerning the pope's
power, since it was not yet established, he says nothing for
or against it.

Collect.
Numb. 15.
　　The articles[67] upon which he made his visitation will be
found in the Collection; and by these we may judge of all the
other visitations over England. "In the preface, he protests
" he had not made his articles out of any secret grudge or dis-
" pleasure to any; but merely for the discharge of his con-
" science towards God and the world. The articles were;
" Whether the clergy did so behave themselves in living,
" teaching, and doing, that, in the judgment of indifferent men,
" they seemed to seek the honour of God, of the church, and
" of the king and queen? Whether they had been married,
" or were taken for married? And whether they were di-
" vorced, and did no more come at their wives? Or whether
" they did defend their marriages? Whether they did reside,
" keep hospitality, provide a curate in their absence? And
" whether they did devoutly celebrate the service, and use
" processions? Whether they were suspect of heresy? Whe-
" ther they did haunt alehouses and taverns, bowling-alleys,
" or suspect houses? Whether they favoured, or kept company
" with any suspect of heresy? Whether any priest lived in the
" parish that absented himself from church? Whether these
" kept any private conventicles? Whether any of the clergy
" was vicious, blasphemed God or his saints, or was guilty of
" simony? Whether they exhorted the people to peace and

---

67 [Fryday the 14th of September were sett out by the bushope of
London to be enquired of thoroughe
out his diocesse by 4 substanciall
persons therto by him appoynted, in
every warde, a boke containing 126
artycles as well towching the mysde-
meynour of the clergie as the layety.
'Chronicle of Queen Jane.' 1850.]

" obedience? Whether they admitted any to the sacrament
" that was suspect of heresy, or was of an ill conversation, an
" oppressor, or evil-doer? Whether they admitted any to
" preach that were not licensed, or refused such as were?
" Whether they did officiate in English? Whether they did
" use the sacraments aright? Whether they visited the sick,
" and administered the sacraments to them? Whether they
" did marry any, without asking the banns three Sundays?
" Whether they observed the fasts and holydays? Whether
" they went in their habits and tonsures? Whether those
" that were ordained schismatically did officiate without being
" admitted by the ordinary? Whether they let leases, for
" many years, of their benefices? Whether they followed
" merchandise or usury? Whether they carried swords or
" daggers in times or places not convenient? Whether they
" did once every quarter expound to the people, in the vulgar
" tongue, the Apostles' Creed, Ten Commandments, the two
" commandments of Christ for loving God and our neighbour,
" the seven works of mercy, seven deadly sins, seven principal
" virtues, and the seven sacraments?" These were the most
considerable heads on which he visited.

One thing is remarkable; that it appears, both by these and
the queen's injunctions, that they did not pretend to reor-
dain those that had been ordained by the new book in king
Edward's time; but to reconcile them, and add those things
that were wanting: which were, the anointing, and giving the
priestly vestments, with other rites of the Roman Pontifical.
In this point of reordaining such as were ordained in heresy or
290 schism, the church of Rome has not gone by any steady rule:
for though they account the Greek church to be guilty both of
heresy and schism, they receive their priests without a new ordination. Yet after the time of the contests between pope Nicolas and Photius, and much more after the outrageous heats
at Rome between Sergius and Formosus, in which the dead
bodies of the former popes were raised and dragged about the
streets by their successors, they annulled the ordinations, which
they pretended were made irregularly.

Afterwards again, upon the great schism between the popes
of Rome and Avignon, they did neither annul nor renew the
orders that had been given: but now in England, though they

No reordination of those ordained in king Edward's time.

only supplied at this time the defects, which they said were in their former ordination, yet afterwards, when they proceeded to burn them that were in orders, they went upon the old maxim, that orders given in schism were not valid; so they did not esteem Hooper nor Ridley bishops, and therefore only degraded them from priesthood, though they had been ordained by their own forms, saving only the oath to the pope: but for those who were ordained by the new-book, they did not at all degrade them, supposing now they had no true orders by it.

Bonner, in his visitation, took great care to see all things were every where done according to the old rules, which was the main thing intended; other points being put in for form.

[Fox, vol. iii. p. 86.]

When he came to Hadham, he prevented the Doctor, who did not expect him so soon by two hours, so that there was no ringing of bells, which put him in no small disorder; and that was much increased, when he went into the church, and found neither the sacrament hanging up, nor a rood set up: thereupon he fell a railing, swearing most intemperately, calling the priest an heretic, a knave, with many other such goodly words. The priest said, all these things should be amended speedily; and, knowing that a good dinner was the best way to temper bishop Bonner, he desired him to go and dine at his house:

Bonner's rage.

but Bonner took it so ill, that Hadham, which was one of his own churches, was an ill example to those about it, that he lost all patience; and reaching at Dr. Bricket (that was the parson's name) to beat him, he misguided the stroke, which fell on sir Thomas Josselin's ear with great force. Feckenham, then

[Ibid. p. 87.]

dean of Paul's in Dr. May's room, studied to appease Josselin, and said to him, that the bishop's being so long in the Marshalsea had so disordered him, that in his passion he knew not what he did; but, when he came to himself, he would be sorry for what he had done. Josselin answered, he thought, now that he was taken out of the Marshalsea, he should be carried to Bedlam. But Bonner continued in his fury: and though he had purposed to stay at his house there some days, and had ordered provisions to be made, yet he would needs be gone, though it disordered the rest of his visitation; for he came to every place sooner than he intended, or had given notice.

The carvers and makers of statues had now a quick trade

for roods and other images, which were to be provided for all places. Bonner had observed, that in most churches the walls were painted with places of scripture; and in many places there were passages written that either favoured the marriage of the clergy, or were against the corporal presence, and the

291 sacrifice of the mass, and the multiplicity of the ceremonies of the church: so he did at his return send out episcopal letters, on the 24th of October, to raze all those paintings. Upon this it was generally said, that the scriptures must be dashed out to make way for the images; since they were so contrary one to another, that they could not decently stand together. There were many ludicrous things every where done in derision of the old forms, and of the images: many poems were printed, with other ridiculous representations of the Latin service, and the pageantry of their worship. But none occasioned more laughter than what fell out at Paul's the Easter before; the custom being to lay the sacrament into the sepulchre at the even-song on Good-Friday, and to take it out by break of day on Easter morning. At the time of the taking of it out, the quire sung these words; *Surrexit, non est hic; He is risen, he is not here:* but then the priest looking for the host, found it was not there indeed, for one had stolen it out, which put them all in no small disorder; but another was presently brought in its stead. Upon this a ballad followed, that their God was stolen and lost, but a new one was made in his room. This raillery was so salt, that it provoked the clergy much. They offered large rewards to discover him that had stolen the host, or had made the ballad, but could not come to the knowledge of it; but they resolved ere long to turn that mirth and pleasantness of the heretics into severe mourning.

[Oct. 25. Fox, vol. iii. p. 88.]

The sacrament stolen. [March 25. ibid. p. 81.]

And thus matters went on to the 11th of November[68], when the third parliament was summoned. In the writ of summons, the title of supreme head of the church was left out, though it was still by law united to the other royal titles: and therefore this was urged, in the beginning of queen Elizabeth's reign, as a good reason for annulling that parliament, since it was not called by a lawful writ. Now was cardinal Pole allowed to

A new parliament. [Nov. 12. Journal of Commons, p. 37.]

---

[68] [This mistake is noticed by Fox, vol. iii. p. 88. as having been made by the printer of Queen Mary's Statutes. The 11th of November fell on Sunday.]

come into England. The emperor had this summer brought him to Flanders, where, to make amends for the rudeness of stopping him on his way, he desired him to mediate a peace between France and him; but that had no effect. It soon appeared, that all things were so well prepared by Gardiner's policy, and the Spanish gold, that it would be an easy matter to carry every thing in this session. The lord Paget and the lord Hastings were sent from the king and queen to bring the cardinal over. At the opening of the parliament, it was an unusual sight to see both king and queen ride in state, and come into it with two swords of state, and two caps of mainte-nance carried before them: the swords were carried, one by the earl of Pembroke, the other by the earl of Westmoreland;

The attainder of cardinal Pole repealed. [Journal of Lords, p. 467.] [Journal of Commons, p. 37.]

and the caps by the earls of Arundel and Shrewsbury. The first bill put into the lords' house was the repeal of the attain-der of [69] cardinal Pole; it began on the 17th, and was sent down to the commons on the 19th, who read it three times in one day [70] and sent it up. This bill being to be passed be-fore he could come into England, it was questioned in the house of commons, whether the bill could be passed without making a session, which would necessitate a prorogation. It was resolved it might be done; so on the 22nd the king and

[Ibid. p. 38.]

queen came and passed it. It set forth, that the only reason of his attainder was, because he would not consent to the un-lawful separation and divorce between king Henry, and his most godly, virtuous, and lawful wife, queen Catharine: there-fore they, considering the true and sincere conscience of the cardinal in that point, and his other many godly virtues and qualities, did repeal that act. 292

He comes to London; [Fox, vol. iii. p. 88.]

On the 24th [71] he came to London, but without the solem-

[69] I have noted under cardinal Pole's picture from Ciaconius and Petramellarius, that he was at last cardinal presbyter (though first only deacon), which will hardly consist with what is said, vol. i. p. 221, that he did not rise above the de-gree of a deacon; though, I sup-pose, cardinals are of equal dignity. [B.]

[70] Thrice in one day. It was read twice on the 19th, and the third time on the 20th. [S.]

[71] ['Item, the 24 of the same monyth came in the cardinalle Powle by watter, and soo came unto the corte at Whythalle; and in the myddes of the brygge the kynge mette hym, and soo eche other sa-lute other goodly and reverently; and soo wente in unto the Qwene, and soo she mett them at hare gret

nities of a legate's entry, because the pope's authority was not
yet set up by law.   What cardinal Pole's instructions were, I
do not know; nor is it fully understood by learned men what
was the power of a legate *a latere* in those days.   But I
found, in the king's paper office, the original bull of cardinal
Beaton's legatine power in Scotland, which it seems was intercepted by some of the king's ships, in the passage by sea thither : or was sent up to London by those who killed him, and
possessed themselves of his castle and goods.   And I having
mentioned this bull to those learned men, by whose direction I
have governed myself in this work, I did, by their advice, give
it a room in the Collection, though it be large ; since no doubt   Collect.
cardinal Pole's bull[72] was in the same form[73].   In it the   Numb. 17.
reader will clearly perceive what authority was lodged in the
legates to overthrow and dispense with almost all the rules and
canons of the church ; only some peculiar things (which were
more conspicuously scandalous) were still reserved to the apostolic see itself, whose singular privilege it has been always
esteemed to dispense with the best things, and allow of the
worst; so the pretenders to those graces paid proportionably
for them : this authority was too sacred to be trusted even to
a legate, it being the prerogative of the popes themselves to
be the most eminent transgressors of all canons and constitutions.

The cardinal first declared what his designs and powers
were to the king and queen ; and then on the 27th a message   [Journal of
was sent to the parliament to come and hear him deliver his   Commons,
legation : which they doing, he made them a long speech,   p. 38.]

chamber and she salutyd hym; and
then they talked a whylle, and he
departyd unto the place at Lambyth
the wyche was preparyd for hym.'
Grey Friars' Chronicle, p. 93.]

[72] [The bull is printed in Wilkins' Concilia, tom. iv. p. 91, dated
8 March, 1554, and headed, ' *Bulla
Papæ Julii III. potestatem concedens
cardinali Polo, Angliam ecclesiæ
Romanæ reuniendi*. Impress. Londini 1685.]

[73] [' We have no such necessity of
borrowing light from Scotland. The

bull of cardinal Pole's legatine
power is entered in the beginning
of his register kept at Doctors'
Commons, which ought in the first
place to have been consulted....
From thence it will appear how
false the conjecture of the historian
is, that Pole's bull was in the same
form with Beaton's bull, which he
pronounceth to be without all doubt.
For in truth they differ altogether
both in matter and form.' Specimen of Errors, p. 140.]

And makes
a speech to
the parlia-
ment.

The queen
is believed
to be with
child.

[Fox, vol.
iii. p. 88.]

inviting them to a reconciliation with the apostolic see; from whence he was sent by the common pastor of Christendom to reduce them, who had long strayed from the enclosure of the church. This made some emotion in the queen, which she fondly thought was a child quickened in her belly: this redoubled the joy, some not sparing to say, that as John Baptist leaped in his mother's belly at the salutation of the Virgin, so here a happy omen followed on this salutation from Christ's vicar. In this her women, seeing that she firmly believed herself with child, flattered her so far, that they fully persuaded her of it. Notice was given of it to the council, who that night writ a letter to Bonner about it, ordering[74] a Te Deum to be sung at St. Paul's, and the other churches of London, and that collects should be constantly used for bringing this to a happy perfection. All that night, and next day, there was great joy about the court and city[75].

On the 29th the speaker reported to the commons the substance of the cardinal's speech; and a message coming from the lords for a conference of some of their house with the lord chancellor, four earls, four bishops, and four lords, to prepare a supplication for their being reconciled to the see of Rome, it was consented to: and the petition being agreed on at the committee, was reported, and approved of by both houses. It contained an address to the king and queen:

The parlia-
ment's pe-
tition to be
reconciled
to the see
of Rome.

" That whereas they had been guilty of a most horrible 293 " defection and schism from the apostolic see, they did now " sincerely repent of it; and, in sign of their repentance, were " ready to repeal all the laws made in prejudice of that see: " therefore, since the king and queen had been no way defiled " by their schism, they pray them to be intercessors with the " legate to grant them absolution, and to receive them again " into the bosom of the church."

So this being presented by both houses on their knees to the

---

[74] [The same order as issued to the dean and chapter of Canterbury is printed in Harmer's Specimen of Errors, p. 175.]

[75] ['The 29 day of November was commandyd by the byshope of London thrughe ys dyosesse that they shuld say the masse of the Holy-Gost with prossessyon and to sing *Te Deum* and ryngyng, and to pray to God to gyffe him thankes of owr gracious Quen of her qwyck-enyng with chyld, and to pray.' Machyn's Diary, p. 76.]

king and queen, they made their intercession with the cardinal,
who thereupon delivered himself in a long speech :

"He thanked the parliament for repealing the act against
"him, and making him a member of the nation, from which
"he was by that act cut off; in recompense of which he was
"now to reconcile them to the body of the church.   He told
"them, the apostolic see cherished Britain most tenderly, as
"the first nation that had publicly received the Christian faith.
"The Saxons were also afterwards converted by the means of
"that see; and some of their kings had been so devoted to it,
"that Offa, and others, had gone to visit the thresholds of the
"apostles.   That Adrian IV, an English pope, had given Ire-
"land to the crown of England; and that many mutual marks
"of reciprocal kindness had passed between that common
"father of Christendom and our kings, their most beloved
"sons: but none more eminent than the bestowing on the
"late king the title of Defender of the Faith.   He told them,
"that in the unity with that see consisted the happiness and
"strength of all churches: that, since the Greeks had sepa-
"rated from them, they had been abandoned by God, and
"were now under the yoke of Mahometans.   That the dis-
"tractions of Germany did further demonstrate this; but most
"of all, the confusions themselves had felt, ever since they
"had broken that bond of perfection.   That it was the ambi-
"tion and craft of some, who for their private ends began it,
"to which the rest did too submissively comply ; and that the
"apostolic see might have proceeded against them for it, by
"the assistance of other princes, but had stayed looking for
"that day, and for the hand of Heaven.   He ran out much
"on the commendation of the queen ; and said, God had sig-
"nally preserved her, to procure this great blessing to the
"church.   At last, he enjoined them for penance to repeal the
"laws they had made; and so, in the pope's name, he granted
"them a full absolution, which they received on their knees:
"and he also absolved the whole realm from all censures."

The cardinal makes a long speech. [Fox, vol. iii. p. 89.]

And grants them absolution. [Nov. 30. Journal of Commons, p. 38.]

[Dec. 2.]

The rest of the day was spent with great solemnity and
triumph : all that had been done was published next Sunday
at Paul's[76].   There was a committee appointed by both houses

[76] [See, for an account of this, Machyn's Diary, p. 77, and the Grey
Friars' Chronicle, p. 93.]

to prepare the statute of repeal, which was not finished before

[Dec. 26.
Journal of
Lords,
pp. 480,
481.]

the 25th[77] of December ; and then, the bishop of London only protesting against it, because of a proviso put in for the lands which the lord Wentworth had out of his bishopric, it was agreed to, and sent to the commons. They made more haste

[Ibid.
p. 484.]

with it ; for they sent it back the 4th of January, with a desire that twenty[78] lines in it, which concerned the see of London and the lord Wentworth, might be put out, and two new provisos added.   One of their provisos was not liked by the lords, who drew a new one ; to which the viscount Montague, and the bishops of London and Coventry, dissented. 294 The twenty lines of the lord Wentworth's proviso were not put out ; but the lord chancellor took a knife, and cut them out of the parchment, and said, " Now I do truly the office of a chancellor :" the word being ignorantly derived by some from *cancelling*.   It is not mentioned in the Journal that this was done by the order of the house ; but that must be supposed, otherwise it cannot be thought the parliament would have consented to so unlimited a power in the lord chancellor, as to raze or cut out provisos at his pleasure.

The act of repealing all laws against that see. [Cap. 8. Statutes, vol. iv. p. p. 246.]

" By the act is set forth, their former schism from the see " of Rome, and their reconciliation to it now ; upon which all " acts, passed since the 20th of Henry VIII. against that see, " were specially enumerated and repealed.   There it is said, " that, for the removing of all grudges that might arise, " they desired that the following articles might, through " the cardinal's intercession, be established by the pope's " authority:

[Ibid.
p. 248.]

1. " That all bishoprics, cathedrals, or colleges, now esta- " blished, might be confirmed for ever.

2. " That marriages made within such degrees as are not " contrary to the law of God, but only to the laws of the

---

[77] [This is a mistake in the Journal of the house of Lords, *Die Mercurii videlicet* 25° *Decembris.* Wednesday fell on the 26th.]

[78] [The Journal states that the bill was accompanied by 'a request that the two clauses containing *nineteen* lines, and concerning the bishops of London, &c., and the lords Wentworthe, &c., should be clearly put out,'.... and adds, that the said nineteen lines were not razed nor taken out of the Act, but the chancellor in the sight of all the lords, with a knife, cut them, saying these words, " I now do rightly the office of a chancellor," p. 484.]

" church, might be confirmed, and the issue by them declared
" legitimate.

3. " That all institutions into benefices might be confirmed.

4. " That all judicial processes might be also confirmed.

" And finally, That all the settlements of the lands of any A proviso
for church-
lands.
" bishoprics, monasteries, or other religious houses, might con-
" tinue as they were, without any trouble by the ecclesiastical
" censures or laws.

" And, to make this pass the better, a petition was procured A petition
from the
convoca-
tion about
it.
[Ibid.
p. 249.]
" from the convocation of Canterbury, setting forth, that
" whereas they, being the defenders and guardians of the
" church, ought to endeavour, with all their strength, to re-
" cover those goods to the church, which in the time of the
" late schism had been alienated; yet, having considered well
" of it, they saw how difficult, and indeed impossible, that would
" prove, and how much it would endanger the public peace of
" the realm, and the unity of the church : therefore they, pre-
" ferring the public welfare, and the salvation of souls, to
" their own private interests, did humbly pray the king and
" queen to intercede with the legate, that, according to the
" powers given him by the pope, he would settle and confirm
" all that had been done in the alienation of the church and
" abbey lands, to which they, for their interests, did consent;
" and they added an humble desire, that those things which
" concerned the ecclesiastical jurisdiction and liberty might be
" reestablished, that so they might be able to discharge the
" pastoral cure committed to them.   Upon this the cardinal
" granted a full confirmation of those things; ending it with
" a heavy charge on those who had the goods of the church in
" their hands, that they would consider the judgments of God
" that fell on Belshazzar for his profane using the holy vessels,
" though they had not been taken away by himself, but by his
" father.   And he most earnestly exhorted them, that at least
" they would take care, that, out of the tithes of parsonages or
" vicarages, those who served the cures might be sufficiently
295 " maintained and encouraged.   This was confirmed in parlia-
" ment; where also it was declared, that all suits about these
" lands were only to be in the queen's courts, and not in the
" ecclesiastical courts : and if any should, upon the pretence of
" any ecclesiastical authority, disturb the subjects in their pos-

[Journal of
Lords,
p. 252.]
" session, they were to fall into a *præmunire*. It was also de-
" clared, that the title of supreme head never of right belonged
" to the crown; yet all writings, wherein it was used, were
" still to continue in force: but that hereafter, all writings
" should be of force, in which, either since the queen's coming
" to the crown, or afterwards, that title should be, or had been
" omitted. It was also declared, that bulls from Rome might
" be executed: that all exemptions, that had belonged to reli-
" gious houses, and had been continued by the grants given of
" them, were repealed, and these places were made subject to
" the episcopal jurisdiction, excepting only the privileges of the
" two universities, the churches of Westminster and Windsor,
[Ibid.
p. 253.]
" and the Tower of London. But, for encouraging any to
" bestow what they pleased on the church, the statutes of
" Mortmain were repealed for twenty years to come; provided
" always, that nothing in this act should be contrary to any of
" the rights of the crown, or the ancient laws of England; but
" that all things should be brought to the state they were in at
" the 20th year of her father's reign, and to continue in that
" condition."

An address
made by
the inferior
clergy.
[Wilkins,
Conc. iv.
95.]
Collect.
Numb. 16.
For understanding this act more perfectly, I shall next set
down the heads of the address which the lower house of convocation made to the upper; for most of the branches of this
act had their first rise from it: I have put it in the Collection,
having found it among archbishop Parker's papers. " In it
" they petitioned the lords of the upper house of convocation
" to take care, that, by their consent to the settlement of the
" church lands, nothing might be done in prejudice of any just
" title they had in law to them: as also, it being said, in the
" grant of chantries to king Edward, that schools and hospitals
" were to be erected in several parts of the kingdom, they de-
" sired that some regard might be had to that; likewise, that
" the statutes of Mortmain might be repealed. And whereas
" tithes had been at all times appointed for the ecclesiastical
" ministry; therefore they prayed, that all impropriations
" might be dissolved, and the tithes be restored to the church.
" They also proposed twenty-seven articles of things meet to
" be considered for the reformation of the church; namely,
" that all who had preached any heretical doctrine should be
" made openly to recant it: that Cranmer's book of the sacra-

" ment, the late service-books, with all heretical books, should
" be burnt; and all that had them should be required to bring
" them in, otherwise they should be esteemed the favourers of
" heresy: that great care should be had of the books that
" were either printed or sold: that the statutes made against
" Lollards might be revived, and the church restored to its
" former jurisdiction: that all statutes for pluralities and non-
" residence might be repealed, that so beneficed men might
" attend on their cures: that simoniacal pactions might be
" punished; not only in the clergy that made them, but in the
" patrons, and in those that mediated in them: that the liber-
" ties of the church might be restored according to the *magna*
" *charta;* and the clergy be delivered from the heavy burdens
296 " of first-fruits, tenths, and subsidies: that there might be a
" clear explanation made of all the articles of the *præmunire;*
" and that none should be brought under it, till there were
" first a prohibition issued out by the queen in that particular;
" and that disobedience to it should only bring them within
" that guilt: that all exemptions should be taken away; all
" usury be forbid; all clergymen obliged to go in their habits.
" The last was, that all who had spoiled churches without any
" warrant might be obliged to make restitution."

The next act that was brought in was for the reviving the
statutes made by Richard the Second, Henry the Fourth, and
Henry the Fifth, against heretics; of which an account was
given in the first book of the former part. The act began in
the house of commons; who, as was observed in the former
parliament, were much set on severities. It was brought in on
the 12th of December, and sent up to the lords on the 15th,
who passed it on the 18th of that month. The commons put
in also another bill, for voiding all leases made by married
priests. It was much argued among them; and the first
draught being rejected, a new one was drawn, and sent up to
the lords on the 19th of December; but they, finding it would
shake a great part of the rights of the church lands, that were
made by married priests or bishops, laid it aside. Thus did
the servile and corrupted house of commons run so fast, that
the bishops themselves were forced to moderate their heats.
They all understood how much the queen was set upon having
the church raised as high as could be, and saw there was

The laws
against
heretics
revived.
[Cap. 6.
Statutes,
vol. iv. p.
244.]
[Journal of
Commons,
p. 39.]
[Journal of
Lords, p.
478.]
[Journal of
Commons,
p. 40.]

nothing so effectual to recommend any to her favour, as to move high in these matters: and though their motions were thought too violent, and rejected, yet their affections were thereby discovered; so that they knew they should be looked on as men deeply engaged in these interests.

An act declaring treasons. [Cap. 10. Statutes, vol. iv. p. 255.] After this, the bill of treasons was brought in. This was also argued for some days in the house of commons, but at last agreed to. By it, any who denied the king's right to the title of the crown, with the queen's, or endeavoured to put him from it, together with them that did several other offences, were to forfeit all their goods, and to be imprisoned during life; and clergymen were to be deprived by their ordinaries: in these cases, the second offence was to be treason. But if any should compass the king's death, and utter it by any overt deed during his marriage to the queen, the first offence of this kind should be treason. It was also enacted, that the parliament having petitioned the king, that if the queen died with any issue, he would take on him the government of them till they came of age; to which he had assented: therefore, if the queen died before her children came to be of age, the government of the kingdom should be in the king's hands; if it were a son, till he were eighteen; or if a daughter, till she was fifteen years of age: and in all that time, the conspiring his death was to be treason. The witnesses were to be brought before the parties, and none was to be tried for any words, but within six months after they were spoken.

Another against seditious words. [Cap. 3. Statutes, vol. iv. p. 240.] Another act passed, upon a report made of some heretical preachers, who had, as was informed, prayed in their conventicles, that God would turn the queen's heart from idolatry to the true faith, or else shorten her days, and take her 297 quickly out of the way: all therefore that so prayed for taking away the queen's life, were to be judged traitors; but if they shewed themselves penitent for such prayers, they were not to be condemned of treason, but put to any corporal punishment, other than death, at the judge's discretion. This was passed in great haste, for it was thrice read in the house of lords, and passed on the 16th of January, in which the parliament was dissolved.

[Ibid. p. 240.] There was another act passed[78], against those that spread

---

[78] [This is part of the same act.]

lying reports of any noblemen, judges, or great officers; that
such as spread them should be imprisoned till they brought
their authors, according to former acts. If any spread such
reports of the king and queen, they were to be set on a pillory, and pay 100*l.* or have their ears cut off, and be three
months prisoners; and they were to pay 100 marks, and suffer
one month's imprisonment, though they had authors for them,
if they reported them maliciously: but if their reports tended
to the stirring of any insurrection, they were to lose their
right hands, and upon a second offence to suffer imprisonment
during their lives; but they were to be proceeded against
within three months after the words so spoken.

All the bills being ended, the parliament was dissolved on
the 16th of January, to Gardiner's no small joy. He had
now performed all that he had undertaken to the queen, or
the emperor: upon which he had the reputation that he was
formerly in, of a great statesman, and a dextrous manager of
affairs, much confirmed and raised; since he had brought
about, in so small a time, so great a change, where the interests of those who consented to it seemed to lead them
another way. To those who had apprehended the tyranny of
Rome, he had said, that, as our former kings had always kept
it under in a great measure, so there was less danger of that
now, since they saw that all princes had agreed to preserve
their own rights entire, against the pope's pretensions. He
shewed them, that therefore all the old laws against provisions
from Rome were still kept in force. And so, upon cardinal
Pole's being called over, there was a commission sent him under
the great seal, bearing date the 10th of November[79], authorizing him to exercise his legatine power in England. By
this he shewed them, that no legate should ever come into

Gardiner is
in great
esteem.
[Journal
of Lords,
p. 490.]

[Wilkins,
Conc. iv. p.
109.]

[79] ["This license bears date on
the 10th of December that year, as
may be seen in the cardinal's own
Register, wherein it is enregistered.
In like manner Pole afterwards obtained a license from the queen,
1555, Nov. 2, to hold a convocation, as the historian relateth, page
324; in virtue of which license he
sent his mandate to Bonner on the
8th day of the same month to summon a convocation. In obedience
to which Bonner summoned the
clergy to meet on the 2nd of December following. Which I observe,
because the historian in speaking of
this convocation hath not fixed the
time of it." Specimen of Errors, p.
142.]

England, to execute any power, till his faculties were seen and approved by the queen. Others thought this was but a vain imagination; for if the papacy were once fully established, and people again brought under the old superstition, of esteeming the popes Christ's vicars, and the infallible heads of the church, it would not be possible to retain the people in their obedience, since all the assistance that the princes of Christendom of this time had from their subjects, in their wars with the popes, flowed chiefly from this, that they generally did no more submit implicitly to their priests. But if once that blind obedience were restored, it would be easy for the priests, by their private dealings in confession, to overturn governments as they pleased.

Great fear about the church lands.

But that which stuck most was, that the church lands were, by the canon law, so indissolubly annexed to the church, that they could not be separated from it. To this it was answered, that they should secure it by a law at Rome, and 298 should confirm all the alienations that had been made, both by consent of the clergy, and by the pope's authority committed to the legate. Yet even that did not satisfy many, who found some laws in the canon so strict, that the pope himself could not dispense with them: if the legate did it, the pope might refuse to confirm it, and then it was nothing; and what one pope did, another often recalled. So it was said, that this confirmation was but an artifice, to make it pass the more easily. Besides, all observed, that, in the cardinal's confirmation of those lands, there was a charge given to all to be afraid of the judgments of God that fell on Belshazzar for using the holy vessels; which was to pardon the thing, and yet to call it a sacrilege, for which they might look for the vengeance of God. So that the cardinal did at the same time both bind and loose; and it was plain, both by that clause, and the repeal of the statute of Mortmain, that it was designed to possess people with the opinion of the sin of retaining church lands. It was thought this confirmation was rather an indemnity and permission to keep them, than a declaring the possessors had any lawful title to them; so that, when men were near death, and could no longer enjoy those lands themselves, it was not to be doubted but the terrors of sacrilege, and the punishments due to it, with the hope of that relief and comfort that soul-

masses might bring them in purgatory, would prevail with many
of them to make at least great, if not entire, restitutions.

This point being carried by those who did not understand what
future danger their estates were in, but considered the present
confirmation, and the other advantages which they were to have
for consenting to this act ; all the rest passed with no opposition.
The act about the proceeding against heretics passed more easily
than any thing that had been proposed : so it seems the opposition that was made to other acts came not from any that favoured the reformation, otherwise this would have found some
resistance. But now it was the only way to the queen's favour,
and to preferment, to run down that which was called heresy.

After the dissolution of the parliament, the first thing taken
into consideration was, what way to proceed against the heretics. Cardinal Pole had been suspected to favour the protestants,
but seemed now to be much alienated from them; and therefore when Tremellius, who had declared himself a protestant,
came to him at Brussels, he would not see him, though he was
his godfather. He came over into England, much changed
from that freedom of conversation he had formerly practised :
he was in reserves to all people, spoke little, and had put on
an Italian temper, as well as behaviour : he brought over two
Italians, Prioli and Ormaneto, who were his only confidants.
He was a man of a generous and good disposition ; but knew
how jealous the court of Rome would be of him, if he seemed
to favour heretics : therefore he expressed great detestation of
them. Nor did he converse much with any that had been of
that party, but the late secretary Cecil, who, though he lived
for the most part privately at his house near Stamford, where
he afterwards built a most sumptuous house, and was known
299 to favour the reformation still in his heart; yet in many
things he complied with the time, and came to have more of
his confidence than any Englishman.

The cardinal professed himself an enemy to extreme proceedings. He said, pastors ought to have bowels, even to
their straying sheep : bishops were fathers, and ought to look
on those that erred as their sick children, and not for that to
kill them : he had seen, that severe proceedings did rather inflame than cure that disease : there was a great difference to
be made between a nation uninfected, where some few teachers

Marginal notes:
Consultations about the way of dealing with heretics.

The cardinal is for moderate courses.

came to spread errors; and a nation that had been overrun with them, both clergy and laity. The people were not so violently to be drawn back, but were to have time given them to recover out of those errors, into which they had been led by the compliance and writings of their prelates. Therefore he proposed, that there should be a strict reformation of the manners of the clergy carried on. He had observed in every country of Christendom, that all the best and wisest men acknowledged, that the scandals and ignorance of the clergy had given the entrance to heresy: so he moved, that there might be a reviving of the rules of the primitive church; and then, within a little time, men might by degrees be brought over. I have not found that he proposed the receiving the council of Trent; which is the more strange, since he had been himself one of the legates at the first session of it: but it seems it was not thought seasonable to propose it till the council were first ended and dissolved.

But Gardiner is for violent ones.

On the other hand, Gardiner, who had no great sense of ecclesiastical matters, but as they served intrigues of state, and being himself of such a temper, that severe proceedings wrought much on him; judged that the executing the laws against the Lollards was that in which they were chiefly to trust: He was confident the preachers then in prison were men of such tempers, that, if they saw they were to be burnt, they would comply; or if they stood out, and were burnt, that would so terrify the rest, that the whole nation would soon change. He remembered well how the Lollards grew in England, only upon cardinal Wolsey's slackening the execution of the laws against them: and upon the passing of the statute of the six articles, many submitted; so that if king Henry had not discouraged the vigorous execution of that act, all had turned. He did not deny, but a reformation of the clergy was a good and fit mean: but said, that all times could not bear such things; and if they went to reform their manners, the heretics would from thence take advantage of raising clamours against a scandalous clergy; which would increase rather than lessen the aversion the people had to their pastors. So Gardiner complained, that Pole, by his intention of coming over too hastily, had almost precipitated all things; and now, by his gentle proceedings, would as much prejudice them another way. All these reasonings were such as became a man of Gardiner's temper, which being servile and abject, made him measure others by himself. He was also at this time highly provoked by the reprinting of his books of True Obedience [80], which he had writ in the time of king Henry, and to which Bonner had made the preface. In these books, Gardiner had not only argued against the pope's supremacy, and for the king's, but had condemned 300 the king's marriage with queen Catharine, calling it often " *incestuous* and *unlawful*; and had justified the king's di-" vorcing her, and marrying his most godly and virtuous wife " queen Anne." This being reprinted in Strasburg, was now conveyed into England; and it was acknowledged to be a handsome piece of spite in the reformed, thus to expose him to the world. But though this nettled him much, yet he was confident enough, and excused himself, that he had erred through fear and weakness, as St. Peter had done; though it was an unreasonable thing to compare an error of near thirty years continuance to the sudden denial of St. Peter, that was presently expiated with so true and sincere a repentance.

Between these two counsels, the queen would have a mean way taken, to follow both in part. She encouraged Pole to go on in the correcting the manners of the clergy; and likewise pressed Gardiner to proceed against the heretics. *To which the queen inclined.*

She also sent ambassadors to Rome; who were, the viscount Montague, the bishop of Ely, and sir Edward Carne, one to represent every state of the kingdom; to make her obedience to the pope, and to obtain a confirmation of all those graces cardinal Pole had granted in his name.

On the 23rd of January, all the bishops went to Lambeth to receive the cardinal's blessing and directions. He wished them to return to their cures, and treat their flocks with all gentleness, and to endeavour rather to gain them that way, than to use extremity and rigour. And on the 25th [81], there was a *1555. [Fox, vol. iii. p. 96.]*

---

[80] [De vera Obediencia. With the preface of Edmunde Boner bisshop of London, translated into English, and printed by Michal Wood: with the preface and conclusion of the traunslatour. From Rome 26 of Octobre, 1553, 16mo.]

[81] [' Item the 25 day of the same

monyth was the Conversione of sent Paulles day, and there was a generall procession with the childerne of all the scolles in London, with alle the clarkes, curattes, and parsons and vikeres, in coppes with their crossis; and the qwere of Powlles in lyke wysse; and dyvers

solemn procession through London; there went first a hundred
and sixty priests, all in their copes, eight bishops next, and last
of all came Bonner himself, carrying the host, to thank God
for reconciling them again to his church; and bonfires were
burning all the night. And, to keep up a constant remembrance of it, it ordered, that St. Andrew's day should be
still observed as the anniversary of it, and be called, *The feast
of the Reconciliation;* and processions, with all the highest solemnities they at any time use, were to be on that day.

They begin
with Ro-
gers and
others,
[Jan. 1.
Fox, vol.
iii. p. 93.]
[Ibid.
p. 96.]
[Ibid. p.
98.]

But now they turned wholly to the prosecution of the heretics. There had been thirty of them taken at a meeting near
Bow-Church, where one Rose, a minister, gave them the communion according to the English book of service; so they were
all put in prison. On the 22nd of January[82], Rogers, with
others, were brought before the council: he had been a prebendary of Paul's, and in a sermon, after the queen was come
to London, had zealously asserted the doctrine he had formerly
preached; and, as it has been shewn, was confined to his house,
upon the tumult that had been at Paul's. He was much pressed
to fly over into Germany; but he would not hearken to it,
though the necessities of ten children were great temptations.
He was esteemed one of the most learned of the reformers; so
that when those of the convocation were required to dispute,
they desired that Ridley and he might be suffered to come and
join with them. It was resolved to begin with him, and some
others, at the council-board, to see if they could be easily
brought over.

He was accordingly brought before the council; where being

byshoppes in their habbettes, and
the bysshoppe of Londone in hys
pontificalles and coppe, berynge the
sacrament under a canyppy, and 4
prebenttes berynge it in their gray
amos; and soo tip unto Ledynhalle
with the mayer and aldermen in
scarlet, with their clokes and alle
the crafttes in their best aray; and
soo came downe agayne on the
other syde and soo to Powlles a-
gayne; and then the kynge with
my lorde cardinalle came to Powlles
and harde masse, and went home
agayne; and at nyght was com-

mandment gevyn to make bonfiers
thorow alle Londone, for joy of the
pepulle that ware convertyd lyke-
wyse as sent Powlle was convertyd.'
Grey Friar's Chronicle, p. 94.]

[82] ['The 22 day of Januarii was
raynyd at my lord chansseler
plasse, by-syd sant Mare Overes, ser
John Hoper, latte bysshope of Glosetur doctur Crome, as the parson of
Wyttyngtun colege, harold Tom-
son, Rogars, parsun or veker of sant
Pulkers, and dyvers odur.' Machyn's Diary, p. 80.]

asked by Gardiner, whether he would knit himself to the [Fox, vol. iii. p. 99.]
301 catholic church, and receive the pope as the supreme head?
he said, he knew no other head of the church but Christ; and Who, re-fusing to comply,
for the pope, he had no more authority in England than any
other bishop, either by the word of God, or the authority of
the church, for four hundred years after Christ.   But they
objecting that he had acknowledged king Henry to be supreme
head; he answered, he never acknowledged him so to be supreme, as to forgive sins, bestow the Holy Ghost, or be a judge
above the word of God.   But as he was going to explain himself, Gardiner pressed him to answer plainly.   He objected to
Gardiner, that all the bishops had for many years preached
against the pope.   Gardiner said, they were forced to it by the
cruelty of the times; but they would argue no more with him:
now mercy was offered; if he rejected it, justice must come
next.   Rogers said, if they had been pressed to deny the pope's
power by cruelty, would they now by the same motives force
others to acknowledge it? for his part, he would never do it.
Other ten were called in, one after another; and only one of
them, by the lord Effingham's favour, was let go upon a general question, if he would be an honest man?   But all the rest
answering resolutely, were sent back to prison, and were kept
much stricter than formerly; none being suffered to come near
them.

On the 28th of January[83], the bishops of Winchester, Lon- Were judged, [Ibid p. 100.]
don, Durham, Salisbury, Norwich, and Carlisle, sat in St. Mary
Overhay's in Southwark; where Hooper was first brought before them.   It needs not to be doubted, but Bonner remembered
that he had informed against him, when he was deprived in
king Edward's time.   He had been summoned to appear before the queen, soon after she came to the crown; and it was
pretended, he owed her great sums of money: many advised
him not to appear, for that it was but a pretence to put him,
and a great many more, in prison, where they would be kept
till laws were made to bring them out to a stake.   But he
would not withdraw: so now he and Mr. Rogers were singled
out and begun with.   They were asked, whether they would

[83] ['The 28 day of January was   Cardmaker, and odur, and Card-
examynyd at sant Mare Overes,   maker recantyd.' Machyn's Diary,
bysshope Hoper, doctur Crom, and   p. 81.]

submit or not? They both refused to submit: Rogers being much pressed, an' continuing firm in his resolutions, Gardiner said, it was vain-glory in him to stand out against the whole church. He protested it was his conscience, and not vain-glory, that swayed him; for his part, he would have nothing to do with the antichristian church of Rome. Gardiner said, by that he condemned the queen and the whole realm to be of the church of Antichrist: Rogers said, the queen would have done well enough, if it had not been for his counsel. Gardiner said, the queen went before them in those counsels, which proceeded of her own motion. Rogers said, he would never believe that. The bishop of Carlisle said, they could all bear him witness to it. Rogers said, they would all witness for one another. Upon that, the comptroller and secretary Bourne, being there, stood up in court and attested it. Then they asked Rogers, what he thought of the sacrament? He said, it was known he had never meddled in that matter, and was suspected by some to be of a contrary opinion to many of his brethren; but yet he did not allow of their corporal presence. He complained, that, after he had been confined half a year in his house, they had kept him a year in Newgate, without any fault; for they could not say he had broken any of their laws, since he had been a prisoner all the while; so that merely for his opinion they were now proceeding against him. They gave Hooper and him time till next morning [84], to consider what they would do: but they continuing in their former resolution, were declared obstinate heretics, and appointed to be degraded, and so to be delivered into the sheriff's hands. Hooper was only degraded from the order of priesthood. Then Rogers desired he might be suffered to speak with his wife, concerning his ten children: they answered, she was not his wife, and so denied it. Upon this, they were led away to Newgate.

On the 4th of February [85], early in the morning, Rogers

[Fox, vol. iii. p. 101.]

302

And condemned. [Fox, vol. iii. p. 102.]

[Ibid. p. 103.]

---

84 [' The 29 day of January wher raynyd at sant Mare Overes for herese, Hoper and Rogers, and cast to be brennt, and from thens cared to Nugatt.' Machyn's Diary, p. 81.]

85 [' The 4 day of Feybruary the bysshope of London went into Nugatt, and odur docturs, to dysgratt Hoper and Rogers, sumtyme vycker of sant Polkers. The same day was Rogers cared betwyn 10 and 11 of the cloke into Smyth-feld, and bornyd for aronyus opinions, with a grett compene of the gard.' Machyn's Diary, p. 81.]

was called upon to make ready for Smithfield: he was so fast
asleep, that he was not easily awakened; he put on his clothes
carelessly, being, as he said, so soon to lay them off. When Rogers'
he was brought to Bonner to be degraded, he again renewed martyr-
his desire to see his wife, but could not obtain it. He was led [Fox, vol.
to Smithfield, where he was not suffered to make any speech iii. p. 108.]
to the people; so, in a few words, he desired them to continue
in that doctrine which he had taught them, and for which he
had not only patiently suffered all the bitterness and cruelty
that had been exercised on him, but did now most gladly resign up his life, and give his flesh to the consuming fire, for a
testimony to it. He repeated the 51st Psalm, and so fitted
himself for the stake. A pardon was brought, if he would recant: but he chose to submit to that severe, but short punishment, rather than put himself in danger of everlasting burnings
by such an apostasy. So the fire was set to him, which consumed him to ashes.

For Hooper, after they had degraded him, they resolved to [Ibid. p.
send him to Gloucester[86]: at which he much rejoiced, hoping 125.]
by his death to confirm their faith, over whom he had been
formerly placed. He was carried thither in three days. After Hooper
he came, he had one day's interval given him, which he spent burnt at
in fasting and prayer. Some came to persuade him to accept Gloucester.
of the queen's mercy, since life was sweet, and death was bitter.
He answered, the death that was to come after was more bitter,
and the life that was to follow was more sweet. As some of his [Ibid. p.
friends parted with him, he shed some tears, and told them, 126.]
all his imprisonment had not made him do so much.

On the ninth he was led out to his execution; where, being
denied leave to speak, but only to pray in the strain of a
prayer, he declared his belief. Then the queen's pardon being [Ibid. p.
shewed him, he desired them to take it away. He prayed 127.]
earnestly for strength from God to endure his torments patiently; and undressed himself, and embraced the reeds.
When he was tied to the stake with iron chains, he desired
them to spare their pains, for he was confident he should not
trouble them. The fire was put to him, but the wood being

---

[86] ['The 5 day of Feybruarii be-   and Sandurs to Couentre, boyth to
twyn 5 and 6 in the mornyng de-   be bornd.' Machyn's Diary, p.
parted master Hoper to Gloceter   82.]

green, burnt ill, and the wind blew away the flame of the
reeds : he prayed oft, *O Jesus, thou son of David, have mercy
on me, and receive my soul;* and called to the people for the
love of God to bring him more fire, for the fire was burning his
nether parts, but did not reach his vitals. The fire was renewed, but the wind still blew it away from rising up to stifle
him, so that he was long in the torment. The last words he
was heard to say were, *Lord Jesus, receive my spirit.* One 303
of his hands dropped off before he died; with the other he
continued to knock on his breast some time after; and was in
all near three quarters of an hour a burning [87].

Sanders burnt at Coventry. [Fox, vol. iii. p. 108.]

Next these, was Sanders condemned, and sent to Coventry
to be burnt, where he suffered on the eighth of February.
He had been made a prisoner for preaching, notwithstanding
the queen's prohibition, and was condemned for refusing to

[Ibid. p. 115.]

conform to the new laws. When he was led out to the stake,
a pardon was likewise offered him : but he said, he held no
heresies, but the blessed gospel of Christ, and that he would
never recant. When he came to the stake, he embraced it,
and said, *Welcome the cross of Christ, welcome everlasting
life.* And so he was burnt.

And Taylor at Hadley. [Ibid. p. 137.]

Dr. Taylor followed next, who was parson of Hadley. Some
of his neighbouring priests came to Hadley, and resolved to
say mass in his church. He went thither, and openly declared
against it, but was by violence thrust out of the church. Gar-

[Ibid. p. 139.]

diner, being informed of this, writ for him to come up. Many
of his friends wished him to go out of the way : he said, he
must follow Christ, the good shepherd, who not only fed his
flock, but died for it. He was old, and thought he should
never be able, at any other time, to do his good God such
service as he was then called to; so he went with much cheerfulness. Gardiner received him with his ordinary civilities of
traitor, villain, heretic, and *knave.* He answered, he was none

---

[87] Here I could have wished your
lordship had taken notice of Hooper's
loyalty, which was very signal, as
appears from his printed apology,
' When she was at the worst, I rode
myself from place to place, as it is
well known, to win and stay the
people for her party. And whenas

another was proclaimed, I preferred
her, notwithstanding the proclamations; I sent horses out of both
shires,' Gloucester and Worcester,
' to serve her in her great danger;
as sir John Talbot, knt., and William Ligon, esq. can testify,' &c.
And more to this purpose. [B.]

of these; and put Gardiner in mind of the oaths he had sworn, both to king Henry and king Edward. Gardiner said, an unlawful oath was not to be kept; and charged him for hindering mass to be said at his church. He said, he was by law parson of Hadley, and no man had a right to come thither, and defile his church and people with idolatry. After some discourse on that head, he was sent to the King's Bench prison; and being carried before the council on the 22nd of January, he refused to turn. After that he was condemned and degraded: and it was resolved to send him to Hadley[88] to be burnt there. All the way he expressed great cheerfulness. When he was brought to the stake, he said to the people, he had taught them nothing but God's holy word, and was now to seal it with his blood; but one of the guard struck him over the head, and made him give over speaking. Then he went to his prayers, and so to the stake, where he was put in a pitch barrel. As the fagots were laying about him, one [Fox, vol. flung a fagot at his head, which broke it, and fetched a great iii. p. 146. deal of blood: but all he said was, *O friend, I have harm* [Ibid. p. *enough, what needed that?* He repeated the 51st Psalm 147.] in English; at which one of the guard struck him over the mouth, and bid him speak Latin. He continued in his ejaculations to God till the fire was kindled, and one of the guard cut him in the head with his halberd, so that his brains fell out. This was done on the 9th of February.

Bradford was also at the same time condemned, but his execution was respited.

Soon after the condemnation of these men, six others were apprehended on the account of heresy.

304   By this Gardiner saw, that what he had expected did not Gardiner is follow; for he thought a few severe instances would have ed. disappointturned the whole nation, but finding he was disappointed, he [Ibid. would meddle no more in the condemning of them; but left [Ibid. the whole matter wholly to Bonner, who undertook it cheerfully, p. 149.] being naturally savage and brutal, and retaining deep resentments for what had befallen himself in king Edward's time. These cruThe whole nation stood amazed at these proceedings, and elties are much censured.

---

[88] [' The 6 day of Feybruarii doctur Tayller was sent into Suffoke, and to be brennt.' Machyn's Diary, p. 82.]

the burning of such men, only for their consciences, without
the mixture of any other thing so much as pretended against
them. And it was looked upon as a horrible cruelty, because
those men had acted nothing contrary to the laws; for they
were put in prison, at first for smaller matters, and there kept,
till those laws were passed, by which they were now burnt.
So that, remembering Gardiner's plea for himself in his imprisonment, when he desired to be first tried, and discharged in
the particular for which he was committed, before new matter
was brought against him; all men saw now how much more
justly those men might have demanded the like at his hands.
But now the spirit of the two religions shewed itself. In king
Edward's time, papists were only turned out of their benefices,
and at most imprisoned; and of those there were but very few:
but now, that could not serve turn, but barbarous cruelties
must be executed on innocent men, only for their opinions.
One piece of severity was taken notice of among the rest: the
council sent for those who were to be burnt in the country; and
required of them a promise to make no speeches; otherwise
they threatened to cut out their tongues immediately: so they,
to avoid that butchery, promised to obey those cruel orders.

[Fox, vol.
iii. p. 146.]

The manner of Hooper's death made those, who judged too
critically of divine providences, reflect on the dissension that
had been raised by him about the vestments; as if he, who had
kindled that fire, had suffered now more than ordinary for
that reason. But all that difference was at an end before this;
for Ridley and he, between whom there had been the greatest
animosity, becoming partners in the same sufferings, were perfectly reconciled to each other. He writ twice to Ridley, who
writ him an answer [89], as soon as he could convey it; in which
he declared, how entirely he was knit to him, though in some
circumstances of religion they had formerly jarred a little: it
was Hooper's wisdom, and his own simplicity, that had divided
them; every one following the abundance of his own sense:
but now he assured him, that in the bowels of Christ he loved
him in the truth and for the truth. He encouraged him to
prepare for the day of his dissolution; after which they should

Reflections
made on
Hooper's
death.

[Ibid. p.
121.]

[89] [The letter is printed in Coverdale's Letters of the Martyrs, fol.
44, in Latin and English, and is
without date. The volume does not
contain Hooper's letters.]

triumph together in eternal glory : he expressed "great joy
" for what he heard of Cranmer's godly and fatherly con-
" stancy, whose integrity and uprightness, gravity and inno-
" cence, was known to the whole nation : and he blessed God,
" that had given, in his reverend old age, such a man to be the
" witness of his truth ; for miserable and hardhearted was he,
" whom the godliness and constant confession of so worthy, so
" grave, and so innocent a man, would not move to acknow-
" ledge and confess his truth."

It had been happy if the fires that consumed those good men
had put an end to these contests : and if those that have been
since engaged in the like, will reflect more on the sense they
305 had of them when they were now preparing for eternity, than
on the heats they were put in concerning them, when perhaps
ease and plenty made their passions keener, they may from
thence be reduced to have more moderate thoughts of such
matters.

If the English nation was dissatisfied with what was done *These burn-*
since the beginning of this reign, it cannot be imagined but *ings were*
their discontent received a great increase by what was now *disliked by*
the nation.
acted. Those that favoured the reformation were awakened to
have more serious thoughts about it ; since they saw those that
had preached it died so patiently and resolutely, rather than they
would deny it. It begot in them greater tenderness to their memories, and a more violent aversion to their persecutors. The rest
of the nation, that neither knew nor valued religion much, yet
were startled at the severity and strangeness of these proceedings ; and, being naturally of relenting and compassionate
tempers, were highly disaffected to the king, from whom they
believed that this flowed. The queen had before declared, she
would force nobody in these points ; so they thought it not
reasonable nor decent to charge her with it. Gardiner, with the
other bishops and privy counsellors, had openly in court purged
themselves of it ; and laid it on the queen, being therein
more careful of their own credit than of her honour. So
now it could fall nowhere but on the king ; the sourness of
whose temper, together with his bigotry for that religion,
made it reasonable enough to impute it to him : besides, he had
been bred in Spain, where the inquisition was let loose on all
that were suspected of heresy, without any restraint : and his

father had, during his whole reign, been always, as far as he safely could be, a persecutor of protestants. Philip could not but see that all was cast on him; and, understanding that thereby he should become unacceptable to the nation, and so not be able to carry on his design of making himself master of England, he was something concerned to clear himself of these imputations. Therefore Alphonsus[90], a Franciscan friar, that was his confessor, in a sermon before him on the 10th of February, preached largely against the taking away of people's lives for religion; and in plain terms inveighed against the bishops for doing it: he said, they had not learned it in scripture, which taught bishops in the spirit of meekness to instruct those that opposed them; and not to burn them for their consciences. This startled the bishops; since it was now plain, that the Spaniards disowned these extreme courses: and hereupon there was a stop for several weeks put to any further severities. But the popish clergy, being once engaged in blood, have been always observed to become the most brutally cruel of any sort of men; so that it was not easy to restrain them: and therefore they resolved, rather than the heretics should not be prosecuted any further, to take the blame of it avowedly on themselves.

There was at this time a petition printed, and sent over from some beyond sea, to the queen, in which they set before her the danger of her being carried away by a blind zeal to persecute the members of Christ, as St. Paul was before his conversion: they put her in mind how Cranmer had preserved her in her father's time; so that she had more reason to believe he loved her, and would speak truth to her, than all the rest of her clergy; whom they compared to Jezebel's prophets. They 306 gathered many passages out of Gardiner's, Bonner's, and Tunstall's writings, against the pope's supremacy, and her mother's marriage; and shewed that they were men that by their own confession had no conscience in them, but measured their actions and professions by their fears and interests: and averred, that it was known that many of that faction did openly profess, that, if they lived in Turkey, they would comply with the religion of the country. They said, that the Turks did tolerate

The king purges himself of them.

[Fox, vol. iii. p. 149.]

But they are prosecuted by the clergy.

A petition against persecution.

---

[90] Alphonsus à Castro, famous for his treatise De Hæresibus. [G.]

Christians, and the Christians did in most places suffer Jews; but the persecution now set on foot was like that which the scribes and pharisees raised against the apostles; for they then pretended that they had been once of their religion, and so were apostates and heretics. They also said, (but by a common mistake,) that the first law for burning in England was made by Henry IV. who, to gratify the bishops that had helped him to depose king Richard II. and to advance himself to the throne, as it were, in recompense of that service, had granted them that law; which was both against all humanity, and more particularly against the mercifulness of the Christian religion.

They remembered her, that in king Edward's time none of the papists had been so used: and in conclusion they told her, she was trusted by God with the sword for the protection of her people, as long as they did well; and was to answer to him for their blood, if she thus delivered them to the mercy of such wolves.

From the queen, the address is turned to the nobility, warning them of the danger of not only losing their abbey-lands, but all their liberties; and being brought under a Spanish yoke, which had ruined many of the best countries in the world: they are told, they must resolve to come under heavy taxes, and a general excise, such as was in the Netherlands; and that all this would come justly on them, who had joined in the reformation, for base ends, to get the church lands; and now, thinking those were secured to them, forsook it: but for all these things they were to answer heartily to God.

From them, it turns to the people, and exhorts them to repent of their great sins, which had brought such judgments on them: and in the end, begs the queen will at least be as favourable to her own people as she had been to the strangers, to whom she allowed a free passage to foreign parts.

This discourse is writ in a strong and good style, much beyond the rate of the other books of that time. Upon this, some were set on work to write in defence of such proceedings; so a book was set out about it, with divers arguments, of which the substance follows:

They said, the Jews were commanded to put blasphemers to death; and those heretics were such, for they blasphemed the *Arguments for persecuting heretics.*

sacrament of the altar, which was the body of Christ, and called it a piece of bread. They noted also, that the heathens had persecuted Christians; and if they had that zeal for their false religion, it became Christians to be much more zealous for theirs: they made use of that expression in the parable, *Compel them to enter in;* and of St. Paul's, *I would they were cut off that trouble you.* They alleged, that St. Peter had, by a divine power, struck Ananias and Sapphira dead; which seemed a good warrant for the magistrate to put such persons to death. They said, that the heretics themselves were for 307 burning, when they had power; and that those that died then by their hands had expressed as much courage in their deaths, and innocence in their lives, as they had ever done. They cited St. Austin, who was for prosecuting the Donatists; and though he had been once of another mind, yet, finding severities had a good effect on them, he changed, and was for fining or banishing of them. These were the arguments for and against those proceedings.

But, leaving them to the reader's judgment, I proceed in the history. I intend not to write a pompous martyrology, and therefore hereafter I shall only name the persons that suffered, with the reasons for which they were condemned: but, except in a very few instances, I shall not enlarge on the manner of their trial and sufferings; which being so copiously done by Fox, there is nothing left for any that comes after him. In some private passages which were brought to him upon flying reports, he made a few mistakes, being too credulous; but in the account he gives from records, or papers, he is a most exact and faithful writer; so that I could never find him in any prevarication, or so much as a designed concealment. He tells the good and the bad, the weakness and passion, as well as the constancy and patience of those good men who sealed their faith with their blood; who were not all equal in parts nor in discretion: but the weaker any of them were, it argued the more cruelty in their persecutors to proceed so severely against such inconsiderable persons.

They pro-
ceed to
burn more.
[Fox, vol.
iii. p. 154.]

The first intermission being over, on the 16th of March, Thomas Tomkins, a weaver in Shoreditch, was burnt in Smithfield[91], only for denying the corporal presence of Christ in the

91 ['The 16 day of Marche was a veyver bornyd in Smythfeld dwell-

sacrament. Bonner kept him many months in his house, hoping to have wrought on him by fair means; but those having no effect, one day he tore out a great deal of the hair of his beard, but, to conceal that, made his beard be clean shaved: and another time he held his hand in the flame of the candle so long, till the sinews and veins shrunk and burst, and spurted in Harpsfield's face, that was standing by, who, interposing with Bonner, got him to give over any further cruelty at that time.

The next that suffered was one William Hunter of Brentwood, an apprentice of nineteen years old, who had been drawn on in discourse by a priest, till he brought him to deny the presence in the sacrament, and then was accused by him. His own father was made to search for him to bring him to justice; but he, to save his father from trouble, rendered himself. Bonner offered him forty pounds if he would change, so mercenary a thing did he think conscience to be: but he answered, if they would let him alone, he would keep his conscience to himself, but he would not change; so he was condemned, and sent to be burnt near his father's house, where he suffered on the 20th of March. [Fox, vol. iii. p. 156.]

On the same day, Causton and Higbed, two gentlemen of good estates and great esteem, were burnt near their own houses in Essex. [March 26. ibid. p. 160.]

On the 28th of March, William Pigot was burnt at Braintree, and Stephen Knight at Malden; and on the 29th John Lawrence, a priest, was burnt at Colchester. [Ibid. p. 163.]

In all their processes, the bishops brought no witnesses against them; but did only exhibit articles to them, according 308 to the way of those courts, called *ex officio*, and required them to make answers; and upon their answers, which were judged heretical, they condemned them: so that all this was singly for their consciences, without the pretence of any other matter.

Ferrar, that had been bishop of St. David's, being dealt with by Gardiner to turn, and refusing to do it, was sent down to Caermarthen; where his successor Morgan sat upon him, and gave him articles about the marriage of priests, the mass, and some other things: to which his answers being found he- [Ferrar, bishop of St. David's, condemned and burnt. [Ibid. p. 165.]

ing in Sordyche, for herese, by 8 of the cloke in the mornyng, ys   name was......' Machyn's Diary, p. 83.]

[Fox, vol. iii. p. 180.] retical, he was condemned. He put in an appeal to cardinal Pole, but it was not received: yet it seems that delayed the execution till they heard from him; for though he was condemned on the 13th, he was not burnt before the 30th of March.

About that time was Rawlins'White, an honest poor fisherman, burnt at Cardiff; it was in March, but the day is not mentioned: he was very ancient, and was put in prison only because he had put his son to school, that he might hear the Bible read by him. After a year's imprisonment, the bishop of Llandaff condemned him, upon articles to which he answered as an heretic.

[Ibid. p. 185.] On the 24th of April, George Marsh, a priest, was burnt at Chester, being judged as the others had been: only at his death there was a new invention of cruelty; a firkin of pitch was hung over his head, that, the fire melting it, it might scald his head as it dropped on it.

After this, one Flower, that had been in orders, but was a rash indiscreet man, went on Easter-day into St. Margaret's church in Westminster, and there, with a knife, struck at, and wounded the priest, as he was officiating. He for some time justified what he had done, as flowing from zeal; but afterwards he sincerely condemned it. Bonner upon this, proceeding against him as an heretic, condemned him to the fire; and he was burnt on the 24th of April in Westminster churchyard[92]. This fact was condemned by all the reformed, who

One wounds a priest at the altar, and is burnt for heresy, himself condemning his former act. [Ibid. p. 199.] [Ibid. p. 203.]

92 [Machyn's Diary, pp. 84, 85, supplies the following particulars: 'The 14 day Aprell, the wyche was Ester day, at Sant Margatt parryche at Westmynster, after masse was done, one of the menysters, a prest of the abbay, dyd helpe hym that was the menyster to the pepull, who wher reseyving of the blessyd sacrament of the Lord Jhesus Cryst, ther cam in to the chyrche a man that was a monke of Elly, the wyche was marryed to a wyff; the sam day ther that sam man sayd to the menyster, What doyst thow gyff them? and as sone as he had spokyn he druw his wod-knyffe, and hyt the prest on the hed, and struck hym a grett blowe, and after ran after hym and struck hym on the hand and cloyffe ys hand a grett way, and after on the harme a grett wond: and then was syche a cry and showtt as has not byne; and after he was taken and cared to presun, and after examynyd wherfor he dyd ytt.

'The 20 day of Aprell was raynyd at Powlles afor the bysshope of London, and many odur, and my lord cheyffe justys, and my lord mayre and the shreyffes; ys name was . . . .; he was a monke of Ely; and there was a goodly

knew that the wrath of man was not the way to accomplish the righteousness of God. In the Jewish government, some extraordinary persons did execute vengeance on notorious offenders; but that constitution was in all its policy regulated by the laws given by Moses, in which such instances were proposed as examples, whereby they became a part of the law of that land; so that in such cases it was certainly lawful to execute punishment in that way: so in some kingdoms, any man that finds an outlawed person, may kill him. But where there is no law warranting such things, it is certainly against both religion, and the laws of all society and government, for private persons to pretend to the magistrate's right, and to execute justice upon any account whatsoever.

There was at this time a second stop put to the execution of heretics; for till the end of May more fires were not kindled: people grew generally so enraged upon it, that they could not bear it. I shall therefore now turn myself to other things, that will give the reader a more pleasing entertainment. The queen resolves to surrender up all the church lands that were in her hands. [Fox, vol. iii. p. 182.]

On the 28th of March, the queen called for the lord treasurer; sir Robert Rochester, comptroller; sir William Petre, secretary of state; and sir Francis Englefield, master of the wards. She said, she had sent for them to declare her conscience to them concerning the church lands that continued still in the crown: she thought they were taken away in the time of the schism, and by unlawful means, therefore she could not keep them with a good conscience; so she did surrender and relinquish them. If they should tell her, that her crown was so poor that she could not well maintain her dignity if she parted with them; she must tell them, she valued the salvation of her soul more than ten kingdoms, and thanked God her husband was of the same mind; and therefore she was resolved to have them disposed as the pope or his legate should think fit: so she ordered them to go with the lord chancellor, to whom she had spoken of it before, and wait on the legate, and signify it to him, together with the value of [Ibid. p. 183.]

309 (margin)

sermon, and after he was cast and condemnyd to have ys hand that hurt the prest cut off, or he shuld suffer, and after dysgracyd, and after cared to Nuwgatt. The 24 day of Aprell was the sam man cared to Westmynster that dyd hurt the prest, and had ys hand stryken of at the post, and after he was bornyd aganst sant Margett chyrche withowt the cherche-yerde.']

those lands. This flowed from the strictness of the queen's
conscience, who then thought herself near the time of her delivery, and therefore would not have such a load lie on her;
of which she was the more sensible, by reason of a bull which
pope Julius had made, excommunicating all that kept any
abbey or church lands; and all princes, prelates, and magistrates, that did not assist in the execution of such bulls.
Some said, this related to the business of England; but Gardiner said, it was only made for Germany; and that bulls had
no authority, unless they were received in England. This did
not satisfy the people much; for if it was such a sin in Germany, they could not see but it was as bad in England: and
if the pope had his authority from Christ and St. Peter, his
bulls ought to take place every where.

Pope Julius
dies,
[March 21,
Sleidan,
p. 441.]
and Mar-
cellus suc-
ceeds.
[April 9.
History of
Council of
Trent, p.
365.]

Pope Julius died soon after this, on the 20th of March;
and, on the 6th of April after, cardinal Marcellus Cervinus
was chosen pope; a man of great gravity and innocence of
life. He continued to keep his former name, which had not
been done a great while, except by Adrian VI. between whose
temper and this man there was a great resemblance. He presently turned all his thoughts (as Adrian had done) to a reformation of the corruptions of that see; and blamed his predecessors much, who had always put it off: he thought nothing
could make the papacy more reverenced, than to cut off their
excessive and superfluous pomp; whereby they would be the
more esteemed all the world over, and might, on surer
grounds, expect the protection of God. He had been one of
the legates at Trent, and there observed what was represented
as the root of all heresy and disorder, that the clergy were
generally corrupted, and had, by many exemptions procured
[Ibid.] .from Rome, broken all the primitive rules. Upon his first
election, he called for the cardinal of Mantua, and, having
observed him to be a man of great probity, told him, he knew
it was ordinary for all popes, at their first coming to the
throne, to talk of reformation; but he would talk little, being
resolved to do more; only he opened his mind to him, that if
ever he went back from it, he might have this check upon him,
that so honest a man as he was would know him to be a knave
and an hypocrite. He would suffer none of his friends that
were in remote parts to come to Rome; nor his nephews, that

were in Rome, to come within the court: he was resolved to
have sent all priests and bishops home to their benefices; and
talked much of their non-residence with great detestation: he
would not change his table, nor his custom of making one read
to him when he was sitting at it. One day, after a long musing
310 at dinner, he said, he remembered the words of Adrian VI.
" That the pope was the most miserable of all men; his whole
" life was bitterness, his chair was full of thorns, and his way
" of briars:" and then, leaning with his hand on the table, he
said, *I do not see how they can be saved that hold this high* [Godwin,
dignity. These thoughts did so affect him, that, on the twelfth p. 351.]
day after he was chosen pope, he sickened, and died ten days
after. These things are reported of him by the learned [April 30.]
Onuphrius, who knew him well: and they will not be thought
impertinent to have a room in this story.

As soon as the news of his death came to England, the [May 30.]
queen writ, on the 29th day of May, to Gardiner, the earl of The queen recom-
Arundel, and the lord Paget, who were then at Calais, mediat- mends car-
ing a peace between the French and Spaniard; which they dinal Pole to the pope-
could not effect, but only procured a truce: she desired them dom upon
to deal with the cardinal of Lorraine, the constable, and the Marcellus' death.
other French commissioners, to persuade their master to set
up cardinal Pole, that he might succeed in that chair. since he
seemed every way the fittest person for it; adding, (as will appear by the letter which is in the Collection,) that she had Collect.
done this without his knowledge or consent. This could not Numb. 18.
come in time to Rome, where, on the 23rd of that month,
Caraffa was chosen pope, who was called Paul IV, and who was as Paul IV.
different from his predecessor as any man could be. He had chosen
put on an appearance of great strictness before, and had set [Sleidan,
up a religious order of monks, called Theatines: but upon his p. 441.]
coming to the popedom, he put on the greatest magnificence
possible, and was the highest spirited and bloodiest pope, that
had been since Julius the Second's time.

He took it for a great honour, that, on the day of his elec- The Eng-
tion, the English ambassadors entered Rome, with a great lish ambas-
train of 140 horse of their own attendants. On the 23rd of come to
June, in the first consistory after he was crowned, they were Rome.
heard. They fell prostrate at his feet, and acknowledged the Council of
steps and faults of their schism, enumerating them all; for so 367.]

the pope had ordered it : confessing they had been ungrateful for the many benefits they had received from that church, and humbly asking pardon for them. The pope held some consultation, whether he should receive them, since in their credentials the queen styled herself queen of Ireland ; that title being assumed by king Henry in the time of schism. It seemed hard to use such ambassadors ill ; but, on the other hand, he stood upon his dignity, and thought it belonged only to his see to erect kingdoms : therefore he resolved so to temper the matter, that he should not take notice of that title, but should

[June 8.] bestow it as a mark of his favour. So, on the 7th of June, he did in private erect Ireland into a kingdom ; and conferred that title on the king and queen, and told them, that otherwise he would not suffer them to use it in their public audience. And it is probable, it was the contest about this that made the audience be delayed almost a month after their arrival. This being adjusted, he received the ambassadors graciously, and pardoned the whole nation ; and said, " That, in token of his " esteem of the king and queen, he gave them the title of the " kingdom of Ireland, by that supreme power which he had " from God, who had placed him over all kingdoms, to sup- " plant the contumacious, and to build new ones." But, in his private discourses with the ambassadors, he complained that 311 the church lands were not restored : which, he said, was by no means to be endured ; for they must render all back to the

The pope presses the restoring of the church lands. History of the council of Trent. [p. 368.] last farthing ; since they belonged to God, and could not be kept without their incurring damnation : he said, he would do any thing in his power to gratify the king and queen ; but in this, his authority was not so large as to profane the things dedicated to God. This would be an anathema, and a contagion on the nation, which would bring after it many miseries ; therefore he required them to write effectually about it. He repeated this to them every time he spake to them ; and told them also, that the Peter-pence must be paid in England, and that he would send a collector to raise it : he himself had been employed in that office when he was young, and he said he was much edified to see the forwardness of the people, especially those of the meaner sort, in paying it : and told them, they must not expect St. Peter would open heaven to them, so long as they usurped his goods on earth.

The ambassadors seeing the pope's haughty temper, that he could endure no contradiction, answered him with great submission; and so gained his favour much: but knew well that these things could not be easily effected; and the viscount Montague was too deeply concerned in the matter himself to solicit it hard; for almost his whole estate consisted of abbey-lands. Thus was this business rather laid over, than fully settled.

But now to return to the affairs in England. There came complaints from all places, that the justices of peace were remiss in the matters of religion; and particularly in Norfolk, that these things were ill looked to: so instructions were sent thither, (which will be found in the Collections,) requiring the justices to divide themselves into ten or twelve districts, that they might more narrowly look into all particulars; that they should encourage the preachers sent to instruct that county, and turn out such as did not come to church, or conform in all things, but chiefly the preachers of heresy; that the justices and their families should be good examples to the rest; that they should have one or two in every parish to be secretly instructed for giving information of every thing in it; and should look strictly to all vagabonds that wandered about, and to such as spread false reports. This was thought to have so much of the inquisition in it, that it was imputed to the counsels of the Spaniards. And they seemed to have taken their pattern from the base practices of those called *delatores*, that are set out by Tacitus as the greatest abuse of power that ever was practised by the ill emperors that succeeded Augustus; who going into all companies, and complying with what might be acceptable to them, engaged men into discourses against the state; and then gave such informations against them, which, without their discovering themselves by being brought to prove them, were made use of to the ruin of the accused persons. This was certainly very contrary to the freedom of the English temper, and helped to alienate them the more from the Spaniards. But it may be easily imagined that others were weary of severities, when Bonner himself grew averse to them: he complained, that the matter was turned over upon him, the rest looking on, and leaving the execution of these laws wholly to him. So when the justices and sheriffs sent up heretics to 312 him, he sent them back, and refused to meddle further. Upon

Side notes: Instructions sent to the justices for searching after all suspected of heresy. Collect. Numb. 19. — [Tacit. Ann.iv.30.] — Bonner grows unwilling to persecute any more;

But is required to proceed by the king and queen. which, the king and queen writ to him, on the 24th of May, complaining of this, and admonished him to have from henceforth more regard to the office of a good pastor and bishop; and when such offenders were brought to him, to endeavour to remove them from their errors; or if they were obstinate, to proceed against them according to law. This letter he caused to be put in his register, from whence I copied it, and Collect. Numb. 20. have placed it in the Collections. Whether he procured this himself, for a colour to excuse his proceedings; or whether it was sent to him by reason of his slackness, is not certain; but the latter is more probable, for he had burnt none during five weeks: but he soon redeemed that loss of time.

The queen's delivery is expected, but in vain. [Strype's Mem. Eccles. Append. No. 87.] At this time the nation was in expectation of the queen's delivery. And on the 3rd of May, the bishop of Norwich writ a letter to the earl of Sussex, of which I have seen the original, that news was brought him from London[93], that the queen had brought forth a noble prince; for which he had Te Deum solemnly sung in his cathedral, and in the other churches thereabout. He adds in the postcript, that the news was confirmed by two other hands. But, though this was without any ground, the queen continued still in her opinion that she was with child: and on the 29th of May, letters were written by the council to the lord treasurer, to have money in readiness, that those who were appointed to carry the joyful news of the queen's happy delivery might be speedily despatched. In the beginning of June she was believed to be in labour, and it flew over London again, that she had brought forth a son. The priests had settled all their hopes on that; so they did every where sing Te Deum, and were transported into no small ecstasies of joy. One more officious than the rest made a sermon about it, and described all the lineaments of their young prince: but they soon found they were abused. It was said, that they had been deceived, and that the queen had no great belly; but Melville in his Memoirs says, he was assured

---

[93] ['The 30 day of Aprell and the last day of Aprell thydynges cam to London that the quen's grace was delivered of a prynce, and so ther was grett ryngyng thrugh London, and dyvers plases Te Deum laudamus songe; and the morrow after, yt was tornyd odurways to the plesur of God. But yt shall be when yt plesse God, for I trust God that he wyll rememmbur ys tru servands that putt ther trust in hym, when that they calle on hym.' Machyn's Diary, p. 86.]

from some of her women, that she did cast forth at several times some moles and unformed pieces of flesh. So now there was small hopes of any issue from her. This increased the sourness of her temper; and king Philip, being so much younger than she, growing out of conceit with her, did not much care for her; but left her some months after. He saw no hope of children; and, finding that it was not possible for him to get England in his hands without that, gave over all his designs about it: so, having lived with her about fifteen months after their first marriage, he found it necessary to look more after his hereditary crown, and less after his matrimonial one; and henceforth he considered England rather as a sure ally, that was to adhere firmly to his interests, than as a nation which he could ever hope to add to his other crowns. All these things concurred to increase the queen's melancholy humours, and did cast her into an ill state of health; so that it was not probable she could live long. Gardiner upon that set himself much to have the lady Elizabeth put out of the way; but, as it was formerly said, king Philip preserved her.

And thus affairs went on, as to civil matters, till the meeting of the next parliament in October following. But I now return to the proceedings against the poor men called heretics; 313 who were again, after a short intermission, brought to new sufferings: John Cardmaker, that had been divinity-reader at St. Paul's, and a prebendary at Bath[94]; and John Warne, an upholsterer in London, were both burnt in Smithfield on the 30th of May[95], for denying the corporal presence; being proceeded agaist *ex officio*. On the 4th of June there was a piece of pageantry acted on the body of one Tooly, who being executed for a robbery, did at his death say something that savoured of heresy: upon which, the council writ to Bonner

Marginal notes:
[Oct. 21.]
Proceedings against heretics.
[Fox, vol. iii. p. 203.]
[Ibid. p. 210.]

---

[94] ['There had been monks in the church of Bath until the dissolution of the monastery. But since that time, neither monks nor prebendaries had any place therein. Cardmaker had been really prebendary of Wells; and in king Edward's Council-book, I find ordered, 1551, Feb. 18, '*A letter to the chapter of Wells in favour* of Mr. John Cardmaker, chancellor of that church.' Specimen of Errors, p. 142.]

[95] ['The 30 day of May was burnt in Smythfeld master Cardmaker, sumtyme veker of sant Bryd, and master Varren, clothworker, dwellyng aganst sant Johns in Walbroke, an hupholster, and ys wyff behyng in Newgate.' Machyn's Diary, p. 88.]

to inquire into it, and to proceed according to the ecclesiastical laws. He thereupon formed a process, and cited the dead body to answer the points objected to him: but he, to be sure, neither appearing nor answering, was condemned and burnt.

[Fox, vol. iii. p. 211.] After this, on the 10th of June[96], Thomas Hawkes, a gentleman in Essex, who had lived much in the court, was also burnt [Ibid. p. 208.] at Coxhall: and on the same day, John Simpson and John Ardeley, two husbandmen, were also burnt in Essex. Thomas [Ibid. p. 222.] Watts, a linendraper, was burnt at Chelmsford. On the 9th[97], [Ibid. p. 231.] Nicholas Chamberlain, a weaver, was burnt at Colchester; and on the 15th, Thomas Osmond, a fuller, was burnt at Manningtree; and the same day William Bamford, a weaver, was burnt at Harwich.

These, with several others, had been sent up by the earl of Oxford to Bonner, because they had not received the sacrament the last Easter, and were suspected of heresy: and articles being given to them, they were upon their answers condemned, The council writ to the lords in Essex to gather the gentry, and assist at these burnings. [June 3. Council Book, p. 259.] and sent to be burnt in the places where they had lived. But upon this occasion, the council, fearing some tumult or violent rescue, writ to the earl of Oxford and the lord Rich, to gather the country, and to see the heretics burnt[98]. The earl of Oxford, being some way indisposed, could only send his people to the lord Rich, who went and obeyed the orders that had been sent him, for which letters of thanks were written to him[99]: and the council understanding that some gentlemen

---

96 ['The 10 day of Juin was delevered owt of Nuwgatt 7 men to be cared into Essex and Suffoke to borne.' Machyn's Diary, p. 89.]

97 [Fox, vol. iii. p. 232, for 9th says 14th.]

98 ['At Hampton Court, the third of June, 1555. ...... A letter to the lord Riche, praying him to be present at Colchester, Manytree, and Harwiche at such time as the offenders that are already condemned for heresy shall be there executed. In consideration whereof he is unburdened from being at Raleigh and other places mentioned in the former letters sent unto him from hence.

A letter to the earl of Oxforde to cause so many of his officers, servants and tenants as his lordship shall think convenient to attend upon the lord Riche at Colchester and Manitrye at the execution of such persons as are there appointed to suffer, for the better execution of justice, Council Book, p. 259.]

99 [The extract is as follows:— 'A letter to the lord Riche, wherein he is required on the king and queen's highnes' behalf to render thanks unto Edward Bery, gentleman, and diverse other of the hundred of Rocheforde in Essex, for coming so honestly and of themselves to Colchester and other places

had come to the burning at Colchester, that had not been writ [June 27.
to, but, as the words of the letter have it, *had honestly and of* Council
Book,
themselves gone thither, writ to the lord Rich to give them p. 273.]
the council's thanks for their zeal. I find in the council-books
many entries made of letters writ to several counties, to the
nobility and gentry to assist at these executions: and such as
made excuses were always after that looked on with an ill
eye, and were still under great jealousy.

After these followed the execution of Bradford in July[1] : Bradford's
martyr-
dom.
he had been condemned among the first, but was not burnt till
now. He had been a prebendary of St. Paul's, and a cele- [Fox, vol.
iii. p. 232.]
brated preacher, in the end of king Edward's days. He had
preserved Bourne in the tumult at Paul's Cross: and that
afternoon, preaching at Bow-Church, he severely reproved the
people for the disorder at Paul's; but three days after was [Ibid. p.
233.]
put in prison, where he lay, removed from one prison to
another, near two years. Wherever he came, he gained so
much on the keepers, that they suffered him to preach and
give the sacrament to his fellow-prisoners. He was one of
those that were carried before the council on the 22nd of
January, where Bonner accused him of the tumult at Paul's;
though all he pretended to prove it by was, that his way
of speaking to the people shewed he thought he had some
authority over them, and was a presumption that he had set
on the sedition. Bradford appealed to God, that saw his innocency, and how unworthily he was requited for saving his
314 enemies, who rendered him evil for good. At last, refusing to
conform himself to the laws, he was condemned with the rest
on the 31st of January, where that rescue was again laid to his
charge, together with many letters he had written over England,
which (as the earl of Derby informed the parliament) had [Ibid. p.
236.]
done more hurt than he could have done, if he had been at
liberty to preach. He said, since he understood that they
acted by a commission which was derived from the pope, he

in the shire, and assisting the sheriff
at the said execution.'—The Council-Book is for several pages chiefly
occupied with letters such as the
author describes in the text.]

[1] ['The furst day of July whent
into Smythfeld to borne master

Bradford, a grett precher by kyng
Edwards days, and a talow-chandler's prentes dwellyng by Nugatt,
by 8 of the cloke in the mornyng
with a grett compane of pepull.'
Mechyn's Diary, p. 91.]

could not answer them, having sworn never to acknowledge that authority: what he had done at Paul's was at Bourne's earnest desire, who prayed him, for the passion of Christ, to speak to the people; upon which he stepped up to the pulpit, and had almost been killed with the dagger that was thrown at Bourne, for it touched his sleeve. But in the points of religion, he professed his faith so constantly, that for that cause he was condemned. Yet the saving of Bourne was so publicly known, that it was thought indecent to proceed against him so quick as they did with the rest. So both Heath archbishop of York, and Day bishop of Chichester, Weston, Harpsfield, and the king's confessor, and Alphonsus a Castro, went to see him, and endeavoured to gain him; but all to no purpose. It looks very ill in Bourne that he never interposed for Bradford, nor came once to visit him: and as, when Bradford was before the council, Bourne's brother, the secretary, was very sharp upon him, so, when he was brought to his trial, Bourne himself, then bishop of Bath and Wells, being present, did not open his mouth for him, though he appealed to him as to the business of the tumult. With Bradford one John Lease[2], an apprentice of nineteen years old, was led out to be burnt, who was also condemned upon his answers to the articles exhibited to him. When they came to the stake, they both fell down and prayed. Then Bradford took a fagot in his hands, and kissed it; and so likewise kissed the stake, expressing thereby the joy he had in his sufferings; and cried, *O, England, repent, repent, beware of idolatry and false antichrists!* But the sheriff hindering him to speak any more, he embraced his fellow-sufferer, and prayed him to be of good comfort, for they should sup with Christ that night. His last words were, *Strait is the way, and narrow is the gate, that leadeth into eternal life, and few there be that find it.*

Now the persecution was carried on to other places, Bonner stopping in it again. But Thornton, suffragan of Dover, Harpsfield, archdeacon of Canterbury, and some others, resolved likewise to shew their zeal. This Thornton had, from the first change made by king Henry, been the most officious and forward in every turn; and had been the first in this reign that had set up the mass at Canterbury. He was much

[Fox, vol. iii. p. 245. sqq.]

[Ibid. p. 253.]

[Ibid. p. 254.]

[Ibid p. 255.]

2 For *Lease* read *Leafe*. [S.]

despised for it by cardinal Pole: but Pole could not hinder
the fury of these men, without drawing on himself the pope's
indignation. The pope was his professed and inveterate enemy;
but knew not how to vent his hatred to him, since he had done
such an eminent service to the church, as the reconciling of
England. Gardiner understanding this, sent secretly to Rome,
to give ill characters of Pole, which the ill-natured pope was
ready enough to receive. Gardiner designed to be made a
cardinal; and to get Pole recalled, and himself made archbishop of Canterbury. The pope was resolved, on the first
occasion, to take the legatine power from Pole, and give it to
Gardiner: but Pole was so much in the queen's favour, that
315 this required some time to bring it about. This made Gardiner [Godwin,
study to preserve Cranmer as long as he lived. It seemed p. 351.]
more reasonable to have begun with him, who had indeed been
the chief author of the reformation, and promoter of that they
called heresy: nor had Gardiner such kindness for him, as to
interpose on his account; but he knew that, as soon as he was
burnt, Pole would be presently invested in the see of Canterbury. Therefore he suggested, that if he could be any way
brought off, it would be the most effectual means possible to
extirpate heresy; for if he, who had so much set on these doctrines, did forsake them, it would confound the whole party,
and bring over at least all that were weak or staggering:
whereas, on the other hand, if he died resolutely for it, his
death would confirm them all very much. This was a colour
good enough to preserve him. But why the see of Canterbury was not declared vacant, since he was now pronounced an
obstinate heretic, I do not so well apprehend: whether there
was any thing in the pall, or the latter inventions of the canonists, that made it necessary not to fill his see so long as he
lived, I know not. Pole being in these circumstances, durst
neither offend those at Rome, nor openly hinder the prosecution of heretics, which it seems he would have done more
steadily, if it had not been for fear of the pope's taking thereby
advantages against him; who had before given out in the conclave, that he was a favourer of heresy, and therefore would
the more easily be induced to believe any thing that might be
written over to Rome to his prejudice.

Those that sat in Canterbury to judge the heretics had four Some burnt

at Canter-
bury.
[Fox, vol.
iii. p. 301.]
men brought before them: two priests, Bland and Frankesh; and Shiterden[3] and Middleton, two laymen. They were condemned upon their answers to the articles exhibited to them, and burnt at Canterbury the 25th of June[4]: and in July

[Ibid. p. 316.]
Margery Polley was burnt at Tunbridge on the like account, who was the first woman that suffered in this reign.

[Ibid. p. 317.]
Christopher Ward[5] was condemned with her, and burnt in Dartford. On the 22nd of July Dirick Carver was burnt at Lewes: and on the 23rd John Launder was burnt at Stoning[6]. They had been taken in London, and brought before Bonner; but he would not meddle with them, and desired they might be sent to their own ordinaries: one of them being of Surrey, was within Gardiner's jurisdiction, who resolved to proceed no more against the heretics; so he procured a letter from the council to Bonner, requiring him to proceed against them, who thereupon presently condemned them.

Pretended plots, and some put to the torture to make discovery.
There were at this time several discoveries of plottings in several counties, especially in Dorsetshire and Essex; but the nature of these plots is not set down in the council-books. Some were taken and put in the Tower. Two or three privy counsellors were sent thither on the 9th of June, with a letter from the council to the lieutenant of the Tower to put them to the torture, according to their discretions: yet nothing following upon this, it is probable these were only surmises devised by the clergy to set on the council more severely against them, whose ruin they were contriving by all the ways they could think on.

There was also an outrage committed on two friars, Peto and Elston, who were Franciscans of the Observance. They had spoken sharply against king Henry in the business of the 316 divorce, and had fled beyond sea on that account: therefore the queen had sent for them, and not only procured the attainder that had passed against them to be repealed in the last parliament, but made Peto her confessor: and, being resolved to

The queen rebuilds
raise religious houses in England again, she had begun with

---

[3] Sheterden. [S.]

[4] 25th of June, read on the 12th of July. [S.] [This date is confirmed by the following extract from Machyn's Diary. 'The 12 day of July was bornyd at Canturbery 4 men for herese, 2 prestes and 2 layemen.' p. 91.]

[5] [Fox calls him Waid.]

[6] *Stoning* read *Stening*. [S.]

their order, the Franciscans of the Observance, and with their
house at Greenwich, which was the first that was suppressed;
as was shewn in the former book: and therefore she ordered
that to be rebuilt this summer. So Elston and Peto going
down by water, there were stones flung at them by some that
were ashore in London. This the queen resented highly; so
she sent the lord treasurer to the lord mayor, requiring him to
make proclamation of a reward to any that should discover
those who had done it: but it could not be found out. She ordered all sir Thomas More's[7] works to be printed together in
one volume, which were in the press this year: and it was
given out as an extraordinary thing, that king Edward had died,
and she succeeded to the crown, that very day in which he was
beheaded. But, in publishing his works, one piece of fraud
has occurred to me since the former part was printed. I have
seen the manuscript out of which his letters were printed,
where the originals of the letters that he writ to his daughter,
Mrs. Roper, are, with the copies of those that he writ to Cromwell.
But among these there is a long letter concerning the Nun of
Kent, in which he speaks fully of her hypocrisy and other vil-
lainies. It contains many remarkable passages concerning her,
of the high opinion he at first had of her; how he was led into
it, and how he was afterwards convinced " that she was the
" most false dissembling hypocrite that had been known, and
" guilty of the most detestable hypocrisy, and devilish dissem-
" bled falsehood: and he believed that she had communication
" with an evil spirit." This letter was at that time concealed,
but not destroyed: so I find the conjecture I made about it in
my former part has proved true; though I did not then hope
to come by the letter itself, as I have done since. It seems it
was resolved to raise the credit of that story; and, since the
Nun was believed to be both a martyr and a prophetess, it is
like she might have been easily gotten to be canonized: and
therefore so great a testimony from such a man was not
thought fit to be left in her way. The letter I have put into
the Collections.

Concerning this edition of sir Thomas More's works, I shall

the Fran-
ciscans'
house at
Greenwich.

Sir Thomas
More's
works
printed.

But his let-
ter about
the Nun of
Kent was
left out.

Collect.
Numb. 21.

---

[7] [The works of sir Thomas More.... written by him in the
English tongue, Lond. fol. 1557.]

recal to the reader's mind what was said in the former part
about his life, pretended to be writ by Rastall; who was now
the publisher of his works, and so much encouraged in it,
that the queen promoted him soon after to be a judge: and so
it is not likely that Rastall ever writ any such book, otherwise he had now prefixed it to this edition. Nor is it probable
that the stories which Sanders vented in his name afterwards
concerning Anne Boleyn, or queen Elizabeth's birth, were then
so much as contrived: otherwise it is not credible that they
should not have been printed at this time; since the lady Elizabeth, being the only object of the fear and jealousy of the
popish party, was now out of the queen's favour, and a prisoner:
so that we cannot doubt but all such stories would have been
very acceptable to the queen, and the clergy would have taken
care to have published them, for the defaming her, and blasting
her title. And therefore these things seem to be afterwards 317
contrived in revenge, when queen Elizabeth began to proceed
severely against that party, after the many and repeated conspiracies they had engaged in against her life.

But now the queen resolved to endow so many religious
houses, as the revenues of the church that were in her hands
could maintain: and about that, and some other particulars, she
writ some directions to the council with her own hand, which
will be found in the Collections. I have seen two copies of
these, that differ a little; but I follow that which seemed to me
to be best derived from the original. She desired, "that those
" who had commission to treat with the cardinal about the
" goods of the church might wait on him once a week, to finish
" that and some other matters that were to be prepared for
" the parliament: she particularly recommended the care of
" having good preaching encouraged, which she wished might
" be well looked to; and she advised a general visitation, both
" of the universities and churches, to be made, by such as the
" cardinal and they should think fit. As for the punishment
" of heretics, she wished it might not be done rashly; yet she
" would have justice done on those who by learning studied to
" deceive the simple: but would have it so managed, that the
" people might see they were not condemned but upon just
" occasions; and therefore ordered that some of the council
" should be present at all the burnings about London, and that

Marginal notes: Rastall published his works, but did not write his life. — The queen restores all the church lands that belonged to the crown. Collect. Numb. 22.

" there should be every where good sermons at those times :
" she also verily believed that many benefices should not be in
" one man's hand; but that every priest ought to look to his
" cure, and reside upon it. And she looked on the pluralities
" over England to be a main cause of the want of good preach-
" ers ; whose sermons, if joined with a good example, would
" do much good; and without that, she thought their sermons
" would profit little."

And now I return to the burnings, from which I am not un- *More here-*
willing frequently to break off, since a continued relation of *tics burnt.*
such things cannot be but an ungrateful entertainment to the
reader. In July one Juxon[9] was burnt at Chichester. On [Fox, vol.
the 2nd of August James Abeys[10] was burnt at Bury in Suffolk. iii. p. 320.]
[Ibid. p.
On the 8th of August, Denley[11] a gentleman, was burnt at 321.]
Uxbridge; and Robert Smith at Weybridge[12]. On the 26th [Ibid.
p. 324.]
George Tankervil[13] was burnt at St. Alban's. And on the 28th [Ibid.
p. 342.]
of August Patrick Packingham also was burnt there. On the [Ibid. p.
31st of August, one Newman was burnt at Saffron Walden in 329.]
[Ibid. p.
Essex ; and Robert Samuel, a preacher, was burnt at Ipswich. 324.]
[Ibid. p.
There were also, in August, six burnt in one fire at Canter- 345.]
bury. Elizabeth Warne burnt at Stratford-le-Bow, Stephen [Ibid. p.
326.]
Whorwood[14] at Stratford, Thomas Fust at Ware, and William [Ibid p.
Hall[15] at Barnet; but of their sufferings, the days[16] are not 328.]
marked[17]. In September, on the 6th day of the month,

9 [Fox calls him Iveson.]
10 ['The 2 day of August was a
shumaker bornyd at sant Ed-
mundebere in Suffolke for herese.'
Machyn's Diary, p. 92. Fox calls
him Abbes.]
11 ['The 8 day of August between
4 and 5 in the mornyng was a pre-
soner delevered unto the shreyff of
Medyllsex to be cared unto Ux-
bryge to be bornyd; yt was the
markett day—out of Nuwgate delevered.' Machyn's Diary p. 92.]
12 For *Weybridge* read *Uxbridge.*
[S.] [Fox also says Uxbridge.]
13 [Tankerfield. Fox.]
14 *Whorwood* read *Harwood.*
[S.]
15 [Fox calls him Hale.]
16 [The date of Elizabeth Warne's

death is recorded in Machyn's Diary
as follows, p. 92. 'The 24 day of
August was bornyd at Stratford of
Bowe in the conte of Mydyllsex, a
woman, wife of John Waren clothworker a huphulster over agaynst
sant John's in Walbroke; the
wyche.... John her hosband was
bornyd with on Cardmaker in
Smythfeld for herese both; and the
same woman had a sune taken at
her bornyng and cared to Nuwgatt
to, his syster for they will borne
boyth.' That of William Hall is
supplied in the following extract
p. 94. 'The 31 day of August
whent out of Nugatt a man of Essex unto Barnett for herese by the
shreyff of Medyllsex, to borne ther.']
17 *After* 'marked' *read,* and in this

[Fox, vol. iii. p. 351.]

George Catmar, and four others, were burnt at Canterbury, On the 20th, Robert Glover, a gentleman, and one Cornelius Bangey, were burnt at Coventry: the same month, but we

[Ibid. pp. 349, 351, 360.]

know not on what days, William Allen was burnt at Walsingham, Roger Coo at Yerford, Thomas Cob in Thetford. Thomas Haywood, and John Garaway, at Lichfield, were also burnt on the same account. On the 16th of October following,

[Thirlby's Register, fol. 81.]

William [18] Wolley and Robert Pigot were burnt at Ely; where Shaxton [19], that had been bishop of Salisbury in king Henry's time, and quitted his bishopric on the account of the six articles, but in the end of that reign recanted, and was now bishop 318 suffragan [20] of Ely, condemned them [21]. It is enough to have named all these, who were burnt merely by the proceedings *ex officio;* for being forced, either to accuse themselves, or to die however, they chose rather plainly to answer those articles that were ministered to them, and so were condemned for their answers.

Ridley and Latimer burnt at Oxford. [Fox, vol. iii. p. 416.]

But on the 16th of October, Ridley and Latimer offered up their lives at Oxford, on which it may be expected I should enlarge a little. The bishops of Lincoln, Gloucester, and Bristol, were sent to Oxford by a special commission from the cardinal to proceed against them. As soon as Ridley heard they proceeded in the name of the pope, by authority from the cardinal, he put on his cap, having stood bareheaded before that, because he would express no sign of reverence to those who acted by such a commission. He said he paid great respect to the cardinal as descended from the royal family, and a man endued with such learning and virtue; that therefore he

month of August Richard Hook suffered at Chichester. [S.]

[18] For Wolley read Wolsey. [S.]

[19] Shaxton could not condemn them, being there only as an assistant. They were condemned by John Fuller, LL.D., Vicarium in spiritualibus Domini Thomæ Episcopi Eliensis — et ejusdem Commissarium — legitime constitutum — ad negotia infra scripta expediendum — in capellâ B. Mariæ Eliensis—assistentibus ei tunc ibidem Reverendo in Christo patre Nicholao — modo suffragano episcopo — Roberto Steward, Decano Eliensi, Joanne Christopherson S.T.B. Decano Norvicensi, &c. Registr. Thyrlby, fol. 81, 82, where the process may be seen. [B.]

[20] Again for suffragan to the bishop of Ely. [G.]

[21] Shaxton did not condemn them, Fuller the bishop's chancellor condemned them. Steward, dean of Ely, and Christopherson, [Fox, vol. iii. p. 358.] Dean of Norwich with others, were in the commission, but the chancellor was the chief. [S.]

honoured and reverenced him; but for his legatine authority from the bishop of Rome, he utterly renounced it: and therefore would shew no reverence to that character, And so, putting off his cap as he spoke of him on other respects, he put it on again when he named his being legate; and being required to put it off, refused to do it on that account; but one of the beadles did it for him. After that, the bishop of Lincoln made [Fox, vol. him a long exhortation to recant, and acknowledge the see of iii. p. 417.] Rome; since Christ had built his church on St. Peter, and the fathers had all acknowledged the preeminence of that see, and himself had been once of that opinion. To which he answered, it was upon the faith which St. Peter confessed, that Christ had founded his church: he acknowledged the bishops of Rome had [Ibid. p. been held in great esteem, both for the dignity of the city, and 418.] the worthiness of the bishops that had sat in it; but they were only esteemed patriarchs of the west; and the church had not then thought of that power, to which they had since advanced themselves: he confessed he was once of their mind, but it was as St. Paul had been a persecutor; he had seen since such [Ibid. p. spots in the church of Rome, that he could never return to it. 419.] Upon this followed much discourse: in conclusion, they objected to him some articles about those opinions which he had maintained a year and an half before that in the schools; and required him to make his answers to them. He began with a [Ibid. p. protestation, that by answering them he did not acknowledge 420.] the pope's authority, and then answered them as he had done before. Latimer used the like protestation and answers. So they were allowed one night's respite to consider better whether they would recant or not: but next day they appearing, and adhering to the answers they had made, were declared obstinate heretics, and ordered to be degraded, and so delivered over to the secular power.

After that, new attempts were made on Ridley to persuade him to accept of the queen's mercy; but all being to no purpose, the writ was sent down to burn them. The night before the [Ibid. p. execution, Ridley was very joyful, and invited the mayor and 429.] his wife, in whose house he was kept, to be at his wedding next day: at which when the mayor's wife wept, he said he perceived she did not love him; but he told her, though his breakfast would be sharp, he was sure his supper would be sweet ·

he was glad to hear that his sister would come and see him 319 die, and was in such composure of mind, that they were all amazed at it. Next morning, being the 16th, they were led out to the place of execution, which was before Balliol college: they looked up to the prison to have seen Cranmer, but he was then engaged in dispute with some friars, so that he was not in his window; but he looked after them with great tenderness, and, kneeling down, prayed earnestly that God would strengthen their faith and patience in that their last but painful passage. When they came to the stake, they embraced one another with great affection, Ridley saying to Latimer, *Be of good heart, brother; for God will either assuage the fury of the flame, or enable us to abide it.*   Dr. Smith was

[1 Cor. xiii.] appointed to preach, and took his text from these words; *If I give my body to be burnt, and have no charity, it profiteth nothing.* He compared their dying for heresy to Judas' hanging himself; and warned the people to beware of them, with as much bitterness as he could express.   The best of it was, the

[Fox, vol. iii. p. 430.] sermon lasted not above a quarter of an hour.   When he had done, Ridley was going to answer him; and the lord Williams, that was appointed by the queen to see the execution, was inclined to hear him: but the vice-chancellor said, except he intended to recant, he was not to be suffered to speak.   Ridley answered, " he would never deny his Lord, nor those truths of his, of which " he was persuaded; God's will be done in him: he committed " himself to God, who would indifferently judge all."   Then he addressed himself to the lord Williams, and said, " Nothing " troubled him so much, as that he had received fines of some " who took leases of him when he was bishop of London, and " these leases were now voided; he therefore humbly prayed, " that the queen would give order, that those might be made " good to the tenants, or that the fines might be restored out " of his goods which he had left in his house, and were of far " greater value than those fines would amount to; and that " some pity might be had of Shipside, his brother-in-law, who " was turned out of a place he had put him in, and had now " attended on him with great care."   Then they both prayed and fitted themselves for the stake; Latimer saying to Ridley, *Be of good comfort, we shall this day light such a candle in England, as I trust by God's grace shall never be put out.*

Then gunpowder being hanged about their bodies in great
quantities to hasten their death, the fire was put to, and Latimer was with the first flame, the powder taking fire, put out
of pain, and died immediately. But Ridley had a more lingering torment; for they threw on the fire so much wood, that
the flame could not break through it: so that his legs were
almost consumed before this was observed; and then one opening the passage to the flame, it put an end to his life.

Thus died these two excellent bishops; the one for his piety,
learning, and solid judgment, the ablest man of all that advanced the reformation; and the other, for the plain simplicity
of his life, esteemed a truly primitive bishop and Christian. Of
his care of his bishopric, the instructions he gave at his visitation, chiefly of the monasteries, will give a good evidence; and
therefore I have put them in the Collection, as they were copied Collect.
from the register of Worcester, by that ingenious and worthy Numb. 23.
counsellor Mr. Summers, who, out of his zeal to the reformation, searched all the books there, that he might gather from
320 them such things as he thought could be of use to this work.
Bonner had made an ill retribution to Ridley for the kindness
he had shewed his friends when he was in possession at London;
for he had made Bonner's mother always dine with him, when
he lived in his country-house of Fulham, and treated her as if
she had been his own mother; besides his kindness to his other
friends.   Heath, then bishop of Worcester, had been kept prisoner a year and a half in Ridley's house, where he lived as if
he had been at his own; and Heath used always to call him
the best learned of all the party; yet he so far forgot gratitude and humanity, that though he went through Oxford when
he was a prisoner there, he came not to see him.   When they
lay in the Tower, both Cranmer and they were, by reason
of the number of prisoners, put into one chamber for some
months; but after they came to Oxford, they could scarce
send messages to one another; and men had laid off humanity
so much, that all the while they lay there, none of the university waited on them. Few that favoured their doctrine were
then left; and of the rest, it is no wonder that none came to
visit them: nor did they supply them with any thing they
needed; for all the charity that was sent to them came from
London.

Suits about
the spoils of
churches. This summer there was a strict search made after all the goods of the church that had been embezzled: and all that had been visitors, either in king Henry or king Edward's time, were brought into suits about it; but many compounded, and so purchased their quiet by an offer to the church of some large gratuity; and according to the greatness thereof, their affection to the church was measured. Many of those did favour the reformation, which made them give the more bountifully, that so they might come under good characters, and be the less suspected.

Gardiner's
sickness
and death.
[Fox, vol.
iii. p. 450.] The parliament was opened on the 21st of October. The chancellor came thither, both then and on the 23rd, but could come no more[22]. It was reported, that he had stayed long for dinner that day that Ridley and Latimer[23] were to be burnt, till one should bring him word that the fire was set to them; but the messenger coming post, did not reach London till four o'clock in the afternoon, and that he then went cheerfully to dine; but was at dinner struck with the illness of which he died. It was a suppression of urine, which held him till the [Nov. 13.] 12th of November, on which he died. He had great remorse for his former life; and Day bishop of Chichester coming to him, and comforting him with the assurance of justification through the blood of Christ; he answered him, " he might speak " of that to him or others in his condition; but if he opened " that gap again, and preached that to the people, then fare-

---

[22] Gardiner's picture [which was placed here in the folio editions]. If your lordship has seen this picture with the seals, &c. it must be Gardiner's; though I have seen two pictures at Trinity College and Trinity Hall, said to be Gardiner's, very unlike this. I have often suspected it to belong to Horn, who was a severe rough sort of a man, and gives the bugle horns for his arms, but without a chevron; which, though they are said to belong to the Gardiners, yet Gardiner, when he was chancellor of Cambridge, gives different paternal arms, as may be seen in the appendix to Archbishop Parker's Antiq. Brit. Poynet his successor describes him thus; ' He had a hanging look, frowning brows, eyes an inch within the head, a nose hooked like a buzzard, wide nostrils like a horse; a sparrow mouth, &c.' And truly by this description it may be Gardiner's. [B.]

[23] [Ridley and Latimer were burnt at Oxford on the 16th of October. Gardiner was in the house of peers on the 21st and the 23rd of October, and of his appearance there Bale says, ' His duobus diebus ita mihi visus est non modo seipsum iis rebus superasse quibus cæteros superare solet ingenio, eloquentia, prudentia, pietate, sed etiam ipsas sui corporis vires.' See his life in Lord Campbells's Lives of the Chancellors.]

" well altogether. He often repeated those words, *Erravi* [Parker,
" *cum Petro, sed non flevi cum Petro* [24] ; I have erred with Antiq.
" Peter, but I have not mourned with him." He was of a p. 511.]
nobler descent than is commonly known; for though he took
the name Gardiner from his supposed father, yet he was then
believed to be the base son of Richard Woodville [25], that was
brother to queen Elizabeth, wife to king Edward the Fourth [26],
so that he was of kin to king Henry the Eighth, in the second
and third degree of consanguinity; which might be the cause
that he was so suddenly advanced to the bishopric of Winchester. This is mentioned by sir Edward Hobbey, in a letter
he writ to one of those that had fled beyond sea, giving him
an account of his death; where he says of him, he was a man
321 of higher descent than he was commonly reputed; and on the
margin it is said, he was nephew to a queen of England. This
explains that which I find objected both to him and Bonner in
one of the books that were written in the defence of the [Poynet,
married clergy; that no wonder they were such enemies to Politic
marriage, since both of them were born in adultery. He was Power,
a man well skilled in the canon and civil laws, and mode- p. 29.]
rately in divinity. He had a good style in Latin, and understood the Greek well; but his strength lay in deep dissimulation, a quickness of apprehension, a great prospect of affairs,
a close and artificial way of concealing his mind, and insinuating himself into the affections and confidences of other persons.
He did comply all Henry the Eighth's time; and would willingly have done the like in king Edward's time, but that
Cranmer knew him too well to be directed by him, and handled
him as he deserved. But the usage he then met with so recovered him with queen Mary, that she put him in the greatest
trusts; and now, when a cardinal's hat was like to fall on his
head, he was carried off, and all his ambitious projects fell
with him. Of his servile compliance in promoting king Henry's

[24] [Negavi cum Petro, exivi cum
Petro, sed nondum flevi cum Petro.]
[25] [' Bishop Godwin delivereth a
more probable relation, which he
affirmeth to have received from a
kinsman of Gardiner, that he was
the base son of Lionel Woodville
bishop of Salisbury; which Lionel
was the son of Richard Wood-

ville mentioned by the historian.
With Godwin agreeth Mills, in
his genealogical catalogue of the
nobility of England.' Specimen of
Errors, p. 143.]
[26] For Edward the Sixth, *read*
Edward the Fourth. [S.] [Alluding
to a misprint in the first edition,
corrected in the second.]

divorce, I have found fresh instances, besides those that are mentioned in the former volume. When he went to Rome, in the year 1529, Anne Boleyn writ a very kind letter to him, which I have put in the Collection. By it the reader will clearly perceive that he was then in the secret of the king's designing to marry her, as soon as the divorce was obtained. There is another particular in that letter, which corrects a conjecture, which I set down in the beginning of the former book, concerning the cramp-rings that were blessed by king Henry; which I thought might have been done by him after he was declared head of the church. That part was printed before I saw this letter. But this letter shews they were used to be blessed before the separation from Rome; for Anne Boleyn sent them as great presents thither. The use of them had been (it seems) discontinued in king Edward's time; but now under queen Mary it was designed to be revived, and the office for it was written out in a fair manuscript, yet extant: of which I have put a copy in the Collection. But the silence in the writers of that time makes me think it was seldom, if ever practised. But to return to Gardiner's officious compliance in the matter of the divorce; I have put in the Collection a letter of his to king Henry, written in such confidence to him, that even cardinal Wolsey was not to see it. In it he sets out the pope's timorousness so plainly, that he writes, he saw nothing but the fear he was in of the emperor's forces kept him from granting what was desired; therefore he advised the king to do the business once in England, and then leave it to the emperor to complain; not doubting but he would be put off by as many delays as were now used in the king's business.

Collect. Numb. 24.

Collect. Numb. 25.

Collect. Numb. 26.

[Jan. 1. 1556. Stow, p. 627.]

Heath, archbishop of York, had the seals in February[27] after; they having been during that interval in the hands of sir Nicholas Hare, then master of the rolls; and he was made chancellor during the queen's pleasure. The queen also, considering that Whitehall had been taken from the see of York[28], had a scruple in her conscience against living in it: but Heath and she agreed it thus: Suffolk-Place, by the duke's attainder, was now in the queen's hands; so she gave that to the see of

27 Heath was appointed chancellor on new year's day. [S.]
28 [Vide Part i. p. 80.]

York, which Heath sold, and converted it to tenements, and
22 purchased another house near Charing-Cross, which from
thenceforward was called York-house.

But for the parliament, it was now much changed; men's _{The temper}
minds were much alienated from the clergy, and also from the _{of the par-}
_{liament is}
queen, who minded nothing else but to raise them to great _{much}
wealth and power again. On the 28th of October it was _{changed.}
_{[Journal of}
moved in the house of commons to give a subsidy, and two _{Commons,}
fifteenths, for paying the debts of the crown; but it was op- _{p. 42.]}
posed with great vehemence. It was said, that the queen had
profusely given away the riches of the crown, and then turned
to the laity to pay her debts: why did she not rather turn to
the spiritualty? But it was answered, that the convocation had
given her a subsidy of six shillings in the pound; and the
queen asked now, after almost three years' reign, nothing but
what she had discharged her subjects of at her first coming to
the crown. Yet the heats grew such, that on the 1st of No- [Oct. 31.
vember, secretary Petre brought a message from her, that she Ibid. p. 43.]
thanked them that had moved for two fifteenths for her: but
she refused it: so the subsidy was agreed on. On the 29th of [Nov. 2.]
November the queen sent for the house of commons. When _{The queen}
_{discharges}
they were come, she said to them, she could not with a good _{the clergy}
conscience take the tenths and firstfruits of spiritual benefices: _{of tenths}
_{and first-}
it was a tax her father laid on the clergy, to support his dig- _{fruits.}
_{[Nov. 19,}
nity of supreme head; of which since she was divested, she _{Journal of}
would also discharge that. Then the legate made a speech to _{Commons,}
_{p. 44.]}
shew that tithes and impropriations of spiritual benefices were
the patrimony of the church, and ought to return to it. The
queen upon that declared, that she would surrender them up [Nov. 20.
likewise to the church. Then one Story of the house of com- _{ibid.]}
mons kneeled down, and said to the queen, that the speaker
did not open to her their desire that licenses might be restrained. This was a great affront to the speaker; so he, returning to the house, complained of Story. This member
thought he might assume more liberty; for in Edward the
Sixth's time, when the bill for the first book of the English
service passed, he spoke so freely against it, with such reflections on the king and the protector, that he was put in the
sergeant's hands, and sent to the Tower. The words he had
said were, *Wo unto thee, O England, when thy king is a* _{Eccles. x.}
_{15.}

child; and an impeachment was drawn against him. But, upon his submission, the house ordered the privy counsellors to declare to the protector, that it was their resolution that he should be enlarged: and they desired that the king would forgive his offence against him and his council. Now he had indiscreetly appeared against all licenses from Rome, thinking he had a privilege to talk .more freely: but he confessed his fault, and the house, *knowing that he spake from a good zeal,* forgave him. He was afterwards condemned for treason in queen Elizabeth's reign.

[Nov. 20.] Journ. Dom. Com. [p. 44.]

[Ibid. p. 45.]

On the 23rd of November, the bill for suppressing the first-fruits and tenths, and the resigning up all impropriations that were yet in the queen's gift to the church, to be disposed of as the legate pleased, for the relief of the clergy, was brought into the house. It was once thought fit to have the surrender of impropriations left out; for it was said, the queen might do that as well by letters patents; and if it were put into the bill, it would raise great jealousies, since it would be understood, that the queen did expect that the subjects should follow her example: but it was resolved, by all means possible, to recover the tithes to the church; so it was put into the bill. It was long argued: some said, the clergy would rob the crown, and the nation both; and that the laity must then support the dignity of the realm. It was particularly committed to sir William Cecil and others, to be examined by them. On the 13th of December the house divided about it; 126 were against it, and 193 were for it.

323

[Dec. 3, Journal of Commons, p. 46.]

There was a bill sent down against the countess of Sussex, who had left her husband and gone into France, where she lived openly in adultery, and bare children to others. A bill was put in, to the same purpose, in the first parliament of this reign to take her jointure from her, and declare her children bastards; and was then cast out by the commons; and had now again the same fate. Another bill was put in against the duchess of Suffolk and others, who had gone beyond sea, to require them to return under severe punishments: but though it was agreed to by the lords, yet, upon a division of the house of

[Nov. 15, Journal of Commons, p. 44.]

[Dec. 5, 1553.]

Against those that had fled beyond sea, rejected.

---

29 The 13th of December. The parliament was dissolved on the 9th of December. [S.]

commons, it was carried in the negative. The greatest and [Dec. 6,
wealthiest of those who favoured the reformation, seeing how Journal of
ill a condition they must be in if they stayed in England, were p. 46.]
gone beyond sea: so it was now endeavoured to force them
to return, or to make them lose their estates. But the commons
thought they had already consented to too severe laws against
them, and therefore would add no more. The duchess of Suffolk had been persecuted while she was in the Netherlands, but
narrowly escaped. Another bill was put in for the incapacitat- [Dec. 7,
ing of several persons from being justices[30] of peace; but was 48.]
cast out by the commons at the first reading. This was chiefly
against such as were suspected of remissness in the prosecuting
of heretics; but the commons would do nothing to encourage
that: nor was it necessary, since it was in the queen's power to
leave out of the commission such as she excepted to: but it
shewed the zeal of some, who had a mind to recommend themselves by such motions.

There was a complaint put into the house of commons, by An act de-
the wife of one Rufford, against Bennet Smith, who had hired barring one
two persons to kill her husband; and which, as the act passed benefit of
about it says, was one of the most detestable murders that had clergy.
ever been known in England. But Smith, that had hired, and Statutes,
afterwards paid the murderers, might by the law claim, and 292.]
have the benefit of clergy. It is, and hath been an ancient custom in this nation, that, for some crimes, those who can read
are not to suffer death. This was at first done with a declaration, that either they had vowed, or were then resolved to enter into orders; which was the cause that no bigamy, that is,
none that had been twice married, or such as married widows,
were capable of it; because such could not receive orders: and
the reading was only to shew that they were in some sort qualified for orders; though afterwards, the reading, without any
such vow or promise, was all that was required to give one the
benefit of clergy. This was granted as an appendix of the ecclesiastical immunity; for the churchmen were not satisfied
that their own persons should be exempted from punishment,
but would needs have all that resolved to come among them be

---

[30]The bill was, that no servants to   should be justices. It was read the
gentlemen, and wearing their clothes   second time on the 12th of Novem-
(except the king and queen's),   ber. [S.]

likewise preserved from the punishment due to those crimes,
which they had formerly committed. So Rufford's wife peti-
tioning that Smith might by act of parliament be debarred
that benefit; they sent her to the queen, to beg that she would 324
order Smith to be brought from the Tower, where he was then
kept, to the bar of their house: which being done, the other
partners and actors confessed all; and though he at first denied,
yet he afterward confessed. So the bill was sent up by the
commons to the lords, where it was much opposed by the
clergy, who would not consent that any diminution should be
made of their ancient privileges: but the heinousness of the
fact wrought so much on the greater part, that it was passed;
the earls of Arundel and Rutland, the bishops of London, Worcester, Norwich and Bristol, the lords Abergavenny, Fitzwater
and Lumley, protesting[31]. Pates was now bishop of Worcester, upon Heath's translation to York. He was (as some
say) designed to be bishop of that see by king Henry upon Latimer's resignation; but being engaged in a correspondence
with the pope and cardinal Pole, he fled beyond sea. But the
truth is, that upon the death of Jerome de Ghinucci, he was at
Rome made bishop of Worcester by the pope, and was thereupon attainted: but his attainder had been repealed by the
former parliament, and so he was restored to that see.

On the 9th of December[32] the parliament was dissolved.
And the day following[33], sir Anthony Kingston, who had been a
main stickler in it, and had one day taken the keys of the
house from the sergeant, which (it seems) was not displeasing
to the major part of the house, since they did nothing upon it,
was sent to the Tower: and that same day, (as it is in the
council-books,) the bishop of Ely delivered to the lord treasurer
the pope's bull, confirming the king and queen's title to Ireland;

Margin notes:
[Nov. 18. Journal of Commons, p. 44.]

[Nov. 22, ibid. p. 45.]

[Dec. 4. Journal of Lords, p. 509.]

Sir Anthony Kingston put in the Tower for his behaviour in the house of commons. Ex Lib. Concil. [p. 329.]

[31] [The journal adds the name of
the bishop of Bangor to the dissen-
tients, and omits that of Lord Abergavenny, p. 509.]

[32] 'The 10 day of Desember was
had to the Towre ser Anthony
Kyngston, knyght, and to the Flett,
and cam owt agayn shortely after.'
Machyns' Diary, p. 98.]

[33] [This day was delivered unto
the hands of the lord treasurer by

the reverend father in God the bishop of Ely, to be safely reposed in
the King and Queen's majesty's
treasury, the Pope's holiness' bull
under lead, touching the erection
and confirmation of their majesty's
title of king and queen in the realme
of Irelande, bearing date at Rome,
1555, Septimo Idus Junii, anno
pontificatûs sui primo. Extract
from Council Book, p. 329.]

bearing date the 7th of June. Kingston lay in the Tower till the 23rd of the month; and then he submitted, and asked pardon, and was discharged. But he was next year accused to have engaged in a design with some others to have robbed the exchequer of 50,000*l*[34]. Whereupon six of them, Udal, Throgmorton, Petham[35], Daniel, Stanton, and White were executed for felony. What evidence was brought against them, I do not know. But Kingston died on his way to London.

From the parliament I turn next to the convocation, where the cardinal was now at more liberty, being delivered from Gardiner's jealousies and opposition. He obtained of the queen, on the 2nd of November, a warrant under the great seal, giving him license to hold a synod. The license he had formerly taken out is made mention of; and, to avoid all ambiguities, which might arise from the laws or prerogatives of the crown, she authorized him to call that, or any other synod after, and to decree what canons he should think fit: she also authorized the clergy to meet, consent to, and obey those canons, without any danger of the law. This was thought safe on both sides; both for preserving the rights of the crown, and securing the clergy from being afterwards brought within the statute of *præmunire*, as they had been upon their acknowledging cardinal Wolsey's legatine power. To this convocation Pole proposed a book he had prepared, which was afterwards printed with the title of The Reformation of England by the Decree of cardinal Pole; and is now put into the volumes of the councils[37].

Cardinal Pole in convocation makes canons for reforming the clergy. Rot. Pat. 1st Par. 3. Reg.

The first decree is, that there should be constantly a remembrance of the reconciliation now made with Rome in every mass; besides, a procession, with other solemnities, on the anniversary of it. He also confirmed the constitutions of Otho and Othobonus, forbidding the reading of all heretical books; and set forth the catholic faith, in the words of that exposition

The heads of Pole's reformation.

325

---

[34] Add — and with it to have made a rebellion. [S.]

[35] *For* Petham *read* Peckham. [S.]

[36] White was not executed; he discovered the conspiracy. For *felony*, read *high treason, and were executed accordingly.* There were

eight who suffered: the three besides those named were Rossey, Bedyl and Dethick. [S.]

[37] [De reformatione, 4to, Rom. 1562. There are several editions of this date, for which see the Bodleian Catalogue.]

of it, which pope Eugenius sent from the council of Florence to those of Armenia.

The 2nd was, for the careful administering and preserving of the sacraments; and for the putting away of all feasting in the festivities of the dedications of churches.

The 3rd exhorts the bishops to lay aside all secular cares, and give themselves wholly to the pastoral office; and to reside in their diocese, under the highest pains. Their canons are also required to reside, and also other clergymen. All pluralities of benefices with cure are simply condemned: and those who had more benefices with cure were required within two months to resign all but one; otherwise it was to be declared that they had forfeited them all.

The 4th is, that whereas the residence of bishops could not be of great use, unless they became truly pastors to their flock; which was chiefly done by their preaching the word of God; that had been, contrary to the apostles' practice, much neglected by many: therefore he requires them to preach every Sunday or holyday; or if they were disabled, to find other fit persons to do it. And they were also in private to instruct and exhort their people, and all the other inferior clergy, and to endeavour to persuade them to the catholic faith; or, if need were, to use threatenings. And because of the great want of good preachers, the cardinal declared he would take care there should be homilies set out for the instruction of the nation. In the mean while, every bishop was to be sending such as were more eminent in preaching over their diocese, thereby to supply the defects of the rest.

The 5th is about the lives of the bishops; that they should be most strict and exemplary; that they should lay aside all pride and pomp; should not be clothed in silk, nor have rich furniture; and have frugal tables, not above three or four dishes of meat; and even so many he rather allows, considering the present time, than approves; that at their table the scriptures, or other good books, should be read, mixed with pious discourses; that they should not have too great numbers of servants or horses. But that this parsimony might appear not to flow from avarice, they were to lay out the rest of their revenues on the poor, and for breeding young scholars, and other works of piety. All the same rules he sets to the inferior clergy, with a due proportion to their stations and profits.

The 6th is about giving orders; they were not to be rashly given, but upon a strict previous *examen*. Every one that was to be ordained was to give in his name a long time before, that there might be time to inquire carefully about him. The bishops were charged not to turn over the examination upon others, and think their work was only to lay on their hands; but were to examine diligently themselves, and not superficially: and to call to their assistance such as they knew to be pious and learned, and in whom they might confide.

The 7th was about conferring benefices, which in some sort came also within that charge, *Lay hands suddenly on no man*. They were to lay aside all partiality in their choice, and seek out the most deserving; and to make such as they put in benefices bind themselves by oath to reside.

326   The 8th was against giving the advowsons of benefices before they were vacant.

The 9th was about simony.

The 10th against the alienations of any of the goods of the church.

The 11th was, that in every cathedral there should be a seminary for supplying the diocese; of whom two ranks were to be made: the one of those who learned grammar; the other, of those who were grown up, and were to be ordained acolyths; and these were to be trained up in study and virtue, till they were fit to serve in the church. And a tax of the fourth penny was laid on the clergy for their maintenance.

The 12th was about visitations.

These were all finished, agreed to, and published by him in February next year.

In these decrees mention is made of homilies, which were intended to be published: and among archbishop Parker's papers I find the scheme he had of them was thus laid: he designed four books of homilies. The first, of the controverted points, for preserving the people from error. The 2nd for the exposition of the Creed and Ten Commandments, the Lord's Prayer, the salutation of the Virgin, and the sacraments. The 3rd was to be for the saints' days, and the Sundays and holydays of the year; for explaining the Epistles and Gospels. And the 4th was concerning virtues and vices, and the rites and ceremonies of the church.

Ex MSS. Coll. C. C. Cant.

Pole's de-
sign for re-
forming the
church.

By all these it may appear, how well-tempered this cardinal was. He never set on the clergy to persecute heretics, but to reform themselves; as well knowing, that a strict exemplary clergy can soon overcome all opposition whatsoever, and bear down even truth itself. For the common people are generally either so ignorant, or so distracted with other affairs, that they seldom enter into any exact discussion of speculative points, that are disputed among divines; but take up things upon general notions and prejudices: and none have more influence on them than the scandals or strict lives of churchmen. So that Pole, intending to correct all those, laid down good rules to amend their lives, to throw out those crying scandals of pluralities and non-residence; to oblige bishops to be exact in their examinations before orders, and in conferring benefices on the most deserving, and not to be biassed by partial affections. In this last thing himself was a great example: for though he had an only brother[38], (so I find him called in one of the cardinal's commissions to him with some others, though I believe he was a bastard brother, David, that had continued all king Henry's time in his archdeaconry of Derby; he, either to punish him for his former compliance, or to shew he had no mind to raise his kindred, did not advance him till after he had been two years in England; and then he gave him only the bishopric of Peterborough, one of the poorest of the bishoprics; which, considering his nearness to the crown, and high birth, was a very small preferment. But above all, that design of his, to have seminaries in every cathedral for the planting of the diocese, shews what a wise prospect he had of the right methods of recovering a church, which was over-run, as he judged, with heresy. It was the same that Cranmer 327 had formerly designed, but never took effect. Certainly, persons formed from their childhood with other notions, and another method of living, must be much better fitted for a holy character, than those that have lived in the pleasures and follies of the world; who, unless a very extraordinary change is wrought in them, still keep some of their old customs about

[38] Cardinal Pole had two brothers, Arthur and Jeffrey, both arraigned in the year 1562 for a conspiracy against queen Elizabeth. David was not his brother, nor a bastard, for there is no bull of dispensation in his favour among those sent over at that time. [S.]

them, and so fall short of that gravity and decency that becomes so spiritual a function.

He shewed the weakness of his spirit in one thing, that,
being against cruel proceedings with heretics, he did not more
openly profess it; but both suffered the other bishops to go
on, and even in Canterbury, now sequestered in his hands, and
soon after put under his care, he left those poor men to the
cruelties of the brutal and fierce popish clergy. In this he was
to be pitied, that he had not courage enough to contend with
so haughty a pope as Paul IV. was; who thought of no other
way of bearing down heresy, but by setting up the inquisition
every where: so Pole, it seems, judged it sufficient for him
not to act himself, nor to set on any; and thought he did
enough, when he discouraged it in private: but yet he granted
commissions to the other bishops and archdeacons to proceed
against those called heretics. He was not only afraid of being
discharged of his legation, and of losing the archbishopric of
Canterbury, which was now ready to fall upon him; but he
feared to be sent for to Rome, and cruelly used by the pope,
who remembered all the quarrels he formerly had with any
of the cardinals, and put cardinal Morone (that was Pole's
great friend) in prison, upon suspicion of heresy. All these
things prevailed with Pole to give way to the persecution: and
it was thought that he himself hastened the execution of Cranmer, longing to be invested with that see; which is the only
personal blemish I find laid on him.

One remarkable thing of him was, his not listening to the
proposition the Jesuits made him of bringing them into England.   That order had been set up about twelve years before
this, and was in its first institution chiefly designed for propa-
gating the doctrines of that church in heretical or infidel countries; to which was afterwards added, the education of children. It was not easily allowed of at Rome, because the
bishops did universally complain of the great numbers of
exempted regulars; and therefore at first it was limited to a
small number; which restriction was soon taken off. They,
besides the vows of other orders, took one for a blind and
universal obedience to the see of Rome; and because they
were much to be employed, they were dispensed with, as to
the hours of the quire, which made them be called a mongrel

order between the regulars and seculars. They have since that time, by their care in educating youth, by their indefatigable industry, and chiefly by their accommodating penances, and all the other rules of religion, to the humours and inclinations of those who confess their sins to them, drawn almost all the world after them; and are raised now to that height both of wealth and power, that they are become the objects of the envy and hatred of all the rest of their own church. They suggested to Pole, that whereas the queen was restoring the goods of the church that were in her hands, it was but to little purpose to raise up the old foundations; for the Benedictine order was become rather a clog than a help to the church: they therefore desired that those houses might be assigned to them, for maintaining schools and seminaries, which they should 328 set on quickly; and they did not doubt but by their dealing with the consciences of those who were a dying, they should soon recover the greatest part of the goods of the church. The Jesuits were out of measure offended with him for not entertaining their proposition; which I gather from an Italian manuscript, which my most worthy friend Mr. Crawford found in Venice, when he was chaplain there to sir Thomas Higgins, his majesty's envoy to that republic: but how it came that this motion was laid aside, I am not able to judge.

[Nov. 30. Fox, vol. iii. p. 458.]
There passed nothing else remarkable this year; but that, in the end of November, John Webbe, a gentleman, George Roper, and Gregory Parke, were burnt all at one stake in Canterbury. And on the 18th of December, Philpot, that had Philpot's martyrdom. [Ibid. p. 459.] disputed in the convocation, was burnt in Smithfield[39]. He was, at the end of that meeting, put in prison for what he had said in it, though liberty of speech had been promised; and the nature of the meeting did require it. He was kept long in [Ibid. p. 462.] the stocks in the bishop of London's coal-house, and many conferences were had with him, to persuade him to change. By what Bonner said in one of them, it appears, that he hoped they should be better used upon Gardiner's death: for Bonner told him, he thought, because the lord chancellor was dead, they would burn no more: but he should soon find his error,

[39] [' The 18 day of Dessember betwyn 8 and 9 of the cloke in the mornyng was cared into Smythfeld to be bornyd, on master,........ gentyllman for herese.' Machyn's Diary, p. 98]

if he did not recant. He continued stedfast in his persuasion, Philpot's
and pleaded, that he had never spoken nor written against martyrdom.
their laws since they were made, being all the while a prisoner, except what he had said in conference with them: yet
this prevailed not with Bonner, who had as little justice as
mercy in his temper. On the 16th of December he was condemned, and delivered to the sheriffs. He was at first laid in
irons, because he was so poor that he could not fee the jailor;
but the next day, these were by the sheriffs' order taken off.
As he was led into Smithfield, on the 18th, he kneeled down,
and said, *I will pay my vows in thee, O Smithfield.* When [Fox, vol.
he was brought to the stake, he said, *Shall I disdain to suffer* iii. p. 498.]
*at this stake, since my Redeemer did not refuse to suffer on
the cross for me?* He repeated the 106th, 107th, and 108th
Psalms, and then fitted himself for the fire, which consumed
him to ashes. So this year ended, in which there were sixty-
seven burnt for religion; and of those, four were bishops, and
thirteen were priests.

In Germany, a diet was held at Augsburg, where the peace 1556.
of Germany was fully settled: and it was decreed, that the Foreign
princes of the Augsburg Confession should have the free li- affairs.
berty of their religion; and that every prince might in his [Thuanus, xvi. 17.
own state establish what religion he pleased; excepting only p. 568.]
the ecclesiastical princes, who were to forfeit their benefices if
they turned. Those of Austria and Ferdinand's other hereditary dominions, desired freedom for their consciences: but
Ferdinand refused it; yet he appointed the chalice to be given
in the sacrament. The duke of Bavaria did the like in his
dominions. At all this the pope was highly offended, and
talked of deposing Ferdinand. He had nothing so much in
his mouth as the authority former popes had exercised, in
deposing princes at their pleasure. He had sworn to the cardinals, before he was chosen, that he would make but four
cardinals in two years: but he created seven within one half
329 year, and would not hear the consistory argue against it, or
remember him of his promise; but said, his power was absolute, and could not be limited. One of these cardinals was
Gropper, the dean of Cologne, a man of great learning and
virtues, but inconstant and fearful; as was shewn in the former

book[40] ; he refused to accept of that dignity, so generally sought after in their church; and was more esteemed for rejecting it, than others were that had by their ambition aspired to it.

Charles the Fifth's resignation. [Thuanus, xvi. 20. p. 570.]

In the end of this year, and the beginning of the next, a memorable thing fell out; of which if I give a large account, I do not fear to be much censured by the reader for it; especially since it is not impertinent to this work, the king and queen being so much concerned in it. It was Charles the Fifth's laying down, first, some of his hereditary dominions in October this year; and the rest, with the empire, not long after. He had now enjoyed the one forty years, and the other thirty-six. He was much disabled by the gout, which had held him almost constantly for several years; he had been in the greatest fatigues that ever any prince had undergone, ever since the seventeenth year of his age: he had gone nine times into Germany, six times into Spain, seven times into Italy, four times into France; had been ten times in the Netherlands, had made two expeditions into Africa, and been twice in England, and had crossed the seas eleven times. He had not only been a conqueror in all his wars, but had taken a pope, a king of France, and some princes of Germany, prisoners, besides a vast accession of wealth and empire from the West Indies. But he now growing out of love with the pomp and greatness of the world, began to have more serious thoughts of another life; which were much increased in him by the answer one of his captains gave him, when he desired leave to retire, and being asked the reason, said, that between the affairs of the world, and the hour of death, there ought to be some interval. He found his fortune turned; his designs in Germany were blasted: in the siege of Metz, he saw he could no more command triumphs to wait on him; for though his army consisted of 100,000 men, yet he was forced to raise his siege with the loss of 40,000 men; and though his wars had been this year more successful both in Italy and Flanders, yet he thought he was too old to deal with the king of France. It was thought his son set this forward, who had left England in discontent; being weary both of his queen, and of holding a

40 [See part ii. book 1, p. 51.]

titular crown only in her right, being excluded from the government.   All these things concurring, made the emperor, in
a solemn assembly at Brussels on the 25th of October, in the [Thuanus,
presence of his son, and Maximilian king of Bohemia, and of the $\begin{smallmatrix} \text{xvi. 20.} \\ \text{p. 570.]} \end{smallmatrix}$
duke of Savoy, and his two sisters, the queens dowager of
France and Hungary, with a vast number of others of lower
quality, first give his son the golden fleece, and so resign the
headship of that order to him; and then, the dukedoms of
Burgundy and Brabant, and the other provinces of the Netherlands.   Two months after that, he resigned all his other hereditary dominions: and the next year he sent a resignation of
the empire to the diet, who thereupon did choose his brother
Ferdinand emperor: to which the pope made great exceptions; for he said, the resignation ought to have been only to
330 him, and that, being made as it was, it was null; and upon
that he would not acknowledge the new emperor.

Charles stayed some time in Flanders in a private house;
for he left all his palaces, and had but little company about
him.   It is said, that when Seld, his brother's secretary, being
sent to him, was leaving him once late at night, all the candles
on the stairs being burnt out, and none waiting to light him
down, the late emperor would needs carry the candle down
after him: the other, as may be well imagined, being much
confounded at it, the emperor told him, he was now a private
man; and his servants, knowing there was nothing now to be
had by attending, did not wait carefully.   He bade him tell
his brother what a change he had seen in him, and how vain
a thing the attendance of courtiers was, since he was so soon
forsaken by his own servants.   He reserved but 100,000
crowns a year for his own use, and sixty servants.   But, at
his coming into Spain, he found even that small pension was
not readily paid; at which he was observed to be much displeased.   He retired to a place in the confines of Castile and
Portugal, which he had observed in his hunting to be fit for a
retreat, by reason of the pleasantness of the situation, and the
temperateness of the air: and there he had ordered a little
apartment of seven rooms, fourteen foot square, to be built for
him.   He kept only twelve servants about himself, and sent
the rest to stay in the neighbouring towns.

He gave himself at first much to mechanical curiosities, and had great varieties of clocks, and some other motions, which surprised the ignorant monks, who were afraid they were the performances of magic; especially his machines of birds of wood, that did fly out and come back, and the representations of armies, that by springs engaged and fought. He also designed that great work of carrying the Tago up a hill near Toledo, which was afterwards done at a vast charge. He gave himself to gardening and used to graft and imp[42] with his own hand; and, keeping but one horse, rid abroad sometimes, attended only by one footman.

The making of clocks was not then so perfect as it is since; so that he could never bring his clocks to strike in the same minute: and he used upon that to say, he saw the folly of endeavouring to bring all men to be of the same mind in religion, since he could not bring machines to agree exactly.

He set himself also much to study; and, in the second year of his retirement, went oftener to the chapel, and to the sacrament, than he had done at first. He used also to discipline himself with a cord, which, after his death, having some marks of the severity he had put himself to, was laid up among his son's chiefest rarities. But amidst all this it was believed he became in most points to be of the belief of the protestants before he died: and as his confessor was burnt[43] afterwards for heresy, so Miranda, the archbishop of Toledo, who used to come often to him, was upon the same suspicions kept long in prison. Near the end of two years, at the anniversary of his mother's funeral, who had died but a few years before, having lived long mad, he took a conceit that he would see an obit made for himself, and would have his own funeral rites performed; to which he came himself, with the rest of the monks, 331 and prayed most devoutly for the rest of his own soul, which set all the company on weeping. Two days after he sickened of a fever, of which he died on the 21st of September 1558: a rare and great instance of a mind surfeited with the pomps and glories of the world, seeking for that quiet in retirement, which he had long in vain searched after in palaces and camps.

Cranmer's trial.   And now I return to the affairs of England. The 21st of

[42 A rare use of this word as a verb. As a noun it is often used for a *graft* or *bud*.]

[43 [He was burnt in effigy only. See Pallavicini, lib. v. p. 426.]

March was Cranmer brought to the end of all his afflictions, and received his crown. On the 12th of September the former [Fox, vol. iii p. 544.] year, Brooks, bishop of Gloucester, came to Oxford as the pope's subdelegate ; and Martin and Story, commissioners from the king and queen, sat with him in St. Mary's to judge him. When he appeared before them, he paid a low reverence to [Ibid. p. 545.] them that sat in the king and queen's name ; but would give none to Brooks, since he sat by an authority from the pope, to which he would pay no respect. Then Brooks made a long speech, to set forth his apostasy and heresy, his incontinence, and finally his treason ; and exhorted him to repent ; and insinuated to him great hopes of being restored to his see upon it. After this, Martin made a speech of the difference between the [Ibid p. 547.] civil and ecclesiastical authority.

When they had done, Cranmer first kneeled down, and said the Lord's Prayer ; next he repeated the Apostles' Creed. Then he told them, he would never acknowledge the bishop of Rome's authority : he owned his allegiance to the crown, ac- [Ibid. p. 548.] cording to the oath he had often sworn ; and the submitting to the pope was directly contrary to that : he could not serve two masters. He said, the bishops of Rome not only set up pretensions that were contrary to the power of princes, but they had also made laws contrary to those made by God : instancing it in the worship of an unknown tongue, the denying the chalice to the people, the pretending to dispose of crowns, and exalting themselves above every creature ; which shewed them not to be the vicars of Christ, but to be antichrists, since all these things were manifestly contrary to the doctrine of Christ, that was delivered in the gospel. He remembered Brooks, that he had sworn to the king's supremacy. Brooks said, it was to king Henry VIII. and that Cranmer had made him swear it. To which Cranmer replied, that he did him wrong in that ; for it was done in his predecessor Warham's time, who had asserted the king's supremacy : and it was also sent to be discussed in the universities, and they had set their hands and seals to it ; and that Brooks, being then a doctor, had signed it with the rest : so that, all this being done before he came to be archbishop, it ought not to be called his deed.

After this, Story made another speech of the authority of [Ibid. p. 549.] the church, magnifying the see of Rome, and enlarging on those arguments commonly insisted on; and desired Brooks would put Cranmer to make a plain answer, and cut off all debates. Then followed a long discourse between Martin and Cranmer: in which Martin objected, that he had once sworn to the pope when he was consecrated; but that, aspiring to be archbishop, he had changed his mind in compliance to king Henry: that he had condemned Lambert of heresy, for denying the presence of Christ in the sacrament, and afterwards turned to that himself. To all this Cranmer answered, pretending, that never man came more unwillingly into a bishopric than he did to his: that he was so far from having aspired to it, that, though the king had sent one post to him to come over to be consecrated, he being then in Germany, yet he had delayed his journey seven weeks, hoping that in all that time the king might have forgot him: that, at his consecration, he publicly explained his meaning in what sense he swore to the pope; so that he did not act deceitfully in that particular: and that, when he condemned Lambert, he did then believe the corporal presence; which he continued to do, till Dr. Ridley shewed him such reasons and authorities as persuaded him to change his mind, and then he was not ashamed to retract his former opinion. Then they objected his having been twice married, his keeping his wife secretly in king Henry's time, and openly in king Edward's reign; his setting out heretical books and articles, and compelling others to subscribe them; his forsaking the catholic church, and denying Christ's presence in the sacrament of the altar, and disputing against it so publicly lately at Oxford. He confessed his living in marriage, and that he thought it was lawful for all men to marry; and that it was certainly better to do so than to lie with other men's wives, as many priests did. He confessed all the other articles; only he said, he had never forced any to subscribe.

After this, Brooks made a long speech to him, with many of the common arguments concerning the pope's power, and the presence in the sacrament: to which Cranmer made another large answer. Then many witnesses were examined upon the points they had heard Cranmer defend in the schools; and, in conclusion, they cited him to appear before the pope within eighty days, to answer for all those things which were now objected to him. He said, he would do it most willingly, if the

[Fox, vol. iii. p. 550.]

332

[Ibid. p. 551.]

[Ibid. p. 552.]

[Ibid. p. 554.]

king and queen would send him; but he could not go, if he were
still detained a prisoner.

After this, he was sent back to prison, where he lay till the [Ibid. p.
14th of February this year; and then Bonner and Thirlby 555.]
were sent down to degrade him. Bonner desired this employment, as a pleasant revenge on Cranmer, who had before deprived him: but it was forced on the other, who had lived in
great friendship with Cranmer formerly, and was a gentle and
good-natured man; but very inconstant and apt to change.
They had Cranmer brought before them; and then they
caused to read their commission, which declared him *contumax*
for not coming to Rome, and required them to degrade him.
They clothed him in pontifical robes, a mitre, and the other
garments, with a crosier in his hand: but the robes were made
of canvass, to make him show more ridiculous in them. Then [Fox, vol.
Bonner made a speech full of jeers: *This is the man that de-* iii. p. 556.]
spised the pope, and is now judged by him: This is the man
that pulled down churches, and is now judged in a church:
This is the man that contemned the sacrament, and is now
condemned before it: with other such expressions. At which
Thirlby was much offended, and pulled him oft by the sleeve,
desiring him to make an end; and challenged him afterwards,
that he had broke the promise he had made to him before, of
treating him with respect. And he was observed to weep
much all the while. He protested to Cranmer, that it was the [Ibid. p.
most sorrowful action of his whole life, and acknowledged the 558.]
great love and friendship that had been between them; and
333 that no earthly consideration, but the queen's command, could
have induced him to come, and do what they were then about:
he shed so many tears, that oft he stopped, and could not go
on in his discourse for the abundance of them. But Cranmer
said, his degradation was no trouble to him at all: he reckoned
himself as long ago cut off from all dependence and communion
with the see of Rome; so their doing it now with so much
pageantry did not much affect him: only he put in an appeal [Ibid. p.
from the pope to the next free general council. He said, he 556.]
was cited to Rome, but all the while kept a prisoner; so there
was no reason to proceed against him in his absence, since he
was willing to have gone thither and defended his doctrine:
he also denied any authority the pope had over him, or in

He is de-
graded.

England; and therefore appealed from his sentence. But, notwithstanding that, he was degraded: and all that ludicrous attire was taken, piece after piece, from him, according to the ceremonies of degradation, which are in use in the church of Rome.

But there were new engines contrived against him. Many had been sent to confer with him, both English and Spanish divines, to persuade him to recant: he was put in hopes of life and preferment again, and removed out of prison to the dean's lodgings at Christ Church; where all the arguments that could be invented were made use of to turn him from his former persuasion: and, in conclusion, as St. Peter himself had with curses denied his Saviour, so he, who had resisted now almost three years, was at last overcome; and human in-

He recants. firmity, the fears of death, and the hopes that were given him, prevailed with him to set his hand to a paper, renouncing all the errors of Luther and Zuinglius, acknowledging the pope's supremacy, the seven sacraments, the corporal presence in the eucharist, purgatory, prayer for departed souls, the invocation of saints: to which was added, his being sorry for his former errors; and concluded, exhorting all that had been deceived by his example or doctrine to return to the unity of the church: and protesting, that he had signed it willingly, only for the discharge of his own conscience.

[Fox, vol.
iii. p. 559.]

Fox, and other later writers from him, have said, that one reason of this compliance was, that he might have time to finish his answer to Gardiner's book, against that which he had written concerning the sacrament: and Fox has printed the letter which he avouches to prove this by. But the good man, it seems, read the letter very carelessly; for Cranmer says no such thing in it; but only, that he had appealed to the next general council, to try if that could procure him a longer delay, in which he might have time to finish his book: and between these two there is a great difference. How long this was signed before his execution, I find it no where marked; for there is no date put to his subscription.

Cranmer's recantation[44] was presently printed, and occa-

---

[44] [All the Submyssions and Recantations of Thomas Cranmer,
lately Archebyshop of Canterburye,
truely set forth both in Latyn and
English. Londini in Ædibus Jo-
hannis Cawodi, 1556. 4to.]

sioned almost equally great insultings on the one hand, and
dejection on the other. But the queen was not at all wrought
on by it: and was now forced to discover, that her private
resentments governed her in this matter, which before she
had disowned. She was resolved he should be made a sacrifice, for giving the judgment of divorce in her mother's marriage; and though hitherto she had pretended only zeal for
religion, yet now, when that could be no more alleged, yet she
persisted in her resolution of having him burnt. She said,
334 since he had been the great promoter of heresy, that had corrupted the whole nation, that must not serve his turn, which
would be sufficient in other cases; it was good for his own
soul, and might do good to others, that he repented; but yet
she ordered the sentence to be executed. The writ went out
the 24th of February, which will be found in the Collection. Collect.
Numb. 27.
Heath took care not only to enrol the writ, but the warrant
sent to him for issuing it, which is not ordinary. It is like he
did it to leave it on record to posterity, that he did it not in
course, as he did other writs, but had a special order from the
queen for it. The long time that passed between the date of
the writ, and the execution of it, makes it probable that he
made the formerly-mentioned recantation after the writ was
brought down; and that the fears of death, then before his
eyes, did so far work on him, that he signed the writing: but
when the second order was sent down to execute the former,
he was dealt with to renew his subscription, and then to write
the whole over again, which he also did; all this time being
under some small hopes of life: but conceiving likewise some
jealousies that they might burn him, he writ secretly a paper
containing a sincere confession of his faith, such as flowed from
his conscience, and not from his weak fears; and, being
brought out, he carried that along with him. He was carried
to St. Mary's, and set on a place raised higher for him to be
more conspicuously seen. Cole, provost of Eton, preached: [Fox, vol.
iii. p. 560.]
he ran out in his sermon on the mercy and justice of God,
which two attributes do not oppose or jostle out one another:
he applied this to princes, that were gods on earth, who must
be just, as well as merciful; and therefore they had appointed
Cranmer that day to suffer: he said, it was he that had dissolved the marriage between the queen's father and mother,

had driven out the pope's authority, had been the fountain of all the heresies in England; and, since the bishop of Rochester and sir Thomas More had suffered for the church, it was meet that others should suffer for heresy: and, as the duke of Northumberland had suffered in More's room, so there was no other clergyman that was equal or fit to be balanced with Fisher but he. Then he turned to Cranmer, and magnified his conversion, which, he said, was the immediate hand of God; that none of their arguments had done it, but the inward working of God's Spirit: he gave him great hopes of heaven; and assured him, there should be dirges and masses said for his soul in all the churches in Oxford.

[Fox, vol. iii. p. 561.] All this while Cranmer expressed great inward confusion, lifting up his eyes often to heaven, and then letting them fall downward, as one ashamed of himself; and he often poured out floods of tears. In the end, when Cole bid him declare his faith, he first prayed, with many moving expressions of deep remorse and inward horror: then he made his exhortation to the people, first, " not to love or set their hearts on the things " of the world; to obey the king and queen out of conscience " to God; to live in mutual love; and to relieve the poor ac- " cording to their abundance. Then he came to that on which, " he said, all his past life, and that which was to come, did " hang; being now to enter either into the joys of heaven, or " the pains of hell. He repeated the Apostles' Creed, and de- " clared his belief of the scriptures: and then he spake to that " which, he said, troubled his conscience more than any thing " he had ever done in his whole life; which was, the subscrib- " ing a paper contrary to the truth, and against his conscience, " out of the fear of death, and the love of life: and, when he 335 " came to the fire, he was resolved that hand that had signed " it should burn first. He rejected the pope as Christ's enemy, [Ibid. p. 562.] " and antichrist: and said, he had the same belief of the sa- " crament which he had published in the book he writ about it."

Upon this, there was a wonderful confusion in the assembly: those who hoped to have gained a great victory that day, seeing it turning another way, were in much disorder; they called to him to dissemble no more. He said, he had ever loved simplicity, and, before that time, had never dissembled in his whole life. And, going on in his discourse with abundance of tears, they pulled him down, and led him away to the stake, which was set in the same place where Ridley and Latimer were burnt. All the way the priests upbraided him for his changing; but he was minding another thing.

When he came to the stake, he first prayed, and then un- *He suffers martyrdom with great constancy of mind.* dressed himself; and, being tied to it, as the fire was kindling, he stretched forth his right hand towards the flame; never moving it, save that once he wiped his face with it, till it was burnt away, which was consumed before the fire reached his body. He expressed no disorder for the pain he was in; sometimes saying, *That unworthy hand!* and oft crying out, *Lord Jesus, receive my spirit!* He was soon after quite burnt. [Fox, vol. iii. p. 563.]

But it was no small matter of astonishment to find his heart entire, and not consumed among the ashes: which, though the reformed would not carry so far as to make a miracle of it, and a clear proof that his heart had continued true, though his hand had erred, yet they objected it to the papists, that it was certainly such a thing, that, if it had fallen out in any of their church, they had made it a miracle.

Thus did Thomas Cranmer end his days, in the sixty-seventh year of his age. He was a man raised of God for great ser- *His character.* vices, and well fitted for them. He was naturally of a mild and gentle temper, not soon heated, nor apt to give his opinion rashly of things or persons: and yet his gentleness, though it oft exposed him to his enemies, who took advantages from it to use him ill, knowing he would readily forgive them, did not lead him into such a weakness of spirit, as to consent to every thing that was uppermost: for as he stood firmly against the six articles in king Henry's time, notwithstanding all his heat for them, so he also opposed the duke of Somerset in the matter of the sale and alienation of the chantry lands, and the duke of Northumberland during his whole government, and now resisted unto blood: so that his meekness was really a virtue in him, and not a pusillanimity in his temper. He was a man of great candour: he never dissembled his opinion, nor disowned his friend; two rare qualities in that age, in which there was a continued course of dissimulation, almost in the whole English clergy and nation, they going backward and forward, as the court turned. But this had got him that esteem with king Henry, that it always preserved him in his days.

He knew, what complaints soever were brought against him, he would freely tell him the truth: so, instead of asking it from other hands, he began at himself. He neither disowned his esteem of queen Anne, nor his friendship to Cromwell and the duke of Somerset in their misfortunes; but owned he had the same thoughts of them in their lowest condition, that he had in their greatest state.

He being thus prepared by a candid and good nature for the searches into truth, added to these a most wonderful dili- 336 gence; for he drew out of all the authors that he read every thing that was remarkable, digesting these quotations into common-places. This begat in king Henry an admiration of him: for he had often tried it, to bid him bring the opinions of the fathers and doctors upon several questions; which he commonly did in two or three days' time: this flowed from the copiousness of his common-place books. He had a good judgment, but no great quickness of apprehension, nor close-ness of style, which was diffused and unconnected; therefore when any thing was to be penned that required more nerves, he made use of Ridley. He laid out all his wealth on the poor, and pious uses: he had hospitals and surgeons in his house for the king's seamen: he gave pensions to many of those that fled out of Germany into England; and kept up that which is hos-pitality indeed at his table, where great numbers of the honest and poor neighbours were always invited, instead of the luxury and extravagance of great entertainments, which the vanity and excess of the age we live in has honoured with the name of hospitality, to which too many are led by the authority of custom to comply too far. He was so humble and affable, that he carried himself in all conditions at the same rate. His last fall was the only blemish of his life; but he expiated it with a sincere repentance, and a patient martyrdom. He had been the chief advancer of the reformation in his life; and God so ordered it, that his death should bear a proportion to the for-mer parts of his life, which was no small confirmation to all that received his doctrine, when they heard how constantly he had at last sealed it with his blood. And though it is not to be fancied that king Henry was a prophet, yet he discovered such things in Cranmer's temper as made him conclude he was to die a martyr for his religion; and therefore he ordered him

[Parker, Antiq. Brit. p. 509.]

to change his coat of arms, and to give *pelicans* instead of *cranes*, which were formerly the arms of his family; intimating withal, that as it is reported of the *pelican*, that she gives her blood to feed her young ones; so he was to give his blood for the good of the church. That king's kindness to him subjected him too much to him; for great obligations do often prove the greatest snares to generous and noble minds. And he was so much overborne by his respects to him, and was so affected with king Henry's death, that he never after that shaved his beard, but let it grow to a great length: which I the rather mention, because the pictures that were afterwards made for him, being taken according to what he was at his death, differ much from that which I have put in my former[45] volume. Those who compared modern and ancient times, found in him so many and excellent qualities, that they did not doubt to compare him to the greatest of the primitive bishops; not only to the Chrysostoms, Ambroses, and Austins; but to the fathers of the first Rate that immediately followed the apostles, to the Ignatiuses, Polycarps, and Cyprians. And it seemed necessary that the reformation of this church, which was indeed nothing else but restoring of the primitive and apostolical doctrine, should have been chiefly carried on by a man so eminent in all primitive and apostolical virtues. And to those who upbraided the reformed with his fall, it was answered, that Liberius, whom they so much magnify, had fallen as foully upon a much slighter temptation, only out of a desire to reenter to his see, from which he had been banished; and that he persisted much longer in it.

337   But now I shall give account of the rest that were burnt this year. On the 27th[46] of January, Thomas Wirtle[47], a priest; Bartlet Green, a gentleman; Thomas Brown, John

Others suffered on the like account [Fox, vol. iii. p. 513.]

---

[45] [There were several portraits in the folio editions to which allusion is often made by the author, as well as in the notes by Fulman, Baker, and others.]

[46] [Machyn's Diary, p. 99, assigns the date January 22. 'The 22 day of January whent into Smythfeld to berne, betwyn 7 and 8 in the mornyng, 5 men and 2 women; one of the men was a gentyllman of the ender Tempull; ys nam master Gren; and they wer all bornyd by 9 at 3 postes; and ther wher a commonment thrughe London over nyght that no yong folke shuld come ther, for ther the grettest number was as has byne sene at shyche a tyme.']

[47] [Whittle. Fox.]

Tudson, and John Went, three tradesmen; Isabel Foster and Joan Warne; having all been presented because they came not to church; articles were put to them, and upon their answers they were all condemned, and burnt in Smithfield at the same stake. And on the 31st of that month, John Lomas, and four women, were burnt at Canterbury. They were presented, because they came not to confession; whereupon articles being given them, they were found guilty of heresy, and burnt in one fire. In the beginning of March, two women were burnt at Ipswich: three tradesmen were burnt in Salisbury on the 24th of March. On the 29th of April[48], Robert Drakes, a priest; William Tyms, a deacon; and four tradesmen, that were sent out of Essex because they came not to church, were condemned, and all burnt together in Smithfield. John Hanpole, and Joan Booek[49], were burnt at Rochester on the first of April; and on the second, John Hallier, a priest, was burnt in Canterbury[50].

Six tradesmen were sent up from Colchester; and the bishop of London, who had hitherto kept his prisoners for some time, to see if he could prevail with them, growing weary of that fruitless labour, and becoming by many acts of cruelty less sensible of those affections which belong to human nature, did without any more ado exhibit the articles to them; and they answering in the way he accounted heresy, he gave them time to consider if they would recant till the afternoon: but they continuing in the same mind, he condemned them, and sent them back to Colchester, were they were all burnt in one fire.

On the 15th of May he gave yet a more astonishing instance of his barbarity[51]. Laverock, an old cripple, a man of sixty-

[Fox, vol. iii. p. 530.]

[Ibid. p. 568.]
[Ibid. p. 569.]
[Ibid. p. 571.]

[Ibid. p. 583.]
[Thirlby's Register, fol. 31.]
[Fox, vol. iii. p. 586.]

[Ibid. p. 587.]

---

[48] [Machyn's Diary, p. 104, says, 'The 24 day of Aprell, in the mornyng betyme was cared to Smythffeld to be bornyd 6 men; and more was cared into the contry to be bornyd.']

[49] [John Harpole and Joan Beach. Fox.]

[50] John Hullier, a priest, was burnt at Cambridge, as appears from Thirlby's register. He is there said to have been vicar of Bad-

burham; of which vicarage he was first deprived and afterwards burnt for maintaining erroneous and heretical opinions. Fox (p. 696.) likewise says he was burnt at Cambridge, as also the letters of the martyrs, p. 517. [B.]

[51] ['The 15 day of May was cared in a care from Nuwgatt thrug London unto Strettford-a-Bow to borne 2 men; the on blyne, the thodur lame; and 2 tall men, the

eight years old, and John Ap-Price, a blind man, were upon the
like account condemned, and burnt in the same fire at Stratford-le-Bow; they comforting one another, that they were now
to be freed of their lameness and blindness. The day after, [Fox, vol.
three women were burnt in Smithfield: another blind man, [Ibid. p.
with a tradesman, were burnt at Gloucester this month. On 589.]
the 21st of the month, three were burnt at Beccles in Suffolk.
On the 6th of June, four men were burnt at Lewes in Sussex. [Ibid. p.
Another was burnt there on the 20th, and one was burnt at 592.]
Leicester on the 26th. But, on the 27th of June, Bonner
made an unheard of execution of thirteen, whereof eleven were
men, and two women, all burnt in one fire in Stratford-le-
Bow[52]. He had condemned in all sixteen; but, by what intercession I do not know, three of them were preserved by a [Ibid. p.
warrant from cardinal Pole. It seems Bonner thought it not 594.]
worth the while to burn those singly, and therefore sent them
in such droves to the stake: but whether the horror of this
action, or the discontent because the cardinal had saved some
of them, wrought on him, I know not; the latter being the
more likely: he burnt no more till April next year.

The 30th of June three were burnt at Bury in Suffolk. On [Ibid. p.
the 16th of July three men were burnt at Newbury. But this 595.]
July there was done in Guernsey an act of as great inhu- [Ibid. p. 615.]
manity, as ever was recorded in any age. A mother and her A strange barbarity
two daughters were burnt at the same stake; and one of them, at Guern-
a married woman, big with child, when she was in the fire, the sey of burn-
violence of it bursting her belly, a boy fell out into the flame, ing a child born in the fire.
338 that was snatched out of it by one that was more merciful than [Ibid. p.
the rest: but after they had a little consulted about it, the 625.]
infant was thrown in again, and there was literally baptized
with fire. There were many eyewitnesses of this, who attested
it afterwards in queen Elizabeth's time, when the matter was
inquired into, and special care was taken to have full and evident proofs of it. For indeed the fact was so unnatural, that
a man must either be possessed with a very ill opinion of the

one was a penter, the thodur a
clothworker; the penter ys name
was Huw Loveroke, dwellyng in
Seythen lane; the blynd man dwellyng in sant Thomas apostylles.'
Machyn's Diary, p. 105.]

[52] [' The 27 day of June rod from
Nuwgatt unto Stretford-a-Bow in
3 cares 13, 11 men and 2 women,
and ther bornyd to 4 postes, and
ther were a 20,000 pepull.' Machyn's Diary, p. 108.]

actors, or be well satisfied about the number and credibility of the witnesses, before he could believe it. But lies and forgeries are seldom made of actions done in the face of the sun, and before so great an assembly as was present at this. Therefore complaint being made of it to queen Elizabeth, the dean of Guernsey was put in prison for it: and afterwards, he and nine more, that were all accessary to it, took out their pardons. So merciful was the government then, to pardon an action of such a monstrous nature, because done with some colour of law: since it was said, the mother was condemned to be burnt, and no exception was made of her belly. On the 18th of July two women and one man were burnt at Greenstead. On the 1st of August Joan Waste, a blind woman, was burnt at Derby. On the 8th of September one was burnt at Bristol; and another in the same place on the 25th of that month. On the 24th four were burnt at Mayfield in Sussex. On the 27th a man and a woman were burnt at Bristol: and on the 12th[54] of October a man was burnt at Nottingham. And thus ended the burning this year: those that suffered were in all eighty-five. All these persons were presented as suspect of heresy, and were required to answer the questions that the bishop put to them; which related to the corporal presence in the sacrament, the necessity of auricular confession, or the sacrifice of the mass: and, upon the answers they made, were condemned to the fire. But none of them were accused of any violence committed on the persons of any churchman, or of any affront put on their religion; and all their sufferings were merely for their conscience, which they kept as private as they could: so that it rather appeared in their abstaining from the communion of a church, which they thought had corrupted the chief parts of worship, than in any thing they had said or done. It was an unusual and an ungrateful thing to the English nation, that is apt to compassionate all in misery, to see four, five, six, seven, and once thirteen burning in one fire; and the sparing neither sex nor age, nor blind nor lame, but making havoc of all equally: and above all, the barbarity of Guernsey raised that horror in the whole nation, that there seems ever since that time such an abhorrence to that religion to be derived

[Fox, vol. iii. p. 627.]

[Ibid. p. 632.]
[Ibid. p. 634.]
[Ibid. p. 636.]

[Ibid. p. 637.]

[54] [Fox speaks of this case as that of a shoemaker at Northampton, October 11.]

down from father to son, that it is no wonder an aversion so deeply rooted, and raised upon such grounds, does upon every new provocation, or jealousy of returning to it, break out in most violent and convulsive symptoms.

But all those fires did not extinguish the light of the reformation, nor abate the love of it. They spread it more, and kindled new heats in men's minds; so that what they had read of the former persecutions under the heathens seemed to be now revived. This made those who loved the gospel meet oft together, though the malice of their enemies obliged them to do it with great caution and secresy; yet there were sometimes at 339 their meetings about 200. They were instructed and watched over by several faithful shepherds, who were willing to hazard their lives in feeding this flock committed to their care. The chief of these were Scambler and Bentham, afterwards promoted by queen Elizabeth to the sees of Peterborough and Lichfield: Foule, Bernher, and Rough, a Scotchman, that was afterwards condemned and burnt by Bonner. There was also care taken by their friends beyond sea to supply them with good books; which they sent over to them for their instruction and encouragement. These that fled beyond sea went at first for the most part to France, where, though they were well used in opposition to the queen, yet they could not have the free exercise of their religion granted them; so they retired to Geneva, and Zurich, and Arau, in Switzerland; and to Strasburg and Frankfort in the upper Germany; and to Emden in the lower.

The reformation spreads for all the persecution.

At Frankfort an unhappy difference fell in among some of them who had used before the English Liturgy, and did afterwards comply with it, when they were in England, where it had authority from the law; yet they thought, that, being in foreign parts, they should rather accommodate their worship to those among whom they lived; so, instead of the English Liturgy, they used one near the Geneva and French forms. Others thought, that when those in England, who had compiled their Liturgy, were now confirming what they had done with their blood, and many more were suffering for it, it was an high contempt of them and their sufferings to depart from these forms. This contradiction raised that heat, that Dr. Cox, who lived in Strasburg with his friend Peter Martyr, went thither;

The troubles at Frankfort among the English there.

[Fuller, lib. viii. p. 30.]

and, being a man of great reputation, procured an order from the senate, that the English forms should only be used in their church. This dissension being once raised, went further than perhaps it was at first intended. For those who at first liked the Geneva way better, that, being in foreign parts, they might all seem to be united in the same forms, now began to quarrel with some things in the English Liturgy; and Knox, being a man of a hot temper, engaged in this matter very warmly; and got his friend Calvin to write somewhat sharply of some things in the English service. This made Knox and his party leave Frankfort, and go to Geneva. Knox had also written in-

[Troubles at Frank-fort, p. 44.]

decently of the emperor, which obliged the senate of Frankfort to require him to be gone out of their bounds. There fell in other contests, about the censuring of offences; which some of the congregation would not leave in the hands of the ministers only, but would have it shared among the whole congregation. Upon these matters there arose great debates, and many papers were written on both sides, to the great grief of Parker and others, who lived privately in England; and to the scandal of the strangers, who were not a little offended to see a company of people fly out of their country for their consciences, and, in-stead of spending their time in fasting and prayer for their per-secuted brethren at home, to fall into such quarrels about mat-ters, which themselves acknowledged were not the substantials of religion, nor points of conscience: in which certainly they began the breach, who departed from that way of worship which they acknowledged was both lawful and good. But there followed too much animosity on both sides, which were the seeds of all those differences that have since distracted this church.

They who reflected on the contests that the Novatians raised, 340 both at Rome and Carthage, in Cyprian's time; and the heats the Donatists brought into the African churches, soon after the persecution was over, found somewhat parallel both to these schisms now during the persecution, and to those afterwards raised when it was over.

Pole is made arch-bishop of Canter-bury.

I now return to the affairs of England. On the 22nd of March, the very day after Cranmer was burnt, Pole was consecrated archbishop of Canterbury by the archbishop of York, the bishops of London, Ely, Worcester, Lincoln, Rochester, and St. Asaph.

He had come over only a cardinal deacon; and was last winter made a priest, and now a bishop. It seems he had his *congé d'élire* with his election, and his bulls from Rome, already despatched before this time. The pope did not know with what face to refuse them, being pressed by the queen on his account, though he wanted only a colour to wreak his revenge on him; to which he gave vent upon the first opportunity that offered itself. It seems Pole thought it indecent to be consecrated as long as Cranmer lived; yet his choosing the next day for it, brought him under the suspicion of having procured his death [54]: so that the words of Elijah to Ahab concerning Naboth were applied to him; *Thou hast killed and taken possession.* On the 28th of that month, he came in state through London to Bow Church; where the bishops of Worcester and Ely, after the former had said mass, put the pall about him. This was a device set up by pope Paschal II. in the beginning of the twelfth century, for the engaging of all archbishops to a more immediate dependence on that see: they being, after they took the pall, to act as the pope's *legates born,* (as the phrase was,) of which it was the ensign. But it was at the first admitted with great contradiction both by the kings of Sicily and Poland, the archbishops of Palermo and Gnesna being the first to whom they were sent; all men wondering at the novelty of the thing, and of the oath which the popes required of them at the delivery of it. This being put on Pole, he went into the pulpit, and made a cold sermon about the beginning, the use, and the matter of the pall, without either learning or eloquence. The subject could admit of no learning; and for eloquence, though in his younger days, when he writ against king Henry, his style was too luxuriant and florid, yet, being afterwards sensible of his excess that way, he turned as much to the other extreme, and, cutting off all the ornaments of speech he brought his style to a flatness that had neither life nor beauty in it.

---

[54] From your lordship's opinion of the cardinal's probity and virtue, p. 370, I think I can clear him from this suspicion from his own letter MS., where he thus accosts Cranmer. 'Ea est mea salutis tuæ cura ac studium, ut si te ab horribili illa quæ tibi nisi resipiscas, impendit, non solum corporis sed animæ etiam mortis sententia ullo modo liberare possem, id profecto omnibus divitiis atque honoribus, qui cuiquam in hac vita contingere possint (Deum testor) libentissime anteponerem.' MS. p. 54. [B.]

Some more religious houses endowed.

All the business of England this year was the raising of religious houses. Greenwich was begun with last year. The queen also built a house for the Dominicans in Smithfield, and another for the Franciscans : and they being begging orders, these endowments did not cost much. At Sion, near Brentford, there had been a religious house of women, of the order of St. Bridget. That house was among the first that had been dissolved by king Henry VIII. as having harboured the king's enemies, and been complices to the business of the Maid of Kent[55]. The queen anew founded a nunnery there. She also founded a house for the Carthusians at Shene, near Richmond, in gratitude to that order for their sufferings upon her mother's account. From these she went to a greater foundation, but that which cost her less : for she suppressed the deanery and the cathedral of Westminster, and in September this year turned it into a monastery ; and made Feckenham, dean of Paul's, the first abbot of it. I have not met with her foundation of it, which perhaps was razed[56] out of the records in the beginning of queen Elizabeth's reign ; for it is not enrolled among the other patents of this year. But on the 23rd of September she gave warrants for pensions to be paid to the prebends of Westminster, till they were otherwise provided : and about that time Feckenham was declared abbot ; though the solemn instalment of him, and fourteen other monks with him, was not done till the 21st of November[57].

341

---

[55] ['The first day of August was the nones of Syon was closyd in by my lorde bysshope of London and my lord abbott of Westmynster, and serten of the consell, and serten frers of that order of shepe color as the shepe bereth ; and thay had as grett a charge of ther leyfvyng, and never to goo forth as longe as they do lyffe, but ever .....' Machyn's Diary, p. 145.]

[56] The king and queen's license or patent, dated Sept. 7. an. 3 and 4. P. and M., may be met with in Reyner (Apostol. Benedict. p. 233.), and as there said, 'habetur 12 parte patentum.' The rest, I suppose, was done by the pope's authority. The cardinal's license towards the suppressing of the college may be met with in the Monasticon, vol. ii. p. 847. [B.]

[57] ['The 21 day of November .. .. was the new abbott of Westmynster putt in, docthur Fecknam, late dene of Powlles and 14 moo monkes shorne in ; and the morow after the lord abott with ys coventt whentt a prossessyon after the old fassyon in ther monkes' wede, in collys of blake say, with 2 vargers carehyng 2 sylver rodes in ther handes, and at evyngsong tyme the verger whent thrugh the clostur to the abbott ; and so whentt into the churche affor

There had been many searches and discoveries made, in the All the for-
former reign, of great disorders in these houses; and at the mer records concerning
dissolution of them many had made confession of their ill lives, them are
and gross superstition; all which were laid up and recorded razed.
in the augmentation-office.   There had been also in that state
of things, which they now called the late schism, many professions made by the bishops and abbots, and other religious men,
of their renouncing the pope's authority, and acknowledging
the king's supremacy : therefore it was moved, that all these
should be gathered together and destroyed.   So, on the 23rd
of September, there was a commission granted to Bonner, and
Cole, (the new dean of Paul's in Feckenham's room,) and Dr.
Martin, " to search all registers, to find out both the profes-
" sions made against the pope, and the scrutinies made in
" abbeys ; which, as the commission, that is in the Collection, Collect.
" sets forth, tended to the subversion of all good religion and Numb. 28.
" religious houses : these they were to gather, and carry to
" the cardinal, that they might be disposed of as the queen
" should give order."   It is not upon record how they executed this commission ; but the effects of it appear in the great
defectiveness of the records in many things of consequence,
which are razed and lost.   This was a new sort of expurga-
tion, by which they intended to leave as few footsteps to posterity as they could of what had been formerly done.   Their
care of their own credits led them to endeavour to suppress the
many declarations themselves had formerly made, both against
the see of Rome, the monastic orders, and many of the old
corruptions which they had disclaimed.   But many things
escaped their diligence, as may appear by what I have already
collected : and, considering the pains they were at in vitiating
registers, and destroying records, I hope the reader will not
think it strange, if he meets with many defects in this work.
In this search they not only took away what concerned themselves, but every collateral thing that might inform or direct
the following ages how to imitate those precedents ; and therefore, among other writings, the commission that Cromwell

the hi auter, and ther my lord   into ys plasse, and contenentt he
knellyd downe and ys coventt, and   begane evyngsong, 22 day of the sam
after ys praer mad was browtt into   monyth, that was santt Clementt
the qwyre with the vergers, and so   evyn last.' Machyn's Diary, p. 119.]

had to be vicegerent was destroyed: but I have since that time met with it in a copy that was in the Cotton library, which I have put in the Collection. How far this resembled the endeavours that the heathens used, in the last and hottest persecution, to burn all the registers of the church, I leave to the reader. The abbey of Westminster being thus set up, some of the monks of Glastonbury, who were yet alive, were put into it. And all the rest of the old monks that had been turned out of Glastonbury, and who had not married since, were invited to return to this monastery. They began to contrive how to raise their abbey again, which was held the ancientest, and was certainly the richest in England; and therefore they moved the queen and the cardinal, that they might 342 have the house and site restored and repaired, and they would by labour and husbandry maintain themselves, not doubting but the people of the country would be ready to contribute liberally to their subsistence. The queen and cardinal liked the proposition well; so the monks wrote to the lord Hastings, then lord chamberlain, to put the queen in mind of it, and to follow the business till it were brought to a good issue; which would be a great honour to the memory of Joseph of Arimathea, who lay there, whom they did heartily beseech to pray to Christ for good success to his lordship. This letter I have put in the Collection, copied from the original. What followed upon it, I cannot find. It is probable, the monks of other houses made the like endeavours, and every one of them could find some rare thing belonging to their house, which seemed to make it the more necessary to raise it speedily. Those of St. Alban's could say, the first martyr of England lay in their abbey; those of St. Edmundbury had a king that was martyred by the heathen Danes: those of Battle could say, they were founded for the remembrance of William the Conqueror's victory, from whence the queen derived her crown: and those of St. Austin's in Canterbury had the apostle of England laid in their church. In short, they were all in hopes to be speedily restored. And though they were but few in number, and to begin upon a small revenue, yet, as soon as the belief of purgatory was revived, they knew how to set up the old trade anew; which they could drive with the greater advantage, since they were to deal with the people by a new motive, be-

[margin notes:]

Collect. Numb. 29.

Endeavours to raise the abbey of Glastonbury.

Collect. Numb. 30.

sides the old ones formerly used, that it was sacrilege to possess the goods of the church; of which it had been robbed by
their ancestors. But in this it was necessary to advance slowly,
since the nobility and gentry were much alarmed at it; and
at the last parliament, many had laid their hands to their
swords in the house of commons, and said they would not part
with their estates, but would defend them. Yet some, that
hoped to gain more favour from the queen by such compliance,
did found chantries for masses for their souls. In the records
of the last years of queen Mary's reign, there are many warrants granted by her for such endowments; for though the
statute of mortmain was repealed, yet for greater security it
was thought fit to take out such licences. This is all I find of
our home affairs this year.

Foreign affairs were brought to a quieter state: for, by the Foreign
mediation of England, a truce for five years was concluded be- affairs.
tween France and Spain; and the new king of Spain was inclined to observe it faithfully, that so he might be well settled
in his kingdoms before he engaged in war: but the violent
pope broke all this. He was much offended with the decree
made at Augsburg for the liberty of religion; and with Ferdinand for ordering the chalice to be given to his subjects; and
chiefly for his assuming the title of emperor without his approbation. Upon this last provocation, the pope sent him word,
that he would let him know to his grief how he had offended
him. He came to talk in as haughty a style as any of all his The pope is
predecessors had ever done, that he would change kingdoms at extravagantly inso-
his pleasure. He boasted that he had made Ireland a king- lent.
dom; that all princes were under his feet, (and, as he said that, [History
of the
he used to tread with his feet against the ground,) and he Council of
Trent, p.]
343 would allow no prince to be his companion, nor be too familiar 370.]
with him; nay, rather than be driven to a mean action, he
would set the whole world on fire. But, to pretend to do
somewhat for a reformation, he appointed a congregation to
gather some rules for the condemning of simony. These he [Ibid. p.
published, and said, having now reformed his own court, he 373.]
would next reform the courts of princes: and because they
had complained much of the corruptions of the clergy and
court of Rome, he resolved to turn the matter on them, and
said, he would gather all the abuses that were in their courts,

and reform them.   But he was much provoked by an embassy that came from Poland to desire of him that they might have the mass in their own tongue, and the communion in both kinds; that their priests might be allowed to marry; that they might pay annates no more to Rome, and call a national council in their own kingdom.   These things put him out of all patience; and, with all the bitterness he could use, he expressed how detestable they were to him.   He then said, he would hold a council: not that he needed one, for himself was above all; but it should never meet in Trent, to which it had been a vain thing to send about sixty bishops of the least able, and forty doctors of the most insufficient, as had been twice done already: that he would hold it in the Lateran, as many of his predecessors had done.   He gave notice of this to the ambassadors of all princes: he said, he did that only in courtesy, not intending to ask their advice or consent, for he would be obeyed by them all.   He intended in this council to reform them and their courts, and to discharge all impositions which they had laid on the clergy: and therefore he would call it, whether they would or not; and if they sent no prelates to it, he would hold it with those of his own court; and would let the world see what the authority of that see was, when it had a pope of courage to govern it.

But after all these imperious humours of his, which sometimes carried him to excesses, that seemed not much different from madness, he was heartily troubled at the truce between the French and the Spaniards.   He hated the Spaniards most, because they supported the Colonnesi, whom he designed to ruin.   And therefore he sent his nephew into France, with a sword and hat which he had consecrated, to persuade the king to break the truce; offering his assistance for the conquest of the kingdom of Naples, to the use of one of the younger sons of France: though it was believed he designed it for his own nephew.   He also sent the French king an absolution from his oath that he had sworn for the maintaining of the truce, and promised to create what cardinals he pleased, that so he might be sure of a creature of his own to succeed in the popedom.   Yet the pope dissembled his design in this so closely, that he persuaded sir Edward Carne, that was then the queen's ambassador at Rome, that he desired nothing so much as a general

History of the Council of Trent, p. 374.]

He breaks the truce between France and Spain, absolving the French king from his oath. [Ibid. p. 376.]

peace; and he hoped, as the queen had mediated in the truce,
she would continue her endeavours till a perfect peace were
made. He said he had sent two legates to procure it; and since he
was the common father of Christendom, God would impute to
him even his silence in that matter, if he did not all he could
to obtain it. He complained much of the growth of heresy in
Poland, and in the king of the Romans' dominions. For the
repressing of it, he said he intended to have a general council;
and in order to that, it was necessary there should be a peace,
344 since a truce would not give sufficient encouragement to those
who ought to come to the council. He said he intended to be
present at it himself, and to hold it in the church of St. John in
the Lateran; for he thought Rome, being the common country
of all the world, was the meetest place for such an assembly;
and he being so very old, could go nowhere out of Rome;
therefore he was resolved to hold it there. But he said, he
relied chiefly on the assistance of the queen, whom he called
*that blessed queen, and his most gracious and loving daugh-
ter;* and, holding her letters in his hand, he said, they were so
full of respect and kindness to him that he would have them
read in the consistory; and made a cross over her subscription.
It was no wonder such discourses, with that way of deportment,
deceived so honest and plain-hearted a man as Carne was; as
it will appear from the letter he writ over upon this occasion to
the queen, which I have put in the Collection. But it soon ap-   Collect.
peared on what design he had sent his legate to France; for   Numb. 31.
he pressed that king vehemently to break the truce and renew
the war. To this the French king, being persuaded by the
cardinal of Lorraine and duke of Guise, consented; though all
the rest about him dissuaded him from such a dishonourable
breach of faith, or meddling more in the war of Italy, which
had been always fatal to their people. The Colonnesi had been
furnished with assistance from Naples; upon which the pope
had it proposed in the consistory, that the king of Spain, by
giving them assistance, had lost his territories: and being then
assured of assistance from France, he began the war, imprisoning the cardinals and prelates of the Spanish faction, and the
ambassadors of Spain and England, pretending they kept correspondence with the Colonnesi, that were traitors. He also
sent to raise some regiments among the Grisons. But when

they came, some told him they were all heretics, and it would be a reproach for him to use such soldiers. He, understanding they were good troops, said, he was confident God would convert them, and that he looked on them as angels sent by God for the defence of his person. Upon this breaking out of the pope's, the duke of Alva, that was then in Naples, being himself much devoted to the papacy, did very unwillingly engage in the war. He first used all ways to avoid it, and made several protestations of the indignities that his master had received, and his unwillingness to enter into a war with him, that should be the common father of Christendom. But these being all to no purpose, he fell into Campania, and took all the places in it, which he declared he held for the next pope: he might also have taken Rome itself, but the reverence he had for the papacy restrained him.

[Ibid. p. 381.]

This being known in England, was a great grief to the queen and cardinal, who saw what advantages those of the reformation would take from the pope's absolving princes from the most sacred ties of human societies; since the breach of faith and public treaties was a thing abhorred by the most depraved nations: and when he, who pretended to be the vicar of Christ, who was the Prince of Peace, was kindling a new flame in Christendom; these things were so scandalous, that they knew they would much obstruct and disorder all their designs. And indeed the protestants everywhere were not wanting to improve this all they could. It seemed a strange thing, that in the same year, a great conqueror, that had spent his life in wars and affairs, should in the 56th year of his age retire to a mo- 345 nastery; and that a bishop at eighty, who had pretended to such abstraction from the world, that he had formerly quitted a bishopric to retire into a monastery, should now raise such a war, and set Europe again in a flame.

1557.
The visitation of the universities.

In the beginning[58] of the next year was the visitation of the universities. To Cambridge Pole sent Scot bishop of Chester,

[58] ['The 26 day of January went to Cambridge Watson bishop elect of Lincoln, Scot bishop of Chester and Christopherson bishop elect of Chichester comyssyoners to the lord cardinal to the chyrche of Sant Mares and thay toke up on Martin Bucer that was bered ther, and Paulus Phagius was taken up at sant Myghelle cherche that was buried there and after brentt boyth.' Machyn's Diary, p. 124.]

his Italian friend Ormaneto, with Watson and Christopherson, [Fox, vol. iii. p. 639.]
the two elect bishops of Lincoln and Chichester, (in the rooms
of White, removed to Winchester, out of which Pole reserved
a pension of 1000*l*., and of Day that was dead,) with some
others. When they came thither, on the 11th of January, [Jan. 9.]
they put the churches of St. Mary's and St. Michael's under an
interdict, because the bodies of Bucer and Fagius, two heretics,
were laid in them. The university orator received them with a [Jan. 11. Ibid. p. 640.]
speech that was divided between an invective against the here-
tics, and a commendation of the cardinal, who was then their
chancellor. They went through all the colleges, and gathered
many heretical books together, and observed the order used in
their chapels. When they came to Clare hall, they found no
sacrament. Ormaneto asked the head, Swinburn, how that
came? He answered, the chapel was not yet consecrated.
Then Ormaneto chid him more for officiating so long in it; but
trying him further, he found he had many benefices in his
hands; for which he reproved him so severely, that the poor
man was so confounded, that he could answer nothing to the
other questions he put to him. But Christopherson himself,
being master of Trinity college, did not escape. Ormaneto
found he had misapplied the revenues of the house, and had
made a lease of some of their lands to his brother-in-law below
the value: Ormaneto tore the lease to pieces, and chid him so
sharply, that he, fearing it might stop his preferment, fell sick
upon it.

Then followed the pageantry of burning the two bodies of
Bucer and Fagius. They were cited to appear; or if any
would come in their name, they were required to defend them:
so, after three citations, the dead bodies not rising to speak for
themselves, and none coming to plead for them, (for fear of being sent after them,) the visitors thought fit to proceed. On [Ibid. p. 645.]
the 26th of January, the bishop of Chester made a speech,
showing the earnestness of the university to have justice done;
to which they, the commissioners, though most unwilling, were
obliged to condescend: therefore, having examined many witnesses of the heresies that Bucer and Fagius had taught, they
judged them obstinate heretics; and appointed their bodies to
be taken out of the holy ground, and to be delivered to the secular power. The writ being brought from London, on the

6th of February their bodies were taken up and carried in coffins, and tied to stakes, with many of their books and other heretical writings, and all were burnt together.   Perne preached at it; who, as he was that year vice-chancellor, so he was in the same office four years after this; when by queen Elizabeth's order, public honours were done to the memories of those two learned men, and sermons and speeches were made in their praise: but Perne had turned so oft, and at every one was so zealous, that such turnings came to be nicknamed from him.   On the feast of Purification, Watson preached at Cambridge; where, to extol the rites and processions of the catholics, and their carrying candles on that day, he said, Joseph **346** and the blessed Virgin had carried wax candles in procession that day, as the church had still continued to do from their example; which was heard not without the laughter of many.

The cardinal did also send Ormaneto, and Brookes bishop of Gloucester, with some others, to visit the university of Oxford.   They went over all the colleges as they had done at Cambridge; and burnt all the English Bibles, with such other heretical books as could be found.   Then they made a process against the body of Peter Martyr's wife, that lay buried in one of the churches: but she being a foreigner that understood no English, they could not find witnesses that had heard her utter any heretical points; so they gave advertisement of this to the cardinal, who thereupon writ back, that since it was notoriously known, that she had been a nun, and had married contrary to her vow, therefore her body was to be taken up, and buried in a dunghill, as a person dying under excommunication [59]. This was accordingly done. But her body was afterwards taken up again in queen Elizabeth's time, and mixed with St. Frideswide's bones, that she might run the same fortune with her in all times coming.

While these things were doing, there was great complaints made that the inferior magistrates grew every where slack in the searching after, and presenting of heretics: they could not find in the counties a sufficient number of justices of peace that

[Fox, vol. iii. p. 646.]

[Ibid. p. 647.]

[Ibid. p. 653.]

Great endeavours used to set forward the persecution most vigorously.

[59] The reason given in the cardinal's letter for raising her body is *Quoniam juxta corpus sanctissimæ*   *Fridesvidæ jacebat corpus Catherinæ uxoris Petri Martyris.* [S.]

would carefully look after it; and in towns they were generally harboured.   Letters were written to some towns, as Coventry and Rye, which are entered in the council-books, recommending some to be chosen their mayors, who were zealous
catholics.   It is probable, that the like letters might have been
written to other towns; for the council-books for this reign
are very imperfect and defective.   But all this did not advance
their design.   The queen understood that the numbers of the
heretics rather increased than abated: so new counsels were
to be taken.   I find it said, that some advised that courts of
inquisition, like those in Spain, might be set up in England.
In Spain the inquisitors, who were then all Dominicans, received private informations; and upon these laid hold on any
that were delated or suspected of heresy, and kept them close
in their prisons till they formed their processes; and, by all the
ways of torture they could invent, forced from them confessions, either against themselves or others, whom they had a
mind to draw within their toils.   They had so unlimited a
jurisdiction, that there was no sanctuary that could secure any
from their warrants; nor could princes preserve or deliver
men out of their hands · nor were their prisoners brought to
any public trial, but tried in secret; one of the advocates of
the court was for form's sake assigned to plead for them; but
was always more careful to please the court than to save his
client.   They proceeded against them, both by articles, which
they were to answer, and upon presumptions; and it was a
rare thing for any to escape out of their hands, unless they
redeemed themselves, either by great presents, or by the discovery of others.   These had been set up first in the county
of Toulouse, for the extirpation of the Albigenses; and were
afterwards brought into Spain, upon Ferdinand of Arragon's
driving the Moors out of it, that so none of those might any
347 longer conceal themselves in that kingdom: who being a false
and crafty sort of men, and certainly enemies to the government, it seemed necessary to use more than ordinary severity
to drive them out.   But now those courts examined men suspected of heresy, as well as of Mahometanism; and had indeed
effectually preserved Spain from any change in religion.   This
made the present pope earnest with all the princes of Christendom to set up such courts in their dominions: and Philip was

so much of the same mind, that he resolved to have them set up in Flanders; which gave the first rise to those wars that followed afterwards there, and ended in the loss of the seven provinces.

A design to set up the inquisition in England. In England, they made now in February a good step towards it. For a commission was given to the bishops of London and Ely, the lord North, secretary Bourne, sir John Mordaunt, sir Francis Englefield, sir Edward Walgrave, sir Nicholas Hare, sir Thomas Pope, sir Roger Cholmeley, sir Richard Read, sir Thomas Stradling, sir Rowland Hall, and sergeant Rastall; Cole, dean of Paul's, William Roper, Randolph Cholmeley, and William Cook; Thomas Martin, John Story, and John Vaughan, doctors of the law, "That since many false rumours were pub-" lished among the subjects, and many heretical opinions were " also spread among them; therefore they, or any three of them, " were to inquire into those, either by presentments, by wit-" nesses, or any other politic way they could devise; and to " search after all heresies; the bringers in, the sellers, or " readers of all heretical books. They were to examine and " punish all misbehaviours or negligences in any church or " chapel, and to try all priests that did not preach of the " sacrament of the altar; all persons that did not hear mass, " or come to their parish church to service; that would not " go in processions, or did not take holy bread or holy water: " and if they found any that did obstinately persist in such " heresies, they were to put them into the hands of their ordi-" naries, to be proceeded against according to the laws: giving " them full power to proceed, as their discretions and con-" sciences should direct them; and to use all such means as " they could invent for the searching of the premises: em-" powering them also to call before them such witnesses as " they pleased, and to force them to make oath of such things " as might discover what they sought after." This commission

Collect. Numb. 32. I have put in the Collection. It will shew how high they intended to raise the persecution, when a power of such a nature was put into hands of any three of a number so selected. Besides this, there were many subordinate commissions issued out. This commission seems to have been granted the former year, and only renewed now: for in the rolls of that year, I have met with many of those subaltern commissions relating to

this, as superior t᷃ them. And on the 8th of March after this,
a commission was given to the archishop of York, the bishop
suffragan of Hull, and divers others, to the same effect; but
with this limitation, that if any thing appeared to them so in-
tricate that they could not determine it, they were to refer it
to the bishop of London and his colleagues, who had a larger
commission. So now, all was done that could be devised for
extirpating of heresy, except courts of inquisition had been set
up; to which, whether this was not a previous step to dispose
the nation to it, the reader may judge.

348   I shall next give an account of the burnings this year. On
the 15th of January six men were burnt in one fire at Canterbury; and at the same time two were burnt at Wye, and
two at Ashford, that were condemned with the other six.
Soon after the fore-mentioned commission, two and twenty
were sent up from Colchester to London[60]: yet Bonner, though
seldom guilty of such gentleness, was content to discharge them.
As they were led through London, the people did openly shew
their affection to them, above a thousand following them.
Bonner, upon this, writ to the cardinal, that he found they
were obstinate heretics: yet since he had been offended with
him for his former proceedings, he would do nothing till he
knew his pleasure. This letter is to be found in Fox. But
the cardinal stopped him; and made some deal with the prisoners to sign a paper, of their professing that they believed
that Christ's body and blood was in the sacrament, without any
further explanation; and that they did submit to the catholic
church of Christ, and should be faithful subjects to the king
and queen, and be obedient to their superiors, both spiritual
and temporal, according to their duties. It is plain, this was so
contrived, that they might have signed it, without either prevari-
cating or dissembling their opinions: for it is not said, "that they
" were to be subject to the church of Rome, but to the church
" of Christ; and they were to be obedient to their superiors,
" according to their duties;" which was a good reserve for
their consciences. I stand the longer on this, that it may appear how willing the cardinal was to accept of any show of
submission from them, and to stop Bonner's rage. Upon this,
they were set at liberty. But Bonner got three men and two

Margin notes: Proceed-ings against the here-tics. [Fox, vol. iii. p. 655.] [Ibid. p. 656.] [Ibid. p. 659.] [Ibid. p. 660.]

[60] [The Chronicle of the Grey Friars, p.98, seems to put this on Sept. 5, 1556.]

women presented to him in London in January [61]; and, after he had allowed them a little more time than he had granted others, they standing still firm to their faith, were burnt at Smithfield on the 12th of April. After that, White, the new bishop of Winchester, condemned three, who were burnt on the 3rd of [62] May in Southwark; one of these, Stephen Gratwick, being of the diocese of Chichester, appealed from him to his own ordinary : whether he expected more favour from him, or did it only to gain time, I know not ; but they brought in a counterfeit, who was pretended to be the bishop of Chichester, (as Fox has printed it, from the account written with the man's own hand,) and so condemned him. On the 7th of May, three were burnt at Bristol. On the 18th of June two men and five women were burnt at Maidstone. And on the 19th, three men and four women were burnt at Canterbury; fourteen being thus in two days destroyed by Thornton and Harpsfield. In which it may seem strange, that the cardinal had less influence to stop the proceedings in his own diocese, than in London : but he was now under the pope's disgrace, as shall be afterwards shewn. On the 22nd of June six men and four women were burnt at Lewes in Sussex, condemned by White; for Christopherson, bishop elect of Chichester, was not yet consecrated. On the 13th of July two were burnt at Norwich. On the 2nd of August ten were burnt at Colchester, six in the morning, and four in the afternoon; they were some of those who had been formerly discharged by the cardinal's orders.

[Fox, vol. iii. p. 660.]

[Ibid. p. 662.]

[Ibid. p. 665.]
[Ibid. p. 667.]

[Ibid. p. 671.]

[Ibid. p. 696.]
[Ibid. p. 698.]

[61 'The 3 day of April five persons out of Essex were condemned for herese 3 men and 2 women, one woman with a staff in her hand to be bornyd in Smythfeld.' Machyn's Diary, p. 130. From the same diary it appears that they were burnt April 6. 'The 6 day of Aprell was bornyd in Smythfeld 5, 3 men and two women for herese; on was a barber dwelling in Lymstrett and on woman was the wyff of the Crane at the Crussyd-frers besyd the Towre hille keping of a in ther. Ibid. p. 131.]

62 [It appears from Fox, from whom the author seems to have taken all this account, that this happened later than the 25th of May. Machyn's Diary says, p. 136, 'The 23 day of May dyd pryche the bysshope of Wynchaster doctur Whytt at sant Mare Overes in Sowthwarke and ther was a heretyke ther for to heare the sermon.' Strype (Eccles. Mem. iii. p. 376) adds, that his name was Steven Gratwick, but gives no authority. Machyn, p. 137, continues, 'The 28 day of May.... was bornyd beyond sant George's parryche 3 men for heresie a dyssyd Nuwhyngtun.' Strype (ibid.) adds that their names were Gratwick, Morant and King.]

But the priests in the country complained, that the mercy
shewed to them had occasioned great disorders among them;
heretics and the favourers of them growing insolent upon it;
and those who searched after them being disheartened. So now,
349 Bonner, being under no more restraints from the cardinal, new
complaints being made that they came not to church, condemned them upon their answers to the articles which he objected to them.

At this time one George Eagle, a tailor, who used to go [Ibid. p.
about from place to place, and to meet with those who stood 700.]
for the reformation, where he prayed and discoursed with them
about religion, and from his indefatigable diligence was nicknamed *Trudge-over*, was taken near Colchester, and was condemned of treason for gathering the queen's subjects together;
though it was not proved, that he had ever stirred them up to
rebellion; but did it only (as himself always protested) to encourage them to continue stedfast in the faith: he suffered as a
traitor. On the 5th of August, one was burnt at Norwich; [Ibid. p.
and on the 20th, a man and a woman more were burnt at Ro- 702.]
chester: one was also burnt at Lichfield, in August, but the [Ibid. p. 703.]
day is not named.

The same month, a complaint was brought to the council, of
the magistrates of Bristol, that they came seldom to the sermons at the cathedral; so that the dean and chapter used
to go to their houses in procession with their cross carried
before them, and to fetch them from thence: upon which,
a letter was written to them, requiring them to conform themselves more willingly to the orders of the church, to frequent
the sermons, and go thither of their own accord.

On the 17th of September, three men and one woman were [Ibid.
burnt at Islington near London[63]; and on the same day two p. 705.]
women were burnt at Colchester. On the 20th, a man was [Ibid. p. 713.]
burnt at Northampton; and in the same month one was burnt
at Laxefield in Suffolk. On the 23rd a woman was burnt at [Ibid. p.
Norwich. There were seventeen burnt in the diocese of Chi- 714.]
[Ibid. p. 716.]

[63] ['The 17 day of September
whent owt of Nuwgatt unto Yslyng-
ton beyonde the buthes towardes the
chyrche in a valley to be bornyd 3
men, on woman, for herese duly
proved; 2 of them was man and
wyff dwelling in sant Donstans
in the Est, of the est syd of sant
Donstons cherche-yerd with master
Waters sargant of armes, and all ther
bornyng was....' Machyn's Diary,
p. 152.]

[Fox, vol.
iii. p. 717.]
[Ibid. p.
719.]
[Ibid. p.
722.]
[Ibid. p.
723.]

chester about this time; one was a priest, thirteen were laymen, and three women: but the day is not marked. On the 18th[64] of November three were burnt in Smithfield. On the 22nd of December John Rough, a Scotchman, was burnt, whose suffering was on this occasion: On the 12th of December there was a private meeting of such as continued to worship God according to the service set out by king Edward, at Islington; where he was to have administered the sacrament according to the order of that book[65]. The new inquisitors had corrupted one of this congregation to betray his brethren; so that they were apprehended as they were going to the communion. But Rough being a stranger, it was considered by the council, whether he should be tried as a native. He had a benefice in Yorkshire in king Edward's days; so it was resolved, and signified to the bishop of London, that he should be proceeded against as a subject. Thereupon Bonner objected to him his condemning the doctrine of the church, and setting out the heresies of Cranmer and Ridley concerning the sacrament, and his using the service set out by king Edward; that he had lived much with those who for their heresies had fled beyond sea; that he had spoken reproachfully of the pope and cardinals, saying, that when he was at Rome he had seen a bull of the pope's that licensed stews, and a cardinal riding openly with his whore with him; with several other articles. The greatest part of them he

64 [This is probably a mistake for the 13th of November. Machyn's Diary, p. 157, says, 'The 12 day of November ther was a post sett up in Smythfeld for 3 that shuld have beyn bornyd, butt boyth wod and colles; and my lord abbott of Westminster cam to Newgatt and talked with them, and so they wher stayd for that day of bornyng.

'The 13 day of November was sant Erkenwald eve, the 4 and 5 yere of king and quen, whent owt of Newgatt unto Smythfeld to be bornyd 3 men, on was Gybsun the sun of sergantt Gybsun sergantt of armes, and of the reywelles, and of the kynges tenstes; and 2 more, the whyche here be ther names — Gybsun, Haliday and Sparow thes 3 men.']

65 ['The 12 day of December being Sunday there met certain persons that were Gospellers and some pretended players at Yslyngtun, takyng serten men and one Ruffe a Skott and a frere for the redyng of a lecture and odur matters; and the communyon was played and should have byne butt the gard came to sune or ever the chief matter was begone.' Machyn's Diary, p. 160.

'The 20 day of Desember was condemnyd for herese ser John Ruffe prest, a Skotte and a woman to be bornyd in Smythfeld for....'

'The 22 day of Desember were bornyd in Smythfeld 2, one ser John Ruffe, the frere and a Skott, and a womanf or herese.' Ibid. p. 161.]

confessed, and thereupon he, with a woman that was one of the congregation, was burnt in Smithfield. And thus ended the burnings this year; seventy-nine in all being burnt.

350   These severities against the heretics made the queen shew less pity to the lord Stourton than perhaps might have been otherwise expected. He had been all king Edward's time a most zealous papist, and did constantly dissent in parliament from the laws then made about religion. But he had the former year murdered one Argall and his son, with whom he had been long at variance: and, after he had knocked them down with clubs, and cut their throats, he buried them fifteen foot under ground, thinking thereby to conceal the fact; but it breaking out, both he and four of his servants were taken, and indicted for it. He was found guilty of felony, and condemned to be hanged with his servants in Wiltshire, where the murder was committed. On the 6th of March they were hanged at Salisbury[66]. All the difference that was made in their deaths being only thus; that whereas his servants were hanged in common halters, one of silk was bestowed on their lord. It seemed an indecent thing, when they were proceeding so severely against men for their opinions, to spare one that was guilty of so foul a murder, killing both father and son at the same time. But it is strange, that neither his quality, nor his former zeal for popery, could procure a change of the sentence, from the more infamous way of hanging, to beheading; which had been generally used to persons of his quality. It has been said, and it passes for a maxim of law, that though

The lord Stourton hanged for murder.

[Godwin, p. 354.]

[Ibid.]

---

[66] ['The 28 day of January was had to the Towre my lorde Sturton for murder of 2 gentyllmen, the father and the sune and ere, master Argylles and ys sune, the wyche was shamfully murdered in ys own plasse.' Machyn's Diary, p. 125. 'The 2 day of Marche rod from the Towre my lord Sturtun with ser Robart Oxinbryge the leyff-tenantt and 4 of my lordes servandes and with serten of the gard, thrugh London, and so to Honsley, and ther lay alle nyght at the seyne of the Angell, and the morow after to Staynes, and so to Bassyngstoke, and so to Sturtun, to sufer deth, and ys 4 men.' Ibid. p. 127. 'The 6 day of Marche .... was hangyd at Salysbere in the markett plasse the lord Sturtun for the deth of old master Argylle and yong Argyll ys sune; the wyche they wher shamfully murdered by the lord, and dyvers of ys servandes; the wyche he mad grett lamentasyon at ys deth for that wyllfull ded that was done, and sayd as he was on the ladder ....' Ibid. p. 128.]

in judgments of treason the king can order the execution to be by cutting off the head, since it being a part of the sentence, that the head shall be severed from the body, the king may in that case remit all the other parts of the sentence except that; yet in felonies the sentence must be executed in the way prescribed by law; and that, if the king should order beheading instead of hanging, it would be murder in the sheriff, and those that execute it: so that in such a case they must have a pardon under the great seal for killing a man unlawfully. But this seems to be taken up without good grounds, and against clear precedents: for in the former reign the duke of Somerset, though condemned for felony, yet was beheaded. And in the reign of king Charles the First, the lord Audley being likewise condemned for felony, all the judges delivered their opinions, that the king might change the execution from hanging to beheading; which was done, and was not afterwards questioned. So it seems the hanging the lord Stourton flowed not from any scruple as to the queen's power of doing it lawfully, but that on this occasion she resolved to give a public demonstration of her justice and horror at so cruel a murder; and therefore she left him to the law, without [March 2.] taking any further care of him. On the last of February he was sent from London, with a letter to the sheriff of Wiltshire, to receive his body, and execute the sentence given against him and his servants; which was accordingly done, as has been already shewn. Upon this, the papists took great advantage to commend the strictness and impartiality of the queen's justice, that would not spare so zealous a catholic, when guilty of so foul a murder. It was also said, that the killing of men's bodies was a much less crime than the killing of souls, which was done by the propagators of heresy; and therefore if the queen did thus execute justice on a friend, for that which was a lesser degree of murder, they who were her enemies, and guilty of higher crimes, were to look for no mercy. Indeed, as the poor protestants looked for none, so they met with very little, but what the cardinal shewed them; 351 and he was now brought under trouble himself for favouring them too much, it being that which the pope made use of to cover his malice against him.

Now the war had again broken out between France and

Spain, and the king studied to engage the English to his
assistance. The queen had often complained to the French
court, that the fugitives, who left her kingdom, had been well
entertained in France. She understood that the practices of
Wiat, and of her other rebellious subjects, were encouraged
from thence; particularly of Ashton, who went often between
the two kingdoms, and had made use of the lady Elizabeth's
name to raise seditions, as will appear by a letter (that is in
the Collection) which some of the council writ to one that Collect.
attended that princess. She was indeed the more strictly kept, Numb. 33.
and worse used upon that occasion. But besides, it so happened, that this year one Stafford had gone into France, and
gathered some of the English fugitives together, and with
money and ships, that were secretly given him by that court,
had come and seized on the castle of Scarborough: from
whence he published a manifesto against the queen, that, by
bringing in the Spaniards, she had fallen from her right to the
kingdom; of which he declared himself protector. The earl
of Westmoreland took the castle on the last of April; and Staf- [Holin-
ford, with three of his complices, being taken, suffered as ${}^{\text{shed, p.}}_{1133.]}$
traitors on the 28th of May. His coming out of France added The queen
much to the jealousy, though the French king disowned that ${}^{\text{becomes}}_{\text{jealous of}}$
he had given him any assistance. But Dr. Wotton, who was then the French.
ambassador there, resolved to give the queen a more certain
discovery of the inclinations of the French, that so he might
engage her in the war, as was desired by Philip: he therefore
caused a nephew of his own to come out of England, whom
when he had secretly instructed, he ordered him to desire to
be admitted to speak with the French king; pretending that
he was sent from some that were discontented in England,
and desired the French protection. But the king would not
see him till he had first spoken with the constable. So Wotton
was brought to the constable; and Melville, from whose Me- [Melville's
moirs I draw this, was called to interpret. The young man ${}^{\text{Memoirs,}}_{\text{pp. 332–}}$
first offered him the service of many in England: that, partly 335.]
upon the account of religion, partly for the hatred they bore
the Spaniards, were ready, if assisted by France, to make stirs
there. The constable received and answered this but coldly;
and said, he did not see what service they could do his master
in it. Upon which he replied, they would put Calais into his

hands. The constable, not suspecting a trick, started at that, and shewed great joy at the proposition: but desired to know how it might be effected. Young Wotton told him, there were a thousand protestants in it, and gave him a long formal project of the way of taking it; with which the constable seemed pleased, and had much discourse with him about it: he promised him great rewards, and gave him directions how to proceed in the design. So the ambassador, having found out what he had designed to discover, sent his nephew over to the queen; who was thereupon satisfied that the French were resolved to begin with her, if they found an opportunity. Her husband king Philip, finding it was not so easy by letters or messages to draw her into the war, came over himself about 352 the 20th of May, and stayed with her till the beginning of July. In that time he prevailed so far with her and the council, that she sent over a herald with a formal denunciation of war, who made it at Rheims, where the king then was, on the 7th of June. Soon after, she sent over 8000 men, under the command of the earl of Pembroke, to join the Spanish army, that, consisting of near 50,000 men, sat down before St. Quintin's. The constable was sent to raise the siege with a great force, and all the chief nobility of France. When the two armies were in view of one another, the constable intended to draw back his army; but by a mistake in the way of it. they fell in some disorder. The Spaniards upon that falling on them, did, with the loss only of 50 of their men, gain an entire victory. 2500 were killed on the place, the whole army was dispersed, many of the first quality were killed, the constable with many others were taken prisoners. The French king was in such a consternation upon it, that he knew not which way to turn himself. Now all the French cursed the pope's counsels, for he had persuaded their king to begin this war, and that with a manifest breach of his faith. This action lost the constable that great reputation which he had acquired and preserved in a course of much success; and raised the credit of the duke of Guise, who was now sent for in all haste, to come with his army out of Italy, for the preservation of his own country. France indeed was never in greater danger than at that time: for if king Philip had known how to have used his success, and marched on to Paris, he could have met

And denounces war.

The great defeat given the French at St. Quintin's. [Aug. 10. Holinshed, p. 1134.]

with no resistance. But he sat down before St. Quintin's, which
Coligny kept out so long, till the first terror was over that so
great a victory had raised : and then, as the French took heart
again, so the Spaniards grew less, as well in strength as reputation; and the English, finding themselves not well used,
returned home into their country.

As soon as the pope heard that England had made war upon
France, he was not a little inflamed with it: and his wrath was
much heightened, when he heard of the defeat at St. Quintin's;
and that the duke of Guise's army was recalled out of Italy;
by which he was exposed to the mercy of the Spaniards. He *The pope is*
now said openly, they might see how little cardinal Pole re- *offended*
with cardi-
garded the apostolic see, when he suffered the queen to assist *nal Pole.*
their enemies against their friends. The pope being thus in-
censed against Pole, sought all ways to be revenged of him.
At first he made a decree (in May this year) for a general revocation of all legates and nuncios in the king of Spain's dominions; and among these, cardinal Pole was mentioned with the
rest. But Carne understanding this, went first to the cardinals, and informed them what a prejudice it would be to their
religion to recal the cardinal while things were yet in so unsettled a state in England. Of this they were all very sensible, and desired him to speak to the pope about it. So, in an
audience he had of him, he desired a suspension might be
made of that revocation. The pope pretended he did it in
general in all the Spanish dominions; yet he promised Carne
to propose it to the congregation of the inquisition, but he was
resolved not to recal it; and said, it did not consist with the
majesty of the place he sat in to revoke any part of a decree
which he had solemnly given. In the congregation, the pope
endeavoured to have got the concurrence of the cardinals, but
353 they were unwilling to join in it. So he told Carne, that
though he would recal no part of his decree, yet he would give
orders that there should be no intimation made of it to cardinal
Pole; and that if the queen writ to him to desire his continuance in England, it might be granted. He also let fall some
words to Carne of his willingness to make peace with king
Philip; and indeed at that time he was much distasted with
the French. Of this, Carne advertised the king, though he
was then so much better acquainted with the pope's dissimula-

tion than formerly, that he did not lay much weight on what
he said to him; as will appear by the despatch he made upon
this occasion, which is in the Collection. Whether the queen
did upon this write to the pope, or not, I do not know. It is
probable [67] she did: for this matter lay asleep till September;
and then the pope did not only recal Pole, but intended to
destroy him. He did not know where to find a person to set
up against the cardinal, since Gardiner was dead, and none of
the other bishops in England were great enough, or sure
enough to him, to be raised to so high a dignity. Peto, the
Franciscan friar, seemed a man of his own temper, because he
had railed against king Henry so boldly to his face; and he
being chosen by the queen to be her confessor, was looked
on as the fittest to be advanced. So the pope wrote for him
into England; and when he came to Rome, made him a cardinal; and sent over his bulls, declaring that he recalled Pole's
legatine power, and required him to come to Rome, to answer
for some accusations he had received of him, as a favourer of
heretics. This might have perhaps been grounded on his discharging that year so many delated of heresy [68], upon so ambiguous a submission as they had made. The pope also wrote
to the queen, that he was to send over cardinal Peto with full
power, requiring her to receive him as the legate of the apostolic see. The queen called for the bulls; and, according to
the way formerly practised in England, and still continued in
Spain, when bulls that were unacceptable were sent over, she
ordered them to be laid up without opening them. It has been
shewn in the former part, how archbishop Chichely, when he
was so proceeded against by pope Martin, appealed to the next
general council; and some that desired to see the form of such
appeals in those ages, have thought it an omission in me, that
I had not published his appeal in the Collection of Records at
the end of that work; therefore, upon this occasion, I shall
refer the reader to it, which he will find in the Collection. But
now, cardinal Pole resolved to behave himself with more sub-

Marginal notes:
Collect.
Numb. 34.

And recals
his lega-
tine power.

Collect.
Numb. 35.

---

[67] The queen and Philip both
wrote to the pope in favour of car-
ninal Pole. The letter is dated
May 21, shewing how serviceable
he had been in restoring religion in
England. The parliament seconded
this by another letter. [S.] [See
both letters in Mem. Eccles. iii. App.
pp. 231–235.]

[68] They were twenty-two in number; their submission is in Fox, p.
1792. [S.]

mission. For though the queen had ordered the pope's breve to him not to be delivered, yet of himself he laid down the ensigns of his legatine power : and sent Ormaneto, who had the title of the pope's datary, and was his friend and confidant, to give an account of his whole behaviour in England; and to clear him of these imputations of heresy. This he did with so much submission, that he mollified the pope : only he said, that Pole ought not to have consented to the queen's joining in war with the enemies of the holy see. Peto had begun his journey to England : but the queen sent him word not to come over; otherwise she would bring him, and all that owned his authority, within the *præmunire*. So he stopped[69] in his journey ; and, dying in April following, enjoyed but a short while his new dignity; together with the bishopric of Salisbury, to which 354 the pope had advanced him, clearly contrary to the old law then in force against provisions from Rome.

[Hist. of Council of Trent, p. 379.]

The queen refuses to admit of cardinal Peto, the new legate.

This storm against Pole went soon over, by the peace that was made between Philip and the pope; of which it will not be unpleasant to give the relation. The duke of Guise having carried his army out of Italy, the duke of Alva marched towards Rome, and took and spoiled all places on his way. When he came near Rome, all was in such confusion, that he might have easily taken it; but he made no assault. The pope called the cardinals together, and, setting out the danger he was in with many tears, said, he would undauntedly suffer martyrdom; which they, who knew that the trouble he was in flowed only from his restless ambition and fierceness, could scarce hear without laughter. The duke of Alva was willing to treat. The pope stood high on the points of honour; and would needs keep that entire, though he was forced to yield in the chief matters : he said, rather than lose one jot that was due to him, he would see the whole world ruined; pretending, it was

A peace made between the pope and the king of Spain. [Hist. of Council of Trent, p. 380.]

---

[69] From the answer to 'English Justice' (supposed to be wrote by sir William Cecil, or by his order) it appears that Peto was now in England, p. 20, 23, &c. Edit. Eat. p. 28; as likewise from the Answer, p. 147, 159. Ciaconius says the same thing, an. Dom. 1557, and Pallavicini, Hist. Conc. Trid. lib. 14, cap. 2, 5, and that he was then an old decrepit man; besides other authorities that might be named if it were material. It was the bulls that were stopped at Calais, with the nuncio or bearer, which may have occasioned the mistake of Godwin and others. [B.]

not his own honour, but Christ's, that he sought.   In fine, the duke of Alva was required by him to come to Rome, and on his knees to ask pardon for invading the patrimony of the church, and to receive absolution for himself and his master. He being superstitiously devoted to the papacy, and having got satis-faction in other things, consented to this.   So the conqueror was brought to ask pardon, and the vain pope received him, and gave him absolution with as much haughtiness and state as if he had been his prisoner.   This was done on the 14th of September ; and the news of it being brought into England on the 6th of October, letters were written by the council to the lord mayor and aldermen of London, requiring them to come to St. Paul's, where high mass was to be said for the peace now concluded between the pope and the king ; after which bonfires were ordered.   One of the secret articles of the peace was the restoring Pole to his legatine power.

The begin-nings of a war be-tween England and Scot-land.

[Buchanan, p. 308.]

War being now proclaimed between England and France, the French sent to the Scottish queen regent to engage Scot-land in a war with England.   Hereupon a convention of the estates was called.   But in it there were two different parties. Those of the clergy liked now the English interest as much as they had been formerly jealous of it ; and so refused to engage in the war, since they were at peace with England.   They had also a secret dislike to the regent, for her kindness to the heretical lords.   On the other hand, those lords were ready enough to gain the protection of the regent, and the favour of France ; and therefore were ready to enter into the war, hoping that thereby they should have their party made the stronger in Scotland, by the entertainment that the queen re-gent would be obliged to give to such as should fly out of Eng-land for religion.   Yet the greater part of the convention were against the war.   The queen regent thought at least to engage the kingdom in a defensive war, by forcing the English to begin with them.   Therefore she sent d'Oyselle, who was in chief command, to fortify Aymouth ; which by the last treaty with England was to be unfortified.   So the governor of Berwick making inroads into Scotland, for the disturbing of their works ; upon that d'Oyselle began the war, and went into England, and besieged Warwick Castle.   The Scottish lords upon this met at Edinburgh, and complained that d'Oyselle was engaging them 355

in a war with England without their consent, and required him
to return back, under pain of being declared an enemy to the
nation; which he very unwillingly obeyed.   But while he lay
there, the duke of Norfolk was sent down with some troops to
defend the marches.   There was only one engagement between
him and the Kers; but, after a long dispute, they were defeated, and many of them taken.   The queen regent, seeing [Buchanan,
her authority was so little considered, writ to France to hasten P. 309.]
the marriage of her daughter to the dauphin; for that he
being thereupon invested with the crown of Scotland, the
French would become more absolute.   Upon this a message
was sent from France to a convention of estates that sat in
December, to let them know, that the dauphin was now coming
to be of age, and therefore they desired they would send over
some to treat about the articles of the marriage.   They sent
the archbishop of Glasgow, the bishop of Orkney, the prior of
St. Andrew's, who afterwards was earl of Murray, the earls of
Rothes and Cassillis, the lord Fleming, and the provosts of
Edinburgh and Montrose, some of every estate, that in the
name of the three estates they might conclude that treaty.

These wars coming upon England when the queen's treasure
was quite exhausted, it was not easy to raise money for carrying them on.   They found such a backwardness in the last
parliament, that they were afraid the supply from thence
would not come easily, or at least that some favour would be
desired for the heretics.   Therefore they tried first to raise
money by sending orders under the privy-seal for the borrowing of certain sums.   But though the council writ many letters
to set on those methods of getting money; yet they being
without, if not against law, there was not much got this way:
so that after all it was found necessary to summon a parliament, to assemble on the 20th of January.   In the end of the
year the queen had advertisements sent her from the king,
that he understood the French had a design on Calais; but
she, either for want of money, or that she thought the place
secure in the winter, did not send those supplies that were
necessary; and thus ended the affairs of England this year.

In Germany there was a conference appointed to bring The affairs
matters of religion to a fuller settlement: twelve papists and of Germany.
twelve protestants were appointed to manage it. Julius Pflugius, [Aug. 14.

Hist of
Council of
Trent, p.
382.]
that had drawn the Interim, being the chief of the papists,
moved, that they should begin first with condemning the heresy
of Zuinglius. Melancthon upon that said, it was preposterous
to begin with the condemnation of errors till they had first
settled the doctrines of religion. Yet that which the papists
expected followed upon this; for some of the fiercer Lutherans,
being much set against the Zuinglians, agreed to it. This raised
heats among themselves, which made the conference break up,
without bringing things to any issue. Upon this occasion, men
could not but see that artifice of the Roman church, which has
been often used before and since with too great success. When
they cannot bear down those they call heretics with open force,
their next way is to divide them among themselves, and to
engage them into heats about those lesser matters in which
they differ; hoping that, by those animosities, their endeavours,
which being united would be dangerous to the common enemy,
may not only be broken, but directed one against another. This
is well enough known to all the reformed: and yet many of 356
them are so far from considering it, that upon every new occasion they are made use of to serve the same designs; never
reflecting upon the advantages that have been formerly taken
from such contentions.

A persecu-
tion of pro-
testants in
France.
[Thuanus,
xix. 15.
p. 664.]
In France the number of the protestants was now increased
much: and in Paris, in September this year, there was a
meeting of about two hundred of them in St. Germains, to receive the sacrament according to the way of Geneva; which
being known to some of their neighbours, they furnished themselves with stones to throw at them when they broke up their
meeting. So, when it was late, as they went home, stones
were cast at some of them; and the enraged zealots forced the
doors, and broke in upon the rest. The men, drawing their
swords, made their way through them, and most of them
escaped; but one hundred and sixty women[70], with some few
men, delivered themselves prisoners to the king's officers that
came to take them. Upon this there were published all the
blackest calumnies that could be devised, of the loose and promiscuous embraces that had been in this meeting; and so
exactly had their accusers copied from what the heathens had

[70] [' Fœminæ atque imbellis sexus   rerum capitalium quæsitori se tra-
numero fere 120 Joanni Martinio   didere.' Thuanus, p. 664.]

anciently charged on the meetings of the Christians, that it
was said, they found the blood of a child, whom they had
sacrificed and eaten among them. These things were confidently told at court, where none durst contradict them for fear
of being judged a favourer of them. But afterwards there was
printed an apology for the protestants. In it they gloried
much, that the same false accusations, by which the heathens
had defamed the primitive Christians, were now cast on them.
Those that were taken were proceeded against; six men and
one woman were burnt. It had gone further, if there had not
come envoys, both from the German princes and the cantons
of Switzerland, to interpose for them: upon which, since the
king needed assistance in his wars, especially from the latter,
the prosecution was let fall. The pope was much troubled
when he heard that the king would exercise no further severity on the heretics: and though himself had hired them in
his wars, yet, he said, the affairs of France could not succeed
as long as their king had so many heretics in his army. That [Hist. of
king had also made two constitutions that gave the pope great Council
offence; the one, that marriages made by sons under thirty, p. 381.]
and daughters under twenty-five, without their father's consent, should be void: the other was, for charging the ecclesiastical benefices with a tax, and requiring all bishops and
curates to reside on their benefices. So scandalous a thing
was non-residence then held, that every where the papists
were ashamed of it. Upon which the pope complained anew,
that the king presumed to meddle with the sacraments, and to
tax the clergy.

The beginning of the next year was famous for the loss of Calais is
Calais. The lord Wentworth had then the command of it; but besieged,
the garrison consisted only of 500 men, and there were not [Stow,
above 200 of the townsmen that could be serviceable in a siege. p. 632.]
The duke of Guise, having brought his army out of Piedmont,
was now in France; and being desirous, when the constable
was a prisoner, to do some great action which might raise him
in reputation above the other, who was his only competitor
357 in France, set his thoughts on Calais, and the territory about
it. There were two forts on which the security of the town depended. The one, Newnambridge, a mile from it, that commanded the avenues to it from the land; from which to the

town there was a way raised through a marsh lying on both hands of it.   On the other side, to the sea, the fort of Risbank commanded the harbour; so that the whole strength of the place lay in those two forts.

[Thuanus, xx. 2. p. 677.]

On the first of January the duke of Guise came and sat down before it. The governor having but a small force within, did not think fit to weaken it by sending such supplies as those forts required; so they were taken without any opposition. Then the town being thus shut up, the enemy pressed it hard, and drew the water out of its current, by which the ditches about the town and castle were drained; and, having prepared devices for their soldiers to pass them without sticking in the mire, they made the assault, after they had opened a great breach by their ordnance: and, when the sea was out, others crossed on that side, and so carried the castle by storm; which the governor had looked on as impregnable, and so had brought his chief force to the defence of the town. Seeing the castle thus unexpectedly lost, he did all he could with his small force to regain it; but, being still repulsed, and having lost 200 of

And taken. [Jan. 8. Ibid. p. 679.]

[Grafton's Chronicle, ii. p. 558. ed. Lond. 4to. 1809]

his best men, he was forced to render the place on the 7th of January. By their articles, all the townsmen and soldiers were to go whither they pleased, only he and fifty more were to be prisoners of war. Thus, in one week's time, and in winter, was so strong a town lost by the English, that had been for many ages in their hands.   It was taken 210 years ago by Edward III. after the battle of Cressy; and was still called the key of France, as long as it continued in English hands.   But now, in a time of war, it was in as ill a condition as if they had been in the profoundest peace: and though Philip had offered to put men into it, yet the English, being jealous that those advertisements were but artifices of his to persuade them to admit a Spanish garrison into it, left it in so naked a condition, that the governor could do little to preserve it.   But yet, that it might appear he had not been too careful of himself, he was content to agree that he should be a prisoner of war.

Guisnes and the rest of that territory taken by the French. [Thuanus, xx. 3. p. p. 680.]

From this the duke of Guise went to Guisnes, commanded by the lord Grey; whose garrison consisted of about 1100 men: but the loss of Calais had much disheartened them.   At the first impression the French carried the town, and the garrison retired into the castle; but Grey, breaking out on the soldiers,

that were fallen to plundering, did beat them out again, and
burnt the town.   The French battered the castle till they
made a breach in the outworks of it, which they carried, after
a long resistance, in which the English lost 300: so the lord
Grey was fain to render it, he and all the officers being made
prisoners of war.   There was another castle in that little
county, Hammes, which lay in such a marsh that it was
thought inaccessible; but the garrison that was in it abandoned it, without staying till the enemy came before them.
The French writers speak more meanly of the resistance made
by the lord Grey than of that made by the lord Wentworth;
for they went out of Guisnes about 800 soldiers, whereas there
went not out of Calais above 300.   But one of our own writers [Stow, p.
magnifies the lord Grey, and speaks dishonourably of the lord 632. refer-
                                                                ring to
358 Wentworth; adding, which was an invention of his own, that Grafton, ii.
he was attainted for the losing of Calais.   All that historian's p. 558.]
ground for it is only this; that there was indeed a mock-cita- [Stow, p. 634.]
tion issued out against the lord Wentworth, to which he could
not appear, being not free from his imprisonment by the
French all this reign; but he came over in the beginning of
the next, when, the treaty of peace being on foot, he obtained
his liberty, and was tried by his peers in the first parliament in
queen Elizabeth's reign, and acquitted.   It was, as he alleged
for himself, his misfortune to be employed in a place, where he
had not so much as a fourth part of that number of men that
was necessary to hold out a siege.   But, in the declinations of
all governments, when losses fall out, they must be cast on those
that are intrusted, to excuse those who are much more guilty,
by neglecting to supply them as the service required.   Among
the prisoners, one of the chief was sir Edward Grimston, the
comptroller of Calais, and a privy counsellor.   He had often,
according to the duty of his place, given advertisement of the
ill condition the garrison was in: but whether those to whom
he writ were corrupted by French money, or whether the low
state of the queen's treasury made that they were not supplied,
is not certain.   It was intended he should not come over to
discover that: and therefore he was let lie a prisoner in the
Bastile; and no care was taken of him, or the other prisoners.
The ransom set on him was so high, that, having lost a great
estate, which he had purchased about Calais, he resolved not

to do any further prejudice to his family by redeeming his liberty at such a rate; and intended either to continue a prisoner, or make his escape. He lay above two years in the Bastile, and was lodged in the top of it. At the end of that time he procured a file, and so cut out one of the bars of the window, and, having a rope conveyed to him, he changed clothes with his servant, and went down on the rope; which proving a great deal too short, he leaped a great way, and, having done that before the gates were shut, made his escape without being discovered. But his beard, which was grown long, made him fear he should be known by it: yet by a happy providence he found in the pockets of his servant's clothes a pair of scissors, and, going into the fields, did so cut his beard, that he could not have been known; and having learnt the art of war in the company of the Scotch guard de Manche, he spake that dialect: so he passed as a Scotch pilgrim, and by that means escaped into England. And there he offered himself to a trial; where, after the evidence was brought, his innocence did so clearly appear, that the jury were ready to give their verdict without going from the bar. So he was acquitted and lived to a great age, dying in his 98th year. He was great grandfather to my noble patron and benefactor sir Harbottle Grimston, which has made me the more willing to enlarge thus concerning him, to whose heir I owe the chief opportunities and encouragements I have had in composing of this work.

Now the queen had nothing left of all those dominions that her ancestors had once in France, but the isles of Jersey, *Sark taken by the French;* Guernsey, Alderney, and Sark. The last of these, being a naked place, only inhabited by some hermits, but having the advantage of a harbour, the French made themselves masters of it. The strength of it consisted in the difficulty of the ascent; the little fort they had being accessible but in one place, where two could only go up abreast. So an ingenious 359 Fleming resolved to beat them out of it: he came thither, and, pretending he had a friend dead in his ship, offered them a *And retaken by an ingenious stratagem.* good present if he might bury him within their chapel. The French consented to it, if he would suffer himself and his men to be so narrowly searched, that they might not bring so much as a knife ashore. This he consented to; and, as he landed

with his coffin, the Frenchmen were to send some to his ship
to receive the present. So the coffin being carried into the
chapel, and the French apprehending nothing from unarmed
men, the coffin was opened, which was full of good arms, and
every man furnishing himself, they broke out upon the French,
and took them all; as their companions in the ship did those
who went aboard to bring the present.

The news of the loss of Calais filled England with great discontent. Those who were otherwise dissatisfied with the conduct of affairs, took great advantages from it to disparage
the government, which the queen had put into the hands of
priests, who understood not war, and were not sensible of the
honour of the nation. It was said, they had drained her
treasury by the restitutions and foundations they got her to
make; and, being sensible how much the nation hated them,
they had set the queen on other ways of raising money than
by a parliament: so that never did the parliament meet with
greater disorder and trouble than now. But that loss affected
none so deeply as the queen herself, who was so sensible of the
dishonour of it, that she was much oppressed with melancholy,
and was never cheerful after it. Those who took on them to
make comments on divine Providence, expounded this loss as
their affections led them. Those of the reformation said, it
was God's heavy judgment upon England for rejecting the
light of his gospel, and persecuting such as still adhered to it.
But, on the other hand, the papists said, Calais could not prosper, since it had been a receptacle of heretics, where the laws
against them had never been put in execution. King Philip,
as soon as he heard of this loss, wrote over to England, desiring them to raise a great force with all possible haste, and
send it over to recover Calais before it was fortified; and he
would draw out his army, and join with them: for if they did
not retake it before the season of working about it came on,
it was irrecoverably lost. Upon which there was a long consultation held about it. They found they could not to any
purpose send over under 20,000 men; the pay of them for five
months would rise to 170,000*l.* Garrisons, and an army against
the Scots, and securing the coasts against the French, would
come to 150,000*l.* The setting out of a fleet, and an army by
sea, would amount to 200,000*l.*; and yet all that would be too

*Great dis-
contents in
England.*

little, if the Danes and Swedes, which they were afraid of, should join against them. There was also great want of ammunition and ordnance, of which they had lost vast quantities in Calais and Guisnes. All this would rise to be above 520,000*l*., and they doubted much whether the people would endure such impositions, who were now grown stubborn, and talked very loosely: so they did not see how they could possibly enter into any action this year. One reason among the rest was suggested by the bishops: they saw a war would oblige them to a greater moderation in their proceedings at 360 home; they had not done their work, which they hoped a little more time would perfect; whereas a slackening in that would raise the drooping spirits of those whom they were now pursuing. So they desired another year to prosecute them, in which time they hoped so to clear the kingdom of them, that with less danger they might engage in a war the year after. Nor did they think it would be easy to bring new raised men to the hardships of so early a campaign; and they thought the French would certainly work so hard in repairing the breaches, that they would be in a good condition to endure a strait and long siege. All this they wrote over to the king on the first of February, as appears from their letter, which will be found in the Collection.

Collect. Numb. 36.

A parliament is called.
[Wilkins, iv. 156.]
[Cap. 10. Statutes, vol. iv. p. 332.]

The parliament was opened on the 20th of January; where the convocation, to be a good example to the two houses, granted a subsidy of eight shillings in the pound, to be paid in four years. In the house of peers, the abbot of Westminster, and the prior of St. John of Jerusalem, took their places according to their writs. Tresham, that had given great assistance to the queen upon her first coming to the crown, was now made prior. But how much was done towards the endowing of that house, which had been formerly among the richest of England, I do not know. On the 24th of January the lords sent a message to the commons, desiring that the speaker, with ten or twelve of that house, should meet with a committee of the lords; which being granted, the lords proposed, that the commons would consider of the defence of the kingdom. What was at first demanded, does not appear; but, after several days arguing about it, they agreed to give one subsidy, a fifteenth and a tenth: and ordered the speaker to let the queen

[Journal of Commons, p. 47.]

[Cap. 11. Statutes, vol. iv. p. 336.]

know what they had concluded; who sent them her hearty thanks for it. Then, complaints being made of some French-men, that were not denizens, it was carried, that they should go out of the kingdom, and not return during the war. The abbot of Westminster, finding the revenues of his house were much impaired, thought, that, if the old privileges of the sanctuary were confirmed, it would bring him in a good reve-nue from those that fled to it; so he pressed for an act to con-firm it. He brought a great many ancient grants of the kings of England, which the queen had confirmed by her letters patents; but they did not prevail with the house, who pro-ceeded no further in it. In this parliament the procurers of wilful murder were denied the benefit of clergy; which was carried in the house of lords by the greater number, as it is in their Journals: the bishops did certainly oppose it, though none of them entered their dissent. Sir Ambrose and sir Ro-bert Dudley, two sons of the late duke of Northumberland, were restored in blood. The countess of Sussex's jointure was taken from her, for her living in adultery so publicly, as was formerly mentioned. In the end of the session, a bill was put in for the confirming of the queen's letters patents: it was de-signed chiefly for confirming the religious foundations she had made. As this went through the house of commons, one Cox-ley[72] said, he did not approve such a general confirmation of those she had given, or might give, lest this might be a colour for her to dispose of the crown from the right inheritors. The house was much offended at this; and expressed such dislike at the imagination that the queen would alienate the crown, that they both shewed their esteem for the queen, and their resolution to have the crown descend after her death to her sister. Coxley[73] was made to withdraw, and voted guilty of great irreverence to the queen. He asked pardon, and desired it might be imputed to his youth: yet he was kept in the ser-geant's hands till they had sent to the queen to desire her to forgive his offence. She sent them word, that at their suit she forgave it; but wished them to examine him, from whence that motion sprung. There is no more entered about it in the

Margin notes:
[Cap. 6. ibid. p. 326.]

[Cap. 4. ibid. p. 322.]

[Journal of Lords, p. 518.]

[Ibid. p. 523.]

[Ibid. p. 527.]

[Cap. 1. Ibid. p. 314.]

[March 5. Journal of Commons, p. 50.]

[Ibid.

361

71 The complaint was made against all the French denizens as well as others, but the act was more favour-able. [S.]

72 Coxley *read* Copley. [S.]

73 Coxley *read* Copley. [S.]

[Nov. 5.]

Journal, so that it seems to have been let fall. The parliament was, on the 7th of March, prorogued to the 7th of November [74].

The king of Sweden treats a marriage with the lady Elizabeth;

Soon after this, the king of Sweden sent a message secretly to the lady Elizabeth, who was then at Hatfield, to propose marriage to her. King Philip had once designed to marry her to the duke of Savoy, when he was in hope of children by the queen; but that hope vanishing, he broke it off, and intended to reserve her for himself. How far she entertained that motion, I do not know: but for this from Sweden, she rejected it, since it came not to her by the queen's direction. But to that it was answered, the king of Sweden would have them begin with herself, judging that fit for him, as he was a gentleman; and her good liking being obtained, he would next, as a king, address himself to the queen. But she said, as she was to entertain no such propositions unless the queen sent them to her; so, if she were left to herself, she assured them she would not change her state of life. Upon this the queen sent sir Thomas Pope to her in April, to let her know how well she approved of the answer she had made to them; but they had now delivered their letters, and made the proposition to her, in which she desired to know her mind. She thanked the queen for her favour to her, but bade Pope tell her, that there had been one or two noble propositions made for her in her brother king Edward's time; and she had then desired to continue in the state she was in, which of all others pleased her best, and she thought there was no state of life comparable to it: she had never before heard of that king, and she desired never to hear of that motion more: she would see his messenger no more, since he had presumed to come to her without the queen's leave. Then Pope said, he did believe if the queen offered her some honourable marriage, she would not be averse to it. She answered, what she might do afterwards she did not know; but protested solemnly, that, as she was then inclined, if she could have the greatest prince in Christendom,

---

[74] [And my lord Chancellor prorogued this parliament unto the *fifth* day of November next. Journal of Commons, p. 51. Dominus Cancellarius ex mandato Dominæ Reginæ præsens Parliamentum prorogavit in quintum diem Novembris proxime futurum. Journal of Lords, p. 534.]

she would not accept of him; though perhaps the queen might Which is rejected by her. think this flowed rather from a maid's modesty, than any settled determination in her: this I take from a letter Pope wrote about it, which is in the Collection. Yet her life at this time Collect. Numb. 37. was neither so pleasant, nor so well secured, but that, if her aversion to a married state had not been very much rooted in her, it is not unlikely she would have been glad to be out of the hands of her unkind keepers; who grew the more apprehensive of her, the more they observed her sister to decay: and, as the bishops did apprehend she would overthrow all 62 that they had been building and cementing with so much blood; so some of them did not spare to suggest the putting of her out of the way. And now that she is so near the throne, in the course of this History, I shall look back through this reign, to give account of what befel her in it.

When she was suspected to be accessary to Wiat's con- She was hardly used all this reign. [Fox, vol. iii. p. 792.] spiracy, the day after his breaking out, the lord Hastings, sir Thomas Cornwallis, and sir Richard Southwell were sent for her to come to court. She then lay sick at her house at Ashbridge; but that excuse not being accepted, she was forced to go: so, being still ill, she came by slow journeys to the queen. She was kept shut up in private at court from the 4th of March to the 16th, and then Gardiner, with nineteen of the council, came to examine her about Wiat's rebellion. She positively denied she knew any thing of it, or of sir Peter Carew's designs in the west, which they also objected to her. In conclu- [Ibid. p. 793.] sion, they told her the queen had ordered her to be sent to the Tower till the matter should be further inquired into: and though she made great protestations of her innocence, yet she was carried thither, and led in by the traitor's gate; all her own servants being put from her. Three men, and as many women of the queen's servants, were appointed to attend on her; and no person was suffered to have access to her. Sir John Gage, who was the lieutenant of the Tower, treated her very severely, kept her closely shut up, without leave to walk either in the galleries, or on the leads; nor would he permit her servants to carry in her meat to her, but he did that by his own servants. The other prisoners were often examined about her, and some were put to the rack, to try if they could be brought any way to accuse her: but though Wiat had done it, when he hoped to have saved his own life by so base an action; yet he afterwards denied that she knew any of their designs; and, lest those denials he made at his examinations might have been suppressed, and his former depositions be made use of against her, he declared it openly on the scaffold at his death. After some days' close imprisonment, upon great intercession made by the lord Chandos, then constable of the Tower, it was granted that she might sometimes walk in the queen's rooms, in the presence of the constable, the lieutenant, and three women; the windows being all shut. Then she got leave to walk in a little garden for some air; but all the windows that opened to it were to be kept shut when she took her walk: and so jealous were they of her, that a boy of four years old was severely threatened, and his father sent for and chid, for his carrying flowers to her. The lord Chandos was observed to treat her with too much respect; so he was not any more trusted with the charge of her, which was committed to sir Henry Bedingfield. About the middle of May she was sent, under the guard of the lord Williams and Bedingfield, to Woodstock. She was so straitly kept, and Bedingfield was so sullen to her, that she believed they intended to put her privately to death. The lord Williams treated her nobly at his house on the way, at which Bedingfield was much disgusted. When she was at Woodstock, she was still kept under guards, and but seldom allowed to walk in the gardens; none being suffered to come near her. After many months' imprisonment, she obtained leave to write to the queen; Bedingfield being to see all she wrote. It was believed, that some were sent secretly to kill her; but the orders were given so strictly, that none of them could come near her without a special warrant: and so she escaped at that time. But after king Philip understood the whole case, he broke all those designs, as was formerly shown; and prevailed to have her sent for to court. When she came to Hampton-Court she was kept still a prisoner. Many of the council, Gardiner in particular, dealt often with her to confess her offences, and submit to the queen's mercy. She said she had never offended her, not so much as in her thoughts; and she would never betray her own innocency by such a confession. One night, when it was late, she was sent for by the queen, before whom she kneeled down, and

[Fox, vol. iii. p. 795.]

[Ibid. p. 796.]

[Ibid. p. 797.]

[Ibid. p. 798.]

36

protested she was, and ever had been, a most faithful subject
to her. The queen seemed still to suspect her, and wished her
to confess her guilt, otherwise she must think she had been
unjustly dealt with. She answered, that she was not to complain, but to bear her burden; only she begged her to conceive a good opinion of her. So they parted fairly, which
king Philip had persuaded the queen to; and, being afraid that
the sourness of the queen's temper might lead her into passion,
he was secretly in a corner of the room, to prevent any further
breach, in case she should have been transported into new
heats: but there was no occasion given for it. Soon after that,
she was discharged of her guards, and suffered to retire into
the country: but there were always many spies about her;
and she, to avoid all suspicion, meddled in no sort of business,
but gave herself wholly to study. And thus she passed these
five years, under no small fears and apprehensions; which was
perhaps a necessary preparation for that high degree to which
she was soon after advanced, and which she held in the greatest
and longest course of prosperity and glory that ever any of her
sex attained to.

The bishops, when the parliament were sitting, did always *The pro-*
intermit their cruelties; but as soon as it was over, they fell *gress of the*
persecu-
to them afresh. On the 28th of March, Cuthbert Simpson, *tion.*
that was in deacon's orders, with two others, were burnt in *[Fox, vol.*
iii. p. 726.]
Smithfield[75]. Simpson had been taken with Rough, that suffered the year before this. He was put to much torture; he
lay three hours on the rack: besides, two other inventions of
torture were made use of, to make him discover all those in
London who met with them in their private assemblies: but
he would tell nothing, and shewed such patience, that the bishops did publicly commend him for it. On the 9th of April *[Ibid. p.*
a man was burnt at Hereford; on the 19th[76] of May three *729.]*
men were burnt at Colchester. At this time, complaints being

---

[75] ['The 21 day of Marche ....
wher browth into the .... afor the
bysshope of London and odur
lernyd men of the temporolte 3
men, the wyche ther opinions wher
shyche that they wher juged and
condemnyd to suffer deth by fyre;
one man was a hossear, dwellyng
in Wodstret, ys name is ....' Machyn's Diary, p. 169.]
[76] For the 19 May *read* 26th;
for three men *read* two men and
one woman. There were indeed
three men burnt on the 19th of
May at Norwich, not at Colchester.
[S.]

made to the queen that books of heresy, treason, and sedition were either brought in from foreign parts, or secretly printed in England, and dispersed among her subjects; she set out on the 6th of June a proclamation of a strange nature: "that "whosoever had any of these, and did not presently burn "them, without reading, or shewing them to any other per-"son, they should be esteemed rebels; and, without any "further delay, be executed by the martial law[77]." On the 27th of that month, when seven were to be led out to be burnt in Smithfield, it was proclaimed in the queen's name, that no man should pray for them, or speak to them, or say, *God help them:* which was thought a strain of barbarity beyond all the example of former times, to deprive dying men of the good wishes and prayers of their friends. But however this might restrain men from giving outward signs of their praying for them, it could not bind up their inward and secret devotions. Those seven had been taken at a meeting in Islington, with many others; of whom some died in prison, and six others were burnt at Brentford the 14th of July. The rest of them were kept by Bonner, who now seemed to have been glutted with the blood of so many innocents, and therefore to have put a stop to the effusion of more; yet those that were kept prisoners by him did not so entirely escape his fury but that he disciplined them himself with rods till he was weary; and so gave over that odd way of pastoral correction, rather to ease himself, than in pity to them whom he whipt. On the 10th of July a minister was burnt at Norwich. On the 2nd or 3rd of August a gentleman was burnt near Winchester. In August, four were burnt at Bury; and in November, three more were burnt there. On the 4th of November, a man and a woman were burnt at Ipswich; at that time a woman was burnt at Exeter. And, to close up all, on the 10th of November three men and two women were burnt at Canterbury, which made in all thirty-nine this year. There had been seventy-nine burnt the former year, ninety-four the year before that, and seventy-two the first year of the persecution; which in all come to two hundred and eighty-four. But he that writ the preface to bishop Ridley's book *De Cœnâ Do-*

[Fox, vol. iii. p. 732.]

[Ibid. p. 733.]

[Ibid. p. 734.]

[Ibid. p. 739. sqq.]

[Ibid. p. 742.]
[Ibid. p. 743.]
[Ibid. p. 744.]

[Ibid. p. 745.]
[Ibid. p. 746.]
[Ibid. p. 750.]

364

---

[77] Martial law. The words of the proclamation are, 'according to the order of the martial law.' [S.]

mini, who is supposed to be Grindal[78], afterwards archbishop of Canterbury, says, that in the two first years of the queen's persecution there were above eight hundred put to most cruel kinds of death for religion: by which it seems Fox, on whom I depend for the numbers I have assigned, has come far short in his account. Besides those that were burnt, many others died in bonds, of whom there are sixty reckoned[79]. There were also great numbers of those who were vexed with long and grievous imprisonment; and though they redeemed their lives by the renouncing, or rather the dissembling of their consciences, yet this being but forced from them, they carried with them their old opinions: and the wound they gave their consciences to save their lives, as it begot in many of them great horror for what they had done, so it raised in them the most mortal hatred to those who had driven them to such straits; so that if that religion was hateful before to the nation, for the impostures and scandals that were discovered in the clergy, and some few instances of their cruelty, the repeated burnings, and other cruelties, of which now they saw no end, did increase their aversion to it beyond all expression.

At first the bishops dealt earnestly with those who were brought before them to recant: and were ready at any time to receive them: the queen's pardon was also sent to them as 365 they were ready to be tied to the stake, if they would then turn. But now it was far otherwise; for in the council-books[80] there

The method of the persecutions of this reign. [Council Book of Mary and Elizabeth, vol. i. p. 131.]

[78] The author of the preface to Ridley's book was William Whittyngham, according to Bale (p. 684, 731.), who knew the man well, as well as his writings. [B.]

[Wood says (an. 1579.), 'The public works that he hath done as to learning are, ... (4) Nich. Rydley's *Declaration of the Lord's Supper*. Genev. 1556.' To which Whittyngham put a preface of his own making.]

[79] Lord Burleigh, in the 'Execution of Justice,' says, there died by imprisonment, torments, famine, and the fire, near 400. On this we may depend. [S.]

[80] [The following is the extract from the Council Book, 'Also to

sir Richarde Pexsall, knight, sheriff of the county of Hampshire, signifying that the queen's majesty cannot but find it very strange that he hath stayed one Bembrigge from execution, being condemned for heresy; and therefore he is straightly commanded to cause him to be executed out of hand, and if he still continueth in the catholic faith as he outwardly pretendeth, then to suffer some such discreet and learned man as the bishop of Winchester shall appoint, who is written unto for this purpose, to have access unto him, and to confer with him for the better confirmation of him in the catholic faith, and to be present with him at his death, for the better aiding of

is an entry made of a letter, written on the 1st of August this
year, to sir Richard Pexsall, sheriff of Hampshire, signifying
" that the queen thought it very strange that he had delayed
" the execution of the sentence against one Bembridge, con-
" demned of heresy, because he had recanted; requiring him
" to execute it out of hand : and if he still continued in the ca-
" tholic faith, which he outwardly pretended, he was then to
" suffer such divines as the bishop of Winchester should ap-
" point to have access to him for confirming him in the faith;
" and to attend on him at his death, that he might die God's
" servant: and as soon as the sheriff had thus burnt him,
" he was to come to the council, and answer for his pre-
" sumption in delaying it so long." The matter of fact was
thus; Bembridge being tied to the stake, and the fire taking
hold on him, he, through the violence of it, yielded, and cried
[Fox, vol.
iii. p. 743.]
out, *I recant.* Upon which the sheriff made the fire be put
out; and Bembridge signed such a recantation as Dr. Seton,
who was near him, writ for him : but for all that, upon this
order of council, he was burnt; and the sheriff was put in the
Fleet. So that now it appeared that it was not so much the
conversion of those they called heretics, as their destruction, that
the bishops desired. And so much were their instruments set
on these severities, that though they saw the queen declining so
fast, that there was no appearance of her living many days;
yet, the week before she died, they burnt, as hath been said,
five together in one fire at Canterbury.

An unhap-
py expedi-
tion against
France.
[Thuanus,
xx. 16. p.
697.]
There was nothing done in the war with France this year,
but the sending out a fleet of 120 ships, with 7000 landmen in
it, under the command of the lord Clinton, who landed at Port
Conquet, in the point of Bretagne; where, after a small resistance made by the French, he burnt the town : but the country
being gathered together, the English were forced to return to
their ships, having lost above 600 of their men. The design
was, to have seized on Brest, and fortified it; which was proposed by king Philip, who had sent thirty of his ships to their
assistance. This the French knowing by some of the prisoners

him to die God's servant. The said
sheriff is also commanded to make
his indelayed repair hither immediately after the execution, to answer
his doing herein. Also to the Bishop of Wynchester for the purpose
aforesaid.] p. 131.

whom they took, went and tortified Brest, and kept a great
body of men together, to resist, in case the English should
make a second impression. But the lord Clinton, seeing he
could do nothing, returned, having made a very expensive and
unprosperous attempt. The English had lost their hearts; the
government at home was so little acceptable to them, that they
were not much concerned to support it; they began to think
Heaven was against them.

There were many strange accidents at home, that struck Strange
terror in them. In July, thunder broke near Nottingham with and unu-
such violence, that it beat down two little towns, with all the sual accidents.
houses and churches in them: the bells were carried a good [Stow, p.
way from the steeples, and the lead that covered the churches 634.]
was cast four hundred foot from them, strangely wreathed.
The river of Trent, as it is apt upon deluges of rain to swell
and overrun the country; so it broke out this year with extra-
366 ordinary violence, many trees were plucked up by the roots,
and with it there was such a wind, that carried several men and
children a great way, and dashed them against trees or houses,
so that they died. Hailstones fell that were fifteen inches
about in other places; and, which was much more terrible, a
contagious intermitting fever, not unlike the plague, raged
every where: so that three parts of four of the whole nation
were infected with it. So many priests died of it, that in many
places there were none to be had for the performing of the
offices. Many bishops died also of it, so that there were many
vacancies made by the hand of Heaven against queen Elizabeth
came to the crown; and it spreading most violently in August,
there were not men enough in many counties to reap the harvest; so that much corn was lost. All these symptoms concurred to increase the aversion the people had to the government; which made the queen very willing to consent to a
treaty of peace, that was opened at Cambray in October; to
which she sent the earl of Arundel, the bishop of Ely, and
Dr. Wotton, as her plenipotentiaries.

The occasion of the peace was from a meeting that the A treaty of
bishop of Arras had with the cardinal of Lorraine at Peronne: peace between Eng-
in which he proposed to him, how much Philip was troubled at land,
the continuance of the war, their forces being so much engaged France,
and Spain.
in it, that they could make no resistance to the Turk, and the [Thuanus,
p. 687.]

mean while heresy increasing and spreading in their own dominions, while they were so taken up, that they could not look carefully to their affairs at home, but must connive at many things: therefore he pressed the cardinal to persuade the king of France to an accommodation. The cardinal was easily induced to this, since, besides his own zeal for religion, he saw that he might thereby bear down the constable's greatness; whose friends, chiefly his two nephews, the admiral and Dandelot, who went then among the best captains in France, were both suspect of being protestants; upon which the latter was shortly after put in prison: so he used all his endeavours to draw the king to consent to it; in which he had the less opposition, since the court was now filled with his dependents; and his four brothers, who had got all the great offices of France into their hands, and the constable and admiral being prisoners, there was none to oppose their counsels. The king, thinking that by the recovery of Calais, and the places about it, he had gained enough to balance the loss of St. Quintin's, was very willing to hearken to a treaty: and he was in an ill state to continue the war, being much weakened both by the loss he

The battle or Gravelines.

suffered last year, and the blow that he received in July last; the marshal de Thermes being enclosed by the count of Egmont near Gravelines, where the French army being set on by the count, and galled with the English ordnance from their ships, that lay near the land, was defeated, 5000 killed, the marshal and the other chief officers being taken prisoners. These losses made him sensible that his affairs were in so ill a condition, that he could not gain much by the war.

The number of the protestants growing in France. [Hist. of Council of Trent, p. 384.]

The cardinal was the more earnest to bring on a peace, because the protestants did not only increase in their numbers, but they came so openly to avow their religion, that, in the public walks without the suburbs of St. Germain, they began to sing David's Psalms in French verse. The newness of the thing amused many, the devotion of it wrought on others, the music drew in the rest; so that the multitudes that used to divert themselves in those fields, instead of their ordinary sports, did now nothing for many nights but go about singing psalms: and that which made it more remarkable was, that the king and queen of Navarre came and joined with them. That king, besides the honour of a crowned head, with the small part of

367

that kingdom that was yet left in their hands, was the first prince of the blood. He was a soft and weak man; but his queen, in whose right he had that title, was one of the most extraordinary women that any age hath produced, both for knowledge far above her sex, for a great judgment in affairs, an heroical greatness of mind, and all other virtues, joined to a high measure of devotion and true piety: all which, except the last, she derived to her son Henry the Great. When the king [Hist. of of France heard of this psalmody, he made an edict against it; Council of and ordered the doers of it to be punished: but the numbers Trent, p. 385.] of them, and the respect to those crowned heads, made the business to go no further.

On the 24th of April was the dauphin married to the queen The dauof Scotland. Four cardinals, Bourbon, Lorraine, Chastillon, phin marries the and Bertrand, with many of the princes of the blood, and the queen of other great men of France, and the commissioners sent from Scotland. Scotland, were present. But scarce any thing adorned it more xx. 8. p. [Thuanus, than the Epithalamium written upon it by Buchanan; which 685.] was accounted one of the perfectest pieces of Latin poetry. After the marriage was over, the Scotch commissioners were [Ibid. p. desired to offer the dauphin the ensigns of the regality of Scot- 686.] land, and to acknowledge him their king: but they excused themselves, since that was beyond their commission, which only empowered them to treat concerning the articles of the marriage, and to carry an account back to those that sent them. Then it was desired that they would promote the business at their return to their country: but some of them had expressed their aversion to those propositions so plainly, that it was believed they were poisoned by the brethren of the house of Guise. Four of them died in France; the bishop of Orkney, and the earls of Rothes and Cassillis, and the lord Fleming. The prior of St. Andrew's was also very sick; and though he recovered at that time, yet he had never any perfect health after it. When the other four returned into Scotland, a convention of the estates was called, to consult about the propositions they brought.

This assembly consists of all those members that make up a A convenparliament; who were then, the bishops, and abbots, and priors, tion of estates in who made the first estate; the noblemen, that were the second Scotland. estate; and the deputies from the towns, one from every town,

only Edinburgh sends two, were the third estate. Anciently
all that held lands of the crown were summoned to parliaments,
as well the greater as the lesser barons. But in king James
the First's time, the lesser barons, finding it a great charge to
attend on such assemblies, desired to be excused from it; and
procured an act of parliament exempting them, and giving them 368
power to send from every county two, three, four, or more, to
represent them: but they afterwards thought this rather a
charge than a privilege, and did not use it; so that now the
second estate consisted only of the nobility. But the gentry
finding the prejudice they suffered by this, and that the nobility
grew too absolute, procured, by king James the Sixth's favour,
an act of parliament restoring them to that right of sending deputies, two from every county, except some small counties that
send only one, but according to the ancient law, none has a
vote in the elections but those who hold lands immediately of
the crown of such a value. The difference between a parliament, and a convention of estates, is, that the former must be
summoned forty days before it sits; and then it meets in state,
and makes laws, which are to be prepared by a committee of
all the estates, called the lords of the articles: but a convention
may be called within as few days as are necessary for giving
notice to all parts of the nation to make their elections: they
have no power of making laws, being only called for one particular emergent; which, during the division of the island, was
chiefly upon the breaking out of war betwixt the two nations,
and so their power was confined to the giving of money for the
occasion which then brought them together.

In the convention now held, after much debate and opposition, whether they should consent to the demand made by the
ambassador sent from France, it was carried, that the dauphin
should be acknowledged their king, great assurances being
given, that this should be only a bare title, and that he should
pretend to no power over them. So the earl of Argyle, and
the prior of St. Andrews, who had been the main sticklers for
the French interest, upon the promises that the queen regent
made them, that they should enjoy the free exercise of their
religion, were appointed to carry the matrimonial crown into
France. But as they were preparing for their journey, a great
revolution of affairs fell out in England.

The parliament met on the 5th of November. On the 7th, A session of parliament in England. the queen sent for the speaker of the house of commons, and ordered him to open to them the ill condition the nation was in: [Journal of Commons, p. 51.] for though there was a treaty begun at Cambray, yet it was necessary to put the kingdom in a posture of defence, in case it should miscarry. But the commons were now so dissatisfied, that they could come to no resolution. So, on the 14th day of [Ibid. p. 52.] November, the lord chancellor, the lord treasurer, the duke of Norfolk, the earls of Shrewsbury and Pembroke, the bishops of London, Winchester, Lincoln, and Carlisle, the viscount Montague, the lords Clinton and Howard, came down to the house of commons, and sat in that place of the house where the privy counsellors used to sit. The speaker left his chair; and he, with the privy counsellors that were of the house, came and sat on low benches before them. The lord chancellor shewed the necessity of granting a subsidy, to defend the nation both from the French and the Scots. When he had done, the lords withdrew; but though the commons entered, both that and the two following days, into the debate, they came to no issue in their consultations.

369   The queen had never enjoyed her health perfectly since the The queen's sickness, false conception that was formerly spoken of; upon which followed the neglect from her husband, and the despair of issue, that increased her melancholy: and this receiving a great addition from the loss of Calais, and the other misfortunes of this year, she, by a long declination of health, and decay of her spirits, was now brought so low, that it was visible she had not many days to live; and a dropsy coming on her, put a conclusion to her unhappy reign, and unfortunate life, on the 17th And death. of November, in the 43rd year of her age, after she had reigned five years, four months, and eleven days.

At the same time cardinal Pole, as if one star had governed Cardinal Pole dies. both their nativities, was also dying; and his end being hastened by the queen's death, he followed her within sixteen hours, in the 59th year of his age. He left his whole estate Thuanus, xx. 21. p. 702.] to Aloysio Priuli, a noble Venetian, with whom he had lived six and twenty years in so entire a friendship, that, as nothing could break it off, so neither was any thing able to separate them from one another's company. Priuli, being invited by pope Julius to come and receive a cardinal's hat, preferred

Pole's company before it; and as he had supplied him in his necessities in Italy, so he left his country now to live with him in England. Pole made him his executor: but Priuli was of a more noble temper than to enrich himself by his friend's wealth; for as he took care to pay all the legacies he left, so he gave away all that remained, reserving nothing to himself but Pole's breviary [81] and diary. And indeed the cardinal was not a man to raise a fortune, being, by the greatness of his birth, and his excellent virtues, carried far above such mean designs. He was a learned, modest, humble, and good-natured man; and had indeed such qualities, and such a temper, that, if he could have brought the other bishops to follow his measures, or the pope and queen to approve of them, he might have probably done much to have reduced this nation to popery again. But God designed better things for it; so he gave up the queen to the bloody counsels of Gardiner, and the rest of the clergy. It was the only thing in which she was not led by the cardinal. But she imputed his opinion in that particular rather to the sweetness of his temper, than to his wisdom and experience: and he, seeing he could do nothing of what he projected in England, fell into a languishing, first of his mind, that brought after it a decay of his health, of which he died. I have dwelt the more copiously on his character, being willing to deny to none of whom I write, the praises that are due to them: and he being the only man of that whole party, of whom I found any reason to say much good, I was the more willing to enlarge about him, to let the world see how little I am biassed, in the account I give, by interest or opinion. So that if I have written sharply of any others that have been mentioned in this reign, it was the force of truth, and my abhorrence of their barbarous cruelties, that led me to it, more than my being of a contrary persuasion to them. It is certain, that Pole's method of correcting the manners of the clergy, and being gentle to the reformed, would in all appearance have been much more fatal to the progress of the reformation; that was set forward by nothing more than by the severities shewed 370 to those that differed from them, and the indulgence of the bishops to the vices of their own party. Yet Pole had a vast

Marginal notes: [Thuanus, xx. 21. p. 703.] His character.

---

[81] Ex quibus Polus Deum precari solitus erat, breviarium vocamus et diurnale. Beccatell. p. 80. [B.]

superstition to the see of Rome; and though his being at the council of Trent had opened his eyes to many things, which he had not observed before; yet he still retained his great submission to that see, and thought it impossible to maintain the order and unity of the church, but by holding communion with it; which carried him, in opposition to many apprehensions himself had of some theological points, still to support the interests of the papacy. His neglect of the offer of it, when it was made to him, shewed this flowed from no aspirings of his own, but purely from his judgment: so that, what mistakes soever his education and heats with king Henry, and the disasters of his family, might have involved him in, it cannot be denied, that he was a man of as great probity and virtue as most of the age, if not all, of that church, in which he lived.

For the queen herself, her character has appeared so manifestly in her reign, that I need make no further description of her. She was a woman of a strict and innocent life, that allowed herself few of the diversions with which courts abound. She was bred to learning, and understood the Latin [82] tongue well; but what further knowledge she had, does not appear to me. She was constant at her devotions, and was as much addicted to the interests and humours of the clergy, as they could have wished her. She had great resentments of her own ill usage in her father's and brother's times; which made her be easily induced to take her revenge, though she coloured it with her zeal against heresy. She did not much mind any other affairs but those of the church; so that if she could have extirpated heresy, she seemed to regard all other things very little; and being given up to follow the dictates of Rome with a nice scrupulosity of conscience, it was no wonder she went on in these designs very vigorously. For as the pope was ever calling on all princes that were under his obedience to set up the courts of inquisition; so the fourth general council of Lateran, to which, with the other general councils, she paid no less reverence than to the scriptures, charged catholic princes to extirpate all heretics out of their dominions: such as were slack must be required to do it by their bishops; and if that prevailed not, they were to be excommunicated by them: and if they continued negligent, and under that censure

The queen's character.

[82] She understood and wrote well both in Spanish and French. [S.]

a year, they were to be deprived by the pope, and their dominions to be given to others, who should take more care to extirpate heresy. The pope had also in February this year published a constitution, to which he had made all the cardinals set their hands, confirming all former decrees and canons against heretics; declaring, that all prelates, princes, kings, and emperors, that had fallen into heresy, should be understood to be deprived of their dominions, without any further sentence; and that any catholics, who would take the forfeiture, should have a good title to all that they invaded and seized. The bishops, besides the other canons binding them to proceed against heretics, were, by the words of the oath of obedience which they swore to the pope at their consecration, engaged to *oppose and persecute the heretics with all their might*: so that their giving severe counsels, and the queen's following 371 them, flowed mainly from the principles of their religion; in which the sourness of her temper made it the more easy to persuade her to a compliance to those courses to which her inclination led her, without any such motives. To conclude, her death was as little lamented as any of all our princes ever was, the popish clergy being almost the only mourners that were among her own people.

Thus lived and died Mary queen of England by inheritance, and of Spain by marriage.

[Feb. 15. Hist. of Council of Trent, p. 383.]

THE END OF THE SECOND BOOK.

THE HISTORY

OF

THE REFORMATION

OF

THE CHURCH OF ENGLAND.

PART II.—BOOK III.

Of the Settlement of the Reformation of Religion in the beginning of Queen Elizabeth's Reign.

QUEEN Mary's death was concealed for some hours. What the secret consultations were upon it is not known; but the issue of them appeared about nine o'clock. Then the lord chancellor went to the house of lords, and first imparted to them the news of the queen's death; which, as it struck the bishops with no small fear, so those counsellors who had been severe in their advices about her sister, did apprehend she might remember it against them. Yet they all agreed to proclaim her queen; and, by the zeal they expressed for her coming to the crown, intended to balance the errors they had formerly been led to, rather in compliance to the late queen's resentments, than out of any ill-will they bore herself. They sent for the house of commons, and the lord chancellor signified to them the queen's death; which, he said, would have been a much more sorrowful loss to them, if they had not such a successor, that was the next and undisputed heir to the crown, Elizabeth, of whose right and title none could make any ques-

Queen Elizabeth succeeds.
[Camden, p. 369.]

tion; therefore they intended to proclaim her queen, and desired their concurrence. This was echoed with many and long repeated cries: *God save queen Elizabeth; Long and happy may she reign.*

And proclaimed queen.
[Nov. 17.
Egerton Papers, p. 28.]

The parliament being declared to be dissolved by the late 374 queen's death, the lords proclaimed Elizabeth queen[1]; and went into London, where it was again done by the lord mayor, and received every where with such excessive joy, that there was no sign of sorrow expressed for the death of queen Mary, but what the priests shewed; who, in so public and universal a joy, were forced to betake themselves to secret groans, since they durst not vent them in public. Never did any before her come to the throne with so many good wishes and acclamations, which the horror of the cruelties, and the reflection of the disasters of the former reign, drew from the people, who now hoped to see better times.

And comes to London.
[Stow, p. 635.]

The queen was then at Hatfield, where having received the news of her sister's death, and of her being proclaimed queen, she came from thence to London. On the 19th, at Highgate, all the bishops met her[2], whom she received civilly, except Bonner, on whom she looked as defiled with so much blood, that she could not think it fit to bestow any mark of her favour on him. She was received into the city, with throngs much greater than even such occasions used to draw together, and followed with the loudest shouts of joy that they could raise. She lay that night at the duke of Norfolk's house in the Charter-house, and next day went to the Tower. There at her entry she kneeled down, and offered up thanks to God for that great change in her condition; that whereas she had been formerly a prisoner in that place, every hour in fear of her life, she was now raised to so high a dignity. She soon

[1] ['The 23 day of November the quen Elsabeths grace toke here gorney from Hadley, beyond Barnett, toward London, unto my lord North's plase, with a M. and mor of lordes, knyghtes, and gentyllmen, lades and gentyllwomen, and ther lay 5 days ...' Machyn's Diary, p. 179.]

[2] The queen was at Hatfield November 20, and yet there November 22, as appears from a register or

council-book, which I have seen. November 24, she was at the Charter-house; it does not appear from thence that she was at the Tower till December 1. [B.]

Queen Elizabeth stayed some days at Hatfield; she came to the Charter-house 24 November. On the 28th she went to the Tower, and came to Westminster on the 23rd of December. [S.]

cleared all people's apprehensions as to the hardships she had
formerly met with, and shewed she had absolutely forgot from
whom she had received them; even Bedingfield himself not
excepted, who had been the chief instrument of her sufferings:
but she called him always her *gaoler*, which though she did in
a way of raillery, yet it was so sharp, that he avoided coming
any more to the court.

She presently despatched messengers to all the princes of
Christendom, giving notice of her sister's death, and her succession. She writ in particular to king Philip a large acknowledgment of his kindness to her, to whom she held herself much
bound for his interposing so effectually with her sister for her
preservation. She also sent to sir Edward Carne, that had *She sends a despatch to Rome.*
been her sister's resident at Rome, to give the pope the news
of her succession. The haughty pope received it in his ordi- *[History of the Council of Trent, p. 385.]*
nary style, declaring, "that England was held in fee of the
" apostolic see; that she could not succeed, being illegitimate,
" nor could he contradict the declarations made in that matter
" by his predecessors Clement the Seventh and Paul the
" Third; he said, it was great boldness in her to assume the
" crown without his consent; for which in reason she deserved
" no favour at his hands: yet, if she would renounce her pre-
" tensions, and refer herself wholly to him, he would shew a
" fatherly affection to her, and do every thing for her that
" could consist with the dignity of the apostolic see." When *But to no effect.*
she heard of this, she was not much concerned at it; for she
had written to Carne, as she did to her other ministers, and
had renewed his powers upon her first coming to the crown,
being unwilling in the beginning of her reign to provoke any
party against her: but hearing how the pope received this
address, she recalled Carne's powers, and commanded him to
375 come home. The pope on the other hand required him not to
go out of Rome, but to stay and take the care of an hospital,
over which he set him: which it was thought that Carne procured to himself, because he was unwilling to return into England, apprehending the change of religion that might follow;
for he was himself zealously addicted to the see of Rome.

As soon as Philip heard the news, he ordered the duke of *King Philip courts her in mar- riage.*
Feria, whom he had sent over in his name to comfort the late
queen in her sickness, to congratulate the new queen, and in

[Camden, p. 370.]

secret to propose marriage to her ; and to assure her, he should procure a dispensation from Rome : and at the same time he sent thither to obtain it. But the queen, though very sensible of her obligation to him, had no mind to the marriage. It appeared by what hath been said in the former book, and by the sequel of her whole life, that though upon some occasions, when her affairs required it, she treated about her marriage, yet she was firmly resolved never to marry. Besides this, she saw her people were generally averse to any foreigner, and particularly to a Spaniard : and she made it the steady maxim of her whole reign, from which she never departed, to rule in their affections as well as over their persons. Nor did she look on the pope's dispensation as a thing of any force to warrant what was otherwise forbidden by God : and the relation between king Philip and her being the reverse of that which was between her father and queen Catharine, it seeming to be equally unlawful for one man to marry two sisters, as it was for one woman to be married to two brothers, she could not consent to this marriage without approving king Henry's with queen Catharine : and if that were a good marriage, then she must be illegitimate, as being born of a marriage which only the unlawfulness of that could justify. So inclination, interest, and conscience, all concurred to make her reject king Philip's motion. Yet she did it in terms so full of esteem and kindness for him, that he still insisted in the proposition ; in which she was not willing to undeceive him so entirely as to put him out of all hopes while the treaty of Cambray was in dependence, that so she might tie him more closely to her interests.

The queen of Scots pretends to the crown of England.

The French, hearing of queen Mary's death, and being alarmed at Philip's design upon the new queen, sent to Rome to engage the pope to deny the dispensation, and to make him declare the queen of Scotland to be the right heir to the crown of England, and the pretended queen to be illegitimate. The cardinal of Lorraine prevailed also with the French king to order his daughter-in-law to assume that title, and to put the arms of England on all her furniture.

The queen's council.

[Camden, p. 369.]

But now to return to England ; queen Elizabeth continued to employ some of the same counsellors that had served queen Mary : namely, Heath, the lord chancellor ; the marquis of Winchester, lord treasurer ; the earls of Arundel, Shrewsbury,

Derby, and Pembroke[3]; the lords Clinton and Howard, sir
Thomas Cheyney, sir William Petre, sir John Mason, sir
Richard Sackville, and Dr. Wotton, dean of Canterbury and
York. Most of these had complied with all the changes that
had been made in religion backward and forward since the
latter end of king Henry's reign, and were so dextrous at it,
that they were still employed in every new revolution. To
them, who were all papists, the queen added the marquis of
376 Northampton, the earl of Bedford, sir Thomas Parr[4], sir Edward Rogers, sir Ambrose Cave, sir Francis Knolles, and sir
William Cecil, whom she made secretary of state; and soon
after she sent for sir Nicholas Bacon; who were all of the
reformed religion. She renewed all the commissions to those
formerly intrusted; and ordered, that such as were imprisoned
on the account of religion should be set at liberty. After this, [Bacon's
a man, that used to talk pleasantly, said to her, that he came Apoph-
to supplicate in behalf of some prisoners not yet set at liberty. thegms,
She asked, who they were? He said, they were Matthew, vol. ii. p.
Mark, Luke, and John, that were still shut up; for the people 387.]
longed much to see them abroad. She answered him as pleasantly, she would first talk with themselves, and see whether
they desired to be set at such liberty as he requested for
them.

Now the two great things under consultation were, religion A consulta-
and peace. For the former, some were appointed to consider the change
how it was to be reformed. Beal[5], a clerk of the council, gave of religion.
advice to Cecil, that the parliaments under queen Mary should iii. p. 819.]
be declared void; the first being under a force, (as was before
related,) and the title of Supreme Head being left out of the
summons to the next parliament before it was taken away by
law: from whence he inferred, that both these were not lawfully held or duly summoned; and this being made out, the
laws of king Edward were still in force. But this was laid
aside as too high and violent a way of proceeding; since the
annulling of parliaments upon little errors in writs, or some
particular disorders, was a precedent of such consequence, that
to have proceeded in such a manner would have unhinged all
the government and security of the nation. More moderate

---

[3] The earl of Pembroke favoured   [4] For Parr *read* Parry. [S.]
the reformation. [S.]   [5] [Fox calls him *Hales*.]

courses were thought on. The queen had been bred up from her infancy with a hatred of the papacy, and a love to the reformation: but yet, as her first impressions in her father's reign were in favour of such old rites as he had still retained; so in her own nature she loved state, and some magnificence in religion, as well as in every thing else. She thought that in her brother's reign they had stripped it too much of external ornaments, and had made their doctrine too narrow in some points; therefore she intended to have some things explained in more general terms, that so all parties might be comprehended by them. She inclined to keep up images in churches, and to have the manner of Christ's presence in the sacrament left in some general words; that those who believed the corporal presence might not be driven away from the church by too nice an explanation of it. Nor did she like the title of Supreme Head; she thought it imported too great a power, and came too near that authority which Christ only had over the church. These were her own private thoughts. She considered, nothing could make her power great in the world abroad so much as the uniting all her people together at home: her father's and her brother's reign had been much distracted by the rebellions within England, and she had before her eyes the instance of the coldness that the people had expressed to her sister on all occasions for the maintaining or recovering of the dominions beyond sea; therefore she was very desirous to find such a temper, in which all might agree. She observed, that in the changes formerly made, particularly in renouncing the papacy, and making some alterations in worship, the whole clergy had concurred, and so she resolved to follow and imitate these by easy steps.

A method of doing it proposed.
Collect.
Numb. 1.

There was a long consultation had, about the method of the 377 changes she should make: the substance of which shall be found in the Collection, in a paper, where, in the way of question and answer, the whole design of it is laid down. This draught of it was given to sir William Cecil, and does exactly

[Camden, p. 371 sqq.]

agree with the account that Camden gives of it. That learned and judicious man has written the history of this queen's reign with that fidelity and care, in so good a style, and with so much judgment, that it is without question the best part of our English history: but he himself often says, that he had

left many things to those who should undertake the history of
the church; therefore, in the account of the beginnings of this
reign, as I shall in all things follow him with the credit that is
due to so extraordinary a writer, so, having met with some
things which he did not know, or thought not necessary in so
succinct a history to enlarge on, I shall not be afraid to write
after him, though the esteem he is justly in may make it seem
superfluous to go over these matters any more.

" It seemed necessary for the queen to do nothing before a The heads
" parliament were called; for only from that assembly could of it.
" the affections of the people be certainly gathered. The next
" thing she had to do was to balance the dangers that threat-
" ened her both from abroad and at home. The pope would
" certainly excommunicate and depose her, and stir up all
" Christian princes against her: the king of France would lay
" hold of any opportunity to embroil the nation; and by the
" assistance of Scotland, and of the Irish, might perhaps raise
" troubles in her dominions. Those that were in power in
" queen Mary's time, and remained firm to the old supersti-
" tion, would be discontented at the reformation of religion:
" the bishops and clergy would generally oppose it; and,
" since there was a necessity of demanding subsidies, they
" would take occasion, by the discontent the people would be
" in on that account, to inflame them: and those who would
" be dissatisfied at the retaining of some of the old ceremonies,
" would on the other hand disparage the changes that should
" be made, and call the religion a cloaked papistry, and so
" alienate many of the most zealous from it. To remedy all
" these things, it was proposed to make peace with France,
" and to cherish those in that kingdom that desired the re-
" formation. The curses and practices of Rome were not
" much to be feared. In Scotland those must be encouraged
" who desired the like change in religion; and a little money
" among the heads of the families in Ireland would go a great
" way. And for those that had borne rule in queen Mary's
" time, ways were to be taken to lessen their credit throughout
" England: they were not to be too soon trusted or employed
" upon pretence of turning; but those who were known to be
" well affected to religion and the queen's person were to be
" sought after, and encouraged. The bishops were generally

" hated by the nation: it would be easy to draw them
" within the statute of *præmunire,* and, upon their falling
" into it, they must be kept under it till they had re-
" nounced the pope, and consented to the alterations that
" should be made. The commissions of the peace, and for the
" militia, were to be carefully reviewed, and such men were to
" be put in them as would be firm to the queen's interests. 378
" When the changes should be made, some severe punishments
" would make the rest more readily submit. Great care was
" to be had of the universities, and other public schools, as
" Eton and Winchester, that the next generation might be
" betimes seasoned with the love and knowledge of religion.
" Some learned men, as Bill, Parker, May, Cox, Whitehead,
" Grindal, Pilkington, and sir Thomas Smith, were to be or-
" dered to meet and consider of the book of service. In the
" mean while the people were to be restrained from innovating
" without authority : and the queen, to give some hope of
" a reformation, might appoint the communion to be given
" in both kinds. The persons that were thought fit to be
" trusted with the secret of these consultations were, the mar-
" quis of Northampton, the earls of Bedford and Pembroke,
" and the lord John Grey. The place that was thought most
" convenient for the divines to meet in was sir Thomas Smith's
" house in Channon-row, where an allowance was to be given
" for their entertainment."

The for-
wardness
in many to
the refor-
mation.

As soon as the news of the queen's coming to the crown was
known beyond sea, all those who had fled thither for shelter
did return into England : and those who had lived in corners
during the late persecution, now appeared with no small assurance ; and these, having notice of the queen's intentions, could
not contain themselves, but in many places began to make
changes, to set up king Edward's service, to pull down images,
and to affront the priests. Upon this the queen, to make some
discovery of her own inclinations, gave order, that the Gospels
and Epistles, and the Lord's Prayer, the Apostles' Creed, and
the Ten Commandments, should be read in English, and that
the Litany should be also used in English; and she forbade
the priests to elevate the host at mass. Having done this, on
the 27th of December she set out a proclamation against all
innovations, requiring her subjects to use no other forms of

[Wilkins,
Conc. iv.
p. 180.]

worship than those she had in her chapel, till it should be otherwise appointed by the parliament, which she had summoned to meet on the 23rd of January. The writs were issued out by Bacon, into whose hands she had delivered the great seal. On the 5th[5] of December she performed her sister's funeral rites with great magnificence at Westminster. The bishop of Winchester being appointed to preach the sermon, did so mightily extol her and her government, and so severely taxed the disorders which he thought the innovators were guilty of, not without reflections on the queen[6], that he was thereupon confined to his house till the parliament met[7].

[Stow, p. 635.]

[Cotton MSS.Vesp. D. xviii. 94.]

One of the chief things under consultation was, to provide men fit to be put into the sees that were now vacant, or that might fall to be so afterwards, if the bishops should continue intractable. Those now vacant were, the sees of Canterbury, Hereford, Bristol, and Bangor; and in the beginning of the next year the bishops of Norwich and Gloucester died: so that, as Camden hath it, there were but fourteen bishops living when the parliament met. It was of great importance to find men able to serve in these employments, chiefly in the see of Canterbury. For this, Dr. Parker was soon thought on. Whether others had the offer of it before him, or not, I cannot tell: but he was writ to by sir Nicholas Bacon on the 9th of December to come up to London; and afterwards on the 30th of December by sir William Cecil, and again by sir Nicholas Bacon on the 4th of January. He understood that it was for some high preferment; and being a man of an humble temper, distrustful of himself, that loved privacy, and was much disabled by sickness, he declined coming up all he could: he

Parker designed to be archbishop of Canterbury.

[Sept. 7, 1558.] [Camden, p. 372.]

[Collect. Numb. 8.]

379

---

[5] For 5th December *read* 13th. [S.]

[6] [This sermon has been printed from the copy amongst the Cotton MSS. by Strype, Mem. Eccles. iii. App. p. 277. It does not contain any reflections on queen Elizabeth. The only allusion to her is in the following passage, p. 286. 'And as we for our parts have received worthily detriment and discomfort upon her departing, so let us comfort ourselves in the other sister whom God hath left, wishing her a prosperous reign in peace and tranquillity, with the blessing which the prophet speaketh of, if it be God's will, *Ut videat filios filiorum et pacem super Israel*: ever confessing that though God hath mercifully provided for them both, yet *Maria optimam partem elegit*; because it is still a conclusion, *Laudavi mortuos magis quam viventes*.]

[7] The council set him at liberty on the 19th of January, and the parliament met on the 25th. [S.]

begged he might not be thought of for any public employment, but that some prebend might be assigned him, where he
might be free both from care and government; since the infirmities, which he had contracted by his flying about in the
nights in queen Mary's time, had disabled him from a more
public station. That to which he pretended, shews how moderate his desires were: for he professed, an employment of
twenty nobles a year would be more acceptable to him than
one of two hundred pound. He had been chaplain to queen
Anne Boleyn, and had received a special charge from her, a
little before she died, to look well to the instruction of her
daughter in the principles of the Christian religion; and now
the queen had a grateful remembrance of those services. This,
joined with the high esteem that sir Nicholas Bacon had of
him, soon made her resolve to raise him to that great dignity.
And since such high preferments are generally, if not greedily
sought after, yet very willingly undertaken by most men, it
will be no unfit thing to lay open a modern precedent, which
indeed savours more of the ancient than the latter times; for
then, instead of that *ambitus*, which has given such offence to
the world in the latter ages, it was ordinary for men to fly
from the offer of great preferments. Some ran away when
they understood they were to be ordained, or had been elected
to great sees, and fled to a wilderness. This shewed they had a
great sense of the care of souls, and were more apprehensive of
that weighty charge, than desirous to raise or enrich themselves
or their families. It hath been shewed before, that Cranmer was
very unwillingly engaged in the see of Canterbury; and now,
he that succeeded him in that see, with the same designs, was
drawn into it with such unwillingness, that it was almost a
whole year before he could be prevailed upon to accept of it:
the account of this will appear in the series of letters both
written to him and by him on that head; which were communicated to me by the present most worthy and most reverend primate[8] of this church. I cannot mention him in this
place without taking notice, that as in his other great virtues
and learning he has gone in the steps of those most eminent
archbishops that went before him; so the whole nation is wit-

[8] [This was first published in 1681, when Sancroft was archbishop of
Canterbury.]

ness how far he was from aspiring to high preferment, how he withdrew from all those opportunities that might be steps to it, how much he was surprised with his unlooked-for advancement, how unwillingly he was raised, and how humble and affable he continues in that high station he is now in. But this is a subject that I must leave for them to enlarge on, that shall write the history of this present age.

380   In the beginning of the next year, the queen having found that Heath, archbishop of York, then lord chancellor, would not go along with her, as he had done in the reigns of her father and brother; and having therefore taken the seals from him, and put them into sir Nicholas Bacon's hand, did now by patent create him lord keeper. Formerly those that were keepers of the seal had no dignity nor authority annexed to their office; they did not hear causes, nor preside in the house of lords, but were only to put the seals to such writs or patents as went in course; and so it was only put in the hands of a keeper but for some short interval. But now Bacon was the first lord keeper that had all the dignity and authority of the lord chancellor conferred on him; and his not being raised to that high title perhaps flowed from his own modesty: for as he was one of the most learned, most pious, and wisest men of the nation; so he retained in all his greatness a modesty equal to what the ancient Greeks and Romans had carried with them to their highest advancement. He was father to the great sir Francis Bacon, viscount St. Alban's, and lord chancellor of England, and will be always esteemed one of the greatest glories of the English nation.

1559.

Bacon made lord keeper.

[Dec. 22, 1558.]

The queen was now to be crowned; and having gone on the 12th of January to the Tower, she returned from thence in state on the 13th. As she went into her chariot, she lifted up her eyes to heaven, " and blessed God that had preserved her " to see that joyful day, and that had saved her, as he did his " prophet Daniel, out of the mouth of the lions. She acknow- " ledged her deliverance was only from him, to whom she offered " up the praise of it." She passed through London in great triumph: and having observed that her sister, by the sullenness of her behaviour to the people, had much lost their affections; therefore she always used, as she passed through crowds, but more especially this day, to look out of her coach cheerfully on

[Jan. 14. Stow, p. 635.]

them, and to return the respects they paid her with great sweetness in her looks; commonly saying, *God bless you, my people;* which affected them much. But nothing pleased the city more than her behaviour as she went under one of the triumphal arches: there was a rich Bible let down to her, as from heaven, by a child, representing Truth; she with great reverence kissed both her hands, and, receiving it, kissed it, and laid it next her heart; and professed she was better pleased with that present than with all the other magnificent ones that had been that day made her by the city. This drew tears of joy from the spectators' eyes. And indeed this queen had a strange art of insinuating herself by such ways into the affections of her people. Some said, she was too theatrical in it: but it wrought her end; since by these little things in her deportment she gained more on their affections, than other princes have been able to do by more real and significant arts of grace and favour. The day following she was crowned at Westminster by Oglethorp bishop of Carlisle, all the other bishops refusing to assist at that solemnity. He, and the rest of that order, perceived that she 381 would change the religion then established, and looked on the alterations she had already made as pledges of more to follow; and observed, by the favour that Cecil and Bacon had with her, that she would return to what had been set up by her brother. They had already turned so oft, that they were ashamed to be turning at every time. Heath, Tunstall, and Thirlby had complied in king Edward's time as well as in king Henry's; and though Thirlby had continued in credit and favour with them till the last, yet he had been one of those who had gone to Rome, where he made such public professions of his respect to the apostolic see; and he had also assisted at the degradation and condemnation of Cranmer; so that he thought it indecent for him to return to that way any more: therefore he, with all the rest, resolved to adhere to what they had set up in queen Mary's time. There were two of king Edward's bishops yet alive, who were come into England; yet the queen chose rather to be consecrated by a bishop actually in office, and according to the old rites, which none but Oglethorp could be persuaded to do. After that she gave a general pardon according to the common form.

On the 23rd of January, being the day to which the parlia-

The queen's coronation, [Jan. 15. Machyn's Diary, p. 186.]

The parliament meets.

ment was summoned, it was prorogued till the 25th[9], and then [Journal of Lords, p. 542.]
it was opened with a long speech of the lord Bacon's, in which
he laid before them " the distracted estate of the nation, both [Journal of Commons, p. 53.]
" in matters of religion, and the other miseries that the wars
" and late calamities had brought upon them: all which he
" recommended to their care.　For religion, the queen desired
" they would consider of it without heat or partial affection, or
" using any reproachful term of papist or heretic, and that
" they would avoid the extremes of idolatry and superstition
" on the one hand, and contempt and irreligion on the other;
" and that they would examine matters without sophistical
" niceties, or too subtle speculations, and endeavour to settle
" things so as might bring the people to an uniformity and
" cordial agreement in them.　As for the state of the nation,
" he shewed the queen's great unwillingness to lay new impo-
" sitions on them; upon which he ran out largely in her com-
" mendation, giving them all assurance, that there was nothing
" she would endeavour more effectually than the advancing of
" their prosperity, and the preserving their affections.　He
" laid open the loss of Calais, with great reflections on those
" who had been formerly in the government; yet spoke of it as
" a thing which they could not at that time hope to recover;
" and laid before them the charge the government must be at,
" and the necessities the queen was in; adding in her name,
" that she would desire no supply but what they did freely
" and cheerfully offer."

One of the first things that the commons considered was,
whether the want of the title of Supreme Head, which the
queen had not yet assumed, was a nullity in the summons for
this and other parliaments, in which it had been omitted: but
after this had been considered some days, it was judged to
382 be no nullity; for the annulling of a parliament, except it had
been under a force, or for some other error in the constitution,
was a thing of dangerous consequence.

But, leaving the consultations at Westminster, I shall now The treaty at Cambray.
give an account of the treaty of peace at Cambray.　That at
which things stuck most was, the rendering of Calais again to [Camden, p. 373.]

---

[9] [A copy of the commission pro-　nuary is in the State Paper Office,
roguing the meeting of parliament　Domestic Series, vol. 2.]
from the 23rd to the 25th of Ja-

the English, which the French did positively refuse to do. For a great while Philip demanded it with so much earnestness, that he declared he would make peace on no other terms; since as he was bound in point of honour to see the English, who engaged in the war only on his account, restored to the condition that they were in at the beginning of it; so his interest made him desire that they might be masters of that place, by which, it being so near them, they could have the conveniency of sending over forces to give a diversion to the French at any time thereafter, as their alliances with him should require. But when Philip saw there was no hope of a marriage with the queen, and perceived that she was making alterations in religion, he grew less careful of her interests, and secretly agreed a peace with the French. But, that he might have some colour to excuse himself for abandoning her, he told her ambassador, that the French had offered him full satisfaction in all his own concerns, so that the peace was hindered only by the consideration of Calais; and therefore, unless the English would enter into a league with him for keeping up the war six years longer, he must submit to the necessity of his affairs. The queen, perceiving that she was to expect no more assistance from the Spaniard, who was so much engaged to the old superstition that he would enter into no strict league with any whom he accounted an heretic, was willing to listen to the messages that were sent her from France, by the constable and others, inducing her to agree to a peace. She on the other hand complained that the queen of Scotland, and her husband in her right, had assumed the title and arms of England: it was answered, that was done as the younger brothers in Germany carried the title of the great families from whence they were descended; and for titles, the queen of England had little reason to quarrel about that, since she carried the title and gave the arms of France.

[Camden, p. 378.]

The queen and her council saw it was impossible for her to carry on the war with France alone. The laying heavy impositions on her subjects in the beginning of her reign might render her very ingrateful to the nation, who loved not to be charged with many subsidies: and when the war should produce nothing but some wastes on the French coasts, which was all that could be expected, since it was unreasonable to look

A peace with France agreed to.

for the recovery of Calais, it might turn all the joy they were
now in at her coming to the crown into as general a discontent.
It was the ruin of the duke of Somerset, that he had engaged
in a war in the beginning of king Edward's reign, when he
was making changes in religion at home : therefore it was
necessary to yield to the necessity of the time, especially since
383 the loss of Calais was no reproach on the queen, but on her
sister. So it was resolved on to make a general peace, that,
being at quiet with their neighbours, they might with the less
danger apply themselves to the correcting what was amiss in
England, both in religion and the civil government. At length [Rymer,
a peace was made on these terms: that there should be free xv. p. 505.]
commerce between the kingdoms of England, France, and [Camden,
Scotland: the French should keep Calais for eight years, and p. 382.]
at the end of that time should deliver it to the English ; and
if it were not then delivered, they should pay to the English
500,000 crowns, for which they should give good security by
merchants that lived in other parts, and give hostages till the
security were given : but if during these years the queen made
war on France or Scotland, she was to lose her right to that
town; or if the French or Scots made war on her, Calais
should be presently restored, to which she was still to reserve
her right : Aymouth in Scotland was to be razed, and a commission was to be sent down to some of both kingdoms to
agree all lesser differences. On these terms a peace was
made, and proclaimed between those crowns; to which many
of the English, that did not apprehend what the charge of a
war for the regaining of Calais would have amounted to, were
very averse ; thinking it highly dishonourable, that they,
whose ancestors had made such conquests in France, should be
now beaten out of the only remainder that they had on the
continent ; and thus make a peace, by which it was in effect
parted with for ever: for all these conditions about restoring
it were understood to be only for palliating so inglorious a
business. But the reformed cast the blame of this on the
papists ; and some moved, that all the late queen's council
should be questioned for their misgovernment in that particular: for it was thought nothing would make them so odious
to the nation as the charging that on them. They on the
other hand did cast the blame of it on the lord Wentworth,

that had been governor of Calais, and was now professedly one
of the reformed, and had been very gentle to these of that
persuasion during his government. But he put himself on a
trial by his peers, which he underwent on the 22nd of April;
and there did so clear himself, that he was by the judgment of
the peers acquitted.

The proceedings of the parliament.

[Journal of Lords, pp. 544. 546.]

The queen's government being thus quieted abroad, she was
thereby at more leisure to do things at home. The first bill
that was put into the house of lords to try their affections and
disposition to a change in the matters of religion, was that for
the restitution of the tenths and first-fruits to the crown. It
was agreed to by the lords on the 4th of February, having
been put in the 30th of January, and was the first bill that
was read: the archbishop of York, the bishops of London [10],
Worcester, Llandaff, Lichfield, Exeter, Chester, and Carlisle,
protested against it: these were all of that order that were at
the session, except the bishops of Winchester, Lincoln, Ely,
and the abbot of Westminster, who it seems were occasionally

[Journal of Commons, p. 54.]

absent. On the 6th of February it was sent down to the commons, to which they readily agreed, and so it had the royal
assent. By it, not only the tenths and first-fruits were again
restored to the crown, but also all impropriated benefices, 384
which had been surrendered up by queen Mary.

They address to the queen for her marrying.

[Ibid. p 54.]

[Camden, p. 375.]

But the commons, reflecting on the miseries in which they
had been lately involved by queen Mary's marriage, had much
debate about an address to the queen to induce her to marry.
On the 4th of February it was argued in the house of commons; and on the 6th the speaker, with the privy counsellors
of the house, and thirty members more, were sent with their
desires to the queen. " They expressed the affections of the
" nation to her, and said, that if they could hope she might be
" immortal, they would rest satisfied; but that being a vain
" imagination, they earnestly besought her to choose such a
" husband as might make the nation and herself happy, and
" by the blessing of God bring such issue as might reign after
" her death, which they prayed God might be very late. She

The queen's answer.

" said, she looked on that as an expression both of their affec-
" tion and respect, since they had neither limited time nor

[10] [The name of the bishop of Winchester has been omitted. See
Journal of Lords, p. 546.]

" place. She declared, that she had hitherto lived in a single
" state with great satisfaction, and had neither entertained
" some honourable propositions, which the lord treasurer knew
" had been made to her in her brother's time, nor had been
" moved by the fears of death that she was in, while she was
" under her sister's displeasure; (of which she would say
" little;) for though she knew, or might justly suspect by
" whose means it was, yet she would not utter it, nor would
" she charge it on the dead, or cast the burden of it wholly
" upon her sister: but she assured them, if ever she married,
" she would make such a choice as should be to the satisfac-
" tion and good of her people. She did not know what credit
" she might yet have with them; but she knew well she
' deserved to have it, for she was resolved never to deceive
' them: her people were to her instead of children, and she
' reckoned herself married to them by her coronation. They
" would not want a successor when she died; and, for her part,
" she should be well contented that the marble should tell
" posterity, HERE LIES A QUEEN THAT REIGNED SO LONG, AND
" LIVED AND DIED A VIRGIN: she took their address in good
" part, and desired them to carry back her hearty thanks for
" the care the commons had of her."

The Journals of the house of lords are imperfect, so that we
find nothing in them of this matter: yet it appears that they
likewise had it before them; for the Journals of the house of [Journal of
commons have it marked, that on the 15th of February there Commons,
was a message sent from the lords, desiring that a committee p. 54.]
of thirty commoners might meet with twelve lords, to consider
what should be the authority of the person whom the queen
should marry. The committee was appointed to treat concerning it: but it seems the queen desired them to turn to
other things that were more pressing; for I find nothing after
this entered in the Journals of this parliament concerning it.

385   On the ninth of February the lords passed a bill for the re- They re-
cognising of the queen's title to the crown. It had been con- cognise her
sidered, whether, as queen Mary had procured a former repeal crown.
of her mother's divorce, and of the acts that passed upon it, [Journal of
declaring her illegitimate, the like should be done now. The 546.]
lord keeper said, the crown purged all defects; and it was [Cap. 3,
needless to look back to a thing which would at least cast a Statutes,
vol. iv. p.
358.]

reproach on her father: the inquiring into such things too
anxiously would rather prejudice than advance her title. So
he advised, that there should be an act passed in general
words asserting the lawfulness of her descent, and her right to
the crown, rather than any special repeal. Queen Mary and
her council were careless of king Henry's honour; but it became her rather to conceal than expose his weakness. This
being thought both wise and pious counsel, the act was conceived in general words, "that they did assuredly believe and
" declare, that by the laws of God and of the realm she was
" their lawful queen, and that she was rightly, lineally, and
" lawfully descended from the royal blood, and that the crown
" did without all doubt or ambiguity belong to her, and the
" heirs to be lawfully begotten of her body after her; and
" that they, as representing the three estates of the realm, did
" declare and assert her title, which they would defend with
" their lives and fortunes." This was thought to be very wise
counsel: for if they had gone to repeal the sentence of divorce
which passed upon her mother's acknowledging a precontract,
they must have set forth the force that was on her when she
made that confession; and that, as it was a great dishonour to
her father, so it would have raised discourses likewise to her
mother's prejudice, which must have rather weakened than
strengthened her title: and, as has been formerly observed,
this seems to be the true reason why in all her reign there
was no apology printed for her mother. There was another
act passed for the restoring of her in blood to her mother, by
which she was qualified, as a private subject, to succeed either
to her grandfather's estate, or to any other's, by that blood.

The acts
that were
passed con-
cerning re-
ligion.
[Journal of
Commons,
pp. 54, 55,
58.]

But for the matters of religion, the commons began; and
on the 15th of February brought in a bill for the English service, and concerning the ministers of the church. On the 21st
a bill was read for annexing the supremacy to the crown
again; and on the 17th of March another bill was brought in,
confirming the laws made about religion in king Edward's
time. And on the 21st another was brought in, that the queen
should have the nomination of the bishops, as it had been in
king Edward's time. The bill for the supremacy was passed

[Journal of
Lords, p.
565.]

by the lords on the 18th of March; the archbishop of York,
the earl of Shrewsbury, the viscount Mountague, and the

bishops of London, Winchester, Worcester, Llandaff, Coventry
and Lichfield, Exeter, Chester, and Carlisle, and the abbot of
Westminster, dissenting.　But afterwards the commons annexed many other bills to it, as that about the queen's making
bishops, not according to the act made in king Edward's time,
but by the old way of elections, as it was enacted in the 25th
386 year of her father's reign, with several provisos; which passed [Journ. of
in the house of lords with the same dissent.　By it, "all the ₅₆₈.]

"acts passed in the reign of king Henry for the abolishing of [Statutes,
"the pope's power are again revived; and the acts in queen ₃₅₀.]
"Mary's time to the contrary are repealed.　There was also
"a repeal of the act made by her for proceeding against he-
"retics.　They revived the act made in the first parliament
"of king Edward against those that spoke irreverently of the
"sacrament, and against private masses, and for communion
"in both kinds; and declared the authority of visiting, cor-
"recting, and reforming all things in the church, to be for
"ever annexed to the crown, which the queen and her succes-
"sors might by her letters patents depute to any persons to
"exercise in her name.　All bishops, and other ecclesiastical [Ibid. p.
"persons, and all in any civil employment, were required to ₃₅₂.]
"swear, that they acknowledged the queen to be the *supreme*
"*governor in all causes, as well ecclesiastical as temporal,*
"*within her dominions; that they renounced all foreign*
"*power and jurisdiction, and should bear the queen faith*
"*and true allegiance:* whosoever should refuse to swear it
"was to forfeit any office he had either in church or state,
"and to be from thenceforth disabled to hold any employment
"during life.　And if, within a month after the end of that
"session of parliament, any should, either by discourse or in
"writing, set forth the authority of any foreign power, or do
"any thing for the advancement of it, they were to forfeit all
"their goods and chattels: and if they had not goods to the
"value of twenty pounds, they were to be imprisoned a whole
"year; and for the second offence, they were to incur the
"pains of a *præmunire;* and the third offence in that kind
"was made treason.　To this a proviso was added, that such [Ibid. p.
"persons as should be commissioned by the queen to reform ₃₅₄.]
"and order ecclesiastical matters, should judge nothing to be
"heresy but what had been already so judged by the author-

" ity of the canonical scriptures, or by the first four general
" councils, or by any other general council, in which such doc-
" trines were declared to be heresies by the express and plain
" words of scripture: all other points, not so decided, were to
" be judged by the parliament, with the assent of the clergy
" in their convocation."

This act was in many things short of the authority that king
Henry had claimed, and the severity of the laws he had made.
The title of *supreme head* was left out of the oath.   This was
done to mitigate the opposition of the popish party.   But besides, the queen herself had a scruple about it, which was put
in her head by one Lever, a famous preacher among those of
the reformation, of which Sandys, afterwards bishop of Wor-

Collect.
Numb. 2.
cester, complained to Parker in a letter that is in the Collection.   There was no other punishment inflicted on those that
denied the queen's supremacy but the loss of their goods ; and
such as refused to take the oath did only lose their employments: whereas to refuse the oath in king Henry's time
brought them into a *præmunire*, and to deny the supremacy

The bi-
shops op-
pose the
queen's
supremacy.
[C. C. C.
Camb.cxxi.
p. 137.
printed in
Strype's
Annals.]
[C. C. C.
Camb. cix.
5. p. 67.
printed in
Parker's
Correspon-
dence, p.
77.]
was treason.   But against this bill the bishops made speeches
in the house of lords.   I have seen a speech of this kind was
said to have been made by archbishop Heath ; but it must be
forgery put out in his name: for he is made to speak of the
supremacy as a new and unheard-of thing, which he, who had
sworn it so oft in king Henry's and king Edward's times, could
not have the face to say.   The rest of the bishops opposed it,
the rather, because they had lately declared so high for the
pope, that it had been very indecent for them to have revolted
so soon.   The bishop of Durham came not to this parliament[11].
There were some hopes of gaining him to concur in the reformation : for in the warrant the queen afterwards gave to some
for consecrating the new bishops, he is first named ; and I
have seen a letter of secretary Cecil's to Parker, that gives
him some hope that Tunstall would join with them.   He had
been offended with the cruelties of the late reign ; and though
the resentments he had of his ill usage in the end of king
Edward's time had made him at first concur more heartily to

387

---

[11] The bishop came not to the
parliament for his presence was
needed in the north, for guarding
the marches against the Scots, and
the French, ready to invade England. [S.]

the restoring of popery, yet he soon fell off, and declared his dislike of those violent courses: and neither did he nor Heath bring any in trouble within their dioceses upon the account of religion; though it is hardly credible that there was no occasion for their being severe, if they had been otherwise inclined to it. The bishop of Ely [12]*was also absent at the passing of this act: for though he would not consent to it, yet he had done all that was prescribed by it so often before, that it seems he thought it more decent to be absent, than either to consent to it, or to oppose it.

The power that was added for the queen's commissionating some to execute her supremacy gave the rise to that court, which was commonly called the high commission court; and was to be in the room of a single person, to whom, with the title of lord vicegerent, king Henry did delegate his authority. It seems the clergymen, with whom the queen consulted at this time, thought this too much to be put in one man's hand, and therefore resolved to have it shared to more persons, of whom a great many would certainly be churchmen; so that they should not be altogether kept under by the hard hands of the laity, who, having groaned long under the tyranny of an ecclesiastical yoke, seemed now disposed to revenge themselves by bringing the clergy as much under them: for so extremes do commonly rise from one another.

The beginning of the high commission.

The popish clergy were now every where beginning to declaim against innovation and heresy. Harpsfield had, in a sermon at Canterbury in February, stirred the people much to sedition: and the members belonging to that cathedral had openly said, that religion should not, nor could not be altered. The council also heard that the prebendaries there had bought up many arms: so a letter was written to sir Thomas Smith to examine that matter. Harpsfield was not put in prison, but received only a rebuke. There came also complaints from many other places of many seditious sermons: so the queen, following the precedent her sister had set her, did in the beginning of March forbid all preaching except by such as had a license under the great seal. But lest the clergy might now

---

[12] The bishop of Ely was absent, being in an embassy at Cambray; but was come over on the 17th of April and joined with the other dissenting bishops. [S.]

in the convocation[13] set out orders in opposition to what the queen was about to do, she sent and required them, under the pains of a *præmunire,* to make no canons: yet Harpsfield, 388 that was prolocutor, with the rest of the lower house, made an address to the upper house, to be by them presented to the queen for the discharge of their consciences. They reduced the particulars into five articles[14]. 1. That Christ was corporally present in his sacrament. 2. That there was no other substance there but his body and blood. 3. That in the mass there was a propitiatory sacrifice for the dead and the living. 4. That St. Peter and his lawful successors had the power of feeding and governing the church. 5. That the power of treating about doctrine, the sacraments, and the order of divine worship, belonged only to the pastors of the church. These they had sent to the two universities, from whence they were returned, with the hands of the greatest part in them to the first four: but it seems they thought it not fit to sign the last; for now the queen had resolved to have a public conference about religion in the abbey-church of Westminster.

The archbishop of York was continued still to be of the council; so the conference being proposed to him, he, after he had communicated it to his brethren, accepted of it, though with some unwillingness. It was appointed that there should be nine of a side, who should confer about these three points: 1. *Whether it was not against the word of God, and the custom of the ancient church, to use a tongue unknown to the people in the common prayers and the administration of the sacraments? 2. Whether every church had not authority to appoint, change, and take away ceremonies and ecclesiastical rites, so the same were done to edification. 3. Whether it could be proved by the word of God, that in the mass there was a propitiatory sacrifice for the dead and the living?* All was ordered to be done in writing. The bishops, as being actually in office, were to read their papers first upon the first point, and the reformed were to read theirs next; and then they were to exchange their papers, without any discourse

Marginal notes: [Fuller, lib. ix. p. 55.] [Wilkins, Conc. iv. p. 179.] [Fuller, lib. ix. p. 56.] [Fox, vol. iii. p. 822.]

---

13 [See Part iii. p. 275.]
14 [The history of this convocation has been preserved in Wilkins, from the Register of Convocation. The articles also may be seen in Fuller, from whom probably the author took his account.]

concerning them, for the avoiding of jangling. The next day
they were to read their papers upon the second, and after that
upon the third head; and then they were to answer one another's papers. The nine on both sides were, the bishops of
Winchester, Lichfield, Chester, Carlisle, and Lincoln, and doctors Cole, Harpsfield, Langdale, and Chedsey, on the popish
side; and Scory, late bishop of Chichester, Cox, Whitehead,
Grindal, Horne, Sandys, Guest, Aylmer, and Jewel, for the
protestants. The last of March was appointed to be the first [Fox, vol.
day of conference, where the privy-council was to be present; iii. p. 823.]
and the lord keeper was to see that they should not depart
from the rules to which they had agreed.

The noise of this drew vast numbers of people to so unusual
a sight; it being expected that there should be much fairer
dealings now, than had been in the disputes in queen Mary's
time. The whole house of commons came to hear it, as no
doubt the lords did also, though it is not marked in their
Journal. At their meeting, the bishop of Winchester said
their paper was not quite ready, and pretended they had mistaken the order; but Dr. Cole should deliver what they had
prepared, though it was not yet in that order that they could
copy it out. The secret of this was, the bishops had in their
private consultations agreed to read their paper, but not to
389 give those they called heretics a copy of it. They could not
decently refuse to give a public account of their doctrine, but
they were resolved not to enter into disputes with any about
it. This seemed to be the giving up of the faith, if they should
suffer it again to be brought into question. Besides, they
looked on it as the highest act of supremacy for the queen to
appoint such conferences; for she and her council would pretend to judge in these points, when they had done disputing.
For these reasons, they would not engage to make any exchange of papers. The lord keeper took notice, that this was
contrary to the order laid down at the council-board, to which
the archbishop of York had in their names consented. But they
pretending they had mistaken the order, Cole[15] was appointed
to deliver their minds, which he did in a long discourse, the
greatest part of which he read out of a book, that will be found

[15] Cole's speech seems to be a reply to Horne, and so should be set
after it. [S.]

in the Collection. For though they refused to deliver a copy of
it, yet Parker some way procured it, among whose papers I found
it. The substance of it was, " That although it might seem that
" the scriptures had appointed the worship of God to be in
" a known tongue; yet that might be changed by the au-
" thority of the church, which had changed the sabbath
" appointed in the scripture, without any authority from
" thence. Christ washed his disciples' feet, and bid them do
" the like; yet this was not kept up: Christ instituted the
" sacrament of his body and blood after supper; and yet the
" church appointed it to be received fasting: so had the church
" also given it only in one kind, though Christ himself gave it
" in both. And whereas the apostles, by authority from the
" Holy Ghost, commanded all believers to abstain from blood,
" yet that was not thought to oblige any now: and though
" there was a community of goods in the apostles' times, it
" was no obligation to Christians to set up that now: so that
" this matter was in the power of the church. And since the
" church of Rome had appointed the Latin service to be every
" where used, it was schismatical to separate from it: for,
" according to Irenæus, all churches ought to agree with her,
" by reason of her great preeminence. Upon which they ran
" out largely to shew the mischiefs of schism, both in France,
" Spain, Germany, and in other countries. And for the Bri-
" tains and Saxons of England, their first apostles, that con-
" verted them to Christianity, were men of other nations, and
" did never use any service but that of their native language.
" All the vulgar tongues did change much, but the Latin was
" ever the same: and it was not fit for the church to be
" changing her service. The queen of Ethiopia's eunuch read
" Isaiah's book, though he understood it not; upon which God
" sent Philip to him to expound it: so the people are to come to
" their teachers, to have those things explained to them which
" they cannot understand of themselves. There were many
" rites in the Jewish religion, the signification whereof the
" people understood as little then as the vulgar do the Latin
" now; and yet they were commanded to use them. The
" people were to use their private prayers in what tongue they
" pleased, though the public prayers were put up in Latin;
" and such prayers may be for their profit, though they un-

" derstand them not, as absent persons are the better for the
390 " prayers which they do not hear, much less understand.
" They said, it was not to be thought that the Holy Ghost
" had so long forsaken his church, and that a few lately risen
" up were to teach all the world. They concluded, that they
" could bring many more authorities; but they, being to de-
" fend a negative, thought it needless, and would refer these
" to the answers they were to make."

When this was done, the lord keeper turned to those of the Arguments
other side, and desired them to read their paper. Horne was against it.
appointed by them to do it. He began with a short prayer to
God to enlighten their minds, and with a protestation, that
they were resolved to follow the truth, according to the word
of God. Then he read his paper, which will be also found in
the Collection. " They founded their assertion on St. Paul's Collect.
" words, who, in the 14th chapter of his First Epistle to the Numb. 3.
" Corinthians, had treated on that subject of set purpose; and
" spake in it, not only of preaching, but of praying with the
" understanding; and said, that the unlearned were to say
" *Amen* at the giving of thanks. From that chapter they
" argued, that St. Paul commanded that all things should
" be done to edification, which could not be by an unknown
" language: he also charged them, that nothing should be
" said that had an uncertain sound; and that, as the sound of
" a trumpet must be distinct, so the people must understand
" what is said, that so they might say *Amen* at the giving of
" thanks. He also required those that spake in a strange lan-
" guage, and could not get one to interpret, to hold their
" peace; since it was an absurd thing for one to be a barba-
" rian to others in the worship of God: and though the speak-
" ing with strange tongues was then an extraordinary gift of
" God, yet he ordered that it should not be used where there
" was no interpreter. They added, that these things were so
" strictly commanded by St. Paul, that it is plain they are not
" indifferent, or within the power of the church. In the Old
" Testament the Jews had their worship in the vulgar tongue;
" and yet the new dispensation being more internal and spi-
" ritual, it was absurd that the worship of God should be less
" understood by Christians than it had been by the Jews. The
" chief end of worship is, according to David, that we may

" shew forth God's praises, which cannot be done if it is in a
" strange tongue. Prayer is the offering up of our desires to
" God; which we cannot do, if we understand not the language
" they are in. Baptism and the Lord's supper are to contain
" declarations of the death and resurrection of Christ, which
" must be understood, otherwise why are they made? The use
" of speech is to make known what one brings forth to another.
" The most barbarous nations perform their worship in a
" known tongue, which shews it to be a law of nature. It is
" plain from Justin Martyr's Apology, that the worship was
" then in a known tongue; which appears also from all the
" ancient Liturgies; and a long citation was brought out of
" St. Basil for the singing of psalms, duly weighing the words
" with much attention and devotion, which, he says, was prac-
" tised in all nations. They concluded, wondering how such
" an abuse could at first creep in, and be still so stiffly main-
" tained; and why those, who would be thought the guides
" and pastors of the church, were so unwilling to return to the
" rule of St. Paul, and the practice of the primitive times."

There was a great shout of applause when they had done. 391
They gave their paper, signed with all their hands, to the
lord keeper, to be delivered to the other side, as he should
think fit: but he kept it till the other side should bring him
theirs. The papists upon this said, they had more to add on
that head; which was thought disingenuous by those that had
heard them profess they had nothing to add to what Cole had
[Friday, said. Thus the meeting broke up for that day, being Satur-
March 31.] day; and they were ordered to go forward on Monday, and
to prepare what they were to deliver on the other two heads.
The papists, though they could complain of nothing that was
done, except the applause given to the paper of the reformers;
yet they saw by that how much more acceptable the other
doctrine was to the people, and therefore resolved to go no
further in that matter. At the next meeting, they desired
that their answer to the paper read by the reformed might be
first heard. To this the lord keeper said, that they had delivered their mind the former day, and so were not to be heard
till they had gone through the other points; and then they
[Fox, vol. were to return on both sides to the answering of papers. They
iii. p. 827.] said, that what Cole had delivered the former day was *extem-*

pore, and of himself ; but it had not been agreed on by them. This appeared to all the assembly to be very foul dealing ; so they were required to go on to the second point. Then they pressed, that the other side might begin with their paper, and they would follow ; for they saw what an advantage the others had the former day by being heard last. The lord keeper said, the order was, that they should be heard first, as being bishops now in office : but both Winchester and Lincoln refused to go any further, if the other side did not begin. Upon which there followed a long debate ; Lincoln saying, that the first order, which was, that all should be in Latin, was changed, and that they had prepared a writing in Latin : but in this, not only the counsellors, among whom sat the archbishop of York, but the rest of his own party, contradicted him. In conclusion, all, except Feckenham, refused to read any more papers : he said, he was willing to have done it, but he could not undertake such a thing alone : and so the meeting broke up. [Fox, vol. iii. p. 829.]

But the bishop of Winchester and of Lincoln said, the doctrine of the catholic church was already established, and ought not to be disputed, except it were in a synod of divines : that it was too great an encouragement to heretics, to hear them thus discourse against the faith, before the unlearned multitude : and that the queen, by so doing, had incurred the sentence of excommunication ; and they talked of excommunicating her and her council. Upon this they were both sent to the Tower. The reformed took great advantage from the issue of this debate to say, their adversaries knew, that, upon a fair hearing, the truth was so manifestly on their side, that they durst not put it to such hazard. The whole world saw that this disputation was managed with great impartiality, and without noise or disorder ; far different from what had been in queen Mary's time : so they were generally much confirmed in their former belief, by the papists flying the field. They on the other hand said, they saw the rude multitude were now carried with a fury against them ; the lord keeper was their professed enemy ; the laity would take on them to judge, after they had heard them ; and they perceived they were already determined in their minds, and that this dispute was only to set off the changes that were to be made with the pomp of a victory : and they blamed the bishops for undertaking it at

The conference between the papists and protestants breaks up.

[Camden, p. 373.]

392

first, but excused them for breaking it off in time. And the truth is, the strength of their cause, in most points of controversy, resting on the authority of the church of Rome, that was now a thing of so odious a sound, that all arguments brought from thence were not like to have any great effect. Upon this whole matter, there was an act of state made, and signed by many privy counsellors, giving an account of all the steps that were made in it; which will be found in the Collection.

Collect.
Numb. 5.

This being over, the parliament was now in a better disposition to pass the bill for the uniformity of the service of the church. Some of the reformed divines were appointed to review king Edward's Liturgy, and to see if in any particular it was fit to change it. The only considerable variation was made about the Lord's supper, of which somewhat will appear from the letter of Sandys to Parker. It was proposed to have the communion-book so contrived, that it might not exclude the belief of the corporal presence; for the chief design of the queen's council was, to unite the nation in one faith; and the greatest part of the nation continued to believe such a presence. Therefore it was recommended to the divines, to see that there should be no express definition made against it; that so it might lie as a speculative opinion, not determined, in which every man was left to the freedom of his own mind. Hereupon the rubric that explained the reason for kneeling at the sacrament, *that thereby no adoration is intended to any corporal presence of Christ's natural flesh and blood, because that is only in heaven*, which had been in king Edward's Liturgy, was now left out. And whereas at the delivery of the elements in king Edward's first Liturgy, there was to be said, *The body or blood of our Lord Jesus Christ preserve thy body and soul to everlasting life;* which words had been left out in his second Liturgy, as favouring the corporal presence too much; and instead of them, these words were ordered to be used in the distribution of that sacrament, *Take and eat this, in remembrance that Christ died for thee, and feed on him in thy heart by faith with thanksgiving; and drink this in remembrance that Christ's blood was shed for thee, and be thankful;* they now joined both these in one. Some of the collects were also a little altered; and thus was

[Lambeth
MSS. 959-
No. 41,
printed in
Parker's
Correspon-
dence.]

the book presented to the house. But for the book of ordination, it was not in express terms named in the act; which
gave an occasion afterwards to question the lawfulness of the
ordinations made by that book. But by this act, the book
that was set out by king Edward, and confirmed by parliament in he fifth year of his reign, was again authorized by
law; and the repeal of it in queen Mary's time was made
void. So the book of ordinations being in that act added to
the book of common prayer, it was now legally in force again;
as was afterwards declared in parliament, upon a question that
was raised about it by Bonner.

393   The bill that was put in on the 15th of February, concerning the new service, being laid aside, a new one was framed,
and sent up by the commons on the 18th of April, and debated
in the house of lords. Heath [13] made a long speech against it,
rather elegant than learned: " He enlarged much on the
" several changes which had been made in king Edward's
" time: he said, that both Cranmer and Ridley changed their
" opinions in the matter of Christ's presence: he called Ridley
" the most notably learned man that was of that way. These
" changes he imputed to their departing from the standard of
" the catholic church: he complained much of the robbing of
" churches, the breaking of images, and the stage-plays made
" in mockery of the catholic religion." Upon all these reasons
he was against the bill. The bishop of Chester spake also to
it: "he said, the bill was against both faith and charity: that
" points once defined were not to be brought again into ques-
" tion : nor were acts of parliament foundations for a church's
" belief: he enlarged on the antiquity of their forms; and
" said, it was an insolent thing to pretend that our fathers
" had lived in ignorace. The prophets oftentimes directed
" the Israelites to ask of their fathers. Matters of religion
" could not be understood by the laity. It was of great con-
" sequence to have their faith well grounded. Jeroboam made
" Israel to sin when he set up a new way of worship; and not
" only the orthodox, but even the Arian emperors ordered, that

Debates
about the
act of uni-
formity.
[Journal
of Com-
mons, p.
60.]
Cotton
MSS. Vesp.
D. xviii.
fol. 87.]

[Cotton
MSS. Vesp.
D. xviii.
fol. 114.
printed in
Strype's
Annals i.
App. pp.
27–34.]

[13] Abbot Feckenham made that
speech, and not Heath. [S.] [The
speech is in the Cotton MSS., from
which it has been printed in the
Appendix to Tierney's edition of
Dodd's Church History, vol. ii. Appendix, p. cclvi.]

" points of faith should be examined in councils. Gallio, by
" the light of nature, knew that a civil judge ought not tò
" meddle with matters of religion. In the service-book that
" was then before them, they had no sacrifice for their sins,
" nor were they to adore Christ in the host; and for these
" reasons he could not agree to it; but if any thought he
" spoke this because of his own concern, or pitied him for
" what he might suffer by it, he would say in the words of
" our Saviour, *Weep not for me, weep for yourselves.*"

After him spake Feckenham, abbot of Westminster: "He
" proposed three rules, by which they should judge of reli-
" gion; its antiquity, its constancy to itself, and the influence
" it had on the civil government: he said the old religion
" began in the time of king Lucius, according to Gildas; the
" book now proposed was not used before the two last years
" of king Edward; the one was always the same, the other
" was changed every second year, as appeared in the point of
" the presence of Christ in the sacrament: there had been
" great order and obedience in queen Mary's reign; but now
" every where great insolences were committed by the people,
" with some very indecent profanations of the most holy
" things. He recommended to them, in St. Austin's words,
" the adhering to the catholic church: the very name *catholic,*
" which heretics had not the confidence to assume, shewed
" their authority. The consent of the whole church in all
" ages, with the perpetual succession of pastors in St. Peter's
" chair, ought to weigh more with them than a few new
" preachers, who had distracted both Germany and England
" of late."

[Cotton
MSS. Vesp.
D. xviii. fol.
8. printed
in Strype's
Annals i.
App. pp.
24-27.]

Thus I have given the substance of their speeches, being all
that I have seen of that side. I have seen none at all on the
other side, though it is not probable but some were made in
defence of the service, as well as these were against it. But
upon this occasion I shall set down the substance of the second 394
paper, which the reformed divines had prepared on the second
point, for the conference about the authority of every particular church to change or take away ceremonies. I do not put
it in the Collection, because I have not that which the papists
prepared in opposition to it. But the heads of this paper were
as followeth:

"It is clear by the Epistles which St. Paul writ to the Co-
"rinthians, and other churches, that every church has power
"in itself to order the forms of their worship, and the ad-
"ministration of the sacraments among them, so as might best
"tend to order, edification, and peace. The like power had
"also the seven angels of the churches, to whom St. John
"writ. And for the first three ages, there was no general
"meeting of the church in synods; but in those times, the
"neighbouring pastors and bishops, by mutual advice rather
"than authority, ordered their affairs : and when heresies
"sprung up, they condemned them, without staying for a
"general determination of the whole church. There were also
"great differences among them in their customs, as about ob-
"serving Lent and Easter. Ceremonies grew too soon to a
"great number. When errors or abuses appeared, private
"bishops reformed their own dioceses : so those who came in
"the room of Arian bishops, even when that heresy was
"spread over all the east, and the see of Rome itself was de-
"filed with it, yet reformed their own churches. Ambrose
"finding the custom of feasting in churches on the anniversa-
"ries of the martyrs gave occasion to great scandals, took it
"away. Even in queen Mary's time, many of the old super-
"stitions of pilgrimages and relics, which had been abolished
"in king Henry's time, were not then taken up again : from
"which they argued, that if some things might be altered,
"why not more? So that if there was good reason to make
"any changes, it should not be doubted but that as Hezekiah
"and Josiah had made by their own power, so the queen
"might make reformations; which were not so much the set-
"ting up of new things, as the restoring of the state of reli-
"gion to what it was anciently; which had been brought in
"by consent of parliament and convocation in king Edward's
"time." The rules they offered in this paper about ceremonies were, that they should not be made necessary parts of
worship ; that they should not be too many, nor dumb and
vain, nor should be kept up for gain and advantage.

These were the arguments used on both sides : but the reformed being superior in number, the bill passed in the house
of lords[14]; the archbishop of York, the marquis of Winches-

[14] [The printed Journal of the
House of Lords omits all notice of
what passed between Saturday,
April 22, and Monday, May 1. It

ter, the earl of Shrewsbury, the viscount Montague, the bishops of London, Worcester, Ely, Coventry, Chester, and Carlisle, and the lords Morley, Stafford, Dudley, Wharton, Rich, and North, and the abbot of Westminster, dissenting. By this act the new book was to take place by St. John Baptist's day.

[Cap. 19. Statutes, vol. iv. p. 381.]

[Journal of Lords, p. 571.]

Another act passed, that the queen might reserve to herself the lands belonging to bishoprics, as they fell void, giving the full value of them in impropriated tithes in lieu of them. To this the bishops dissented on the 7th of April, when it passed in the house of lords. But when this came to the commons, there was great opposition made to it. Many had observed, that in Edward the Sixth's time, under a pretence of giving some endowments to the crown, the courtiers got all the church lands divided amongst themselves; so it was believed the use to be made of this would be the robbing of the church, 395

[Journal of Commons, p. 60.]

without enriching the crown. After many days' debate, on the 17th of April, the house divided, and 90 were against it, but 133[15] were for it; and so it passed.

[Cap. 24. Statutes, vol. iv. p. 397.]

On the 5th[16] of May another bill passed with the like opposition. It was for annexing of all religious houses to the crown. After that, there followed some private acts for declaring the deprivation of the popish bishops in king Edward's time to have been good. When they were restored by queen Mary, the sentences passed against them were declared to have been void from the beginning; and so all leases that were made by Ridley, Poynet, and Hooper, and the patents granted by the king, of some of their lands, were annulled.

appears from the Journal of the House of Commons (p. 60), that 'the bill for the unity of service in the church and administration of the sacraments was read the third time April 20, and passed to the lords with eight other bills, April 25.' The particulars are supplied by sir Simonds D'Ewes (p. 27), who says, that the fifth of the nine bills, which were read for the first time in the house of lords on the 26th of April, was 'touching the uniformity of common prayer and service in the church, and administration of the sacraments;' and

that it was read a second time on the following day, and the third time on the 28th of April, being opposed by the peers mentioned in the text, and also by the bishops of Llandaff and Exeter, (p. 29). He gives the said catalogue of names as *dissentientes* (p. 28), and in both instances omits the name of the abbot of Westminster.]

[15] [The number was 134, as appears from the Journal, p. 60.]

[16] [The bill was read the third time, April 29. Journal of Commons, p. 61.]

It was particularly remembered in the house of commons, that Ridley had made the confirming of these leases his last desire, when he was going to be tied to the stake. The ground on which the sentences were declared void was, because the parties had appealed; though in the commission, by virtue of which the delegates deprived them, they were empowered to proceed notwithstanding any appeal. To this, not only the bishops, but the marquis of Winchester, and the lords Stafford, Dudley, and North, dissented.

It shews the great moderation of this government, that this marquis, notwithstanding his adhering to the popish interest in the house of lords, was still continued lord treasurer: which employment he held fourteen years after this, and died in the 97th year of his age, leaving 103 issued from his own body behind him. He was the greatest instance of good fortune and dexterity that we find in the English history; who continued lord treasurer in three such different reigns as king Edward's, queen Mary's, and queen Elizabeth's were.

There was a subsidy, and two tenths and two fifteenths [Cap. 21. given by the parliament, with the tonnage and poundage, for ibid. p. the queen's life; and so on the 8th of May it was dissolved. 384.]

There were three bills that did not pass in the house of Bills that commons; but upon what account they were laid aside, it does were proposed, but not appear. The one was for the restoring of the bishops that not passed. had been deprived by queen Mary. There were but three of these alive, Barlow, Scory, and Coverdale: the first of these had resigned, and the last, being old, had no mind to return to his bishopric [17]: so perhaps it was not thought worth the while to make an act for one man's sake, especially since there were so many vacant bishoprics in the queen's hands, and more

[17] I suppose Coverdale might have other reasons, for in a book entitled *Part of a register,* I find him ranked with those that then, or soon after, were styled Puritans, p. 12, 23, 25, &c.; and having been of the English congregation at Geneva, might probably there receive a tincture that he could not be brought to consent to impositions. (Troubles of Frankfort, p. 188. 215.) This further appeared by his practice at archbishop Parker's consecration, where *togá laneá talari utebatur;* and if he would not use the episcopal habits on such an occasion, I am fully persuaded he never would. However, it was very well in your lordship to treat him with tenderness, he having been a peaceable good man, and a very useful instrument in the reformation. [B.]

were like to fall. The other bill was, for the restoring of all persons that were deprived from their benefices because they were married. This the queen ordered to be laid aside, of which Sandys complained much in his letter to Parker: but yet the queen took no notice of the laws formerly made against their marriage, and promoted many married priests, particularly Parker himself. There was no law now in force against clergymen's marrying; for queen Mary had only repealed the laws of Edward the Sixth, which allowed it, but had made none concerning that matter: so there was nothing but the canon law against it; and that was resolved to be condemned, by continuing that article of religion concerning the lawfulness of their marriage among those that should be set out. The next bill that came to nothing was, a new act for giving authority to thirty-two persons to revise the ecclesiastical laws, 396 and digest them into a body; it was laid aside at the second reading in the house of commons, and has slept ever since.

The bishops refuse the oath of supremacy. Vit. Parkeri, [ap. Antiq.Brit. p. 535.] When the parliament was over, the oath of supremacy[18] was soon after put to the bishops and clergy. They thought, if they could stick close to one another in refusing it, the queen would be forced to dispense with them, and would not at one stroke turn out all the bishops in England. It does not appear how soon after the dissolution of the parliament the oath[19] was put to them; but it was not long after, for the last collation Bonner gave of any benefice was on the 6th of May this year. The oath being offered to Heath archbishop of York, to Bonner of London, Thirlby of Ely, Bourne of Bath and Wells, Christopherson of Chichester[20], Bayne of Lichfield, White of Winchester, and Watson of Lincoln, Oglethorp of

[18] [The letters patent directing the lord keeper and seventeen others to receive, the oaths of the clergy and others, are dated 23 May, 1559, and are printed in Rymer, xv. 518. It is remarkable, that there are letters patent directed to four others to receive the oath from Bourne, bishop of Bath and Wells, dated Oct. 18, 1559, and to inform of his refusal to do so, without delay. These are also printed in Rymer, xv. 545.]

[19] The oath was tendered to them in July. [S.] See note (21), from which it appears that this remark of Strype's applies only to Heath of York and Thirlby of Ely. Strype takes his statement from Stow, p. 639.]

[20] Christopherson died before the parliament met. [S.] [He was buried Dec. 28, 1558, according to Leneve. See also Machyn's Diary, p. 184, for an account of his funeral.]

Carlisle, Turberville of Exeter, Pole of Peterborough, Scot of Chester, Pates of Worcester, and Goldwell of St. Asaph, they did all refuse to take it : so that only Kitchin bishop of Llandaff took it. There was some hope or Tunstall ; so it was not put to him till September : but he being very old, chose to go out with so much company, more for the decency of the thing, than out of any scruple he could have about the supremacy, for which he had formerly writ so much[21]. They were upon their refusal put in prison for a little while; but they had all their liberty soon after, except Bonner, White[22], and Watson. There were great complaints made against Bonner, that he had in many things, in the prosecution of those that were presented for heresy, exceeded what the law allowed ; so that it was much desired to have him made an example. But as the

---

[21] [The dates of the deprivation have been preserved in Machyn's Diary, as follows : ' The 29 day of May was depreved of ys byshoperyke of London doctur Boner, and in ys plasse master Gryndall, & ... electyd dene of Powlles, and the old dene depreved, master ...' p. 200.
' The 21 day of June was 5 bysshopes deprevyd, the bysshope of Lychfeld and Coventre, and the bysshope of Carley, the bysshope of Westchester, the bysshope of Landaffh, and the bysshope of ....' Ibid. p. 201.
' The 26 day of June ...... was deprevyd of ther bysshoprykes the bysshope of Wynchestur and the bysshope of Lynckolne at master Hawse the kyng shreyff in Mynsyon lane, and the bysshope of Wynchester to the Towre agayne, and the bysshope of Lynckolne delevered away.' Ibid. p. 201.
' The 5 day of July was deposyd of ther byshoperykes the archebyshope of Yorke doctur Heth, and the bysshope of Ely docthur Thurlbe, at my lord treysorer plasse at Frers Augustyne.' Ibid. p. 203.
' The 20 day of July the good

old the bysshope of Durham cam rydyng to London with three-score hors, and so to Sowth .... unto master Dolman howsse, a talow-chandler, and ther he lys aganst the chene gatte.' Ibid. p. 204.
' The 28 day of September was Myghellmas-evyn, was the old bysshope of Durram doctur Dunstall was deposyd of hys bysshope-pryke of Durram, because he shuld not reeseyff the rentes for that quarter.' Ibid. p. 214.]
[22] [The bishop of Winchester was afterwards liberated, and died in January of the following year, as appears from Machyn's Diary : 'The 7 day of July was sant Thomas of Cantebere day, my good lord of Wynchastur doctur Whytt came owt of the Towre, with the leyftenantt ser Edward Warner, by 6 in mornyng, and so to my lord keper of the brod selle, and from thens unto master Whyt, John, altherman, and ther he lys,' p. 203. 'The 12 day of January ded good master docthur Whyt, latt byshope of Wynchestur in Hamshyre, at ser Thomas Whytes plasse, the wyche ded of a aguw, and he gayff myche to ys servandes.' Ibid. p. 223.]

queen was of her own nature merciful, so the reformed divines had learned in the gospel not to *render evil for evil*, nor to seek revenge; and as Nazianzen had of old exhorted the orthodox, when they had got an emperor that favoured them, not to retaliate on the Arians for their former cruelties; so they thought it was for the honour of their religion to give this real demonstration of the conformity of their doctrine to the rules of the gospel, and of the primitive church, by avoiding all cruelty and severity, when it looked like revenge.

The queen's gentleness to them.

All this might have been expected from such a queen, and such bishops. But it shewed a great temper in the whole nation, that such a man as Bonner had been, was suffered to go[23] about in safety, and was not made a sacrifice to the revenge of those who had lost their near friends by his means. Many things were brought against him, and White, and some other bishops; upon which the queen promised to give a charge to the visitors, whom she was to send over England, to inquire into these things; and after she had heard their report, she said, she would proceed as she saw cause: by this means, she did not deny justice, but gained a little time to take off the edge that was on men's spirits, who had been much provoked by the ill usage they had met with from them.

[Camden, p. 376.]

Heath was a man of a generous temper, and so was well used by the queen; for as he was suffered to live securely at his own house in Surrey, so she went thither sometimes to visit him. Tunstall and Thirlby lived in Lambeth with Parker with great freedom and ease; the one was learned and good natured, the other was a man of business, but too easy and flexible. White and Watson[24] were morose sullen men, to which their studies as well as their tempers had disposed them; for they were much given to scholastical divinity, which 397

[23] Bishop Andrewes, who gives a very particular account of the treatment of the several bishops, has this account of Bonner: 'Bonerus autem Londinensis qui regnante Mariâ cum lanienæ præesset in odium venerat omni populo (ut nec tutum esset ei prodire in publicum, ne saxis obrueretur) ille quidem in carcere consenuit.' Tortura Torti, p. 146, 147. [B.]

[24] Watson, who was fellow and master of St. John's college, was noted for polite learning; I suppose it was Dr. John Watson, that was given to scholastical divinity, styled *Scotist* by Erasmus. [B.] [The account is taken from Godwin, who however does not speak of White as he does of Watson, who, he says, was 'of a stiffness in his humour, next to sullen or morose].'

inclined men to be cynical, to overvalue themselves, and despise others. Christopherson was a good Grecian, and had translated Eusebius and the other church-historians into Latin, but with as little fidelity as may be expected from a man violently addicted to a party. Bayne was learned in the Hebrew, which he had professed at Paris in the reign of Francis the First. All these chose to live still in England; only Pates, Scot, and Goldwell, went beyond sea. After them went the lord Morley, sir Francis Englefield, sir Robert Peckham, sir Thomas[25] Shelley, and sir John Gage; who, it seems, desired to live where they might have the free exercise of their religion: and such was the queen's gentleness, that this was not denied them, though such favour had not been shewed in queen Mary's reign. Feckenham, abbot of Westminster, was a charitable and generous man, and lived in great esteem in England. Most of the monks returned to a secular course of life; but the nuns went beyond sea.

[Fuller, ix. p. 58.]

Now the queen intended to send injunctions over England; and in the end of June they were prepared. There was great difficulty made about one of them: the queen seemed to think the use of images in churches might be a means to stir up devotion, and that at least it would draw all people to frequent them the more; for the great measure of her counsels was, to unite the whole nation into one way of religion[26]. The reformed bishops and divines opposed this vehemently: they put all their reasons in a long writing which they gave her concerning it; the preface and conclusion of which will be found in the Collection. "They protested they could not "comply with that, which, as it was against their own con-"sciences, so it would prove a snare to the ignorant: they "had often pressed the queen in that matter, which it seems "stuck long with her: they prayed her not to be offended "with that liberty they took thus to lay their reasons before "her, it being a thing which Christian princes had at all times "taken well from their bishops. They desired her to commit "that matter to the decision of a synod of bishops and divines,

A visitation and injunctions ordered by the queen.

Collect. Numb. 6.

The queen inclined to retain images in churches.

25 *For* Thomas *read* Richard. [S.] [The author apparently copies the mistake from Godwin. Fuller, lib. ix. p. 59, calls him Thomas Shelley, esq.]

26 This matter belongs to the year 1560 or 1561. [S.]

" and not to do such a thing merely upon some political consi-
" derations; which as it would offend many, so it would reflect
" much on the reign of her most godly brother, and on those
" who had then removed all images, and had given their lives
" afterwards for a testimony to the truth.

Reasons
brought
against it.   " The substance of their reasons (which for their length I
" have not put in the Collection) is, that the second Com-
" mandment forbids the making of any images, as a resem-
" blance of God.   And Deut. xxvii. there was a curse pro-
" nounced on those *who made an image, an abomination to*
" *the Lord, and put it in a secret place;* which they ex-
" pounded of some *sacraria* in private houses: and Deut. iv.
" among the cautions Moses gives to the people of Israel to
" beware of idolatry, this is one, *that they do not make an*
" *image;* for the use of these does naturally degenerate into
" idolatry : the Jews were so sensible of this after the cap-
" tivity, that they would die rather than suffer an image to be
" put in their temple.   The Book of Wisdom calls an image,
" *a snare for the feet of the ignorant.*   St. John charged those
" he writ to, to *beware of idols.*   So Tertullian said, it was
" not enough to beware of idolatry towards them, but of the
" very images themselves.   And as Moses had charged the
" people not to lay a stumblingblock in the way of the blind;
" so it was a much greater sin to leave such a trap for the 398
" weak multitude.   This was not for edification, since it fed the
" superstition of the weak and ignorant, who would continue
" in their former dotage upon them, and would alienate others
" from the public worship; so that, between those that would
" separate from them if they were continued, and the multi-
" tude that would abuse them, the number of those that would
" use them aright would be very inconsiderable : the outward
" splendour of them would be apt to draw the minds of the
" worshippers, if not to direct idolatry, yet to staring and dis-
" traction of thoughts.   Both Origen and Arnobius tell us,
" that the primitive Christians had no images at all.   Irenæus
" accused the Gnostics for carrying about the image of Christ.
" St. Austin commends Varro, for saying that the old Romans
" worshipped God more chastely, without the use of any
" images.   Epiphanius tore a veil with an image on it; and
" Serenus broke images in Gregory the Great's time.   Valens

" and Theodosius made a law against the painting or graving
" of the image of Christ: and the use of images in the eastern
" churches brought those distractions on that empire, that laid
" it open to the invasions of the Mahometans."

These reasons prevailed with the queen to put it into her
injunctions, to have all images removed out of the church.

The injunctions given by king Edward, at his first coming [Wilkins,
to the crown, were all renewed, with very little variation.   To ${}^{\text{Conc. iv.}}_{\text{p. 185.]}}$
these some things were added, of which I shall give account.

" It was no where declared, neither in the scriptures, nor The heads
" by the primitive church, that priests might not have wives; ${}^{\text{of the in-}}_{\text{junctions.}}$
" upon which many in king Edward's time had married.   Yet
" great offence was given by the indecent marriages that some
" of them then made.   To prevent the like scandals for the
" future, it was ordered, that no priest or deacon should marry
" without allowance from the bishop of the diocese, and two
" justices of the peace, and the consent of the woman's parents [Ibid. p.
" or friends.   All the clergy were to use habits according to ${}^{186.]}$
" their degrees in the universities; the queen declaring, that
" this was not done for any holiness in them, but for order
" and decency.   No man might use any charm, or consult with
" such as did.   All were to resort to their own parish churches,
" except for an extraordinary occasion.   Inn-keepers were to
" sell nothing in the times of divine service.   None were to
" keep images or other monuments of superstition in their
" houses.   None might preach but such as were licensed by
" their ordinary.   In all places they were to examine the causes
" why any had been in the late reign imprisoned, famished, or
" put to death, upon the pretence of religion; and all registers
" were to be searched for it.   In every parish the ordinary
" was to name three or four discreet men, who were to see
" that all the parishioners did duly resort on Sundays and [Ibid. p.
" holydays to church; and those who did it not, and upon ad- ${}^{187.]}$
" monition did not amend, were to be denounced to the ordi-
" nary.   On Wednesdays and Fridays the common prayer and
" litany was to be used in all churches.   All slanderous words,
" as *papist*, *heretic*, *schismatic*, or *sacramentary*, were to be
" forborne under severe pains.   No books might be printed
" without a license from the queen, the archbishop, the bishop
399 " of London the chancellor of the universities, or the bishop

[Wilkins, Conc. iv. p. 188.]
" or archdeacon of the place where it was printed. All were
" to kneel at the prayers, and to shew a reverence when the
" name of Jesus was pronounced. Then followed an explana-
" tion of the oath of supremacy, in which the queen declared,
" that she did not pretend to any authority for the ministering
" of divine service in the church, and that all that she chal-
" lenged was that which had at all times belonged to the im-
" perial crown of England ; that she had the sovereignty and
" rule over all manner of persons under God, so that no foreign
" power had any rule over them ; and if those who had for-
" merly appeared to have scruples about it, took·it in that
" sense, she was well pleased to accept of it, and did acquit
" them of all penalties in the act. The next was about altars
" and communion-tables : she ordered, that, for preventing of
" riots, no altar should be taken down but by the consent of
" the curate and churchwardens ; that a communion-table
" should be made for every church, and that on sacrament-
" days it should be set in some convenient place in the chancel ;
" and at other times should be placed where the altar had
" stood. The sacramental bread was ordered to be round and
" plain, without any figure on it, but somewhat broader and
" thicker than the cakes formerly prepared for the mass.
" Then the form of bidding prayer was prescribed, with some
" variation from that in king Edward's time : for whereas to
[Ibid. p. 189.]
" the thanksgiving for God's blessings to the church in the
" saints departed this life, a prayer was added, *that they with*
" *us, and we with them, may have a glorious resurrection ;*
" now those words, *they with us,* as seeming to import a prayer
" for the dead, were left out."

Reflections made on the injunc-tions.   For the rule about churchmen marrying, those who reflected on it said, they complained not of the law, but, as St.
Jerome did in the making a law in his time, they complained
of those that had given occasion for it. Ministers wearing
such apparel as might distinguish them from the laity was
certainly a means to keep them under great restraint, upon
every indecency in their behaviour laying them open to the
censures of the people ; which could not be, if they were habited so as that they could not be distinguished from other
men : and human nature being considered, it seems to be a
kind of temptation to many, when they do but think their

disorders will pass unobserved. Bowing at the name of Jesus was thought a fit expression of their grateful acknowledging of our Saviour, and an owning of his divinity : and as standing up at the Creed, or at the Gloria Patri, were solemn expressions of the faith of Christians ; so, since Jesus is the name by which Christ is expressed to be our Saviour, it seemed a decent piece of acknowledging our faith in him, to shew a reverence when that was pronounced ; not as if there were a peculiar sanctity or virtue in it, but because it was his proper name, Christ being but an appellation added to it. By the queen's care to take away all words of reproach, and to explain the oath of supremacy, not only clearing any ambiguity that might be in the words, but allowing men leave to declare in what sense they swore it, the moderation of her government did much appear; in which, instead of inventing new traps to catch the weak, which had been practised in other reigns, all possible care was taken to explain things so, that they might be as comprehensive to all interests as was possible. They 400 reckoned, if that age could have been on any terms separated from the papacy, though with allowance for many other superstitious conceits, it would once unite them all; and in the next age they would be so educated, that none of those should any more remain. And indeed this moderation had all the effect that was designed by it for many years, in which the papists came to church, and to the sacraments. But afterwards, it being proposed to the king of Spain, then ready to engage in a war with the queen upon the account of her supporting of the United Provinces, that he must first divide England at home, and procure from the pope a sentence against the queen, and a condemnation of such papists as went to the English service ; and that, for the maintaining and educating of such priests as should be his tools to distract the kingdom, he was to found seminaries at Douay, Louvain, and St. Omer's, from whence they might come over hither, and disorder the affairs of England : the prosecution of those counsels raised the popish party among us, which has ever since distracted this nation, and has oftener than once put it into most threatening convulsive motions, such as we feel at this day.

After the injunctions were thus prepared, the queen gave out commissions for those who should visit all the churches of England : in which they lost no time, for the new book of ser- The first high commission.

vice was by law to take place on St. John Baptist's day; and these commissions were signed that same day. One of those commissions, which was for the archbishopric and province of York, is put into the Collection. It was granted to the earls of Shrewsbury and Derby, and some others, among whom Dr. Sandys is one.

Collect.
Numb. 7.

The preamble sets forth, "that God having set the queen "over the nation, she could not render an account of that "trust, without endeavouring to propagate the true religion, "with the right way of worshipping God, in all her dominions: "therefore she intending to have a general visitation of her "whole kingdom, empowered them, or any two of them, to "examine the true state of all the churches in the northern "parts; to suspend or deprive such clergymen as were un- "worthy, and to put others into their places; to proceed "against such as were obstinate by imprisonment, church cen- "sure, or any other legal way. They were to reserve pen- "sions for such as would not continue in their benefices, but "quitted them by resignation; and to examine the condition "of all that were imprisoned on the account of religion, and "to discharge them; and to restore all such to their benefices "as had been unlawfully turned out in the late times."

This was the first high commission[27] that was given out; that for the province of Canterbury was without doubt of the same nature. The prudence of reserving pensions for such priests as were turned out was much applauded; since thereby they were kept from extreme want, which might have set them on to do mischief; and by the pension which was granted them upon their good behaviour, they were kept under some awe, which would not have been otherwise. That which was chiefly condemned in these commissions was, the queen's giving the visitors authority to proceed by ecclesiastical cen- sures, which seemed a great stretch of her supremacy: but it was thought, that the queen might do that as well as the 401 lay-chancellors did it in the ecclesiastical courts; so that one abuse was the excuse for another.

[Camden,
p. 376.]

These visitors having made report to the queen of the obe- dience given to the laws and her injunctions, it was found, that

---

[27] This was not a high commis- sion warranted by act of parlia- ment; but a commission for a royal visitation by virtue of the queen's supremacy. [S.]

of 9400 beneficed men in England, there were no more but [Fuller, ix.
fourteen bishops, six abbots[28], twelve deans, twelve archdea- p. 59.]
cons, fifteen heads of colleges, fifty prebendaries, and eighty
rectors of parishes, that had left their benefices upon the account of religion: so compliant were the papists generally.
And indeed the bishops after this time had the same apprehension of the danger into which religion was brought by the
jugglings of the greatest part of the clergy, who retained their
affections to the old superstition that those in king Edward's
time had: so that, if queen Elizabeth had not lived so long as
she did, till all that generation was dead, and a new set of
men better educated and principled, were grown up and pnt
in their rooms, and if a prince of another religion had succeeded before that time, they had probably turned about again
to the old superstitions as nimbly as they had done before in
queen Mary's days.   That which supported the superstitious
party in king Edward's time most was, that many great bishops
did secretly favour and encourage them: therefore it was now
resolved to look well to the filling of the vacant sees.

It has been said before, that Parker was sent for to London Parker's
by the queen's order, and the archbishopric of Canterbury unwilling-
was offered him: he was upon that cast into such a perplexity cept of the
of mind, that he was out of measure grieved at it.   As soon as ric of Can-
he was returned home, he writ a letter to the lord keeper; terbury.
which, with all the other letters that passed in this matter, I
have put into the Collection.   " He professed he never had Collect.
" less joy of a journey to London, and was never more glad to Numb. 8.
" get from it, than upon his last being there.   He said, it was
" necessary to fill that see with a man that was neither arro-
" gant, faint-hearted, nor covetous: an arrogant man would
" perhaps divide from his brethren in doctrine, whereas the
" whole strength of the church depended on their unity; but
" if there should be heart-burnings among them, and the pri-

---

[28] [Fuller, from whom this is probably taken, says, 'six abbots and
abbesses.'   The houses are enumerated as follows by Stow, p.640, 'Also
the houses of religion by queen Mary,
at the priory of St. John of Jerusalem by Smithfield, the nuns and
brethren of Sion and Shene, the

black friars in Smithfield, and the
friars at Greenwich, were all suppressed; the abbots and monks of
Westminster were put out, a dean,
prebends, and canons placed there,
and so named the college of Westminster founded by queen Elizabeth.']

" vate quarrels, that had been beyond sea, should be brought
" home, the peace of the church would be lost, and the success
" of all their designs would be blasted : and if a faint-hearted
" man were put in, it would raise the spirits of all their adver-
" saries : a covetous man was good for nothing. He knew
" his own unfitness both of body and mind so well, that though
" he should be sorry to offend him and secretary Cecil, whom
" he honoured above all men in the world, and more sorry to
" displease the queen ; yet he must above all things avoid
" God's indignation, and not enter into a station, into which
" he knew he could not carry himself so as to answer it either
" to God or the world for his administration. And if he must
" go to prison for his obstinate untowardness, (with which it
" seems they had threatened him,) he would suffer it rather
" with a quiet conscience, than accept of an employment which
" he could not discharge. He said, he intended by God's
" grace never to be of that order, neither higher nor lower.
" He knew what he was capable of : he was poor, and not
" able to enter on such a station ; he had a rupture, which
" made him that he could not stir much ; therefore he desired
" some place in the university, where he might wear out his 402
" life tolerably. He knew he could not answer their expecta-
" tion, which made him so importunate not to be raised so
" high. He said, he had great apprehensions of differences
" like to fall out among themselves ; which would be a pleasant
" diversion to those of the church of Rome. He saw some
" men were men still, even after all their teaching in the
" school of affliction. He protested he did not seek his own
" private gain or ease ; he had but two or three years more
" of life before him, and did not intend to heap up for his
" children." This he writ the first of March.

The business of the parliament made this motion to be laid
aside till that was dissolved ; and then, on the 17th of May,
the lord keeper wrote to him concerning it : he told him, that
he saw, by a resolution taken that day in the queen's presence,
that it would be very hard for his friends to get him delivered
from that charge. For his own part, if he knew a man to
whom the characters in his letter did agree better than to
himself, he should be for preferring of such a one ; but knowing
no such, he must be still for him. On the 19th, after that, the

lord keeper and secretary Cecil signed a letter in the queen's
name, requiring him to come up; and after that they sent a
second command to him to come to court on the 28th of the
month. He came up, but again excused himself. Yet at last,
being so often pressed, he writ to the queen herself, "protest-
"ing that extreme necessity forced him to trouble her, both
"out of conscience to God, and regard to her service: he
"knew his great unworthiness for so high a function; there-
"fore as on his knees he humbly besought her to discharge
"him of that office, which did require a man of more learning,
"virtue, and experience, than he perfectly knew was in him-
"self. He lamented his being so meanly qualified, that he
"could not serve her in that high station; but in any other
"inferior office he should be ready to discharge his duty to
"her in such a place as was suitable to his infirmity." But
in the conclusion he submitted himself to her pleasure. In
the end he was with great difficulty brought to accept of it.
So on the 8th [29] day of July the *congé d'élire* was sent to Canterbury; and upon that, on the 22nd of July, a chapter was
summoned to meet the first of August; where the dean and
prebendaries meeting, they, according to a method often used
in their elections [30], did by a compromise refer it to the dean
to name whom he pleased: and he naming doctor Parker, according to the queen's letter, they all confirmed it, and published their election, singing *Te Deum* upon it. On the 9th [Rymer,
of September [31] the great seal was put to a warrant for his xv. p. 541.]
consecration, directed to the bishops of Durham, Bath and
Wells, Peterborough, Llandaff, and to Barlow and Scory,
(styled only bishops, not being then elected to any sees,) requiring them to consecrate him. From this it appears, that
neither Tunstall, Bourne, nor Pole were at that time turned
out: it seems there was some hope of gaining them to obey
the laws, and so to continue in their sees.

This matter was delayed to the 6th [32] of December. Whe- He is consecrated

---

[29] Mason has it the 18th of July.
[S.]

[30] There had been but one election since the prior and monks
were changed into a dean and prebendaries. [G.]

[31] [A copy of the queen's letter
is in the State Paper Office, Domestic, vol. vi. 41.]

[32] [A copy of this commission
is in State Papers, Domestic, vol.
vii. 56.]

archbishop
of Canter-
bury.
[Rymer,
xv. 549.
Wilkins,
iv. 198.]
ther this flowed from Parker's unwillingness to engage in so
high a station, or from any other secret reason, I do not know.
But then, the three bishops last named refusing to do it, a new
warrant passed under the great seal, to the bishop of Llandaff;
Barlow, bishop elect of Chichester; Scory, bishop elect of 403
Hereford; Coverdale, late bishop of Exeter; Hodgkins, bishop suffragan of Bedford; John, suffragan of Thetford; and
Bale, bishop of Ossory; that they, or any four of them, should
consecrate him. So by virtue of this, on the 9th of December,
Barlow, Scory, Coverdale, and Hodgkins, met at the church
of St. Mary-le-Bow; where, according to the custom, the *congé
d'élire*, with the election, and the royal assent to it, were to
be brought before them: and these being read, witnesses were
to be cited to prove the election lawfully made; and all who
would object to it were also cited. All these things being performed according to law, and none coming to object against
the election, they confirmed it according to the usual manner.
On the 17th of December Parker was consecrated in the
chapel at Lambeth by Barlow, Scory, Coverdale, and Hodgkins, according to the book of ordinations made in king Edward's time: only the ceremony of putting the staff in his
hands was left out of the office in this reign. He being thus
consecrated himself, did afterwards consecrate bishops for the
[Dec. 21.]   other sees: namely, Grindal, bishop of London; Cox, that had
been king Edward's almoner, bishop of Ely; Horne, bishop of
Winchester; Sandys, bishop of Worcester; Meyrick, bishop
[Jan. 21,   of Bangor; Young, bishop of St. David's; Bullingham, bishop
1560.]   of Lincoln; Jewel, bishop of Salisbury, (the great ornament
of that age for learning and piety;) Davis, bishop of St. Asaph;
[Mar. 24.]   Guest, bishop of Rochester; Berkeley, bishop of Bath and
[July 14.]   Wells; Bentham, bishop of Coventry and Lichfield; Alley,
[Feb. 16,   bishop of Exeter; and Par[33], bishop of Peterborough. Barlow
1561.]   and Scory were put into the sees of Chichester and Hereford.
And some time after this, in February 1561, Young was translated from St. David's to York, there being now no hopes of

[33] For Scambler. Thomas Davis
of St. Asaph, and Richard Cheney
of Gloucester, being some of the
first set of bishops, should have
been remembered, though enumerated a while after. [G.]   [Thomas

Davis was not consecrated till May
26, 1561, nor Richard Cheney till
April 19, 1562. The author has
omitted mention of Parkhurst of
Norwich, consecrated Sept. 1, 1560.]
For Par, *read* Scambler. [S.]

gaining Heath to continue in it; which it seems had been [Camden,
long endeavoured, for it was now two years that that see[34] p. 377.]
had been in vacancy. In like manner, after so long waiting
to see if Tunstall would conform[35], there being now no more
hope of it, in March 1561, Pilkington was made bishop of [Mar. 2.]
Durham. Best[36] was afterwards made bishop of Carlisle, and
Downham bishop of Chester.　　　　　　　　　　　　　　　[May 4.]

　　I have given the more distinct account of these promotions, The fable of
because of a most malicious slander, with which they were the Nag's-
aspersed in after-times. It was not thought on for forty head con-
years after this. But then it was forged, and published, and futed.
spread over the world, with great confidence, that Parker
himself was not legally or truly consecrated. The author of it
was said to be one Neale, that had been sometime one of Bonner's chaplains. The contrivance was, that the bishop of
Llandaff being required by Bonner not to consecrate Parker,
or to give orders in his diocese, did thereupon refuse it: upon
that the bishops elect being met in Cheapside, at the Nag's-head
tavern, Neale, that had watched them thither, peeped in through
an hole of the door, and saw them in great disorder, finding
the bishop of Llandaff was intractable. But (as the tale goes
on) Scory bids them all kneel, and he laid the Bible upon every
one of their heads or shoulders, and said, *Take thou authority
to preach the word of God sincerely;* and so they rose up all
bishops. This tale came so late into the world, that Sanders,
and all the other writers in queen Elizabeth's time, had never
heard of it: otherwise we may be sure they would not have
concealed it. And if the thing had been true, or if Neale had
404 but pretended that he had seen any such thing, there is no
reason to think he would have suppressed it. But when it
might be presumed that all those persons were dead that had
been present at Parker's consecration, then was the time to
invent such a story; for then it might be hoped that none could

---

[34] May, dean of St. Paul's, was
elected archbishop, but died before
he was consecrated. [S.] [He died
Aug. 12, 1560. See Leneve.]
　　[36] [Tunstall died on the 18th of
November, 1559. Vid. State Paper
Office, Domestic, vol. vii. 39, and
Antiq. Brit. p. 468. The queen is-
ued letters patent Feb. 27, 1566,

authorizing Robert Tempeste to receive the rents, &c., during her
pleasure: in them it is stated that
the bishopric was vacant by the deprivation of Cuthbert, late bishop
deceased. Vid. Rymer, xv. 569.]
　　[36] [Best was consecrated on the
same day with Pilkington, March 2,
1561.]

contradict it. And who could tell but that some who had seen bishops go from Bow-church to dine at that tavern with their civilians, as some have done after their confirmation, might imagine that then was the time of this *Nag's-head consecration.* If it were boldly said, one or other might think he remembered it. But as it pleased God, there was one then living that remembered the contrary. The old earl of Nottingham, who had been at the consecration, declared it was at Lambeth, and described all the circumstances of it, and satisfied all reasonable men, that it was according to the form of the church of England. The registers both of the see of Canterbury, and of the records of the crown, do all fully agree with his relation. For as Parker's *congé d'élire*, with the queen's assent to his election, and the warrant for his consecration, are all under the great seal; so, upon the certificate made by those who consecrated him, the temporalities were restored by another warrant, also enrolled; which was to be shewed in the house of lords when he took his place there. Besides that the consecrations of all the other bishops made by him shew that he alone was first consecrated without any other. And, above all other testimonies, the original instrument of archbishop Parker's consecration lies still among his other papers in the library of Corpus Christi College at Cambridge, which I saw and read. It is as manifestly an original writing as any that I ever had in my hands: I have put it in the Collection, for the more full discovery of the impudence of that fiction. But it served those ends for which it was designed. Weak people hearing it so positively told by their priests, came to believe it; and I have myself met with many that seemed still to give some credit to it, after all that clear confutation of it made by the most ingenious and learned bishop Bramhall, the late primate of Ireland. Therefore I thought it necessary to be the larger in the account of this consecration; and the rather, because of the influence it hath into all the ordinations that have been since that time derived down in this church.

Some excepted against the canonicalness of it, because it was not done by all the bishops of the province, and three of the bishops had no sees when they did it, and the fourth was only a suffragan bishop. But to all this it was said, that after a church had been overrun with heresy, those rules, which were

[Reg. Parker, fol. 3.]

Collect. Numb. 9.

[Bramhall's Works, p. 1045.]

to be observed in its more settled state, were always superseded;
as appears particularly when the Arian bishops were turned out
of some great sees; for the orthodox bishops did then ordain
others to succeed them, without judging themselves bound by
the canons in such cases. And bishops that had been rightly
consecrated could certainly derive their own character to others,
whether they were actually in sees or not. And a suffragan
bishop, being consecrated in the same manner that other bishops
were, though he had a limited jurisdiction, yet was of the same
order with them. All these things were made out with a great
deal of learning by Mason, who, upon the publishing of that
fiction, wrote in vindication of the English ministry.

405   Thus were the sees filled, the worship reformed, and the
queen's injunctions sent over England. Three things remained
yet to be done. The first was, to set out the doctrine of the church
as it had been done in king Edward's time. The second was,
to translate the Bible, and publish it with short notes. And
the third was, to regulate the ecclesiastical courts. The bishops
therefore set about these. And for the first, though they could
not by public authority set out the articles of the church till
they met in a convocation; yet they soon after prepared them.
And for the present, they agreed on a short profession of their
doctrine, which all incumbents were obliged to read and publish
to their people. This will be found in the Collection, copied Collect.
from it as it was then printed.   Numb. 11.

In the articles made in king Edward's reign, which I have
put in the Collection, the reader will find on the margin the
differences between those and these marked. In the third
article, the explanation of Christ's descent to hell was left out.
In that about the scriptures, they now added an enumeration
of the canonical and apocryphal books; declaring, that some
lessons were read out of the latter for the instruction of the
people, but not for the confirmation of the doctrine. About the
authority of the church, they now added, that the church had
power to decree rites and ceremonies, and had authority in
controversies of faith; but still subordinate to the scripture.

In the article about the Lord's supper, there is a great deal
left out; for instead of that large refutation of the corporal
presence, from the impossibility of a body's being in more
places at once; from whence it follows, that since Christ's body

is in heaven, the faithful ought not to believe or profess a real or corporal presence of it in the sacrament; in the new articles it is said, *That the body of Christ is given and received after a spiritual manner; and the means by which it is received is faith.* But in the original copy of these articles, which I have seen subscribed by the hands of all that sat in either house of convocation, there is a further addition made. The articles were subscribed with that precaution which was requisite in a matter of such consequence; for before the subscriptions there is set down the number of the pages, and of the lines in every page of the book, to which they set their hands.

MSS. C. Cor. Christ. Cant. [CXXI. p. 233.]

In that article of the eucharist, these words are added; *Christus in cœlum ascendens, corpori suo immortalitatem dedit, naturam non abstulit: humanæ enim naturæ veritatem, juxta scripturas perpetuo retinet, quam uno et definitō loco esse, et non in multa vel omnia simul loca diffundi, oportet: quum igitur Christus in cœlum sublatus, ibi usque ad finem sœculi sit permansurus, atque inde, non aliunde, (ut loquitur Augustinus,) venturus sit ad judicandum vivos et mortuos, non debet quisquam fidelium, carnis ejus et sanguinis realem et corporalem (ut loquuntur) præsentiam in Eucharistiá, vel credere vel profiteri.* In English thus; "Christ, when he "ascended into heaven, made his body immortal, but took not "from it the nature of a body; for still it retains, according to "the scriptures, the verity of a human body, which must be "always in one definite place, and cannot be spread into many, "or all places at once. Since then Christ, being carried up to "heaven, is to remain there to the end of the world, and is to "come from thence, and from no place else, (as says St. Austin,) **406** "to judge the quick and the dead; none of the faithful ought "to believe or profess the real or (as they call it) the corporal "presence of his flesh and blood in the eucharist."

An explanation of Christ's presence in the sacrament.

But it is suppressed.

But this in the original is dashed over with *minium;* yet so, that it is still legible. The secret of it was this: the queen and her council studied (as hath been already shewn) to unite all into the communion of the church: and it was alleged, that such an express definition against a real presence might drive from the church many who were still of that persuasion; and therefore it was thought to be enough to condemn transubstantiation, and to say, that Christ was present after a spiritual manner, and received by faith ; to say more, as it was judged superfluous, so it might occasion division. Upon this, these words were by common consent left out : and, in the next convocation, the articles were subscribed without them, of which I have also seen the original.

This shews that the doctrine of the church, subscribed by the whole convocation, was at that time contrary to the belief of a real or corporal presence in the sacrament ; only it was not thought necessary or expedient to publish it. Though from this silence, which flowed not from their opinion, but the wisdom of that time, in leaving a liberty for different speculations as to the manner of the presence, some have since inferred, that the chief pastors of this church did then disapprove of the definition made in king Edward's time, and that they were for a real presence.

For the translating of the Bible, it was divided into many parcels. The Pentateuch was committed to William Alley, bishop of Exeter. The books from that to the second of Samuel were given to Richard Davis, who was made bishop of St. David's when Young was removed to York. All from Samuel to the second book of Chronicles was assigned Edwin Sandys, then bishop of Worcester. From thence to the end of Job to one whose name is marked A. P. C[37]. The book of the Psalms was given to Thomas Bentham[38], bishop of Coventry and Lichfield. The Proverbs to one who is marked A.P.[39] The Song of Solomon to one marked A. P. E[40]. All from thence to the Lamentations of Jeremy was given to Robert Horne. bishop of Winchester. Ezekiel and Daniel to Bentham[41]. From thence to Malachi to Grindal, bishop of London. The Apocrypha, to the book of Wisdom, was given to Barlow. bishop of Chichester ; and the rest of it to Parkhurst, bishop of Norwich. The Gospels, Acts, and Epistle to the Romans, were given to Richard Cox, bishop of Ely. The Epistles to the Corinthians

[37] A. P. C. stands for Andrew Pierson, Cantuar. [S.]

[He was chaplain to archbishop Parker and prebendary of Canterbury.]

[38] [The initials T. B., which appear at the end of the Psalms, have been thought to indicate Thomas Becon, as Bentham would probably have signed with the initial letters of his see.]

[39] [The initials are A. P. C. and mean probably Andrew Pierson.]

[40] A. P. E. stands for Andrew Perne, Eliensis [S.]

[41] [The initials here are T. C. L. meaning Thomas Coventry and Litchfield.

T t 2

to one marked G. G[42]. I know not to whom the rest of the New Testament was assigned. All these allotments I gather from the Bible itself, as it was afterwards set out by Parker. What method they followed in this work, I cannot discover ; unless the rules afterwards given in king James' time, when the translation was revived, were copied from what was now done : which rules, for the curiosity of the thing, I shall put in the Collection, as I copied it from Bishop Ravis' paper. They were given with that care that such a matter required. There were many companies appointed for every parcel of the scripture, and every one of a company was to translate the whole parcel : then they were to compare these together ; and when any company had finished their part, they were to communicate it to the other companies. So, it is like, that at this time those several bishops, that had undertaken the translation, did associate to themselves companies, with whose assistance they perfected it afterwards : and when it was set out, at the end of every section, the initial letters of his name that had translated it were printed, as W. E., E. W. for Will. Exon. and Edwin Wigorn. ; and so in the rest. In what year this was first printed, I am not so well assured : for I have not seen the first impression of it ; but I believe it was in the year 1561[43], or soon after it ; for the almanack prefixed for the moveable feasts begins with that year.

Collect. Numb. 10.

407

As for the canons and rules of the church government, they were not so soon prepared. There came out some in the year 1571, and more in the year 1597, and a far larger collection of them in the first year of king James' reign. But this matter has yet wanted its chief force ; for penitentiary canons have not been set up, and the government of the church is not yet brought into the hands of churchmen. So that in this point the reformation of the church wants some part of its finishing in the government and discipline of it.

[Wilkins, Conc. IV. pp. 263, 352.]

Thus did queen Elizabeth again recover the reformation of religion : and it might have been expected, that, under such moderate and wise counsels, things should have been carried

The beginnings of the divisions of this church.

---

[42] C. G. stands for Christopher Goodman [S.] [the initials are G. G. and stand for Gabriel Goodman Dean of Westminster.]

[43] The new translation of the Bible was not printed before the year 1572. [S.]
[It appeared in the year 1568.]

with that temper, that this church should have united in its
endeavours to support itself, and become the bulwark of the
reformation, and the terror of Rome.   But that blessing was,
by the sins of the nation, the passions of some, the interests of
others, and the weakness of the greatest part, in a great
measure denied us.   The heats that had been raised beyond
sea were not quite forgotten; and as some sparks had been
kindled about clergymen's habits in king Edward's reign, so,
though Hooper and Ridley had buried that difference in their
ashes, it broke out again concerning the vestments of the
inferior clergy.   Other things were also much contested; some
were for setting up ecclesiastical courts in every parish, for the
exercising of discipline against scandalous persons; others
thought this might degenerate into faction.   These lesser differences were craftily managed by some who intended to improve
them so far, that they might have the church lands divided among
them; and they carried these heats further in queen Elizabeth's
reign, than one would imagine, that considers the temper of
that government.   But since that, still by many degrees, and
many accidents in the civil government, they are now grown to
that height, that, though, considering the grounds on which
they have been, and still are maintained, they appeared to be
of no great force or moment; yet if the animosities and heats
that are raised by them are well examined, there is scarce any
probable hopes left of composing those differences, unless our
lawgivers do vigorously apply themselves to it.

The reformation in Scotland.

Having given this account of the establishment of the reformation here in England under queen Elizabeth, I have in some
sort discharged myself of the design of my engagement in this
work; but since the settlement of religion in Scotland was
408 made the same year, I shall next give some account of that;
which I do with the more assurance, having met with several [Melville's
important things relating to it in Melville's Memoirs[43], that Memoirs, p.77.sqq.]

44 [The author has referred to
these Memoirs, supra, pp. 204, 209,
and 214, and elsewhere. They have
been published by the Bannatyne
club, 4to Edinburgh, 1827, with the
title, 'Memoirs of his own life by

sir James Melville of Halhill, 1549
—1593, from the original manuscript.'   See the preface to this
volume, p. 3, where the editor gives
his opinion that the descendant alluded to at p. 205, was George Scott

are in none of the printed books. When the treaty began for
a peace between the two crowns of France and Spain, the
secret reason of making it was, to root out heresy; so much
was expressed in the preamble to it, that to extirpate heresy,
to have a general council called, and the church fully reformed
both from errors and abuses, those princes had entered into a
firm peace.

The cardinal of Lorraine writ to his sister, the queen regent
of Scotland, that now, since they were making peace, they
were resolved to purge the world of heresy. He also writ to
the archbishop of St. Andrew's to the same effect. The queen
regent was much confounded at this. She was now forced to
break her faith with those who had served her interests
hitherto; and to whom she had often promised, that they
should not be troubled for their consciences. The danger was
also very great from their combination, since the queen of
England would certainly assist them; both because the religion was the same in both countries, and because, by dividing
that kingdom, she would secure the north of England from the
mischief Scotland could do it, if moved and set on to it by
France. But the bishops in Scotland, shutting their eyes upon
all dangers, resolved by some signal instance to strike a terror
into the people.

The archbishop of St. Andrew's, having gathered a meeting
of many bishops, abbots, and divines, brought before them one
Walter Mill, an old decrepit priest, who had long given over
saying mass, and had preached in several places of the country.

Mill's mar-
tyrdom.

They had in vain dealt with him to recant; so now, he was
brought to his trial. They objected articles to him, about his
asserting the lawfulness of priests' marriages; denying the
seven sacraments; saying the mass was idolatry; denying the
presence of Christ's flesh and blood in the sacrament; and condemning the office of bishops, speaking against pilgrimages,
and teaching privately in houses.

[Spots-
wood, p.
96.]

To these he answered beyond all their expectation; for he
was so old and infirm, that they thought he could say nothing.
He said, "he esteemed marriage a blessed bond, and free for
" all men to enter into it; and that it was much better for

of Pitlochrie, a younger son of sir   garet Melville, one of sir James'
John Scott of Scotstarvet, and Mar-   daughters.]

" priests to marry, than to vow chastity and not keep it, as
" they generally did. He said, he knew no sacraments but
" baptism and the Lord's supper; the rest he left to them.
" He said, the priest's sole communicating was as if a lord
" should invite many to dinner, and ring a bell for them to
" come ; but when they came, should turn his back on them,
" and eat all himself. He said, that Christ was only spiritually
" in the sacrament ; and that there was no other sacrifice but
" that which he offered on the cross. He held, that they were
" bishops indeed who did the work of a bishop, and not they
" who sought only their sensual pleasures, and neither re-
" garded the word of God, nor their flocks. He knew pilgrim-
" ages had been much abused, and great uncleanness was
" committed under the colour of going to them ; but there was
" no ground for them in scripture."

Upon these answers he was required to recant; but he said,
he knew he was to die once, and what they intended to do
409 with him, he wished they would do it soon. Upon this, he
was declared an obstinate heretic. But the country was so [Bucha-
alienated from them, that they could not find a man to burn nan, p.
310.]
him ; and he that had the jurisdiction in that regality refused
to execute the sentence. Yet at last, one of the archbishop's
servants was gotten to undertake it : but in the whole town
they could find none that would sell them a cord to tie him to
the stake ; so they were forced to put it off till the next day ;
and then, since none other could be had, the archbishop sent
the cords of his own pavilion for that use. When Mill was
brought to the stake, he said, he would not go up of his own
accord, because he would not be accessary to his own death ;
but if they would put their hand to him, they should see how
cheerfully he should do it. That being done, he went up, and
said, *I will go in to the altar of God.* He exhorted the
people to be no more seduced by the lies of their priests, but
to depend upon Christ and his mercy ; for whose doctrine, as
many martyrs had offered up their lives, so he blessed God
that had so honoured him to call him to give this testimony,
for whose glory he most willingly offered up his life. When
the fire was set to him, he called to the people to pray for him,
and continued to cry, *Lord, have mercy on me,* till he could
speak no more.

The nation
was much
provoked
by it.
[Spots-
wood, p.
97.]
His suffering was much resented by the inhabitants of St. Andrew's, who raised a great heap of stones in the place where he was burnt, for a memorial of it; and though the priests scattered them often, they renewed them still, till a watch was set about it.

In all parts of Scotland, and especially in the towns, and in the families of the nobility and gentry, the reformation had been received, and secretly professed. So they began now to consult what to do. They had many meetings in several places; and, finding their interest was great over the kingdom, they entered into confederacies to maintain the true religion.

[Spots-
wood, p.
119.]
Before the parliament met last year, they had sent a petition to the queen regent, "that the worship of God might be in the "vulgar tongue, and the communion might be given in both "kinds: that there should be great care taken in the election "of ministers, that it might be according to the custom of the "primitive church, and that scandalous ministers might be "removed, and more worthy men put in their places."

But the queen regent, to keep them in hopes till the dauphin should be acknowledged king of Scotland, promised they should not be hindered to have prayers in their own tongue, so they would keep no public assemblies in Edinburgh and Leith.

In the parliament, they proposed the abrogating of the laws for churchmen's proceedings against heretics, and that none should be condemned of heresy but according to the word of God; with some other limitations of the severities against them. But the queen still gave them good hopes; only she said, she could not agree to those things, by reason of the opposition that would be made by the spiritual estate: but she suffered them to read a protestation in parliament, declaring their desires of a reformation; and that, if, upon the denial of it, abuses were removed violently, they were not to be blamed, who had begun thus in a modest way to petition for it.

[Spots-
wood, p.
120.]
[Ibid. p.
121.]
This year it was become visible that she resolved to proceed 410 to extremities. She ordered all the reformed preachers to appear at Stirling the 10th of May. When this was done, the earl of Glencairn went to her in the name of the rest, and asked her the reason of that way of proceeding. She answered him in passion, "that maugre them, and all that would take

" part with them, the ministers should be banished Scotland,
" though they preached as soundly as St. Paul did." Upon
this he remembered her of the promises she had often made
them : to which she answered, " that the promises of princes
" should be no further strained than seemed convenient to
" them to perform." Glencairn replied, " If she would keep
" no promises, they would acknowledge her no more, but re-
" nounce their obedience to her."

That very night she heard, that in the town of St. Johnstoun A revolt
the people had sermons openly in their churches. Upon that began at
she ordered the lord Ruthven to go and reduce that town : he toun.
answered, he could not govern their consciences : upon which, [Bucha-
she vowed she would make him and them both repent it. The 313.]
ministers were coming from all parts, accompanied with many
gentlemen, to appear on the day to which they were cited.
The queen hearing that, sent word to them to go home, for
she would not proceed in the citation. Many of them upon
that returned to their homes, but others went to St. Johnstoun : yet, upon their not appearing, she made them all be
declared rebels, contrary to her promise : this made many
leave her, and go over to them at St. Johnstoun. The people
began there first to break images ; and then they fell into the
houses of the Franciscans and Dominicans, where they found
much more wealth than agreed with their pretended poverty.
They also pulled down a great house of the Carthusians with
so much haste, that within two days there was not one stone
left to shew where it had stood ; but yet the prior was suffered
to carry away the plate. All that was found in these houses,
besides what the monks carried away, was given to the poor.
The queen hearing this, resolved to make that town an example, and sent over all the kingdom to gather the French soldiers together, with such others as would join with her in this
quarrel. But the earl of Glencairn, with incredible haste, [Bucha-
came to their assistance with 2500 men ; and there were nan, p.
gathered in all, in and about the town, 7000 men. The queen, Spots-
seeing it now turned to an open rebellion, employed the earl of wood, p.
Argyle and the prior of St. Andrew's to treat with them. An 122.]
oblivion for what was past was agreed on : the queen was to
come to St. Johnstoun without her Frenchmen ; and the mat-

ters of religion were to be referred to a parliament. Upon this she went thither : but carried Frenchmen with her, and put a garrison in the town; and proceeded to the fining of many, and the banishing of others. Being pressed with her promise, she said, " the promises of princes ought not to be " strictly urged; and those were not to be kept that were " made to heretics : she declared, that she would take it on " her conscience to kill and undo all that sect, and make the " best excuse she could when it was done." Upon this, all the nation forsook her : and in many other places they went on to cleanse the churches, and pull down monasteries.

When the news of this came to the court of France, it was at first not rightly understood. The queen regent represented **411** it as if it had been a design to shake off the French power; and desired a great force to reduce them. The king then saw, too late, that the constable had given him good advice, in dissuading the match with Scotland, and, fearing to be entangled in a long chargeable war, he resolved to send one thither to know the true occasion of these stirs. So the constable proposed to him the sending of Melville, by whom he had understood, that the reason of all their disorders was the queen's breaking her word to them in the matters of religion. He carried Melville to the king, and in his presence gave him instructions to go to Scotland, and see what was the true cause of all these disorders; and particularly how far the prior of St. Andrew's (afterwards the earl of Murray) was engaged in them; and if he, by secret ways, could certainly find there was nothing in it but religion, that then he should give them assurances of the free exercise of it, and press them not to engage any further till he was returned to the French court, where he was promised to find a great reward for so important a service : but he was not to let the queen regent understand his business. He found, upon his going into Scotland, that it was even as he had formerly heard, that the queen regent was now much hated and distasted by them; but that, upon an oblivion of what was past, and the free exercise of their religion for the future, all might be brought to peace and quiet. But before he came back, the king of France was dead, the constable in disgrace, and the cardinal of Lorraine governed

The French king intends to grant liberty of religion.
[Melville's Memoirs, p. 78 sqq.]

But is killed.

all: so he lost his labour and reward, which he valued much
less, being a generous and virtuous man, than the ruin that he
saw coming on his country.

The lords that were now united against the queen-mother
came and took St. Johnstoun. From thence they went to
Stirling and Edinburgh; and every where they pulled down
monasteries: all the country declared on their side; so that
the queen regent was forced to fly to Dunbar Castle. The
lords sent to England for assistance, which the queen readily
granted them. They gave out, that they desired nothing but
to have the French driven out, and religion settled by a parliament. The queen regent, seeing all the country against
her, and apprehending that the queen of England would take
advantage from these stirs to drive her out of Scotland, was
content to agree to a truce, and to summon a parliament to A truce
meet on the 10th of January. But the new king of France in Scot-
sent over M. de Croque with a high threatening message, that land.
he would spend the whole revenue of France, rather than not [July 24, Buchanan,
be revenged on them that raised these tumults in Scotland. P. 317.]
The lords answered, that they desired nothing but the liberty
of their religion; and that being obtained, they should be in all
other things his most obedient subjects. The queen regent,
having gotten about 2000 men from France fortified Leith,
and in many other things broke the truce. There came over
also some doctors of the Sorbonne to dispute with the minis- [Ibid. p.
ters, because they heard the Scottish clergy were scarce able 318.]
to defend their own cause. The lords gathered again, and,
seeing the queen regent had so often broke her word to them,
they entered into consultation to deprive her of her regency.
Their queen was not yet of age; and in her minority, they
pretended that the government of the kingdom belonged to the
412 states: and therefore they gathered together many of her
mal-administrations, for which they might the more colourably
put her out of the government. The things they charged on The queen
her were chiefly these: "that she had without law begun a deposed.
" war in the kingdom, and brought in strangers to subdue it;
" had governed without the consent of the nobility; embased
" the coin to maintain her soldiers; had put garrisons in free
" towns, and had broke all promises and terms with them.
" Thereupon they declared her to have fallen from her re-

" gency, and did suspend her power till the next parliament."
So now it was an irreconcilable breach. The lords lay first
at Edinburgh, and from thence retired afterwards to Stirling :
upon which the French came and possessed themselves of the

[Spots-
wood, p.
140.]

town, and set up the mass again in the churches. Greater
supplies came over from France under the command of the
marquis of Elbœuf, one of the queen regent's brothers; who,
though most of his fleet were dispersed, yet brought to Leith
1000 foot, so that there were now above 4000 French soldiers
in that town. But what accession of strength soever the queen
regent received from these, she lost as much in Scotland : for
now almost the whole country was united against her; and the
French were equally heavy to their friends and enemies. They
marched about by Stirling to waste Fife, where there were
some small engagements between them and the lords of the
congregation.

The Scots
implore the
queen of
England's
aid.

But the Scots, seeing they could not stand before that force
that was expected from France the next spring, sent to queen
Elizabeth to desire her aid openly ; for the secret supplies of
money and ammunition, with which she hitherto furnished
them, would not now serve the turn. The council of England
apprehended that it would draw on a war with France : yet
they did not fear that much ; for that kingdom was fallen into
such factions, that they did not apprehend any great danger
from thence till their king was of age. So the duke of Norfolk
was sent to Berwick to treat with the lords of the congregation, who were now headed by the duke of Châtelherault. On
the 27th of February they agreed on these conditions : " They
" were to be sure allies to the queen of England, and to assist
" her both in England and Ireland, as she should need their
" help. She was now, on the other hand, to assist them to
" drive the French out of Scotland : after which they were
" still to continue in their obedience to their natural queen.
" This league was to last during their queen's marriage to the
" French king, and for a year after : and they were to give
" the queen of England hostages, who were to be changed
" every six months."

[Bucha-
nan, p.
321.]
[Spots-
wood, p.
142.]

[Ibid. p.
143.]

[Ibid. p.
p. 144.]
[April 5.]

This being concluded, and the hostages given, the lord Grey
marched into Scotland with 2000 horse and 6000 foot. Upon
that, the lords sent and offered to the queen regent, that, if she

would send away the French forces, the English should likewise be sent back, and they would return to their obedience.

This not being accepted, they drew about Leith to besiege *Leith is*
it. In one sally which the French made, they were beaten *besieged*
by the
back with the loss of 300 men. This made the English more *English.*
secure, thinking the French would no more come out: but *[Spots-*
wood, p.
they, understanding the ill order that was kept, sallied out *145.]*
again, and killed near 500 of the English. This made them
413 more watchful for the future. So the siege being formed, a
fire broke out in Leith, which burnt down the greatest part of
the town: the English playing all the while on them distracted
them so, that, the soldiers being obliged to be on the walls,
the fire was not easily quenched. Hereupon the English gave
the assault, and were beaten off with some loss: but the duke
of Norfolk sent a supply of 2000 men more, with the assurance of a great army if it was necessary; and charged the
lord Grey not to quit the siege till the French were gone.
Ships were also sent to lie in the Frith, to block them up by
sea. The French, apprehending the total loss of Scotland, sent *[Ibid. p.*
over Montluc, bishop of Valence, to London, to offer to restore *146.]*
Calais to the queen of England, if she would draw her forces
out of Scotland. She gave him a quick answer on the sudden
herself, that she did not value that fish-town so much as she did
the quiet of Britain. But the French desiring that she would me- *[Bucha-*
diate a peace between them and the Scots, she understood that, *nan, p.*
324.]
and sent secretary Cecil and Dr. Wotton into Scotland to conclude
it. As they were on the way, the queen regent died in the *The queen*
castle of Edinburgh, on the 10th of June [45]. She sent for some of *regent of*
Scotland
the chief lords before her death, and desired to be reconciled to *dies.*
them; and asked them pardon for the injuries she had done *[Spots-*
wood, p.
them. She advised them to send both the French and English *146.]*
soldiers out of Scotland; and prayed them to continue in their
obedience to their queen. She also sent for one of their
preachers, Willock, and discoursed with him about her soul,
and many other things, and said unto him, that she trusted to
be saved only by the death and merits of Jesus Christ; and so

---

[45] [Cecil and Wotton, writing to   Illustrations, vol. i., p. 329.
Elizabeth, inform her of the death   The date in the text is taken
of the queen dowager having taken   from Spotswood, p. 146.]
place on the 11th of June. Lodge's

ended her days : which if she had done a year sooner, before these last passages of her life, she had been the most universally lamented queen that had been in any time in Scotland. For she had governed them with great prudence, justice, and gentleness; and in her own deportment, and in the order of her court, she was an example to the whole nation : but the directions sent to her from France made her change her measures, break her word, and engage the kingdom in war ; which rendered her very hateful to the nation. Yet she was often heard to say, that if her counsels might take place, she doubted not to bring all things again to perfect tranquillity and peace.

A peace is concluded. [Spotswood, p. 147]

The treaty between England, France, and Scotland, was soon after concluded. The French were to be sent away within twenty days; an act of oblivion was to be confirmed in parliament; the injuries done to the bishops and abbots were referred to the parliament; strangers and churchmen were no more to be trusted with the chief offices, and a parliament was to meet in August for the confirming of this.. During the queen's absence, the nation was to be governed by a council of twelve ; of these the queen was to name seven, and the states five. The queen was neither to make peace nor war, but by the advice of the estates, according to the ancient custom of the kingdom. The English were to return, as soon as the French were gone : and for the matter of religion, that was referred to the parliament; and some were to be sent from thence to the king and queen, to set forth their desires to them : and the queen of Scotland was no more to use the arms and title of England. All these conditions were agreed to on the 8th of July; and soon after, both the French and English left the kingdom.

[Buchanan, p. 326.]

Reformation is settled in Scotland by parliament. [Aug. 1. Acts of Parl. of Scoland, vol. ii. p. 525.]

In August thereafter the parliament met, where four acts 414 passed : one, for the abolishing of the pope's power : a second, for the repealing of all laws made in favour of the former superstition; a third, for the punishing of those that said or heard mass; and the fourth was a confirmation of the confession of faith, which was afterwards ratified and inserted in the acts of parliament, held anno 1567. It was penned by Knox, and agrees in almost all things with the Geneva Confession.

[Spotswood, p. 150.]

Of the whole temporalty, none but the earl of Athol, and the lords Somerville and Borthwick, dissented to it : they

said, they would believe as their fathers had done before
them. The spiritual estate said nothing against it. The
abbots struck in with the tide, upon assurance, that their abbeys should be converted to temporal lordships, and be given
to them. Most of the bishops, seeing the stream so strong
against them, complied likewise; and, to secure themselves,
and enrich their friends or bastards, did dilapidate all the
revenues of the church in the strangest manner that has ever
been known: and yet, for most of all these leases and alienations, they procured from Rome bulls to confirm them; pretending at that court, that they were necessary for making
friends to their interest in Scotland.

Great numbers of these bulls I myself have seen and read:
so that, after all the noise that the church of Rome had made
of the sacrilege in England, they themselves confirmed a more
entire waste of the church's patrimony in Scotland; of which
there was scarce any thing reserved for the clergy. But our
kings have since that time used such effectual endeavours
there, for the recovery of so much as might give a just encouragement to the labours of the clergy, that universally the
inferior clergy is better provided for in no nation than in Scotland; for in glebe and tithes, every incumbent is by the law
provided with at least 50*l.* sterling a year; which, in proportion to the cheapness of the country, is equal to twice so much
in most parts of England. But there are not among them
such provisions for encouraging the more learned and deserving
men as were necessary. When these acts of the Scottish parliament were brought into France to be confirmed, they were
rejected with much scorn; so that the Scots were in fear of a
new war. But the king of France dying in the beginning of
December, all that cloud vanished; their queen being now
only dowager of France, and in very ill terms with her mother-
in-law, queen Catharine de Medici, who hated her because she
had endeavoured to take her husband out of her hands, and to
give him up wholly to the counsels of her uncles. So she,
being ill used in France, was forced to return to Scotland, and
govern there in such manner as the nation was pleased to submit to.

Thus had the queen of England separated Scotland entirely
from the interests of France, and united it to her own: and,

Francis the
Second
died. [Dec.
4. Bucha-
nan, p.
327.]

being engaged in the same cause of religion, she ever after this had that influence on all affairs there, that she never received any disturbance from thence during all the rest of her glorious reign. In which, other accidents concurred to raise her to the greatest advantages in deciding foreign contests that ever this crown had.

The civil wars of France. [July 8.] In July, after she came to the crown, Henry the Second of 415 France was unfortunately wounded in his eye at a tilting, the beaver of his helmet not being let down; so that he died of it soon after. His son, Francis the Second, succeeding, was then in the 16th year of his age, and assumed the government in his own name; but put it into the hands of his mother, the cardinal of Lorraine, and the duke of Guise. The constable was put from the court, the princes of the blood were not regarded, but all things were carried by the cardinal and his brother; between whom, and the queen-mother, there arose great misunderstandings, which proved fatal to the queen of Scotland: for she, being much engaged with her uncles, and having an ascendant over her husband, did so divide him from his mother, that before he died she had only the shadow of the government. This she remembered ever after against her daughter-in-law, and took no care of her afterwards in all her miseries.

But the prince of Condé, with the admiral, and many others, resolving to have the government in their hands, engaged some lawyers to examine the point of the king's majority. These writ several books on that subject to prove, that two and twenty was the soonest that any king had been ever held to be of age to assume the government: and that no strangers nor women might be admitted to it by the law of France, but that it belonged to the princes of the blood, during the king's minority; who were to manage it by the advice of the courts of parliament, and the three estates. So that the design now concerted between these great lords, to take the king out of their hands who disposed of him, was grounded on their laws: yet, as this design was laying all over France, papists and protestants concurring in it, it was discovered by a protestant, who thought himself bound in conscience to reveal it. Upon this, the prince of Condé and many others were seized on; and [Dec. 4.] had not the king's death, in the beginning of December 1560, saved him, the prince himself, and all the heads of that party, had suffered for it.

But upon his death, Charles the Ninth, that succeeded him, being but eleven years old, the king of Navarre was declared regent; and the queen-mother, who then hated the cardinal of Lorraine, united herself to him and the constable, and drew the weak regent into her interests. Upon this some lawyers, examining the power of the regents, found, that the other princes of the blood were to have their share of the government with him; and that he might be checked by the courts of parliament, and was subject to an assembly of the three estates.

In July, the next year, there was a severe edict passed against the protestants, to put down all their meetings, and banish all their preachers. The execution of it was put into the hands of the bishops; but the greater part of the nation would not bear it.

So in January thereafter another edict passed, in a great assembly of the princes of the blood, the privy counsellors, and eight courts of parliament, for the free exercise of that religion; requiring the magistrates to punish those who should hinder or disturb their meetings. Soon after this, the duke of Guise and his brother reconciled themselves to the queen-mother, and re-416 solved to break that edict. This was begun by the duke of Vassy; where a meeting of the protestants being gathered, his servants disturbed them: they began with reproachful words; from these it went to blows and throwing of stones, and by one of them the duke was wounded; for which his men took a severe revenge, for they killed sixty of them, and wounded two hundred, sparing neither age nor sex. After this, the edict was every where broken. Many lawyers were of opinion, that the regent could not do it; and that the people might lawfully follow the next prince of the blood in defence of the edict.

Upon this his brother, the prince of Condé, gathered an army. In the beginning of the war, the king of Navarre was killed at the siege of Rouen; so that, by the law, the prince of Condé ought to have succeeded him in the regency: and thus the wars that followed after this could not be called rebellion; since the protestants had the law and the first prince of the blood of their side, to whom the government did of right belong.

Thus began the civil wars of France, which lasted above thirty years; in all which time the queen of England, by the assistance she sent them, sometimes of men, but for the most part of money and ammunition, did support the protestant interest with no great charge to herself. And by that she was not only secured from all the mischief which so powerful a neighbour could do her, but had almost the half of that kingdom depending on her.

The wars of the Netherlands. The state of the Netherlands afforded the like advantages in those provinces; where the king of Spain, finding the proceedings of the bishops were not effectual for the extirpation of heresy, their sees being so large, intended to have founded more bishoprics, and to have set up the courts of inquisition in those parts; and apprehending some opposition from the natives, he kept garrisons of Spaniards among them, with many other things, contrary to the *lœtus introitus* that had been agreed to, when he was received to be their prince.

The people, finding all terms broken with them, and that by that agreement they were disengaged from their obedience if he broke those conditions, did shake off his yoke. Upon which followed the civil wars of the Netherlands, that lasted likewise above thirty years. To them the queen gave assistance; at first more secretly, but afterwards more openly: and as both they and the French protestants were assisted with men out of Germany, which were generally led by the brave, but seldom fortunate, Casimir, brother tò the elector palatine, so the money that paid them was for the most part furnished from England.

And thus was queen Elizabeth the arbiter of all the neighbouring parts of Christendom. She at home brought the coin to a true standard: navigation prospered: trade spread, both in the northern seas to Archangel, and to the East and West Indies: and, in her long wars with Spain, she was always victorious. That great armada, set out with such assurance of conquest, was, what by the hand of Heaven in a storm, what by the unwieldiness of their ships and the nimbleness of ours, so shattered and sunk, that the few remainders of it returned with irrecoverable shame and loss to Spain again, She reigned

in the affections of her people; and was admired for her
417 knowledge, virtues, and wisdom, by all the world. She always
ordered her counsels so that all her parliaments were ever
ready to comply with them; for in every thing she followed
the true interest of the nation. She never asked subsidies but
when the necessity was visible; and when the occasions that
made her demand any vanished, she discharged them.

She was admired even in Rome itself, where Sixtus the
Fifth used to speak of her and the king of Navarre, as the
only princess that understood what it was to govern; and pro-
fanely wished he might enjoy her but one night, hoping they
would beget a new Alexander the Great between them [46]. But
if that had been, and the child had taken after the father, it
would have been more like Alexander the Sixth.

Vita di Sisto V. [Tom. ii. p. 60.]

Notwithstanding all the attempts of Rome against her person and government, she still lived and triumphed. In the
first ten years of her reign, all things were carried with such
moderation, that there was no stir about religion. Pope Pius
the Fourth, reflecting on the capricious and high answer
his mad predecessor had made to her address, sent one Parpaglia [47] to her, in the second year of her reign, to invite her to
join herself to that see, and he would disannul the sentence

[May 5, 1560.]

---

[46] [Gregorio Leti, whose work is
here alluded to, is an author of no
credit. He has earned the name of
the Italian *Varillas* for his want of
historical truth and accuracy. With
regard to the book quoted for this
anecdote, he himself observed,
'*qu'une chose bien imaginée faisait
beaucoup plus de plaisir que la vé-
rité quand elle n'était pas mise dans
un beau jour.*]

[47] [See this letter in English in
Fuller, lib. ix. p. 68. Fuller adds,
'What private proposals Parpaglia
made to her majesty on condition
she would be reconciled to Rome, is
uncertain. Some conceive the pope
might promise more than he meant
to perform; but would he perform
more than he did promise, nothing
had been effected. A bargain can
never be driven, where a buyer can
on no terms be procured. Her ma-

jesty was resolute and immoveable
in her religion. And yet some not
more knowing of councils, but more
daring of conjectures than others,
who love to feign what they cannot
find, that they may never appear to
be at a loss, avouch that the pope
promised to revoke the sentence
against her mother Anne Boleyn's
marriage, to confirm our English
liturgy by his authority, to permit
the English the communion under
both kinds, provided she would own
the pope's primacy, and cordially
unite herself to the Catholic church.
Yea, some thousands of crowns,
but all in vain, were promised to
the effectors thereof, wherein his
holiness, seemingly liberal, was
really thrifty, as knowing such his
sums, if accepted, would within one
year return with a hundredfold increase,' p. 69.]

against her mother's marriage, confirm the English service, and the use of the sacrament in both kinds: but she sent the agent word to stay at Brussels, and not to come over. The same treatment met abbot Martinengo [48], who was sent the year after with the like message. From that time, all treaty with Rome was entirely broken off. Pius the Fourth proceeded no further; but his successor, Pius the Fifth, resolved to contrive her death, as he that writ his Life relates [49].

[Cotton MSS. Julius F. fol. 163.]
Catena,
[Vita di Pio V.
p. 113.]

The unfortunate queen of Scotland, upon the wars in her country, was driven to seek shelter in England, where it was at first resolved to use her well, and to restore her to her crown and country; as will appear by two papers, which, for their curiosity, being originals, I have put into the Collection. The one is the advice that sir Henry Mildmay gave about it: the other is a long letter written concerning it by the earl of Leicester to the earl of Sussex. They were given me by that most ingenious and virtuous gentleman, Mr. Evelyn; who is not satisfied to have advanced the knowledge of this age, by his own most useful and successful labours about planting, and divers other ways, but is ready to contribute every thing in his power to perfect other men's endeavours.

[Collect.
Numb. 12.]

But while the English council intended to have used the queen of Scotland well, her own officious friends, by the frequent plots that were in a succession of many years carried on, sometimes by open rebellion, as in the north of England and in Ireland, but more frequently by secret attempts, brought on her the calamities of a long imprisonment, and death in the conclusion.

Vita di
Sisto V.
[Tom. ii.
p. 274.]

Her death was the greatest blemish of this reign, being generally censured by all the age, except by pope Sixtus the Fifth, who was a man that delighted in cruel executions, and

---

[48] [See Tierney's edition of Dodd's Church History, vol. ii. App. No. 48. for 'A note of the consultation had at Greenwich, May 1, 1561, by the queen's majesty's commandment upon a request made to her majesty by the king of Spain's ambassador, that the abbot Martinengo, being a nuncio from the pope, and arriving at Brussels, might come into the realm with letters from the pope and other princes to the queen's majesty.' Taken from a MS. in the State Paper Office.]

[49] [Catena (Girolamo.) Vita del Papa Pio V. dedicata al santissimo Signor nostro, Sisto Quinto. Rom. 1586, 4to, and again Rom. 1587, 8vo.]

so concluded her to be a happy woman, that had the pleasure
to cut off a crowned head. But queen Elizabeth's own pre-
418 servation from the many designs that were against her life,
made it in some sort, if not necessary, yet more excusable in
her : especially that unfortunate queen having herself cherished
the plot of Babington and Ballard, and having set her hand to
the letters that were written to them about it, though she still
denied that, and cast the blame of it on her secretaries, who,
as she said, had gotten her hand to them without her knowledge. The pope had deposed the queen, (as will appear by
his sentence, which I have put in the Collection,) and the Collect.
queen of Scotland being the next heir to the crown, and a Numb. 13.
zealous papist, those of that religion hoped, by destroying the
queen, to set her in her room ; which put England in no small
disorder, by associations, and other means that were used for
preserving the queen, and destroying the popish interest. The
rebellions and plots in England and Ireland were not a little
supported by the assistance of king Philip of Spain, who did
all he could to embroil the queen's affairs at home, though still
without success. But the steps of the queen's proceedings,
both against papists and puritans, are so set out by her great
and wise secretary, sir Francis Walsingham, in so clear a manner, that I shall set it down here as a most important piece of
history ; being written by one of the wisest and most virtuous
ministers that these latter ages have produced. He wrote it
in French to one monsieur Critoy, a Frenchman, of which
I have seen an English copy, taken, as is said, from the
original.

" Sir,

" Whereas you desire to be advertised touching the pro- Walsing-
" ceedings here in ecclesiastical causes, because you seem to ham's letter con-
" note in them some inconstancy and variation, as if we in- cerning
" clined sometimes to one side, and sometimes to another ; and the queen's
proceed-
" as if that clemency and lenity were not used of late, that ings
against
" was used in the beginning : all which you imputed to your both pa-
" own superficial understanding of the affairs of this state, pists and
puritans.
" having notwithstanding her majesty's doings in singular re-
" verence, as the real pledges which she hath given unto the
" world of her sincerity in religion, and of her wisdom in go-

" vernment, well meriteth. I am glad of this occasion to im-
" part that little I know in that matter unto you, both for
" your own satisfaction, and to the end you may make use
" thereof towards any that shall not be so modestly and so
" reasonably minded as you are. I find therefore her ma-
" jesty's proceedings to have been grounded upon two prin-
" ciples.

" The one, that consciences are not to be forced, but to be
" won and reduced by force of truth, with the aid of time, and
" use of all good means of instruction and persuasion.

" The other, that causes of consciences, when they exceed
" their bounds, and grow to be matter of faction, lose their
" nature ; and that sovereign princes ought distinctly to punish
" their practices and contempt, though coloured with the pre-
" tence of conscience and religion.

" According to these principles, her majesty, at her coming
" to the crown, utterly disliking the tyranny of Rome, which
" had used by terror and rigour to settle commandments
" of men's faiths and consciences ; though as a princess of 419
" great wisdom and magnanimity she suffered but the exercise
" of one religion ; yet her proceedings towards the papists
" was with great lenity ; expecting the good effects which time
" might work in them : and therefore her majesty revived not
" the laws made in the 28th and 35th of her father's reign,
" whereby the oath of supremacy might have been offered at
" the king's pleasure to any subject, so he kept his conscience
" never so modestly to himself ; and the refusal to take the
" same oath, without further circumstances, was made treason.
" But contrariwise, her majesty, not liking to make windows
" into men's hearts and secret thoughts, except the abundance
" of them did overflow into overt and express acts or affirma-
" tions, tempered her law so, as it restraineth every manifest
" disobedience, in impugning and impeaching, advisedly and
" maliciously, her majesty's supreme power, maintaining and
" extolling a foreign jurisdiction. And as for the oath, it was
" altered by her majesty into a more grateful form ; the hard-
" ness of the name and appellation of *Supreme Head* was re-
" moved, and the penalty of the refusal thereof turned only
" to disablement to take any promotion, or to exercise any
" charge, and yet of liberty to be reinvested therein, if any

" man should accept thereof during his life. But after, when
" Pius Quintus excommunicated her majesty, and the bulls of
" excommunication were published in London, whereby her
" majesty was in a sort proscribed, and that thereupon, as
" upon a principal motive or preparative, followed the rebel-
" lion in the north; yet, because the ill humours of the realm
" were by that rebellion partly purged, and that she feared at
" that time no foreign invasion, and much less the attempt of
" any within the realm, not backed by some potent power and
" succour from without, she contented herself to make a law
" against that special case of bringing in and publishing of
" any bulls, or the like instruments; whereunto was added a
" prohibition upon pain, not of treason, but of an inferior de-
" gree of punishment, against the bringing of the *Agnus Dei's*,
" and such other merchandise of Rome, as are well known not
" to be any essential part of the Romish religion, but only to
" be used in practice, as love-tokens, to enchant and bewitch
" the people's affections from their allegiance to their natural
" sovereign : in all other points her majesty continued her
" former lenity. But when, about the twentieth year of her
" reign, she had discovered in the king of Spain an intention
" to invade her dominions; and that a principal part of the
" plot was, to prepare a party within the realm, that might
" adhere to the foreigner; and that the seminaries began to
" blossom, and to send forth daily priests and professed men,
" who should by vow taken at shrift reconcile her subjects
" from their obedience, yea, and bind many of them to attempt
" against her majesty's sacred person; and that, by the poison
" which they spread, the humours of most papists were altered,
" and that they were no more papists in conscience, and of
" softness, but papists in faction; then were there new laws
" made for the punishment of such as should submit them-
" selves to such reconcilements, or renunciation of obedience.
" And because it was a treason carried in the clouds, and in
" wonderful secrecy, and come seldom to light; and that there
420 " was no presuspicion thereof so great as the recusancy to come
" to divine service, because it was set down by their decrees, that
" to come to church before reconciliation was to live in schism,
" but to come to church after reconcilement was absolutely
" heretical and damnable. Therefore there were added laws

" containing punishment pecuniary, *videlicet*, such as might
" not enforce consciences, but to enfeeble and impoverish the
" means of those about whom it resteth indifferent and ambi-
" guous, whether they were reconciled or not. And when,
" notwithstanding all this provision, the poison was dispersed
" so secretly, as that there was no means to stay it, but by
" restraining the merchants that brought it in; then, lastly,
" there was added a law, whereby such seditious priests of new
" erection were exiled, and those that were at that time in the
" land shipped over, and so commanded to keep hence upon
" pain of treason. This hath been the proceeding, though in-
" termingled, not only with sundry examples of her majesty's
" grace towards such as in her wisdom she knew to be papists
" in conscience, and not faction and singularity, but also with
" extraordinary mitigation towards the offenders in the highest
" degree, committed by law, if they would but protest, that if
" in case this realm should be invaded with a foreign army, by
" the pope's authority, for the catholic cause, as they term it,
" they would take part with her majesty, and not adhere to
" her enemies.

" For the other party, which have been offensive to the
" state, though in another degree, which named themselves
" *reformers,* and we commonly call *puritans,* this hath been
" the proceeding towards them; a great while, when they in-
" veighed against such abuses in the church as pluralities,
" nonresidence, and the like, their zeal was not condemned,
" only their violence was sometime censured. When they re-
" fused the use of some ceremonies and rites, as superstitious,
" they were tolerated with much connivancy and gentleness;
" yea, when they called in question the superiority of bishops,
" and pretended to a democracy into the church, yet their pro-
" positions were here considered, and by contrary writings
" debated and discussed. Yet all this while it was perceived
" that their course was dangerous, and very popular: as, be-
" cause papistry was odious, therefore it was ever in their
" mouths, that they sought to purge the church from the relics
" of papistry; a thing acceptable to the people, who love ever
" to run from one extreme to another.

" Because multitude of rogues and poverty was an eyesore,
" and a dislike to every man; therefore they put into the

" people's head, that if discipline were planted, there should
" be no vagabonds nor beggars ; a thing very plausible. And
" in like manner they promised the people many of the impos-
" sible wonders of their discipline : besides, they opened to the
" people a way to government, by their consistory and pres-
" bytery ; a thing, though in consequence no less prejudicial
" to the liberties of private men than to the sovereignty of
" princes, yet in first show very popular. Nevertheless this,
" except it were in some few that entered into extreme con-
" tempt, was borne with, because they pretended in dutiful
" manner to make propositions, and to leave it to the provi-
" dence of God and the authority of the magistrate.

421   " But now of late years, when there is issued from them
" that affirmed, the consent of the magistrate was not to be
" attended ; when, under pretence of a confession, to avoid
" slander and imputations, they combined themselves by classes
" and subscriptions ; when they descended into that vile and
" base means of defacing the government of the church by
" ridiculous pasquils ; when they began to make many sub-
" jects in doubt to take oaths, which is one of the fundamental
" parts of justice in this land, and in all places ; when they
" began both to vaunt of their strength, and number of their
" partisans and followers, and to use comminations that their
" cause would prevail through uproar and violence ; then it
" appeared to be no more zeal, no more conscience, but mere
" faction and division : and therefore, though the state were
" compelled to hold somewhat a harder hand to restrain them
" than before, yet was it with as great moderation as the
" peace of the state or church could permit. And there-
" fore, sir, to conclude, consider uprightly of these matters,
" and you shall see, her majesty is no more a temporizer in
" religion : it is not the success abroad, nor the change of
" servants here at home, can alter her ; only, as the things
" themselves alter, she applied her religious wisdom to me-
" thods correspondent unto them ; still retaining the two rules
" before mentioned, in dealing tenderly with consciences, and
" yet in discovering faction from conscience, and softness from
" singularity. Farewell.

" Your loving friend,

" F. Walsingham."

THUS I have prosecuted what I at first undertook, the progress of the reformation, from its first and small beginnings in England, till it came to a complete settlement in the time of this queen: of whose reign, if I have adventured to give any account, it was not intended so much for a full character of her and her counsels, as to set out the great and visible blessings of God that attended on her; the many preservations she had, and that by such signal discoveries, as both saved her life, and secured her government; and the unusual happiness of her whole reign, which raised her to the esteem and envy of that age, and the wonder of all posterity. It was wonderful indeed, that a virgin queen could rule such a kingdom, for above forty-four years, with such constant success, in so great tranquillity at home, with a vast increase of wealth, and with such glory abroad. All which may justly be esteemed to have been the rewards of Heaven, crowning that reign with so much honour and triumph, that was begun with the reformation of religion.

THE END OF THE THIRD BOOK, AND OF THE HISTORY OF THE
REFORMATION OF THE CHURCH OF ENGLAND.

CONTENTS

OF THE

SECOND PART OF THE HISTORY.

[The pages referred to are those of the first and second folio editions, as printed in the inner margin of this edition.]

BOOK I.

Of the life and reign of king Edward the Sixth.

BOOK II.

The life and reign of queen Mary

BOOK III.

*Of the Settlement of the Reformation of Religion in the beginning of
queen Elizabeth's reign.*